DEATH TO ORDER

DEATH TO ORDER

A Modern History of Assassination

SIMON BALL

YALE UNIVERSITY PRESS
NEW HAVEN AND LONDON

Copyright © 2025 Simon Ball

All rights reserved. This book may not be reproduced in whole or in part, in any form (beyond that copying permitted by Sections 107 and 108 of the U.S. Copyright Law and except by reviewers for the public press) without written permission from the publishers.

All reasonable efforts have been made to provide accurate sources for all images that appear in this book. Any discrepancies or omissions will be rectified in future editions.

For information about this and other Yale University Press publications, please contact:
U.S. Office: sales.press@yale.edu yalebooks.com
Europe Office: sales@yaleup.co.uk yalebooks.co.uk

Set in Adobe Garamond Pro by IDSUK (DataConnection) Ltd
Printed and bound in the UK using 100% renewable electricity at CPI Group (UK) Ltd

Library of Congress Control Number: 2025936355
A catalogue record for this book is available from the British Library.
Authorized Representative in the EU: Easy Access System Europe, Mustamäe tee 50, 10621 Tallinn, Estonia, gpsr.requests@easproject.com

ISBN 978-0-300-25804-2

10 9 8 7 6 5 4 3 2 1

To Helen

CONTENTS

List of Illustrations		ix
Preface and Acknowledgements		xi
Acronyms and Abbreviations		xv
	Introduction	1
1	Murder as an Instrument of Policy: The Sarajevo Assassination, 1914–1930	14
2	The Monopoly of Legitimate Violence: European Assassinations, 1917–1923	34
3	The Rules of the Game: Assassination and the Greatest Empire, 1909–1940	47
4	Death to the Presidents: Assassination and the USA's Near Abroad, 1901–1950	75
5	Government by Assassination: China and Japan, 1928–1941	96
6	Sabotage Applied to Individuals: Totalitarians and Democrats, 1923–1945	119
7	Last Rites: Assassination and the Fall of Empires, 1944–1973	146
8	Dangerous in Conception and Execution: The US Experiment with Assassination, 1952–1976	170
9	Splinter Groups: Denial, 1971–1979	192

CONTENTS

10	London Killing: Acceptance, 1980–1990	217
11	Very Very Important People: Security, 1991–2001	234
12	Who Should Pull the Trigger? Assassination in the Twenty-First Century	250
	Conclusion	282
	Notes	*287*
	Bibliography	*365*
	Index	*393*

ILLUSTRATIONS

1. Assassination of Orlando Letelier, Peter Bregg, 1976. Associated Press / Alamy.
2. Still from *The Day of the Jackal*, 2024. FlixPix / Alamy.
3. Statue of Benoy Basu Badal Gupta and Dinesh Gupta in Kolkata, Sujay25, 2013. CC BY-SA 4.0.
4. Luis Segura Vilchis facing a Mexican firing squad, with the body of Father Miguel Agustín Pro next to him, 1927. World History Archive / Alamy.
5. Ceremony of the presentation of the Sarajevo plaque as a trophy in the armory, Unter den Linden in Berlin, Pincornelly, 1941. United Archives / M-Verlag Berlin / Pincornelly.
6. Wanted poster for Matthia Erzberger's assassins, Heinrich Schulz and Heinrich Tillessen, 1921. Bundesarchiv Plak 002-009-021.
7. Benito Mussolini wounded on the nose, 1926.
8. Assassination of Zhang Zuolin, near Mukden in Manchuria, 1928. Image courtesy of Special Collections, University of Bristol Library (http://www.hpcbristol.net). CC BY-SA 4.0.
9. Assassination of Alexander I of Yugoslavia, 1934. Pictorial Press Ltd / Alamy.
10. *Joseph Stalin at Sergei Kirov's Coffin*, Nikolai Rutkovsky, 1934. Bridgeman.

ILLUSTRATIONS

11. *Man Hunt* film poster, 1941. Album / Alamy.
12. *Assassination of Heydrich*, Terence Cuneo, 1939–46. © The National Archives.
13. Adolf Hitler giving a speech at Heydrich's state funeral in Berlin, 1942. Bundesarchiv Bild 146-1969-052-69.
14. British assassination kit. © Royal Armouries.
15. Leslie Coffelt shot in front of Blair House during an assassination attempt, 1950. Harry S. Truman Library & Museum.
16. Secret Service agents subdue a gunman after an attempted assassination of Ronald Reagan, Ron Edmond, 1981. Associated Press / Alamy.
17. Ian Gow's wrecked car, 1990. Bill Cross / ANL / Shutterstock.
18. Tahir Jalil Habbush holding up a picture of Abu Nidal's corpse, 2002. Karim Sahib / AFP via Getty Images.
19. Explosion scene after the assassination of Rafiq Hariri, Mahmoud Tawil, 2005. Associated Press / Alamy.
20. Active shooter exercise at Stewart Air National Guard Base, Staff Sgt Julio Olivencia Jr, 2016.
21. MQ-9 Hellfire launches in the desert, Airman 1st Class Victoria Nuzzi, 2023.
22. Body of Qassem Soleimani, 2020.
23. Vladimir Putin greets Vadim Krasikov at Vnukovo International Airport, Mikhail Voskresensky, 2024. Associated Press / Alamy.
24. Attempted assassination of Donald Trump, 2024. SOPA Images Limited / Alamy.

PREFACE AND ACKNOWLEDGEMENTS

Death to Order is the result of curiosity-driven research. It began as a side project of a side project. Initially, I planned only to write an article on attempts to control the global proliferation of modern firearms from the Edwardian era to the outbreak of the Second World War. That project was designed to keep my research wheels turning while I served as the head of history, and then of humanities, at the University of Glasgow. Reading the papers of the British government's 1917 Islington Committee in the National Archives, however, I was struck by a remark which the politician Sir Mark Sykes made about self-loading pistols: 'Any fool can shoot a Viceroy or a police inspector.' I decided to investigate further.

I have received a great deal of help in turning that germ of an idea into a book. My first thanks go to Joanna Godfrey at Yale University Press. Jo remembered a conversation we had had years previously, in a different context, and asked if I would be interested in writing about assassination for Yale. I would like to thank the team at YUP in London for taking such good care of my work. Yale's anonymous readers were exemplary: they were most encouraging, while writing detailed reports that made me think hard about many tricky issues of interpretation and fact.

I am fortunate to work in the supportive and intellectually stimulating environment of the School of History at the University of Leeds. The School awarded me a semester of research leave so that I could carry

PREFACE AND ACKNOWLEDGEMENTS

out research for this book. The Faculty of Arts, Humanities and Cultures matched that semester with another through its competitive research leave scheme. Leeds University Library subscribed to several digital archive collections that I found extremely useful. Members of the School and the Faculty laid aside their own work to help me with mine. For discussion, ideas, references and encouragement I would very much like to thank my colleagues in the School of History, Professor Shane Doyle, Professor James Harris, Professor Elisabeth Leake (now Tufts University), Dr Will Jackson, Dr Jonathan Saha (now Durham University), Dr Eline van Ommen and Dr Matt Woolgar. I would also like to thank my colleagues from the School of Languages and Cultures, Professor Alison Fell (now Liverpool University), Dr Jim House and Dr Stephan Petzold for similarly offering advice, support and ideas. Throughout the research for *Death to Order*, I was delving into countries and cultures in which my interlocutors were the experts: they were universally tolerant and helpful as I tapped their scholarly knowledge and resources. Not only did my colleagues put up with my questions, but some of them also read parts of the manuscript of *Death to Order*. I am very grateful indeed for the comments and emendations offered by my readers, Professor Nir Arielli, Professor Sanjoy Bhattacharya, Professor Claire Eldridge, Professor Will Gould and Dr Yuexin Rachel Lin. I usually, but not always, took their excellent advice: they are without spot if any reader should feel I have made errors of fact, language or judgement.

Beyond Leeds I drew intellectual sustenance from a community of – I fear I must now call them distinguished – historians and political scientists. For all their help and support I would like to thank Professor Richard English of Queen's University Belfast, Professor Peter Jackson of the University of Glasgow, Professor Phil O'Brien of the University of St Andrews and Professor Martin Thomas of the University of Exeter.

I also got inspiration from outside the universities. Omer Mohammedalamin very generously translated documents from Arabic for me. I collaborated with Mark Alden on the assassination episode of his ITN documentary series, *Secrets of the Spies*. My former student Dr Lucy Slater organised a very well-attended and lively round table in Leeds, bringing together undergraduates from the Schools of History, Languages, and Communications with documentary film makers, at which Mark, Matthew Dunn and I attempted to field questions about assassination, making me think how best to present the subject.

Those beyond the University of Leeds did not escape my search for readers. I am very grateful to Professor Sönke Neitzel of the University of Potsdam for commenting on the portions of the manuscript that related to Germany. Andy Scott and Lucy Scott kindly read my draft chapter on the twenty-first century. Professor Richard Aldous of Bard College read the whole manuscript. Richard drew double duty, acting as my unpaid research assistant at the Franklin D. Roosevelt Presidential Library and Museum at Hyde Park, NY. I could not have wished for a more agreeable batter-about of ideas.

Books like *Death to Order* would be impossible to write without the tireless work of the librarians and archivists who preserve and make available the documentary record. I would like to thank the staff of the The National Archives, London, the Asian & African Reading Room at the British Library, London, the Cambridge South Asian Archive at the Centre of South Asian Studies, the Churchill Archives Centre at Churchill College, Cambridge, the Archives and Modern Manuscripts Department of Cambridge University Library, Special Collections in the Brotherton Library, University of Leeds, and Special Collections in the Bodleian Library, Oxford University. I would particularly like to thank three archivists who I know took much trouble over my searches and requests: Debbie Usher at the Middle East Centre Archive, St Antony's College, Oxford; Lavinia Cyrillo at the Royal Anthropological Institute, London; and Gillian Long of the School of Slavonic and East European Studies Library, University College London. The world of archival study has become increasingly digitised over the past decade: beyond the archives I visited in person, I am grateful to those who have curated digital platforms for the papers they hold. I used extensively and with great profit the President John F. Kennedy Assassination Records Collection at the US National Archives; the Department of State Freedom of Information Act Virtual Reading Room; CIA Freedom of Information Act Electronic Reading Room; FBI Freedom of Information Act Digital Library; Abhilekh Patal of the National Archives of India; the United Nations Library & Archives, Geneva; the Clinton Digital Library from the William J. Clinton Presidential Library & Museum;

PREFACE AND ACKNOWLEDGEMENTS

DiscoverLBJ from the Lyndon Baines Johnson Presidential Library and Museum; Digitized Archives, Ronald Reagan Presidential Library & Museum; the Margaret Thatcher Foundation Archive; Online Collections at the Harry S. Truman Presidential Library and Museum; Presidential Oral Histories, Miller Center, University of Virginia; Middle East & Islamic Studies Collections, Durham University Library; and the Wilson Center Digital Archive.

For help of a very different nature, I am immensely grateful to Kirsteen Hardie for corresponding with me about the assassination of Duncan Stewart, her father, and Martin Norris for corresponding with me about the assassination of Percy Norris, his father. I am very aware that my academic interest is somebody else's flesh-and-blood tragedy.

My greatest thanks go to Helen, my wife. She has tried to introduce some rigour into my thought and expression even though assassination is not her favourite subject. This book is dedicated to her, with all my love.

University of Leeds, December 2024

ACRONYMS AND ABBREVIATIONS

ACJM	Asociación Católica de la Juventud Mexicana (Mexico)
ADC	aide-de-camp
AFPFL	Anti-Fascist People's Freedom League (Burma)
ANC	African National Congress (South Africa)
AWB	Afrikaner Weerstandsbeweging (South Africa)
BAO	Bureau d'Action Opérationnelle (France)
BBC	British Broadcasting Corporation (UK)
BKA	Bundeskriminalamt (Germany)
BSB	Brigade Speciale Beveiligingsopdrachten (Netherlands)
CCB	Civil Co-operation Bureau (South Africa)
CCP	Chinese Communist Party (China)
CCTV	closed-circuit television
CDU	Christlich Demokratische Union Deutschlands (Germany)
CENTCOM	Central Command (USA)
CIA	Central Intelligence Agency (USA)
CID	Criminal Intelligence Department (India)
CID	Criminal Investigation Department (various)
CNI	Centro Nacional de Informaciones (Chile)
CNM	Cuban National Movemement (USA)

ACRONYMS AND ABBREVIATIONS

CORDS	Civil Operations and Revolutionary Development Support (USA)
CT	counter-terrorism
DBB	Dienst Bewaken en Beveiligen (Netherlands)
DCI	Director of Central Intelligence (USA)
DINA	Dirección de Inteligencia Nacional (Chile)
DNA	deoxyribonucleic acid
DPG	Diplomatic Protection Group (UK)
DS	Diplomatic Security Service (USA)
DS	Durzhavna Sigurnost (Bulgaria)
EOKA	Ethniki Organosis Kyprion Agoniston (Cyprus)
EPRLF	Eelam People's Revolutionary Liberation Front (Sri Lanka)
EPS	Executive Protective Service (USA)
ESR	Egyptian State Railways (Egypt)
ETA	Euskadi Ta Askatasuna (Spain)
FAAD	Front algérién d'action démocratique (France)
FBI	Federal Bureau of Investigation (USA)
FLN	Front de libération nationale (Algeria)
FPL	Fuerzas Populares de Liberación Farabundo Martí (El Salvador)
FSB	Federal'naya sluzhba bezopasnosti Rossiyskoy Federatsii (Russia)
FSO	Federal'naya sluzhba okhrany Rossiyskoy Federatsii (Russia)
GCHQ	Government Communications Headquarters (UK)
GOS	Government of Sudan (Sudan)
GRU	Glavnoye razvedyvatel'noye upravleniye (Soviet Union)
HMG	His or Her Majesty's Government (UK)
HRD	Hindu Rashtra Dal (India)
HSCA	House Select Committee on Assassinations (USA)
HSRA	Hindustan Socialist Republican Association (India)
HUR	Holovne upravlinnia rozvidky Ministerstva oborony Ukrainy (Ukraine)
ICS	Indian Civil Service (India)
IDF	Israel Defense Forces

ACRONYMS AND ABBREVIATIONS

IPI	Indian Political Intelligence (UK)
IPS	Indian Police Service (India)
IPS	Institute of Policy Studies (USA)
IRA	Irish Republican Army (Ireland)
IRGC	Iranian Revolutionary Guard Corps
ISF	Forces de Sécurité Intérieure (Lebanon)
JCAG	Justice Commandos of the Armenian Genocide (various)
KGB	Komitet gosudarstvennoy bezopasnosti (Soviet Union)
KMT	Kuomintang (China)
MK	uMkhonto weSizwe (South Africa)
MNA	Mouvement National Algérien (Algeria)
MRLA	Malay Races Liberation Army (Malaya)
MVD	Ministerstvo vnutrennikh del SSSR (Soviet Union)
MVSN	Milizia volontaria per la sicurezza nazionale (Italy)
NID	Naval Intelligence Division (UK)
NKVD	Narodnyy komissariat vnutrennikh del SSSR (Soviet Union)
NSA	National Security Agency (USA)
NSC	National Security Council (USA)
NTS	Narodno-trudovoy soyuz rossiyskikh solidaristov (Soviet Union)
NYPD	New York Police Department (USA)
OAS	Organisation armée secrète (France)
OC	Organisation Consul (Germany)
OGPU	Obyedinyonnoye gosudarstvennoye politicheskoye upravleniye (Soviet Union)
OSS	Office of Strategic Services (USA)
OVRA	Opera Vigilanza Repressione Antifascismo (Italy)
PDFLP	Popular Democratic Front for the Liberation of Palestine (various)
PFA	Policía Federal Argentina (Argentina)
PFLP	Popular Front for the Liberation of Palestine (various)
PIRA	Provisional Irish Republican Army (UK)
PLO	Palestine Liberation Organization (various)
PNR	Partido Nacional Revolucionario (Mexico)

ACRONYMS AND ABBREVIATIONS

PPF	Palestine Police Force (Palestine)
PPP	Pakistan People's Party (Pakistan)
PRU	Provincial Reconnaissance Unit (USA–Vietnam)
PSB	Public Safety Bureau (China)
PUK	Patriotic Union of Kurdistan (Iraq)
RAF	Rote Armee Fraktion (Germany)
RAVEC	Royal and VIP Executive Committee
RDC	Revolutionary Development Cadre (USA)
RIC	Royal Irish Constabulary (UK)
RSD	Reichssicherheitsdienst (Germany)
RSHA	Reichssicherheitshauptamt (Germany)
RSO	Regional Security Officer (USA)
RSS	Rashtriya Swayamsevak Sangh (India)
RUC	Royal Ulster Constabulary (UK)
SA	Sturmabteilung (Germany)
SADF	South African Defence Forces (South Africa)
SAP	South African Police (South Africa)
SAS	Special Air Service (UK)
SAU	Special Action Unit (Vietnam)
SBS	Special Boat Section (UK)
SBU	Sluzhba bezpeky Ukrainy (Ukraine)
SCIRI	Supreme Council of the Islamic Revolution in Iraq (Iraq)
SD	Sicherheitsdienst (Germany)
SDECE	Service de documentation extérieure et de contre-espionnage (France)
SIM	Servizio Informazioni Militare (Italy)
SIS	Secret Intelligence Service (UK)
SMC	Shanghai Municipal Council (China)
SMP	Shanghai Municipal Police (China)
SOE	Special Operations Executive (UK)
SPD	Sozialdemokratische Partei Deutschlands (Germany)
SPG	Special Protection Group (India)
SR	Partiya sotsialistov-revolyutsionerov (Russia)
SS	Schutzstaffel (Germany)
SUV	sports utility vehicle

ACRONYMS AND ABBREVIATIONS

SVR	Sluzhba vneshney razvedki Rossiyskoy Federatsii (Russia)
SY	Office of Security (USA)
TNT	trinitrotoluene
UAE	United Arab Emirates
UKUSA	United Kingdom–USA
UMRO	Vatreshna Makedonska Revolyutsionna Organizatsiya (various)
UN	United Nations
USAF	United States Air Force
USN	United States Navy
USPD	Unabhängige Sozialdemokratische Partei Deutschlands (Germany)
USSS	United States Secret Service
UVOD	Ústřední vedení odboje domácího (Czechoslovakia)
VIP	Very Important Person
VVIP	Very Very Important Person

INTRODUCTION

Some assassinations are still hard to unravel; others, however, are not. The best way to understand the anatomy of assassination is to draw on well-documented examples, rather than agonising about those that remain elusive. The assassination of Orlando Letelier on 21 September 1976, for example, is well understood, not least because of the decade-and-a-half of investigation carried out by US government authorities, concerned citizens and an international commission. While US politicians were still arguing feverishly about the assassinations of the 1960s, notably those of John F. Kennedy, Robert F. Kennedy, Martin Luther King, Rafael Trujillo, Patrice Lumumba and Ngo Dinh Diem, what became possibly the best documented assassination of the 1970s took place in central Washington, DC. On the orders of the dictatorial president of Chile, Augusto Pinochet, the Chilean intelligence service, DINA, in collaboration with the anti-leftist Cuban National Movement, assassinated Letelier, a former Chilean interior minister. The investigators of the murder subsequently dissected the four common elements of assassination: the procurers of assassination, the assassins, the tools of the trade, and the cover-up.

The principal procurer of the Letelier assassination was General Augusto Pinochet. Pinochet was a military dictator. Like many dictators he saw threats all around him: what he had done to others could be done to him. Also like many dictators Pinochet was a narcissist. In his case, the narcissistic personality was expressed in a conviction that he was the saviour of the Chilean army, the Chilean nation, Latin America and the world from Communism. Pinochet was sensitive to criticism, any criticism. He was particularly sensitive to criticism from secular liberals. They presented no immediate threat to his rule, but he loathed them.[1]

Orlando Letelier was one such critic. Letelier had been Chilean ambassador to the United States between 1970 and 1973. He was briefly a minister in the Chilean government that had been overthrown by Pinochet in September 1973. After imprisoning and torturing Letelier, Pinochet had expelled him from Chile.

Letelier's cardinal sin, in Pinochet's eyes, was that he became a prosperous and articulate exile. Letelier arrived back in Washington in late 1974 to become the spokesman for the Institute of Policy Studies. The IPS was an anti-Pinochet lobbying organisation, well funded by money from private sources. That stuck in Pinochet's throat: he knew that the cosmopolitan Chilean elite laughingly looked down on him.[2]

Every morning Augusto Pinochet had breakfast with his fellow general, Manuel Contreras.[3] It was not just a social event. Contreras was the head of the Chilean Directorate of National Intelligence, Dirección de Inteligencia Nacional, or DINA. DINA billed itself as Chile's senior intelligence agency: everyone knew it was the secret police. Pinochet told Contreras to have Letelier killed: that is exactly what Contreras did.

The assassination was not a simple task. Assassinating an enemy in the capital of your superpower backer was rather more challenging than putting a bullet into the brain of a student in Santiago. Indeed, the United States' diplomatic and intelligence community was not only caught by surprise by the assassination, but also initially refused to believe that Pinochet was either so daring or so stupid as to have taken the risk.[4]

Enter the assassins. Luckily, from Contreras's point of view, he had already built an organisation that regularly carried out assassinations beyond Chile. In late June 1976, Contreras's deputy, Colonel Pedro Espinoza, ordered two experienced DINA assassination specialists to

INTRODUCTION

murder Orlando Letelier. Armando Fernández was a standard-issue right-wing Chilean army officer. His partner, Michael Townley, was more exotic. Townley was an American: his father had come to Chile to run the Ford Motor Company's operations in the 1950s. Townley had joined DINA in 1974. His ability to appear 'American' made him a useful operative, perhaps even more so than his right-wing politics and seeming unconcern at killing to order.

In 1974 and 1975, Espinoza, Townley and Fernández had collaborated on a range of assassinations in Europe and Latin America, with cover and support from Chilean diplomats.[5] In October 1975, for instance, one of their death squads had badly wounded the leader of Chile's Social Democrats and his wife in Rome. Bernardo Leighton may have survived but he went completely silent, uttering not one word of criticism of Augusto Pinochet, even in private, thereafter.[6]

Espinoza, Fernández and Townley's modus operandi was to ally with right-wing thugs, indigenous or émigré, so that DINA did not need to take the risk of sending a large party to carry out its assassination. Their preferred partner was the Cuban National Movement, or CNM. The CNM comprised Cubans who had fled Cuba after Castro's seizure of power in 1959, or the children thereof. Most of the group were US citizens.[7]

On 26 August 1976, Fernández flew to the United States: accompanying him was a female DINA officer, known as 'Liliana Walker'. Walker was more than another assassin; she was Manuel Contreras's particular confidante. Walker had the additional advantage for the mission of being female – given the social mores of Washington in the 1970s, a woman could pass unnoticed. Fernández and Walker's job was to document the life of Orlando Letelier: where he lived, where he worked, how he moved around Washington.[8]

In Santiago, Colonel Espinoza told Townley that the assassination was 'on' and ordered him to contact the leaders of the CNM in the USA. Townley flew into John F. Kennedy airport, New York, on 9 September 1976. Fernández met him at the airport to pass over a map of Letelier locations, the surveillance notes he had prepared, and the bankroll for the mission. Townley then travelled to New Jersey to meet his long-time CNM collaborator Virgilio Paz. Paz set up meetings with the leaders of the CNM, Guillermo Novo and Dionisio Suárez. They agreed to take part in the assassination. In practical terms, the joint DINA–CNM murder conspiracy began on 15 September 1976.[9]

It was at this stage that the third element of assassination – the tools of the trade – became crucial. The tools that Townley chose were particularly redolent of the 1970s. Before 1970, explosives had been very unreliable assassination weapons. They tended to kill bystanders rather than the intended target. As the 1970s progressed, however, plastic explosive, originally used for military demolitions, became a reliable alternative to the handgun. Stable military-grade plastic composite was still difficult to obtain, however. The South American technique was to combine it with more primitive explosives.[10]

Even before he left Chile, Townley had decided he would use a remotely detonated car bomb to kill Orlando Letelier. He smuggled detonators through JFK. However, the main body of the bomb had to be supplied by the CNM: they could only acquire a limited amount of plastic explosive, so it had to be supplemented by more old-fashioned TNT. According to the CIA, 'the plastic bomb was expertly designed to concentrate its force upward into the driver's seat'.[11]

On 15 September 1976, Townley and Paz drove from New Jersey to Washington with the explosives in the trunk. They also had a modified remote electronic paging device. In Washington, they went shopping in Sears and Radio Shack to acquire further car bomb-making components: tins, tape and a battery pack for the remote-controlled device. On 18 September 1976, Suárez arrived with more detonators. With a complete set of components, Townley immediately built a bomb. On the same day, he attached the bomb to the underside of Orlando Letelier's car.

On 19 September 1976, Townley left Washington and flew to Miami, to await events in a safe house owned by the CNM. On 20 September 1976, Virgilio Paz and Dionisio Suárez, who had remained behind in Washington, waited for Orlando Letelier to get into his car and attempted to detonate the bomb strapped under the vehicle. However, the trigger mechanism malfunctioned and there was no explosion: Letelier drove safely about his business. Later that day, the two Cubans removed the bomb from under the car, corrected the fault

INTRODUCTION

and reinstalled the weapon. On 21 September 1976, they waited for Letelier to leave work at the IPS and assassinated him by detonating the bomb. Letelier's young female assistant, Ronni Moffitt, was also killed in the explosion.

In Miami, Michael Townley sat watching American TV news broadcasts reporting the explosion. Once he was sure that Letelier was indeed dead, he caught a flight from Miami to Santiago on 22 September 1976.

The fourth element of a 1970s assassination, the cover-up, then swung into action. The cover-up did not begin with Letelier's death. It was integral to the whole planning of the murder. General Contreras and Colonel Espinoza had originally hoped to fulfil Pinochet's instruction by having Townley persuade the CNM not only to kill Letelier but also to make the killing look like an accident, or even better, suicide. Townley told them that from both a technical and human relations standpoint this level of cover-up was impracticable. Because their orders were so clear, the leaders of DINA decided to press on regardless – 'the bottom line was that Letelier had to be killed, and Townley was specifically authorized to use a bomb if necessary.'[12]

Even if a complete cover-up was impossible, there were plenty of other gambits available. In July 1976, Townley and Fernández had travelled to Paraguay to pick up Paraguayan passports with US visas, as cover for their journey to the United States. This part of the cover-up went wrong. In the short term, US embassy sources in Asunción tipped off the US ambassador to Paraguay, George Landau, that something dodgy was afoot: Landau had no inkling of an assassination plot, but he revoked the US visas, rendering the passports useless for their intended purpose. Of subsequent importance, Contreras and Espinoza had liaised directly with their opposite numbers in Paraguayan intelligence to arrange the passports and visas. Paraguayan intelligence subsequently shopped the Chileans. This direct intervention in the mechanics of the operation would allow US prosecutors to tie the two men directly to the assassination in later years.[13]

In the short term, however, Contreras and Espinoza turned the Paraguayan setback into part of their deception operation. Two other DINA officers were sent to the USA with Chilean papers made out in the names of the revoked Paraguayan passports. The two Chilean officers tooled around the eastern United States for a fortnight, doing nothing in particular, solely with a view to confusing post-assassination investigations. Captains Riveros and Mosquiera left the USA on 22 August 1976, four days before Fernández and Walker, also using Chilean passports under false names, arrived in the country.[14]

The passport ploy did indeed sow much confusion. By the end of the 1970s, US intelligence was still unable to identify 'Liliana Walker'. She was only finally unmasked at the end of the investigation in 1990.[15] The US embassy in Santiago had issued the visas for the Chilean passports used in the operation at the request of the Chilean government in August 1976. The Chilean foreign ministry official who had made the official request for the visas was murdered in October 1977: the single pistol shot to the centre of his forehead made the assumption that he had been assassinated by DINA inevitable.[16]

Townley also covered his tracks within the USA. When he left Washington on 19 September 1976, having planted the bomb in Orlando Letelier's car, he did not head directly to his actual destination, Miami. Instead, he flew to Newark airport, New Jersey, where Alvin Ross Diaz of the CNM met him. Townley drove from Newark to JFK in New York. At Kennedy airport he submitted a false immigration form to show that his fake identity had departed for Spain. He then drove back to Newark and boarded a flight from there to Miami.[17]

The cover-up took a long time to unravel. The Pinochet government used their prepared deceptions to deny, lie and dissimulate. Other actors could be encouraged to claim responsibility, and there were plenty of conspiracy theorists ready to believe them in the absence of hard information. Anyone could be sacrificed – willingly or not – to keep Pinochet's hands clean. In the autumn of 1977, DINA changed its name to the Centro Nacional de Informaciones (CNI): its brand was so toxic that even other Latin American security services did not want to be seen associating with it.[18] In November 1977, Pinochet sacked Contreras as the head of the CNI, albeit 'with considerable reluctance'.[19] In March 1978, Pinochet dismissed Contreras from the army for 'lying' to him. The 'new' CNI mendaciously promised to help the Americans investigate the Letelier assassination. They threw Townley to the wolves.

INTRODUCTION

Although the CNI handed Townley over to the FBI, they immediately launched a virulent campaign of denunciation, painting him as a rogue mercenary, who had worked for the CIA, just as much as for them.[20] It became a persistent theme of Chilean propaganda to claim that the assassins had been working for the CIA.[21]

The Chileans most spectacularly muddied the waters by linking the Letelier assassination with 'Operation Condor'. Contreras warned the CIA that they could easily be tarred with the Condor brush since they had genuinely worked so closely with the multiple Latin American intelligence services involved. He was right.[22]

In the summer of 1975, US intelligence agencies had started picking up 'rumors' about 'Operation Condor', an agreement between 'Southern Cone' states – Chile, Argentina, Uruguay and Bolivia – for 'government planned and directed assassinations within and outside the territory of Condor members'. The Ford administration immediately recognised the jeopardy, warning its representatives that 'even in those countries where we propose to expand our exchange of information, it is essential that we in no way finger individuals who might be candidates for assassination attempts'. It was an admittedly nice distinction: give intelligence to the 'good' Condor – an anti-Communist intelligence alliance – but withhold the same intelligence from 'bad' Condor – the assassination conspiracy.[23]

The US intelligence on 'Condor' as an assassination conspiracy was declared firm a few days after the Letelier assassination.[24] As a result of such exposure, Condor had largely shut up shop by the end of 1976.[25] By the time Contreras made his threat, however, investigative journalists were well on the trail of the now defunct organisation.[26] Some US agencies bluntly referred to Condor as an assassination consortium in public.[27] Nevertheless it remained a sore point: in 1979, American embassies in South America were instructed to lie about US knowledge of Condor.[28]

By the end of the 1970s, the Americans had worked out that DINA was behind the Letelier assassination and that they had used the Cubans as cat's-paws.[29] In 1978, CIA agents in the Chilean military confirmed that Pinochet had been personally responsible for the assassination.[30] The problem was proving what turned out to be, on the whole, accurate intelligence. Contreras himself twitted the CIA that, whatever they might believe, there was 'insufficient evidence against him to either extradite him or to convict him in a Chilean court'.[31]

In August 1978, the US Department of Justice laid formal charges in front of a federal court, stating that DINA was the agency responsible for the murder of Orlando Letelier. In Justice's precise legal terminology, there had been an assassination conspiracy and 'members of the conspiracy would and did perform different functions and operate at different levels of responsibility. All the participants in the conspiracy were aware that the conspiracy would encompass and depend upon the combined, coordinated efforts of two organizations – DINA and the Cuban Nationalist Movement.'[32] The prosecutors had little difficulty proving their case to a US court – Townley had confessed in return for a plea bargain: they had, they concluded, no chance of making it stick in Chile while Pinochet was in power.[33] It was only after the fall of Pinochet that the Chilean government itself brought Contreras to book. He was convicted of the murder of Letelier in 1993: he served time in prison until his release in 2001. He was subsequently rearrested and convicted of crimes committed in Chile: Contreras died in prison in 2015.[34] Pinochet was never charged for the killing of Oscar Letelier. It was Operation Condor, where American collusion had once seemed to be a shield, that revealed him in his true colours in a court of law as a multiple procurer of international assassination.[35]

The study of assassination is akin to running a razor blade down the history of international politics: the cut is narrow, but long and deep. Assassination reveals statesmen and their servants at their most authentically vulnerable moments – they are, after all, often the people with the most to lose. Assassination: personal, violent, widely reported, strips back layers of self-deception like few other acts. At the same time, it reveals the 'hinterland of political argument where deliberately treacherous ambiguities of quasi-appropriation, quasi-repudiation and subtle evasion took a central place in political culture'.[36] Assassination makes states answer uncomfortable questions about violence, appeasement, collaboration and persuasion. In other words, the actual exercise of power in international politics.

INTRODUCTION

Death to Order focuses on the impact of assassination on international politics since 1914. It thus has two major themes: the use of assassination as a political instrument and the reaction of states to assassination. Assassination over the past one hundred and ten years has been fundamentally a phenomenon related to states. That is not to say that states were always behind assassination – although they sometimes were, as in the case of Letelier – but rather that the reaction of states, and particularly great powers, to assassination has given modern political murder its potent charge.

It fell mainly to officials of the state to work out the nature of assassination conspiracies within a politically relevant timeframe. By its very nature, conspiracy has as its essential element relatively small groups working in secret to commission an act that is usually illegal and almost certainly illicit. The definition of the conspiracy was central to the response to assassination. In framing the scope of the conspiracies affecting them, politicians, civil servants, policemen and intelligence officers worked repeatedly with imperfect information. The nature of any conspiracy was rarely self-defining: 'Greek or Arab?' Henry Kissinger demanded upon hearing of the 1975 assassination of Richard Welch, the CIA's chief of station in Athens, for instance.[37] Policymakers often had a genuine choice about how widely to define the groups involved in an assassination, ranging from dismissing a murder as little more than 'the work of a lone nutter' or a 'crazy loner', in the idiolect of British diplomats, to seeing it as emblematic of an enemy within or without.[38] The definition of the conspiracy, in turn, calibrated the activity that might flow from an assassination. Those shaping assassination response might, for instance, choose to cage 'the monkeys but let the organ-grinders go free'.[39] They might also start a war.

Beyond a concentration on the leaders of great powers making consequential decisions, *Death to Order* tackles the task of charting how assassination has affected the organisation and political culture of such states. Pinning down the impact of assassination has hitherto proved especially elusive for the study of democratic states. The age of assassination that began in 1914 also marked the start of the great but violently contested age of liberal democracy. Studying the burden of assassination for political systems high in capability – sophisticated, stable, rich democracies – is not without its challenges. The changes wrought on democratic states by assassination have rarely been spectacular, unlike in some fragile or failing states. Assassination has nevertheless been the moment when the citizens of capable states glimpsed either the precariousness of their supposedly high-functioning systems or the resilience of those systems. Merely because the changes assassination wrought in democracies were subtle does not mean they were unimportant: just because theorising has taken place based on limited empirical evidence does not mean that such evidence is not recoverable, and goes far beyond mere public commentary.

Nevertheless, one must always acknowledge that available evidence on assassination is both complex and fractured and needs to be unravelled with care. As might be expected, archives related to assassination have often received particularly rigorous scrubbing during any declassification process. Lost, destroyed, retained, weeded and redacted files litter the historical record. Some officials might be 'reluctant' to suppress material that 'someone, somewhere, will doubtless find of great interest' but they do so, albeit with 'regrets'.[40] Some countries, most notably the USA and India, have developed a habit of inquiry into assassination. The twinned investigation of the assassinations of President John F. Kennedy in 1963 and Martin Luther King in 1968, for example, was the most expensive Congressional inquiry of the twentieth century.[41] The Congressionally mandated publication of all JFK assassination-related documents by the US National Archives is a cornucopia. However, it has taken a quarter of a century. The assassination itself took place six decades ago.[42]

What has reached the public domain in most cases is incomplete and fragmented. This situation has significant consequences for how historical investigation can proceed. There are limits to how far it can go as a step-by-step history of decision-making. First, decisions are often made 'off stage'. The general direction of travel and the reverberations of decisions may be observable, but the moment of decision itself is often cloaked. Second, it is not always possible to identify specific actors within a state bureaucracy. Third, the agencies releasing records do not necessarily represent the importance of those agencies in policy-making. Officials in foreign ministries, for instance, collected a great deal of material on assassination, even when they were not the primary drivers of events. Fourth, the records for any given assassination case are rarely complete. Most of the case histories contain dry wells.

However, it is the aggregate of cases that yield the important trends. There are many hundreds of thousands of pages of government records on assassination available in the archives. Histories of *an* assassination are necessarily concerned with the specificities of the event and its time, rather than the phenomenon of assassination per se. What the archives reveal most clearly are the standard operating procedures and modes of thought – sometimes clearly stated, but often merely implied – through which states functioned.

Death to Order attempts to filter out some of the 'noise' that surrounds assassination. Assassination itself has been (and is) a notoriously slippery term. In the Anglophone tradition, assassination is normally used as the word for political murder. The classic American political-science definition of assassination is 'the deliberate, extra-legal killing of an individual for political purposes'.[43] In the Francophone tradition, by contrast, assassination is the word for premeditated murder, not necessarily political, with, until the mid-1990s, a particular stress on the use of an ambush, including emotional ambushes, lures and false friendship. 'Political assassination' is a tautology in the English tradition (or means something that has nothing to do with murder) but a necessary descriptor in the French. The two traditions have often been elided. In the twentieth century, international lawyers tried to pick their way through such elision, but their frequently strained definitions of assassination achieved little clarity. The lawyers themselves recognised the futility of their efforts. By the later twentieth century, they were excising the term assassination from many treaties.[44] Instead, some great powers had the state's own employees define assassination and claimed that their national definition was applicable outside state boundaries. In 2010, lawyers of the US Department of Justice declared that when state authorities carried out a deliberate extra-judicial killing of a specific named individual as a matter of raison d'état, that was not an assassination because 'killings in self-defense are not assassinations'.[45] Thankfully, the historian does not have to accept the American admonition, that even using the word assassination is a 'conclusion masquerading as narrative'.[46] Edge cases are often highly revealing.

There are other significant generators of noise that need tuning down, too. The development of assassination over time has often been obscured by an intense fascination with assassins and their motivations. Assassins are, necessarily and usually, the starting point for investigators trying to trace the threads of a conspiracy. They become much less significant once the conspiracy has been unravelled. Nevertheless, in the west, assassins – at least in fictional form – have become a staple of popular entertainment: think of James Bond or Jason Bourne and their imitators. In former imperial possessions, and in the hands of post-colonial writers, on the other hand, some assassins have been hailed as the heroes who exposed the sham of western liberal democracy, revealing the coercive viciousness that was its true nature. Indeed, the fact that for much of the twentieth century many of the most powerful, constitutional, strongly rooted and stable nation-states were at the same time authoritarian empires remains one of the most potent factors in shaping how assassins have been remembered. Governments of now independent states such as India, Ireland and Israel repatriated the bodies of fallen killers, awarded pensions to the surviving murderers and built monuments to commemorate their deadly acts.[47]

Some commemorations of assassins simply lose touch with the reality of historical events. The Serbian playwright Biljana Srbljanović, for instance, admitting that she was 'not very much into history and utterly not interested in World War I', wrote a play about the Sarajevo assassins of June 1914 because 'I suddenly fell in love with . . . Princip and the guys'.[48]

Sadly, few societies, whether subject to external domination or not, have struggled to find assassins: fanatics, mercenaries, conscripts, the mentally disturbed or some combination thereof. Even the isolated Himalayan kingdom of Bhutan produced assassins in the 1960s.[49]

Equally, the history of assassination told through its victims has pitfalls. Victimology is another important tool for criminal investigators. It is also important for political science. To quantify assassination, political scientists have tightly defined its scope, usually by means of the political office held by the victim. Historically, however, such hierarchies of assassination rarely matched those subsequently assigned to them. 'Any fool,' a witness in a 1917 British inquiry observed, 'can shoot a Viceroy

INTRODUCTION

or a police inspector.'[50] In many environments the effective police officer was much harder to replace than the politician. In some circumstances, the lowest of the low, the police informer, was more significant still. The British authorities in 1920s India were painfully aware of how reliant they were on a relatively small number of police agent-runners, mainly Indian. Forty years later the British position in Aden nearly failed when the 'systematic assassination of members of the Arab Section of the Special Branch' destroyed its intelligence system.[51] As a French expert on counter-revolutionary warfare wrote in the 1950s, 'the murders of a general, a *caïd*, a *bachaga* or a prefect, would not affect the population whereas the assassination of a park warden concerns them enormously.'[52]

In addition, the study of victims can sometimes topple over into victim blaming.[53] Certainly, assassins killed some evil people. Candidate One is probably Reinhard Heydrich, the architect of the Holocaust. Often, however, victims were killed for simply doing their job.

Finally, the fate of victims is all too often a tempting lure for the counter-factualist. What if German officers had succeeded in killing Hitler in July 1944? They didn't, so no-one knows. American officials described Helmut Kohl, Chancellor of West Germany, as indulging in little more than 'wishful thinking' when he gave speeches in the 1980s about what would have happened if the officers had succeeded.[54] What if Gavrilo Princip's shot had not killed Franz Ferdinand in June 1914? It did, so no-one knows. Assassinations have observable effects: an historian's time is more fruitfully spent on those effects rather than fantastical non-happenings. *Death to Order* is a history of the observable effects of assassination in the modern age.

1

MURDER AS AN INSTRUMENT OF POLICY
The Sarajevo Assassination, 1914–1930

'Assassination,' the Victorian statesman Benjamin Disraeli remarked, 'has never changed the history of the World.'[1] Before 1914, assassination was the preserve of disgruntled individuals, plotters in royal courts, or small groups of fanatics pursuing lost causes. Even those who approved of Anarchist assassination admitted that most state officials regarded an assassin of this type as little more than a 'brute, resembling a hyena rather than a man . . . an odious malefactor, impelled by hatred and passion for notoriety'.[2] The western powers noticed assassination in the Balkans, but paid it little heed: it was considered something to be expected in a region recently ruled by the Ottoman empire. After Sarajevo, statesmen could never again afford to be quite so confident. The catastrophic consequences of the assassination of Archduke Franz Ferdinand made 1914 the starting point for a new age of assassination. It was impossible for pre-war politicians and officials still operating in the post-Great War world to escape the shadow of Sarajevo.[3]

Within days of the archduke's death the great powers established how the assassination had been carried out and by whom. Members of the assassination squad were captured alive in the immediate aftermath of the murder. Four years later, and after the minimum of a further eleven million deaths, the impact of the assassination was also clear: the

MURDER AS AN INSTRUMENT OF POLICY

collapse of four great empires, the Austro-Hungarian, the German, the Russian and the Ottoman.

It is useful to disaggregate the story of the assassination of the archduke and its aftermath into two parts: what participants in the events of June and July 1914 knew and how they acted on their information; and what statesmen in the years after 1914 came to understand about Sarajevo, and how it shaped their view of assassination. States and individuals tried to cover up the assassination conspiracy and other individuals, sometimes in cahoots with a state, sometimes working disinterestedly, unearthed enough material to create a tolerably accurate narrative by the early 1930s. Thus, not only was Sarajevo the most important assassination of them all, it was also the archetype for how the understanding of an assassination could enter the public domain.

Some assassinations were meticulously investigated by competent authorities. The murder of Franz Ferdinand was not one of those assassinations. Nearly everything the Habsburg regime turned its hand to in 1914 and subsequently was slovenly. The fate of the pistol that fired the fatal shots – a Browning Model 1910 – was indicative of the random nature of the preservation of evidence. The pistol was taken by the priest who gave the archduke the last rites. Under a nom de plume – Pharos – he was one of the prime rumourmongers of the early 1920s.[4] The Serbian government investigation was corrupt from day one. Historians thus have a relatively fragile yardstick by which to measure the factual content of the ex post facto accounts. This is even though most of the assassins stood trial.

The basic facts of the assassination, however, are clear enough. A seven-man assassination squad killed Franz Ferdinand and his wife on the morning of 28 June 1914 in Sarajevo. At about ten in the morning the archduke left the Habsburg military garrison outside the town and was driven towards Sarajevo town hall. This was a planned and publicised journey. The assassins were standing along the route in town, most of them to the south of the roadway. When the car passed, the first assassin, Muhamed Mehmedbašić, failed to act. The second assassin, Nedeljko Čabrinović, stationed opposite Mehmedbašić, on the north side of the road, threw a bomb at the archduke's car. The bomb clipped the rear of the car, fell onto the road and exploded, injuring an Austrian officer and several passers-by. The assassin then jumped into the river Miljacka in a failed attempt to escape. The archduke's driver accelerated along the road, effectively taking the remaining five assassins out of play, since they were prepared for a slow roll-by.

One of the assassins, Gavrilo Princip, crossed the road to the north side. The archduke's party regrouped in the town hall, where they stayed for over an hour. They decided to cut short the planned tour of Sarajevo and instead to drive back to the garrison along the same road by which they had entered town. In the only additional security measure, one of the archduke's aides stood on the car's running board to shield him. As the archduke's car returned along the road it stopped, due to some confusion about the agreed route. Princip fired two rounds. He hit the archduke in the neck and his wife in the stomach. Neither died instantaneously but both wounds rapidly proved fatal.

The two assassins who had carried out the actual attack, the shooter Princip and the bomb-thrower Čabrinović, were captured almost immediately after their attacks. Four of the remaining five assassins were also caught. The one assassin who escaped was Mehmedbašić, whose failure to attack gave him a head start. None of the assassins denied their guilt when questioned. All were quite clear that they had killed Archduke Franz Ferdinand to strike a blow against the Habsburg annexation of Bosnia, wishing Bosnia to be joined with Serbia. The oldest of the assassins, a schoolmaster, proved the most talkative. He revealed that the assassins had come from Belgrade. Their weapons had been supplied by two officials of the Serbian government, Miko Ciganović, who worked for the state railway company, and Vojislav Tankosić, a major in the Royal Serbian Army. Tankosić was a man of some celebrity in Serb *komitadji* – freedom fighter – circles, having been a notable leader of these irregular forces in the recent Balkan war. Tankosić procured the weapons; Ciganović handed them over to the assassins. Friendly Serb frontier officers helped the assassins over the Serb–Bosnian border at the end of May 1914.

It was clear that the radicalised Bosnian men *wanted* to kill Franz Ferdinand. They were not pressganged. Equally clearly, there had been a terrorist infrastructure supporting them. If one wanted to kill an Austrian, it was not hard to find someone who would help you in

Belgrade. This terrorist infrastructure included Serbian military intelligence, the *komitadji* and a secret society.

Tankosić and Ciganović were both members of a Serbian secret society known as the Black Hand, formed in 1911. The friendly frontier officers were members of Serbian military intelligence and many of them were also members of the Black Hand. The head of Serbian military intelligence was the effective leader of the Black Hand in Belgrade. One of the main roles of these Serb military intelligence officers was liaison with anti-Habsburg revolutionary groups in Bosnia. They arranged weapons training for Bosnian radicals, including pistol shooting. Tankosić brought the plan for this specific assassination attempt in Sarajevo to the head of military intelligence, his Black Hand superior, Colonel Dragutin Dimitrijević, usually known by his nickname, Apis, 'The Bull'. The Bull approved the plan and told Tankosić to supply the plotters with the weapons that they needed, a feature of the plot that Tankosić confirmed to the Serb government when he was arrested in July 1914.

The Serbian government was aware of the activities of the Black Hand, its own military intelligence apparatus, the *komitadji* and the wider terrorist network. Serbia was deeply factional, and the factions watched each other like hawks. Although there was general agreement about aspirations for Greater Serbia, a much bigger state that would supplant the Habsburg empire in the Balkans, this was matched by ruthless struggles for power within the existing state. The two main power centres of Serbia – the Radical government, led by Nikola Pašić, and the Royal Family, both King Peter and his son, Crown Prince Alexander – had deliberately incubated the terroristic, although to some extent deniable, infrastructure. There is no evidence that either Pašić or Crown Prince Alexander ordered this specific assassination, although demonstrably neither was averse to terrorism as a general principle.

As a result of factional rivalries, border officers, hostile to those who had helped the assassins, reported that bombs had been smuggled across the frontier a few days after the squad crossed. The interior minister issued an order that border officers should halt weapons smuggling. The minister of war immediately questioned his military intelligence chief, Apis, about what was going on. Apis submitted a formal report confirming the border activity but claimed that the weapons smuggling had been a cover for couriers servicing military intelligence's subversive network in Bosnia. The minister was not convinced. That was how matters stood when the assassination took place.[5]

The assassination at Sarajevo became the new archetype for assassination because of the way in which the affected state defined the conspiracy. It was not as if the Habsburgs were unused to dealing with assassinations. In 1898, the emperor's wife had been assassinated by an Anarchist in Geneva. In 1906, Franz Ferdinand had been present during an Anarchist assassination attempt on the king of Spain. In Sarajevo itself, the Governor-General of Bosnia, Marijan Varešanin, had survived an assassination attempt in June 1910. The young assassin had shot himself to cover up any wider conspiracy. His suicide was 'greatly admired by the whole revolutionary party [in Belgrade] as he then destroyed all possibility of the origin of the crime being traced'.[6] In 1912, a Croatian nationalist MP tried to assassinate the prime minister of Hungary, Count Tisza, in the Hungarian parliament building.[7] In June 1912, two days after the Tisza shooting, the Ban (governor) of Croatia was subject to a further assassination attempt: the Bosnian assassin missed the Ban but killed his secretary, who was sitting next to him in a car. All of these attempts had been dealt with calmly.[8]

The response to the Sarajevo assassination was not calm. On the afternoon of 28 June 1914, the Imperial and Royal Government of Austria-Hungary, orchestrated by the emperor's chief and foreign minister, Leopold, Count Berchtold, had three plausible theses about the assassination conspiracy before it. The assassination was plainly the work of a conspiracy since there had been two attacks on Franz Ferdinand and the bomber and the shooter were already in custody.

The *Mlada Bosna* – Young Bosnia – thesis was that a gang of Bosnian Serb fanatics had assassinated the archduke on their own cognisance. The *Narodna Odbrana* – People's Defence – thesis was that the assassination had been sponsored by a Belgrade-based Great Serb propaganda organisation formed in 1908. The third – Serb State – thesis was that Franz Ferdinand's killing had been a state-sponsored assassination involving both prime minister Pašić and Prince Regent Alexander.

A fourth thesis – that the heir to the imperial throne had been murdered by his Austrian enemies in a court conspiracy – could be dismissed because the Austro-Hungarian decision-makers knew they were not guilty. A fifth – Black Hand – thesis was not considered by the Austrians because, due to the weakness of imperial intelligence, they did not know about the Black Hand. The Serbian government knew the Black Hand was responsible for the assassination as, probably, did the Russian government, but neither the Austrians nor any of the other great powers could take the Black Hand into account.[9]

There are more than enough contemporary documents to allow a reconstruction of how the imperial government weighed up those theses. There are also plentiful sources showing how other powers assessed the imperial process. None of this meant that the Austro-Hungarian imperialists approached their assessment of the assassination conspiracy in an open-minded fashion.[10]

At the time of the assassination, Berchtold already had on his desk a memorandum, written by one of his officials, outlining the campaign waged by the Serbians and their proxies to undermine the empire and recommending violent action against Serbia. That seemingly prophetic document was to serve as the basis for all future imperial analyses. Berchtold returned to it on 28 June and started adapting the wording, incorporating the assassination of the archduke, with a view to sharing the plan with Vienna's allies in Berlin.[11] As Berchtold worked, he was lacking hard information, as opposed to strident advice. The military governor of Bosnia-Herzegovina, Oskar Potiorek, the man who had made such a mess of the archduke's security, offered rhetoric rather than analysis. 'Firm action in the domain of foreign policy,' Potiorek warned, was desperately necessary to 'restore peace and normality to Bosnia Herzegovina.' In Vienna, the chief of the imperial general staff, Conrad von Hötzendorf, was frothing with Wagnerian frenzy. 'War, War, War,' he wrote to Berchtold the day after the assassination.[12] Hötzendorf believed in a kind of *Götterdämmerung* in which the empire would go down in glorious final battle rather than succumb to the pinpricks of dwarfs. An attack on Serbia would probably ignite a more general war, a 'sheer gamble' for the empire. But it would be worth it.[13]

The first element of what could be characterised as an attempt to analyse the available theses arrived from the imperial chargé d'affaires in Belgrade on 29 June 1914. Baron von Giesl did not have any hard information, thus he 'would not yet be so bold as to accuse the Belgrade [government] directly of the murder'. However, the empire's man on the spot continued, the government of Serbia was 'surely indirectly guilty, and the ringleaders are to be found not just among the uneducated masses, but in the Propaganda Department of the Foreign Ministry, among those Serbian university professors and newspaper editors who for years have sown hatred and now reaped murder.'[14] Von Giesl put his finger on a key problem the imperialists were going to have throughout the Sarajevo crisis: they might wish to believe that the Serbian government had been the procurer of the assassination but they would struggle to prove it to anyone else. That was one of the reasons that the People's Defence thesis became attractive to Vienna. Berchtold took these thoughts to the emperor on 30 June. They agreed that if they could gather enough evidence to link Belgrade to the assassination there should be an 'action programme' against Serbia. They had to do something spectacular.[15]

From the beginning, other powers took an interest in the theses. Just because imperial intelligence was poor did not mean that others did not have assets surprisingly close to the action. Russian military intelligence, the *Razvedka*, of course, was exceptionally close to Serbian military intelligence. The Russians also had a long track record of independently seeding the Balkans with their own agents. The Russians, however, were *parti pris* and were hardly likely to share their thoughts with others. They assured the Austro-Hungarians that they would never get to the bottom of the assassination.[16] However, even the seemingly distant British had intelligence assets on the ground in Sarajevo, with British intelligence running its operations out of the British consulate in the city. The British had been fishing in much the same talent pool for agents as everybody else, including the assassins.[17] On 29 June 1914, the British consul in Sarajevo reported that the assassination was most likely to have been carried out by 'Servian irredentists, preconcerted long ago'. He dismissed any chatter about the traditional slayers of royalty, Anarchists.[18] Looking over the reports, the British ambassador in Vienna, Sir Maurice de Bunsen, was convinced that the assassins were 'members of the terrorist Great Servian organisation' which was guilty of a 'carefully prepared plot . . . against the Archduke'.

De Bunsen conceded, however, that the imperialists had a credibility problem. In 1908 and 1909, they had put Great Serb nationalists on trial in Zagreb, claiming a 'widespread irredentist Servian plot'. It was not that the imperialists had been wrong in their suspicions, but they had shamelessly falsified evidence in the case, which had collapsed in public contumely once malpractice was revealed. The imperialists were the boy who had cried wolf. No other power could 'accept without adequate proof wholesale denunciations of the Servian patriotic societies which may now be expected to be made'.[19] Other powers reached much the same conclusion.

The imperial leader who saw the empire's credibility problem most clearly was the prime minister of Hungary, Count Tisza. Since the empire was a dual monarchy, and Tisza was the dominant political force in its eastern domains, he had an effective veto on adopting the Serb State thesis and the armed response that would flow therefrom. Tisza put the situation with what proved to be perfect accuracy. 'We have,' he told the emperor, 'as yet no sufficient evidence at our disposal to justify us holding Serbia to account and in provoking war with her . . . We would, therefore, have the worst possible *locus standi*, would be branded before the whole world as peace breakers and start a great war under the worst possible conditions.'[20]

Berchtold, however, was proceeding on the basis that the assassination itself supplied 'indubitable proof of the insurmountable differences between the Monarchy and Serbia'. As long as they could convince Germany of such a thesis, the empire would be able to settle accounts with the Serbs.[21] Nevertheless, the chief minister was willing to concede to Tisza that they needed to build a better case on responsibility before an imperial war effort could be launched. He hoped that investigators in Sarajevo would produce such evidence and sent his own personal representative to report as soon as there was something to go on. The emperor too said he wanted to see some proof of Serbian complicity – as well as rock-solid German support – before he would give permission for any military action. In public, on the occasion of Franz Ferdinand's burial, he even seemed to endorse something akin to the Young Bosnia thesis: the assassination was the 'madness of a small group of misguided persons' which could not 'loosen the sacred ties attaching him to his [Bosnian] people'.[22]

On 2 July 1914, Berchtold and Franz Joseph wrote down their case for the benefit of the Germans. 'The researches made to the present have shown that the bloody deed of Sarajevo is not the work of a single individual but the result of a well-organised plot, the threads of which reach to Belgrade, and though it may be impossible to prove the complicity of the Servian government, there can be no doubt whatever that this government's policy, intent as it is to unite all South-slavs under the Servian flag, must encourage such crimes and if it is not stopped, it will proved a lasting danger to my house and my countries.' Again, there was the rhetorical elision: they had no proof that the Serbs had assassinated Franz Ferdinand, merely the fact that their whole foreign policy pointed to such a conclusion.[23]

Luckily, in the short term, the Germans were happy to overlook the lack of specific evidence. Berchtold's representative, Count Hoyos, was on the rails to Berlin even as the obsequies for Franz Ferdinand were taking place in Austria – the Kaiser having declined to attend the funeral on the grounds that he might be assassinated. Hoyos commented that, 'through his death, he [the archduke] has helped us to the decision, which he would never have taken, as long as he lived'.[24] The next day Hoyos was able to report that his reception was all he could have wanted. The Kaiser had declared that 'if we had really recognised the necessity of warlike action against Serbia, he would regret it if we did not make use of the present moment, which is all in our favour'. The Austrian ambassador in Berlin was able to report the next day that the German chancellor, Theobald von Bethmann-Hollweg, was fully of a mind with his royal master. It was these two messages that constituted what later became known as the 'blank cheque'. It was immediately clear to foreign diplomats in Vienna that the Austrians had their blood up.[25]

On 7 July 1914, with the German assurances in hand, Berchtold and the emperor agreed that there would be strong action against Serbia. Berchtold summoned the common ministerial council later in the day and put it to them 'whether the moment has not come when a show of force might put an end to Serbia's intrigues once and for all?' Tisza replied, 'no'. Perhaps, Tisza conceded, the interrogation of the assassins in Sarajevo was yielding firmer information. They had two usable pieces of information that had not been available in the immediate aftermath of the assassination. First, the assassins' bombs could be traced back to the Serbian state arsenal at Kragujevac. Second, the plotters had been helped across the Serb–Bosnian border by Serb officials who had provided them with fake passports.[26]

But, Tisza observed, they were no further forward in convincing anyone who was not already committed to the anti-Serb cause. The glee with which the Serbs were plainly celebrating the assassination grated on him as much as anyone else. On the other hand, it was not as if anyone in Hungary cared about Franz Ferdinand's death. They just disliked Serbs.[27] His colleagues were living in cloud cuckoo land if they believed that war would solve much. There were no circumstances in which the empire would be allowed to obliterate Serbia, the implied goal of his colleagues, albeit wrapped in more diplomatic language. Even if it was militarily possible to take over Serbia, Tisza argued, the other powers would not allow it. In the best-case scenario, Serbia would be temporarily cowed and the empire could achieve some minor territorial gains along the border. The risks to be run for that mess of pottage were enormous.[28]

Tisza's observations on the weakness of the Serb State thesis were amply confirmed by Berchtold's own man in Sarajevo. On 13 July 1914, he reported that the Sarajevo investigators had been unable to confirm the Serb State thesis. 'There is nothing to prove or even to suppose that the Servian government is accessory to the inducement for the crime, its preparation or the furnishing of weapons,' Friedrich von Wiesner telegraphed. 'On the contrary, there are reasons to believe that this is altogether out of the question.' Unfortunately, the bomb evidence was less useful than it had at first seemed: there was nothing to prove that the weapons had come directly from the Serbian state for the purpose of this assassination. Similar explosives had been widely issued to irregular fighters (*komitadji*) during the Balkan wars. They could have come from any number of sources. Wiesner doubted that the imperial government could even prove the People's Defence thesis. The investigators had assembled a lot of information on *Narodna Odbrana* but nothing that obviously linked it to the assassination. Perhaps a careful sifting of that information might turn up something more sinister, but that would take a long time to carry out. The most telling piece of information, in Wiesner's view, was that the assassins had received direct aid from Tankosić and Ciganović. These two men had 'jointly provided bombs, Brownings, ammunition and prussic acid'. With this last point Wiesner was, of course, getting near the nub of the matter. Tankosić and Ciganović were the keys to the Black Hand conspiracy. But because neither the investigators in Sarajevo nor anyone in Vienna knew about the Black Hand, no-one could make the link.[29]

The facts of the case, as known to the Austrian authorities, and widely understood by the other powers, were, however, no longer relevant. The decision had already been made for war. In the face of anger from his fellow ministers, the military high command, the emperor and the empire's German allies, Tisza withdrew his objections. There was no point being correct if one could not convince anyone else of one's argument. On 15 July 1914, Tisza went before the Hungarian parliament to argue that, although there was no existential threat to the empire, 'the revolutionary societies and the schools were the field of a dangerous agitation, which must be resolutely put down'. In that sense, the assassination of Franz Ferdinand was over on 14 July 1914. It no longer really mattered who had assassinated him, why or how. There was now a great power crisis predicated on military mobilisation and the looming imperial invasion of Serbia. The British Foreign Secretary, Sir Edward Grey, wrote that he really couldn't care less about the details of the assassination – this was now all about the 'peace of Europe'.[30]

The assassination persisted, however, in a half-life of political propaganda. The imperialists accepted Tisza's advice that they still needed to make the best possible case about Serbia's guilt.[31] Austrian diplomats attempted to win over the press in western capitals to the justice of the imperial cause in the face of deadly provocation.[32] The Serbians themselves showed some discomfort in the face of the Austrian campaign. The Serbian government arrested Major Tankosić on the grounds that he was part of a plot to discredit Prime Minister Pašić and his Radical Party. Miko Ciganović mysteriously disappeared from Belgrade when his identity as a conspirator began to be bruited in the press.[33]

The imperialists completed their final statement on the matter on 20 July 1914. In the end they went with the People's Defence thesis, leavened with a strong dose of Serb State complicity. Serbia had 'allowed officers and officials to take part in subversive plans . . . the depositions and confessions of the criminal perpetrators of the plot of 28th June prove, that the murder of Sarajevo was prepared in Belgrade, that the murderers had received weapons and bombs, with which they were armed, from officers and officials belonging to the *Narodna Odbrana* and that the conveyance of criminals and weapons to Bosnia had been prepared and carried through by Servian frontier organs.'[34] However, in the end, the imperialists admitted that 28 June 1914 was not the key date in their case. Rather, the important date was 31 March 1909, when Serbia had consciously set out to subvert the empire. The assassination was merely the inevitable end of that course. Surely, everyone could understand 'the love of plotting, which is peculiar to Servian politicians, and whose bloody results can be traced in the annals of Servian history'.[35] Austria's statements, commented one of Grey's senior officials, Sir Eyre Crowe, 'concerning Servia's misdeeds rest for the present on no evidence that is available for the Powers whom the Austrian Government has invited to accept those statements'.[36] Thus unconvinced about the assassination, Europe entered a major conflict when Austria declared war on Serbia on 28 July 1914. The trial of Archduke Franz Ferdinand's assassins eventually opened in Sarajevo, to very little interest, on 12 October 1914.[37]

In a broad sense, no-one seriously doubted that the pistol shot at Sarajevo was significant. 'What effects that pistol shot has had and will have!', wrote Britain's future official historian of the origins of the War in 1914.[38] Stefan Zweig's literary simile remains the most poignant: 'in a single second', he wrote in 1942, the dependable world was 'smashed into a thousand pieces like a hollow clay vessel'.[39] Belief in the measurable political significance of Sarajevo, however, was out of fashion for more years than it was in during the century after the assassination. Stress on the pivotal importance of the Sarajevo assassination only came back into vogue with the centenary commemorations of the outbreak of the First World War in 2014.[40] Nevertheless, despite all the conspiracy theories of the post-1914 decade, by the 1930s western politicians and journalists had a shrewd idea of what had happened. The post-Great War investigation into the Sarajevo assassination proceeded most thoroughly in Berlin – led by men who were far from disinterested – and London, where there was at least a sliver of genuine curiosity about the death of Franz Ferdinand.[41] The most assiduous of the London investigators was the British folklorist and Balkan traveller Edith Durham, although she herself feared she was nothing but a 'Cassandra'.[42]

The eventual unwinding of the Sarajevo assassination conspiracy shaped the shared imaginative space of world statesmen. That imaginative space took about fifteen years to properly form.[43] In the decade after Sarajevo, few probed too deeply into the assassination. In 1923, when Winston Churchill wrote *The World Crisis*, he thought the details of Sarajevo so unimportant that he devoted one line to the assassination, getting both the name of the victim and the method of killing wrong.[44] Historians were legitimately sceptical of how much politicians knew about history.[45] Before the digging started in earnest, there was a darkness surrounding Sarajevo; the assassination was the spark, but any spark would have done.[46]

It needed something compelling to catch anyone's attention and, in many ways, in trying to conceal their own actions and glorify the achievement of the Great Serb dream, Yugoslavia, it was the Serb government itself that offered up interesting information. In 1918 the Serbs needed to say very little about Sarajevo.[47] Even before the powers met at Versailles, they had told the Germans that there would be no investigation of the assassination of Franz Ferdinand. 'All documents' 'incontestably' established German guilt for the outbreak of the War.[48] Once the leaders of the victorious powers arrived in Versailles they did appoint an expert Commission on Responsibility: Serbia had a representative on the commission but he sat almost mute throughout its proceedings – the great power representatives did all the work for him. The one piece of evidence on Sarajevo that the commission cited was the emperor's public statement following the burial of his heir, which could be, and was, taken as an endorsement of the Young Bosnia thesis. The final text of the commission's report read: 'On the 28th June, 1914, occurred the assassination at Sarajevo of the heir apparent of Austria. "It is the act of a little group of madmen," said Francis Joseph. The act, committed as it was by a subject of Austria-Hungary on Austro-

Hungarian territory, could in no way compromise Serbia, which very correctly expressed its condolences and stopped public rejoicings in Belgrade. If the Government of Vienna thought there was any Serbian complicity, Serbia was ready to seek out the guilty parties. But this attitude failed to satisfy Austria and still less Germany, who, after their first astonishment had passed, saw in this royal and national misfortune a pretext to initiate war.'[49]

The Serbs did not say much at Versailles, but they had prepared the ground thoroughly beforehand. They had a network of fellow-travellers and propagandists in Allied countries devoted to the Great Serb ideal.[50] The most effective Serb propagandist in the English-speaking world was a Scot, Robert Seton-Watson. Seton-Watson was the kind of self-financed intellectual who thought it a fine thing to fall in love with a country other than one's own and make its cause, in this case a Great Serb Yugoslavia, yours. Seton-Watson, and his ilk, were – in a phrase coined in the 1920s – 'organic intellectuals'. The organic intellectual's goal was to shape the future rather than to analyse the past. Not that Seton-Watson, who became a highly significant figure in shaping the memory of Sarajevo, saw it like that, of course.[51] His admirers portrayed him as the cynosure of the disinterested historical method.[52] He was the leading inter-war exponent of the Young Bosnia thesis.[53] He was the Serbs' useful idiot.[54]

The Serbs had also taken even more direct action to cover their tracks. In June 1917, the Serbian government-in-exile executed those – Colonel Apis and his main intelligence operative in pre-war Austria-Hungary, Rade Malobabić – who knew all about the Sarajevo assassination.[55] The 'first assassin' at Sarajevo, Muhamed Mehmedbašić, was forced to turn state's evidence to save his own life, and was subsequently immured in silence.[56] Technically, the Serb government, still led by Pašić as prime minister and Alexander as Prince Regent, executed Apis and Malobabić as assassins. However, the assassination was an attempt on Prince Alexander in August 1916 rather than the actual assassination of Archduke Franz Ferdinand in June 1914. Supposedly, Apis had ordered the assassination and Malobabić and Mehmedbašić had tried to shoot Alexander in his car. They were clearly capable of such an act, but Apis didn't order the hit and Malobabić and Mehmedbašić didn't fire the shots: the charges were made up.⁵⁷ Really at issue was a vicious power struggle within the Serbian government-in-exile on Corfu. Seton-Watson liked to claim that he and Allied intelligence authorities made some attempt to save Apis and Malobabić but this was not really the case.⁵⁸ Through both official and secret channels, some former British officials appealed to Prince Alexander to issue a royal pardon, but in the main, no-one cared much about an internal Serb dogfight.⁵⁹

The dogfight did, however, leave behind one scrap. The prosecutors and judges – in a rigged military court – were determined to prevent Apis from airing any information about Sarajevo in his defence. In an attempt to save the lives of Malobabić and Mehmedbašić, Apis agreed to say nothing in return for being allowed to write an account of Sarajevo for the archives. Apis's 'confession' was buried deep in those archives after his death and did not emerge for decades, but there were enough rumours about its existence to pique the interest of investigators.⁶⁰

The most ardent observers of the Serbian internal conflict were to be found in the *Wilhelmstrasse*, the German foreign office. German officials and politicians were just as involved in dirty tricks as the Serbs. From the beginning they had a coherent programme of subverting the Versailles accusations, not paying any reparations and secretly rearming. Sarajevo was merely part of German propaganda. However, when it came to the assassination, they had plenty of genuine material to lace in with their lies. In 1919 the *Wilhelmstrasse* created its own 'war guilt' section – the *Kriegsschuldreferat* – to co-ordinate overt and covert propaganda.⁶¹ The section had three agencies: one was charged with publishing a – carefully selected and shaped – edition of German diplomatic documents; the second – the Centre for the Study of the Causes of War – with seducing foreign academics to tell the story the Germans wanted told; and the third to co-ordinate the patriotic associations, who were all too passionate about funding and proclaiming German innocence but needed to be corralled to do so without sounding like the swivel-eyed loons they were.⁶²

In 1921 the Chancellor of Germany, Joseph Wirth, a Catholic politician who was by then a reluctant expert on the realities of assassination, gave his direct encouragement to the *Kriegsschuldreferat*'s semi-subterranean activities. His government was happy with how the campaign was going: 'discussions between German and foreign personalities is to be encouraged in every way'. British intellectuals, he added, seemed particularly useful targets.[63] The Americans – who received similar attention – were crawling over the origins of the Great War, too, but the British seemed peculiarly fascinated by the mechanics of the assassination conspiracy itself.[64]

The Germans judged that their campaign had come to fruition in 1927, when the president of the republic publicly disclaimed German responsibility for starting the Great War. As the Chief Historian of the Foreign Office, Seton-Watson's friend and former boss James Headlam-Morley, conceded, if one squinted, the Germans did have a point.[65] Knowing about Apis, the Black Hand and the Serbian government did 'explain a good deal'.[66] Britain's official historians started using the Black Hand material in their work.[67] They had come round to the view that that 'history cannot be written entirely on the basis of diplomatic documents'. It had to consider emotions. Assassinations tended to generate intense emotion.[68]

The inevitable response of Serb apologists to assassination investigators was that they were creatures of the Germans.[69] The *Kriegschuldreferat*'s second agency certainly attempted to encourage Edith Durham. Her primary motivations, however, were a loathing of the Serbs and a dislike of lies. She was also not without supporters within the British elite. She was encouraged to write about the assassination by two retired British diplomats, Sir Maurice de Bunsen and Sir John de Salis, the Foreign Office's representative to Montenegro before and during the war.[70] De Bunsen and de Salis knew that the official line taken by their former colleagues on the assassination was hogwash. As de Bunsen commented, 'the Serbs themselves, it seems, glory in the deed which precipitated the war. I have always thought the Austrians fully justified in their determination to resist.'[71] De Salis and Durham had first compared notes on the assassination as early as 1916; 'he was full of indignation with the Serbs and I told him how certain I was that the Serb Govt was guilty of the Serajevo [sic] murders,' Durham recorded.[72] These gentry were too squeamish of their own reputations and perquisites to criticise their contemporaries in officialdom in public but they were delighted to egg on Edith Durham to do it for them.[73]

Ramsay MacDonald, the leader of the Labour Party, and in 1924 prime and foreign minister, was also one of Durham's fans. MacDonald ordered the Foreign Office to investigate their own archives on the assassination, particularly Serbian guilt.[74] At the end of 1924 the new Foreign Secretary, Austen Chamberlain, commissioned two official historians, Harold Temperley and George Gooch, to do just that.[75] However, Temperley did not think the assassination was anything to get worked up about; Gooch admitted he had spent the summer of 1914 having a 'nervous breakdown', and didn't remember much about it.[76] Behind the scenes, they collaborated with Seton-Watson.[77]

These shadow manoeuvres might have mattered relatively little if the Yugoslavs had not revealed further information. For obvious reasons, the tendency of most commentators was to see the assassination at Sarajevo as special and unique: it certainly was in its consequences. However, it became increasingly clear in the 1920s and early 1930s that assassination was merely business as usual in Yugoslavia. The disappearance of Habsburg imperialism – supposedly the underlying cause of political violence – had made very little difference. The Salonika assassination attempt of August 1916 may have been a sham, but it was telling that no-one observing the Serbs thought it was implausible. In 1921 Bosnian Communists assassinated the former Radical interior minister Milorad Drašković.[78] A few months later, Yugoslav security exposed a conspiracy to assassinate now King Alexander of Yugoslavia at his own wedding. In this case, the would-be procurers of the assassination were exiled Croatian nationalists who hated Great Serb-Yugoslavia. In both cases, Alexander took the opportunity to consolidate royal power. Most spectacularly of all, in June 1928 a Serb assassin shot and killed the charismatic leader of parliamentary Croat nationalism, Stjepan Radić, in the Belgrade parliament building itself. It was the crisis following this assassination that allowed King Alexander to suspend parliament, ban political parties and abolish the Constitution, all under powers granted to him after the Drašković assassination.[79] Those interested in Serb government complicity in the Sarajevo assassination certainly pointed out that the Serb MP who shot and killed Radić was a former operative of the now late Serb Radical leader Pašić.[80] The *Manchester Guardian* commented that the old conspirators for 'Greater Serbia' were alive, well and still killing.[81]

Although assassination in Serbia, often cross-communal, was the background, the unveiling of evidence on the assassination in Sarajevo was largely the product of intra-Serb hatreds. The old supporters of the Black Hand version of the Great Serb dream retreated into exile in places such as Vienna and Paris. Serbs in exile with information to sell could expect a call from the *Kriegsschuldreferat*. The most notable taker was Miloš Bogićević, who had been the Serb Minister in Berlin in 1914. The Yugoslav government tried to head off that trouble by getting a well-disposed historian to publish an account in German, debunking the old *Narodna Odbrana* thesis, trumpeting the new Black Hand thesis, but vigorously denying the Serb State thesis.[82]

But former Serb allies fell out and became rivals, most notably Prime Minister Pašić and his former Radical cabinet minister Ljuba Jovanović. In the summer of 1924 Jovanović wrote an article in Serbian to mark the tenth anniversary of the assassination. He now admitted that the Pašić cabinet had been informed by its interior minister that assassins were heading for Sarajevo to kill the archduke and that border officials were colluding to get them and their weapons over the border in safety. This admission that the Austrian accusations of July 1914 had been accurate was a key moment in the unravelling of the conspiracy. Edith Durham immediately translated the article into English, as did the only Serbian speaker in the Foreign Office on the instructions of the Foreign Secretary.[83] The Foreign Office had its version anonymously published in the journal of Chatham House.[84] Seton-Watson set off to Belgrade to receive assurances from his Serb friends that Jovanović was lying.[85] In April 1926, in one of his last significant political acts, Pašić did indeed denounce Jovanović as a liar, and reiterated the line that 'the murder of the Archduke was merely a favourable excuse for Austria to settle accounts with Serbia'.[86]

However, after Pašić's death, Alexander's dictatorship revealed the truth by putting up a plaque in Sarajevo in honour of Gavrilo Princip. It read, 'Princip proclaimed freedom on Vidovdan (15) 28 June 1914.' Plenty of people understood the symbolism: Vidovdan was the official Serb national day which celebrated a medieval assassination. King Alexander, the Prince Regent of 1914, was giving the imprimatur of the Serb state to the assassination. The *Daily Mail* called the act a 'World

Affront'.⁸⁷ *The Times*, quite changing its tune from what it had written on the tenth anniversary of the assassination six years previously, declared that the assassination was 'the immediate cause of the Great War, of its attendant horrors, and of the general suffering which has been its sequel'.⁸⁸ Even Seton-Watson blanched. 'The worm will turn,' Edith Durham noted with great satisfaction.⁸⁹

After 1930, the argument was less about the commissioners of the assassination and more about who was to blame for the response. In the 1930s, when the Italian politician and historian Luigi Albertini set out to write the 'definitive' history of the assassination, he found, in the observation of a British MI5 officer and historian, that there was not much more to tell.⁹⁰

The journalist Winston Churchill – taking a remunerative break from his day job as prime minister – summed up the revised understanding of Sarajevo on the assassination's twenty-seventh anniversary in June 1941. Churchill's popular writing revealed how the thinking of a statesman had evolved thanks to the revelations of the 1920s. In the summer of 1914, he said, Britain's 'friendship with Austria was of long standing, and our relations with Germany had entered on a new and cordial phase'.⁹¹ Europe was, in fact, entering a period of 'hope'. However, 'the guilty men' turned the assassination of Franz Ferdinand from a family tragedy into a world catastrophe. The actual assassins should only 'share responsibility for that fatal day at Sarajevo'. The real villains were the Black Hand, 'to whom murder was an instrument of policy'. The Black Hand 'were connected at many points with Serbian governing circles'. Churchill named Crown Prince Alexander and Pašić among the 'guilty men'. It was hard going, Churchill admitted, wading through the lies and obfuscations of 1914 and later but, he declared, 'there is little doubt that Dimitriyevitch was the organiser of the crime in Sarajevo'.

Since the outbreak of the Great War, records had flooded into the public domain. It must be overwhelming for the ordinary reader, Churchill commiserated, but there were a 'few gleaming points of truth' that everyone should remember. Responsibility for the disaster lay first with the assassination conspirators, second with the Kaiser for giving the Habsburg imperialists permission to react with overwhelming force, and third with those imperialists for their reckless violence. The assassination conspirators and the states that acted on the conspiracy bore 'the direct concrete responsibility for the loosing on mankind of incomparably its most frightful misfortune since the collapse of the Roman Empire before the Barbarians'.[92]

2

THE MONOPOLY OF LEGITIMATE VIOLENCE
European Assassinations, 1917–1923

Given the catastrophic detonator effect of the Sarajevo assassination, it was always likely that the assassinations that followed would pale into insignificance: it was impossible to imagine an assassination that might be more consequential. Nearly every subsequent account of post-war political violence quoted Churchill's valediction: 'The war of the giants has ended: the quarrels of the pygmies have begun.'[1] Nevertheless, it can be argued that the most enduring effect of the post-Sarajevo assassinations was to shape the entire conception of the modern state.

Assassination helped define the final statements of the most significant political theorist of the twentieth century. Max Weber was working in Munich when 'Red Bavaria' declared itself independent of Germany in 1918. At the end of January 1919, he addressed students on the topic of 'politics as a vocation'. Although his lecture was a characteristically Weberian sweep through human history, he constantly returned to the current situation, stressing to his audience when he was specifically focusing on the political transformation of 'now' rather than great historical forces. It was 'now' that the entire nature of the modern state had been laid bare by the highly visible and 'particularly intimate' relationship between that state and violence. According to Weber, a modern state could only succeed if it secured 'the monopoly of legitimate physical violence within a certain territory'. The test that Weber proposed in

1919 remained thereafter the most accepted measure of a viable state in western political thought and practice. It thus became very hard to dismiss assassination, which delegitimised political regimes, demonopolised violence and transgressed territorial boundaries, as a force in politics.[2]

In 1919 political legitimacy had been dangerously narrowed, Weber observed, so that it rested uneasily in the hands of a few – and thus highly vulnerable – charismatic demagogues who were all too likely to fall 'prey to political intoxication'. As was rapidly demonstrated in Munich itself, in such conditions assassination could be a potent weapon. Although he did not name him, Weber's political target was plainly the leader of the Bavarian Republic, the left socialist Kurt Eisner.[3] Eisner certainly saw himself as Weber's butt and immediately bit back with an address of his own, proclaiming that the true 'vocation of politics' was to construct a new society. Ten days after Eisner delivered his rebuttal of Weber he was assassinated.[4] Eisner was on his way to parliament to hand over power to a Social Democrat government when he was shot by a young aristocrat. Further shots were fired in the parliamentary session when Eisner's death was announced, leaving the SPD leader Erhard Auer badly wounded. A far-left government seized power and declared martial law, claiming a widespread rightist plot. Weber was hardly sorry to see Eisner gone. The final version of 'Politics as a Vocation' was prepared for publication after Eisner's assassination with its snideries intact.[5]

The second assassination that provided the immediate context for 'Politics as a Vocation', and its revision for publication, took place in Berlin. The chief reviser, Weber's wife, Marianne, was herself one of the liberal representatives at the first constituent assembly of the new German Republic. At the beginning of 1919 the enemies of the constitutional republic were manifested in a left-wing paramilitary militia, known as the Spartacists, and a multiplicity of right-wing uniformed paramilitary militias. The militias and warbands certainly murdered numerous people, of whom they did not approve. Some of these killings were arbitrary or even random. Scattered among the massacres, nevertheless, were planned assassinations of senior politicians. Ex-officers assassinated Karl Liebknecht, the leader of the Spartacists, along with his right-hand woman, Rosa Luxemburg, in January 1919. Liebknecht was the founder, too, of the left Social Democrats, the USPD, of which Kurt Eisner had also been a leader.

Convinced by warnings of imminent peril, Liebknecht and Luxemburg had half-heartedly gone undercover, abandoning their homes, sofa-surfing around the apartments of friends in Berlin. In somewhat obscure circumstances they were rousted out of such an apartment by a 'civilian defence league' in the suburb of Wilmersdorf. The militiamen handed Liebknecht and Luxemburg into the army headquarters at the Hotel Eden in central Berlin. The army called in a death squad made up of former naval officers. On the pretext of moving the victims to the central prison in Moabit in northern Berlin, the death squad took Liebknecht instead to the Tiergarten and killed him with three shots from close range. Luxemburg they didn't even bother to take out of the transport, shooting her in the back of the vehicle.[6]

Constitutional politicians immediately came to the support of the army. On the evening of the murders, Philipp Scheidemann, about to become the republic's first elected chancellor, told an SPD rally that Liebknecht and Luxemburg had 'fallen victim to their own bloody terror tactics'. 'I must use my weapon against him [the Spartacist leader] because then it is not just about me but about the lives of many others,' he declared. When Scheidemann appointed Gustav Noske defence minister in his government, Noske announced that 'the gruesomeness and bestiality of the Spartacists fighting against us forces me to issue the following order: every person who is encountered fighting against government troops with a weapon in hand is to be immediately shot.'[7] The Social Democrats agreed to the army's cover stories for the assassination, first that Liebknecht had been killed trying to escape and eventually that both Liebknecht and Luxemburg had been murdered by a soldier, acting entirely on his own, in a fit of madness, at the Hotel Eden.[8]

There were other major assassinations that preceded the publication of 'Politics as a Vocation' They emanated from both the left and the right. A notable shrug of the shoulders greeted the assassination of Karl von Stürgkh, the chief minister of Austria, shot while he blamelessly took lunch at a hotel in Vienna in 1917. The assassin was the son of the leader of the empire's Social Democrats. No-one tried to blame the father or his party: indeed, the father tried to have his son committed as a dangerous lunatic. The young man would have none of it, assured the examiners that he was a dedicated political murderer and demanded to be tried for his crime. He was allowed to mount a full political defence in court in May 1917, claiming that Austria was being led to disaster in the war, by many of the same men – including Stürgkh – whose reaction to Sarajevo had caused the conflagration in the first place. Other than by an act of violence like his, 'the eleven men in the ministry are unreachable, so the question I place is, what way is left open when there is no institution by which we call the eleven people to responsibility? What way is there left except force?' Fritz Adler demanded.[9] Given his own admission of guilt, the court had little alternative but to sentence him to death – unlike the Sarajevo assassins, he was old enough for capital punishment. However, Adler's execution was put off and Emperor Charles pardoned him in 1918.[10]

A fortnight after Adler's trial, Count Tisza was ousted as chief minister of Hungary, demonstrating that Adler in fact spoke for many in the war-weary empire, even those who disapproved of his methods.[11] The most notable victim of assassination in Austria-Hungary was Tisza himself. History knows Tisza as the one major imperial politician who tried to prevent the Sarajevo assassination turning into armed conflict. Many of his contemporaries, however, saw Tisza as the prime architect of the attack on Serbia, supposedly to advance even further the Magyar grip on power within the empire. At the end of October 1918, the 'Red Count', Mihály Károlyi, overthrew the government of Hungary, near bloodlessly apart from the assassination of István Tisza, who was shot in his home. The assassins were dressed as soldiers and reportedly declared, 'We have come to make our reckoning with you, for it is you who have brought about the World War.'[12] Notably, Tisza's murder did not unleash any further violence. Neither was the assassination properly investigated.[13]

Weber tended to lump in the Russian and Hungarian revolutionaries with their contemporaries in Bavaria and Germany. He did not see events in Russia as being of especial significance. The assassination of the archduke had sparked the Great War, the Great War had changed Germany's destiny, post-war assassination was important since it shaped

Germany's future.¹⁴ There had been a burst of assassinations in Russia between 1905 and 1910. A particular revolutionary organisation, the Socialist-Revolutionary Party – the SRs – formed in 1901, generated the highest volume of murder, arming its assassins with Browning semi-automatic pistols.¹⁵ According to their own testimony, the Sarajevo assassins had been very aware of the Russian example. However, assassination in Russia between 1905 and 1910 had been 'terrorism in one country'. It had been contained and defeated long before the outbreak of the Great War by a reformed secret police organisation using means both brutal and cunning, not least the infiltration of informers.¹⁶

There had been a spectacular assassination in wartime St Petersburg, but no observer could treat it as anything other than an aberration. As the representative of the British secret service – then known as C – wrote of the murder of the mad empress-whispering monk, Rasputin, 'the moujik's uncontrollable appetite for debauch left him defenceless before his enemies. . . . True to his nickname it was at an orgy that Rasputin met his death.'¹⁷ The procurers and perpetrators of the crime were the Grand Dukes of the imperial family, who had indulged themselves as orgiasts to shoot the hated charlatan multiple times before dumping his body in the Neva. Their intention seems to have been that he would never be seen or heard of again, with the 'whole matter in the hands of the family'. The Grand Dukes would be sadly disappointed in that hope, but there was little that outsiders could do other than shrug and dismiss the affair as Russian imperialists baring their oriental souls.¹⁸

The Bolsheviks spoke out of both sides of their mouth when it came to assassination. In theory, Lenin was not enthusiastic because he feared assassination was more likely to disrupt his revolutionaries than their enemies. In practice, the Bolsheviks did carry out assassinations but tried to conceal their authorship. Their most prominent pre-war victim had been Ilia Chavchavadze, the 'father' of modern Georgian nationalism, in 1907. At the time Rasputin was assassinated in St Petersburg, Lenin was issuing orders to the Bolsheviks in the city to start carrying out assassinations but on the proviso that murders must be passed off as the acts of individuals rather than those of the Bolshevik vanguard. The collapse of the Tsarist government a couple of months later meant that this plan was never put into action. As Lenin had predicted, Bolsheviks could be more effective as rabble-rousers than assassins.[19]

Weber commented that the Bolsheviks were notable for their willingness to co-opt rather than kill officials to keep the state machine running.[20] When targeted killing was called for, the bureaucratic machine could be turned upon itself.[21] As the Bolsheviks executed remnants of the old regime with a show of legality, the Bolshevik leaders concluded that they, personally, had a lot more to lose from assassination than to gain.

In March 1918, the Bolsheviks switched Russia's allegiance from Britain and France to Germany, signing a peace treaty that removed Russia's hold on Eastern Europe: not all revolutionaries supported this deal with the Devil. The revolution had created its own secret police, the Cheka, and many newly minted Chekists were old SRs. In July 1918, two SR Chekists assassinated Germany's ambassador in Moscow, Wilhelm von Mirbach. The assassins escaped from the scene by car and headed for the safety of their Cheka building. Hours of panic followed: when the Bolshevik head of the Cheka, Felix Dzerzhinskii, attempted to arrest his own men, and the rest of the SR leadership, they instead captured him and his guards. The Bolsheviks retaliated by seizing all the SRs they could find. The matter was not settled until the Bolsheviks' Latvian shock troops stormed SR HQ on the next day. Lenin declared that the assassination of von Mirbach had been the signal to launch a counter-revolution intended to drag Russia back into a war with Germany. Trotsky proclaimed, counter to what Dzerzhinskii had found, that the SRs were collectively responsible for the assassination: the SR leaders upon whom the Bolsheviks could lay their hands, including Dzerzhinkii's deputy in the Cheka, were executed.[22]

The Bolsheviks had come out on top, but they knew that assassination remained dangerous. At the beginning of August 1918, they arrested the British representative in Moscow, Robert Lockhart, along with the secret service officers who operated under cover of his mission. Lockhart and C were certainly plotting against the Bolsheviks, many of their hopes resting on the familiar figure of Boris Savinkov, who was leading SR opposition north of Moscow in Yaroslavl. Savinkov had not forgotten his old calling and made sure to target Bolshevik commissars.²³ The C officers who had eluded the Bolsheviks by disguising themselves as Russians went under cover. One of those officers, Sidney Reilly, hatched a plan to assassinate the Bolshevik leadership. He believed that the Latvian troops whom the Bolsheviks had used to attack the SRs were mere mercenaries who could be turned against their masters. His interlocutor was the commander of the Latvians Colonel Berzin. Unfortunately for Reilly, Berzin was an agent provocateur who would later go on to be one of the leaders of Soviet intelligence.²⁴

On 30 August 1918, veterans of Savinkov's pre-war SR Combat Organisation shot, first, Moishe Uritskii, the head of the Cheka in St Petersburg, and, secondly, Lenin himself in Moscow. Uritskii died; Lenin, although wounded in the neck and the shoulder, survived. Once more, the insecurity provided by the Cheka was exposed. Within an hour of Lenin's shooting, Jacob Sverdlov, the Bolshevik who had once been the leader most enthusiastic about assassination as a revolutionary tactic, announced that the assassination attempt on Lenin had been another SR counter-revolution. The Bolsheviks ordered the arrest and purge of anyone associated with the SRs, the first step of what became the Red Terror of 1918, as the revolution began to eat itself.

The Cheka rearrested Lockhart and Bolsheviks trumpeted the attack on Lenin as the SRs working in cahoots with the British imperialists. Although both the SR and British plots were real enough, they were not closely related, apart from revealing that those of widely different political persuasions thought that the assassination of Bolshevik leaders was an end greatly to be desired.²⁵ The British feigned disgust and astonishment that anyone could believe its representatives capable of plotting assassination. Subsequently, they concocted the story that Reilly was a corrupt Jew, a habitual consort of assassins, with 'no British blood in his veins' who had penetrated their intelligence service during the exigencies of war.²⁶

The second wave of post-war assassination post-dated the publication of 'Politics as a Vocation'. Weber had seen the threat to the state coming from all sides but was most fearful of the far left. Those who wrote on assassination during the second wave were much less important political thinkers than Weber but largely succeeded in fixing the view that assassination was particularly a phenomenon of the far right. The right, according to the German and Hungarian left, relied on assassination because it was congenitally incapable of raising the masses, and thus to bring revolutionary mass violence.[27] This might have been an arguable point of view, taking only events in Hungary and Germany between 1920 and 1923 into account; however, the general theory of an unpopular far right was a canard. The Nazis might have been a small group of farcical putschists in 1923, but they subsequently proved that the far right could win the hearts and minds, then shape the actions, of the masses. Elsewhere, very traditionalist far-right movements, such as the French Catholic and monarchist *Croix de Feu*, also proved highly effective at mass mobilisation.[28]

In Hungary, the Whites, under Admiral Horthy, seized power in November 1919. The head of Horthy's paramilitary bodyguard, Pál Prónay, claimed to have organised an assassination squad to remove dangerous opponents but that it never went into action. The 'White Terror' seems to have been a more decentralised affair, with aristocratic warband leaders exacting various forms of retributive violence on those they saw as responsible for the despoliation of their land.[29] About fifteen hundred people were killed in Hungary, by both sides, in 1919–20. It would be hard to claim too many of these deaths as assassinations, as opposed to massacres of perceived class enemies.[30] It was certainly the case that those who tried to publicise and oppose the murders subsequently became victims of assassination: most notably the Social Democrat journalist Béla Somogyi, who was assassinated in March 1920.[31]

The post-war assassination threat played out most threateningly in the German Republic. In the German case, a would-be democratic Social Democrat government mounted a sustained three-year campaign against assassins of both the far left and the far right. The German government's position was further complicated by assassinations related to the collapse of its erstwhile ally, the Ottoman empire, playing out on the streets of Berlin. By the extraordinary exertion of state power, the republic survived, albeit at a cost. The government itself had to use extreme force to enforce its monopoly on legitimised violence. This placed it in hock to an embittered German army. The counter-assassination campaign also revealed for all to see that a significant portion of the civilian administrative state had colluded with the assassins.[32]

The main contemporary account of assassination in Germany was written from the far left, by Emil Julius Gumbel, an academic mathematician and USPD political activist. One of the reasons that assassination in post-war Germany was, and remained, so well known was Gumbel's relentless statistical reckoning of political murder.[33] Gumbel's single-minded desire to prove that the right was the commissioner of nearly all political murder, however, made his statistics rather less revealing than is sometimes assumed. He counted 354 assassinations carried out by far-right 'assassination organisations' between late 1918 and late 1922. However, he classified assassinations mainly by their 'cover story'.[34] Most of what he reported were massacres by paramilitaries. Only about ten of the killings seem to have been assassinations in the sense of an organisation setting out to murder a specific individual. In Gumbel's own view, a true assassination, as opposed to semi-random murder of a 'social pest', could be identified because 'murder is made plausible to the public beforehand. The victim must be so suspect that his murder is seen as a liberating step, as a heroic act.'[35]

Over the summer of 1920, under severe pressure from the victorious Allied powers, the government turned the army on the right-wing paramilitaries. The last organised attempt to overthrow the government was the Kapp Putsch of March 1920. It was after the crackdown on anti-government militias that the remnants of some reconstituted themselves as underground terrorist organisations, with the specific goal of eliminating those they believed had betrayed them.[36] The most important of these groups was the *Freikorps* led by Hermann Ehrhardt. Dissolved by the government in 1920, members reorganised as the underground Organisation Consul, or OC. Consul did not act at once, not least because it was still in part funded by the German foreign ministry, which wanted to keep Ehrhardt's personnel on hand in Upper Silesia, which had voted to join Germany rather than Poland in a May 1921 plebiscite, the campaign for which had itself spawned assassination.[37]

Due to the Silesian interlude, the assassinations that grabbed the headlines in Berlin between the summer of 1920 and the summer of 1921 were not those of OC but those related to the former Ottoman empire. In Turkey, the emergent military dictatorship of Kemal Atatürk most definitely deployed assassins to eliminate its opponents, including former Ottoman officials.[38] In return, Ottoman loyalists called for the assassination of Atatürk.[39] In Germany, however, the assassins were Armenians and the victims were Ottomans. In March 1921 an Armenian assassinated the former Grand Vizier of the Ottoman empire, Talaat Pasha, in the western Berlin district of Charlottenburg, explicitly in revenge for the Armenian genocide of 1915, of which Talaat had been an architect.[40] A month later, two further Armenian assassins shot and killed the leader of Ottoman exiles in Germany, Behaeddine Shakir, the man who had read the eulogy for Talaat, and Cemal Azmi, the so-called 'Butcher of Trebizond'.[41] Talaat's assassin had been caught by the prompt action of civilian witnesses who dragged him to the ground. Indeed, civilian Europeans showed considerable bravery when faced by armed assassins at this period.[42] However, beyond the assassination site itself, far from demonising these foreign assassins in their midst, the German press celebrated the assassinations. Senior German lawyers provided Talaat's assassin with a formidable defence team, and the judge in the case overruled the prosecution to allow a full rehearsal of the crimes Talaat had committed against the Armenians. The jury acquitted. Following the acquittal, a third group of Armenian assassins murdered Talaat's predecessor as Ottoman Grand Vizier, Said Halim Pasha, also in Berlin.[43]

It was only in the wake of the Silesian victory, with their usefulness to the central government waning, that OC started serious planning aimed at ridding Germany of prominent 'traitors'. In June 1921, Philipp Scheidemann, the now former SPD chancellor of the republic, who had applauded the assassinations of Liebknecht and Luxemburg, survived an acid attack while out walking in forests near his home in Kassel.[44] A few days later, Karl Gareis, a USPD member of the Bavarian assembly, was shot dead outside his apartment in Munich. In August 1921, OC killed one of the most influential politicians in Germany, Matthias Erzberger of the Catholic Centre Party.[45] Two of its assassins ambushed Erzberger on another woodland walk, this time in the Black Forest. The obese Erzberger tried to run but they brought him down with ease. As he lay on the forest floor, the former officers emptied the magazines of their semi-automatic pistols into his body, ensuring that he could not survive.

The thorough investigation carried out by the Baden police revealed how sophisticated and widespread an organisation Ehrhardt and his officers had created. In May 1922 their police colleagues in Frankfurt developed an informant within OC who was able to confirm that the same people had planned the assassinations of both Scheidemann and Erzberger.[46] The OC cell that killed Erzberger had hidden behind a front organisation known as the Bavarian Wood Disposal Company.[47] The assassins themselves were spirited out of Germany to safe exile in Hungary.[48] Those who had planned the attack hired a strong team of lawyers who secured their acquittal in June 1922.[49]

The Erzberger trial was still in progress when the OC began planning their most outrageous coup of all: the assassination of the foreign minister of the republic, Walther Rathenau. Rathenau was not only an exceptionally powerful figure within the government; he was a European political celebrity. A secular Jew – which merely exacerbated OC's hatred – he was reputedly the richest man in Germany. Although Rathenau was no friend of western Europe, he was nevertheless seen by foreigners as the best hope for the reintegration of Germany among the great powers.[50] The assassins were not the only ones who understood Rathenau's value. The Chancellor, Joseph Wirth, on whose desk the reports of assassinations old and new accumulated, urged Rathenau to take care and offered him police bodyguards. Rathenau declined, declaring that he would continue to live the life of a free man. In June 1922, as he did most mornings, he set off from his villa in the Berlin suburb of Grunewald to drive himself into the foreign ministry. The OC assassination squad, which had been stalking him for weeks, overtook his car in their own. One assassin opened fire with a sub-machine gun; the second killer lobbed a hand grenade into Rathenau's sports car. Rathenau died quickly from five bullet wounds and a back broken by the explosion in the confined space. The assassins made their escape.[51]

The response to the Rathenau assassination was complex. Given existing police intelligence and political calculation, the German politicians were not surprised by the fact of the assassination, even if the circumstances had been shocking. The most visible show of support for the republic was the massive turnout in Berlin for Rathenau's funeral. The crowd was estimated at half a million. In private, reaction was more mixed: many politicians expressed dislike for Rathenau and a lack of real sorrow for his elimination, although only to their own diaries.[52]

Nevertheless, state action was decisive. The government already assumed that Organisation Consul were the villains.[53] The police pursued them with energy and skill. The assassination squad was tracked down to a castle in Halle. One was killed in the ensuing gunfight and the other committed suicide.[54] The Wirth government successfully moved legislation in the Reichstag to give itself extraordinary powers to crush Consul.[55] The death penalty was extended to anyone who was convicted of planning assassinations, rather than to just the killers themselves. Such cases were to be tried in front of a special tribunal. The government gained authority to censor the press, controlling any journalism that seemed to encourage or celebrate assassination.[56]

Even when the Wirth government fell in November 1922, its policies were continued by the succeeding Cuno coalition. Although the German Republic was marked by frequent changes of government coalitions, it remained firm in its response to assassination. The former SPD chancellor, now president, Friedrich Ebert, constantly used constitutional powers that allowed him to invoke martial law and rule as a virtual dictator with army support. With the police temperamentally and the army situationally loyal, it was possible for the state to energetically pursue OC. As the SPD politician, and soon to be chief of police in Berlin, Albert Grzesinki, remarked in the wake of the Rathenau assassination, 'If we don't create order, our people and our country will be gone.'[57] In December 1922, Hermann Ehrhardt was seized by the police and carried off to Leipzig, where the special tribunal sat, safe in the SPD stronghold of 'Red Saxony'.[58]

There were notable attempted assassinations in Germany after the killing of Rathenau. Barely a week after Rathenau's death, the journalist Maximilian Harden was attacked, also in Grunewald. As late as 1924, Franz Josef Heinz-Orbis, a Palatinate nationalist leader who favoured separation from Germany, was shot and killed in Speyer by assassins from an OC remnant.[59] The OC could now be portrayed as anti-French resistance fighters in the west as the trials of their comrades proceeded in the east.[60] For all its eventual energy in the face of assassinations that threatened the physical survival of the republican political elite, the government placed limits on itself. Its vulnerability remained its own dishonest political conduct. Both prosecution and defence lawyers at the OC trials of 1924 knew that the accused had information that could reveal activities damning to the reputation of Rathenau and his successors in the eyes of the western powers. The defendants in the east could testify that the German state was working at every level to do all the things that the French government claimed, not least rearming and retraining the German armed forces with the aid of Russia. This political problem was exacerbated by a court system that remained fundamentally hostile to the republic, with judges who regularly failed to convict those with even a thin screen of deniability between themselves and an assassination. Therefore, the lawyers and judges colluded with the defendants to say very little in return for light sentences with no jail time. The government issued a general amnesty to procurers of assassination in December 1925. With that, the Rathenau case was effectively closed and forgotten.[61]

Across Europe, assassins had challenged the emerging post-war status quo. The post-Sarajevo assassinations had, however, done little to change the political direction of any country. Whatever the political character of the various post-war European states – and they ranged from the extreme left to the extreme right, with Germany, a country of strong democratic traditions, in the middle – the assassins had been put in their place. Even the weakened and destabilised post-war European polities had political leaders with survival instincts.

Nevertheless, assassination and assassins had entered the post-war political bloodstream. Unlike the pre-Sarajevo age, assassins were part of the state. Anarchists and court assassins of royalty were not completely things of the past, but they were now of passing importance. They had been replaced by soldiers and national patriots, whom many politicians and journalists in some sense admired. The commissioners of assassination had worked for the state in the past and would do so again in the future. Even those who most energetically denounced assassination usually had some ideological axe to grind, being all too ready to leap to the defence of violence perpetrated by their political soulmates.

3

THE RULES OF THE GAME
Assassination and the Greatest Empire, 1909–1940

In 1914 a successful empire had no need to panic about assassination. Contemporaries did not have to look very far to see imperialists acting very differently from the hysterical Austro-Hungarians. Despite the recent trend in writing about the British empire to stress 'panic', the 'insecurity state' and 'imperial overreaction', in 1914 the rulers of the British empire were in the process of dealing with assassination in a hard-headed and cold-hearted fashion.[1]

It was certainly the case that governing British imperialists held two visions of empire in their minds at the same time. On one level, there was the serene civilisation of imperial propaganda. At both a more informed, and yet a more visceral, level, however, imperialists knew running an empire was a dirty business. Classically trained rulers knew all about the *faex Romuli*. The British ruling elite was not naive: they understood the nature of empire.[2] As one commentator wrote when the Christian prime minister of Egypt was assassinated in February 1910, his 'British "advisers" . . . certainly understand that they are not there for the love of the Copts or any other sentimental reasons, but for the strengthening and consolidating [of] British power, or British interests, and of British world influence'.[3] Some amount of violent opposition to imperial oppression was inevitable. The British never fell into the trap of thinking that they were trusted or loved by those they ruled, despite the flowery condolence letters from civic and voluntary bodies that clogged the files after each assassination attempt. No bystanders would wrestle assassins to the floor; no help would be forthcoming.[4]

It is relatively easy to find examples of Britons who panicked about assassination. The press in these years was rarely free of some worthy suggesting brutal collective punishments or fearing the collapse in the moral fibre of the governing elite. On the latter score, it is possible to find evidence of a real culture of fear within imperial civil services under attack. That evidence comes from near the front line, and none of these civil services broke down. On the whole, however, the assassination evidence demonstrates that the British approach to imperial 'politics as a vocation' was slow boring on hard boards. Unlike the Austrians, they believed time was on their side. On the eve of the First World War, while Habsburg investigators conducted a hapless appraisal of the Sarajevo assassination, British investigators were putting the finishing touches to a two-year-long inquiry into a major assassination conspiracy that had attacked the Viceroy and Governor-General of India, Lord Hardinge, the personal representative of the monarch and the chief executive of the Indian government. The British government had already dealt with the irruption of Indian assassination onto the streets of the imperial capital, London.

Britain's first imperial assassination of the twentieth century took place in July 1909. Madao Lao Dhingra, a 25-year-old Punjabi Hindu student studying at University College, University of London, assassinated the India Office official Sir Curzon Wyllie, shooting him as he left a meeting at the Imperial Institute in South Kensington.[5] The question of who Dhingra was, and what he represented, immediately fed into an existing debate about the nature of imperial rule. Months before Wyllie's assassination, *The Times*'s Valentine Chirol had submitted a series of despatches warning of a conspiracy that fused Hindu fundamentalism with western assassination techniques. Small groups of young high-caste Hindus – disgusted at the Raj's failure to recognise their divinely ordained superiority and right to rule as well as its mocking dismissal of their masculinity, even – formed Hindu cultural associations at the turn of the century. The associations, in turn, spawned terrorist cells that mastered both bomb-making and the use of pistols for assassination.⁶ The first high-profile Hindu extremist assassination attempt was made against the Lieutenant-Governor of Bengal, Sir Andrew Fraser, in December 1907.⁷

In 1908 two assassins attempted to assassinate Bamfylde Fuller, lieutenant-governor of East Bengal, and Douglas Kingsford, chief presidency magistrate of Calcutta, in Muzzaffarpur, a holiday resort in western Bengal. Instead, they threw a bomb into the carriage of the Kennedy family, killing mother, daughter and coachman. One assassin shot himself with his Browning self-loading pistol; the other was captured, tried and hanged. He was hailed as a hero by the Hindu extremists, and the name of Kshudiram Bose remained as well known in India as Gavrilo Princip would be in Europe.⁸ Little was remembered of the solicitor, Pringle Kennedy, who lost his family.⁹

The Hindu extremists demonstrated that the assassination of police intelligence officers, prosecution lawyers or even informers – known in India as approvers – could be just as damaging as the loss of a high-ranking official. Assassins ambushed sub-inspector Nanda Lal Banarji in Calcutta, shot dead deputy superintendent Shamsul Alam as he listened to evidence in the High Court in Calcutta, shot and killed the Alipore public prosecutor Ashutosh Biswas as he left the Police Court, and murdered the approver Norendra Nath Gossain in Alipore jail. The Viceroy, Lord Minto, described the whole affair as a 'fiasco'.¹⁰ Alam's murder lay heavily on the minds of the British elite. Minto told the Secretary of State for India that the 'gloom of his assassination' permeated the Viceroy's Council.¹¹ Other assassinations followed.¹²

The Wyllie assassination moved the Liberal prime minister, Herbert Asquith, to pronounce obiter dicta on the threat of Indian assassination. Campaigning at Southport, Lancashire, on the day after Wyllie's death, he inserted in his speech the assessment that the 'character and methods of the conspiracy' were 'happily confined to a small number of people, but desperate and determined in its methods'.¹³ Asquith's formulation satisfied neither the people interested in the details of Indian assassination nor the supporters of Indian political reform. It became, however, the standard response of the British government to assassination. Asquith's view on assassination could be broken down into three parts. First, there was an organised assassination conspiracy.

Second, very few people were involved in the conspiracy. Third, the conspiracy was dangerous because of the violence of its methods, not because it represented the tip of the iceberg. Asquith created a kind of 'liberal script' for the British state's response to assassination. It proved memorable: when faced with political murder in future, ministers specifically referred to the Asquithian script as 'precedent'.[14]

It must not be thought that Asquith's response merely rested on vague rhetoric. From 1909 onwards, the British state set about improving its Indian intelligence apparatus. These improvements stretched from the CIDs (Criminal Investigation Departments) of the Presidencies to a new intelligence organisation in London, Indian Political Intelligence (IPI). IPI's role was to collate intelligence on the threat to and from India, and to run agents in the Indian diaspora.[15] The Government of India passed a slew of legislation in 1910 criminalising incitement to violence, controlling the trade in explosives and making it easier to convict terrorists to inoculate itself against assassination. The government was thus disappointed that it was caught by surprise once more by the formation of a cell of Hindu extremists in the capital of India, Delhi.[16]

In December 1912 the viceroy made a ceremonial entrance to Delhi only to be on the receiving end of a spectacular assassination attempt. King George V and the British royal household were 'keenly interested' in the assault on their vicegerent.[17] This was the assassination case with which the British were grappling at the time of Sarajevo. Both Delhi in December 1912 and Sarajevo in June 1914 were examples of imperial representatives being attacked while showing themselves in a ceremonial procession. There were plenty of contrasts, however. The viceroy was riding in a howdah on top of an elephant. Crucially, the Delhi assassins only used bombs, and did not follow up with firearms. His mode of transportation saved Hardinge: the howdah partition protected him from the fierce blast; his umbrella bearer was killed. The British response was to assemble their counter-terrorism experts – already at work on multiple cases from the Presidencies – under the leadership of David Petrie of the intelligence bureau of the Government of India.[18]

The contrast with Sarajevo is again clear. The British had terrorism experts whom they could assemble. Their problems were, nevertheless, still serious. Police officers and indeed the investigators themselves became targets for assassination.[19] Potential witnesses greeted investigators with silence.[20]

The slowness of the police effort certainly led to frustration and anger among Indian government leaders. Sir Harcourt Butler, a member of the Viceroy's Council, denounced the Indian police, calling for the importation of 'men of real detective ability' from Scotland Yard in London, and even from Paris.[21] General Creagh, the Commander-in-Chief of the Indian Army, agreed that the IPS (Indian Police Service) was poor but went much further: the time had come to 'shed the kid gloves and come to business . . . Delhi must suffer – the innocent with the guilty.'[22] The political head of the Home Department, Sir Reginald Craddock, feeling beleaguered from all quarters, said the only way to control assassination was mass deportation of suspected persons, 'the last refuge of the helpless'.[23] On the other side, the procurers of the assassination were delighted. They decided against a second attempt on Hardinge because their near miss was sowing exactly the confusion in which they revelled.[24]

However, the result was not the unleashing of Creagh and his troops to visit violence on the inhabitants of Delhi or mass deportation. Rather, the investigation continued as Petrie wanted.[25] The budget for 'secret service' – running agents and informers – was doubled. The Bengal CID set up a well-financed Special Branch.[26] They began to crack the case in November 1913 when the head of Special Branch raided a Hindu extremist meeting house in Calcutta only to discover their bomb factory. The police started to recruit informers within the assassination conspiracy. In February 1914 the investigators identified the procurer of the Delhi attack.[27] They estimated – and the Indian government accepted – that the conspiracy encompassed about three hundred members with approximately fifty hard-core assassins.[28]

From February 1914 onwards, the Government of India was sure of the threat and its targets. The Hindu extremist conspiracy looked exactly as Asquith had described it 1909, small in numbers but extraordinarily deadly.[29] Given that, the question remained of how Delhi could square its determination to crush the assassins in Bengal – what Craddock described as 'a bolt from the blue, and not a wild and blind vengeance on the morrow of an outrage' – with London's preference for the 'liberal script'.[30]

The official British position on response to assassination at the time of Sarajevo was that the answer lay in continued, long-term police work to identify, arrest and try the assassins and the commissioners of assassination. That did not mean that Britain was in the least bit forgiving of assassination. Whatever the supplications and threats of anti-British Indian politicians – and Mohandas Gandhi himself had been in London in 1909 to plead for clemency for Dhingra – assassination plotters could expect deportation to an unpleasant island camp at best, and more likely execution after a short trial.[31] The chief organiser of the Delhi assassination was a fugitive and no longer a threat – he escaped to Japan to live out a long powerless exile; the Delhi assassin had been caught and executed, and the government had the measure of 'a problem which so long defied all attempts at solution'. 'We must rest content,' David Petrie concluded.[32]

In a sense, the Great War rendered the assassination problem moot. Britain introduced stringent security legislation to protect the UK from the Germans for the duration. That security legislation was easily extended to India, giving the Indian government more powers than even its most draconian members would have dreamt of asking for in peacetime. The Defence of India Act 'forged [a] . . . weapon in the hands of police'. They could detain the people they wanted and, as police officials frankly admitted, treat them much as they wanted. That treatment included both financial inducements to turn informer and brutal interrogation: assassination plotters could expect little quarter from either the British or the Indian officers who had been their potential victims. These interrogations yielded a very full picture of the assassination cells, their networks reaching across much of northern India, and how they communicated.[33] The police identified eighteen assassination cells. They detained slightly over eight hundred individuals. One hundred and fifty members of the assassination network made full confessions. They included some of the leading figures who had both planned and carried out killings – although the assassination societies had tried to keep the hands of their organisers 'clean'.[34] Seven of the men were tortured into confessing.³⁵ The breaking of the assassination ring was held up at the time and since as evidence of imperialist oppression. However, it was hard to see Indian police and intelligence officials as particularly different from their opposite numbers in Britain who had little compunction in using interrogation to obtain confessions that led to the execution of spies. The British were proud of their work in both instances.

Towards the end of the Great War the security establishments in neither India nor Britain were keen to give up their powers.³⁶ In the short term, the hardliners got their wish with new legislation, usually known as the Rowlatt Act. However, London remained as sceptical of draconian legislation in 1918 as it had been in 1914. In defending the Rowlatt Act in the House of Commons, the Coalition Liberal Secretary of State for India, Sir Edwin Montagu, said, 'it was not intended to be a permanent measure and would not be used except to cope with . . . the murder of innocent citizens and the assassination of those who gave evidence against the murderers'.³⁷ Many in London, Delhi, Calcutta and Bombay hoped that the Hindu extremist assassination conspiracy was a thing of the past.³⁸ The Government of India released nearly all detainees in the immediate post-war period, including some notorious procurers of assassination.³⁹

Indeed, British fear of assassination lay elsewhere than India in the immediate post-war period. Egypt too had suffered from the foundation of assassination societies, both Anglophobe Muslim – forming a wing of the Watani Party – and pan-Islamists. It was the Anglophobes who assassinated the prime minister, Boutros Ghali, in 1910 and the pan-Islamists who plotted to assassinate both the British Consul-General – General Kitchener – and the Khedive in 1912.⁴⁰ The Khedive was eventually wounded by an assassin in Constantinople in July 1914, but the Ottoman authorities claimed the attack was 'not the result of a plot but an isolated act of a madman'.⁴¹ There was much more to it than that, with links leading back to the 1912 plotters, assisted by collaborators within the Ottoman police and intelligence services. Nevertheless, it was easy for a government – in the month between Sarajevo and the outbreak of the Great War – to brush off an assassination attempt against a politically important royal when they wished to do so.⁴²

The files on these conspiracies remained open for years, but nothing much was done.⁴³ In 1914 the British overthrew the Khedive, installed a Sultan and the military battened down Egypt against the Ottoman threat. As a result, when the half-forgotten assassination societies re-emerged in 1919, they took the British civil authorities largely by surprise.⁴⁴ The first prominent Briton to lose his life was Alexander Pope, the British inspector of prisons in Egypt who was travelling from Luxor to Upper Egypt. Pope was actually torn apart by a mob, along with a number of British soldiers.⁴⁵ On further investigation, however, the British began to suspect that the mob had been deliberately set on Pope by operators from Cairo.⁴⁶ The assassins notably targeted Egyptian politicians and effective Egyptian police officers as much as they did Britons.⁴⁷ In 1920 the police and intelligence services began to pick up preliminary indications that, as the star of the pre-war Watanists faded, its secret societies were collaborating with the newer champion of Anglophobe nationalism, the Wafd Party led by the Egyptian notable Saad Zaghlul.⁴⁸

Assassination was a minor weapon in Zaghlul's arsenal. His strength was his ability to bring out the masses to demonstrate their hatred of the English. The British in the end decided that they would have to get along with Zaghlul. In February 1922, the government in London transformed the political status of Egypt by issuing a unilateral declaration of independence for the country, inevitably making Zaghlul its political leader.

While addressing the threat of mass violence, however, the 1922 declaration merely spurred on the assassins, who saw Britons still controlling the Egyptian state. A few days before independence, a respectably dressed assassin – wearing a suit and tarbush – shot Richard Aldred Brown, the Controller-General of Administration in the Department of Education in Cairo. Brown died of his wounds in hospital a few hours later. On the same day a less respectably dressed assassin – clad in a traditional galabieh – shot Mr Peach of the Egyptian State Railways (ESR) in the back as he and his wife were walking in suburban Cairo.⁴⁹ Peach survived but was so traumatised that he resigned from ESR and retreated to Malton in the North Riding of Yorkshire. In 1922, the assassins particularly targeted the engineers and managers of ESR. This was an effective tactic: the railway was very vulnerable to the loss of Europeans, who, its general manager admitted, were following Peach out of the door.[50] More generally, too, the British voted with their feet, having witnessed thirty-two attempted assassinations: the retirement rate for officials sextupled.[51]

The British community in Egypt was bitter in its public reproaches of the mild response of the British government in London and its representative in Cairo to the real threat of assassination under which they worked. The High Commissioner, Lord Allenby, was the man, after all, who had conquered the Ottoman empire only four years previously. To many Britons he did not seem to be living up to his nickname, 'Bull'.[52] Allenby told London that overreaction to assassination would 'ruin any chance of our coming to a friendly understanding' and would 'put a sudden and sharp check on the progress of HMG's policy in Egypt'.[53]

The police did not seem any better to the potential victims.[54] As the commandant of the Cairo police, Tom Russell, admitted, as in India very few Egyptians had the least interest in helping the British. In May 1922, assassins killed Russell's deputy, Bimbashi Cave, in front of three shops and a school. No-one would admit to having seen or heard a thing. The only person who did come forward was a young British woman and her name was immediately leaked to the Egyptian press. A few days later a paid police spy heard two schoolboys boasting that they had seen the whole thing. One of the schoolboys turned out to be the son of an official in the Public Security Department of the Ministry of the Interior.[55] The only real recourse the British had was to arrest suspects under martial law, a holdover from London rule with which they were hoping to dispense.[56]

In the end, Allenby's answer was to reconstitute part of his old military intelligence service with the sole purpose of using martial law powers to investigate assassination, cutting Egyptian officials out of the loop. What resulted was the detention without trial of about sixty militants. By July 1923, when martial law was finally abolished, the various efforts of former military intelligence, British police officers and government officials had seemingly crimped the assassination campaign. These men were under no illusions, however, that they had destroyed the secret societies or even deterred those who directed the assassination campaign from within the Wafd.[57]

Much closer to home than Egypt, the post-war government of David Lloyd George faced a parallel but not dissimilar assassination campaign in Ireland. Although British commentators on Ireland made frequent references to one of the most notorious assassinations of the nineteenth century, the stabbing to death of Lord Frederick Cavendish as he walked in Phoenix Park, Dublin in 1882, the thought of assassins using knives now seemed almost quaint.[58]

The Easter Rising of 1916 in Dublin had no truck with such methods: it was an armed insurrection using modern high-powered weaponry, crushed by the British army's even heavier weapons. The return to assassination was a product of the failure of the German-supported wartime revolution.[59] The IRA was only formally created out of the surviving militant groups in 1917. Its assassination campaign was a deliberate tactic devised by its so-called 'director of intelligence', Michael Collins, and launched in July 1919. As others had done elsewhere, he created a designated assassination squad. Collins's purpose was to kill the police and intelligence officers who could directly threaten the IRA. By March 1920, there had been fifteen assassinations.[60] Spectacular assassinations of high-profile individuals were less central to his plan.[61] However, as in India, in Ireland the most tempting target would always be the viceroy, the symbolic repository of British power. In December 1919, the IRA ambushed the viceroy, Lord French, as he was driven down his familiar and regular route from a Dublin railway station to the viceregal lodge. This was a very serious effort since up to two dozen assassins took part. It differed from the other assassinations of the age in that French had a military escort whereas most targets were unprotected. The assassins were not only numerous but also well-equipped. The one assassin killed in the attack was carrying a semi-automatic pistol, a revolver and a hand grenade. The assassination attempt failed but it was a close-run thing for French: four bullets hit his car; a policeman was wounded.[62]

As in India and Egypt, there was little secret about the anger that these assassinations aroused in those who were threatened. The Special Branches of the Royal Irish Constabulary and the Dublin Metropolitan Police had been hollowed out during the long Irish peace: once formidable institutions of control were already shadows of their Victorian selves before the IRA assassins started their assault. Morale all but collapsed. However, there were other organisations, also under threat, that were more likely to strike back, such as the Home Office's Directorate of Intelligence, run by Basil Thomson, also with control over the Metropolitan Police's Special Branch, and military intelligence. They in turn could draw on a reserve of former police and army officers. In the spring of 1920, the British started to operate identifiable 'death squads'. Their most prominent victim was the Lord Mayor of Cork and senior IRA commander, Tomás MacCurtain, assassinated by a group of former RIC officers in March 1920.[63]

British counter-assassination was not very successful. Because the death squads killed episodically and collected little worthwhile intelligence, the IRA assassins had several recourses. The most violent were MacCurtain's former followers in the Cork Brigade. They responded with a large-scale campaign against those they regarded as informers. Since the Cork IRA's intelligence was just as poor as the British authorities', their assassinations amounted to little more than random terror. Between 1920 and 1923 they murdered over two hundred people.[64]

At this stage, Lloyd George was playing a double game. He was willing to allow the men on the ground very considerable latitude to see if they could whittle down the IRA. On the other hand, he knew that the very intelligence personnel who might become involved in assassination, notably Thomson, could also act as his intermediaries with the Sinn Féin leadership. Thomson put out feelers to Sinn Féin on the prime minister's behalf in June 1920. In May 1920, Lloyd George replaced the men running security in Ireland from the nerve centre of British rule in Dublin Castle. Separately from Thomson, the Dublin Castle men established a secure back channel to Collins in September 1920. The official in charge of this back channel became so closely associated with Lloyd George that he subsequently left the civil service and joined the, by then former, prime minister's political office.[65]

Lloyd George's manoeuvres were bitterly resented by the police and army because he was looking to compromise with the assassins at the very moment their officers were at a high risk of assassination. The Chief of the Imperial General Staff, Sir Henry Wilson, described Liberal politicians' hypocrisy as 'the most . . . shameful, that I ever saw . . . I wonder they [Lloyd George and Winston Churchill] did not hide their heads in shame'.[66] By far the most threatening conspiracy for the British was Collins's in Dublin. In November 1920, his assassins murdered fourteen British officers and wounded a further six. The IRA claimed that all the officers were significant figures in British military intelligence, but they knowingly worked off a ramshackle approximation. Nevertheless, many of the men killed were the 'most efficient members' of British intelligence. Tellingly, their killers branded them the 'Cairo Gang' to underline that Ireland was as much part of the British empire as Egypt – formally it was not, but part of the United Kingdom. Less noticed was that, in November 1920, British counter-assassination intelligence in Cairo was notoriously bad. So too was it in Dublin. Military intelligence's own assessment of the assassinations was that they 'temporarily paralysed the special branch [of Dublin District]'.[67]

The most notorious military response to the assassination came on the afternoon of the murders themselves. Troops entered the sporting and cultural centre of anti-British nationalism, Croke Park in Dublin, and opened fire, killing thirteen spectators. This was not the first time that British troops had run amok. The army in India had launched a similar attack on its perceived enemies as recently as April 1919, in Amritsar in the Punjab. On both these occasions, soldiers had been under the firm and secure command of their officers. These were official actions of the state. The murders were evidence of imperial panic writ large. Both at the time and ever since, the killings were a gift to nationalist propagandists.[68]

However, in neither the case was massacre the whole story. In Ireland the army and civil authorities rapidly rebuilt their intelligence system to such effect that it was much better than the one that had failed on Bloody Sunday, 1920. In rebuilding in Ireland intelligence officers had every intention of using intelligence – increasingly based on captured documents and prisoner interrogation as well as paid informants – to hunt down and presumably kill the commissioners of assassination.

The intelligence officers thought they were doing the nation's work but in truth they were doing the work of the man some had come to regard as a slippery devil. Lloyd George merely wanted a negotiating position that would enable him to strike a deal with the chief procurer of assassination – Collins. This his subordinates achieved relatively quickly. November 1920 proved the highpoint for Collins's assassins. Thereafter, the leaders of the IRA were hunted men. Their followers had to rely on mass, rather than targeted, terror attacks to keep up the levels of killing. In May 1921, Lloyd George offered Collins a deal through the Dublin Castle back channel, and via other intermediaries: after a relatively brief period of negotiation, Sinn Féin and the British government agreed a truce in early July 1921.[69]

Whatever else it achieved, the Anglo-Irish truce, and the subsequent peace treaty that the sides signed at the end of 1921, did not bring an end to assassination, although it changed the targets. Most of the killings now occurred within Irish republicanism as Sinn Féin and the IRA violently split over the Collins deal. On the British side the truce allowed the government in London to reassert its low-key response to assassination.

Lloyd George offered the IRA a deal in the same month that the IRA's 'director of operations' for the mainland, Rory O'Connor, started procuring assassinations. The London IRA attempted to murder Londoners who had some connection with the Royal Irish Constabulary, including shooting at a party playing golf in Ashford, Kent. The campaign soon petered out.[70] In June 1922, however, Field Marshal Sir Henry Wilson was gunned down as he entered his home in Eaton Square. The two assassins tried to fight their way away from the scene through Belgravia and Pimlico, firing their large-calibre Webley revolvers at unarmed police, seriously wounding pursuers, until they were overwhelmed by weight of numbers. The murder was announced in the House of Commons by a visibly shaken Asquith.[71]

There were voices raised in parliament, and outside, who wished to portray the assassination as evidence that the whole 'Irish [Catholic] race' was addicted to assassination.[72] Winston Churchill, speaking for the government, on the other hand, argued that the assassination was the work of a 'rebellious faction'.[73] The assassins were 'Rory O'Connor Republicans'. O'Connor now led the faction of IRA fighters which had launched a violent insurrection against the new government in Dublin. Collins and Lloyd George were tacit collaborators.[74] Lloyd George and his ministers reached a 'general agreement . . . to bring the prisoners to trial and to convict them as soon as possible; to avoid anything which would give the appearance of a great political trial'.⁷⁵ The only official intervention of Collins's Provisional Government in Dublin was a lukewarm plea that the assassins should not be executed because it would complicate their own prosecution of civil war. The assassins went to the gallows as traitors to both Britain and Ireland.⁷⁶

Making Irish assassination an Irish problem gave the British little respite from assassination as a broader imperial problem, however. When Britain elected a new Conservative government in the autumn of 1924, that government was immediately faced with the recrudescence of assassination in both Egypt and India. At first sight, assassination in Egypt seemed the greater threat. To some it also appeared that a right-of-centre democratic government might be willing to abandon the 'liberal script'. There was, in the event, no change of approach in Egypt, and the British dealt with the assassination campaign in what one might now speak of as their traditional manner. Indeed, some of the men following tradition had done much to create that tradition in the first place. Winston Churchill, a defector from Liberal to Conservative, had served as senior minister under Asquith. By chance, Asquith himself was lodging with the British High Commissioner in Cairo in the winter of 1924.⁷⁷

In November 1924, assassins shot down Sir Lee Stack, Sirdar of the Egyptian Army and Governor-General of the Sudan, as he was getting into his car. Stack's shooting was different from what had gone before.⁷⁸ First, Britain could directly blame the government of an independent state, Egypt, for commissioning the assassination. Second, Britain had ready-made, damaging and achievable punishments for Egypt.⁷⁹ The British would accept blood money, but they would also irrevocably sever Sudan from Egypt.⁸⁰ Third, and crucially, Britain had an imperial proconsul, Bull Allenby, now willing to operate outside the usual framework of checks and balances.⁸¹ Allenby held the prime minister, Saad Zaghlul, whom he described as 'that wicked old man', personally responsible for the assassination.⁸² Allenby's officials in the British High Commission drew up a charge sheet. Its title, 'Points establishing Saad Zaghlul's direct responsibility for the murder of Sir Lee Stack' was an accurate indication of its purpose and conclusions.⁸³

There was room for manoeuvre in defining the conspiracy. The contents of the High Commission's charge, if not its conclusions, could easily have led to a more cautious approach. As it was, Allenby was relentless in his personal pursuit of Zaghlul, leading to a rate of action that London found disturbing in its pace, if not its direction. The High Commissioner tracked down the prime minister to deliver an ultimatum before Zaghlul's government had the chance to resign.[84] He was seen off on his mission by Asquith and accompanied by an impressive bodyguard of mounted lancers.[85]

The British had a trump card to play in the form of an informer – a real informer, not some 'pervert student', in the phrase of the commandant of the Cairo police – inside the assassination gang. He led British officials to the Zaghlulist politician, once a Watanist, Shafiq Mansur.[86] Mansur confessed to his crimes.[87] His evidence in turn led directly to ministers in the Zaghlul government, Mahmoud Nakrashi and Ahmed Maher.[88] However, the brio with which Allenby issued threats backed by shows of British might, including the menacing overflights of bombers, turned the Foreign Secretary against his turbulent proconsul. Allenby was effectively forced out. The end of his term of office marked a return to the, by now, traditional tendency to narrow an assassination conspiracy as much as possible.[89] At the height of the crisis, the government despatched an obsessively conformist diplomat, Nevile Henderson, to act as Allenby's minder.[90] Whereas Allenby had wanted to use Mansur, alive and talking, to destroy the Wafd, Henderson advised the immediate execution of Mansur and his band.[91] As a result, Nakrashi and Maher were found not guilty at trial in May 1926.[92]

Assassination in India proved an even more intractable problem than assassination in Egypt but here, too, the traditional response dominated. In India, too, the imperial government tried to limit the extent of conspiracy. The Viceroy of India, Lord Reading, formally announced that the pre-war Hindu extremist organisations, the Anusilan Samiti and the Jugantar, had reformed and were killing again a few weeks before the assassination of Lee Stack in Cairo. The new twist that Reading added to his announcement was the use of the phrase 'Red Bengal', suggesting that a veneer of Bolshevism had been applied to Hinduism.[93] British officials were always half-hearted about this characterisation, however: they knew that, although the Bolsheviks would certainly make trouble if they could, Communism was a sideshow.[94] Just as before the war, British officials realised that India would require slow boring work. Their approach was to localise any special legal measures to Bengal, most notably in the Bengal Criminal Law Amendment Ordinance, then Act. Behind the scenes, and based on previous experience, they started building out long-term intelligence networks, without which any legal remedies would be toothless.[95]

Indian nationalists – of all stripes – naturally denounced the Bengal legislation as monstrous: it reintroduced internment without trial, specifically for 158 individuals. British policymakers saw the law as a middle course. The last thing they wanted was 'panic among the Europeans of Calcutta'.[96] The Governor of Bengal, Lord Lytton, was 'quite prepared to discuss with Gandhi terms under which internees can be released but he must have the ordinance in the background . . . on the last occasion . . . when the men were released, some went back on their promises and the whole conspiracy was set up again.'[97]

This dull administrative approach was somewhat obscured in the post-war period since so much of the public action revolved around the character of an unusual type for the British empire, the celebrity policeman. The Commandant of the Calcutta City Police, Mike Tegart, was as an energetic pursuer of assassins. Tegart combined effectiveness with an undoubted element of showmanship.[98] He avidly read his reviews in the pro-assassination Hindu press.[99] An assassin 'killed' Tegart in the Chowringhee district of central Calcutta in January 1924 only to find he had shot dead an 'innocent Sahib' – a schoolteacher named Ernest Day – instead.[100] The assassins repeated the performance in Chittagong a few months later, killing a police officer they mistook for Tegart.[101] Tegart met personally with Gandhi to try and persuade him that the British would genuinely prefer those attracted by assassination conspiracies to become anti-British political activists instead. The British had plenty of evidence that the assassins received support and funding from inside Gandhi's own movement but they did not intend to make an issue of it.[102] They stuck to that line.[103] In September 1928 the Bengal Government released all the detainees held under the Bengal Criminal Law Amendment Act and Ordinance.[104]

The British faced another recrudescence of assassination in 1929, both in the Punjab and in Bengal.[105] There was no doubt that these assassins were very dangerous.[106] An assassin shot and killed Police Assistant Superintendent Saunders, in Lahore, in another case of mistaken identity since he had wanted to kill Police Superintendent Scott, although he professed himself satisfied with the more junior officer.[107] Thanks to the intelligence services' ability to place informers close to terrorist leaders, they were able to work out what had happened.[108] Assassins had come into the Punjab from the United Provinces to assist with the killing of Scott/Saunders: the police matched a Mauser pistol cartridge recovered at the scene with ammunition from a train robbery near Lucknow.[109]

Politicians, too, preferred a watching brief rather than precipitate action. It took a shift of tactics by the assassins away from police officers and towards spectaculars to get much in the way of an overt response.[110] In November 1929, the Delhi-based HSRA (Hindustan Socialist Republican Association) attempted to blow up the viceroy's train.[111] Lord Irwin had been on his way to meet Gandhi for further political negotiations with the nationalists. This was a moment when the HSRA and Gandhi were in close contact.[112] The latter was notably unsympathetic when he met Irwin after the attempt. Even after his own brush with death, however, Irwin was unwilling to take overt action against the assassins. In April 1930, the Bengal Government deliberately allowed the Bengal Criminal Law Amendment Act to lapse once again.[113]

It was only when a group of revolutionaries seized the government armoury in Chittagong in May 1930 that the viceroy agreed that Bengal should reimpose the Bengal Act.[114] He also declined to reprieve Saunders's assassins.[115] Immediately thereafter, the assassination threat worsened.[116] In August 1930, two assassins tried to murder Tegart in Calcutta's Dalhousie Square. A bomb penetrated the rear door of his car, injuring the driver, a beggar sitting on the pavement, a rickshaw coolie and a Muslim passer-by. It wounded one of the assassins. Tegart gave chase, brandishing his own semi-automatic pistol. He went through the assassin's pockets, looking for evidence, as the man bled out on the street.[117]

Tegart did not leave matters there. Coming up to retirement after thirty years in India, he planned and carried out one final long-desired coup. He led a group of volunteer Bengal police officers across the border into French Chandernagore and personally seized the procurers of assassination who had long evaded him. Tegart's were an unlikely group of special forces raiders, some bespectacled, most wearing shorts that revealed a few somewhat pudgy bellies, and equipped with a missorted armoury of personal weapons. Nevertheless, aided by the complaisance of French officials who had no love for their violent cuckoos-in-the-nest, their coup succeeded.[118] The legend of Tegart's 'charmed life' grew on both sides.[119]

Others were not so lucky. In the same month as Tegart's raid, the Inspector-General of Police for Bengal, Francis Lowman, and Superintendent Eric Hodson were both shot as they visited a friend in a Dacca hospital: Lowman died.[120] In December 1930 the assassin who had murdered Lowman shot and killed Lieutenant-Colonel Norman Simpson, the Inspector General of Prisons, in his Calcutta office. The news arrived in London as the Round Table Conference on a future constitutional settlement for India was in progress.[121] Simpson's successor barely escaped the same fate when his would-be assassins murdered Inspector Tarini Mukharji instead.[122] Sir Geoffrey Montmorency, the Governor of the Punjab, took two bullets from an assassin. A police officer was killed during the attack.[123] Some officials, not 'particularly keen on being shot', such as the Lahore judge, Alan Gordon Walker, got on a first-class boat to Britain and left India.[124]

Irwin's response was largely to ignore the threat to pursue political negotiations with Gandhi. Their 'pact', signed in March 1931, lifted press controls, allowing both vernacular and English-language newspapers to celebrate the assassins and their work. Both Irwin and his intelligence officers thought there was a long game to be played. Congress might be 'contemptible', but if it enjoyed some political successes, assassination might seem less plausible as a tactic.[125]

This came at a time when the Midnapore district, where there were close links between the Hindu extremists and the Congress Party, emerged as the epicentre of assassination in Bengal.[126] Tegart said that entryism by the procurers of assassination into Congress was the most challenging threat for him to disentangle.[127] The first District Magistrate of Midnapore to be assassinated, James Peddie, had been effective in opposing Congress's violent intimidation of Midnapore's part-time village policemen. He had also directly criticised Gandhi.[128]

The Midnapore assassination campaign generated the clearest example of both European private citizens and government officials losing confidence in the 'liberal script'. The matter was not helped when an assassin attempted to kill Edward Villiers, the president of the European Association in Calcutta. Villiers was loud in demanding savage reprisals.[129] In fact, the man who had shot him was sentenced to ten years in prison for attempted murder.[130] When a young female assassin murdered the District Magistrate of Tippera, G.C.B. Stevens, a group of his ICS (Indian Civil Service) colleagues asked the Bishop of Calcutta to intercede with the viceroy to express their view 'that they are being killed off one by one and the Government cannot protect them. They say it was not part of their contract that they should be shot at.'[131] In contrast to Peddie in Midnapore, Stevens was regarded by his colleagues as an ICS officer who was all for India for the Indians.[132]

Two assassins killed another District Magistrate of Midnapore, B.E.J. Burge, at a football match, part of a series he had organised to improve intercommunity relations.[133] The investigation of Burge's assassination provided the police with a clear picture of the whole conspiracy, since one of the assassination gang turned approver. The murder of successive District Magistrates had been a definite strategy since 1928. The assassins were recruited from a Hindu school in Midnapore which was finally closed after Burge's death.[134]

A senior ICS officer, indeed, a future governor of both Bengal and Assam, put it directly to the Government of India that the time had come to abandon the intelligence-led counter-assassination policy and adopt a policy of full-blooded reprisal. Specifically, he proposed removing all British officials from Midnapore and encouraging Muslims and Hindus to massacre one another.[135] The *Manchester Guardian*'s correspondent in India wrote that 'not since the Mutiny has British opinion in India been so stirred'. He had heard British officials blaming Irwin's indulgence of Gandhi for unleashing 'the degenerates who control Congress, mostly worshippers of the bloodthirsty goddess Kali'.[136]

Such expostulations gained very little traction. Bengal's chief intelligence officer dismissed the press's obsession with Kali: the assassins, he commented, were primed with a quick political lecture, not a long religious ritual.[137] Nevertheless, the Director of the Delhi Intelligence Bureau – the all-India intelligence co-ordination centre – did acknowledge that 'depression' was spreading in the police and civil officials stationed in the 'worst districts of Bengal'. These districts included Midnapore, Dacca and Alipore.[138] A judge, Ralph Garlick, was shot in the head and died instantly at his own bench in his own courtroom. The Commissioner at Dacca, Cassells, took a bullet in the thigh and Inspector Khan Bahadur Maulvi Ahsanullah was shot dead in Chittagong.[139]

It was Ahsannullah's death that led to the most worrying loss of control. The police took their own measures following the murder of the 'popular Muhammadan Inspector by a Hindu youth after a football match'. The Bengal government severely censured the officers who had beaten suspects and ransacked their houses. One of those officers shot himself after receiving the rebuke. Directives flew out to all magistrates and police officers warning them that, although understandable, letting their men off the leash was 'prejudicial to Government'.[140]

It was the worry about the state apparatus starting to crack that finally moved the Bengal and Indian governments, and ultimately their masters in London. Between late October 1931 and early 1932 the Bengal government strengthened the Bengal Criminal Law Amendment Act and its associated ordinances. In an abandonment of the pretence that assassination was simply a Bengali problem, the Punjab also introduced similar legislation. In March 1932, a familiar face in the world of assassination arrived in Bengal. The government appointed Sir John Anderson, the man who had been sent to run Dublin Castle by Lloyd George a dozen years previously, as governor. Just before Anderson's arrival a female assassin attempted to shoot his outgoing predecessor. In a rather unusual apprehension, she was grappled into submission by the vice-chancellor of the University of Calcutta. A hard-bitten terrorist who had been involved in the plots against Tegart, she pleaded that she had been 'overcome by womanly emotion'. Even London thought that the Indian courts had gone soft in the head when they exercised clemency.[141]

One of Anderson's first acts was to reach agreement with his equally new opposite number, the commander-in-chief of the Army's Eastern Command, Sir Norman MacMullen, to deploy troops in Bengal. This meant also that military intelligence officers would join the hunt for assassins alongside their much put-upon police opposite numbers.[142] By the time military intelligence arrived, the government of Bengal had already detained two thousand. That left about another two thousand to find. This was plainly a world away from the one hundred and fifty would-be members of assassination squads the government had targeted during the Great War era.[143] British administrations in India were often chided for panicking but a more realistic charge may have been complacency.[144]

There was no doubt that Anderson's appointment marked a major change of tack in London. However, the Secretary of State for India, Sir Samuel Hoare – the secret service officer who had written the report on the assassination of Rasputin – was forever vigilant about pushing counter-terrorist violence too far.[145] Like Irwin, he did not wish assassination to affect political reform in India. It was enough for men like Hoare and Irwin that Congress was willing to publicly criticise assassination. In September 1931, Jawaharlal Nehru called for the abandonment of the dual-track strategy of sponsoring both terrorist violence and mass political protest. Gandhi condemned assassination as a political tactic in January 1932, although he accused the Government of India of 'terrorism' in the same breath.[146]

To nobody's surprise, Anderson himself quickly became a target for assassination. In May 1934, six assassins made a 'bold attack' on the governor's box at the Lelong races in Darjeeling. They had a clear shot but missed with all their rounds before security surged around Anderson. One attacker was killed, and another was captured on the course. The British around Anderson had harsh words to say about Congress speaking out of two sides of its mouth, but there was never any suggestion that they would cease talking directly to its leaders, especially Gandhi.[147] In large part, this was because Anderson and his officers were confident that they were getting on top of terrorism. Personally, they were just as much at risk, but the combination of intelligence and detention worked. The police had by now seeded the assassination organisations with informers; once they had names and locations, the military picked up the terrorists and shipped them to remote prison camps.[148] In August 1934, Anderson pushed through a new law making the power of detention permanent.[149] However, assassination proved no bar either to striking a deal with the Indian parties or to pushing that deal for a new Indian constitution through the British parliament.[150]

Thus, the last and late spectacular assassination, of what was by then the inter-war period, was dismissed as nothing more than a politically irrelevant tragedy.[151] When the former Lieutenant-Governor of the Punjab, Sir Michael O'Dwyer, was shot and killed, and the Secretary of State for India, Lord Zetland, was injured, at the Caxton Hall, London, in March 1940, the act was dismissed as that of a crazed individual. 'This fanatic,' *The Times* commented when Udham Singh was condemned to death, 'was resorting to terrorist methods which have long been discredited and discarded by many schools of Indian Nationalism. As Mr. Gandhi said on the morrow of the crime, "such acts have been proved to be injurious to the causes for which they are committed."'[152] Nehru's spokesmen 'earnestly hoped' that the assassination 'would not have far-reaching repercussions on the political future of this country'. The one prominent nationalist who wanted to turn the assassination trial into a political showpiece was Congress's man in London, Krishna Menon, and even he wanted to enter an insanity plea, and reportedly genuinely believed the assassin was crazy.[153] Not that the British imperial state took the crazed individual theory on trust: it used its now very well-established procedures to investigate. The behind-the-scenes inquiry revealed Singh was a bit more than a mere 'lingerie salesman'. He had a long record as a would-be assassin in the Punjab. Unlike the Bengalis who had attacked John Anderson, the Punjabi was a good shot. He hit Sir Louis Dane and Lord Lamington as well as O'Dwyer and Zetland. The prosecution and the judge, however, agreed to co-ordinate to keep politics out of the trial.[154]

Singh was swiftly convicted and executed. It was three decades since the last Indian assassination in London. The killing of Sir Curzon Wyllie had seemed pregnant with potential menace; that of Sir Michael O'Dwyer was not. The Indian government reported that assassination had faded into oblivion. Many former procurers of assassination had been absorbed into the political blocs, particularly Congress. A few clung in thought, but not in action, to the old ways but, under close police watch, they had little success in recruiting others in the old hot spots, including the Punjab.[155]

This reading of the 'Calcutta rules', as part of an Asquithian script written in London, should come with two caveats. First, to obviate systemic panic within the ICS and IPS, some compromise had to be reached between London's sang froid and the hot fear and anger in the *mofussil*, the badlands. That compromise was a specifically Indian personal security system. Second, neither the security system nor the more general architecture of Indian counter-assassination was easily replicable.

Until 1930, the standard response to assassination in both Britain and the empire had been broadly similar: protect only reluctantly and in response to severe need.[156] How different India became was perhaps best symbolised by the fact that two Special Branch bodyguards escorted Gandhi home from London after the second Round Table Conference of 1932. This may not have sounded like oppressive security, but it was the same level of protection that Special Branch gave the prime minister in 'exceptional' situations.[157] Other ministers rarely had any protection: it was a matter for comment if they did. When Sir Samuel Hoare spoke about the Midnapore murders to the Oxford University Conservative Association, it was 'the first time a speaker at a University meeting has had a police guard'.[158]

The ad hoc approach was apparent in assassination hot spots. During the Egyptian crisis of 1919, the commandant of the Cairo Police, Tom Russell, although receiving intelligence that he would soon be a target, drove around by himself – albeit very fast – and relied on his own sidearm for protection.[159] Russell believed that 'one of the factors that has made the assassins' task an easy one, has been the innate dislike of the Englishman of going about armed, and his unwillingness to take reasonable precautions.'[160] Many Britons, however, were ill suited to bear arms. One official badly wounded himself when he pulled the trigger of a revolver while reaching into his mackintosh to retrieve his handkerchief.[161] The assassins were much more adept with the manual of arms. Lee Stack's assassin used a handy .32 semi-automatic pistol loaded with modified expanding bullets. Stack survived the actual shooting with the relatively small-calibre weapons but died from internal injuries caused by the doctored rounds. Stack had no bodyguards. The assassins shot his chauffeur and military ADC, and they played no effective role in the Sirdar's defence. An unarmed policeman, who happened to be in the area, gave chase: he was also shot.[162]

In the 1920s, India had been little different from Egypt. Following the attempted assassination of Hardinge in 1912, the police did devise a new security regime for close protection, but it was lifted as soon as possible.[163] Prominent Indian intelligence officers who, it was realised, were the most exposed officials, retained their bodyguards, but men pressed into the protection role were not specialists.[164]

The Indian police did pull together large task forces of armed police on an ad hoc basis for high-profile visitors. David Petrie was put in charge of an 'all-India' team for the visit of the Prince of Wales in 1921. He was told to make security discreet, however: the purpose of the visit was to have the future King-Emperor surrounded by adoring crowds. Petrie put two squads of detectives in cars, one behind and one in front of the royal vehicle. However, the 'pilot car' had to keep 800 yards distant, making it pointless if there was any threat. Security relied entirely on the 'tail car' fifty yards to the rear.[165] In the much more dangerous circumstances of 1927, the 'all-India' team protecting the members of the Simon Commission – charged by the British government to consider constitutional reform in India – comprised two hundred armed plainclothesmen.[166]

As late as 1930, there was no regular system.[167] The most sought-after target in India, Mike Tegart, like Tom Russell in Cairo, preferred to rely on his wits, his sidearm and his rejection of all routine, an approach that his colleagues regarded as a reflection of his personality.[168] Such an approach worked for Tegart but, as in Egypt, was not always a good bet for others.[169]

This kind of showmanship could not go on forever. The assassination of Norman Simpson in December 1930 forced significant change.[170] Simpson was working in his office in the Writers' Building in Calcutta. Three assassins, wearing smart European suits, breezed in as if they were on legitimate business. They entered Simpson's office and shot him dead. The threat was only ended when a senior police officer, who had his office nearby, rushed in and shot an assassin. In any case, the assassins themselves were intent on committing suicide.[171] At this point Irwin started cancelling public engagements.[172]

The 'permanent' protection system for the viceroy and the governors comprised a close-protection detail in two security cars, one in front and one behind. Each car had a driver and a four-man security detail, at least two of whom always had their hands on the butts of their revolvers. The cars drove everywhere fast. When they had to stop, another protection team of armed plainclothes police officers would surround the VIP. That team comprised thirteen men. A much wider perimeter was created by local uniformed police and troops.[173]

Lower down the scale, judges, magistrates and 'superior' police officers now also had visible protection. This protection was mainly provided by Indian constables, although some police officers employed British sergeants. A given district could have up to fifteen officials who qualified for protection. That meant thirty policemen on permanent bodyguard duty, with a two-man team for each official, so that there was 'always one gun-man on duty with each officer'.[174] The police recruited these 'gun-men' from a pool of Indians who had served in the army, mainly from groups regarded as 'trustworthy', particularly Punjabi Muslims. Officials were impressed by the quality of their bodyguards, but the government feared that the new system might well prove 'endless'.[175] The introduction of the formal protection system had a visible and significant impact on both policing and governance. The burden of personal protection was the creation of a barrier between the authorities and the people.[176]

The non-replicability of the Indian system was demonstrated by attempts to do so in Palestine. India was a long-established dominion, with a large army, administrative class, civil service, police service and court system. One of the legal measures used for the control of plotters was a Bengal law dating back to 1818. The intelligence department traced its roots back as far as 1838. Palestine, on the other hand, had been an imperial possession only since 1918. Technically, it was not even British but a League of Nations Mandate. The new territory formed the Palestine Police in 1922. Outwardly, Palestine quickly gained the features of colonial governance common across the empire. But this was just show. The police and civil service was jerry-built.[177] As one long-serving mayor in northern Palestine commented, the Ottoman empire had many faults but, having ruled the Near East since 1516, it did security better than the British.[178]

Despite claims to the contrary, and as Mike Tegart found to his cost, few were willing or able to reproduce Calcutta rules elsewhere.[179] In December 1937, Tegart and David Petrie agreed to come out of retirement to advise on reversing the near collapse of law and civil governance in Palestine. In December 1938, assassins ambushed Tegart's car on the Jerusalem road. His luck held, and 'his remarkable escape' was but 'one more to the many'.[180] His companion, Deputy Superintendent G.D. Sanderson, who had recently transferred to the Palestine Police from the IPS, was not so fortunate. Sanderson died next to Tegart before the car could make it to Ramallah.[181]

Palestine was not the India Tegart and Petrie had left.[182] Even after the experiences of India, the High Commissioner for Palestine, Sir Arthur Wauchope, and the head of the British forces in the country, Sir John Dill, failed to strike the same deal that Anderson and MacMullen had managed four years previously in Bengal.[183] In the end, Britain had to pour many more troops – about two-and-a-half times as many – into Palestine as it had into Bengal. Palestine's conflict was much more militarised than Bengal's ever had been. Bengal was about seven times the size of Palestine and had a population twenty-eight times as big.[184] According to Tegart's interviewees, the Inspector General of the Palestine Police Force (PPF), R.G.B. Spicer, who survived an assassination attempt in June 1937, had tried to turn the PPF 'into a military machine' and, while failing at that, had ensured that it could not function in its counter-terrorism role either, with a 'total lack of reliable police intelligence'.[185] Unlike in Bengal, counter-assassination was not a joint army–police operation. Military intelligence ran their own networks and shared nothing with the civilian authorities.[186] The new police force that Petrie and Tegart helped redesign was, nevertheless, much closer to Spicer's vision than anything produced in Bengal.[187]

One matter in which India and Palestine were similar was the festering of assassination societies, though in Palestine, of course, the assassins were Muslim and Jewish fanatics.[188] At the head of the Supreme Muslim Council of Palestine, the Grand Mufti of Jerusalem, Hajj Amin al-Hussein, was a virulent Anglophobe and antisemite. He became even more outspoken about killing Britons and Jews once he escaped from Jerusalem and found a safe haven in French-controlled Beirut.[189]

The Mufti and those he inspired mixed random shooting of Britons in uniform with genuine targeted murders of named officials. The Palestine Police was prepared for neither, despite the lessons of India. The first fully attested assassination target was Alan Sigrist, an assistant superintendent of police. Two Palestinian assassins, one armed with a semi-automatic pistol and the other with a revolver, ambushed Sigrist's car on the Jericho road in Jerusalem. Contrary to the practice of an experienced officer in assassination country, he was driving slowly with a rifle-armed constable in the passenger seat. The guard could not bring his unwieldy weapon to bear. Although the guard did subsequently manage to shoot an assassin with his revolver, Sigrist had already been hit twice. He survived but left the PPF.[190]

Such assassination attempts, including the attack on Spicer, continued, but the attack that finally spurred London into a frontal attack on Palestinian Arab political institutions, proscribing the Arab Higher Committee and introducing large-scale detention without trial, was the murder of Lewis Andrews, the District Commissioner of Galilee, in Nazareth in late September 1937.[191] Andrews did have a British bodyguard, but the bodyguard was killed in the attack. The police forensic investigation established that the assassination weapon had previously been used to assassinate a highly effective Palestinian police superintendent, Halim Basta, in Haifa five months earlier.[192] The leadership of the Palestine police made a fetish of catching the Andrews assassins.[193] Their more damaging operational losses attracted very much less notice. The third Muslim Palestinian police intelligence inspector in Haifa, Saado Arab, was assassinated in December 1937. None of the Palestinian intelligence inspectors had any form of protection.[194] Unlike in India, where Indian police officers were trusted to hunt the assassins, the British disarmed nearly all Palestinian policemen, fearing that they would side with the rebels. The Palestinians were replaced by hastily recruited Britons from England and Jewish settlement police.[195]

In October 1938, an assassin, disguised as a blond hunchback, killed W.S.S. Moffat, the assistant district commissioner in Jenin. British soldiers beat a resident who suffered from curvature of the spine to death.[196] In a statement endorsed by the High Commissioner, Sir Harold MacMichael, Donald MacGillivray, a junior official who would later rise high in colonial service, wrote: 'punitive measures, adopted against persons against whom there are no reasonably good grounds for suspicion . . . [are] prejudicial to our interests.' The British were terrorising people 'for refusing to commit virtual suicide by giving information or assistance against their own flesh and blood'. No protection from revenge assassination was, or could be, offered in return.[197]

The best-known, and best-organised, example of violent counter-assassination was the army's creation of the 'special night squads' in Galilee. British officers led Jewish settlers and turned them on Arab villages: their goal was terror rather than the pursuit of specific suspects. The Palestine police acted as the clean-up crew for the bodies. The army could only tolerate the irregulars for four months.[198] The feeling many officials had of being out of control was palpable.[199] There was an assassination panic in Palestine.

However, Palestine was not particularly representative of the British empire. British politicians and officials proved remarkably wedded to Asquith's script for dealing with assassination. Assassination should not be interpreted as broad opposition to British rule. It was the preserve of a few violent fanatics. British imperial authorities should deal with the assassins rather than overreacting, killing large numbers of their subjects and provoking a crisis that posed a genuine threat to the legitimacy and security of British rulership.

4

DEATH TO THE PRESIDENTS
Assassination and the USA's Near Abroad, 1901–1950

In the first half of the twentieth century, the Americans usually told the story of assassination in the US in terms of infection from Europe: anarchy in the USA, so to speak.[1] Every threat to a President was met with inevitable suspicion that the assassin was an Anarchist.[2] If assassins were not Anarchists, they were inbred madmen. 'An essential difference,' wrote a *Washington Post* correspondent in 1934, 'between assassinations in the New World and the Old is that here it is attempted or carried out most frequently because of imagined grudges, madness or primary dementia praecox.'[3]

Patient Zero was President William McKinley, shot and killed by an American-born assassin of Polish descent in the Temple of Music, Buffalo, NY, in September 1901. Presidential assassination was hardly a twentieth-century phenomenon in America, Presidents Lincoln and Garfield both having been murdered in office, but nineteenth-century assassination had been nativist murder, killings by disappointed office holders or political rivals of exemplary breeding.[4] McKinley's assassin, armed with a short-barrelled revolver, passed through fifteen guards hired by the Temple of Music, ten uniformed Marines, two Buffalo police department detectives and three Secret Service bodyguards.[5] It was not that the President was unprotected, it was that his protection was, as befitted the location, a tragicomic opera. One of the Secret

Service men did wrestle the revolver from the assassin's hand after he had fired, only to be set upon by the crowd, who thought he was the assassin, and beaten so badly that he never recovered his health.[6]

The pro-Democrat *North American Review* gave a platform to America's most famous detective to make the point that the US state was not very effective. Robert Pinkerton argued that the public sector was laughably amateur.[7] The Secret Service were political appointees, not properly trained professionals. The first thing professionals would do was organise some proper threat analysis – this was a call that would echo through American politics for the next century.[8] In 1906, Congress gave the Secret Service the statutory duty of guarding the President, a role extended to the President-elect in 1908. The Department of Justice created its own Bureau of Investigation to fill some of the gaps created by the Treasury Department Secret Service's new role.[9]

The most telling element of the McKinley assassination, however, was the broader reaction of government authorities. McKinley died a week after being shot. Fifty Anarchists, including their best-known representative, the Lithuanian-born Jew Emma Goldman, were arrested and detained for three weeks. It would have been entirely reasonable for the New York and federal authorities to have claimed that McKinley's murder was not an assassination, but rather the act of a crazed individual born in Detroit. Instead, they insisted it *was* an assassination and did everything to make the case that the murder was the direct result of the infection of the American body politic by Eastern European proselytes. The *North American Review* commented: 'We see that the anarchists of this country, and especially those of the class to which [Leon] Czolgosz [the assassin] belongs – Slavs, Polish and Russian Jews – are in no sense a product of American conditions, but rather a growth transplanted from the Old World.'[10]

Pinkerton weighed in with two proposals. Internally, 'Reds' should be 'marked for constant surveillance and on the slightest excuse made harmless' and, externally, new laws should allow the deportation of any individual who threatened the state. Both suggestions were accepted by the political elite.[11] The 1907 Immigration Act included a clause that allowed the secretary of commerce to deport any immigrant who expressed support for the 'assassination of public officials'. That was only if such views were articulated after entry; it was mandatory to deny entry to anyone who had previously spoken favourably of assassination in Europe. These provisions were restated in the 1917 Immigration Act.

There is no evidence that the very specific linkages made between assassination and immigration in American legislation had any practical impact on assassination in America. The few assassinations that could be traced back to Europe were organised by the Soviet Union, not incubated by Anarchists.[12]

McKinley's successor, Teddy Roosevelt, served as President from 1901 to 1909 as a Republican, then formed his own party to run in 1912, then ran in the Republican primaries in 1916. He rather theatrically proclaimed that he could wield a pistol to guarantee his own security. He did not want protection and would not have any.[13] The record suggested something rather different. In September 1903 Roosevelt took a special train from his home at Oyster Bay in Long Island to Syracuse, New York, accompanied by 'a cavalcade of Secret Service men, mounted police, and Central Office detectives'.[14] Roosevelt was both lauded and derided for the attention he paid to his personal security. He 'fully realized the danger to which a public man of his prominence was exposed, particularly at times of popular excitement when cranks and Anarchists were likely to seek notoriety by attempting assassination. No President was ever guarded more closely by Secret Service men than Col. Roosevelt. He regarded ... these guards as a necessity.' When Roosevelt was shot on the 1912 campaign trail, the attacker proved to be a crank rather than an Anarchist, albeit one born in Germany.[15]

By the time of President Wilson's second inauguration in 1917, the German threat had been added to the Anarchist and crank threats on the list of presidential worries. Those worries were reasonable enough although there was no specific threat. Deadly German special operations in the USA were well documented by 1917.[16] The justification for pulling out all the stops on security was that everyone realised that the USA had reached a 'turning point' in international relations. With his second inauguration, Wilson had the political freedom to choose if the United States would declare war on Germany. As the *New York Times* described the political theatre, 'not since the first inauguration of Abraham Lincoln [by which time the Civil War was inevitable] ...

have there been such precautions as were taken today to guard the life [of] an incoming President of the United States. Secret Service men, troops of the regular army, detectives, and policemen formed a hollow square about President Wilson as he rode to and from the Capitol building. . . . The President literally rode to the Capitol and back again through a lane of armed men. Surrounding the President's carriage . . . were thirty-two Secret Service men. Eight walked ahead of the carriage, eight behind and eight on each side . . . outside the ranks of the Secret Service men . . . fifteen troopers rode abreast at the head of the carriage and as many more immediately behind. A half dozen troopers, in single file, rode nearer the curbing on each side of the President's carriage . . . closely following the President, were twenty-five plain-clothes policemen from Washington and other cities.'[17] Despite Calvin Coolidge's attempts to reset practice to more modest levels in the 1920s, the 1917 showpiece provided the pattern for what should happen around presidents on state occasions for decades to come.[18]

However, such outward display tended to mask the reality of American assassination. Assassination in the United States was closely related to assassination elsewhere in the Americas. The United States was unusual in comparison to the European great powers (bar France) in having an elected head of state. However, presidential rule was the norm throughout the Americas. Admitting the similarity of the US to its 'near abroad' contrasted with the normal sentiment that American presidents personified the 'Anglo-Saxon ideal of freedom'; southern American presidents did not – they were perceived as Latin despots, analogous to the 'Oriental despot'.[19] Even some Latinos, such as the Mexican politician José Vasconcelos, seemed to concede the point for their American audience; southern American politics could produce 'abominable tyrannies of the Asiatic type'.[20] Assassinations counted for less in Latin America than if 'similar terrible events had occurred in the United States' because 'human life is held rather cheap'.[21]

The distinguished war correspondent Frederick Palmer acknowledged that North Americans regarded Latin American politics as 'opera bouffe'. He believed, nevertheless, that such opinions were misguided: conditions elsewhere in the Americas told Americans about themselves.[22] Assassins, commissioners of assassination and victims of assassination – often the same persons – flowed in and out of the United States on a constant basis. Vasconcelos, for example, sought refuge in the USA in fear of his life.[23] The potential victims of the so-called 'Roosevelt of the South', President Cabrera of Guatemala, famed for his ability to survive assassinations and notorious for the fervour with which he commissioned the same, sought refuge in the USA and asked for protection while there.[24] This throughput of Latin American politicians rarely fell afoul of US immigration laws. Those who did stood out. Cipriano Castro, the former president of Venezuela, charged with organising the attempted assassination of his successor in 1909, was detained on Ellis Island in 1912. However, Castro was notably attempting to enter the US after spending three years in Germany.[25]

Due to US military interventions in Central America, the US government was not infrequently accused of being implicated in assassination. The highest-profile of these assassinations was the killing of the Nicaraguan leftist leader Sandino in 1934. In 1931, the US decided to get its troops out of Nicaragua, whence they had been sent by President Coolidge in 1926. At the time, the US Secretary of State, Henry Stimson, denounced the 'mythical patriot' Sandino as a dangerous procurer of assassination.[26] President Hoover was even blunter: Sandino was a 'cold-blooded murderer' and therefore 'outside the civilized pale'.[27] In January 1934, Sandino himself was assassinated by the American-financed National Guard as he drove away from an amicable dinner with the president of Nicaragua.[28] The head of the National Guard, Anastasio Somoza, effectively admitted that he had organised the killing.[29] Some of Sandino's followers publicly blamed the US Minister in Managua, Arthur Bliss Lane, as the 'principal person responsible for the cowardly assassination', the 'true Chief of the Guardia Nacional of Nicaragua'.[30] There was no evidence that the US government had directly participated in the killing; however, Sandino's murder showed that assassination could be an effective technique against a populist irregular fighter who had humiliated the US military. In 1935, the Roosevelt government refused to aid the Nicaraguan government in dismissing Somoza for the 'assassination of innocent persons'.[31]

The Sandino case would recrudesce in the 1980s, but in the first half of the twentieth century itself the most significant threads that linked the USA to assassination in the Americas ran to and from Mexico City, Havana and San Juan. The USA had militarily occupied both Cuba and Puerto Rico during the Spanish–American War of 1898, and Puerto Rico was declared US territory in perpetuity. Mexico was the most important site of assassination in the trans-Great War period, Cuba in the early 1930s and Puerto Rico in the late 1930s. Assassination emanating from Puerto Rico generated the last 'pre-Cold War' assassination crisis of the American half-century.

Looked at in the wider American context, the protective screen thrown around Wilson in 1917 was by no means new. The comparison with the ancient history of Abraham Lincoln was superfluous when one could just compare Wilson with his immediate predecessor. In 1909, the threat had been a joint assassination aimed at the presidents of the United States and Mexico, William Taft and Porfirio Díaz.

The American frontier might have rhetorically closed in 1893 but, in reality, it just went south. As former president Teddy Roosevelt observed, with conscious reference to Sarajevo, 'Mexico is our Balkan Peninsula'.[32] The Díaz regime in Mexico was welcoming to US capitalists; but capitalism on the frontier was famously rough on all sides. Its most notorious practitioner was William Jenkins of Tennessee, who arrived in 1901 and certainly included murder among his regular business practices.[33] Jenkins was only arrested by the Mexicans in 1919.[34] An American mine manager was accused of engineering the assassination of a Mexican politician as late as 1938.[35] No real harm came to such violent *yanquis*. The rough capitalists, who often employed private military and security contractors, had deep links with influential politicians from the south-western USA.[36]

President Taft arranged a grand cross-border summit with President Díaz in the autumn of 1909. In fact, the Taft–Díaz summit was the first time that a US president had travelled outside the USA to meet any opposite number. Three weeks before the meeting, Mexican police discovered dynamite hidden in a building near where Díaz and Taft were due to meet in Ciudad Juárez.[37] Both sides denied that this was the precursor of an assassination plot aimed at the presidents. The head of the Secret Service, John Wilkie, described any such suggestion as 'rot'.[38] The Mexicans claimed that the dynamite was to be used in one of the regular assassinations aimed at lower-level officials. Nevertheless, not only did the Mexicans flood Ciudad Juárez with police and soldiers but the Americans did the same in El Paso, directly across the border. The US Army deployed three thousand troops to protect the president.[39] The Americans arrested many Mexicans on their side of the border as a precaution. Indeed, the Americans arrested many more Mexicans in assassination cases than they ever touched Anarchists.[40]

Taft underestimated how far the Díaz regime had crumbled by 1909. Assassinations were but one symptom of its incipient collapse. Díaz's partisans, however, were under few illusions about how dangerous the US border was to their prospects. The Díaz regime created a secret service specifically to operate against its enemies sheltering in the USA.[41] In May 1911, nevertheless, Taft realised his mistake, withdrew support from Díaz and reluctantly transferred it to his rival and supplanter as president, Francisco Madero. Madero inherited the secret service.[42] Mexican leftists said of Madero that he used a 'phalanx of mercenary filibusters, who without law, without honor, and without conscience have been assassinating our brothers'.[43]

Ten days before Taft demitted office in 1913, Madero and his deputy were assassinated by their erstwhile supporter General Victoriano Huerta. Huerta's officers shot Madero as he was being arrested by the army. Taft dismissed the assassination as 'deplorable from a humanitarian standpoint' but a matter of purely 'Mexican domestic concern'. On 25 February 1913, the outgoing Taft administration formally accepted Huerta's story that Madero had been killed by an out-of-control mob.[44] Huerta's cover story for the assassination enjoyed considerable mileage in Washington because the murders might plausibly be seen as 'in accord with Mexican traditions to satisfy hatred by killing'.[45] When Henry Lane Wilson, Taft's ambassador in Mexico City, arrived back in the US, he claimed that 'the Government of Provisional President Huerta of Mexico is as legal as the Government of Roosevelt when he succeeded to the Presidency after the assassination of President McKinley'.[46] The Mexican politician Ramón Prida, an exile in New York, riposted that Huerta had been in the room when Lane Wilson drafted his telegram clearing the general of murder.[47] Lane Wilson was more than a fool: he 'knew of and consented to the assassination of President Madero'.[48]

'Throughout official and Congressional circles,' the *New York Times* commented, 'the general view was that the ex-President and the ex-Vice President had been the victims of a cold-blooded assassination, directed by some of those in control of the Mexican Government.' That was most certainly the view of Taft's successor, Woodrow Wilson.[49] As soon as practicable, he removed Lane Wilson. Not trusting Lane Wilson, Woodrow Wilson sent his own investigator, the journalist William Bayard Hale, to Mexico. On 1 August 1913, Wilson announced that 'he was against the recognition of an Administration founded on murder'. The chairman of the Senate Committee on Foreign Relations chimed in that the USA would never recognise Huerta since 'it would be an incentive to every revolutionary leader to assassinate the head of the nation'.[50] A few days later Hale told the Mexican government that the USA knew it had assassinated Huerta.[51]

The assassination of President Madero formed the basis of Wilson's subsequent 'moral crusade' in Mexico.[52] The US invaded Mexico in 1914 and 1916. It was by no means inevitable that Sarajevo would become the most important assassination for 'Wilsonian internationalism'; in many ways that was an ex post facto retrofit made in the 1920s.[53] The intensely Teutonophile Hale, for instance, was delighted to do Wilson's dirty work in Mexico, but turned on him virulently over the war. Assassination in Mexico was a much more intimate affair for American politicians and opinion-formers than assassination in Bosnia. Just before Wilson's inauguration, a steamship had docked in New York, bringing the Madero family into exile in the United States. They joined former President Díaz and his family. In due course too they would be joined by General Huerta and his family.[54]

Huerta was driven from power by Venustiano Carranza, with American help, in mid-1914. Wilson recognised Carranza as the legitimate president of Mexico in 1915. Carranza plunged Mexico into a civil war, the chaos and bloodiness of which made assassination seem the least of either Mexico's or the United States' problems. One consequence of the civil war was the rise of charismatic, populist bandit-politicians.

These warlords allied with and betrayed political factions on a regular basis. The two most famous were Pancho Villa and Emiliano Zapata. It was Villa who led his forces across the border in March 1916 to raid Columbus, New Mexico, thus provoking the second American invasion of Mexico. Conventional military force, whether wielded by Mexicans or Americans, proved effective against neither Villa nor Zapata. Assassination was effective against both. Zapata was assassinated in April 1919, Villa in July 1923. Villa was finally undone by General Plutarco Calles, who managed to hide an assassination squad of seven men armed with bolt-action rifles in his house in Chihuahua. When Villa drove his car near enough to the house, they cut him down along with his bodyguards.[55] Once Zapata and Villa were safely dead, the generals who had killed them co-opted the glamorous warlords as heroes of the revolution.[56]

Carranza did much to rebuild the Mexican secret services in the United States. Indeed, he formally created the Mexican Secret Service as a division of the Ministry of Foreign Relations, with the sole goal of acting against the president's enemies in the United States.[57] Carranza's own precautions did him little good, however. He was assassinated during a military coup, in much the same way as his old boss, Madero, had been, in May 1920.[58] The commander of Carranza's bodyguard fled to the United States and described the killing in detail.[59]

The three men who killed Carranza themselves feared assassination, even in the United States. Adolfo de la Huerta, Carranza's former secretary and successor, having fallen out with the other members of the triumvirate, Plutarco Calles and Álvaro Obregón, fled to the United States. There he claimed that their assassins were stalking him. The District Attorney in Webb County, Texas, opened cases against Calles and Obregón for the murder of two Mexican army officers in Laredo in June 1922.[60] De la Huerta left New York, believing that his life in the city made him too vulnerable.[61] The former Mexican president eventually relocated to Los Angeles, where he said he would have no regret if his former allies were themselves assassinated.[62]

Obregón was nearly assassinated when he visited the United States in 1926. In that year devout Catholic Mexicans, the *Cristeros*, rose in revolt against the godless 'Bolshevik revolutionary generals'. The Catholic revolt in Mexico was a major political issue in the USA. Many

Catholic leaders fled into exile in the United States. The insurgents were supported by the US Catholic hierarchy, most notably the Archbishop of Baltimore, and primate of the United States, Michael Joseph Curley.[63] Curley was the main power behind a Catholic lay order, the Knights of Columbus.[64] A Knight of Columbus broke into Obregón's sleeping compartment on the Los Angeles–Tucson train and emptied a revolver into the bunk where the former President of Mexico and his assistant were lying. The gunman proved to be a Catholic fanatic, radicalised by the Knights but in no way directed by them.[65]

Obregón made light of the risk of assassination when he was in the US, but not when he returned to Mexico. He raised a bodyguard of six hundred men.[66] A few days previously, Obregón's rival in the upcoming presidential campaign, Francisco Serrano, had been murdered on the road to Mexico City on the orders of President Calles.[67] Obregón's caution was justified. While driving through the Bosque de Chapultepec, a wooded 1700-acre park in Mexico City, in November 1927, he was ambushed by 'clerical reactionary assassins' in another car. The attackers threw a dynamite bomb at his vehicle, and then opened fire with pistols, albeit their aim was terrible.[68]

Obregón's aides were able to wound and capture one of the assassins. This meant that the assassination conspiracy could be quickly unravelled. The men behind the assassination were all Catholic militants of the ACJM (Asociación Católica de la Juventud Mexicana) and included a priest. Within days, President Calles ordered them summarily executed, launching the priest, Miguel Agustín Pro, on the road to sainthood.[69] The Knights of Columbus rapidly mobilised to cover up Church responsibility, hiring an Irish journalist to write a hatchet job on the investigators, or 'vampires'.[70]

As it was, the Catholic militants finally killed Obregón in July 1928 in a restaurant in the Mexico City suburb of San Ángel. The successful assassin was a young political cartoonist who made a seemingly respectful approach to Obregón's table and then shot him five times with a pistol concealed in his hat. Despite the attempts of Catholic propagandists on both sides of the border to obfuscate, the nature of the assassination was immediately clear: Obregón's followers once more captured the assassin. He was personally interrogated by President

Calles, confessed his motivations and was then brutally tortured – swung by his testicles, among other torments – by the Mexican police to make sure of his story. The Catholic counter-story was that Calles himself had had Obregón killed. Calles sent his daughter and son-in-law, an American, to New York to try and counter the rumours.[71]

The US Secretary of State, Frank Kellogg, refused to take an official position on the assassination. Obregón had been in talks with the US Ambassador, Dwight Morrow, on the day he was killed.[72] Calles and Obregón had brought 'American–Mexican relations to the most auspicious stage since the days of President Diaz'. Morrow later said that every time there was an improvement in US–Mexican relations, it was erased by an assassination.[73] On the other hand, Kellogg could not give the two generals a clean bill of health, 'because of the concern with which American Catholics have regarded the Mexican government'.[74]

The US government was dragged directly into the furore when the Mexican government claimed that the assassination weapon had come from north of the border. The US Justice Department admitted that this was not an unlikely scenario, but slow-rolled the request to extradite suspected plotters. The Americans danced around the question of extradition. If the assassination was political, the suspects were protected by the 1898 US–Mexican extradition agreement. If the men had assassinated Obregón for religious reasons, they were fair game. Predictably, the Mexican plotters were long gone from the Spanish-speaking colony in the Chelsea district of Manhattan when the FBI came to call.[75]

With regard to the conspiracy to assassinate Obregón, President Calles, who had learnt from his mistakes in the Bosque de Chapultepec assassination investigation, insisted that the prosecution should take its time and play out its case in public.[76] Even the most sceptical international observers had to admit that the assassin was a fanatical Catholic, because that is what he maintained throughout. Numerous witnesses had seen him shoot Obregón and he admitted he had done so.[77]

The whole affair came to pivot on the guilt of the procurers of assassination, especially the nun, Concepción Acevedo de la Llata, universally known as Madre Conchita. ACJM members testified that they met at her house to conspire, but they provided no evidence of a direct plan for this assassination. The former head of the Mexico City police investigative bureau said that Madre Conchita had confessed, but Calles had removed him from his post for notorious corruption. It was the assassin, José Toral, who effectively condemned the woman who was his spiritual adviser and rumoured to be his lover. According to the assassin, he had wanted to kill Obregón from the moment Father Pro was executed for the Bosque de Chapultepec attack. Madre Conchita told him that religious persecution could only be ended by the deaths of Obregón and Calles. A previous plan had been to assassinate Obregón and Calles together when they attended a ball.[78] Madre Conchita confirmed the conversation but denied that she had instructed Toral to kill Obregón.[79] The male assassin was sent to his death; the woman was convicted and sent to prison.[80]

President Portes Gil, who won the presidency after the death of the president-elect, refused to pardon Obregón's assassin. Portes Gil was then almost immediately the target of a complex Catholic assassination plot. As his special presidential train – 'one of the finest in the world' – passed through the high-altitude ravine of Guanajuato, about 160 miles north of Mexico City, the assassins blew the bridge. The train was derailed and the fireman in the cab killed, but Gil, in the presidential car further back, survived.[81]

Calles declared enough was enough. In September 1928 he had told his fellow revolutionaries that they must create a unified, institutionalised political machine that would insulate its leaders from the threat of further assassinations. Believers in the Mexican Revolution could not rely solely on 'necessary men', the *caudillaje*, like him and Obregón. The assassins had to understand that the revolution had robust succession planning. The irony of Calles's proposal was not lost on his audience. An Obregonista interrupted the president to say that they did not need any lessons in assassination from an 'assassin'. Calles dismissed him as a 'masturbator'. The tone was not high-brow, but the plan to create the Permanent Revolutionary Party – the PNR – went ahead.[82] The assassination attempts not only on Gil but on his successor, President-elect Ortiz Rubio, who was shot in the jaw, reinforced the point of the exercise.[83]

In the medium term, Calles was the political victim of his own insight. He became the superfluous rather than the necessary man of

Mexican politics. The PNR sent Calles into exile in the United States in April 1936. The party was done with Calles, but Calles was not entirely done with assassination. He settled in a mansion in San Diego surrounded by private security guards. In January 1937, an assassin attempted to blow up the house with Calles within. The weapon was a large, but crude, bomb, and the bodyguards negated the threat by the simple expedient of pulling out the fuse. Thereafter, Calles's private security was reinforced with American policemen.[84]

The eventual quietening of Mexico did not remove assassination from US political culture, it merely shifted the geographical focus.[85] Well-educated splitters would point out that the Spanish-speaking Caribbean was very different territory from Spanish-speaking Mexico, but lumpers were in charge in Washington. Wilsonian internationalists would never forget Mexico, but Wilson's Democratic successor, Franklin Delano Roosevelt, was pulled east rather than south: Florida rather than Texas.

Roosevelt nearly died in Florida. Having won the 1932 presidential election, he took a fishing holiday in Floridian waters. When the president-elect made landfall at Miami's Bay Front Park, he gave a short speech from his open-topped car to the crowd that had come to greet him. Barely had Roosevelt sat down when an attacker fired five shots from a .32 revolver.[86] Under the post-McKinley law, Roosevelt was being protected by a Secret Service detail, although they did little to defend him: the shooter was overwhelmed by the crowd and local police. The post-attack reports were largely reflective of the Secret Service's attempt to run a public relations defence of the penetration of the 'most effective protective system in the world'.[87] This customary claim was plainly ignorant nonsense, if the comparator, for instance, was the highly professional system for the Viceroy of India: the Secret Service seemed to think that they were measuring themselves against Panama, where the president was vulnerable because he drove himself around the country alone.[88]

In truth, the Miami attack was a very close call: the shooter's aim was not bad; he was able to fire all the rounds in his chamber, hitting those standing near the president-elect, with the Mayor of Chicago, Anton

Cermak, fatally wounded. The American state went into full performance mode in a fashion that was very comparable to what happened in contemporary Latin America. 'Hosts of blue-coated policemen and grim-faced detectives and secret service men, aggregating nearly 1,000', met Roosevelt's train at Jersey City, escorting him across into New York.[89] The New York City Police Commissioner assigned '150 picked uniformed patrolmen to remain on duty constantly at the Roosevelt [residence]'.[90]

Although investigators ran through every conspiracy that they could imagine in the hours after the attack, including a link to Cuban revolutionaries, the garrulous Italian-born shooter soon convinced his interrogators that he was a lone idiot.[91] Only a few months after sympathising with Roosevelt over his brush with assassination in Miami, however, President Gerardo Machado of Cuba came to Florida seeking refuge from assassination in a deal brokered by now-President Roosevelt's favourite diplomat, Sumner Welles.[92]

In the 1920s, Machado enjoyed a reputation for good relations with the United States not dissimilar to that of Plutarco Calles. He undertook a successful tour of the United States in 1927, during which he was fêted by bankers and industrialists. It was others who accused Machado of running a regime based on the assassination of opponents. One of Machado's rivals for the presidency fled to New York in 1929, 'where he declared that "countless assassinations have been perpetrated by orders of the government through its agents".' The most notable victim was the student revolutionary Julio Antonio Mella, assassinated in Tampico, Mexico.[93]

However, at the turn of the decade, the hunters began to be hunted: 'the assassination of Mella was one of those things' that had acted with 'a boomerang effect'.[94] In February 1931, there was a double attempt on Machado's life. An assassin brandished pistols as Machado dedicated Havana's new capitol. A large bomb also exploded in the presidential palace. The bombers had hoped to kill Machado as he abluted. The presidential guard, whom they suborned to plant the bomb, made a mistake and rigged the president's son-in-law's bathroom instead. The result was spectacular but ineffective.[95] In this case, the assassin was an incompetent dynamiter-for-hire. The investigation into the explosion revealed, however, that treachery ran deep in the presidential guard and some officers were still working for Machado's predecessor.[96]

In August 1931, troops loyal to Machado put down a rising against his government. Some of the rebels, led by Carlos Mendieta, a future president, and a former president, Mario Menocal, went underground and formed an assassination ring. Their aim was to weaken the government by killing reliable officials before a second uprising. The ring carried out only one successful assassination – that of the head of the Rural Guards, who was killed by a letter bomb – before the judicial police in Havana broke it up.[97]

However, the struggle between police and assassins was by no means one-way. Former University of Havana students comprised the hard core of the revolutionary movement. They banded together in the openly terrorist ABC. A parallel group known as the Directorio Estudiantil was equally committed to assassination. The ABC assassinated Captain Miguel Calvo, head of the Cuban secret police in July 1932. Calvo was Machado's most effective, if brutal, counter-assassination officer. He had barely survived an ambitious plot in January 1932. The ABC had lured Calvo to a building in Havana with a false tip-off; the building was pre-rigged with explosives that the assassins detonated as the police entered. On that occasion, Calvo survived but other policemen were killed.[98] The ABC's assassination squad succeeded with more conventional means. They intercepted Calvo's car as he was driven from his home to the police headquarters accompanied by bodyguards. A big green touring car drew up alongside as Calvo's driver slowed at the bottom of an incline and the occupants killed Calvo with a shotgun slug. Slug-firing shotguns became the weapon of choice for assassins in Havana. Machado told reporters that 'I knew it was coming. They have been after me, after him and after all the men in my government.'[99]

The former students also assassinated Machado's second most effective assassin/counter-assassin, the leader of *la Porra* militia, Leopoldo Ros. Ros had created 'the Bludgeon', a supposedly civilian political party that received arms, IDs and salaries from the government. In effect, *la Porra*'s members were Machado's storm troopers. At the time of his death, Ros had supposedly retired from politics, although no-one believed that retirement to be permanent. Like Calvo he was shot with a shotgun slug from a car.[100]

In September 1932, the Directorio Estudiantil killed Machado's ally and expected successor, Vázquez Bello. This was another car-borne assassination: the student assassins shot Vázquez Bello ten times as his car pulled away from his estate. Investigators found fifty-seven bullet holes in the vehicle. The assassins had used a machine gun to generate the volume of fire that made sure of their kill.[101]

In a macabre twist, Vázquez Bello left instructions with his followers that they were to murder three named opposition politicians in the event of his death. They did their best, killing two, and missing the third only because he took refuge in the British Legation. Vázquez Bello's own family fled to the United States, where his brother served as Cuba's consul-general in New York.[102] America's senior diplomat in Cuba, Edward Reed, explained that every political 'boss' in Cuba had an entourage: if that 'boss' was killed, 'these persons suffer the consequences which may entail the ruin of all their hopes and aspirations. It was, therefore, not unnatural that Vázquez Bello's henchmen should have sought to avenge his murder on the persons of his political enemies.'[103] In fact, the assassinations were not the work solely of a grief-stricken gang, they took place under the direction of Octavio Zubizarreta, Machado's minister of the interior, the 'brains' behind the whole system of assassination.[104]

As Reed summed up the atmosphere in Havana, 'the feeling of personal insecurity exists not only among adversaries of the Government; it extends as well to high officials of the administration . . . I have received innumerable requests from anxious relatives and friends to intervene for the protection of persons . . . whose lives are believed to be in jeopardy.' The fear was palpable.[105] According to the *New York Times*'s special correspondent in Havana, Russell Porter, 'perhaps, President Machado would welcome an adjustment of the present impasse which would permit him to take ship from Havana, possibly under the protection of the Stars and Stripes.' 'For the past few years,' Porter wrote,

> President Machado has been guarded by his police and soldiers as a gang leader is guarded by his gunmen. It is an entirely different

atmosphere from that which surrounds the normal protection afforded a ruler. Lately the President has seldom appeared in public. He spends his time either in the Presidential Palace in Havana, now become a fortress with soldiers and police swarming on every floor and machine gunners and riflemen on the roof, or at his estate outside the city, surrounded by barbed wire and bristling with machine guns and light artillery, a veritable armed camp. When he rides from one place to another, it is in an armored car, preceded and followed by armored cars filled with soldiers. He travels at a high rate of speed along a route guarded by rows of police.

A 'Negro officer' guarded the entrance to Machado's office; 'there was something ferocious about the look in this man's eyes – something impersonal but coldly savage . . . the most cruel expression I had ever observed upon any human countenance'.[106]

Something clearly had to give. On 11 August 1933, Welles offered Machado a deal. The United States would get him out of Cuba on a 'leave of absence' from the presidency and guarantee him his safety. The deal, Welles told Washington, 'offers security to President Machado for the lives and property of himself and of the members of the present Government as well as the members of his family. The fear of assassination is in my judgment the fundamental obstacle to President Machado's refusal to relinquish office.'[107] Machado flew out to Miami on 12 August. Welles could save Machado, but with regard to anyone else he spoke only empty words.[108] As he admitted a few days later, 'it appears hardly likely that a so called revolutionary government composed of enlisted men of the Army and radical students who have occupied themselves almost exclusively during the last 10 days with the assassination of members of the Machado Government can form a government "adequate for the protection of life, property and individual liberty".'[109]

Assassination in Cuba did not subside with Machado's departure: there was another wave in 1936.[110] By that time, however, Roosevelt's focus had shifted nearer home. The most serious assassination of the 1930s had occurred in September 1935. Roosevelt labelled both the victim and his death 'un-American'.[111] The populist politician Governor

Huey Long was assassinated in the Louisiana State House. The still-obscure murder – Long's bodyguards killed the assassin – providentially removed Roosevelt's most dangerous Democratic rival before the 1936 presidential campaign had really begun. There was a notable lack of federal involvement in the investigation of Long's death. An unimpressive state inquest concluded that the dead shooter had had a personal grudge against Long.[112]

The part of the United States where federal action was felt most heavily was Puerto Rico. As in Cuba and Mexico, there was a strain of anti-American militant nationalism in Puerto Rico, which the American authorities, much like the Cuban and Mexican, roughly suppressed. The American authorities, like their British cousins, expressed surprise and horror that Puerto Ricans were not grateful for the manifest material benefits that imperial rule had brought to the island. They characterised the nationalists as 'an exceedingly small group' of perverted individuals: 'youngsters . . . attracted by secret meetings, flags, uniforms and golden promises, they have been putty in the hands of leaders ingenious in reconstructing history to bolster their hopes for the island's independence.'

The police killed four Puerto Rican nationalists near the pro-American University of Puerto Rico in October 1935. The nationalist leader Pedro Albizu Campos, himself a product of Harvard, called the male students at the University of Puerto Rico 'sissies' and its co-eds 'drunkards'. When Roosevelt visited Puerto Rico, Albizu Campos said that he should be greeted with 'bullets not flowers'.[113]

On 24 February 1936, the Governor of Puerto Rico, Blanton Winship, met his police chief, Colonel Francis Riggs, to discuss the threat of nationalist violence. Riggs was against the immediate arrest of militants on the dual grounds that there was not enough evidence to try nationalist leaders for serious violent offences and because he did not want to make 'a Sandino' out of Albizu Campos. It was a fatal mistake: the nationalists assassinated Riggs later in the day. Their methods were similar to those used by the Cubans. Riggs made his regular attendance at Mass and his car was ambushed by another vehicle as he left. In this case, the shots fired from the assassins' car missed; Riggs and his police escort gave chase and were lured into an ambush. A waiting assassin stepped up to the window of Riggs's car and shot him three times.

The reaction of the Americans was also similar to that of the Cubans. The assassins were murdered in police custody soon afterwards. Winship argued that Puerto Rico was hobbled by its 'sissy' approach to law and order; there was no point in offering the protection of US law to those who plainly did not wish to be American.[114] Like the British, the Americans used the tactic of physical removal. Albizu Campos and the other nationalist leaders were sent out of Cuba to serve their sentences in Atlanta, Georgia.[115] Like the Roosevelts, Winship 'laughed' at threats to his own life: like them he maintained a strong police bodyguard.[116] He was right to be cautious. The judge who oversaw the trial of the conspirators in the Riggs case was himself marked for assassination. In June 1937, assassins fired 'a dozen' bullets at him but missed.[117] They made an even more spectacular attempt on Winship himself as he attended the celebrations of the fortieth anniversary of the American occupation in the city of Ponce in July 1938. Up to nine assassins opened fire on Winship as he stood on a platform. Once more, the assassins missed their intended target, although they did kill and wound those standing nearby.[118] The attack certainly fixed Roosevelt's attention on Puerto Rico. He sacked Winship, a Republican politician for whom he did not much care, for his indulgence of police brutality.[119] He sent in the man he always trusted with his most difficult assignments, Admiral William Leahy. Within days of the outbreak of the Second World War, the president's main military adviser was heading to San Juan.

This disjuncture between what the world thought US presidents should be focused upon and their practical lived experience of assassination was nowhere more apparent than in the last of the 'pre-Cold War' conspiracies that brushed very near the US presidency. The first oddity of this attempt was that it took place seemingly out of time in 1950. On 1 November 1950, two Puerto Rican nationalists attacked Blair House, the official presidential residence while the White House was being refurbished. Their plan was to shoot their way into the building by surprising the White House police at their guard posts. The attack was not too far from success. The assassins were armed with

9mm semi-automatic pistols and thus outgunned the guards, who carried revolvers. Unlike the White House, Blair House was a townhouse with a front door on the street and no grounds. The front door was open. President Truman was dressing in his bedroom on the second floor. Reportedly, he looked out of his window clad only in boy's ventilated drawers during the shooting. As it was, the decoy shooter who was supposed to draw the police and Secret Service towards him failed when his pistol jammed. The lead assassin was killed by a policeman as he headed towards the main door. Both sides shot over thirty rounds in a short but deadly gun battle.[120]

Truman had nearly suffered for the general failure of the United States to place American assassination in its actual context. He had no worthwhile intelligence on the threat from Puerto Rico. The Blair House attack exposed presidential security as largely performative, configured mainly to keep madmen away. Truman was preparing to attend an event. As he always did, he would have walked directly out of the front door of Blair House, with two Secret Servicemen in attendance, to get in his car parked at the kerb. On being told of the attack, the head of the Secret Service White House detail, and later head of the Secret Service, futilely ran around looking for his tommy gun.

Nearly all contemporary and subsequent coverage of the Puerto Rican conspiracy to assassinate President Truman spoke of it as if it was unhinged from any real-world context. Truman was confronting the Soviet Union, developing the H-bomb, fighting the Korean War. Those were the things that mattered. The key policy issue on the President's docket on 1 November 1950 was the mounting evidence that Communist China had sent a large army into Korea. The attempt to murder Truman in Washington referred to none of those weighty matters. Assassination was working to a different timeline from the expectations of international politics. One of the White House correspondents who arrived on the scene a few minutes after the attempt found 'utter confusion'; no-one knew the identity of the attackers. Those present assumed 'that these must be agents of a foreign Communist power'. There was not even a hint that they were Puerto Ricans.[121]

The whole Truman assassination plot, of course, made a lot more sense to those who knew that the Puerto Rican nationalist leaders, rounded up and taken to continental USA in the 1930s, had been released in the 1940s. Albizu Campos had lodged with one of the would-be assassins upon his release. The US National Commission on the Causes and Prevention of Violence later commented that the Puerto Rican nationalists were the only true assassins of the American Century: other would-be murderers of presidents had been madmen.[122]

5

GOVERNMENT BY ASSASSINATION
China and Japan, 1928–1941

Between the late 1920s and the outbreak of the Second World War, the most intense use of assassination as political tool was found in East Asia. Journalists coined the phrase 'government by assassination' to describe the phenomenon in the mid-1930s.[1] In no particular order, Communists assassinated members of the KMT – the Chinese nationalists. The KMT assassinated Communists. The KMT assassinated its own members. The KMT assassinated warlords. Warlords assassinated warlords. The Japanese assassinated warlords. Koreans assassinated Japanese. The Japanese assassinated each other. Thrown into the mix were assorted Anarchists, cultists and narco-assassins, and a subculture of professional hitmen.

The assassination complexes of Japan and China became closely aligned in the late 1920s. They remained closely intertwined in the early 1930s, although China was often pushed into the background in discussion of Japanese assassination, with both assassins and government fixating on the insular origins of killing. Chinese and western observers, and even the Japanese political police, doubted, however, that a frequently proclaimed mission to protect the 'national essence' was at the root of assassination in Japan.[2] More prosaically, Japan had a weak civilian state and an overweening army with ambitions of empire in China.[3] Once Japan launched its full-blooded attempt to conquer

China in the summer of 1937, the interweaving of assassination conspiracies was once more on very public display. Many of the conspiracies manifested in Shanghai, and from Shanghai, were broadcast to the Occident. Shanghai became the very public assassination capital of the world.

The result was confusion. No-one produced a convincing master narrative. As a result, later investigators came to see the assassinations as merely the prelude to the events that interested them, the triumph of the Chinese Communist Party in the Chinese civil war in 1949 or the spread of revolutionary movements in post-Second World War Southeast Asia.[4] In the 1930s, however, there were more pressing issues for participants, not least staying alive.[5] For example, when the Chinese general Zhang Xueliang, known as the Young Marshal, visited the seaside resort of Beidaihe for a holiday in 1930, 'he and his staff occupied two trains, the former being filled with plain-clothes men to the number of 500, while the second train was of the armoured variety.' The Young Marshal, journalists observed, was probably safe from a Communist drive-by shooting, but treachery was another matter.[6]

The assassination of the Young Marshal's father, the Old Marshal, the Manchurian warlord Zhang Zuolin, in 1928 was one of the most consequential of the twentieth century. Zhang senior's death weakened Japanese democracy and made the conquest of Manchuria feasible. Yet Zhang's assassination is an event forgotten by all but specialists.[7] He does not fit into the world view espoused by anyone in contemporary Beijing, Tokyo or Taipei. Indeed, the very word 'warlord' is a derogatory term meant to belittle those soldier-politicians who 'failed' to embrace the 'whole China' visions of Nationalists, Communists or Japanese imperialists.[8]

At the time of his assassination, however, Zhang Zuolin had ruled Manchuria – north-eastern China – for eighteen years. Over those years, he had both fought and co-operated with most other factions, including Japan, which had an army in Manchuria, technically protecting its railway concessions under a 1905 agreement with the old Chinese imperial government.[9] Like all the other factions, the Old Marshal had great ambition: he had conquered Beijing but was forced to retreat from the capital by his rivals in 1927. Nevertheless, in 1927 he seemingly had a reliable ally in the newly installed prime minister of Japan, Tanaka Giichi. Tanaka had another Chinese general, Chiang Kai-shek, in his sights, not the Old Marshal. Chiang's KMT regime in Nanjing had allowed the sack of the Japanese consulate and businesses by a mob. It was the Nanjing Incident that had precipitated the fall of the Japanese government in Tokyo and brought Tanaka to power. The official policy of the Japanese government was the creation of 'fortress Manchuria', ruled by the Old Marshal with Japanese military support.[10]

Unfortunately for Tanaka's scheme, someone blew up the Old Marshal's armoured train on a railway bridge near Mukden, the capital of Manchuria. Prime Minister Tanaka himself was the target of an attempted assassination a few days later as he too went to board a train, although the police easily dealt with the nationalist fanatic who tried to stab him.[11]

In the hours immediately after the assassination of the Old Marshal, neither western observers nor rival factions could define the conspiracy that had felled Zhang. The Japanese government in Tokyo was equally baffled, not least because Japanese army officers and diplomats in China lied relentlessly to their masters.

The list of plausible assassins was long: Manchurian gangsters, the KMT, jealous underlings, rival generals. A British investigative journalist, Lenox Simpson, came closest with a Sarajevo parallel. Simpson believed the assassins were a secret society working for the Japanese Army: 'There have long been in Japan organisations similar to the Serbian organisation which carried out the Sarajevo crime,' Simpson wrote.[12] Simpson himself was assassinated in Tianjin in 1930, 'thus suffering,' Miles Lampson, the British government's diplomatic representative in China wrote, unfeelingly, of an acquaintance, 'the extreme penalty which Fate has on occasion meted out to other foreigners who were unwise enough to enter the arena of Chinese internal political strife'.[13]

The Japanese government did eventually work out the conspiracy, having sent the head of the *Kempeitai* – the military police – to investigate: the Japanese army had assassinated the Old Marshal. In doing so it had had no compunction in also killing its own officers: Japanese military liaison officers were with the Old Marshal on the train. One of them carried the Marshal out of the wreckage: the death of the Japanese left behind in the train was regarded as merely another useful layer of deception by their 'comrades'. The actual assassins were a regular Japanese army engineer unit using military explosives with professional skill.[14]

The government in Tokyo decided it was too weak to challenge the army in China. It therefore covered up the assassination, leaving the rest of the world to suspect and speculate for decades to come.[15] When the Americans investigated the Old Marshal's assassination, they managed to produce an amalgam of nearly every cock-and-bull story told: the assassination was a Japanese–Chinese conspiracy (false); the actual assassins were Chinese (false); the Japanese behind the assassination were the Secret Service Organisation (false); the chief Chinese conspirator was the Old Marshal's chief of staff (false), subsequently murdered by the Young Marshal (true).[16] In December 1928, Tanaka told Emperor Hirohito that the army had assassinated the Old Marshal and that this would be kept secret in perpetuity. Hirohito sacked the man but retained the plan. The assassins were quietly retired. Tanaka's initial instinct to purge the army of disloyal officers was quickly forgotten.

The procurer of the assassination was the chief of staff to the director of army intelligence in China, Colonel Komoto Daisaku. Komoto was in turn part of a network of army officers who believed in a 'Greater Japan': Japanese rule, over Manchuria first and China subsequently, and the liberation of the army itself from the control of politicians and plutocrats. 'Greater Japan' was only possible if army officers took direct action outside the corrupted chain of command; Tanaka himself was a general. Komoto and his collaborators were not the only group of army officers who intended to assassinate the Old Marshal. The Japanese army had a nascent special services unit for such missions, the Secret Service Organisation, but Komoto derailed it by setting the military police upon the secret service men.[17]

Before the Old Marshal's death, assassination had not been unknown in post-Great War Japan. A Korean nationalist assassinated the prime minister of Japan, Hara Takashi, in 1921. His successor was 'seldom seen in public, and then only surrounded by a bodyguard of from ten to twenty policemen, soldiers and plain-clothes officers'. Premier Takahashi did not want to be murdered by '[a] station master's half-wit helper'.[18] As crown prince in 1924, Hirohito had been shot at by a Korean nationalist.[19] More forebodingly, in the context of later developments, 'the Rockefeller of Japan', Yasuda Zanjiro, had been murdered in his villa a few weeks before the death of Prime Minister Hara, in 1921. The assassin committed ritual suicide at the scene.[20]

Assassination in the wake of the Old Marshal cover-up, however, took on a quite different tenor, not least because the assassins expected, literally, to get away with murder. In October 1930, Lieutenant-Colonel Hashimoto Kingoro – another Japanese Army intelligence officer who had moved in the same circles as Komoto Daisaku in the 1920s – formed the Cherry Blossom Society. The explicit aim of the Cherry Blossom was to bring assassination back home to Japan and turn it against Japan's leaders. The Cherry Blossom was a short-lived but influential integrating organisation. It absorbed several already existing military societies: it also brought in civilian nationalist societies. Indeed, it was the civilians who struck first, shooting the prime minister, Hamaguchi Osachi, in November 1930.

Hamaguchi's injuries paralysed his government: he finally had to resign in April 1931, dying in August 1931. The emperor's chief adviser, Prince Saionji Kinmochi, pointed out that His Imperial and Divine Majesty had to allow the flailing administration to continue, with or without Hamaguchi, or every future prime minister was sure to be assassinated. The Cherry Blossom had succeeded in its mission to spread fear and confusion.[21] Saionji himself visited Tokyo less and less. When he did come to the capital, he insisted on 'extraordinary precautions for his safety'.[22]

The government's weakness in the summer of 1931 suited the military. In September 1931, the Army took over in Manchuria, declaring it a country separate from China under Japanese tutelage, sparking the most extensive world crisis of the early 1930s. Less than a month later, the army, specifically General Araki Sadao, the godfather of the 'Greater Japan' movement, dispensed with the Cherry Blossom, arresting Hashimoto and the other leaders.[23] However, the Cherry Blossom's members merely relocated into other societies.[24]

Other powers began to take a serious interest in the Tokyo assassination complex when the Cherry Blossom's demise was simply followed by more assassination. It was, however, hard for outsiders to make out what was going on. The British ambassador, Sir Francis Lindsay, remarked in frustration that the assassinations 'present a situation which Western observers have difficulty in understanding'.[25] American officials convinced the US Secretary of State, Henry Stimson, that the assassins might eventually overthrow constitutional government in Japan.[26] Stimson, however, found comfort in the thought that such a collapse of democracy would only be a problem 'in the next generation'.[27]

Much of the assassination plotting took place in private members' clubs; the personal rivalries and back-biting among the plotters were vicious and incessant; everyone drank heavily. Diplomats relied for much of their information on 'old Japan hand' journalists, the most notable of whom was the Tokyo correspondent of both the London *Times* and the *New York Times*, Hugh Byas. Byas took a particular interest in the societies and managed to bring out his research when he finally fled Japan as war approached in 1941. He published his findings in September 1942. He became an adviser on Japan for America's wartime secret service, the OSS.[28] Even for Byas, however, much remained confusing and closed. As he commented, his informants were mainly drawn from the 'other Japan' that regarded the assassination complex and the assault on democracy with horror.[29] It took decades for first the post-war occupation forces and then Japanese scholars to piece together the full story. Despite all the uncertainties, however, the main contours were clear enough to those who chose to notice: 'Assassination and ruthless imperialism are what you would expect . . . and what you get in Japan,' as the *Manchester Guardian* put it in 1932.[30]

In February 1932, the Young Blood Brotherhood assassinated first the Japanese finance minister, Junnosuke Inoue, and then, in early March, the new 'Rockefeller of Japan', Takuma Dan, the managing director of Mitsui. The Young Bloods were a civilian society formed by a self-anointed Shinto monk, Nissho Inouye. They were, however, closely linked with the armed forces, the monk's shrine being located next door to a naval air station.[31] Both naval and military societies supplied the Young Blood with weapons. The assassins used Browning semi-automatic pistols.[32] They were sheltered and encouraged by the model patriotic society, the Black Dragon, which was intertwined with both Army and Navy intelligence and of which General Araki was a member.[33] Nissho himself had spent ten years in China as a *ronin* – gun-for-hire – and knew Araki from the latter's time in military intelligence.[34] The monk personally instructed his assassins on technique: the Brownings were to be fired using a single-handed grip.[35]

Nissho and the Young Bloods gave themselves up after the assassinations, in the confident and accurate expectation that they would not be heavily punished. They covered everyone else's tracks by claiming to have acted alone for pure patriotic and religious motives. Even though the members gleefully admitted their full guilt, the trial dragged on for two years because the government and judiciary were terrified of reaching the 'wrong' verdict. The British ambassador in Tokyo noted, 'I have little doubt that many public men in this country are going about in fear of their lives.'[36] The Young Blood members who remained free, like the Cherry Blossom's, merely relocated into other societies.[37]

The fear among Japanese politicians was reasonable since the surviving Young Bloods helped the naval base officers assassinate the prime minister, Inukai Tsuyoshi, in May 1932.[38] This was 'the first time that officers in uniform have taken part in a deliberate outbreak of violence against the constituted authorities'.[39] When the shocked politicians reconvened after the shooting, they agreed that they were all likely to die if elected civilian rule persisted: they chose formally to share power with the armed forces, because the military were the only people who could offer them some protection.[40] After prolonged wrangling, the emperor appointed Admiral Saito Makoto prime minister of Japan with General Araki Sadao as minister of war, thus bringing to an end party government and even any pretence of democracy.[41]

However, the collapse of Japanese democracy hardly sated the assassins. Indeed, a study by the Japanese Ministry of Justice found it had merely whetted their appetite.[42] Araki's promotion to the cabinet was not enough to appease them. His colleagues forced him out of office in January 1934 because he was incapable of calling off the assassins. Many radicalised young officers denounced Araki as too soft, a compromiser, a careerist, like all the rest. He was fit only to run a 'women's committee'.[43]

Araki got off lightly. In August 1935, a lieutenant-colonel assassinated Major-General Nagata Tetsuzan, the Director of the Military Affairs Bureau of the war ministry, who was regarded as insufficiently sympathetic to the cause of the radical officers. To make sure that other senior officers got the message that their 'more honourable' comrades could kill them at will, the assassin used a sword to murder his superior and then calmly waited with the weapon for help to arrive, knowing it would be too late for Nagata.[44] The military police knew that more assassinations were coming; the civilian police knew that there were more assassinations coming; even as far away as Beijing, American intelligence was told that 'there would occur more assassinations within the Japanese Army'.[45] In order to persuade a general to take over as minister of war – the incumbent having resigned immediately after Nagata's death – all the other generals had to promise to protect him.[46]

General Watanabe Jotaro, the new inspector-general of military education – one of the traditional triumvirate that ran the army – was the most senior military leader to fall to an assassin's bullet. Even forewarned, the military-dominated Japanese government was too weak to protect itself. In February 1936, the young officers tried to kill all their civilian and military targets in what amounted to a three-day coup. Apart from Watanabe, the assassins finally killed Admiral Saito, along with Takahashi Korekiyo, the finance minister.[47] They missed the prime minister, Okada Keisuke, but killed his brother-in-law whom he resembled: for some days many people thought Okada was dead. It was the emperor who finally ordered the Tokyo garrison to stop the killing, after the officers tried to seize him at the imperial palace.[48]

The American ambassador, Joseph Grew, by now with long experience of Japanese assassination, warned Washington that no-one should delude themselves the assassins had lost. Yes, they had been arrested, but they had achieved their aim of cowing all potential opponents. The prime minister had survived but resigned, as did his ministers, many of whom had been wounded or terrified by the multiple attempts to kill them. Prince Saionji eluded his assassins but effectively withdrew from politics.[49] The message was understood: the State Department's leading Japan expert, Stanley Hornbeck, wrote that 'the perpetrators of last week's assassination were expressing a view and making a political move which was not original with or exclusive to them. They represented the desire of many people, in many walks of life, that the restrictions on the military . . . be done away with, and the views of the military be given the ascendancy.'[50] Thereafter, the Americans always understood that no Japanese interlocutor would, or could, speak in good faith because of the fear of assassination.[51] The head of the British Foreign Office merely noted in his diary, 'I wish the little savages would kill each other.'[52]

The assassination of the Old Marshal demonstrated that the Japanese and Chinese assassination complexes were tightly intertwined.[53] Emperor Hirohito's confidant Kido Koichi said that rather than having the army threaten and assassinate their way up as far as the imperial household, it was better to indulge assassination safely over the sea in China.[54] Both Japan and China institutionalised their assassination capabilities in the late 1920s, in the wake of the Mukden Incident.[55] The Japanese army's special services had reason to be aggrieved by the bureaucratic politics of the Mukden Incident, since they had been manipulated by Komoto Daisaku. Such humiliation led to reorganisation of the Army Special Services Section (SSS or *Tokumu Kikan*), 'an organization designed to promote what is now termed fifth-column activity'.[56] It in turn spawned semi-autonomous units. For instance, the *Ume Kikan* was hived off to operate in Nanjing and Shanghai, where it was known by its Chinese name, Plum Blossom Society. The Plum Blossoms had the dual role of protecting collaborators from Chiang Kai-shek's assassins, while assassinating his supporters.[57]

The SSS and the military police – the *Kempeitai* – were close collaborators. The *Kempeitai*'s counter-espionage organisation collected the intelligence needed for the assassination of Chinese Nationalists and Communists; its investigation organisation took care of surveillance. *Kempeitai* officers were frequently seconded for detached service with the SSS.[58] The Imperial Japanese Navy had its own special services organisation. They were rumoured not to get on with their Army counterparts.[59] There was, however, evidence for their joint training of assassins.[60]

On the Chinese side of the hill, Chiang Kai-shek created a formal Nationalist assassination bureau in February 1932. He fashioned what became known as the Blue Shirt paramilitary organisation from his former students at the Whampoa Military Academy as a personal vanguard organisation.[61] The Blue Shirts were quite capable of organising political violence – indeed, that was their purpose – but within the organisation lay its special services section commanded by Chiang's enforcer, Dai Li.[62] It specialised in assassination. Indeed, it was the fear that Dai Li's assassins inspired in others that sparked Chiang's gravest crisis: he was temporarily kidnapped by allied army commanders, led by the Young Marshal, in fear of their own lives, at Xi'an in 1936.[63]

Dai Li was not just a fascistic thug, he was double-hatted in the military as head of the Second Section of the KMT Military Affairs Commission's Bureau of Investigation and Statistics, usually known simply as 'military statistics' or *Juntong*. The Second Section carried out assassinations under its own banner as well as that of the Blue Shirts. The situation was formalised in 1938 when the Blue Shirts faded and the *Juntong* became the entire Military Statistics Bureau.[64] In 1938, Dai Li set out his rules of assassination in a handbook for *Juntong* cadres. The priority of the *Juntong* was actually counter-assassination: it existed to prevent anyone killing Chiang Kai-shek. As for carrying out *Juntong* assassinations, the trick, according to Dai Li, was to keep everything simple: choose the right location – usually a road – make sure that every member of the assassination squad knew their role and was personally suited to that task, check the assassination weapon, be punctual and the hit would succeed often. A June 1933 assassination in the French Concession of Shanghai was used as a training exercise to show how everything should work.[65]

Chiang, however, was not fool enough to leave intelligence and special operations to one potentially overmighty and deadly organisation. He established another KMT special services group under Dai Li's rival, Chen Lifu, as well: 'central statistics' or *Zhongtong*.[66] In addition, the KMT Public Safety Bureau of Shanghai had its own assassination organisation, the 'Red Squad' of its Special Services Group, created in 1930.[67]

Major Chinese political leaders were quite capable of procuring assassination without any reference to Japan. The two most important leaders of Chinese nationalism in the 1930s – the general-politician Chiang Kai-shek and the civilian politician Wang Jingwei – were both steeped in assassination.⁶⁸ Indeed, much of Wang's early political celebrity derived from his fame as a patriotic assassin. In March 1910, he had attempted to assassinate the Prince Regent of imperial China with an 'electro-bomb' packed with 50 pounds of dynamite placed under a Beijing bridge.⁶⁹

However, a new phase of Chinese Nationalist assassination was almost exactly coeval with the integration of the assassination societies in Tokyo in the spring of 1930.⁷⁰ In February 1930, assassins shot to death Wang Leping in Shanghai's French Concession. Wang, a former member of the KMT's Central Committee, was Wang Jingwei's most senior follower and had served as his liaison with the KMT. It was a particularly spectacular assassination since seven assassins armed with Mauser pistols but dressed in traditional Chinese long robes — Republicans tended to wear western suits — shot their way into Wang Leping's meeting house, killing not just him but his advisers.⁷¹ Wang Jingwei immediately accused Chiang of being behind the assassination.⁷² The notorious assassin Wang piously remarked that 'the pistol as a political argument is unconvincing'.⁷³

Sweeping changes in the Chinese political landscape brought Chiang and Wang back together by the end of 1931. First a group of Chinese generals in the south denounced Chiang's KMT regime, with its capital at Nanjing, as illegitimate and set up their own government. In the north, the Japanese had taken over Manchuria. In January 1932, Wang rejoined the KMT's central leadership in Nanjing, becoming prime minister. In 1933, he also acted as foreign minister. The very fact that assassination was such an important tool in the political repertoire of Chinese politicians made them willing to overlook, at times, the scorpion-in-a-bottle nature of their relationships.⁷⁴

On 1 November 1935, however, an assassin, posing as a photographer, shot Wang three times in Nanjing, seriously wounding and very nearly killing him. Wang said that when he saw his colleagues peering down on him on the ground, 'I thought I could not escape death.'⁷⁵ Indeed, in one sense, he was right. Although Wang eventually died of pneumonia in November 1944, his doctors had no doubt that the underlying cause of his persistent illnesses and eventual death was the assassin's bullets.⁷⁶ The exact mechanisms of the plot remained unclear.

According to British intelligence in Hong Kong, the southern generals in Guangdong (Canton) and Chiang Kai-shek were talking about reconciliation and Wang appeared as a stumbling block. The British thought that the Cantonese were the immediate procurers of the assassination.[77]

Wang himself was convinced that Chiang had tried to kill him. Chiang had been due at the same photoshoot but had called off at the last moment.[78] In December 1935, Wang pronounced himself too badly wounded to carry on in leadership and handed the presidency of the KMT to Chiang. His suspicions about the true source of the attempt on his life were reinforced when the pattern of 1930 repeated itself. An assassin killed Tang Youren, Wang's ally and former deputy foreign minister, who had resigned alongside his boss. Tang had just returned from a visit to Wang's bedside in Shanghai when he was murdered.[79]

Thereafter, Wang's actions were shaped largely by a search for safety and adequate medical treatment.[80] In February 1936, he travelled to Germany to recuperate, a positive experience that, he said, made him view the Germans most favourably.[81] He returned to China in January 1937, in time to witness the launch of the Japanese attempt to conquer China, including their capture of Shanghai in November 1937. Along with Chiang and the rest of the KMT leadership, Wang evacuated Nanjing before the Japanese arrived and went to their newly proclaimed safe-haven capital in Chongqing in south-west China. Once more fearing assassination by Chiang, however, Wang finally abandoned the KMT in December 1938. With the help of the Japanese intelligence services, he secretly fled Chongqing with his family and entourage and flew to Hanoi. Somewhat predictably, Chiang tried to have him assassinated. For the third time, Wang lost his right-hand man: his private secretary, Zeng Zhongming, a former KMT minister, was killed when assassins broke into their apartment to murder Wang.[82] Wang now threw in his lot fully with the Japanese, flying first to Japanese-controlled Shanghai, and finally, in June 1939, to Japan itself.[83]

Wang recognised that if he was to be anything more than a Japanese puppet he had to have some independent means of wielding deadly force. Assassins offered that opportunity. The main man of violence in Wang's following, Zhou Fohai, recruited former members of Chiang's assassination squads who had fallen out with him, or merely believed that, with Japanese aid, Wang would come out on top. Even before the Japanese proclaimed Wang leader of China in March 1940, his assassins had launched a campaign to cow or eliminate as many of Chiang's supporters as they could reach.[84]

The reach of these assassination organisations stretched across China, and sometimes beyond, but it was experienced intensely by the occidental powers in Shanghai. The occidentals viewed East Asia mainly through their own 'windows'. In the nineteenth century they had carved out a series of 'Treaty Ports' along the Chinese coastline. These ports included Guangzhou in the south and Tianjin in the north, both the scenes of notable assassinations. The greatest and most deadly of the Treaty Ports by the 1920s, however, was Shanghai on the Huangpu, a tributary of the Yangzi. Shanghai was China's largest port and most prosperous city. It was about three times as big as the US West Coast's boom city, Los Angeles. It was also a nightmare of cross-cutting jurisdictions: the International Settlement led by the British; the French Concession that had broken away from the International Settlement in a quarrel between Victorian imperialists; the Western Roads, not conceded by treaty but arrogated by the imperial powers, and where the English-speaking elites had built their great mansions; the Chinese Old City; and the unincorporated Chinese city, often under military control, initially Chinese then Japanese. Both Chinese and Japanese wished to seize control of Shanghai from the westerners.

Shanghai was also the home to a vibrant press, both English-language and Chinese.[85] As a result, it became not only a physical prize but also took on a metaphorical existence as a precarious island of civilisation in a sea of depravity.[86] The Nanjing warlord Sun Chuanfang, later assassinated while living as a Buddhist monk in Tianjin, commented in May 1926, 'I am ashamed every time I cross the border from the foreign settlements into ours as I see the contrast between their good and our bad management.'[87] However, even 'efficient' Shanghai's grasp on civilisation was visibly tenuous compared even to other dangerous imperial territories: there were 'so many revolutionary and counter-revolutionary movements,' the senior Indian Police Service officer G.H.R. Halland remarked, 'that a state of internal chaos had come to be regarded as a more or less normal feature of existence.'[88] Shanghai's assassination complex, declared British and American officials, was 'a blot on civilization'.[89] 'I am appealing to the conscience of the civilized world,' the head of Shanghai Municipal Council wrote when the assassinations reached their highest intensity. 'Shanghai is a prey.'[90]

Shanghai had been the most visible site of Chiang Kai-shek's attack on his former allies, the Communists. The 'Shanghai Massacre' of 12 April 1927 was just that, the mass killing of suspected Communists, including public beheadings. For his executioners, Chiang relied on the Green Gang, a criminal syndicate that dominated Shanghai's drug trade. Until 1924, the head of the Green Gang had been the chief of Chinese detectives for the French Concession. Although he had been toppled as *capo di tutti capi* by the KMT, anxious for a larger cut of the opium trade, he retained his post as chief of detectives with the French. These arrangements were well known; they had been exposed by Lenox Simpson, another black mark against him in the eyes of the KMT.[91] Despite the surprise and shock of the massacre, it did not necessarily displease the elite of Shanghai. Between 1921 and 1927, the Communists had controlled Shanghai's trade unions, and that was very bad for business.[92]

In general, the western municipal authorities wanted to return to 'business better than normal'. This was seemingly achieved when the KMT created the Special Municipality for Chinese Shanghai in July 1927 with its own police force, the Public Safety Bureau (PSB). The PSB was an explicitly anti-occidental organisation. According to Chiang, its role was to pave the way for the reclamation of the International Settlements for China. Behind the scenes, however, the PSB went out of its way to form a close operational alliance with the Special Branch of the Shanghai Municipal Police and the Service de la Sûreté of the French Concession police.[93]

All the Shanghai authorities regarded the Communists as a dangerous threat, not least because of the arrest of the Comintern agent Jakob Rudnik with three crates of papers which revealed the continuing reach of their networks.[94] The main threat of assassination came from the Communists, now driven underground.[95] The CCP (Chinese

Communist Party) had indeed created its 'Dog-Killing Corps' in 1927.[96] The 'nice Communist' Zhou Enlai led this assassination organisation in the 1930s.[97] In September 1927, the Dog Killers carried out their first notable assassination, that of Yang Jiamo, an inspector with the Compagnie Française de Tramways et d'Éclairage Électrique de Shanghai.[98] This was followed by a failed attempt on Wu Chaoshu, a former foreign minister of the Nanjing government, in February 1928. Their biggest coup, however, was the assassination of a prominent 'dog', the former Communist Bai Xin, along with four KMT officials in the French Concession.[99]

However, the constant pressure from the three police forces had an effect. In September 1931, the general secretary of the CCP, Wang Ming, left Shanghai for Russia. His successor, Bo Gu, began drawing in the party's horns. In November 1931, disaster struck when the KMT found and arrested Bo and the head of party security. The security chief turned informer and the entire CCP leadership had to flee from Shanghai. The PSB passed on some of their intelligence to the Shanghai Municipal Police, who arrested nearly three hundred cadres, including another former Party general secretary.[100]

It was not that the Communists were rendered entirely toothless, however.[101] The detective of the Shanghai Military Garrison Police, who had carried out the arrest of the senior Communists in the Chinese city, was assassinated in his rickshaw, an increasingly vulnerable form of travel in the Shanghai of the 1930s, in April 1932.[102] Communist assassins killed the two most senior detectives of PSB special services in the summer of 1933. The assassins trapped the head of special services, Yang Quan, in the lift of a luxury hotel in the French Concession and shot him to death along with his bodyguard.[103] The PSB, the Service de la Sûreté and the SMP (Shanghai Municipal Police) only really cracked the assassination ring in the autumn of 1934, when the assassins forced their way into the Lester Chinese Hospital in the International Settlement to finish off a policeman whom they had previously wounded. Other patients died in the shoot-out. The gunfight yielded important forensic information: pistols dropped by the assassins could be tied to other murders. The SMP arrested ten Communists in a safe house; the Communists proved to be very well armed with an arsenal of twenty-seven pistols, including ten powerful 'Broomhandle' Mausers. It was these arrests that revealed the 'Dog-Killing Corps' to the western authorities.[104]

Alarm bells only started jangling in earnest for the western authorities when the assassination threat became less about Communists and more about the KMT.[105] Even more spectacular than the assassination of Wang Leping was the attempted assassination of the KMT finance minister, and Chiang Kai-shek's brother-in-law, T.V. Soong (Song Ziwen), at Shanghai North railway station in July 1931.[106] Five assassins sent by the Canton breakaway regime ambushed Soong and his party with pistols and bombs as he got off the morning train from Nanjing. According to Soong's own account, 'I threw away my white sun helmet which was conspicuous in the gloom of the station hall, and I ran into the crowd, drew my revolver, and dodged behind a pillar. Scarcely had I reached the pillar when I heard two bomb explosions. . . . There was confused firing from all sides . . . when the smoke cleared away, my secretary, Mr Tang [Yulu] . . . was found lying shot [dead].'[107]

The Japanese invaded Shanghai with a naval landing party in January 1932 – the so-called Shanghai Incident – introducing an even more unstable and deadly dynamic into the city. Indeed, the assassins who had attacked Soong were later arrested for assassinating Japanese.[108] The arrival of the Japanese, both as targets and assassins, also brought the assassination of *hanjian*, Chinese regarded by the KMT as collaborators. Indeed, the Japanese authorities noted that assassination ordered by Chiang Kai-shek was not merely a tactic but the 'core of his anti-Manchukuo [Sino-Japanese Manchurian state], Resist Japanese Policy'.[109] In September 1932, the Shanghai Coal Association announced that it had formed a 'suicide squad' to deal out 'iron and blood' to any merchant who traded with the Japanese. The anti-*hanjian* assassination policy put a target on the backs not only of businessmen but also of prominent figures in the Chinese cultural elite.[110]

Although the British, Chinese and Japanese were able to paper over their differences at a diplomatic level, this made little difference to the assassination complex. Talks in the British consulate led to the withdrawal of the naval landing party in May 1932 but essentially left the Japanese in control of the Hongkou district of the International

Settlement.[111] In response to the assassination of a Japanese marine in the Chinese city in November 1935, the Japanese sent two thousand marines back into Shanghai. Inevitably, when the Japanese launched their attempt to conquer China, they seized Chinese Shanghai. The battle of Shanghai lasted from August to November 1937. The fighting was on an enormous scale: the Nationalists lost hundreds of thousands of men. The Japanese deployed heavy artillery and aerial bombing against the city: refugees sought sanctuary in the relatively untouched International Settlement and French Concession and the population of those areas temporarily tripled. The area to the west of the International Settlement, where rich Shanghailanders had taken advantage of cheap land to build luxurious homes with extensive grounds, became known instead as the 'Badlands'. With Japanese encouragement the opium trade boomed. Assassination was an important feature of Shanghai politics before the occupation: now factions in Shanghai regarded it as a reasonable response to large-scale misery.[112]

Even before the Japanese set up their own Chinese 'Reformed Government of the Shanghai Municipality', often known as the *Dadao*, in March 1938, the assassinations had already started.[113] In June 1938, the Nationalists assassinated Chen Deming, notable as a former detective of the SMP who had joined the *Dadao*. The Chen assassination was another rickshaw murder. It was also the fifth assassination recorded by the SMP in eleven days. It was clear to them that 'a powerful assassination gang is now operating in the city'. A few weeks later the assassins killed the senior SMP Chinese detective Lu Liankui. This was the 'first instance in the history of the Municipal Police in which a high ranking officer had been assassinated'.[114]

Anyone associated with the *Dadao* got the message and became exceptionally 'cautious in their movements'. None dared 'show their faces'. Some refused to enter the city centre, staying in 'Pootung [east of the Huangpu], Nantao [around the Old City] or north of Soochow Creek [the Japanese-dominated area of the International Settlement]'. Those who did move were 'accompanied by bodyguards, in armoured cars'.[115] On occasion, the cars worked. When two assassins fired nine shots at the *Dadao* official Shao Shijun, his 'heavy investment in the bullet-proof machine stood up to the test, and not a single bullet pierced the armoured plate'. Even in his expensive Buick, Shao travelled infrequently, and always by devious routes. He was only intercepted because, following Dai Li's instructions, the KMT deployed several large assassination teams with assassins posted on all roads leading to Shao's destination, the Continental Bank Building.[116]

The assassins moved their way up the social scale. In December 1938, the victim was the chairman of the Chamber of Commerce, Wang Zhulin, who was assassinated in the French Concession in Tianjin. Two months later it was Marquis Li Guojie, a long-time celebrity, albeit of dubious reputation.[117] Marquis Li's decision to throw his lot in with the *Dadao* proved one misstep too many for this wily operator.[118] An even bigger catch for the *Juntong* was the foreign minister of the Nanjing government, Chen Lu, assassinated while on a visit to Shanghai. The assassins forced their way into a dinner in his honour, easily overpowered his numerous bodyguards and shot Chen to death. One calculation put him as the fifty-third assassination of a Japanese-aligned Chinese, another as the eightieth, in the Shanghai area over an eighteen-month period. Observers struggled to keep up.[119]

The occidental powers expected Chen's assassination to provoke a showdown with the Japanese in Shanghai. They admitted that 'we should have little or no means of resisting effectively'. If the Japanese were intent on invading the International Settlement to root out the assassins, then a massacre was likely.[120] In the event, the expected dénouement happened in the southern Treaty Port of Xiamen (Amoy) and the northern Treaty Port, Tianjin (Tientsin). In April 1939, the *Juntong* assassinated Cheng Xigeng, the Superintendent of Customs at Tianjin while he was attending the theatre in the British Concession. A few weeks later, the Japanese simply invaded the Amoy International Settlement when the chairman of the Amoy Chamber of Commerce, Hong Lixun, was assassinated.[121] The situation in Tianjin was more complex. In the late 1930s, the British were now in the position vis-à-vis the Japanese as the French had found themselves vis-à-vis the British over their micro-colony in India, Chandernagore, in the 1920s.

'The events' at Amoy, the British ambassador Sir Archibald Clark Kerr reported, 'are a pointer to what may happen at Tientsin and then at Shanghai.'[122] The Tianjin Concession police had captured the assassins, who had also murdered a Swiss as they attempted to escape. The municipal authorities and the British Consul-General badly wanted to hand over the killers to the *Kempeitai*.[123] Clark Kerr refused to make a decision, 'a decision from which I confess I flinch'. He just wanted everybody to be clear that they would be 'handing over these four men to be killed'. It was left to London to instruct that the men should not be handed over unless an appropriate face-saving solution could be found.[124] The British handed over the assassins when the Japanese promised them a 'fair trial'.[125]

Despite the temporary shift of attention to other ports, Shanghai was always the main prize. Some occidentals believed that the KMT wanted the Japanese to seize Shanghai by force because they believed – wrongly – that such an act of aggression would force Britain and America into a war with Japan.[126] Of course, the KMT had no way of knowing that Germany would invade Poland on 1 September 1939 to start a war in Europe. Their actual tactic over the summer of 1939 was the assassination of those Chinese police officials who posed a threat to the operations of the assassination squad in Shanghai itself. In April 1939, two assassins fatally shot Xi Shitai, the Secretary of the Police Bureau of the *Dadao*, the force that had replaced the KMT's Public Safety Bureau, as he emerged from his house.[127] Lu Ying, the chief of *Dadao* police, a former chief of detectives for the old Public Safety Bureau, survived the ambush of his car by assassins dressed as coolies.[128] The head of Chinese police in the French Concession Sûreté was not so lucky: he died instantly when shot in the back.[129] The assassination of Detective Inspector Lu Gensheng and Superintendent Tan Shaoliang, the 'most valuable Chinese member of the SMP', rapidly followed.[130]

The Japanese did not invade the International Settlement. Instead, they sponsored an assassination campaign of their own, which rapidly grew to rival that of the *Juntong*. In 1938, the Japanese army had demanded that the SSS should up its game in Shanghai.[131] The specialist Nanjing–Shanghai squads of the *Tokumu Kikan* carried out assassinations on behalf of Wang Jingwei while also committing their own murders. They were particularly active against White Russians who defied them. They assassinated both the leader of the Russian community, Charles Metzler, and the senior Russian detective of the French Concession police who tried to investigate the crime.[132]

GOVERNMENT BY ASSASSINATION

In 1939, Wang Jingwei created his own assassination bureau in Shanghai, known as Jessfield Road from its headquarters. Jessfield Road was the epicentre of the 'the Badlands'.[133] The Jessfield Road bureau launched its first high-profile assassinations in August 1939. Its initial targets were Shanghai journalists and editors who had dared to write things that fell short of fawning adulation of Wang Jingwei. An assassin killed Zhu Xinggong, the editor of the Chinese-language edition of the *Shanghai Evening Post*, Wang Jilu, the manager of the *Eastern Times*, and an American journalist, Tug Wilson. The assassins were effective enough, although they were judged less professional than the *Juntong*. Zhu's killer was captured with the murder weapon, an old .38 Japanese revolver.[134]

No-one doubted that Jessfield Road's predations would get worse. When war was declared in Europe, Europeans themselves became Jessfield Road's main targets. In early January 1940, a joint Sino-Japanese assassination squad shot up the car of Godfrey Phillips, the secretary of the Shanghai Municipal Council, using high-power Mausers.[135] Phillips survived, but Europeans started to adopt the kind of security previously reserved for the *Dadao*.[136] The French Concession police put a military-style armoured car outside Phillips's house; its crew was armed with tommy guns. When Phillips was at work, two armed Chinese SMP detectives accompanied him. His own car was armoured with 'attaché case shields'. Phillips was expected to carry a revolver and fight off assassins himself.[137] This possibility became even starker a few weeks later when the SMC (Shanghai Municipal Council) was bullied by the Japanese into removing the police guards, 'an insult to the Japanese Army, and consequently the Japanese Emperor himself', and into paying protection money to Wang Jingwei instead, for a 'friendly understanding' with Jessfield Road.[138]

This 'friendly understanding' amounted to little more than an attempt to take over the SMP and the French Concession police (FCP). The two officers who resisted most strongly – Lieutenant Blanchet of the FCP and Reginald Yorke, Deputy Commissioner and head of Special Branch for the SMP – were both on the receiving end of assassination attempts. Yorke saw 'two Chinese, immaculate in white foreign clothes', draw their pistols as they approached the rear of his car and he emptied the clip of his own pistol at them: three of the assassins' own bullets hit the car but none penetrated. The Blanchet attack was attempted in the same fashion.[139] The KMT also began assassinating European civilian officials in the French Concession.[140]

Jessfield Road also assassinated Chinese civilians, including the chairwoman of the Shanghai Vocational Women's Society, a teacher and a former policeman. SMP forensics worked out that the same semi-automatic pistol had been used in each murder. They knew the serial number of the pistol because it had once been legally registered. They knew the owner was an inhabitant of Jessfield Road.[141] In a gesture of contempt, Jessfield Road gave them the pistol once the SMC had agreed to pay protection money.[142]

One killing stood out to occidentals as 'a peculiarly cold-blooded one'. Jessfield Road threatened the local manager of Imperial Chemical Industries (ICI), whose facility was in the Badlands, and who was regarded as not paying enough protection money. George Haley, the ICI executive, was one of the few who retained their SMP bodyguards. So Jessfield Road killed William Carine, the facility's nightwatchman, instead. Carine was one of Shanghai's seldom-glimpsed 'poor Brits', a fifty-three-year-old unemployed man, married to a Chinese woman, who had been delighted to get a job with ICI.[143]

In August 1940, the British Consul-General in Shanghai attempted to work out the relative balance of assassinations in Shanghai. By his calculation, between December 1937 and February 1940 there had been ninety-seven political assassinations in the city, with responsibility divided roughly equally between the KMT and Japanese-backed factions. In the six-month period between February and August 1940, there were thirty-nine further assassinations. Although Wang Jingwei and the Japanese liked to exaggerate the KMT responsibility for assassination, they were on reasonably firm ground in their accusations.[144] Nineteen of the victims had been aligned with Wang, twelve with the KMT, with the allegiance of the remaining eight unclear. In addition, there had been eleven attempted assassinations: six of Wang supporters, three of KMT supporters, with two unclear.[145]

Almost as soon as the ink was dry on the British analysis, the *Juntong* further increased the tempo of their assassination campaign. In October

1940, they finally succeeded in murdering their most prized target, the head of the *Dadao*, the mayor of Shanghai since October 1938, Fu Xiaoan.[146] Fu's house in the French Concession was a 'miniature camp' after a previous assassination near miss in the Civic Centre in November 1938.[147] Then Fu had been guarded by Chinese police and the *Kempeitai*. Indeed, a Japanese *Kempeitai* sergeant had deliberately stepped into the line of fire and was killed by a bullet to the chest.[148] Fu's arrangements thereafter were regarded as virtually impregnable: apart from hard fortifications, he always maintained a permanent protection force with twenty guards on duty, including four trusted White Russians as his close protection. In the event, he was stabbed to death with a meat knife by one his Chinese servants. The assassin escaped.[149]

The KMT also tried the new tactic of assassinating Japanese members of the *Kempeitai*.[150] According to the *New York Times* journalist Douglas Robertson, 'It is now apparent that the virtually continuous assassinations of Japanese officers are part of the Chinese plans for harassing the Japanese and preventing the accomplishment of further Japanese adventures.' 'Foreign residents in Shanghai,' he observed, 'are no longer astonished or shocked ... to learn of another assassination. In fact, such killings have become more or less routine.'[151] The *Juntong* even managed to feed numerous new assassins into Shanghai to reinforce those already operating. By the spring of 1941, the KMT had four large active assassination squads in the city.[152] Their killings suggested that, for all their criticism of the occidental authorities in Shanghai, the Japanese too might struggle to control assassination.[153] However, the Japanese were scrupulous in gathering intelligence. When they took over Shanghai on the outbreak of the Pacific war in December 1941, the Japanese rolled up the KMT organisation.[154]

In 1933, Miles Lampson, Britain's senior diplomat in China, had suggested that assassination by both Japanese and Chinese was a good thing for the occidental great powers, especially Great Britain. He hoped it would achieve Chinese unification under a regime with which the UK could do business. Lampson characterised the Shanghailanders as whiners who could not accept the semi-colonial era of the Treaty Ports was ending, to be replaced by a modern system of state-to-state relations. Although it gave them little satisfaction, the Shanghailanders could point out that Lampson had been talking poppycock. Relentless assassination brought chaos not stability.[155]

By 1941, Shanghai had left observers numbed by assassination. The city plainly had no major role in international – as opposed to Chinese internal – politics after 1938. No-one was going to ride to the rescue from the west. The only conclusion that anyone – other than the most obsequious KMT supporter – could reach was that assassination was pointless. There seemed little virtue in individual acts of bravery, such as the attempt by a young Briton, Paul Kaye, to capture the assassin who had just shot a Wang Jingwei supporter and his wife. What made Kaye's action 'pointless' was that the female victim was German, an enemy.[156] 'If the past three years have taught . . . anything at all,' the *North-China Herald*, the most reliable of the English-language Shanghai newspapers, editorialised, 'it must surely have been that assassination as a political weapon achieves no results save the death of a few men unfortunate to encounter the assassin's bullet. The murder of political figures has not prevented successors taking their place.'[157] In part, the numbing effect made occidentals view Shanghai, and China more generally, as a place apart, with little meaning for the wider conduct of international politics. However, that was not necessarily how the Chinese factions viewed the matter. Both the KMT and the Chinese Communist Party embraced the concept of 'patriotic assassination' as both practice and propaganda. Albeit by a different road, occidentals very soon afterwards accepted the notion of the 'honourable assassin'. Their special services employed former members of the Shanghai Municipal Police to teach them to fight dirtily in a noble cause.[158]

6

SABOTAGE APPLIED TO INDIVIDUALS
Totalitarians and Democrats, 1923–1945

For some western observers of the 1930s, assassination was still merely a feature of Churchill's 'struggles of pygmies' happening in 'parts of Europe where the influence of the Orient remains . . . a matter-of-fact procedure . . . not altogether comprehensible to the Western mind'.[1] It was all a bit like an Eric Ambler novel: exotic, tawdry and very confusing.[2]

The most threatening of democracy's enemies, the 'totalitarians' – Mussolini coined the term in the 1920s – were disappointingly irregular practitioners of assassination. It was not that assassination was an unimportant element in the totalitarians' toolbox; it demonstrably was. It merely was that assassination failed to reveal any greater depth of perfidy than anything else that totalitarians did or said. As Fascist propagandists scoffed at the Nazis before they reconciled their differences, 'A National-Socialist is an assassin and a pederast.'[3] The totalitarians' specialism was mass violence. They could exert terror much more effectively through the organs of the state than through individual acts of savagery.[4]

In part, of course, the seemingly relatively minor part assassination played in the totalitarian regimes was an illusion. State and Party assassins often covered their tracks. The NKVD – Soviet secret police – killer who assassinated Leon Trotsky in August 1940 spent twenty years in a Mexican prison claiming that he was a disillusioned Trotskyite from Belgium, rather than an agent of the organisation that lay at the core of the Stalinist assassination apparatus.[5]

Investigators put a lot of time and effort into unravelling these various lies. That very necessary work of subsequent investigation, however, also obscured the two most significant features of the European assassination regime. First, the totalitarians were primarily the *victims* rather than the perpetrators of assassination. Assassination played a central role in the totalitarian theatre of paranoid victimhood. Second, the experience of the 1930s convinced the democrats that the assassins were on to something. There was such a thing as the 'honourable assassin'. It was a small step from there to the belief that a strong democratic power should have the capability of carrying out its own assassinations. This was the war that the totalitarians won: it was the most profound shift in assassination in the twentieth century.

That is not to say that some western countries had not previously fumbled around the edges of assassination.[6] Their threat might even have made Stalin more paranoid. Until the end of 1924, the Soviet leader was in the habit of walking the streets of Moscow. It was only then that Felix Dzerzhinskii persuaded him that there was a real threat from émigré assassins, aided by British intelligence based in the Baltic states.[7] Thereafter, Stalin would always be accompanied by his OGPU – secret police – security detail. Indeed, the key function of the Soviet intelligence services was securing the leaders of the revolution. By the 1930s, that function was being shown off to westerners.[8]

In May 1927, a new group of émigrés, trained and equipped by the British SIS, crossed the border from Finland and managed to let off bombs in Leningrad and Moscow. In June 1927, Stalin commented to Vyacheslav Molotov that 'the course towards terror taken by London's agents changes the situation fundamentally'. In accordance with Stalin's line, the foreign intelligence service of the OGPU reported that the main purpose of the Anglo-Russian organisation in Finland was to assassinate Stalin. They manufactured much of the 'evidence' for this assertion themselves. The extent of British, or French, involvement with the Whites was significantly exaggerated. Most certainly there was no British or French secret service plan to kill Stalin.[9] The Whites attempted very few assassinations. The most prominent actual White

SABOTAGE APPLIED TO INDIVIDUALS

assassination was that of Pyotr Voykov, the Soviet plenipotentiary in Warsaw, who was murdered in June 1927. Following the Voykov assassination, the Soviet regime staged a public show trial in September 1927 to expose Captain Ernest Boyce, SIS's head of station in Helsinki, as the organiser of anti-Bolshevik assassination. With his cover blown, Boyce had to be withdrawn. Stalin used the momentum generated by his accusations of assassination plots to mount a coup within the party against his rivals Trotsky, Grigory Zinoviev and Lev Kamenev in November 1927.[10]

The most consequential Soviet assassination of the 1930s, as could be predicted from the above, was all about Soviet victimhood. In December 1934, the Leningrad Party boss, Sergei Kirov, was murdered. Shockingly, Kirov was shot in the back of the head, with a Russian revolver, as he approached his office within the Leningrad Party building itself. Stalin immediately ordered a review of his own security in the Kremlin and inevitably found that the party had become complacent about his survival.[11]

The Kirov assassination has always been recognised as significant: for decades, it was the most-debated assassination in Soviet history.[12] Now, however, it is the best-documented, due to the availability of the documents from the NKVD's exhaustive investigation of the crime. Despite the wealth of detail, of course, it should not be thought that the NKVD were conventional assassination investigators. They wrote what Stalin wanted them to write and changed conclusions as soon as Stalin decided that they should be changed. But the detail is nevertheless telling in its own way, not least because those close to Stalin believed the assassination had a profound effect upon him.[13]

Kirov was murdered by a disgruntled minor Party official, acting alone, who fantasised that everyone would thank him for the cleansing deed. The murderer freely admitted this during his first interrogation by the NKVD.[14] However, when Stalin rushed to Leningrad, he declared the murder an assassination, and no-one was ever going say anything different. Stalin ruled that the assassination had to be a conspiracy because individuals never acted without someone pulling the strings. In the first few days after the killing, Stalin, the NKVD and the Party genuinely struggled to define their conspiracy. The NKVD both flattered and tortured the murderer until he confessed that he had been working for the Latvians.[15] However, they also flattered and tortured him into confessing he had been working for Trotskyites within the Leningrad Party.[16] Nine days after the murder, Stalin put Nikolai Yezhov personally in charge of finding and punishing the conspirators. Nearly nine hundred people were arrested over the next few weeks.[17]

The investigation did not stop there. On the anniversary of Kirov's murder, Stalin ordered the NKVD to do better. In August 1936, Stalin charged his former rivals Zinoviev and Kamenev with a conspiracy to assassinate him. Supposedly, the plot had been hatched in Kamenev's apartment in the summer of 1934. The plotters had agreed to collaborate with the Nazi regime in Germany. Kirov had merely been their first victim. All of this was palpable nonsense and seen as such at the time: 'I have not been convinced from what I saw at the trial or from a careful study of the evidence presented that the accused were really implicated in a specific plot to kill Stalin, Kirov, or other prominent Soviet leaders, that Trotski ever gave instructions to his adherents to assassinate Stalin, or that the German police had connections with any of the defendants,' reported Loy Henderson, the US chargé d'affaires in Moscow. The other western diplomats in Moscow and its press corps agreed with him.[18] Nevertheless, no-one doubted Stalin's murderous intent.[19]

Stalin feared that the assassins he had set on others might be turned against him. In the late 1920s, the OGPU's assassination operation had been institutionalised in the 'Administration for Special Tasks'.[20] Stalin had nevertheless ordered the killing of the OGPU's own best-known assassin as early as 1929.[21] For his loyal work on the Kirov assassination, Stalin not only appointed Yezhov to lead the NKVD but also turned him loose on its supposedly unreliable foreign intelligence service, as well as the linked foreign service of the *Razvedupr*, Soviet military intelligence.[22]

The best-documented of the overseas assassinations of Soviet agents in the 1930s was that of Ignace Reiss, a veteran intelligence officer who had served with the *Razvedupr* before joining OGPU. Based in Paris, Reiss had nurtured plenty of contacts with Trotskyites in the west. The NKVD's Paris residency ordered Reiss's assassination in June 1937, but he got wind of the plot and fled to Switzerland. Reiss did not know whom he could trust, and he chose the wrong person. His female

SABOTAGE APPLIED TO INDIVIDUALS

contact led a four-person Special Tasks assassination squad to him in Lausanne in September 1937. Reiss was lured to a suburb of the city where he was killed with nine pistol shots.[23] The operation was plainly of high importance since 'this dramatic end to his career had the effect of bringing a large number of OGPU [personnel] to the attention of the police authorities in Western Europe and [has] dislocated the work of that organisation to some extent'.[24] Not least, Reiss's assassination caused his friend, and *Razvedupr* colleague, Walter Krivitsky, to defect and become the west's best source on Soviet intelligence.[25]

An NKVD team like the one that had killed Reiss failed to find Krivitsky in Paris.[26] None of this stopped the NKVD assassination squads closing in on either Krivitsky or the ultimate prize, Trotsky. There was a notable continuity of personnel on the Krivitsky and Trotsky teams. If the assassins missed, they were expected to regroup and try again.[27] In order to increase effectiveness, yet another new head of the NKVD, Lavrentiy Beria, appointed the organisation's most experienced officer-assassin Pavel Sudoplatov head of Special Tasks and deputy head of foreign intelligence in March 1939. From Sudoplatov we have an insider's view of the assassination effort since he, miraculously, survived into the post-Cold War era. According to Sudoplatov, Stalin summoned him in person to make sure he knew exactly who should be killed.[28]

The team that Sudoplatov sent to Mexico comprised three assassination squads. The first squad got into Trotsky's villa in May 1940, posing as Mexican police officers, with the help of one of his security guards whom the team had previously planted. Although they opened fire determinedly, the NKVD gunmen missed Trotsky himself. The treacherous security guard was instead assassinated by the second squad to keep him quiet. In August 1940, the third squad got a lone assassin into the villa armed with his subsequently famous ice pick, an unusual field extemporisation. The team leader had recruited the assassin by seducing his mother. The assassin in turn had seduced Trotsky's secretary. He managed to impale Trotsky's skull with the pick.[29]

The eventual death of Krivitsky was more mysterious. Once he had reached seeming safety in the United States, Krivitsky became outspoken in denouncing Stalin as a procurer of assassination. In June 1939, he publicly floated the theory that Stalin had been behind the assassination of Kirov: the assassination secured his twin objective of removing a charismatic rival and acting as the springboard for the Purges. It seems that Krivitsky was wrong about the first part but, given Trotsky's fate, Krivitsky's speculation seemed highly plausible to western intelligence services.[30] He also caught the ear of Congressman Martin Dies, the chairman of the House Un-American Activities Committee, who had him testify before Congress. In November 1940, the NKVD reported that Krivitsky's statements were disrupting their operations in the USA.[31] In February 1941, Krivitsky was found dead in his room in the Bellevue Hotel in Washington. He died from a single shot to his head. The bullet came from a .38 pistol that lay near his hand. The medical examiner ruled the death a suicide: that remained the official verdict.

Behind the scenes, however, the American state scrambled to define the conspiracy. US officials did not understand the nature of the Soviet regime, wished it would go away and were primarily interested in covering their own backsides. Krivitsky's lawyer claimed that his client had been assassinated; that Krivitsky had known he was being hunted and by whom; and that he had asked for protection from the FBI, from the State Department and from the NYPD. Martin Dies believed him and published the name of the assassin – the same man who had led the Special Tasks team that had assassinated Ignace Reiss.[32] J. Edgar Hoover, on the other hand, announced that 'The Bureau is doing absolutely nothing in connection with the death of Krivitsky.'[33] What he did do was order a 'very discreet' investigation that confirmed that the FBI had brushed off Krivitsky when he came to them with his assassination story. What was certainly the case, FBI agents subsequently realised, was that in the months before his death Krivitsky had had contacts with NKVD agents, some of whom were on file as assassins.[34] For what it was worth, the NKVD recorded that it had been mounting an operation against Krivitsky – who was codenamed 'Enemy' – which ended because '"Enemy" took his own life'.[35] Krivitsky's death soon faded from the immediate headlines but popped up again in Washington discussion of the Soviet enemy for decades thereafter.[36]

If assassination was important for defining the anti-democratic Left in the 1920s and 1930s, it was even more significant in defining the

SABOTAGE APPLIED TO INDIVIDUALS

anti-democratic Right. The end of the 'Versailles process' had been marked by the Treaty of Lausanne, signed in July 1923. The supposed European order thus created lasted a month before it was derailed by an assassination. In August 1923, assassins ambushed the cars of the League of Nations border commission that was responsible for demarcating the line between Greece and Albania. The assassins killed the head of the commission, an Italian general, Enrico Tellini. Fortuitously, or unfortunately, depending on one's point of view, the car carrying the Greek members of the commission had broken down: the assassins only targeted the Italians and Albanians. Mussolini, seeing this as the perfect opportunity to demonstrate Fascist victimhood, blamed the Greeks and invaded Corfu. The study commissioned for the incoming secretary-general of the UN in 1945, on 'the moral and political reasons why the League of Nations was not successful', blamed the Corfu crisis for hamstringing the League from the outset.[37]

Unsurprisingly, given that he was the leader of an anti-democratic, violent revolutionary movement, Mussolini was mired in assassination. He used it when it suited him, while being aware that those who saw murder as 'a school, a system or, worse still, an aesthetic' could be as much a threat as an aid to his consolidation of power.[38] When he had his only charismatic rival on the Left, Giacomo Matteotti, assassinated in June 1924, he wanted it to look like an act of chaotic gang violence. The Milanese assassins ambushed Matteotti near the Tiber in Rome, stabbed him to death and dumped his body 20 miles outside the city. The Italian police arrested the assassins two days after the killing, their car still drenched in Matteotti's blood, but his body was not discovered until August. The Milanese were working for the 'Ceka del Viminale', a sort of secret police squad organised by Mussolini from gangs of Fascist thugs – *squadristi* – in 1921 on the grounds that 'all governments undergoing a transition need certain illiberal branches to take care of their adversaries'.[39]

When the Fascists won the general election of April 1924, Mussolini had reiterated, 'The violent ones? I need them as well!'[40] The 'Ceka' were nested in the Milizia volontaria per la sicurezza nazionale (MVSN). The head of this Fascist militia was also the police chief in charge of investigating Matteotti's killing. Thus, the assassins' claim that they were kidnappers whose abduction for ransom had gone terribly wrong dovetailed perfectly with the police case that they had broken a crime ring. Few in Rome believed this cock-and-bull story. Indeed, it was the relentless ridicule of the Fascist regime from all non-Fascist quarters that led to Mussolini proclaiming the death of parliamentary government and the birth of a totalitarian state in January 1925.[41]

Totalitario was consolidated through a series of four assassination plots. The first was a complete fraud. In November 1925, police arrested a socialist parliamentary deputy and accused him of preparing to shoot Mussolini with a rifle as the Duce greeted the crowds from the balcony of the Palazzo Chigi. The deputy, his desire to kill Mussolini, and the rifle were real enough, but the plot itself was largely the work of Fascist agents provocateurs. The police were in on the con from the outset and arrested the would-be assassin hours before Mussolini was due to make his appearance. There was never any real threat to the Fascist leader. Nevertheless, Mussolini used the pretext of the assassination to pass laws destroying freedom of association, subordinating all state employees to the Fascist regime and awarding himself enormous powers to govern by decree.

The second assassination attempt, of April 1926, was, by contrast, not choreographed. An Anglo-Irish aristocrat living in Italy, Violet Gibson, shot Mussolini in the face on her own initiative. On this occasion, the threat to the dear leader was only flaunted for propaganda purposes. Mussolini chose not to define the attempted murder as an assassination, but the act of one with a totally infirm mind, deporting Gibson back to England.

In September 1926, a man hit Mussolini's car with a bomb, with the usual predictable result: no-one inside was hurt but eight passers-by were wounded. This attempt was used to highlight the threat of political exiles, a subject that obsessed Mussolini as much as Stalin. The death penalty was reintroduced for the offence.

In October 1926, Mussolini was shot in the neck while riding in his car. The mob turned on the boy believed to have fired the gun and beat him to death. In response, Mussolini created the OVRA, a proper secret police to replace the semi-formal 'Ceka'.[42] In January 1927, he declared

SABOTAGE APPLIED TO INDIVIDUALS

that, as a result, 'the state is equipped with all necessary means of prevention and repression'.[43] Mussolini's own behaviour changed. Although Fascist propaganda made much of his coolness under fire and his insouciance in the aftermath, foreign diplomats noticed that his 'entourage have strenuously avoided exposing him to the danger of assassination, which makes it difficult for him to go to a foreign country'.[44] The new security regime executed a fifth supposed assassin, a US citizen, in 1931, although he was arrested, in bed with a dancer, nowhere near Mussolini.[45]

Like Mussolini, Hitler too thought that assassins were a mixed blessing. The US ambassador in Berlin said of Hitler's assumption of presidential authority in 1934 that it was wishful thinking to believe that his hold on power was anything other than rock solid. Assassination was about the only thing that 'might strike him low'. Hitler tended to agree. As Mussolini had observed of the *squadristi*, Hitler said of the SA that it was full of 'permanent revolutionaries . . . [who had] completely lost touch with the human social order'.[46] His most public use of assassination, the 'Night of the Long Knives', 30 June 1934, was more like a massacre, setting one gang of Nazi thugs, the SS, on a rival gang of Nazi thugs, the SA. Officers of Britain's MI5 and SIS in Berlin had noted that the old Organisation Consul had found a comfortable home in the SA.[47] One well-known assassin of the 1920s was specifically added to the SS's death list.[48]

When Hitler drove past the British embassy in Berlin in the wake of the 'Night', the British ambassador noted that he seemed worried about assassination. 'The Dictator,' Eric Phipps wrote, 'debouched from the empty Wilhelmstrasse' followed by 'several motors with S.S. guards.' 'The police,' the ambassador continued, 'had cleared the street and had even forbidden the people to open their windows. The public were herded behind a cordon of police at a respectable distance from the Adlon Hotel.' Hitler was already an 'unbalanced being' and it seemed safe to assume that fear of assassination was making him 'still less normal'. The Italians claimed that Hitler was petrified of assassination and had told Mussolini 'that such acts were catching'.[49]

Thanks, in part, to Hitler and Mussolini themselves, 1934 did, at first sight, seem a foreboding year for European heads of government.[50] On 25 July 1934, Austrian Nazis, encouraged by Hitler, stormed the

Federal Chancellery in Vienna and shot Chancellor Engelbert Dollfuss. When the Austrian army failed to rally to the cause of the coup, they allowed the chancellor to bleed to death while they negotiated safe conducts for themselves.[51] The Austrian government's weakness in granting that safe conduct to Germany proved a 'fatal blow' to the viability of the Austrian state. The fact that the authorities welched on the deal once the assassins surrendered, keeping them in Austria, hardly made things any better.[52]

When Croats and Macedonians assassinated the dictator of Yugoslavia, King Alexander, and the foreign minister of France, Louis Barthou, in Marseilles in October 1934, it was, of course, 'impossible not to recall that other terrible assassination at Serajevo twenty years ago'. The *Manchester Guardian* phoned Edith Durham with the news of Alexander's death and asked for a comment: 'he asked for it', she replied.[53]

The impact of the assassination of the Serb monarch was heightened because it was the first to be caught on moving film. Alexander and Barthou were driving through Marseilles in a motorcade when the assassins shot them. What was less obvious was that subsequent civilian casualties were caused by the French police indiscriminately opening fire. Within days, the murder was playing to cinema audiences around Europe.[54]

Mussolini was a procurer of the assassination. So too was the Hungarian dictator, Admiral Horthy. When Serbian assassins had murdered the Croat nationalist leadership in the 1920s, they unwittingly facilitated the rise of a demagogic journalist, Ante Pavelić. Beyond modelling himself on another demagogic journalist, Mussolini, Pavelić sought an alliance of convenience with the Italians. Founded in 1930, his *Ustasha* (Insurgents) sought safe havens in Italy and Hungary. Not that Mussolini thought much of his Croat clients, 'a useless and dangerous mob'. The Macedonian nationalists of UMRO were essentially a predatory criminal gang. Based in Bulgaria, where they dominated parts of the countryside, they had, by the 1930s, established themselves as a kind of Murder, Inc. The addition of a Macedonian specialist to the *Ustasha* assassination squad certainly added to its effectiveness.[55]

It was left to the French to define the conspiracy. Their foreign minister was dead. They had captured the four assassins. The deed was on film. The spaghetti-like conspiracy left plenty of choices in the apportionment of blame: the Croats, the Macedonians, the Hungarians, the Bulgarians and, of course, the Italians. Few played straight with the French investigation. The Yugoslavs blamed the Croats and the Italians, choosing to ignore the Hungarians. Police reports spoke of a mixture of stonewalling and outright deceit from their opposite numbers in Rome and Budapest.[56] Under the decisive leadership of their prime minister, Pierre Laval, the French decided to cover up as much as they could.[57] The last thing that Laval desired was a quarrel with Italy. He preferred to cultivate Mussolini as a potential counterweight to Hitler. His answer was to try the assassins quickly, not seek further extraditions, blame the Hungarians – with whom France had no border – and kick the matter into the League of Nations which then spent four years pointlessly discussing an anti-terrorist convention. 'I don't care about the irregularities and illegalities in this criminal trial where reasons of state come into play. I need these three [Croat] heads out of necessity for Yugoslavia and quickly,' Laval is reported to have said.[58]

Mussolini was certainly not abashed by the international scrutiny of Italy in the wake of the assassination. He remained confident of his ability to endlessly play a thimblerig of death and evasion with the French. In June 1937, Mussolini's son-in-law and foreign minister, Galeazzo Ciano, ordered the Italian military intelligence service, SIM, to assassinate the exiled leader of the Giustizia e Libertà party, Carlo Rosselli. SIM recruited the *cagoulards* of the far-right Action Française to carry out the killing in Normandy. The assassination had some commonality in method with that of Matteotti, in that Rosselli was ambushed and stabbed to death in a car. Assassination bureaux did not need to provide their killers with traceable firearms when they could use tools available from a hardware store. It is probable that Rosselli's assassination was but one among many. The various Fascist security services claimed to have murdered up to fifty political opponents in the late 1930s, mainly linked to the Spanish Civil War. Once again, the French government chose to cover up Italian involvement in the assassination for *raison d'état*.[59]

There was no Sarajevo-like general crisis of 1934. The assassinations merely illustrated the deliquescence of the European legal order. As the disgruntled Rumanian foreign minister remarked of Europe's inability to contain assassination, it was 'monstrous that men like himself who were striving to consolidate peace should have to live under [the] constant threat of [a] trained assassin's pistol'.[60] Rumanian politicians had every right to fear assassination since they had to deal with the 'christofascists' of the Legion of the Archangel Michael, otherwise known as the Iron Guard, the 'mad assassins', who saw assassination as some kind of holy rite.[61] The Guard had assassinated the prime minister of Rumania, Ion Duca, in December 1933. Not that the Rumanian government was restrained in matching assassination with murder. In 1938, the leader of the Iron Guard, Corneliu Codreanu, was strangled, alongside the assassins of Duca, by their prison guards.[62]

However, the chancelleries of Europe were not quivering before the threat of assassination after 1934, much less were Mussolini, Hitler or Stalin hysterically perturbed by that threat. In 1934, the German government instructed Daimler-Benz to design new assassination-proof cars for the Führer's use. The upgraded vehicles entered service in 1938, which hardly spoke to a crash development programme. Hitler was well guarded, nevertheless. What had previously been a specialist police unit to protect the head of government became a free-standing organisation, whose personnel were members of the SS. The Reichssicherheitsdienst (RSD) reported directly to Hitler's office. He also had a uniformed SS bodyguard, the Begleit-kommando. At this stage, however, they could still be bossed around by a forceful and ambitious Wehrmacht officer like Erwin Rommel.[63] When Reinhard Heydrich reviewed Nazi anti-assassination security in early 1940, he thought it was lax, a view in which the head of the Gestapo concurred.[64] Unlike former Weimar Republic officials schooled in the world of Organisation Consul, a dedicated Nazi had 'a certain arrogant pride and sporting attitude'.[65] That attitude was only ended with Heydrich's own assassination in 1942.[66]

Hitler, Mussolini and Stalin were much more concerned with mass control than with small terrorist cells. They shared an irrational belief in their own protective genii.[67] Assassination was still more of an opportunity than a threat. For Hitler, that opportunity came when a Polish Jew shot and killed the German diplomat Ernst vom Rath in Paris.[68] The

SABOTAGE APPLIED TO INDIVIDUALS

Nazis were delighted. Goebbels issued instructions that the assassination 'must completely dominate the front pages'.[69] The result was *Kristallnacht*, the massive escalation of mob violence against German Jews in November 1938. 'Following the assassination of a Secretary at the German Embassy in Paris by a frenzied Polish-Jewish youth of 17, whose parents had been maltreated,' the Irish League of Nations official Seán Lester recorded, 'the Nazis launched a pogrom, burning synagogues and destroying houses and shops and imprisoning thousands of poor wretches. . . . The world has been aghast – horrified once more by the monster.'[70]

In 1939, Geoffrey Household, who described himself as a 'civilized European who lies, half a litre below the surface, in the average introverted Englishman', suggested that the best way to tackle 'the monster' was by assassination. Household had an unusual long-term connection to assassination: he had been on a schoolboy visit to Sarajevo when the archduke was murdered. His adult fictional representation of assassination, however, was very much a product of the late 1930s. Household's third novel, *Rogue Male*, was the tale of a keen English sportsman who takes it upon himself to assassinate a European dictator – anonymous, but plainly Hitler. Household started writing *Rogue Male* after the Munich Crisis of October 1938 when he imagined 'how much I'd like to kill him [Hitler]'. The story's hero has the Dictator in his sights when he is thwarted by the secret police. At the end of the novel, the nameless assassin is lining up a second attempt. He now understood, 'one should always hunt an animal in its natural habitat; and the natural habitat of man is – in these days – a town.' The ethics of assassination were the same as the ethics of war, the narrator claims: 'unless you are a conscientious objector you cannot condemn me.' Nevertheless, the hero wished to stress that he is indeed 'rogue' and 'there can never again be any possible question of the complicity of HM Government'. In real life, Household became a British special operations officer. Indeed, he was already undercover in Rumania when *Rogue Male* was published.[71]

As the example of Household – intellectual, writer, man of direct action, minutely informed about violence in Europe (he spoke Rumanian from a posting in the 1920s) – suggests, something changed in the English imaginary in the autumn of 1938. Decades later, the British military attaché in Berlin in 1938, Noel Mason-MacFarlane, claimed that he had proposed to London that the British secret services should assassinate Hitler, albeit in the sure knowledge that he would be rebuffed.[72] Hitherto, assassination had been seen as immoral, unnecessary and a sign of political failure. And the official position – both publicly and internally – remained just that. It was as predictable that loyal servants of the British state – leaving aside rogues with 'no British blood' – would not wish to be associated with attempts to assassinate its enemies, as it was that Hitler would play the victim. Both sides of that equation were apparent in the Venlo-Munich Affair of November 1939.

There were two quite separate elements to the affair. A German anti-Nazi did try to assassinate Hitler. George Elser spent thirty nights wiring the beer cellar in Munich where Hitler returned each year to meet former comrades: it was one of the most important occasions in the Nazi calendar. In the end, Hitler was not in the cellar when the bomb went off: eight random Nazis were killed instead. The Munich cellar bomb pointed to the low priority that the pre-war Nazi state accorded to the threat of assassination.

At the same time as Elser was preparing his solo attack on Hitler, however, the SD – the intelligence and security agency of the SS – was running an entrapment operation against the British secret services. The SIS, the Foreign Office and the prime minister, Neville Chamberlain, thought they were negotiating with a group of German generals to overthrow Hitler. Although never explicitly stated, it was clear that the German military was expected to do the dirty work of killing the Führer. Instead, the SD and the Gestapo kidnapped two SIS officers at the Venlo crossing on the Dutch–German frontier. German propaganda had a field day with their coup, claiming that the captured officers had been behind the attempted assassination of Hitler in Munich. In London, SIS, in their attempts to deny that they had anything to do with assassination, was forced to admit to the press that the captured officers were genuine British spies.[73] At the same time, Neville Chamberlain had to go cap in hand to his French opposite number, Édouard Daladier, to apologise for running such an operation without telling his allies, and then royally cocking it up. Daladier was gracious

SABOTAGE APPLIED TO INDIVIDUALS

about the whole thing: after all, he had overseen the Rosselli cover-up in 1937.[74]

Geoffrey Household was certainly representative of the 'have a go hero' mentality abroad in British intelligence in 1939: plans and units for 'unconventional warfare' sprouted up all over the place – SIS, the Foreign Office and military intelligence. The world of 1939 was thus very different from the world of 1914 when, despite a public spy scare, the whole emphasis had been on recruiting volunteers into regular military units. Spies were supposed to collect intelligence, not kill people. Looking back, Ian Fleming, an important wartime official in the Naval Intelligence Division (NID), wrote of his fictional assassin, 'Bond is not in fact a hero, but an efficient and not very attractive blunt instrument in the hands of government, and though he is a meld of various qualities I noted among secret service men and commandos in the last war, he remains, of course, a highly romanticised version of the true spy. The real thing is another kind of beast altogether.'[75]

No-one was really talking seriously about assassination in 1939, however: sabotage, black propaganda and subversion were the order of the day. On the other hand, it might be possible to see such preparations as the matrix from which even 'directer action' could spring. There was an obvious impediment: the direct-action enthusiasts were, in the main, useless. Churchill, a long-time enthusiast for unconventional warfare, came to that conclusion in July 1940 when he ordered that the whole business should be started anew with the creation of Special Operations.[76] SOE was still regarded as useless by most, corrupt by many, and a menace by some, as late as April 1942.[77]

It was their own sense of failure and humiliation that appears to have nudged British officials into wanting to ape their totalitarian betters. Until 1942, British intelligence had no real understanding of their German opposite numbers. It was thus that British intelligence officers turned their attention to a direct-action state that they felt they knew much better: the Soviet Union. In July 1941, SO2, the direct-action arm of the Special Operations Executive, asked SIS to hand over the debriefings of the recently slain Krivitsky, in order that they might study 'Soviet methods' and pass them on to their instructors and trainees.[78]

British intelligence also noted that no meaningful acts of resistance, especially assassination, occurred in formerly democratic Europe until Germany invaded the Soviet Union in June 1941. In August 1941, two Communists murdered a German sailor at a Paris metro station. This act immediately kicked German victimhood into high gear. The German commander in France, General Otto von Stülpnagel, announced that all French prisoners were now to be regarded as hostages.[79] Stülpnagel was, however, feeling his way. He observed to his superiors in Berlin that the Communist resistance was tiny: no real threat to German rule. There did not seem much point in falling for the classic revolutionary use of assassination to provoke a violent reaction and thus wider resistance. Stülpnagel suggested that a good alternative to the execution of French hostages would be the mass deportations of Jews and Communists to concentration camps. This, he was sure, would be very popular in France.[80]

Stülpnagel's argument was rapidly undone by the first assassination of a specifically targeted senior officer, the Wehrmacht Feldkommandant of Nantes, Lt-Col. Fritz Hotz, in October 1941. The Germans initially thought that the British were behind the assassination – overrating them in the same way that the British overrated the Germans. However, Hotz's murder was rapidly followed by that of the counsellor to the Feldkommandant in Bordeaux by a member of the Central Committee of the French Communist Party: Stülpnagel executed forty-eight prisoners in retaliation. That effectively ended the assassination campaign. Stülpnagel's plan for labelling the mass deportation of Jews an 'anti-assassination' measure was adopted by Berlin. Although the French Communist assassination effort in the late summer–autumn of 1941 had been brief, it showed some promise as a 'detonator'.[81]

That thought certainly occurred in London. SOE wanted to be seen to do something. So too did the Czech government-in-exile in London, which feared that if the Communists were the only visible resisters, it would rapidly become superfluous. In fact, there was a relatively effective non-Communist resistance movement – UVOD – in Czechoslovakia in 1941: it merely, sensibly, concentrated on gathering and passing intelligence to the British and the Soviets. It had become less effective, however, with the appointment of Reinhard Heydrich, head of the

SABOTAGE APPLIED TO INDIVIDUALS

security organisation of the SS, the RSHA, as the Reich Protector of Bohemia and Moravia in September 1941. Communist sabotage in Czechoslovakia was much more effective than anything that was happening in France. Nevertheless, Heydrich's view on the situation was not dissimilar to that of Stülpnagel: violent Communists were a problem to be dealt with but the hearts and the minds of much of the population were winnable.[82] When he was blown up, as the Gestapo noted, Czech civilians rushed to his aid and even tried to stop the assassins from escaping from the scene.[83]

The dual need of SOE and the Czechs to 'do something' merged on 3 October 1941 when Sir Frank Nelson, Executive Director of SOE, and Colonel František Moravec, head of Czech intelligence, agreed on a 'spectacular assassination'. The Czechs would provide the assassins; the British the weapons, training and the aircraft needed to fly the assassination squad into Czechoslovakia. Technically, the assassination attempt was carried out under the auspices of the Czech President Edvard Beneš, whose followers Edith Durham had once characterised as the 'Black Hand's best friends'.[84]

However, the Gestapo officers who investigated the assassination were, from the first, in no doubt who was behind the conspiracy: 'British submachine gun, British ammunition, British bombs with British explosives, British detonating caps, British detonators, British insulating tape'.[85] The final report on the investigation merely reiterated, with additional evidence, that 'the order, the tools, the weapons, the execution and finally the responsibility for the assassination of SS Obergruppenführer Heydrich were: "Made in England"'.[86] As the deputy head of SOE's Czech Section wrote after the infiltration but before the killing, 'the two agents have been trained in all methods of assassination known to us'.[87]

The assassins were parachuted into Czechoslovakia in December 1941. On 27 May 1942 they ambushed Heydrich as his chauffeur drove him to work, unescorted, in Prague Castle. The assassination method was little changed from Sarajevo – gun and bomb – although, unusually, the gun failed and the bomb eventually killed the target – Heydrich died from the wounds it inflicted on 3 June 1942.

The Germans deployed much the same two-track approach to defining the conspiracy as they had in France: a thorough and very well-resourced investigation combined with insensate bloodlust. Since the assassins had been living with the resistance for six months before the attack, and took refuge with them in its wake, the investigation was able to uncover almost the entire UVOD network. The case broke in mid-June 1942, when another of the SOE parachutists betrayed the whole conspiracy to the Gestapo. The SS stormed the Borromeo Church in Prague: everyone hiding in the crypt, including the assassins, was either killed or committed suicide.[88]

The investigators used the foulest tortures in their search for the hideout.[89] The most public victims of the bloodlust, however, were the inhabitants of the village of Lidice. The assassins had never gone anywhere near Lidice: it was home village of members of a resistance network which had sheltered an SOE radio operator.[90] The SS murdered all the men of the village in June 1942, and the women were sent to a concentration camp: 'Aryan' children were given to German families and the remainder killed.[91] At the same moment, the performance of totalitarian victimhood was reaching its apogee in Berlin. Heydrich's wife was too heavily pregnant to be flown to Germany. Instead, his young children were petted by the Nazi elite as the centrepiece of his state funeral.[92]

The precise reaction in London to its handiwork was curiously elusive. There was seemingly very little post-operational discussion of the mission within the organisation. The assassination garnered SOE some unwanted respect within the inner councils of the SS. Moravec never wavered from the view that he had engineered a heroic triumph of self-sacrificial national will. After the attack, but before Lidice, the operational head of SOE, Colin Gubbins, told Moravec that the British and Czechs should do more assassinations together.[93] After Lidice and the Borromeo church massacres, Lord Selborne, the government minister overseeing SOE, wrote that 'SOE agents have earned the gratitude of mankind'.[94]

However, propaganda from London in June 1942 played down the sacrifice and claimed that the Germans had not been able to capture the assassins, so had shot random innocent Czechs.[95] Someone in the Ministry of Information thought it was a good idea to commission a heroic oil painting of the assassination.[96] Two feature films celebrating the event – *Hangmen Also Die* and *Hitler's Madman* – were released in 1943, but the wartime line was that the assassins had been members of an indigenous resistance movement. It was not until June 1945 that the British press reported that the assassins had flown in from Britain, only contacting the resistance when they landed.[97]

The internal history of SOE Czech section described the assassination as an 'effective' action that owed its success to SOE's 'very full preparation'. Nevertheless, it assessed the assassination as 'disastrous' for SOE, given the effectiveness of the German response.[98] The internal history of SOE, written at the end of the war, concluded that 'for SOE the disaster was almost complete . . . [but] the extent of these disasters was perhaps hardly realised at the time'. It used the strangest term for the future of Czech resistance: *insaisissable*, vanishing. Relations between Czech intelligence and SOE were tense. SOE wanted to claim that they had urged and equipped the Czechs to assassinate Heydrich but had no responsibility for the killing.[99]

Even though the Heydrich assassination had been a remarkable demonstration of operational capability – indeed, the only one that SOE had to show for at least another year – it was allowed to pass without much comment. The implicit conclusion seems to have been: technical success, operational disaster.

SOE officers were involved in other assassination plots at the same time as the Heydrich *attentat*, but in a much more tangential fashion. One employed members of the Zionist Irgun to assassinate Iraqis in a 'dangerous and ill-conceived' scheme in 1941.[100] Other SOE officers in the Middle East provided the erroneous intelligence that the German commander in the theatre, Erwin Rommel, was staying at a villa on the Libyan coast. The intelligence galvanised the entire 'special forces' complex in Cairo. Cairo was the breeding ground of 'private armies', a feature that had done much to bring SOE into disrepute. In November 1941, British army commandos, aided by the SAS and the SBS, landed on the coast on a mission to kill Rommel. The raid was a fiasco. Rommel was not at the villa; he wasn't even in Libya. The Germans protecting what was, in fact, a logistics planning facility killed or captured most of the raiders. Although there was no direct link between the Heydrich assassination and the Rommel raid – which was planned by the devolved military command in the Middle East – they were most certainly coeval. There was clearly an atmosphere of assassination within the British have-a-go community in late 1941.[101]

Any enthusiasm there had been for assassination appears to have waned by mid-1942, and the dangers of playing with this kind of operation were confirmed by the second very high-profile assassination of the year, that of the effective ruler of Vichy France, Admiral François Darlan, in December 1942. In preparation for the Allied invasion of Morocco and Algeria in November 1942, the Americans had put a great deal of effort into trying to subvert Vichy forces in the North African territories. The unexpected presence of Darlan in Algiers at the time of the invasion led to some swift extemporisation, negotiations, and agreement by Darlan to switch his allegiance from the Axis to the Allies if his personal rule would be guaranteed by the latter. Everything seemed to have been settled nicely when Darlan was assassinated on Christmas Eve 1942. The somewhat optimistic first report from General Eisenhower in Algiers was that the assassin was a young student, who claimed 'no affiliation [to] any party and insisted to [a] priest [that he] act[ed] on his own without accomplices'.[102]

The reality was, predictably, somewhat messier. The assassin was the product of a training camp run by SOE and its American opposite number, the Office of Strategic Services (OSS), outside Algiers.[103] The few French recruits that the camp had been able to attract were appalled by the Allied deal with the Vichyite Darlan. The British senior officer at the camp had not been discreet in his support for such elements. Less than a fortnight before the assassination, he had been warned that 'if SOE afford any assistance to anti-Darlan or pro-Gaullist elements in North Africa General Eisenhower will order the removal of the mission'. SOE promised that 'we shall of course be careful not to burn our fingers': which they promptly did. SOE regarded the assassination of Darlan as a technical success for one of their trainees, a real boon to their operations, and a political relief.[104]

The conspiracy to assassinate Darlan was hatched by a small group of monarchist fanatics. From the outset, however, there were suspicions in Algiers that it had been orchestrated by the special services of General Charles de Gaulle, the leader of the Free French. No-one wanted an investigation. The leaders of the French factions in Algiers met in immediate conclave. Careful to make no contact with the Allies, they had the killer executed. The most senior figure ever directly connected to the conspiracy was the head of the Algiers police, brother of de Gaulle's representative in the city. There was nothing to suggest that SOE or OSS knowingly commissioned the assassination. Nevertheless, many were the voices calling for the 'hidden hand' to be purged as it did more harm than good to the Allied war effort.[105]

Once more, responses to the Darlan assassination in Washington and London were elliptical. President Roosevelt's chief adviser, William Leahy, recently returned as ambassador from Vichy, urged that the 'President make a statement <u>this evening</u> to the effect that the President "strongly deprecates assassination to achieve political ends".'[106] Little was done: instead, Roosevelt personally extended hospitality and healthcare to the Darlan family at his resort in Warm Springs, Georgia.[107] The British ambassador in Washington reported that although most American officials greeted Darlan's assassination with 'relief', their political masters 'appeared to be somewhat upset, and a series of quite unnecessarily fulsome messages about the merits and achievements of Darlan were sent to his widow by the President and others'.[108] The British censored a West End play about events in Algiers, *The Assassin*, not because it might embarrass de Gaulle, but because it showed the Americans in a poor light.[109]

When the OSS field manual on special operations subsequently came to outline the use of assassination, its authors resorted to synecdoche. They explicitly made the claim that assassination fell under the category of 'Special operations not assigned to other governmental agencies and not under direct control of theater commanders'. Some OSS technical researchers experimented with poisons and pathogens in the hope that they might be able to assassinate opponents but make the death appear to be by 'natural causes'.[110] Such research was largely irrelevant to OSS officers in the field. Assassination was an official role of the OSS nested within its authority to commit acts of sabotage: 'Sabotage applied to individuals includes liquidation,' the field manual authors wrote. Sabotage was also to be the cover story for assassination: 'political and public physical sabotage covers the liquidation of . . . political and administrative leaders'. This formulation meant that the extensive documentation of special operations in the late war period merely needed to discuss sabotage.[111]

Nevertheless, part of the OSS discussion of assassination was already in the public domain. At the end of 1943, the OSS officer Saul Padover published an academic article on the subject. Padover was a social scientist, specialising in propaganda, stationed in London.[112] He argued that in the era of the Great War, assassination had been a 'paltry affair' in face of 'the supreme value of large-scale-organization in killing'. However, in the inter-war years, 'Europe's assorted Chekas, Iron Guards, Blackshirts, and Gestapos showed the world how to liquidate opponents with skill and dispatch.' He maintained that, in future, the assassin could function 'both in tyrannies and democracies, and in neither'. 'Governmental forms and structures, as such,' Padover wrote, 'do not determine assassination.' In the long term, it might be possible for democracies to 'devalue the deed in the public mind' but that would take 'more time than the life span of the average administrator'. In the short term, America should expect to deal with a burst of assassination in liberated Europe. More than that, 'assassination is not only common to political societies everywhere; it also has a long and not dishonorable history'. OSS had to be prepared to play in the assassination field.[113]

Padover subsequently had the chance to demonstrate how this might be done in practice. In line with his prediction, the SS did start to plan to use assassination in liberated Europe. Allied intelligence first picked up hints of such an interest in March 1944.[114] Fear of German assassins peaked in December 1944 and January 1945 when German special forces dressed in Allied uniforms appeared during the Battle of the Bulge.[115]

In January 1945, Padover was operating as an intelligence officer in Aachen, the only major German city to have fallen to the Allies. He concluded that Oberbürgermeister Franz Oppenhoff was a diehard right-wing conspirator just as hostile to the Americans as to the Nazis. Padover therefore began feeding the press stories detailing the extent of Oppenhoff's anti-Nazism and the extent of his collaboration with the occupiers. In March 1945, SS assassins parachuted into Aachen and killed Oppenhoff. The causal link between Padover's propaganda operation and Himmler's decision to order the assassination of Oppenhoff

SABOTAGE APPLIED TO INDIVIDUALS

is not clear: the RSHA had plenty of its own sources about collaborators.[116] However, Padover got the result he wanted.[117]

In London, whence Padover had deployed, there was relatively little direct mention of assassination in SOE until after D-Day. In late June 1944, however, the head of SOE air operations said that the organisation should really try to assassinate Hitler.[118] His colleagues took the proposal seriously. The head of German operations, Ronald Thornley, was told to commission a feasibility study and SOE's leader, Colin Gubbins, went off to discuss the possibilities with the head of SIS, Sir Stewart Menzies.[119] A few days later, one of British intelligence's best agents, the German journalist Klop Ustinov, in Lisbon, who often had an inside track with the German intelligence services, reported that there was already a 'big plot' afoot in Germany to assassinate Hitler.[120] The OSS picked up similar information.[121]

In the intelligence services' view, carrying out assassinations was less straightforward than speculating about assassinations.[122] Nazi leaders no longer relied upon the hand of providence to protect them by 1944, as they might have done in 1939.[123] Heydrich's assassination had been followed by the Soviet assassination of Gauleiter Wilhelm Kube, Generalkommissar for Belorussia in Minsk in September 1943. Kube was assassinated by his maid, who planted a timed bomb under his bed. There was also a plot to kill Kube's opposite number in Kiev, Erich Koch, by having his Russian domestic staff poison his food: the servants were rumbled before they could act.[124] The Soviets barely missed Kube's successor in Minsk, Curt von Gottberg. A German Luftwaffe officer, who had been captured and turned by the Soviets in 1941, gained an audience with von Gottberg but failed to shoot him as planned.[125]

When Hitler appeared in public, he had a close escort of 450 men. Even beyond major events, Hitler was guarded by eleven RSD officers and ten Begleitkommando men. The RSD protective detail accompanied Hitler even within his fortified residences. This factor seems to have played on the minds of the men who plotted to assassinate Hitler in 1944: they doubted if they would have time to draw a pistol before the RSD officers shot them.[126]

Nevertheless, the indigenous German conspiracy to assassinate Hitler was real enough. The July Plot, although unsuccessful, would go on to be one of the building blocks of the post-war Federal Republic of Germany: there had been Germans who had violently opposed the Nazis. The assassination attempt was, however, at best an ambiguous advertisement for the 'honourable assassin'.[127] In the wake of the assassination, both the Gestapo and Anglo-American intelligence went to very considerable pains to build up a detailed picture of the German opposition.[128] They concluded that 'no danger involved in analysis of German opposition to Hitler is more tempting nor at the same time more misleading than that of pressing too far the significance of purely religious or humanitarian revolt.'[129]

For a group of trained soldiers, the army officers were not good assassins.[130] The officers mounted their first serious assassination attempt at Smolensk in March 1943. Two Wehrmacht officers planted a bomb on Hitler's aeroplane while he was meeting his commanders. The bomb on the aircraft failed to explode. Another Wehrmacht officer from the same group made a second attempt at the Zeughaus in Berlin a few days later: once again, the attempt failed because of the lack of an appropriate fuse and Hitler's unpredictable movements. In part, the problem with fuses stemmed from the assassins' extreme caution: they knew how pervasive the Gestapo security system had become and constantly feared betrayal.[131]

Similar considerations shaped the bomb that went off. In this case, the organiser of the assassination was chief of the Allgemeines Heeresamt, the inspector-general of the Home Army, Friedrich Olbricht, and the assassin, one of the most famous of the twentieth century, the chief of staff of the Home Army, Claus von Stauffenberg. The plan was for Stauffenberg to plant a timed bomb under Hitler's map table in his compound in East Prussia. He would then return to Berlin. The Home Army headquarters in the Bendlerblock, Berlin, would announce that the SS had assassinated Hitler and call on the Wehrmacht to destroy the threat.

The bomb did go off – Stauffenberg used a British detonator.[132] Stauffenberg did get back to Berlin. The Führer's death was proclaimed in the Bendlerblock. But very few army or intelligence officers acted. Hitler's headquarters was able to communicate with the Army, the SS and the propaganda authorities in Berlin, and vice versa, because the

SABOTAGE APPLIED TO INDIVIDUALS

Reichspost refused to co-operate with the plotters.[133] Soldiers in the Bendlerblock seized their own commanders: 'a collection of twelve armed clerks arrested them all', as one survivor put it.[134] The head of the Home Army executed the procurers of the assassination, and then the SS and the Gestapo swept in, to arrest, torture and execute anyone against whom they could find any evidence.[135]

In the wake of 20 July 1944, western intelligence services returned to the utility of assassination. What they found was not encouraging. The OSS concluded that 'the collapse of Germany may be retarded and the future formation of a centralized non-Nazi government for the purpose of surrendering, made difficult by the coup and the purge.'[136]

The leaders of SOE had their most extended recorded discussion about the assassination of Hitler *after* the German attempt. In presenting the feasibility study to the SOE Council, Ronald Thornley made a strong pitch for assassination. The Germans had failed 'to carry out this operation for us': the British should do the job for them instead. The likely result, he admitted, was unclear. In a perfect world, the Wehrmacht and the SS would fall upon one another, and the Germans would start killing each other. Thornley dismissed 'one of the commonest arguments' within SOE against assassination, that the victim would become a martyr, on the grounds that 'Hitler will become a legendary figure and his mode of death will not materially alter the situation'.[137]

Air Vice-Marshal Ritchie, who had originally proposed the assassination, chimed in to say that, as the OSS had already written into their handbook, it was the ability to carry out high-profile assassinations that marked out secret services as 'strategic services', never to be shackled to military theatre commanders. There the case rested, with an agreement to proceed with the assassination plan. As late as March 1945, SOE was still searching for an officer 'for a high priority assassination task which would require his lying low in Germany for [a] considerable period collecting necessary intelligence to enable him to do the job'.[138]

SOE also attempted assassinations lower down the food chain. In Italy it claimed that 'assassinations were not conducted or controlled'. However, the Italian networks that they supported 'carried out the assassination of several informers, torturers, etc. . . . entirely on their own volition'. The one assassination which SOE directly attempted, on military orders, was that of Joachim Lemelsen, the commander of the German 10th Army. A British officer was 'nominated' as the assassin, 'but despite searching for three weeks in the occupied zone dressed in British uniform and riding a bicycle, he was unable to find the person'.[139]

What a late war assassination plan might look like in detail was most clearly explained in another SOE German directorate operation. At the beginning of 1945, the Germans launched their last submarine offensive, with new U-boats that the Allies struggled to detect. By this stage in the war, SOE was regularly parachuting agents, nicknamed 'Bonzos', into Germany. The plan in this case was to parachute an assassin, a German left-wing activist, who had deserted from the Wehrmacht, into Hamburg.[140] In the autumn of 1944, he had been taught 'special killing methods' and had proved an able pupil.[141] Once on the ground in Hamburg, he was to 'observe the movements of U-boat officers, find out what cafes and places of amusement they visit, where they live and try to kill as many of them as possible'.[142] The assassination method would be close-range pistol shots. The agent was equipped with a specialist assassination kit: an advanced integrally silenced pistol with a standard semi-automatic pistol as a back-up. The ammunition between the two weapons was interchangeable and he carried one hundred rounds.[143]

In one sense the mission went well. The agent successfully parachuted into Hamburg in April 1945. Once there, however, he made no attempt to assassinate anyone. Rather, he contacted his left-wing friends, then exfiltrated himself to a British SAS unit, with lists of men who would collaborate with the British. That political role had not been part of the agent's mission briefing: in the changed end-of-war context, however, his handlers were pleased enough with the results.[144]

Assassination made no significant impact on the course, conduct, result or end of the Second World War. The Second World War, on the other hand, had a very significant impact on assassination. The 'honourable assassins' that had existed only in fantasy in 1939 existed in reality by 1945. Behind them lay a web of recruiters, trainers, armourers, logisticians, handlers, propagandists and theorists. They were exceptionally proud of themselves. Although both the British and American governments chose to wind up their specifically designated special operations agencies at the end of the Second World War, those decisions had nothing to do with an aversion to assassination. In Britain, SIS absorbed the special operations functions of SOE, and its new special operations division commanded one-fifth of the budget of the state's most costly intelligence agency.[145] When the CIA was eventually formed in 1947, its special operations budget grew exponentially to corner half of the agency's expenditure.[146]

7

LAST RITES
Assassination and the Fall of Empires, 1944–1973

The Second World War transformed assassination for empires, even though the perpetrators and their techniques were often familiar. Assassination remained much the same, but empire changed. Britain, for instance, had for long traced the filaments of assassination plots beyond its areas of imperial control. That international dimension of assassination had been, however, an irritant rather than a major threat. The empires could deal with terrorists. However, the imperial powers could no longer rely on 'superpowers' taking their side.

It was not that either Britain or France gave up on their empires. However, the danger of assassination for an imperial power was greatly amplified by geopolitical change. The results were a fear of a being assassinated in a cause that seemed increasingly futile, a sense that the new leaders with whom the imperial powers wanted to do business would probably be murdered, followed by weary cynicism as the parade of death continued.

Although the themes of post-war imperial assassination unfolded to a degree sequentially, all were already plain in the 1940s, most notably during the collapse of British rule in Palestine. The government of Palestine had always been weak, and it became weaker because of poor security and determined assassins. The assassination gangs achieved their mature form in the summer of 1940 when the 'Fighters for the

Freedom of Israel' – the Stern Gang – broke away from the 'National Military Organisation' – the Irgun. Having assassinated his main rival in the group, Yitzhak Shamir took over the effective leadership of the Stern Gang in 1943.[1] In some ways the British, with eyes on important wartime prizes, nurtured the assassins, wrongly believing that even violent Zionists would privilege anti-Nazism over anti-imperialism.[2] Instead, the Stern Gang despised Britain as a 'declining power' ripe for the plucking.[3] The persecution and then slaughter of the Jews of Europe brought even more of a desire to attack anyone who challenged the very specific vision of Zionism espoused by the assassins. Menachem Begin, the leader of the Irgun from 1945, arrived in Palestine from Europe during the war but was never identified by the British security services.[4] As Begin explained, the Irgun held underground court trials for British officials 'regarded as criminal' and sentenced them to death in absentia.[5] As the head of security intelligence in Palestine conceded in 1945, there was 'some blame on our own shoulders'.[6]

The Irgun and the Stern Gang openly launched their terrorist campaign against the British in early 1944, with the Stern Gang in particular concentrating on assassination. Their first spectacular was an attempt to assassinate the High Commissioner of Palestine, Sir Harold MacMichael. In early August 1944, MacMichael was being driven from Jerusalem to Jaffa. A squad of Stern Gang assassins, posing as a road survey party dressed in British army uniforms, attacked his car with automatic weapons, hand grenades and Molotov cocktails. MacMichael was wounded in the arm and the leg: his ADC took a bullet in the lung. The assassins ran off into a nearby Jewish settlement and disappeared.[7] Soon thereafter the leader of the MacMichael attack assassinated the head of Special Branch's Jewish section, Tom Wilkin. Wilkin proved a much easier target than MacMichael. He was walking unaccompanied in Jerusalem and was shot eleven times at short range.[8]

The British in Palestine were fairly certain they knew the identity of the attackers – they had an informer in the Stern Gang – but were stymied in taking the investigation much further forward.[9] Two things were clear: London – currently in the person of the Colonial Secretary, Oliver Stanley – had no wish to depart from the long-established precedent of downplaying the importance of assassinations: the official representatives of Jews in Palestine had no intention of helping the British against their co-religionists.[10] One official compared the reaction of 'official Zionism' to the MacMichael attack to that of official Nazism to the assassination of Dollfuss.[11] MacMichael's badly wounded ADC bitterly complained that the Jewish settlers who had sheltered the assassination squad were left unmolested.[12]

One of those suggesting to London that assassination was a serious problem for Palestine was the British cabinet minister resident in the Middle East, Walter Moyne, himself a former colonial secretary. In early 1944, two Stern Gang assassins ambushed Lord Moyne at the entrance of his official residence in Cairo. They killed both Moyne and his driver. Moyne had chosen to forgo any form of protection.[13] In this case, however, the assassins, who attempted to flee on bicycles, were trapped on a bridge and captured. Two days later, although the real identities of the assassins were still unclear, they confessed to the Egyptian authorities that 'we are members of the Fighters for the Freedom of Israel organisation and what we have done was done on the instruction of this organisation'.[14] One went on to say that 'the assassinations which are being carried on at present are the initial stages of a universal rising and that the Stern group can see no other way of supporting what he called "the war" other than by these political assassinations'.[15] By the next week a forensic examination had established that the Nagant revolver and the Luger semi-automatic pistol used by the killers were multiple assassination weapons that had been used in a string of murders of British officials carried out by the Stern Gang in Palestine since February 1944, including Wilkin.[16]

By the time the investigation in Cairo had precisely established the nature of the conspiracy, however, the decision had already been taken in London not to concentrate on the 'masters' of the assassins lest, in doing so, 'drastic action . . . should be directed against the whole Jewish community in Palestine'.[17] Instead, all attention was to be concentrated on the two assassins.[18]

In public, Churchill's rhetoric was harsh: 'if our dreams for Zionism are to end in the smoke of assassins' pistols, and our labours for its future to produce only a new set of gangsters worthy of Nazi Germany, many like myself will have to reconsider the position we have maintained so consistently and so long in the past.' Yet despite the hard line taken by Churchill on the punishment of the gunmen, he was sedulous in avoiding moves against the wider Zionist movement. He said no to those who demanded that the response to the assassination should be on a par with the punishment of the Egyptians after the Stack assassination. Egypt had lost a land it claimed as its own, the Sudan: the Jews should not, Churchill ruled, suffer the same fate.[19]

The Jewish Agency's willingness to arrest some members of the Irgun, the so-called Season, was regarded as sufficient co-operation. According to the High Commission in Jerusalem, the 'condemnation of terrorists by leaders and the press was forceful and genuine enough, probably inspired by the realisation that the Zionist cause was in jeopardy'.[20] 'In practice,' however, John Shaw, the Acting High Commissioner in Palestine, told London, 'supporters of the terrorists are to be found in all sections of the Yishuv.'[21] Moyne's grieving former officials commented, through gritted teeth, 'our whole policy at the moment is based on the assumption that there are "good" Jews . . . and that these "good" Jews are the official leaders and the vast majority of the Zionist movement; and that the people who organised the murder of Lord Moyne are a tiny and execrated minority. (Whether it is a true assumption is another matter; but having adopted a policy, we are entitled to follow it through).'[22] As officials in Jerusalem and Cairo had accurately predicted, all the Jewish terrorist groups soon reached an agreement for a joint campaign.[23]

The British in London were unwilling to make much of assassination. Moyne's son, Bryan Guinness, insisted that there should be no public mourning in Britain and that 'everything in England should be of a private and family nature only'.[24] Even Miles Lampson, not hitherto noted for his sympathy towards assassination victims, was moved to note that it was 'rather grisly for the poor boy sitting in a wicker chair alone with his father's coffin' in an aircraft hangar.[25] The British in Jerusalem were reluctant to start protecting their officers: 'it was [so] damaging to British prestige that it would be preferable to leave things as they were and take the risk.'[26] The 1946 assassination season was thus unsurprising yet deadly.[27] The assassins were particularly relentless.[28] When the Stern Gang set out to murder Major Doran, the area security officer for Tel Aviv, they dressed in their customary disguise of British soldiers and carried sub-machine guns. They shot the guard on the front door of the building where Doran was based on the Tel Aviv to Jaffa road, then wounded Doran himself. He managed to escape into his house which was at the rear of the office. The assassins blew up the house, killing Doran inside.[29] Some casualties were less visible but still significant. Sir John Shaw, now the second-ranking British official in Palestine as chief secretary, became so fearful of assassination that he had to be withdrawn.[30]

The British only really started thinking about a serious response to assassination once their morale had begun to fail. In February 1947, the Foreign Secretary, Ernest Bevin, announced that the British government could not resolve the future of Palestine and it would turn the search for solutions over to the UN. At the same time, the government approved a plan by the head of the Palestine Police's counter-terrorist cell to create 'flying squads'. The squads would be led by army officers seconded to the police, since 'there is in the Army a small number of officers who have both technical and psychological knowledge of terrorism, having themselves been engaged in similar operations on what might be termed the terrorist side in countries occupied by the enemy in the late war.'[31] Thus it was that Deputy Superintendent Roy Farran, formerly of the SAS, 'a young officer . . . with a fine military record . . . doing most valuable and successful work against terrorists', beat an unsuspecting member of the Stern Gang to death with a rock on the streets of Jerusalem in early May 1947.[32]

The clash of opinion between various British officials over this incident was revealing: some thought it was about time to use wartime techniques, but the majority opinion regarded the killing as a crime. Putting his SAS skills to good use, Farran promptly deserted and fled to Syria, only being lured back by the promise of a soft court martial. The assassination that followed on directly from the Farran case was that of Roy Farran's brother, Rex, slain by a Stern Gang parcel bomb at the family home near Wolverhampton in May 1948. This was the actual murder that the Stern Gang managed to commit in the UK. They had previously circled British-based government ministers but had made no attack on individuals who might have the power to retaliate.[33] Special Branch caught the bombmaker: he was convicted of an explosives offence, released and was able to emigrate to the new State of Israel in 1950.³⁴

For British officials, leaving Palestine behind was not the same as leaving assassination behind. Many of those who had served in Palestine were subsequently transferred elsewhere to face other assassination complexes. They, and their political and official superiors in London, took the existing mindset with them to new locations. Even Shaw returned to the fray in 1949 as head of MI5's new overseas division.³⁵ In the two-year period after Shaw's appointment, the British governors of Sarawak and Malaya were assassinated: both had been senior officials in Palestine.

In December 1949, Duncan Stewart, formerly financial secretary of the government of Palestine, the new Governor of Sarawak, was stabbed by Malay youths in Sibu. He was flown out to Singapore but died of his wounds. In October 1951, the car of Sir Henry Gurney, High Commissioner in Malaya, Shaw's successor as Chief Secretary of Palestine, was ambushed on its way from Kuala Lumpur to Fraser's Hill, about 60 miles north of the city. Gurney was shot and killed by a pistol-calibre bullet.

In the case of the Stewart assassination, the British government acted forcibly to narrow the published scope of the conspiracy. The rare use of knives in the killing and the exotic remoteness of Sarawak made the conspiracy appear ramshackle and primitive. The two youthful assassins were arrested and identified as 'members of an association, a small part of which has continued to show opposition to the cession of Sarawak to the Crown'.³⁶ The transfer of Sarawak to Britain, in 1946, had been made by the last 'White Rajah', a descendant of James Brooke, the Victorian adventurer who had carved out a personal empire in Borneo. The assassins were members of the Malay minority, fighting, it seemed at first glance, for the return of a quixotic British dynast.³⁷

The organiser of the assassination was arrested, tried and executed within months. He was portrayed as 'a discredited civil servant' with a notorious record of collaboration with the Japanese.³⁸ The centrepiece of the prosecution case was his correspondence with the secretary-general of the Malay National Union. What was deliberately not stressed in public was the evidence that the Malay National Union was a front organisation for Indonesia. 'These letters provide proof of what we have long suspected,' the Colonial Office informed the Foreign Office; 'though the rank and file of the anti-cession movement may think they are merely asking for the return of a Brooke Rajah under British Protection, the leaders are working for "independence" in the Indonesian sense of the term and for ultimate incorporation into the Indonesian Republic.'[39] Just before Stewart had arrived in Sarawak, the Colonial Office official administering the government, C.W. Dawson, had suppressed KRIS, an Indonesian paramilitary organisation in the territory.[40] After the assassination, Dawson reported that there was very considerable support for the assassins among Malay groups, despite public statements of revulsion. 'One rather disquieting feature of the matter,' he noted, 'is the religious (Islamic) ingredient.' The assassins had taken oaths on the Koran to carry out the deed.[41]

Extreme care was exercised not to explore Malay support for the assassination.[42] At senior governmental levels, a very clear decision was made to avoid all mention of the Indonesian origins of the assassination. 'We have hitherto taken the line that this agitation is by a self-seeking small clique who have lost their privileged position under the Rajahs,' London instructed Sarawak, 'and to introduce any publicity revealing direct anti-British or pro-Indonesian feeling would provide yet another handle for our critics. . . . The whole "anti-colonial" world would seize happily on this evidence that one more colonial people is embarking on the struggle against British imperialism.'[43] The Commissioner-General in Southeast Asia, and former Colonial Secretary, Malcolm MacDonald, and the current Colonial Secretary, Oliver Lyttelton, agreed that the Indonesians should not even be given cause to think that the British suspected them.[44]

Defining the conspirators in Gurney's assassination was much more straightforward. Britain had declared an Emergency in 1948 so that it might resist the Malayan Communist Party and its military wing, the Malay Races Liberation Army (MRLA). In Malaya, the identity of the conspirators was easy to discover – the assassins left their plan of attack at the scene: its handwriting was that of a known commander of an MRLA guerrilla band.[45]

The definition of the conspiracy, on the other hand, was politically dangerous. In days before his death, Gurney himself had expressed the view that the ethnic Chinese community was collectively responsible for Communist violence. 'Everyone knows,' he had expostulated, 'that with a few notable exceptions the Chinese themselves have done absolutely nothing to help their own people to resist Communism, which is today rampant in schools and among the young uneducated generation. . . . Leading Chinese have contented themselves with living in luxury in Singapore etc. and criticising the Police and security forces for causing injustices.'[46] M.V. del Tufo, Gurney's deputy, and Malcolm MacDonald struggled to get Malay leaders to attend a post-assassination meeting because 'they felt that, as Chinese would be present, they would not be able to speak freely on . . . the complete failure in their eyes of the Chinese community to play its proper share in the effort to end the emergency'. Although this attempt to blame a rival ethnic group merely accorded with Gurney's view, the British immediately recognised that the sentiment 'will become dangerous if it is allowed to develop unchecked'. Even before intervention from London, officials on the ground, while arguing that they had a 'Chinese problem', were not willing to go too far down the road towards collective guilt.[47] The intervention from London occurred with the personal arrival of Oliver Lyttelton and his subsequent dismissal of nearly all the senior officials in Malaya. The positive concept of winning Chinese 'hearts and minds' became the centrepiece of British policy. Assassination was not the danger: the real danger was popular support for assassination.[48]

The command of popular support was of increasing importance. The Britons assassinated in the 1940s and early 1950s were bureaucrats. In parallel to their deaths, however, ran those of charismatic leaders. Many of those leaders were staunch anti-imperialists, but at least they were open to an order in which traditional lines of influence could be maintained. The assassination complex that demonstrated this development most clearly was the Raj. The assassination of British officials played no role in the collapse of British rule on the Indian subcontinent. The British policed the assassination threat while they were in power. On the other hand, assassins rapidly slew Britain's preferred leaders in Burma, India and Pakistan.

In Burma, the British faced two nationalist leaders, U Saw and Aung San, both former collaborators with the Japanese, each of whom suspected the other – reasonably enough – of trying to assassinate him.[49] U Saw survived an attempt on his life from jeep-riding assassins dressed in British army uniform in September 1946, although he nearly lost his eyesight to shattered windscreen glass.[50] In August 1947, he retaliated: a squad of assassins, once more dressed in British army uniform, arrived at the building where Aung San's Executive Council, the proto-government to which the British intended to hand power, met. They walked in unopposed because Aung San did not like being guarded by the British. Bursting through the door of the council chamber, the assassins opened fire on Aung San with sub-machine guns.[51]

It was subsequently discovered that the assassins had set out from, and returned to, U Saw's house. Rather embarrassingly, corrupt British officers had assisted U Saw to obtain a veritable arsenal of automatic small arms, as well as the uniforms the assassins used as their disguise.[52] More than any other colony, Burma seemed a honeypot for down-on-their-luck British adventurers.[53]

The British and Aung San's surviving followers rapidly agreed, however, that it was in their joint best interests to cover up the extent of the assassination conspiracy. The British feared that if the Burmese unleashed Aung San's Anti-Fascist People's Freedom League (AFPFL) on their small forces, there would be a massacre. The AFPFL did not want to attack the British, who seemed willing to facilitate a smooth transfer of power to themselves. Their joint plan was 'to pin the guilt to some person or persons' as quickly as possible.[54] Aung San's successor Thakin Nu issued a statement exonerating the British from any involvement in the assassination.[55]

British and Burmese co-operated to arrest U Saw. He was on trial when the formal Anglo-Burmese treaty was signed in November 1947. Everyone was very on edge. Fearing an assassination attempt, Thakin Nu's bodyguard shot and killed a young British soldier. That had to be covered up, despite the heartfelt pleas of the boy's father as to why his son had died unrecorded in a dead empire. U Saw was condemned to death in December 1947; his British arms suppliers received lesser sentences: officials breathed a sigh of relief that the affair was over.[56]

British imperial rulers had an intimate knowledge of all the players in the Aung San assassination saga; they were similarly intimate with the players in the assassination of Gandhi in newly independent India in January 1948. The British High Commission in New Delhi was across the street from Gandhi's home and political centre in Birla House. The inhabitants of the High Commission watched his death in near real time.[57] When a Hindu extremist let off a bomb in the Birla House compound, Edwina Mountbatten, the wife of the former viceroy and current Governor-General, Lord Mountbatten, hurried across the road to check that Gandhi was unhurt. When the bomber's partner-in-assassination fatally shot Gandhi with a Beretta semi-automatic pistol in the Birla House prayer room ten days later, Lord Mountbatten went across himself to tell the Indian Prime Minister, Jawaharlal Nehru, that Gandhi had complained to the governor-general about the government's indulgence of Hindu extremism.[58]

Just because Hindu assassins had played little role in the overthrow of British rule in India did not mean they had disappeared.[59] Although fascistic Hindu societies were now a minor threat to the British, the war had proved a golden age for their formation: they had grown 'like mushrooms'.[60] The most active assassination society, known as the HRD, had been formed by the president of the Hindu Maha Sabha, V.D. Savarkar.[61] The Hindu Maha Sabha was, in turn, linked with the paramilitary RSS, which specialised in murdering Muslims under the Congress banner. In the wake of Gandhi's assassination, barely six months after independence, Nehru, fearing for his own safety, effectively reintroduced the old 'Bengal protective protocols'.[62]

The bitter argument between Nehru and his home minister, Vallabhbhai Patel, over the assassination mirrored those that had taken place in British India. Patel took the classic 'Asquithian' stance of blaming the assassination on a very small conspiracy, dangerous for its methods rather than mass support.[63] Nehru, on the other hand, detected a 'wide conspiracy and organisation behind' the assassins.[64] He complained of 'lack of real effort in tracing the larger conspiracy'. He insisted that the RSS and the Hindu Maha Sabha should be targeted as much as the HRD, who were the actual assassins.[65] Nehru feared that the Hindu extremists had thoroughly infiltrated provincial governments. Assassination speech of the kind that he had once defended was to be suppressed.⁶⁶ In light of the assassination, it was 'futile and dangerous to the peace of India to try experiments in democracy'.⁶⁷

Nehru had little truck with the argument that V.D. Savarkar should be spared because of his 'sacrifice and suffering in the past' – long imprisonment by the British for the assassination conspiracies of 1909.⁶⁸ In the event, the Gandhi assassination trial was very similar to those held in British India. The assassins were convicted and hanged, five others were found guilty of conspiracy, but two of those decisions were reversed on appeal. The procurer of the assassination, V.D. Savarkar, was acquitted. No-one was satisfied and the Indian government returned to the investigation thirteen years later, after Patel and Savarkar's deaths. The subsequent investigation confirmed many of Nehru's suspicions that there had been a much wider plot by Hindu extremists to assassinate Gandhi.⁶⁹

The supposed justification for Gandhi's assassination had been his friendly talks with the Prime Minister of Pakistan and leader of the Muslim League, Liaquat Ali Khan. Khan was the last of the three national fathers of the dismembered Raj to be assassinated. The assassin in this case was an Islamist fanatic. He shot Khan three times with a Luger semi-automatic pistol at a rally in Rawalpindi in October 1951.⁷⁰ It proved hard to trace the true nature of assassination conspiracy beyond that because the crowd at the rally Khan was addressing lynched the shooter. Somewhat unconvincingly, the Pakistani investigation rejected the 'religious fanatic' line on the ground that the assassin's actions were 'completely lacking in the essentials of a Mussalman's conduct'. It was, the investigator claimed, 'as likely for an honest Muslim to get killed by another Muslim as to be bitten by a rabid dog or snake'. Therefore, there must have been a political conspiracy unlinked to religion.⁷¹

Once more, this was familiar territory. The assassin had been identified as an extremist under the Raj. A British police officer was the first to Liaquat's side when he was shot. In the end, the Pakistan government asked an MI5 officer, who had previously led the Bombay CID, to investigate the assassination.⁷² To the displeasure of Liaquat's family, he reinstituted the verdict of assassination by a religious fanatic.⁷³

It was not the causes of assassination that mattered to the western powers; the Indian subcontinent had, after all, just yielded assassinations of a Buddhist, a Hindu and a Muslim by Buddhists, Hindus and Muslims: it was the fact of relentless assassination that was so worrying. Such killings were by no means confined to South Asia: three months before the death of Liaquat Ali Khan, another Muslim fanatic had assassinated King Abdullah of Jordan in Jerusalem. The assassination was traced back to the former Grand Mufti of Jerusalem in Cairo. Once more, it was hard to investigate properly: the king's bodyguards killed the assassin at the site of the murder and the regency council executed all suspected conspirators they could lay their hands on in Amman.[74]

Of course, even weakening imperial states could pursue different goals at the same time. While parts of the state were lamenting and investigating assassination, even offering services to try and keep potential victims safer, others might applaud or even encourage assassinations. In 1953, a SIS delegation to Washington proposed to their opposite numbers in the CIA that it might be a good idea to overthrow the government of Iran. Neither secret service directly mentioned assassination but the whole context of their discussion was the March 1951 assassination of the Prime Minister of Iran, Ali Razmara.[75] It was Razmara's successor as prime minister, Mohammed Mossadeq, whom the British had in their sights.[76] Mossadeq was hardly unalert to the threat to his person. He was very well guarded and lived in a fortified compound.[77] In the end, the former Iranian army officers whom the Anglo-Americans recruited to their cause satisfied themselves with the assassination of the chief of the Iranian police, Mahmud Afshartus, in April 1953.[78] The Iranian generals did launch a coup, with full CIA–SIS support, in August 1953, but there were no assassinations: Mossadeq survived.[79]

The Iran non-assassination is the best documented instance of the British toying with assassination in the post-war imperial context. Much else is decidedly tenuous. Thanks to the posthumously published testimony of George Young, the SIS controller for the Middle East in the 1950s, and vice-chief of the organisation at the beginning of the 1960s, we know that he personally was enamoured by the idea of assassination. The CIA's head of clandestine operations, and a prime mover in well-documented CIA assassinations, Richard Bissell, later testified under oath that: 'I know of no way in which it is possible to operate a secret intelligence agency or a secret service unless it has at least a number of employees who are willing to and can be depended upon to carry out orders involving acts of this sort [assassination]. . . . I think definitely it has been used by MI6.'[80] Much of the rest is undocumented gossip.[81] According to the diary of the assistant under-secretary for the Middle East at the Foreign Office, Queen Elizabeth II commented of the troublesome Egyptian leader, Colonel Nasser, in July 1955 that 'she was surprised nobody had found means of putting something in his coffee'. Conversationally, the diplomat agreed that the removal of Nasser was 'a good idea which ought to be applied to a number of people in the Middle East' and promised to keep her updated. However, no-one has seriously suggested that Her Majesty was a proponent of assassination. The British intelligence services launched covert operations against Nasser on a scale that dwarfed their campaign against Mossadeq. But in Egypt, as it had been in Iran, the main British technique was black propaganda rather than assassination. In any case, SIS's most highly placed agent was in fact working for the Egyptian security services.[82]

The imperial power for which assassination is very well attested is France rather than Britain. In 1955, France and Britain both faced new assassination threats: France from North Africa, Britain from Cyprus. The leader of EOKA – Greek nationalists demanding that Cyprus should become part of Greece – George Grivas ordered his followers to form assassination squads in May 1955.[83] The problem for France first manifested itself in Morocco when an assassin murdered the businessman and political fixer Jacques Lemaigre-Dubreuil in June 1955.[84] France had an even bigger problem, however. Algerian terror groups launched a campaign to murder French settlers in August 1955.[85] Algeria was over 250 times bigger than Cyprus. In 1956, France had sixteen times as many troops in Algeria as the British had in Cyprus. Although the British campaign in Cyprus was actually larger than pre-war military operations in Bengal and Palestine, the stakes were even higher for France. Legally, Algeria was not a colony: it was as much part of France as Pyrénées-Atlantiques.[86]

The government of France decided to launch an assassination counter-offensive. For the simple bureaucratic purpose of securing funding, SIS's French counterpart, SDECE, kept a list of the murders its Service Action branch committed between 1956 and 1958. This is an instance where there is more evidence of practice than of motivation. SDECE's first recorded victim was Ben Moulaid Mostaffa, an Algerian rebel who was killed using a booby-trapped radio set in March 1956. Given the number of combatants on all sides involved in Algeria, such an obscure murder was truly a pinprick. SDECE subsequently shifted its tactics to assassinations in Europe. In September 1956, Service Action attempted to assassinate the arms dealer Otto Schlüter in Hamburg. The assassination team blew up his premises, killing one person and wounding Schlüter. They returned in June 1957 for a second attempt: this time a car bomb killed Schlüter's mother. Similarly, SDECE made two attempts on an arms dealer called Leopold in Geneva. In August 1957, the assassin's silenced semi-automatic pistol jammed when he tried to ambush the arms dealer. He returned to the same staircase in an apartment building the next month and shot Leopold dead. Many of the assassination attempts ran into problems. Two Service Action assassins blew themselves up in Tunis.[87]

When Charles de Gaulle seized power in France in 1958, he placed the operations under the supervision of his close aide Jacques Foccart, but there was no change in policy.[88] Foccart gave permission for the assassination of a German running a desertion network for soldiers of the Foreign Legion from Tétuan.[89] In November 1958, Service Action missed the political representative of the rebel provisional government of Algeria in Bonn. The German police and intelligence services worked out who was responsible for the attack. With a shrug, European politicians accepted the French campaign. The Germans set up a liaison link with SDECE to ensure that the allies did not end up killing each other's assets.[90] The one area into which the French government was reluctant to tread was the assassination of well-known political targets. It cancelled a planned attack on Algeria's most famous revolutionary, Ben Bella, in Cairo in July 1956. It also vetoed a plan to assassinate the Egyptian leader, Colonel Nasser, with a bomb in Port Said in December 1956.[91]

For both Britain and France, it remained very much the case that the risk of assassination was a more serious concern than the challenge of carrying out assassinations. Here again, it was the French who suffered the most serious difficulties. An innovation in the Cyprus struggle was that Britain, counter to previous imperial practice, was willing to exfiltrate some of its indigenous collaborators to England. In May 1956, EOKA began collecting the names of such 'traitors' so that its assassins might pursue them to London. However, Archbishop Makarios, the true leader of the rebellion, vetoed the plan soon after he returned from enforced exile under the Anglo-American Bermuda agreement in March 1957.[92] As a result, the risk of assassination in Cyprus remained very high while the threat of assassination in Britain remained only a theoretical possibility.[93]

By contrast, in July 1956, the Front de libération nationale (FLN) political and military leadership agreed that the destruction of its rival insurgent group, the Mouvement national algérien (MNA), by assassination was as much a priority as the struggle against France.[94] The assassinations were to take place in France as much as in Algeria.[95] The FLN's 'shock groups' assassinated their first senior MNA leaders, Ahmed Bekhat and Abdal Fillali, who headed the trade union for Algerian migrant workers in France, a year later. The MNA retaliated in kind, producing a deadly assassination war. About 150 assassinations took place in southern France, with comparable numbers around Paris.[96] These murders were embedded in political rituals. Often the death squad would kidnap the victim first, read out the death sentence proclaimed by their underground courts and then throw the corpse into a canal.[97]

At the very moment in 1958 that EOKA called a temporary halt to assassination, the FLN decided to assassinate not just fellow Algerians but French officials in France. In late August 1958, FLN assassins attempted to kill the most visible Franco-Algerian politician, Jacques Soustelle, whom de Gaulle had just named as his minister of information.[98] The FLN carried out its first successful assassination of the new campaign in September 1958 when a member of a 'shock group' shot and killed sous-brigadier Armand Soudon as he was walking to his car in Lyons.[99]

While Algeria remained the bloody focus of assassination for France, assassination panic manifested itself in a very unexpected place for the

British. At the end of 1958, a defeated EOKA declared an end to their armed struggle, thus lifting the threat of assassination from imperial Britons.[100] Three years previously, Sir Robert Armitage had been removed as governor of Cyprus because he had been ineffective in opposing EOKA. He had been sent instead to govern the 'safe' small African colony of Nyasaland. Exactly a month after EOKA gave up on assassination, Nyasaland Special Branch discovered that Nyasaland nationalists were much more dangerous than had been thought. They had conceived a 'murder plot' to assassinate the governor, senior British officials and 'Quislings'. 'Naturally, a great number of people were sceptical that such a plot was planned,' Armitage subsequently conceded.[101] 'The Murder Plot', the Colonial Secretary in London, Alan Lennox-Boyd, remarked, could easily be portrayed as a fantasy assassination 'invented in order to provide the white community . . . with an excuse to take repressive action against black people.'[102]

Armitage declared a state of emergency in Nyasaland in March 1959, turning security over to the military. As Lennox-Boyd had feared, the subsequent report into the state of emergency published in July 1959 accused Britain of using a made-up assassination plot as the excuse to create a 'police state' in Nyasaland. The Devlin Commission concluded that 'by contrast with the sparseness of the positive evidence in favour of the plot, there is a vast quantity of negative evidence. . . . No attempt at assassination was ever made . . . no European was ever killed.' Devlin essentially dismissed any possibility that the plot was real on the grounds that the Nyasaland African Congress leaders were 'intelligent men who must have known that they could not succeed in taking over the government of the country by assassinating the Governor and his Council'. Devlin went on to say that, although he had no evidence to support the assertion, he believed that the putative assassination 'may have affected the attitude of mind of the policy-makers towards the members of the organisation which they were suppressing and it may have affected too the attitude of those who had to execute the operations . . . [and] might explain any unnecessary degree of violence [in carrying out arrests] that was used after 3rd March'.[103]

Devlin's 'Jesuitical' reasoning provoked anger among those accused, not least Armitage. He accused Devlin of trying to discredit the assassination plot in an attempt to downplay the other modes of violence that Congress employed. 'What was important from my point of view,' ran Armitage's version, 'was not whether there was talk of killing Europeans or talk of cold-blooded, or for that matter hot-blooded, assassination or massacre, but whether there was a real threat to the lives of Europeans and Africans as a result of the adoption by Congress of a policy of violence.' Armitage's response was as rhetorical, and lacking in evidence, as Devlin's report.[104] Armitage's defence was hobbled because ministers would not let him use the – ambiguous – intelligence reports that had made him fear imminent assassination.[105]

Although the mechanics of the assassination threats they faced were quite different, it is notable that the leaders of the governments in London and Paris reached the conclusion that enough was enough at almost the same moment. Although he shared the thought with few, least of all the electorate, Harold Macmillan led the Conservative Party to a convincing victory in the October 1959 general election with the firm intention of abandoning British colonies, keeping only useful bases. Of course, this nice distinction did not make much difference to the determined assassin. Britain would face one last late imperial assassination campaign, a 'very skilful operation of the Egyptian Intelligence Service', in Aden, where it planned to decolonise but retain a base.[106]

In September 1959, without spelling out the full implications of how he planned to abandon the Algerian war, President de Gaulle declared that the Muslim population of Algeria had the right to choose independence from France. As de Gaulle said at the time, it would be much more difficult for him to walk away from his empire than it was for Macmillan to walk away from his. He attributed this to the 'not very bright' French emotionalism about empire in contrast to the cold blood of the English.[107] Unlike Macmillan, de Gaulle was consciously putting himself at risk of assassination. Macmillan was able to tour Africa at very little personal risk – while famously declaring that the days of the white man were done: when de Gaulle went to Algeria also in 1960 many thought him reckless given the genuine plans to kill him by groups of settlers in cahoots with soldiers of the French army.[108]

The fact that one part of de Gaulle's state wanted to kill the president did not mean that he ceased using other – and very closely related –

parts of the same state to carry out assassinations. The SDECE co-located their Service Action assassins with the Force de Police Auxiliaire, made up of pro-French Algerians at Fort de Noisy in south-west Paris. They were joined by the Front algérién d'action démocratique (FAAD), an SDECE false-flag organisation meant to replace the Algerian nationalist rivals whom the FLN had assassinated. Overseeing the complex was Jacques Foccart, representing de Gaulle and his prime minister, Michel Debré. The three organisations shared intelligence and tactics, probably assassinating well over one hundred targets during 1960.[109]

The next year, the assassinations expanded as the Paris police, under its head, Maurice Papon, who had previously been dismissed from Morocco in 1955 for implication in the Lemaigre-Dubreuil assassination, killed suspects. Papon was particularly exercised by the assassination of brigadier Pierre Grandjouan by the FLN in September 1961. It became almost impossible to keep the murders secret because bodies were regularly pulled from the Seine by the river authority.

At the same time, deserters from the French army began organising what would become the OAS, the 'secret army' that would oppose and kill representatives of de Gaulle's 'false state'. From its inception, the OAS had a formal death squad organisation, the Bureau d'Action Opérationnelle (BAO). The BAO used many of the same rituals as the FLN, issuing formal *bulletins de renseignements* – death warrants – to add a sheen of officialdom to their killings.[110] The official assassination complex at Fort de Noisy exchanged information with the unofficial BAO.

Just as the FLN targeted police officers, so too did the OAS, given that police intelligence officers were a danger to both. In May 1961, it killed two senior policemen in Algiers, commissaire Roger Gavoury and inspector René Joubart. Two linked assassination squads stabbed Gavoury to death in his apartment in Algiers and used a sub-machine gun to kill Joubart as he celebrated his planned return to France. In September 1961, the minister of the armed forces complained to de Gaulle and Debré that parts of the French state demanded much of other parts by their 'collusion with assassins'.[111] In May 1962, one of Debré's advisers formally wrote that complicity in assassination amounted to the abrogation of the state's claim to monopolise *legitimate* violence. A state that took the route of secret assassination risked becoming a failed state. Of course, neither de Gaulle nor Debré needed any of this spelt out to them by their underlings since they were the font of the complicity.[112] In March 1962, a final reckoning-up of assassination in Algeria concluded that in 1957 France had been faced by a serious assassination threat from the FLN but there was hope. In 1962, FLN assassination was over 200 per cent worse and it was being matched, killing for killing, by the OAS. The French government had allowed a fivefold increase in assassination and extinguished hope.[113]

Once de Gaulle and Debré had achieved their broader goal – a negotiated settlement with the FLN for an independent Algeria – in May 1962, they turned off the anti-Algerian repressive state. Instead, they turned its force on the OAS and its collaborators.[114] It executed Roger Gavoury's assassins in June 1962 and the head of the BAO in October 1962.[115] The culmination, but also the finale, of the assassination threat was the OAS's ambush of de Gaulle's Citroën DS20 as it drove through the Parisian suburb of Petit-Clamart in August 1962. The assassins used a full-bore military machine gun mounted in the back of a van as their murder weapon. The assassins hit the car multiple times, but no-one was hurt except a passer-by. De Gaulle's driver sped away and there was no back-up ambush. Notably, de Gaulle had no protection: he was with his wife and son in the car. CIA observers noted that, whatever the risks to de Gaulle, there was little hope for the OAS now their sanctuary in Algeria was no more.[116] The leader of the assassination squad was, indeed, caught in metropolitan France with relative ease. His execution in March 1963 was the last of the Algerian assassination campaign.[117]

It says something for the skilful obfuscations of the French state over assassination that, outside France, it did not even generate the most notorious assassination conspiracies of the early 1960s. That distinction went to the Belgians, who took the decision to abandon colonial rule at the same time as the British and the French. The Belgians formally granted independence to the Congo in June 1960. They left behind a network of security officials in the hope that they would be able to bind Congo, with its enormous mineral resources, economically to the mother country. They also left behind a group of intensely ambitious Congolese politicians vying to be the man sitting atop the money pile.

These men habitually befriended and betrayed one another and had no compunction about contemplating murder. The most notable of them were Joseph Kasa-Vubu, who became Congo's first president, Moishe Tshombe, who was willing to lead Congo's mineral-rich southern province of Katanga into secession if he could not be national leader, Joseph-Désiré Mobutu, whom the CIA pegged as their most desirable leader, and Patrice Lumumba, by far the most popular and charismatic of the quartet, and Congo's first prime minister. It was Lumumba's popularity that led the other three to turn on him first.[118]

Kasa-Vubu and Mobutu first combined to arrest Lumumba. Not trusting their own troops, they sent him to Tshombe in Katanga. Tshombe saw Lumumba in person, taunted him with his impending death and then instructed his trusted Belgian police officers to take him, and his two followers, Maurice Mpolo and Joseph Okito, to a remote place and kill them. Tshombe watched the execution take place. There were various attempts to hide the bodies until the Belgian officers finally dissolved them in acid. However, the killing was public knowledge by the next morning. A UN investigation discovered what had happened with tolerable accuracy.[119]

In the face of international scepticism, the government of Katanga claimed that the three men had escaped and had been killed by random men in the bush. 'I am going to speak frankly and bluntly, as I always do,' Godefroid Munongo, Tshombe's deputy, announced as he delivered a pack of lies. 'We shall be accused of murdering them. My reply is: prove it.' That was the rub, since the definitive evidence in the case did not become available in Belgium until the twenty-first century.[120]

Katanga's reputation as a dangerous place for politicians was further boosted when the UN Secretary-General Dag Hammarskjöld died in an aeroplane crash on his way to meet Tshombe. There were immediate suspicions that he had been assassinated by the Katanganese, their allies in the government of the British Central Africa Federation, or indeed the British themselves. Unlike in the case of Tshombe, however, a UN investigation found no convincing evidence of murder and merely left assassination as a possibility. The Lumumba assassination was a near certainty, the Hammarskjöld assassination a mere rumour.[121]

There was a strong element of performativeness that swirled round these deaths. A group of American leftists, including the young Black writer Maya Angelou, had interrupted a sitting of the UN Security Council in New York discussing Lumumba's death to denounce the west as 'Assassins!' and to chant, 'Get Hammarskjöld!'[122] No-one much, with the possible exception of St Antony's College, Oxford – of which the organiser of the assassination was an honorary fellow – seemed to care when the prime minister of Belgium's other Central African territory, Prince Rwagasore of Burundi, also a 'tinder box', was assassinated in October 1961.[123]

Given the sordid reality of assassination at the end of empire, it is hardly surprising that it left a legacy of cynicism. The western powers were certain that politicians in recently independent nations would try to assassinate each other. They no longer cared much if they did. Despite a few flurries of concern, newly independent countries did not often threaten western leaders.[124] Equally, politicians in new nations were bound to accuse western intelligence services of being behind assassinations.[125]

A great deal of both cynicism and the peddling of false accusation in the early 1960s clustered around the Ghanaian leader Kwame Nkrumah. The western interest in Ghana as a 'model' for Africa was disproportionately high.[126] Nkrumah, haunted by a belief that his enemies were out to get him, was in many ways the most notable inheritor of the Nyasaland assassination panic of 1959.[127] In August 1961, his opponents struck. He had just got out of his car in Kulungugu near the intersection of the borders of Ghana, Togoland and Upper Volta when an assassin threw a British No. 36 grenade at him.[128] He survived because his ADC deliberately shielded the president and took the brunt of the blast. Four other people were killed and seventy-seven wounded. Nkrumah was hit by shrapnel in the back. 'Nkrumah,' American diplomats reported, 'remained transfixed, shaking, whining "they want to kill me, they want to kill me".' Nkrumah was badly affected by the assassination attempt. He became 'even more suspicious of those around him' and refused to meet even his own supporters as he bunkered down in the presidential palace.[129]

The problem for investigators was that there were so many people who wanted to kill Nkrumah. The most likely candidates were his own ministers, Ghanaian refugees in Togoland, or local politicians in eastern

Ghana.[130] The actual investigation, with a great deal of technical assistance from Britain, led to a non-commissioned officer in the Ghanaian army. However, the NCO jumped, or was thrown, out of a high window during police investigation, closing down serious inquiry.[131] Having toyed with blaming the British, Nkrumah plumped for his own ministers as the culprits, imprisoning several and declaring a state of emergency.[132] The arrests neither lessened Nkrumah's fear nor the hatred felt for him by his Ghanaian enemies. He was attacked again in January 1964.[133]

Elsewhere, assassination remained a feature of politics whatever the western powers did, or did not do. Assassination was a weapon in the internal power struggles of the FLN rulers of Algeria. The FLN assassinated its defalcating former treasurer, Mohammed Khider, one of the 'historic nine' leaders of the independence struggle, in Madrid in January 1967. The assassin shot Khider five times with a pistol.[134] In 1968, an Algerian army officer who had been involved in Khider's death, and who had previously acted as the regime's strongarm man, attempted to assassinate Houari Boumedienne, Algeria's second president, the FLN leader on whose behalf he had previously acted. The assassins, dressed in the uniforms of the presidential guard, machine-gunned Boumedienne's car as it left the Palais du Gouvernement in Algiers, killing one of his bodyguards but only wounding the president. The assassins were captured and tortured, leading to a clear account of the attempt.[135] 'I fear,' the British Foreign Office official charged with monitoring Algeria briefed the prime minister, 'that the country may have taken a long step towards becoming the police state which its critics declare it already to be. Algeria is ruled by a small group of frightened men, isolated from their people.'[136]

Assassination remained central to post-independence Cypriot politics: Archbishop Makarios was the president, former assassins were his ministers.[137] Somewhere to be found near the heart of most assassination conspiracies in Cyprus was Polycarpos Georghadjis, once the EOKA intelligence chief who had directed the assassination of Special Branch officers. By the late 1960s, he was Cyprus's defence and interior minister. Georghadjis resigned after the Greek government found evidence that he had been instrumental in organising an assassination attempt on the head of its military junta, Colonel Papadopoulos. The assassins planted explosives in a drain under the road down which Papadopoulos was to drive.[138] Greek intelligence told the head of SIS station in Athens that Georghadjis, whom they had supported to the hilt in his assassination of Britons, scared them because he seemed to have a 'natural liking for killing'.[139] In the end, Georghadjis turned against Makarios too. In March 1970, assassins attempted to shoot down Makarios's helicopter as it was taking off. A week later, Georghadjis was found dead in his car. He had been shot.[140] With Georghadjis dealt with, the Cypriot government gave the captured assassins, some of whom were police officers, a 'very fair' trial and remarkably light sentences.[141]

The messy transition from the colonial assassination complex to a new era was best exemplified by what might be described as Britain's last imperial assassination.[142] The assassination of Sir Richard Sharples, the Governor of Bermuda, in March 1973 was on one level treated as a post-imperial tragicomedy. Sir Richard and his ADC were shot and killed in the grounds of Government House as they took a stroll after dinner. The assassins also killed Sir Richard's dog. The murders seemed very professional since the assassins only expended three shots to murder their three victims. Sharples's ADC had a holstered revolver but died without even touching the flap. The main topic of conversation in the press was that Sharples had taken the same walk accompanied by the Prince of Wales only a fortnight previously, and that Princess Margaret was due to visit soon.[143]

Bermuda was seen as little more than a sinecure. Sir Richard had been a Tory politician of minor note. His murder was, however, the second high-profile assassination in Bermuda within months, the Commissioner of Police, George Duckett, having been murdered in September 1972. Although Duckett's assassination had been carefully planned and carried out, until Sharples's death the British government had preferred to believe that it had something to do with his 'volatile' personal life.[144] Despite the previous assassination, British officials described Sharples's murder as an 'isolated incident': Sharples's successor stuck to the line that it had no political implications.[145] Indeed, he continued to suppress speculation that the assassination was a political crime, even as detectives sent from London were themselves being threatened with assassination if they proceeded any further with their investigation.[146]

In fact, the investigators rapidly identified fifteen individuals as being part of both assassination conspiracies.[147] Intelligence sources traced close links between a Black power movement, the 'Black Berets', and the Bermudian political opposition parties.[148] When the detectives did conclusively identify the assassins, demonstrating that they were part of a politico-narcocrime conspiracy to dominate the island, the British response resembled earlier colonial encounters with assassins. The Bermudian authorities had run the Sharples case in parallel with the investigation of two purely criminal murders the assassins had later committed. Although parliament had effectively abolished the death penalty in the UK in 1965, the assassins were executed in 1977. Formally, they were punished for the murders rather than the assassinations, although everyone recognised this was little more than a convenience. The executions were the last carried out in British-controlled territory.[149]

8

DANGEROUS IN CONCEPTION AND EXECUTION
The US Experiment with Assassination, 1952–1976

In 1967, the CIA admitted to themselves that they had an assassination problem. Down in New Orleans a rogue, but publicity-savvy, district attorney was claiming that the CIA was implicated in the assassination of John F. Kennedy.[1] The mafioso whom the Agency had once hired to assassinate Fidel Castro of Cuba was fighting deportation.[2] America's leading syndicated newspaper columnist was publishing stories about those CIA attempts to assassinate Fidel Castro. His stories were so on the mark that the Director of Central Intelligence, Richard Helms, believed that the former head of the CIA's assassination bureau was leaking to the press.[3]

The problem, in the view of the CIA's leaders, was not that the Agency carried out assassinations. In 1967, the CIA was just as committed to assassination as it had been in earlier years. The problem was not even that so many people knew about the CIA's assassination programmes. They included current and former CIA officers, other current and former officials of the US government, CIA contractors, émigré groups with whom the CIA had worked, private investigators, gangsters and journalists. The real problem was that, for anyone not schooled in OSS/CIA verbiage, once one started writing down what had been done in clear English, it read as very, very ugly. Also, it read as very, very stupid. For it was clear that no-one had given much intelligent thought to assassination.

DANGEROUS IN CONCEPTION AND EXECUTION

Something that struck and bothered the 1967 investigators was the 'frequent resort to synecdoche' by CIA officers. The unwillingness to disentangle the specificities of assassination from other parts of an operation left everything based on a loose series of unchallenged assumptions: circumlocuted or unspoken. CIA's newly appointed head of 'Executive Action Capability' had remarked in January 1961, the month before he started his job, that assassination was the 'last resort beyond the last resort and a confession of weakness'.[4] The Deputy Director of Central Intelligence observed around the same time that 'action of this kind is uncertain of results and highly dangerous in conception and execution'.[5] In their 1967 post-mortem, the CIA officers stressed again and again that the 'elimination of the dominant figure in a government . . . will not necessarily cause the downfall of the government'. Assassinations were likely to get out of control and end up with results that were directly contrary to the interests the US had been pursuing by suborning murder.[6]

In 1967, the CIA were relatively confident that they could ride out any wave of criticism that came their way. However, their hopes were undone by the intensity of interest in murders for which they had no responsibility. In most meaningful senses of the word, the murders of President John F. Kennedy, the civil rights campaigner Martin Luther King and the presidential candidate Bobby Kennedy were not assassinations. The murders were carried out by emotionally unbalanced – although not legally insane – individuals, not self-evidently in the service of a political cause. However, the US state's regular attempts to define assassination conspiracies out of existence proved to be spectacular failures. In 1978, the House Select Committee on Assassinations (HSCA) found that the murders of JFK and MLK were both assassination conspiracies.[7]

Even laying aside the wilder conspiracy theories that stuck to assassination like flies to dung, the CIA, in its own attempted defence, succeeded in defining the parameters of debate about overseas murders in some odd ways. The post-1967 CIA line on assassination, endlessly iterated in various combinations, comprised four main contentions. First, yes, the CIA planned and prepared for assassinations. Such assassinations almost always involved an attempt to corral an indigenous or émigré group to carry out the assassination on the CIA's behalf. Second, however, very few, if any, assassinations took place. The chosen instruments of assassination were usually incompetent. The only operations they seemed capable of carrying out were botched kidnappings which led to the death of the target. Oddly, these groups never used the weapons which the CIA had supplied. Other, more competent groups often succeeded in assassinating the target. The CIA had no or minimal contact with such competent assassins. Third, one should not focus too much on the CIA. Other agencies, especially the Department of Defense and the White House staff, were just as keen on assassination. It warped the picture to constantly harp on about the CIA. Fourth, the CIA was ordered to carry out assassinations by superior authorities, specifically by direct presidential order. Sometimes, these orders were off the record and not fed through the covert operations machinery. If one wished to understand assassination, the most important factor was the conspiratorial personalities of Presidents Kennedy, Johnson and Nixon.[8]

All in all, the CIA succeeded in painting a very unflattering picture of itself in attempting to get off the assassination hook. Of the four directors of Central Intelligence who came over to CIA from the wartime OSS – Allen Dulles, Richard Helms, William Colby and Bill Casey – three – Dulles, Helms and Colby – were effectively dismissed. In two of those cases – Helms and Colby – assassination played a material role in destroying their careers and muddying their reputations. No-one could trust a word they said after so many lies had been told.[9]

However, despite the headline role taken by former OSS Europe, which had formalised assassination as a legitimate aspect of special operations, investigators kept circling back to the fact that the US was still part of its long-established Latin American assassination complex. In 1947, the CIA had inherited the clandestine intelligence service of its predecessor, the CIG. The service had itself been a merger of the remnants of the old OSS with the SIS, the FBI's overseas intelligence service that had operated solely in Latin America. The first Congressional investigation into the CIA and assassination focused on Latin America.

DANGEROUS IN CONCEPTION AND EXECUTION

Initially, assassination in post-war Latin America had little to do with the CIA. The assassination of the chief of Guatemala's armed forces – strong man and probable next President, Francisco Arana – in July 1949 resulted from a falling-out among the putschists who had seized power in 1944. The people behind the assassination were the President of Guatemala, Juan Arévalo, and its leading left-wing politician, and soon-to-be president, Jacobo Árbenz. An assassination squad, led by Guatemala's deputy police chief, intercepted Arana's car: both Arana and the police chief were killed in the subsequent gun battle.[10]

Nevertheless, the Arana assassination did have consequences for the CIA. The CIA's first, subsequently notorious, formal assassination training manual was created as part of a project to overthrow Árbenz's government. The manual was an odd and revealing document. It was written around the premise that a CIA officer would be leading or stirring up a resistance movement. However, the only example of a resistance movement attempting to assassinate a political leader examined in any detail was the German resistance's failed attack on Hitler in July 1944. There was no mention of any of the resistance movements that the OSS had genuinely supported, even though both Frank Wisner, the head of covert operations, and Dick Helms, the leading figure in clandestine intelligence, had spent the war specifically working with such resistance movements.

The author of the assassination handbook claimed to have made an historical study of assassination to build his appreciation. The modern assassinations, and attempted assassinations, he cited were a heterogeneous group: Franz Ferdinand, Rasputin, Mussolini, Madero, Roosevelt, Kirov, King Alexander of Yugoslavia, Huey Long, Trotsky, Heydrich, Hitler, Aung San, King Abdullah of Jordan, Ali Razmara of Iran and President Truman. The oddity in the modern list was 'Benes'. President Beneš of Czechoslovakia had died of natural causes, albeit a broken man. Presumably, the author was thinking of Jan Masaryk, the Czech foreign minister, defenestrated during a Communist coup in February 1948. Certainly, the document was obsessed with the mechanics of defenestration. After several calculations, the handbook advised that the 'most efficient' means of killing a target was to drop them from at least 75 feet 'onto a hard surface'. Classifying all suspicious falls as potential assassinations proved to be one of the rocket fuels of post-Second World War assassination conspiracy. In truth, a decent thriller writer could have done better than the CIA's technical expert. Indeed, thriller writers did do better.

Upon this rather shaky historical base, the document built an analytical typology of assassination. The typology worked along two axes: security and publicity. Along the security axis, assassinations were to be classified as 'simple' (the victim was unaware of the threat and unguarded), 'chase' (the victim was aware of the threat but unguarded), 'guarded' (victim was both aware and guarded) and 'lost' (a suicide mission for the assassin, but not for his handler). The publicity axis ran: 'secret' (the assassination was staged as an accident or a natural death), 'safe' (the assassin could be reliably exfiltrated), 'open' (the concealment of the assassination was immaterial) and 'terroristic' (the assassination required publicity to achieve its goal). There is no evidence that the CIA ever adopted these terms: it might have helped their contemplation of assassinations if they had. As it was, the preference remained for leaving most things unsaid, and therefore unanalysed.

The handbook did address the issue of not saying. It assumed that assassination would 'never be ordered or authorized by any US Headquarters, although the latter may in rare instances agree to its execution by members of an associated foreign service. This reticence is partly due to the necessity for committing communications to paper. No assassination instructions should ever be written or recorded.' Consequently, 'the decision to employ this technique must nearly always be reached in the field'. The CIA may have wished this was the case: in reality, it combined inarticulacy with regular fretting, and thus recording.

Assuming the decision to order an assassination would rest with a case officer in the field, the handbook had some thoughts on the psychology of assassination. Murder was in no way morally justifiable. On the other hand, 'killing a political leader whose burgeoning career is a clear and present danger to the cause of freedom may be held necessary'. As a result, 'assassination can seldom be employed with a clear conscience'. The handbook concluded piously that 'persons who are morally squeamish should not attempt' assassination.

DANGEROUS IN CONCEPTION AND EXECUTION

It was clear that the author was less interested in moral philosophy than in hardware and technique. He was notably hostile to the use of pistols in assassination, despite the fact that 'many well-known assassinations have been carried out with pistols'. His objection was that 'the assassin usually has insufficient technical knowledge of the limitations of weapons, and expects more range, accuracy and killing [power] than can be provided with reliability'. As a result, pistol attacks 'fail as often as they succeed'. On the other hand, he was very enthusiastic about the use of hunting rifles: 'public figures or guarded officials may be killed with great reliability and some safety if a firing point can be established prior to an official occasion,' the handbook claimed. It warned against the use of military firearms for the task: standard ammunition did not expand in the body but 'altering military ammunition to expand courts unreliability'. There were two problems with this analysis. It was almost unsupported by the historical case studies cited. The use of the rifle as an effective assassination weapon was vanishingly rare. However, second – assassination by long-range rifle was about to come into vogue. Both John F. Kennedy and Martin Luther King were assassinated by rifles fired from ambush; the CIA's most credible plot to assassinate Fidel Castro also involved the use of a rifle. No-one seemed to pay much attention to the author's overpenetration worry. JFK's killer, Lee Harvey Oswald, used a military surplus rifle; Fidel Castro's would-be assassin, Rolando Cubela, was supplied with a modern military rifle by the CIA. Only James Earl Ray, the killer of Martin Luther King, used a hunting rifle.[11]

None of this should detract from the seriousness of the CIA mission in Guatemala – for which the handbook was written – in its intent to kill people.[12] In February 1952, it drew up a 'death list' of over fifty Guatemalan individuals to be subject to 'executive action'. In February 1954, the CIA sent in '2 assassination specialists' to fine-tune the training of General Carlos Castillo's 'K team'.[13]

The next month, the CIA wondered if the best way forward was to bring in some '*pistoleros*' from the Dominican Republic to assassinate Árbenz's leadership cadre. By this time tempers were beginning to fray, both within the CIA team and between the CIA and the State Department. Everybody agreed 'elimination was part of the plan and could be done' but some officers doubted that bringing in Dominican mercenaries would be of much assistance. Their main problem was that Castillo's 'army resistance movement' was, in their view, useless.[14]

The CIA country team even wondered if they might stage a 'false flag' assassination in Honduras. They would plant a bomb under the car of President Juan Gálvez (allowing him to get out before setting it off) and hand the assassin over to the Honduran police with his pockets stuffed with documents showing that he had been sent by Árbenz with the aid of Soviet intelligence. This was supposed to provoke retaliation and force Castillo to finally launch his coup.[15] They need not have worried. The army did overthrow Árbenz in July 1954. He was not assassinated.[16]

The CIA's one-time potential partner in the Árbenz assassination – the man with the *pistoleros*, President Rafael Trujillo of the Dominican Republic – was, however, assassinated. In April 1960, the US ambassador in the Dominican Republic requested that the CIA should overthrow Trujillo. He was under no illusion that their putative Dominicano collaborators would insist on Trujillo's assassination. William Pawley, the leading American oilman in the Dominican Republic, openly said that Trujillo should be assassinated. In this case, the oilman was not a random blowhard.[17] In 1954, Pawley had sat on President Eisenhower's investigation panel into the covert operations of the CIA. After closely examining the Guatemalan operation, the panel had concluded that it was a model for the future: one of the key roles of the CIA should be to provide the USA with 'an aggressive paramilitary organisation more effective, more unique and, if necessary, more ruthless than that employed by the enemy.'[18] Pawley had remained covertly enmeshed with CIA ever since.[19]

The State Department endorsed assassination over a full revolt in June 1960. They wanted the USA 'to provide a small number of sniper rifles or other devices for the removal of the key Trujillo people from the scene . . . [but not] to send arms, equipment, or paramilitary experts to assist the underground to accomplish a revolt'.[20] As Henry Dearborn, the acting head of mission, reiterated to State in March 1961, 'political assassination is ugly and repulsive but everything must be judged in its own context'.[21] The operation was signed off in CIA by Dick Helms as acting head of the clandestine and covert service.

The plan hit some headwinds. After much discussion, the CIA head of station reported that the Dominicano resistance plan to assassinate

DANGEROUS IN CONCEPTION AND EXECUTION

Trujillo was 'fatal[ly] childish'. They wanted to intercept his entourage and kill him with small arms and grenades. 'That type [of] attack [is] precisely what bodyguards appear best qualified [to] cope with,' the head of station opined. Thus challenged, the CIA's collaborators came back with a demand for more American firepower. They would wait for an opportunity when Trujillo had few bodyguards, slaughter any he did have with automatic weapons, and then finish him off at leisure.[22] The CIA case officer and Washington were both happier with this plan.[23] In the first instance, the station provided the Dominicanos with carbines and ordered some sub-machine guns from CIA store. The State Department, however, baulked at the thought of machine guns committing mass murder. They had been looking forward to the 'clinical' sniper shot of the CIA handbook and fiction.

Despite the CIA's failure to supply fully automatic weapons, in May 1961 the Dominicanos went ahead with the assassination according to the plan that they had discussed with their handlers. Instead of tackling Trujillo's bullet-proof Chrysler with its fleet of accompanying bodyguard cars, they waited until the dictator sloped off to have sex with his mistress. Eight assassins in three cars intercepted Trujillo's unarmoured Chevrolet, in which he was only accompanied by his chauffeur. They killed Trujillo with semi-automatic pistols, revolvers and sawed-off shotguns. This was the standard Latin American assassination toolkit dating back to the 1930s. Some of the assassins were carrying the CIA-supplied semi-automatic carbines, in case more firepower was needed: it was not. Based on that technicality, the CIA claimed that it had not been involved with the assassination of Rafael Trujillo. None of its weapons had fired the fatal shot. Unfortunately, the man who had picked up the carbines from his CIA handlers and handed them over to the assassination squad claimed at trial that one of the weapons had been used to kill Trujillo.[24] Things went badly for the assassins in a much less technical fashion. Trujillo's brother, Héctor, and the head of his military intelligence service, 'one of the most ruthless of the Trujillo hatchetmen', killed their leader. All opposition collapsed under the Trujillianos' ruthless counter-offensive.[25] The State Department ordered its diplomats to weed its documents to show that it had always been resolutely opposed to assassination.[26] The CIA rapidly evacuated its head of station and the assassination case officer from Colombia lest they in turn became the targets for assassination.[27]

It is worth tracing the Trujillo case, and the CIA's subsequent attempt to justify itself under the Johnson administration, because Trujillo was actually assassinated, the request for the assassination had come from the diplomatic side of the Eisenhower administration, the US was intimately involved with planning the assassination, and the CIA provided weapons to ensure that the attempt had the best chance of success. All of this was very clearly documented internally. The *New Republic* accurately reported on the CIA's role, including that of armourer, in April 1963. It is thus possible to trace the four classic elements of assassination – procurer, assassins, tools and the cover-up – with some certainty.

The assassination attempts that followed Trujillo's death were arguably more consequential and stirred much greater public interest; however, they were either unsuccessful or, arguably, murders wrongly pulled into the assassination phenomenon. However, it would be wrong to think that the Trujillo plot was unusual or compartmented. It was intertwined with other assassination attempts, most notably those aimed against Fidel Castro and his associates. It was also the precursor of an effort to put assassination on a much more general footing within the Agency. Notably, both developments were top-down.

The moving force behind both the attempts on Castro and the formalisation of the assassination organisation in CIA was Richard Bissell, the Deputy Director of Plans, a deliberately bland title for the head of the clandestine and covert service. Bissell was not an old OSS sweat. He had joined the CIA in 1954, was regarded as one of the most brilliant officers anywhere in US government and was close to the Kennedy circle.[28] One of Bissell's first acts when Kennedy became president was to create a command staff for 'Executive Action Capability'.[29] He appointed William Harvey to run the assassination effort. Harvey's office was subsequently known as Task Force W and then the Special Affairs Staff.[30] At first blush, the appointment of the CIA's best-known bugging specialist as its head of assassination seemed a leap, but Bissell had his reasons: Harvey's former outfit – Division D – was responsible for many of the CIA's black-bag tasks such as high-risk breaking and entering. Harvey had a lot of useful contacts and was a 'very venturesome officer'. Harvey's office covered the world, but it was born out of the Latin American assassination complex.[31]

It was no secret that the US government wished that Fidel Castro would die, and his Cuban revolution would consume itself. It was equally no secret that many Cubans wanted Castro dead. In July 1960, the Castro regime announced that it had unearthed a plot within the Cuban army to assassinate Castro.[32] The first serious discussion of the US taking a hand in the assassination of Castro occurred in August 1960. The question was posed by the State Department as to 'whether any real planning has been done for taking direct positive action against Fidel, Raul [Castro, Fidel's brother] and Che Guevara'. It thought that 'without these three the Cuban Government would be leaderless and probably brainless'. The best solution was to kill all three men at the same time or in quick succession. This démarche came six weeks after the State Department had asked for the assassination of Trujillo: there was a pattern of thought and conduct.[33]

The CIA's admission that it did not have the ability to kill the leaders of the Cuban revolution with any certainty was what prompted Bissell to formalise an assassination office six months later. However, the CIA was on the case even before the creation of Harvey's outfit. Bissell's extemporaneous attempt to solve the problem had been to ask the head of the Office of Security, Sheffield Edwards, who had the requisite contacts, to approach the Mafia and request that they assassinate Castro.

For reasons that should have been obvious at the time, this subsequently became the most infamous CIA assassination plot, the father of so many conspiracy theories. Edwards recruited Robert Maheu, private investigator for the reclusive mogul Howard Hughes, to set things up. Maheu often did such tasks for the CIA.[34] And the Mafia were not the only candidates as assassins. In early August 1960, a Cuban exile sponsored by the CIA had landed in Cuba. He got out in November 1960, claiming that he 'had made some progress' on the 'assassination of prominent Cuban Communist members in the Castro entourage'.[35] His debriefers in the Western Hemisphere Division of the CIA's clandestine service drew up a 'must go' list of Cuban leaders: it comprised eleven individuals plus their wives.[36]

The plotting was not particularly subtle. The CIA and their collaborators were watched with interest by the large Cuban intelligence and security apparatus, of which Raúl Castro was in overall charge. They were also monitored by the Castros' friends, the intelligence agencies of the Soviet Union.[37] In July 1961, the Cubans and the Soviets had a detailed discussion on the matter. They concluded, with some accuracy, that 'the internal and external counterrevolution essentially have no other way out left, and they are hanging on to the idea of assassination as the only and last means to smother the Cuban revolution'. This didn't seem to the Cubans and Soviets a particularly convincing way of going about things, but one could never be too careful. Fidel Castro stressed that 'he personally' and the other Cuban revolutionary leaders attached 'importance to their security protection'. However, Castro also made clear his preference that 'acts of terrorism might first of all be turned against their organisers'. The Cubans would tighten their security, but they really preferred to kill their enemies.[38] As the Americans could see and hear from their own sources, this was no empty threat.[39]

The Soviet intelligence records and the US intelligence on Cuban operations make a nonsense of any contention that Castro could not possibly have known that the US government in general, and the CIA in particular, were targeting him for assassination.[40] The *New Republic*'s April 1963 article about Trujillo specifically linked his death with CIA-sponsored assassination plots against Castro.[41] In August 1963, the *Chicago Sun-Times* published the story that the CIA was collaborating with the Mafia to kill Castro.[42] A month previously, the Mafia had supplied a Cuban counter-revolutionary group in the US with one hundred silenced Beretta 7.65 mm pistols with which to assassinate Cuban officials.[43]

On Allen Dulles's last day in office, the CIA concluded that Castro's 'loss now, by assassination or by natural causes, would have an unsettling effect, but would almost certainly not prove fatal to the regime'.[44] That warning did not make the American government any less keen on assassinating him. In some ways it merely enflamed their desire to do so. Robert Kennedy personally approved the revivification of the plan to have the Mafia assassinate Castro.[45] However, following the Bay of Pigs – the failed Cuban exile attempt to invade Cuba in April 1961 – the

Kennedys, their confidence in the CIA dented, preferred a 'whole of government' effort. When administration leaders met to launch that effort in August 1962, it was Robert McNamara, the Secretary of Defense, who tabled the motion for the 'liquidation' of Castro. The overall responsibility for the project – codename Mongoose – was placed in the hands of the Deputy Assistant Secretary of Defense for Special Operations, Brigadier Edward Lansdale. Lansdale submitted a plan of operations three days after the decision meeting.[46] The CIA were predictably sniffy about his military approach. Lansdale had written explicitly that the 'elimination of leaders' by the US would be a major part of the effort to overthrow the Cuban revolution. Harvey struck the phrase out of the document, denouncing the 'inadmissibility and stupidity of putting this type of comment in writing'.[47] Nevertheless, Dulles's successor as DCI, John McCone, told all relevant stations in April 1963 to do everything possible to bring down the Cuban regime. There things rested at the time of John F. Kennedy's murder.[48]

Although the origins of US assassination were to be found in the combination of the resistance operations of the OSS with American assassination culture, the Kennedy murder very clearly demonstrated that it was now the Soviet Union that dominated assassination calculation. As William Harvey explained, 'assassination is obviously a two-pronged subject, ours and theirs. We spent countless hours over the years trying to determine the parameters of how far the Soviet service was willing to go. This [was] partly a question of assessment, this was partly a question, to put it just as bluntly, of self-protection.'[49]

As Harvey observed, Soviet assassination was indeed active in the 1950s. In the 1940s, Soviet 'special tasks'' main role had been consolidating Communist rule in Eastern Europe. It was only in 1951 that it pushed west in earnest. Initially, 'special tasks' seemed particularly noticeable around Italy.[50] The west, however, had its 'first real insight' into the Soviet apparatus in early 1954 when Nikolai Khokhlov, a Soviet assassin in Germany, defected to the Americans. Khokhlov was an operative of the 9th Department of the Second Chief Directorate of the MVD, the then current manifestation of 'special tasks'.[51] He had set out on his mission to assassinate Georgiy Okolovich, the leader of the

Russian émigré organisation NTS, in late 1953. He had an 'assassination squad' that he had recruited, trained and equipped from among German Communists. The United States made much of the defection, organising a press conference in Germany in April 1954, which focused as much on Otdel 9's 'assassination kit', specifically a specialised semi-automatic pistol with integral silencer, as the assassins.[52] In May 1954, Khokhlov was transferred to the US, appearing before Congress, the press and TV. Not everyone was impressed: although British SIS had been in on the defection with the Americans, Churchill forbade them to take any part in the public festivities. Churchill objected to lionising an assassin: he was a 'traitor', not a 'hero'.[53] However, Khokhlov's credibility was buffed by the subsequent defection of a KGB intelligence officer in 1955.[54]

The KGB was established in March 1954. The first clearly established KGB 'special task' was the abduction of another NTS leader in Berlin in April 1954.[55] Khokhlov himself collapsed with suspected thallium poisoning at an NTS event in Frankfurt in 1957, only being saved by 'special treatment' in a US military hospital.[56] Subsequent defectors continued to confirm just how committed the KGB was to assassinating its own 'traitors'.[57]

Khokhlov's intelligence was even more amply confirmed four years later when a KGB assassin, Bogdan Stashinsky, defected *after* he had carried out his killing. The victim was the Ukrainian émigré leader Stepan Bandera. The killing ground was again Germany, this time Munich. Bandera himself was no assassination neophyte: in 1934, he had been sentenced to life imprisonment for an attempt to assassinate the Polish interior minister. He was thus appropriately suspicious of assassins. In October 1959, Bandera's neighbours found him in the hallway of his apartment block clutching at his right armpit where he usually kept his shoulder-holstered pistol. Stashinsky also claimed responsibility for assassinating a previous Ukrainian émigré leader, Lev Rebet, in October 1957. In both cases he had used a 'pistol' that sprayed poison.

The use of poison in the Khokhlov, Rebet and Bandera cases initially succeeded in bamboozling the CIA.[58] In the first instance they rejected Stashinsky and handed him over to the West Germans, who believed him and tried him for murder.[59] By the autumn of 1961, however, the

US intelligence community was firmly – and correctly – convinced that they had witnessed a 'vicious' and sustained Soviet assassination campaign. This reassessment was carried out at exactly the moment that the CIA was rebooting its own post-Bay of Pigs assassination plan for Cuba. The CIA admitted that its intelligence of Soviet assassination was 'fragmentary' but believed that a long-established mechanism for carrying out assassinations had outlived Stalin. The Soviets were clearly innovative when it came to the successful use of poison, rather than the traditional pistol, or kidnapping followed by murder at leisure. Rifles played no role in Soviet assassination tradecraft.[60] It was on this basis that the DCI briefed the president at the end of 1961.[61]

Until November 1963, the tracking of Soviet assassination – and the development of propaganda about its evils – was something of a specialist interest. However, the Soviet assassination beat became of existential importance when the President of the United States, John F. Kennedy, was shot and killed in Dallas. Indeed, defining the Soviet part in the conspiracy was really the only important issue in November 1963. There were many subsequent theories about the murder that came to have a much more pervasive grip on the political and public imagination. However, the possibility that America's main adversary had assassinated its head of government and commander-in-chief made state response a potentially very dangerous business indeed.

The people who were equally aware of the threat were the Soviets themselves. After all, Lee Harvey Oswald, the man who had killed Kennedy, had spent several years living in the Soviet Union, was married to a Russian and was a fanatical Communist. Oswald had also recently spoken to an undercover KGB officer in Mexico City, who was a member of what was now the KGB's 'special tasks' department, the 13th. He had previously met with an officer from the same department who was undercover in the UN Secretariat in New York. The Soviet leadership might have been even more worried if they had known that the CIA was running a very successful operation bugging Soviet diplomatic buildings in Mexico City.[62]

As it was, the Soviet ambassador in the United States, Anatoliy Dobrynin, felt able to report to Moscow on the day of the assassination that 'there is nothing that compromises us'.[63] Khrushchev sent Anastas

Mikoyan, his close ally on the Presidium, to the United States to reassure the Americans that the Soviet Union had had no role whatsoever in Kennedy's death. Interspersed with Kennedy funeral obsequies, Mikoyan met with Llewellyn Thompson, generally acknowledged as the Americans' best interpreter of the Russian mind after his critical role at Kennedy's right hand during the Cuban Missile Crisis. Mikoyan reported that, thankfully, 'the US government does not want to involve us in this matter'. Thompson's main message was that President Johnson would not blame the Soviets, but that the Soviets could end up blaming themselves if they continued a drumbeat of propaganda about a right-wing assassination conspiracy.[64] Both sides agreed to be careful, and the Soviets handed over their official correspondence with Oswald.[65] The Soviets and the Americans continued occasional high-level contact thereafter about avoiding nuclear war triggered by an assassination.[66]

The Johnson administration was willing to believe Soviet reassurances because they could be verified against the Mexico City records. At the end of the 'Kennedy assassination crisis', the CIA signalled its Mexico station that 'your [intelligence and] analyses were major factors in the quick clarification of the case, blanking out the really ominous spectre of foreign backing'.[67]

On the other hand, the Johnson administration was no less keen on assassination than its predecessors. Immediately after he took over from Kennedy, President Johnson asked the DCI 'how we planned to dispose of Castro' and told him to 'evolve more aggressive policies'.[68] Richard Bissell and Bill Harvey had left their posts well before Kennedy was assassinated, but Bissell's successor, Dick Helms, retained Harvey's 'Special Affairs Staff', now under Desmond FitzGerald. The Special Group of the NSC, which oversaw covert operations, reauthorised a campaign against Cuba in February 1964, albeit with the caveat that they had no expectation that such operations would bring down the Communists.[69] The CIA was a little more circumspect than it had been formerly. The plots against Castro continued unabated, however: if anything, those of the Johnson years were more credible than those under Kennedy, inasmuch as they included individuals who were much closer to Castro.[70]

That such plots eventually amounted to little was more to do with Cuban counter-measures than lack of will. Not only was Cuba itself a police state but the Cuban intelligence services repeatedly penetrated Cuban émigré groups in Miami. The assassination plots were regularly betrayed. In December 1963, the CIA recruited the Castro family's former physician. He had lost his position upon the death of Castro mère. At the time of his recruitment by the CIA, the medic informed his handlers that he was already deeply immersed in a plot to assassinate the Castro brothers and Che Guevara.[71] His co-conspirator was a former head of police intelligence under the Batista regime. The CIA supplied the former policeman with pistols and revolvers. Both men were arrested in Cuba in mid-1965 and accused, accurately, of plotting to assassinate Castro. It then became clear that the doctor was a regime collaborator.[72]

The CIA's most promising recruit, however, was Rolando Cubela.[73] Notably, Cubela had a track record as an assassin. In 1956, he had taken part in the assassination of Lt-Col. Antonio Blanco Rico, the chief of Cuban military intelligence.[74] Cubela was not only a genuine revolutionary but had close links to the Castros, being a protégé of Raúl Castro. Raúl had appointed him head of the Cuban student movement, with a brief to take over Havana University, a hotspot of political ferment in Cuba going back to the 1930s. Cubela succeeded, but in doing so he fell out with the Communists, who made much of his being a drunk and a womaniser. He was sacked and his bitterness made him ripe for recruitment, in the spring of 1961.[75] Cubela was keen to kill. However, the CIA did not want him to go off half-cocked, so preferred him as an intelligence source in the near term.[76] Nevertheless, the CIA trained Cubela in France. In November 1963, they equipped him with plastic explosive, hand grenades and pistols. They also gave him a silenced military-grade rifle, optimised for assassination in 1964.[77] Like all the others, however, Cubela was a blown agent. He re-entered Cuba in February 1965 and was almost immediately captured.[78] The regime put him on trial in 1966.[79] In the words of the 1967 internal investigation, 'the AMLASH [Cubela] project was probably as widely known within the Clandestine Service as any other project of a similar nature.'[80]

American attempts to assassinate Fidel Castro petered out largely because they ran out of credible collaborators. The last gasp of the post-war Latin American assassination adventure was taken in Chile in 1970. This was a relatively new theatre, but the attitude and methods were by this stage completely predictable. In 1970, General René Schneider, the head of the Chilean army, declared that he was unwilling to prevent a left-wing government coming to power if they won the upcoming democratic elections. President Nixon and his National Security Advisor, Henry Kissinger, were horrified: they also wanted all the privileges of power that had been granted Eisenhower, Kennedy and Johnson. They told the CIA to stop the rise of the Chilean Left. Reverting to standard operating procedure, the Agency immediately began planning a military coup, known as Track Two. There were treacherous generals in Chile with whom the CIA might collaborate. Those generals saw Schneider as a roadblock to their ambitions. They asked the CIA for the correct equipment to remove him: the CIA station in Santiago obliged. The CIA also despatched two 'deep cover' agents, or 'false flaggers', to assist the Chilean putschists. On 20 October 1970, Santiago station signalled CIA HQ that thanks to the 'vigorous effort' of the 'false flaggers' the coup was on.[81] On 22 October, the traitors used the CIA equipment to assassinate General Schneider. The CIA's excuse that they would have preferred a kidnap to an assassination was acknowledged to be pathetic.[82]

Democrats later took pleasure in watching Nixon, Kissinger and the CIA twist in the wind, something about which all three felt particularly bitter.[83] Democrats tended to swerve away from the fact that the most sustained US experiment with assassination in the twentieth century took place, with Johnson's enthusiastic endorsement, nowhere near Latin America. Although it certainly became a cause célèbre in left-wing circles, the widespread use of assassination in Vietnam was drowned out by the general disaster that was the Vietnam War. The war managed to bring into disrepute all mainstream politicians, the armed forces and the intelligence community. Amid so much killing, it may have seemed that a few more lives, especially of individuals who were never known in the west, were neither here nor there. In that context, the 'it wasn't our fault' line could gain more traction. To personalise assassination, investigators had, as ever, to return to the compelling dramatic irony of the Kennedy presidency. Kennedy had, after all,

DANGEROUS IN CONCEPTION AND EXECUTION

specifically said that his actions in Latin America and Vietnam were intimately connected.[84]

In November 1963, the Vietnamese army assassinated the President of Vietnam, Ngo Dinh Diem, and his brother, Ngo Dinh Nhu, the power behind the throne, as part of a military coup. One of the putschist officers, acting on the orders of the general leading the coup, hustled the brothers into a military vehicle and shot them.[85] The coup leaders killed the two brothers because they wanted their power and wealth. The Americans egged them on to do so because they thought that the men were ineffective at fighting Communists. Despite attempts to cover up the assassination – the first story to emerge was that the devout Catholics had committed suicide in despair at their incipient overthrow – the deaths looked suspicious from the outset.[86]

Subsequently, the responsibility for US involvement in the assassination was laid at the feet of a colourful, but in fact relatively junior, CIA officer, a re-recruit from the old OSS, Lucien Conein. Conein was but one part of a team which included his CIA superiors, the embassy in Saigon, the State Department and the White House. He was not making it up as he went along. This was especially evident given how copybook the American manoeuvres were. The Vietnamese generals first approached the CIA station's liaison officer with the South Vietnamese army in August 1963 to tell him they wanted to get rid of the Ngos.[87] At that time their plan was to assassinate Nhu and launch a coup. Diem was only specifically marked for death later in the planning.[88] CIA headquarters told their head of station in Saigon to tone down his enthusiasm for the assassination because he was making the US specifically responsible for the murders rather than letting events take their desired course.[89] The CIA, however, continued to egg the plotters on, challenging their courage and demanding to know what they were waiting for.[90] When Henry Cabot Lodge, the US ambassador in Saigon, went to congratulate the coup leaders, both the Vietnamese and American sides were grinning as they agreed that 'assassination [was] . . . the kind of thing which will happen in a coup d'etat when order cannot be guaranteed everywhere'.[91]

In 1963–4, the Americans were in Vietnam as 'advisers'. In 1965, as the Vietnamese struggled to combat an insurgency run from North

Vietnam, President Johnson committed a large American expeditionary force to the country. The North Vietnamese and the Viet Cong (VC) were determined exponents of 'pinpointed assassination'. Their assassination targets were the provincial and local Vietnamese officials who were supposed to get life back into working order once their area had been 'cleared' by regular military units. The VC tended to use four-man assassination squads for this task. In March 1967, the squads assassinated nearly two hundred officials.[92] Some of the best and brightest Vietnamese were killed in this fashion. The response was a sort of escalating assassination tit for tat between the Viet Cong's Special Action Units (SAU) and the CIA's Provincial Reconnaissance Units (PRU). In one province, the PRU managed to target and kill eight successive provincial SAU chiefs, while losing three of their own. There was essentially a 'blood feud' between assassination teams.

This sanguinary struggle of assassins was important enough to reach presidential level. In May 1967, President Johnson replaced most of his team in Saigon. As part of a more general clean-out, he created a new organisation known as CORDS (Civil Operations and Revolutionary Development Support). As Kennedy had done over Cuba five years previously, Johnson's creation of CORDS meant putting the Department of Defense rather than the CIA in charge. The architect and new head of CORDS, Robert Komer, was an outspoken champion of what he called 'rifle shot' operations against specific individuals. Komer reported to the US military high command in Saigon. However, the action teams of CORDS were the same PRUs that the CIA was already running. These teams remained under direct CIA control. Bill Colby was seconded from the CIA as deputy head of CORDS. To make things even more complex, the new leader of South Vietnam in 1967, General Thieu, responded by creating a mirror-image organisation known as Phung Hoang, usually called Phoenix for the convenience of Anglophones. The same CIA organisation that served CORDS served Phoenix, merely rebadged as the Revolutionary Development Cadre (RDC). As the RDC expanded in 1968, it too was transferred to the Department of Defense. It was, however, still run by the CIA on behalf of CORDS, of which Colby became head. These bits of Washington HR management were the justification Colby later gave for saying that the CIA had not run assassination in Vietnam. The bureaucratic double-speak could not disguise what this organisation did. In 1969, it claimed 11,700 'neutralisations' of 'priority targets': assassinations of specific individuals. CIA officers were even more blunt in private. The Secretary of the Army came away from a briefing in Vietnam with the phrase 'political assassination' firmly lodged in his mind.

Like many things in Vietnam, the obsession with numbers in Phoenix clouded results. The Americans struggled to find and reach the Vietnamese leaders they wanted to kill. Phoenix lacked 'quality'. In the event, Phoenix did not last very long, because of waning Vietnamese enthusiasm for the whole idea. Becoming the assassin of senior Vietnamese Communists rapidly became a less attractive option when it became clear that the Americans were pulling out. There were some nasty misunderstandings in the field, such as an incident when a Green Beret officer serving in a PRU killed his own agent in the belief he might betray him to the North Vietnamese. By the time Robert Komer visited Vietnam in the summer of 1970, Phoenix was effectively dead. Komer told Nixon that the whole thing was a 'fiasco'.[93]

It is hard to see what advantage the United States derived from assassination. Guatemala was an assassination hot spot before and after the overthrow of Árbenz. The US's collaborator was himself assassinated, as were, eventually, the head of the US military aid group and its ambassador. The United States invaded the Dominican Republic four years after the assassination of its leader. The United States sent a huge military expeditionary force to Vietnam two years after the assassination of its leader. The leader whom they had encouraged to kill his predecessor had already been overthrown in a coup. The campaign of assassination against Communist activists produced few results – apart from a lot of corpses. The assassination of the chief of the Chilean army disrupted the plans of military officers to prevent the leftist Salvador Allende coming to power. The officers overthrew and killed Allende in 1973, but evidence of direct US participation in those events is less clear-cut than the 1970 intervention. Nevertheless, it was widely assumed at the time that the US was behind the murder of Allende. The United States used proxy forces to invade Cuba before its assassination plots matured. Cuba then placed itself under the Soviet security umbrella. The American officials organising attempts to assassinate the Cuban leadership acknowledged that success would throw the Communist regime off balance, but it was unlikely to collapse. The Cuban intelligence services penetrated the plots, thus undermining the threat and revealing significant weaknesses in the US political and security system. The American state was not very good at assassination.[94]

Assassination certainly brought the American political and security elite much grief. 'It was like being a prisoner in the dock,' William Colby remarked of his appearance before Congress: 'there was a real interrogation. All the questions were on assassination and it was like "when did you stop beating your wife?"'[95] The spot of assassination stained nearly everyone it touched. As the Senate investigation of assassination in 1975 noted with both surprise and glee, 'there were more relevant contemporaneous documents [about assassination] than we expected'. The American state was a complex bureaucracy, and it acted like one. It regarded assassination as both legal and official. Assassination, in fact, became about the best-known activity of the American secret state.[96] According to the State Department, 'the impression is created that the US was preoccupied with plotting the removal of foreign leaders'.[97]

The Americans couldn't talk plainly on assassination for the fear that they would no longer be able to portray themselves as the good guys. In the White House, President Gerald Ford's advisers agreed that 'official acknowledgement of assassination plotting by successive Administrations of the USG [United States Government] would have an appalling and shattering impact in the international community. Without question, it would do grave damage to our ability to play a positive role of leadership in world affairs. It would provide profoundly harmful leverage to our adversaries and the resultant humiliation we would suffer would deal a serious blow to our foreign policy from which we could recover only with difficulty.' Assassination had to remain a conspiracy.[98]

The age of American assassination officially ended when Gerald Ford finally signed an Executive Order in February 1976 banning American officials from committing 'political assassination'.[99] Ford signed the 1976 order out of political necessity. Its drafting revealed Ford's real thinking. 'We need,' he told his inner circle, 'to strike a sensible balance between the need for durable standards and sufficient flexibility to enable me and future Presidents to react appropriately. . . . We must never bind our hands so tightly that we become a helpless giant in a very real and very hostile world.'[100] The American political theatre of assassination nevertheless now included not only the threat of assassination but the threat that a president might be discredited for procuring an assassination. The assassination ban was, claimed Henry Kissinger, 'an act of insanity and national humiliation'.[101] Anyone who criticised the procurers of assassination should be in a 'nut house'.[102]

9

SPLINTER GROUPS
Denial, 1971–1979

From the longer perspective, it is possible to look at a case study such as the assassination of Orlando Letelier in 1976 and well understand the anatomy of assassination in the 1970s; but many in the 1970s did not. For western governments, foreign ministries and intelligence agencies, the pieces of the puzzle only began to click into place at the end of the decade. The west's response to assassination in the 1970s had its own quality. It was markedly dissimilar to either the preceding or following decades. 1970s assassination culture had three defining characteristics: obsession with the past, confusion about the present and lax security.

Much more time and effort were expended on disinterring the assassinations of the 1960s, different in kind and context, than in addressing the assassinations of the 1970s. In the public sphere it was almost impossible to discuss a contemporary assassination without that conversation being derailed back to the 1960s. The assassinations of the 1960s were just more interesting to audiences of the 1970s than news of their own times.

This obsession with the past was a direct result of the genuine confusion felt by political leaders about the assassination conspiracies that they faced. It took until the end of the decade for most governments to admit that they even had an assassination problem. It suited many political leaders to remain confused: then they were freed of the necessity of making unpalatable choices. However, it is now plain that western intelligence agencies, the supposed experts on assassination, were also confused. In part, this was due to the elision of assassination with mass-casualty terrorism in intelligence, political, journalistic and academic circles. It was the massacre of Israeli athletes at the Munich Olympics of September 1972 that most focused attention. It was not the case that the 'hard men of intelligence' – to use John le Carré's 1977 phrase – knew all along what was going on but lied to their political masters. Much of the best intelligence work on assassination dated from the 1980s or later; reading it back into the 1970s is apt to be misleading. This view of western intelligence as floundering is borne out by poor security. Like assassination intelligence, assassination security did not begin to evolve in any serious fashion until the end of the decade.

American political culture was not well prepared for the actual assassination threat that emerged from the Middle East in the 1970s. The matrix for that assassination culture was initially Palestinian, first manifested in the creation of a terrorist organisation known as Black September within the Fatah faction of the Palestine Liberation Organisation.

Named after the events of 1970 when the Jordanian government had violently expelled the PLO from its country, Black September assassinated the Prime Minister of Jordan, Wasfi Tal, in November 1971. This was the first time the CIA had heard of Black September, just another group of '*fedayeen* of some stripe'.[1]

Black September did not stay in Jordan. The month after the assassination of Tal, a Black September assassin attempted to kill Zaid al-Rifai, the Jordanian ambassador to the UK, in Kensington.[2] The assassin raked the ambassador's Daimler with a sub-machine gun. Al-Rifai was lucky to escape with only a wounded arm. The British secret services were about as clueless as the CIA, to whom they turned for help with little success. Both Britain and America believed that the attack was the work of anti-Fatah Palestinians in the Popular Front for the Liberation of Palestine (PFLP) or the Popular Democratic Front for the Liberation of Palestine (PDFLP).[3] That is not to say that those two groups were not just as keen as Fatah on assassination. The PFLP's subsequently famous terrorist 'Carlos the Jackal' attempted to assassinate the British Zionist and part-owner of Marks & Spencer, Teddy Sieff, in December 1973. 'The Jackal' got into Sieff's London home and shot him in the face, although he survived. 'The Jackal' was not identified until 1975.[4] In 1972, the London *Spectator* had better intelligence on the Palestinian factions than the CIA or SIS, thanks to commissioning an informed Arab observer to write about them.[5] It was left to the Jordanian General Intelligence Directorate and al-Rifai himself to put the British and the Americans straight about what was going on.[6]

In March 1973, Black September seized the Saudi Arabian embassy in Khartoum. Their main target was not the Saudis, but the Americans. The *fedayeen* captured the American ambassador, Cleo Noel, and his deputy, George Moore. They then murdered both men. Documents recovered from the embassy revealed that the 'terrorists were apparently under external control and did not murder Ambassador Noel and Moore or surrender to GOS until receiving specific codeword instructions'.[7] Nevertheless, Kissinger advised 'against conditioning our future diplomatic involvement on a crackdown on Black September: that would play into Black September's hands because they would like to prevent a negotiated solution' to the Palestinian–Israeli conflict.[8] Nixon and Kissinger wanted as little to do with the assassination as possible. In Kissinger's words, 'this is a bunch of Arabs': the Americans 'had no control over that'. Nixon confined himself to demanding, 'let's just show that we're caring about it'.[9] In the end, Nixon placed sanctions on Sudan for failing to try the assassins.[10]

Western nations really did not want to believe that Fatah was behind a wave of assassination.[11] A few months after the Khartoum murders, the assistant Israeli military attaché to the USA, Yosef Alon, was assassinated on the driveway of his suburban home in Chevy Chase, Maryland. He was 'the first diplomat accredited to Washington to be killed in recent memory'.[12] US law enforcement agencies assumed that Black September was behind the shooting: the FBI had warned that there was a Black September murder squad on the loose before the attack, but the assassination was never properly solved.[13] Although the press reported that there was a 'fierce underground war between Israeli agents and Arab partisans in cities all over the world', it was more convenient for western governments to assume that assassination was the work of small 'splinter groups'.[14]

Both the US and the British concluded – prematurely – that Fatah had abandoned assassination in 1975.[15] However, the scenario that western authorities had wanted to be true – assassination driven by Palestinian groups other than Fatah – only actually came to pass during 1976.[16] It was with something akin to relief that Kissinger reported that when the US ambassador to Lebanon, Francis Meloy, was assassinated in June 1976, 'it was done without PLO involvement'.[17] When the Palestinian terrorist Abu Nidal launched his anti-PLO Black June assassination organisation over the summer of 1976, perversely he gave western governments something they had wished for.[18]

In any case, some agencies, such as the Metropolitan Police Special Branch, believed the most dangerous assassination threat came from the Israeli Mossad: PLO leaders in London should be treated as potential victims rather actual perpetrators.[19] Mossad assassinated Black September's co-ordinator in Paris in June 1973.[20] Specialist intelligence and security agencies kept returning to the Israeli threat in the 1970s, but their work tended to be smothered for political reasons. In Britain, the issue came to a head in early 1979. In January 1979, Mossad assassinated Abu Hassan, the head of Fatah security, in Beirut.[21] The assassination weapon was a car bomb. Also killed in the explosion was a British schoolteacher, Susan Wareham. The British investigated the assassination in collaboration with Fatah. They rapidly traced the assassination of Hassan and the murder of Wareham back to London.[22] One Mossad assassin was an Israeli using a fake British passport; the second assassin was also an Israeli but was travelling under her genuine British passport. The British passed information about the identity of the assassins to the PLO.[23]

Britain then made a very lukewarm protest to the Israeli government about its involvement in a 'conspiracy to murder'.[24] The gravamen of British complaints about the Israeli killings in the 1970s was that the use of British passports associated Britain with the assassinations. The British, however, had no desire to push their investigation of the broader conspiracy any further. The Israeli Prime Minister, Menachem Begin, was himself a well-known assassin. Britain had long since swallowed the fact that they dealt with a man who had murdered and tortured British soldiers. The government officials around Begin, with whom British diplomats dealt, were known Mossad operatives, some organisers of assassination, and cared not one whit about who knew it.[25] Above all, Begin was on the brink of making peace with President Anwar Sadat of Egypt – the single most important act in the Arab–Israeli conflict since 1948. The British had no desire to complicate the Camp David negotiations and would have received a dusty response from the United States if they had attempted to do so. Thus, the Israeli propensity for assassination was filed as merely a series of unfortunate incidents.[26]

Even in the Middle East, the potentially most worrying assassination, as far as the western powers were concerned, had, arguably, little to do with the Israeli–Palestinian tit-for-tat assassinations. The most important Middle Eastern power was Saudi Arabia. In March 1975, one of King Faisal of Saudi Arabia's nephews, also Faisal, drew a pistol at a family meeting and shot him dead. Prince Faisal claimed he killed his uncle in revenge for the death of his older brother, killed by the police while protesting about the introduction of television into Saudi a decade before. This was what the British ambassador labelled as an assassination of an 'oriental Court'.[27] Many in that court would have loved to blame 'international Zionism' for the assassination, but even the most virulent anti-Zionists rapidly admitted there was no evidence for that whatsoever.[28] The Americans were more nervous of being framed than the Israelis because Prince Faisal had just returned from studying at Berkeley.[29]

The most convenient explanation, and one that the Saudis tried to push, was that the killer was simply insane. However, their interrogations suggested otherwise: he was an Islamist fanatic who stood out even in a country of Islamists. A quick trial convicted him not only of murder but also, in a deliberate act of delegitimisation, of apostasy – conversion to Christianity. The royal family's religious advisers 'suggested that the traditional penalty for apostasy should be exacted, i.e. the accused's right hand and left leg should be chopped off, then he should be beheaded, and finally his body should be pinned up on a pole. However, the authorities considered that this would not quite be the right thing.' The Saudis confined themselves to publicly beheading Prince Faisal.³⁰

In the event, the al-Sauds arranged the succession very smoothly with King Khalid as a figurehead and 'the Strong Man of Saudi Arabia', Prince Fahd, as the real ruler.³¹ All the Saudis' oil customers were appropriately fawning in ways that were seen in no other assassination of the 1970s. In Britain, in a departure from precedent, flags on government buildings were flown at half-mast.³² The British even attempted to get the author Jan Morris to write a hagiography of King Faisal, while 'shuddering to think' what the 'Ulema might say if they found out the truth about him/her!'³³

In the early and mid-1970s, powers with global interests, such as the US and Britain, were as interested in 'old-style' assassination in their traditional stamping grounds as they were in 'new-style' assassination, usually emanating from Beirut but spreading inexorably into the cities of America and Europe. American interest was still drawn towards Latin America. Britain remained fascinated by South Asia. South American and South Asian assassins, like the Israelis, used London, with its excellent transport links and relaxed security, as a planning and logistics hub.³⁴

Juan Perón, the Argentine populist president, died in May 1974. The Marxist People's Liberation Army, or *Montoneros*, 'declared war' on his widow and successor Isabel Perón in September 1974 and launched an assassination campaign aimed at her senior military and police officials.³⁵ A 'state of siege' was precipitated when the *Montoneros* assassinated the head of the Federal Police – the PFA, or *federales* – Alberto Villar by blowing up his yacht.³⁶ They missed his successor Luis Margaride in December 1974. The attempt on Margaride was both primitive and frighteningly sophisticated. The *Montoneros* used a type of Claymore, originally an American design for an above-ground anti-personnel mine firing ball bearings in a limited directional arc. The invention was copied by the Vietnamese and passed on to the *Montoneros* by the Cubans. The copyists had long since realised that they could fabricate a usable facsimile Claymore by 'making use of black powder and other explosives (fertilizer based) which can be easily combined and manufactured in their own workshops'.[37] The *Montoneros* assassinated Margaride's successor, Cesáreo Cardozo, when a female assassin placed a bomb under his bed in June 1976. It was these assassinations that persuaded the Argentine military and police that, in the interests of their own survival, they should launch a coup against Perón. In March 1976, the *Montoneros* attempted to assassinate the head of the Argentine army, Jorge Videla, with a car bomb. Videla led the coup that overthrew Isabel Perón ten days after his narrow escape. The *Montoneros* made a second attempt on now President Videla in October 1976.[38] Under Videla, Argentina's right-wing 'death squads', first created in 1973 as 'a dynamic security organisation' in the Ministry of Social Welfare, became fully an arm of the state.[39]

The *Montoneros* also assassinated Yankees. Their first victim was an executive of the Ford Motor Company, James Swint, in November 1973. The attack that really made waves in Washington, however, was the kidnap, then assassination, of a US consular official, John Egan, in the city of Córdoba in February 1975.[40] The Americans reduced the size of their embassy in Buenos Aires, and most American employees of multinational corporations left with the diplomats, a retreat which all parties saw as a humiliation.[41] The pressure was partially relieved in the autumn of 1975 when the *Montoneros* disclaimed the assassination of Americans.[42] US businesses had bought their safety by paying protection money.[43]

The driving force for an alliance of leftist South American assassins came from Argentina.[44] The Argentine government killed the brains behind the terrorist alliance, Roberto Santucho, in 1976. Between October 1975 and May 1977, the 'Condor' alliance systematically assassinated the rest of the leadership of the terrorist groups. The CIA concluded that 'terrorism requires the use of small units to commit spectacular incidents, and individuals' personal qualities often play a decisive role in the ultimate success or failure of the entire organization. When the opposing security forces succeed in putting a few key terrorists out of action, the results can be significant.'[45] Of course, it did not stop there. Individuals such as Orlando Letelier and Bernardo Leighton were members of the democratic opposition.

Although exposure had largely shut down Condor by the end of 1976, there were plenty of significant individuals left outside the

Argentina-Chile-Uruguay-Bolivia quadrilateral. The problem for the Americans rapidly shifted from southern to central Latin America. In May 1977, the left-wing Salvadorean FPL assassinated Mauricio Borgonovo, the foreign minister of El Salvador, one of the few Latin American political leaders the international community admired for his competence and commitment to civilian rule. Within a day of his death, right-wing death squads, known colloquially as the White Warriors, started committing 'counter assassinations'.[46]

El Salvador was bad enough, but its southern neighbour Nicaragua became notorious. In January 1978, Major Anastasio Somoza, son of the dictator Tachito Somoza, organised the assassination of the critical newspaper editor Pedro Joaquín Chamorro.[47] Chamorro's supporters massed in huge anti-government demonstrations and burnt down Somoza's export firm Plasmaferisis. Five captured assassins testified that they had been hired for the Chamorro assassination by the general manager of the company, a US citizen of Nicaraguan descent who had since taken refuge in Miami. The remaining managers of Plasmaferisis fled into the US embassy. The US ambassador sent up a distress flare telling Washington that 'the clear implications of USG protecting possible killers of Chamorro' might be the storming of the embassy and the slaughter of its inmates.[48]

At the same time as American diplomats battened down the hatches in Nicaragua, their opposite numbers in El Salvador's northern neighbour, Guatemala, were doing the same thing. In January 1978, the Guatemalan leftist leader Alberto Fuentes was assassinated, and the Americans thought that 'a series of retaliatory killings in Guatemala would not be unlikely'.[49] They were slightly comforted by the thought that Fuentes had not been a 'major force on the left'. The other main leftist leader in Guatemala, Manuel Colom, was 'a far more charismatic and hence more "dangerous" figure' in the eyes of the Guatemalan government.[50] Assassins killed Colom in March 1979.[51]

Commentary on assassination in Latin America read remarkably similarly to comment on the Arab–Israeli assassinations: single-issue activists placed the blame on whichever political alignment – left or right – they found most detestable. In fact, it was clear that Southern and Central America were very dangerous for both their own political leaders and visiting westerners. Most governments just wanted to duck and weave and not become too involved.

In South Asia, meanwhile, a wave of assassination was also building in hard-to-understand ways. The full impact of these assassinations would only become clear in the 1980s, when they had undermined the possibilities for westernising regimes in India, Pakistan, Bangladesh, Afghanistan and Sri Lanka. The population of India made the global statistics for citizens living under democratic regimes look relatively healthy. The tension between democracy and assassination in India was thus particularly significant.

In January 1975, a grenade-throwing assassin killed India's railways minister, L.N. Mishra, in Samastipur, Bihar. At the time of his death, Mishra's position in Indian politics was rather more central than his specific ministerial portfolio initially suggested. He was the main adviser to Indira Gandhi, the leader of the Congress Party which had governed India since independence. It proved very hard for the Indian government to define the conspiracy against Mishra, since there was little evidence that the police or security services could find.[52] Indira Gandhi herself talked darkly about the assassination being the 'rehearsal' for a 'bigger plot'. She thought the threat serious enough to establish an investigatory commission – the Mathew Commission – on the same basis as that which had investigated Mahatma Gandhi's death.[53] In July 1975, the Gandhi government proclaimed a state of emergency in India. Its claim was that 'opposition parties and fascist organisations of the extreme right and left have sought to destroy the democratic set up'. However, the sole act of targeted political violence that the government could cite was Mishra's murder. Other deaths had certainly occurred, but they tended to be in mass protests over prices.[54]

The government implied that the assassin was in some way connected to Jayaprakash Narayan's agitation in Bihar against the shameless and endemic financial corruption of Congress, which Mishra had personified. However, by the time Mathew reported in 1977, the Congress government had gone, to be replaced by the Janata party which Narayan had been instrumental in creating.[55] The new government was willing to acknowledge that 'Mr Mishra had been a victim of a well-designed plot', but it was uninterested in probing any further.[56] Mrs Gandhi stuck firmly to the view that Narayan and the leftist proto-Janata in Bihar had procured the assassination of her friend. She added for good measure that she feared too for her own life.[57]

Just after the Indian government declared its 1975 state of emergency, assassination dealt a major blow to its foreign policy. In 1971, India had fought a major conventional war against Pakistan to sever West Pakistan from East Pakistan, which became the new state of Bangladesh. In January 1972, the pro-Indian East Bengali/Bangladeshi opposition leader Sheikh Mujibur Rahman entered Dacca and took control of the government. The army assassinated Sheikh Mujibur as part of a coup in August 1975. A force of junior and middle-ranking army officers stormed Mujib's house, killing not only him but his entire family. Mujib's strong personal guard had put up a 'stiff resistance' but had been overwhelmed when the army brought up tanks. Despite his own strong Islamic credentials, Mujib had been a champion of 'secular principles' on the Indian model. He and his followers also admired the corruption of Congress, although they took their peculation to even more spectacular levels.[58] Oddly, the Islamist assassins – disgruntled army officers who had been repatriated from West Pakistan – cited the despoliation of the Red Cross as a particular grievance.[59] Both Indian and western intelligence were caught completely by surprise. Western intelligence was equally caught off guard when the assassins of August were themselves overthrown in another military coup in November.[60] No-one was brought to book for Mujib's murder.[61]

Britain paid close attention to events in the subcontinent, not least because of emigration to the UK.[62] By contrast, few saw assassination in Afghanistan as a prelude to more important things to come.[63] In fact, President Mohammad Daoud was murdered and overthrown in a Communist coup in April 1978, a few days after he had procured the assassination of Mir Akbar Khyber, the Communists' own leader. The attention of the west was only fully caught in February 1979 when the US ambassador in Kabul was assassinated. Adolph Dubs was carjacked and taken to the Kabul Hotel in the centre of the city. By the time US embassy officials arrived on the scene, hoping to negotiate their boss's release, the Afghan police were already deployed with their Soviet 'security advisers'. The Afghans proceeded to storm the room in which Dubs was held, in a spectacularly inept operation during which the ambassador was shot dead: who fired the fatal shot, the kidnappers, the Afghan security forces or the police, was uncertain. As the Indians put it, there was 'good reason to believe that the Afghan authorities used maximum force a little impatiently, without giving adequate consideration to saving the life of the US Ambassador'.[64]

On one level, the Americans were minded to treat the Dubs killing as a strange and unusual murder. However, interest in assassination was sharpened in the west by the suspicion that the Soviet special tasks operation might be coming back to life.[65] Most notoriously, an assassin had murdered Georgi Markov, a Bulgarian émigré, in September 1978 as he crossed Waterloo Bridge in London. The murder weapon was unusual: a poisoned umbrella. The Markov assassination generated more column inches than any of the other London killings of the 1970s. It took the British state by surprise. It had believed that the Soviets were bound by a 'code of conduct' in western cities.[66] The investigation into the Markov case concluded, correctly, that the Soviets had franchised assassination to the Bulgarians.[67] Despite a great deal of speculation, limited progress was made in understanding what had gone on.[68]

This was, on one level, hardly surprising since the background to the killing was incredibly tangled. The KGB's in-place assassination capability had been severely disrupted in 1971 when one of its operatives in London, Oleg Lyalin, had defected to the British. In February 1976, the Politburo decided that 'special tasks' should be incorporated into the KGB's Illegals Directorate, as its 8th Department. The 8th Department comprised about 6 per cent of the strength of the Illegals Directorate. As its head mournfully observed, 'we move paper from place to place, that's all we do.' However, it was very possible to understate the Soviets' continuing interest in assassination. Lyalin and his comrades in London had certainly been on the lookout for Soviet defectors to kill. Both the KGB and the GRU – military intelligence – were investing heavily in their so-called *spetsnaz* special forces units in the 1970s. One of their roles was assassination in the context of a major war.

In terms of more classical assassination, other Eastern Bloc governments suffered from few of the inhibitions of the Soviet Politburo. Of these, the most enthusiastic was the Bulgarian Durzhavna Sigurnost (DS), tasked by the Communist dictator Todor Zhivkov. Like Pinochet in Chile, Zhivkov ran a cult of personality and was very sensitive to slights from the Bulgarian intelligentsia. The DS claimed to have carried out ten undetected assassinations of Bulgarian émigrés before they targeted Markov because he had been 'slandering Comrade Zhivkov'. This was not a Bulgarian freelance operation, however. From the beginning, the head of the DS, Dimitar Stoyanov, turned to the KGB for permission and assistance. The decision to go ahead was taken in Moscow by the chairman of the KGB, Yuriy Andropov. In particular, the KGB offered the services of its poison laboratory in the Operational Technical Directorate. The Soviet technicians made the assassination weapon by converting the end of an umbrella into a silenced gun capable of firing a tiny pellet containing a lethal dose of ricin.[69]

The inflection point in the British understanding of assassination can be dated reasonably precisely to 1978. In 1978, the British government of James Callaghan admitted that, over the past decade, it had completely misunderstood the nature of assassination. Since the days when Callaghan had been Home Secretary, the British state had dealt with assassinations as a series of isolated incidents. Assassinations had been conceptualised as an occasional phenomenon, somehow distinct from the mainstream of international politics. In terms of foreign policy and diplomatic practice, it had become a regular reflex to 'let sleeping dogs lie'.[70] However, as the British government belatedly acknowledged, over the past decade assassination had become a regular and endemic challenge not only to British interests but also to the broader political system. The time had come to pore over events since 1968 and retrofit them into an analytical pattern.[71] Having done that, the British state had to prepare itself for more of the same.[72]

A great deal of credit for the change of heart over assassination can be given to the Palestinian Abu Nidal and his main sponsor, the ruler of Iraq, Saddam Hussein. Although Saddam only became formal leader of Iraq in 1979, he had effectively been in charge since 1975: he had been the dominant figure in the state's security apparatus since the Baath revolution in 1968. Thus the intelligence services of Iraq and Abu Nidal's Black June group were intimately intertwined.[73]

In a very direct fashion, it became hard for the British government to ignore Abu Nidal's Black June and Iraqi intelligence. In 1977, the British and American intelligence communities, to the despair of their opposite numbers in the Gulf States, were dismissive of Black June.[74] Their eyes were instead fixed on another Baghdad-based group, the PFLP, the killers of Francis Meloy.[75] After all, 'The Jackal' was a PFLP assassin.[76] In January 1978, however, Black June shot and killed the PLO's representative in London, Said Hammami, in his office in Green Street, near West Ham's Upton Park football stadium. In quick succession, it also assassinated the PLO representatives in Kuwait and Paris.[77]

Six months after the Hammami killing, Iraqi intelligence similarly assassinated, by shooting, Saddam Hussein's long-term rival, Razzak al-Naif, in the Intercontinental Hotel, Hyde Park. The al-Naif assassination really clarified matters for the British because they managed to catch the assassin.[78] As their Fatah intelligence contacts commented, 'London should be considered a good place for assassinations.'[79] The Metropolitan Police admitted that London 'was an attractive target area for Arab assassins because of both the ease of air travel from the Middle East and numbers of Arabs already resident, who could provide cover and support. In Britain there were, for example, some 8,000 Palestinian students and [a] similar number of Iraqis.'[80] Their breakthrough in the al-Naif case hardly made the British police and secret services happy: once a trial had found the shooter guilty of murder, they concluded gloomily, 'we will be in the situation [vulnerability to further attacks] that almost all Western governments finding themselves with alien terrorists on their hands have tried desperately to avoid.'[81]

The other main Middle Eastern entrepreneur of assassination was Colonel Muammar Qaddafi. Qaddafi's long-term commitment to assassination often puzzled western observers because of his seeming recklessness. At core, however, Qaddafi was pursuing a violent policy of regime survival and aggrandisement as seen in other dictatorships. He loathed and feared opponents to his rule, especially those who prospered in western countries. He sought to terrorise such opponents. At the same time, he could threaten other regional leaders with his assassins, especially if he appeared to be closely associated with non-Libyan terrorist organisations to whom he could franchise violence. Finally, he was convinced that he could get away with assassination in the west if he trimmed from time to time. For a long time, that seemed a realistic calculation.[82]

Like the Palestinians and the Iraqis, the Libyans had a very strong foothold in London.[83] Qaddafi had supplied the sub-machine gun used to attack Zaid al-Rifai, the weapon having been sold to him by the British a few months previously.[84] He was caught red-handed supplying arms to the IRA in 1973.[85] In March 1973, the Irish government intercepted a ship smuggling arms from Libya to the Provisional IRA. The Irish recovered weapons and arrested a senior member of the PIRA on board.[86] The interception of the ship did not immediately cool Colonel Qaddafi's public enthusiasm for supporting the IRA. He made his last major public statement to that effect in November 1974.[87]

To be fair to Qaddafi, the British and Americans had considered removing him in a classic assassination wrapped up in a coup, although little was done since potential collaborators were judged incompetent at best or likely to be even more hostile to the west at worst.[88] Nevertheless, Qaddafi had been badly shaken by two assassination attempts by domestic rivals in the autumn of 1971: in an attack on his car, members of his escort were killed, and a few months later a bomb was found on his flight from Cairo to Tripoli.[89]

The British government was about as keen to understand the fact that the charismatic Libyan dictator was the architect of multiple assassinations as it had been to investigate Yasser Arafat or Saddam Hussein. People who tried to convince the British Prime Minister Edward Heath that Qaddafi was a prime mover behind assassination in Europe were told they were 'wasting his time'.[90] In September 1977, Roy Mason, the Secretary of State for Northern Ireland in the Callaghan government, attended the tenth anniversary celebration of the coup that had brought Colonel Qaddafi to power. Mason's attendance upon the Libyans signalled to the diplomatic community that the British government had accepted that Qaddafi's well-documented supply of weapons to the Provisional IRA had ceased, as he now claimed.[91]

It was well understood in the west that Qaddafi was a serial commissioner of assassination: but if he confined his assassination squads to his own neighbours, no-one was inclined to do much about the threat.[92] Continental European nations were much more caught up with soul-searching about home-grown assassins. In April 1977, the West German Red Army Faction (RAF) assassinated the country's attorney general, Siegfried Buback.[93] The assassins were able to practise their ambush unmolested in the idyllic Baden wine town of Sachsenheim. They were subsequently tracked down to another small town, Singen on the Rhine. The RAF followed up the Buback assassination by kidnapping the industrialist Hans Martin Schleyer in Cologne, murdering him at their sadistic leisure. The Buback and Schleyer assassinations allowed the Germans to agonise about their favourite subject, their own past: 'modern German history, particularly the Weimar Republic period, which was rife with political assassinations, has left an imprint in the German psyche that continues to play a role in German behavior today,' American diplomats concluded.[94]

The Federal Criminal Investigation Office's (BKA) statements on the RAF were little more than 'propaganda', overstating its roster of active assassins by a factor of thirty.[95] The historical comparison was crass – the Weimar Republic had been racked by financial crises and economic instability, whereas West Germany was prosperous to the point of envy – but that did not stop the Germans attempting to 'assign social blame'.[96] They took some solace from the fact that German assassins were deadly because they were Germans, with 'brains, planning, dedication and awesome ability to achieve goals'. There was, therefore, the Germans maintained, no comparison to be made between home-grown assassination and whatever murders Arabs might commit.[97] The growing list of assassinations of Middle Eastern exiles in Europe could be written off as mere 'inter-Arab skirmishes'.[98]

Equally, the Western European states dismissed the experiences of 'pariahs'. The prime minister of Spain was the most senior European politician assassinated in the 1970s. In 1973, Basque assassins rented an apartment in the building opposite the back door of the church in which Luis Carrero Blanco worshipped daily. The flat came with a cellar, from which the assassins tunnelled under the street to place a huge mine. They watched for the prime minister's arrival from the apartment, ready with a trigger that ran down to the cellar. The explosion was so intense that it blew Carrero Blanco's car up to the roof of a six-storey building. The car hit the eaves and landed on the terrace over the courtyard of the church. Blanco had been prepared for a street-level gun attack, not this. His two police bodyguards were killed alongside him. Of course, being a Fascist, Carrero Blanco's death did not count in democratic Europe. In the rather cruel humour of the British Foreign Office, he was merely 'Spain's first man in space'.[99] The incipient failure of the Franco regime was, if anything, regarded as a boon.[100]

Those other pariahs, the British, found no takers when they wanted European Community ministers to discuss counter-assassination.[101] In the 1970s, Belfast was the assassination capital of Europe. The scale of assassination in Ulster dwarfed anything to be found elsewhere in Europe, although assassination often merged with random sectarian murders.[102] As the Northern Ireland Office commented in July 1975, assassination was 'a constant feature of Northern Ireland life'.[103]

In 1975, however, the assassination wave began to spread outside Northern Ireland. Under new leadership, the Provisional IRA decided to switch from low-status, high-volume murder in Ulster to high-value assassination elsewhere.[104] It carried out its first assassinations in London. The assassination of the television personality and Unionist political activist Ross McWhirter in November 1975 was the highest-profile of these murders. The PIRA assassins shot McWhirter on his own doorstep in Enfield, north London.[105] The police captured the PIRA assassination squad in London not long after the McWhirter killing. The security forces also recovered their assassination target list, including details of British government ministers.[106]

In July 1976, the Provisional IRA assassinated the British ambassador in Dublin, Christopher Ewart-Biggs, by means of a culvert bomb – 200 pounds of explosives planted under the road along which the diplomat commuted.[107] The attack took the Irish authorities by surprise.[108] Given the lack of security, Ewart-Biggs's former colleagues in the British Foreign and Commonwealth Office found the reaction to his death in Ireland slightly nauseating in its sentimentalism.[109]

At least in their own telling, the British received precious little help or consideration in facing Irish assassination. Not only did the Dutch and the Belgians mount 'fruitless' investigations into the assassination of the British ambassador in The Hague, Sir Richard Sykes, in March 1979, but also they rapidly lost interest in those investigations, regarding the assassination as 'an event extraneous to the Netherlands'.[110] The Belgians were a little more engaged, because the PIRA had simultaneously murdered a British SIS officer's Belgian next-door neighbour. Even then the British were unable to make a narrative about an IRA assassination campaign in continental Europe stick.[111] Despite the death of the unfortunate M. Michaux, the neighbour in Brussels, in practical terms Irish assassins posed a 'very low' threat to anyone but the British.[112]

Even when the threat was repeatedly shown to be very real, this attitude persisted, not least because the British failed to prove many links to assassination conspiracies that had valency for other powers. A few days after the PIRA assassinated Sykes, another Irish terrorist group, the Irish National Liberation Army (INLA), assassinated a Conservative MP with an in-car bomb that detonated in the car park of the Houses of Parliament. The intelligence services could not pin down stories that 'Irish terrorists received training in the Middle East'. Even if that were true, the real base for Republican assassins was 'in the Republic of Ireland'.[113] Police forces in both Britain and Ireland had known for years that the IRA had a rolling series of plots to kill the elderly Lord Mountbatten – former viceroy of India, former chief of the defence staff and a member of the royal family – in the Republic of Ireland, where he spent much time.[114] When the PIRA assassins finally murdered Mountbatten in August 1979, MI5 'tried and failed to find evidence that any member of this team has visited Libya'.[115] Even if the intelligence services had been able to tie Irish assassination to the Middle East, it was doubtful that would have made much difference. Irish assassins received a spread in *Paris Match*.[116] European politicians and journalists seemingly had some sentimental sympathy for assassins who murdered 'British imperialists'.[117]

In fighting back against the PIRA, the British risked casting themselves as not only unworthy victims but actual assassins. Republican propagandists certainly made the claim that the British special forces, first deployed in Northern Ireland in 1975, were assassins and found willing audiences in both North America and Europe. They focused on three cases. In April 1976, the SAS captured an 'officer' of the PIRA Crossmaglen 'battalion': he was shot and killed attempting to escape. An inquest returned an ambiguous 'open' verdict in January 1977. In December 1977, and again in June 1978, PIRA terrorists attempted to carjack vehicles containing SAS troopers. In both cases the terrorists were summarily killed.[118]

The issue only came starkly into public focus in July 1978, however, when the SAS reported a very successful operation that had taken place near the village of Dunloy in County Antrim. Working on intelligence supplied by Royal Ulster Constabulary (RUC) Special Branch, a four-man SAS team had lain in wait for the PIRA in a graveyard in which the terrorists had previously buried a cache of firearms and explosives. When four terrorists arrived, they shot two of them dead and captured the others.[119] Very little of the SAS's initial report was true. They had shot the sixteen-year-old son of the local farmer. The RUC disavowed the SAS. The family's local MP — as luck would have it, the populist leader of militant Protestant Unionism, Ian Paisley — demanded justice for 'a decent Roman Catholic family'. It was Paisley who released the detail that the dead teenager had been shot in the back.[120] Despite behind-the-scenes pleas to act otherwise, the Director of Public Prosecutions for Northern Ireland, a Protestant and a former army officer, prosecuted two SAS troopers for murder. Hearing the case, the Lord Chief Justice of Northern Ireland denounced one of the troopers as an 'unreliable witness' and made it very clear that he believed that the SAS had carried out a deliberate execution. He ruled, however, that since there was no direct proof of intent, the SAS men could not be found guilty of murder. He pointedly refused to consider a charge of manslaughter since, whatever happened in that cemetery, it was not an accidental death.[121] Officials in London and Belfast had no need of the formal proceeding to understand the import of the killing: as soon as they read the corrected intelligence reports, they realised that was the end of SAS covert operations in Northern Ireland and a 'victory' for the PIRA.[122]

Given the trouble western governments had in defining the assassination conspiracies being launched against them, it is perhaps unsurprising that their response was weak and inchoate. Assassinations were affecting democracies from many directions but there was a tendency to dismiss each killing as a singular event, disconnected from regular politics. Part of the problem was that assassination cut directly against how these governments had imagined the world would be. Assassination was supposed to be a problem for other people; it was not supposed to happen in democracies. Perhaps, some conceded, it was a fruit of colonialism, but colonialism was dead. The new capitalist world was to be one of open cities and easy travel for prosperous and well-educated citizens.[123]

If broader societal trends militated against inoculation, then the alternative was better security in a narrower sense. However, many states were reluctant to address this issue either. The gold standard of western counter-assassination security was popularly believed to be in the United States. From the moment he won the Republican nomination as its presidential candidate in 1968, Richard Nixon enjoyed a very different degree of protection from the one that he would have received if he had won the presidential election of 1960.[124]

In 1970, Nixon decided that members of his cabinet too should be allowed 'adequate personal security'. His main worry was that they might be embarrassed by an assault from a Black radical or a militant student. The Ohio National Guard had shot several students at Kent State University, Ohio, and feelings against the American state were running high on university campuses.[125] Nixon ruled, however, that members of the cabinet should not fall under the 'special' Secret Service umbrella. Rather, each department was to create, and pay for, its own 'in-house' security service.[126]

In 1970, very few people received any state security. For instance, it was the task of the NYPD, not the federal government, to protect visiting dignitaries in New York, the HQ of the UN and recognised as potentially the most dangerous place in the US for assassination. There were over four thousand accredited diplomats working in New York, multiplied many times over by the expat communities that clustered around them. In total, nearly 140,000 people might have some claim to protection.[127]

In April 1970, when Taiwan was still seated at the UN as China, a Formosan nationalist attempted to assassinate Chiang Ching-kuo, heir apparent to his father, Chiang Kai-shek, at the Plaza Hotel on Fifth Avenue in Manhattan. In classic movie mob hit style, the assassin – a Cornell student – trapped Chiang in the hotel's revolving doors, but one of the two NYPD detectives who were escorting the Taiwanese vice-premier grabbed the assassin's arm, upsetting his aim sufficiently that, although his pistol round hit the glass door, it missed Chiang. The Secret Service renamed the White House Police, its uniformed branch, the 'Executive Protective Service' (EPS) and widened its remit. In 1971, Congress gave the President permission to deploy the EPS to New York to protect diplomatic missions.[128]

However, when the Fatah leader – and known procurer of assassination – Yasser Arafat addressed the UN in November 1974, there was virtually no preparation for his arrival. The Libyans chartered a jet to fly him into JFK airport and a helicopter to take him to the UN building in Manhattan. His staff came in a NYPD road convoy. The federal government merely arranged for the arrest of one Jewish Defense League official who had 'publicly threatened to murder Arafat'.[129]

Although the UN presented the Americans with a unique problem, other countries were wrestling with similar issues. The Jordanian ambassador, Zaid al-Rifai, had no protection as he drove around London.[130] Metropolitan Police Special Branch only offered him bodyguards after the assassination attempt.[131] The Metropolitan Police deployed armed officers outside the Jordanian embassy in London, and the Met and Surrey Police created a guard system for King Hussein's children who were at school in Britain.[132] The British government, very reluctantly, accepted the importation of armed Jordanian embassy guards.[133] All of these ad hoc arrangements were to be strictly temporary.[134] King Hussein did not think much of Britain's efforts: he removed his children, and sent them to the USA, where he could organise armed private security. He 'no longer trusted British security'.[135] The British were relieved, 'without', of course, 'any suspicion of *schadenfreude*', when the Jordanian delegate to the UN in New York was attacked in October 1972, since it confirmed 'that the problem was not confined to the UK'.[136]

British counter-assassination security during the Heath government was, literally, a joke.[137] Less than a month after the assassination attempt on al-Rifai in London, Edward Heath himself travelled to Brussels to sign the treaty for Britain's accession to the European Economic Community. Heath regarded the ceremony at the Palais d'Egmont as a personal triumph. Triumph turned to farce when a woman known to be mentally unwell attacked the prime minister with a bottle of ink. One Metropolitan Police Special Branch officer had accompanied the prime minister to Brussels. Unfortunately, the British embassy in Belgium had failed to arrange a pass for that officer. He was denied entry to the Palais by the Belgians: Heath was assaulted as his bodyguard was barging his way in.[138]

A subsequent review of this embarrassing cock-up revealed that Special Branch protection officers never bothered to prepare overseas trips. They merely travelled with the prime minister and trusted that the local authorities had everything under control. Just as surprisingly, it emerged also that foreign security officers rarely did any preparatory visits to London either.[139] Other ministers got even less than the prime minister. When the cabinet minister John Davies attended the funeral of Carrero Blanco in 1973, he was judged not worthy of a Special Branch bodyguard.[140]

The question of protection for the prime minister and for foreign diplomats in London became intertwined.[141] Heath explicitly drew the parallel between his own experience and that of al-Rifai: they had both been poorly served, in his view.[142] Heath ordered the establishment of a mobile unit of the SAS so that the Army could take over from the police anywhere in the UK in a crisis. The SAS counter-terror unit rapidly became the centrepiece of Britain's response to threat. Revealingly, senior politicians in London cared less about the Dunloy Incident limiting the use of the SAS in Northern Ireland and more about jeopardising its CT security on the mainland.[143] Security forces began to hold meetings to discuss best practice, finding that their cultures differed greatly.[144]

In late 1972, the British Metropolitan Police and Home Office sent an investigative mission around the capitals of Europe plus the USA to find out what western nations did to protect diplomats. They found that 'in Paris and Bonn the availability of almost unlimited manpower by the use of para-military bodies to supplement the local police made any results obtained by these Forces of little value in solving the problem of protection in London'. They rejected the 'Belgian model' of high-visibility, but ineffective, protection of embassies, sarcastically wondering whether they could use unpaid special constables, 'because they already have a uniform'.[145] When its team returned from the US, the mission decided to try and create a 'hybrid Washington-Hague system'. The 'Hague' bit of the system was the wide use of 'panic buttons'. In the main, the British decided to copy what the Americans had already done. The Diplomatic Protection Group (DPG) was created within the Metropolitan Police on the model of the US EPS.[146] Once established, both the EPS and the DPG were inundated with demands for increased security that they could not satisfy.[147]

In the British case, the experience of trying to protect diplomats flowed back into prime ministerial protection. In 1974, Edward Heath lost the general election: the victor, Harold Wilson, retired as prime minister in April 1976. Thus, two recent prime ministers ceased to enjoy high office, and the protection it entailed, in quick succession.[148] Before 1976, such former prime ministers had expected relatively few post-office privileges. The state only protected serving prime ministers, the leader of the opposition, and very senior ministers because 'until very recently ex Ministers were not regarded as at risk'. Wilson, however, demanded, on security grounds, that he – and Heath – should keep his government car, his chauffeur, his security detail, and have all his security organised and paid for by the state.[149] Callaghan agreed to Wilson's demands. Heath and Wilson also got official 'panic buttons' on the same model as ambassadors.[150]

Initially, officials hoped that the extension of counter-assassination security would be little more than a short-term response to an immediate threat.[151] But when the police tried to withdraw protection, the two ex-prime ministers objected.[152] They argued that high-value individuals should be protected constantly from the threat of assassination, and in perpetuity.[153] Once more, Callaghan agreed. Assassination protection outside the chain of constitutional command became a permanent feature of the British political system some dozen years later than it had in the United States.[154]

Some pressures also came from overseas. It occurred to Richard Nixon in 1973, following the assassination of Cleo Noel, that Americans overseas might need, and want, security. 'I just wonder,' he said of US ambassadors and 'people in critical posts', 'if you can just frankly expect these poor bastards to go over there.'[155] Henry Kissinger believed that there was now 'an argument for concentrating . . . on the security of our officials.'[156] However, when the State Department appointed its first Security Coordinator in 1975, he was 'primarily concerned with the protection of foreign officials' in the USA.[157]

Kissinger, on the other hand, as the President's National Security Advisor, was very particular when it came to his own personal security. In the spring of 1972, the White House Counsel, John Dean, set out to establish Secret Service protection for Kissinger, about whom the USSS was not, legally, supposed to concern itself. The relevant 1970 statute had a clause 'permitting the Secret Service, at the direction of the President, to protect the person of official representatives of the United States performing special missions abroad'. The Office of Security in the Department of State had a broader authority to 'protect official representatives . . . of the United States attending international conferences, or performing special missions'. The law allowed one department to ask another department for assistance. If Kissinger was grandfathered in as a State Department protectee – he, after all, performed plenty of 'special missions' abroad – the State Department could then ask the Treasury for Secret Service help in protecting him: but this would only cover 'special missions', not the 'routine protection' Kissinger wanted. The best that the White House legal team could offer was an arguable, if tortured, defence for giving Kissinger Secret Service protection of the kind enjoyed by Vice President Agnew.[158] On that basis, Kissinger got his Secret Service detail. He made sure that he kept it. When Kissinger himself became Secretary of State in 1973, thus explicitly qualifying for protection from the State Department Office of Security, he didn't consider that protection was good enough for him.[159]

Kissinger retained his Secret Service protection until he left office in 1977. It was a sore point in Washington. As the director of the Secret Service remarked, 'I find it pretty well common knowledge there is not actual authority for the Secret Service to serve you in this capacity.'[160] Kissinger's successors as national security advisor, notably Zbigniew Brzezinski, were refused Secret Service protection details; his successors as secretary of state reverted to State Department security.[161]

SPLINTER GROUPS

Apart from Kissinger, the American government provided little protection to officials working overseas on its behalf, despite the palpable sense of danger that many US diplomats expressed.[162] The Soviet ambassador in Buenos Aires – which Kissinger visited in early 1975 – made the habit of mocking both the Americans' need for security and their failure to provide it.[163]

The Argentines, very well versed in the technicalities of assassination, observed that the Americans did not use properly armoured vehicles and drove around as if they were on a meet-and-greet mission.[164] British investigations into the assassination of Sir Richard Sykes, ambassador in The Hague, in 1979 confirmed that an official without effective protection was a sitting duck.[165] Sykes was in the ambassadorial Rolls-Royce, along with his chauffeur and a female secretary, when he was murdered. The PIRA used equipment much less advanced than that deployed by assassins in Argentina: two handguns, a Colt revolver and a 9mm self-loading pistol. The assassins fired eight shots. 'The Embassy Rolls,' Sykes's shocked deputy reported, 'was generally regarded here as "bullet-proof". This description is quite wrong ... the door panels were fitted with armour plating. These are designed to stop almost any bullet; yet the windows of the car were only "bullet resistant". Even to describe them in this way would be inaccurate, as I can testify from seeing the Rolls after attack. The glass had no effect on the force of the bullets fired.'[166]

In 1976, when the US ambassador Francis Meloy was assassinated in Beirut – probably the most dangerous posting for a US diplomat in the world – he had no effective protection. He was being driven in a standard saloon car by a Lebanese chauffeur/bodyguard armed with a 9mm pistol. Subsequent investigations suggested that even that single bodyguard had probably been working for the assassins (although they murdered him to cover their tracks).[167] It was the British who had to get Meloy's corpse out of Beirut in a heavily armed convoy variously protected by the PLO, the Libyans, and Syrian-backed irregulars known as the Saiqa.[168]

It was only under the Carter administration that new protocols were developed for the protection of an ambassador under 'extraordinary' threat. Such an ambassador was to have an armoured car and a team of four State Department security – SY – agents, in a similarly armoured follow car.[169] At the same time, the Callaghan government in Britain hired a private security firm, founded by former SAS personnel, to take over the security of ambassadors judged to be at extraordinary risk. At the end of 1979, those were the ambassadors in Beirut, The Hague, Kampala and San Salvador, each with a two- or four-man team.[170]

The 1970s was a decade in which much happened but little was done. By the end of the decade, senior politicians and officials were willing to admit they had a problem; they just didn't have many good solutions. One solution that had implicitly been adopted was the old imperial ideal of doing little. The price of leadership in a liberal, open, democratic society was an acceptable level of assassination. The advantages for the many far outweighed the demerits for the few. However, this no longer seemed convincing to those who saw themselves as being under direct threat. It was left to new leadership in the 1980s to make western society less open but the political and administrative elite more secure.

10

LONDON KILLING
Acceptance, 1980–1990

For the west, the assassination world shifted most profoundly in the 1980s. Faced with an increasing number of assassination conspiracies, the western political elite changed its own status, way of living and structural relationship to other citizens.[1] The western approach to assassination in the 1980s was to secure the elite while leaving the populace not much better protected against mass casualty terrorism. These changes were not often broadcast: the 1980s was a decade of action rather than words. Kenneth Baker attested that, by the time he became Home Secretary in 1990, five of his friends in British Conservative politics – Richard Sharples, Ross McWhirter, Airey Neave, Anthony Berry, his bridge partner, and Ian Gow, his near neighbour in Sussex – had already been assassinated. Baker claimed that none of the assassinations changed government policy, not reflecting that, by right of his specific cabinet positions, he played a significant role in transforming security over the decade.[2]

The 1980s also marked the effective end of the Sarajevo era. Some states abandoned their reluctance to make assassination a cause of war. Israel invaded Lebanon in 1982 on the grounds that Palestinians had attempted to assassinate its ambassador in London. The United States attacked Libya in 1986, and attempted to assassinate its leader, because Libya had been behind a series of attacks targeting America and its allies.

In neither case did the real cause of the conflict map on to the titular casus belli. However, both the Israelis and the Americans made the same calculation as the Austro-Hungarians of 1914: assassination would give them good cover for the disproportionate application of force. They were, of course, on rather firmer ground than the Habsburg empire. The Israelis calculated that they had already cowed regional powers enough to ensure that none would risk war for the sake of either Lebanon or the PLO. The Americans were confident that no other power would risk challenging a superpower on behalf of Libya. In these regards their gambles proved successful. Despite appearances, what emerged from the Middle East crises of 1982 and 1986 was not division but rather a shared understanding of the threat of assassination and the security system needed to deal with such. This understanding spread to other democracies, most notably India. Indeed, the challenges faced in South Asia did much to leaven western bickering about policy in the Middle East.

Britain was the most likely western power, other than the USA, to be willing to confront assassination. By contrast, when President Mitterrand of France was elected in May 1981, he initiated the policy of 'sanctuary' for assassins. He granted amnesty to domestic political murderers from Corsica and Brittany as part of a terrorism amnesty law.[3] In 1982, his government struck a deal with Abu Nidal to refrain from assassinations in France in return for very light sentences for the assassins who had killed the PLO's representative in Paris, Izz ad Din Khalaq, in March 1978. Italy and Germany pursued similar policies.[4]

However, there were strict limits to even Britain's willingness to tweak the nose of international procurers of assassination. The British government's analysis of assassination conspiracies involved the explicit, if reluctant, admission that Britain, like all the other European powers, had become a vulnerable and penetrated society. The diplomat Sir Anthony Parsons famously remarked to Margaret Thatcher, in the context of Black June, that 'our principal liability is that we have no leverage over any of the parties to any of the disputes which bedevil the Middle East'.[5] Mrs Thatcher herself admitted that she 'was not sure how much influence we can realistically bring to bear'.[6]

In June 1982, a Black June assassin shot the Israeli ambassador in London, Shlomo Argov: he survived but was paralysed for life. There seemed no doubt that Britain had a Black June assassination team working for Iraqi intelligence on its hands.[7] Nevertheless, the Thatcher government chose to stick to the line that Saddam Hussein was not the architect of the Argov assassination.[8] In December 1982, the British government declared that neither SIS nor MI5 had been able to establish 'clear proof of a direct link between the group and the Iraqi Embassy'.[9] The prosecution of Argov's attackers was carefully orchestrated to prove that there had been an assassination conspiracy organised by the 'Abu Nidal group' while not mentioning that the assassination weapon had been supplied by Iraqi intelligence.[10] There was little mileage, British officials pointed out, in denying Saddam Hussein a veil of respectability, lest someone 'might reasonably argue . . . we should do something about it'.[11]

Although the Americans were often critical of British pusillanimity, President Reagan was in truth content.[12] Both governments wished to cosy up to Barzan Tikriti, Saddam's brother, the head of Iraqi intelligence and Abu Nidal's controller.[13] With the British adopting a supine posture, it was the Americans who took the Black June issue to its short-term conclusion.[14] In early October 1983, the State Department issued a public statement that it had 'no reason to believe that the Government of Iraq has supported acts of international terrorism'. Iraq would thus be eligible to buy arms for use in its war against Iran.[15] In response, Saddam announced that he would end all Iraqi subsidies to Black June and expel Abu Nidal from Iraq.[16] In December 1983, Donald Rumsfeld, the former secretary of defense, arrived in Baghdad to inaugurate a new era in cordial US–Iraqi relations. The British accepted that the Baghdad–Black June nexus had been broken.[17] The news 'was very welcome in London'.[18]

However, British intelligence did warn that Abu Nidal at bay probably meant more rather than fewer assassinations.[19] In 1984, Black June assassinated two British diplomats, one in Athens and one in Bombay. In both cases, there was contemporary speculation – including by the Greek and Indian police – that the murdered men were SIS officers acting under diplomatic cover, although the British state always denied this was the case.[20] Indeed, the British government attempted to say as little about these cases as was possible, including in intelligence-service-to-intelligence-service exchanges.[21]

In March 1984, Kenneth Whitty – an official of the British Council in Athens who was dual-hatted as the first secretary (cultural affairs) in the British embassy – was giving his colleagues a lift home in his Ford Fiesta. The Fiesta was not a vehicle an official would choose if they felt threatened. An assassin stepped up to the car and shot Whitty three times at short range with a 9mm pistol. Another British Council employee in the car subsequently also died of their wounds. The Greek security police's recovery of the pistol in August 1984 – and confirmation that it had been bought in London in 1977 from a gun dealer well known for equipping terrorists – did stir the British intelligence agencies out of their 'let sleeping dogs lie' attitude.[22] Not that it did them much good since they had gathered no useful intelligence by the time of the next assassination.[23]

Assassins shot Percy Norris, British Deputy High Commissioner in Bombay, also in his car, also with a 9mm pistol, in November 1984. In the Norris case, his driver was weaving through Bombay traffic, at relatively high speed, as he took Norris from his home to work.[24] London warned British missions overseas 'that a well trained and effective terrorist organisation capable of carrying out professional operations in widely divergent areas' was at work.[25] Like the Greeks, the Indians pulled out 'all the stops' in tracing the assassins to the Middle East. As with Whitty, as with Norris, the British government was only marginally grateful for the effort. The Abu Nidal problem had been 'solved' and they did not wish any publicity otherwise.[26]

Given the west's deep reluctance to make a public spectacle of assassination conspiracies in the early 1980s, Muammar Qaddafi had to work diligently to create such a spectacle. The Qaddafi problem was supposed to have been solved at the end of the 1970s. At the beginning of the 1980s, when they were not focused on Iraq, US eyes were on much more pressing assassination issues than those involving Qaddafi.[27] Assassination in Latin America devoured media attention in 1980.[28]

Despite this year of focus on Central America, Qaddafi still succeeded in making assassination the defining characteristic of his regime.[29] His new representatives in London charged that the British were harbouring

1. State Assassination: Orlando Letelier was assassinated by a Chilean intelligence service in-car bomb, Washington, DC, September 1976.

2. Fantasy Assassin: the actor Eddie Redmayne plays the part of the Jackal, a fictional professional assassin, 2024.

3. Celebrated Assassins: a post-independence statue commemorating the assassins who killed Lieutenant-Colonel Norman Simpson in Calcutta, December 1930. The statue stands outside the office building where Simpson was murdered.

4. Martyred Assassins: the Mexican state executed those involved in an attempted assassination of Álvaro Obregón, November 1927. The men shot included Miguel Agustín Pro, SJ: Pope John Paul II beatified Pro in 1988.

5. Repurposed Assassin: the controversial plaque celebrating Gavrilo Princip, who had assassinated Archduke Franz Ferdinand in Sarajevo in 1914, was removed by the German occupiers of Yugoslavia and taken to Berlin as a trophy of war in 1941, where it was presented with considerable ceremony.

6. Hunted Assassins: a wanted poster for the assassins who had murdered the German politician Matthias Erzberger in the Black Forest, Germany, in August 1921.

7. Theatre of Victimhood: Benito Mussolini sported a plaster in public after being shot in the face by a would-be assassin in April 1926.

8. Consequential Assassination: the scene near Mukden in Manchuria after the Japanese army had assassinated Marshal Zhang Zuolin by blowing up his train, June 1928.

9. The Wages of Assassination: the body of King Alexander of Yugoslavia after he was assassinated in Marseilles, October 1934.

10. Theatre of Totalitarianism: Nikolai Rutkovsky's 1937 Soviet propaganda portrait of Stalin mourning at the open casket of the assassinated Sergei Kirov who had been killed in Leningrad in December 1934.

11. Honourable Assassin: a poster for the 1941 Hollywood movie adaptation of Geoffrey Household's 1939 thriller, *Rogue Male*. In the novel, an Englishman attempts to assassinate a fictional European dictator – plainly meant to be Hitler – and then has to evade the secret policeman hunting him in turn.

12. Assassination as Propaganda: Terence Cuneo's painting for the British Ministry of Information celebrating the assassination of the head of the Nazi RHSA and Deputy Reich Protector of Bohemia and Moravia, Reinhard Heydrich in Prague, May 1942.

13. Theatre of Totalitarianism Again: Hitler presides over Heydrich's state funeral in Berlin, June 1942.

14. Tools of the Trade: British assassination kit comprising a Welrod integrally silenced pistol and an Astra 300, both in .32 calibre. A kit of this kind was issued for at least one operation in Germany in 1945.

15. Price of Protection: the body of Leslie Coffelt, a White House Police officer, shot by Puerto Rican assassins attempting to reach President Truman in Blair House, Washington, DC, November 1950.

16. Performing Protection: US Secret Service agents piled onto a would-be assassin after he had shot and badly wounded President Reagan, Washington, DC, March 1981.

17. Soft Target: Ian Gow, a Conservative MP, was assassinated by the PIRA with a bomb in his car, which was parked in the driveway of his house in Sussex, July 1990.

18. Death of an Assassin: the head of the Iraqi intelligence service, Tahir Jalil Habbush, holding up a photo of Abu Nidal's corpse, August 2002. As head of the eponymous Abu Nidal Organization, the Palestinian had organised many assassinations.

19. Hard Target: the scene in Beirut after Hezbollah had assassinated Rafiq Hariri, the former prime minister of Lebanon, with a large external car bomb triggered by a suicide bomber, February 2005.

20. Protective Detail: armoured men debussing from a Lenco Bearcat, by the 2000s the standard backup vehicle for a personal protective detail operating in a high-threat environment, during an active shooter drill.

21. The Name Says It All:
a US Reaper drone launching a Hellfire missile.

22. Personality Target: purportedly a photograph of the burning corpse of Qassem Soleimani taken by US Special Operations Forces after a US drone strike, Baghdad, January 2020.

23. Return of the Assassin: President Putin and an honour guard welcoming the GRU assassin Vadim Krasikov back to Russia after his release from a German jail in a prisoner swap, August 2024.

24. Assassination Survivor: Donald Trump after being shot and wounded by a sniper, Butler, PA, July 2024.

Libyan dissidents with plans to assassinate the colonel. They produced a 'target list' of such dangerous dissidents in the UK. At the same time, his supporters attacked the US embassy in Tripoli.[30] Both the British and Americans assumed that Qaddafi was posturing and that, after a flurry of activity, he would want 'to build a better relationship'. The Carter government soon changed its mind. In February 1980, it withdrew its chargé, Bill Eagleton, from Libya because he was at risk of assassination. In April 1980, the State Department expelled two Libyan diplomats from the USA in 'light of intelligence suggesting intimidation and possible violence against Libyan students in the US'.[31] The British took no such action, although they possessed similar intelligence. A few days later, a gunman assassinated the journalist Mustafa Mohammed Ramadan at Regent's Park mosque: Ramadan's name had been one of those featured on the 'target list' of November 1979. The assassins carried documents that described them as 'government officials'.[32]

Mrs Thatcher's senior ministers all agreed that the assassination of Ramadan had been 'instigated by the Libyan authorities through their mission here'. They counselled, however, against challenging the head of the Libyan People's Bureau, an operative of Qaddafi's secret service, Musa Kusa. Instead, they cooked up a plan to send the head of the Joint Intelligence Committee to Libya to ask Qaddafi to call off his assassins. On the day that Mrs Thatcher agreed to the plan, the Libyans assassinated a second dissident in London, Mahmoud Nafa.[33] The British envoy was despatched anyway, and in public the government described the double assassination as 'harassment'.[34]

In response to the assassinations in London, however, the Reagan administration expelled six Libyans from the US on the grounds that they were part of an 'international campaign of terrorism'. In issuing the order, the State Department noted that 'scores' of Libyan students in the USA had been threatened with 'extermination'.[35] In London itself, it was Musa Kusa, rather than the British government, who engineered his own expulsion. He told the press that 'Libyan Revolutionary Committees based in Britain had decided to kill two of Colonel Qadhafi's opponents in London and that he approved of this'.[36] At that point, ministers felt they had little choice but to declare him persona non grata.[37]

In October 1980, a Libyan dissident, Faisal Zagallai, was attacked in the college town of Fort Collins, Colorado. Despite being shot twice in the head from close range, Zagallai survived the assassination attempt. The assassin proved to be an associate of Edwin Wilson and Frank Terpil, former CIA officers who worked for Libya.[38] The CIA rogues ran much of their operation out of the UK.[39] The FBI arrested the would-be assassin. A few days later, President Reagan approved the decision to close the Libyan People's Bureau in Washington. Reagan and his advisers saw the closure as part of a plan, 'meant to put Qadhafi on notice that the US is taking a new and more forceful approach to our dealings with Tripoli'.[40]

In this plan, the assassination strand and the geopolitical strand were seen as distinct. The State Department's Director of Policy Planning, Paul Wolfowitz, was particularly insistent on this point.[41] The assassination of an American ambassador would help 'dramatize' the need for action against Libya, but putting too much stress on assassination risked narrowing 'the frame of reference of "provocation" and "response" to such an extent that we leave ourselves open to the politically costly charge of having overreacted'.[42] The Reagan government chose to challenge Libya because it had 'become a strategic threat to US interests both in the Middle East and Africa'.[43] Whereas the British were reluctant to take any significant action against assassination, the Americans saw assassination as a potential excuse for taking such action.[44]

The US provoked an airborne incident over the Gulf of Sidra in August 1981, shooting down Libyan air force jets with ease. In the short term, as even those keenest to smell out Libyan malfeasance admitted, the assassinations did indeed largely stop.[45] This was despite black propaganda to the contrary.[46] The Americans faked a Libyan assassination squad targeting President Reagan.[47] The 'major disadvantage of the bold approach, however disguised' was that it risked scaring off 'some Western European allies'.[48] These allies included Margaret Thatcher's Britain. When Reagan's Secretary of State, Al Haig, outlined the 'Reagan assassination plot' to the British Foreign Secretary, Lord Carrington, the latter was 'dismissive'.[49] As President Reagan remarked, neither allies nor the American public believed what American intelligence agencies said about assassination.[50]

Meanwhile, other genuine assassinations temporarily deprived both Qaddafi and his enemies of the oxygen of publicity. In May 1981, a Turkish assassin shot and badly wounded Pope John Paul II with a 9mm pistol. Initially, the Italians declared that this was no conspiracy, but rather the act of a 'fanatical, unrestrained and crazy terrorist who committed the assassination attempt on the head of the church as a lone actor'. The Italian courts, however, rejected that claim in September 1981, declaring that there had plainly been a well-organised conspiracy.[51] The trouble was that no-one succeeded in unravelling that conspiracy.[52]

Islamist extremists linked to the Egyptian Muslim Brotherhood definitely assassinated the president of Egypt, Anwar Sadat, in October 1981. Like the Pope, Sadat was a core US foreign policy ally.[53] As Sadat was taking the salute at a military parade in Cairo, four soldiers jumped off one of the parade trucks and shot him in the neck and face at close range. As everyone ducked for cover, a soldier ran into the stands and emptied the magazine of his assault rifle into Sadat's body. Unlike the attack on the pope, few were surprised at the attempt on Sadat's life, although many were horrified by the method and the feebleness of supposedly overwhelming Egyptian security.[54]

In 1983, the leader of another of the United States' allies, Ferdinand Marcos of the Philippines, procured the assassination of his main political rival, Benigno Aquino, as the latter attempted to return from exile.[55] No-one believed Marcos's story that Aquino had been assassinated by Communists, except the CIA.[56]

The next month, the leader of North Korea, Kim Il Sung, attempted to procure the assassination of yet another of America's key allies, President Chun Doo-hwan of South Korea, when he visited Burma. The North Korean assassins attempted to use the mausoleum of an assassinated leader – Aung San – as their murder weapon, planting a bomb in the roof with the aim of collapsing the structure on Chun. In the event, it was the South Korean foreign minister, Lee Beom-seok, who was slain.[57] Unlike the baroque cover-up in the Philippines, the Burmese conducted a swift and effective investigation, catching the assassins and laying the conspiracy at the door of the North Koreans to near-universal international acceptance.[58]

However, even against such stiff competition, Qaddafi managed to push himself forward once more as the face of international assassination. His assassination campaign visibly restarted in February 1984 when a 'Committee of Revolutionary Students' took over the Libyan People's Bureau in London. As the State Department's intelligence department commented, 'England, with the largest Libyan population in Europe, was the natural place for Qadhafi to make his point.'[59] On 7 March 1984, the British intelligence services issued a specific warning that the 'LPB may have assassins at its disposal and [a] stock of weapons'.[60] Officials assessed the most likely threat as a rerun of the 1980 assassinations.[61]

However, the actual murder that tipped Anglo-Libyan relations into crisis was that of a young British policewoman, Yvonne Fletcher, who was controlling a dissident demonstration outside the LPB: she was killed by a shot from within the building.[62] Margaret Thatcher was in Lisbon at the time of the shooting but called London to instruct her ministers that the best solution was to put 'all the Libyan staff on an aircraft to Libya'. She had no confidence that the police and intelligence services would be able to identify the shooter, or at least identify him in a way that would stand up in a court since much of her intelligence came from intercepted communications.[63] The Home Secretary, Leon Brittan, denounced the murder as a 'barbaric outrage', while making the proposal in private that the Libyans should be able to take their weapons with them when they went.[64] The gap between British rhetoric and action was not lost on the press who pointed out to Brittan that he was letting the Libyans off 'scot-free'.[65] The problem throughout for the British government was that the Libyans were holding British embassy staff in Tripoli as hostages for the release of its assassination squad. The crisis was resolved, as Thatcher had initially instructed: the British returned to London and the Libyans returned to Tripoli.[66]

This was the context in which, over the spring and summer of 1985, the Reagan administration attempted to weave together a coherent account of assassination, as the key to understanding contemporary world affairs. This attempt operated on multiple levels: bilateral intelligence exchanges, multilateral diplomacy and public rhetoric.[67] The account was relatively straightforward. Assassination was not 'simply the erratic work of a small group of fanatics'.[68] In the past five years it had become 'an attack on all western civilization', co-ordinated by malign state actors.[69] Of those malign state actors, Libya was the most vulnerable. Libya was thus the 'crucial candidate for deterrent retribution . . . irrespective of whether an immediate linkage' was established between its activities and a particular assassination.[70]

The problem with this account was that very few policymakers outside the United States accepted it. There was widespread acceptance among western governments that assassination was an escalating threat. No-one had any trouble in believing that Colonel Qaddafi had assassinated numerous Libyan exiles and had tried to assassinate rival political leaders in the Middle East and Africa. However, Libya was not behind assassination on a global level: emulation was as plausible an explanation as direct influence. Most damaging of all, as Margaret Thatcher pointed out, America played favourites in defining the global assassination conspiracy.[71]

In the end, it was the shift of the Libyan regime from assassination to mass casualty attacks that finally tipped President Reagan's hand on the decision to launch a direct assault on Libya.[72] The Americans acted only with the support of the British government.[73] Most members and supporters of the Thatcher government nevertheless believed that an American air attack on Libya, launched from British soil, would increase rather than decrease the risk that 'British targets will be singled out by Libyan hit-men'.[74] Indeed, in the wake of the American bombing of Tripoli in April 1986, terrorist groups in Beirut murdered both their British and American hostages.[75] Colonel Qaddafi also supplied the PIRA with large quantities of the plastic explosive Semtex in direct retaliation for the Tripoli raid: the first attack with the new weapon was the assassination of Sir Maurice Gibson, Lord Chief Justice of Northern Ireland.[76]

There is little doubt that US NSC officials conceived the attack on Libya itself as an assassination attempt on Qaddafi. They were supported by members of Reagan's cabinet, including the Secretary of State, George Shultz, who said he wanted Qaddafi 'put in a box'.[77] To their frustration, they were thwarted by other parts of the US system. As was so often the case, amateurs thought of assassination as a 'surgical strike'.

In 1986, the USAF and the other US armed forces begged to differ. They designed a classic air operation that privileged defence suppression and force reduction: they did not want any pilots being shot down and captured over Libyan territory. For months, they were less than 'responsive on the targeting issue'.[78]

In the end, Qaddafi was not attacked, although members of his family were among the casualties of US bombing. In the public sphere, the US received no support from its allies, apart from Britain. The Italian government denounced the attack and, like the British, argued that it was likely to lead to deadly retaliation, not least because Abu Nidal was working for Libya after his temporary exit from Baghdad. Germany piously rejected the use of force. The French government accused the Americans of perpetuating 'cycles of violence'.[79]

However, when it came to counter-assassination, those responses were apt to be misleading. The attack on Libya did not derail the growing integration of the western counter-assassination community, and probably hastened its consolidation. French military counter-terrorist leaders sent back-channel messages of support to the Americans: 'congratulations; great job; well done'.[80] In June 1986, a French counter-terrorism delegation came to Washington for a broad-ranging discussion about co-operation against the Libyans, the Palestinians and the Iranians.[81] In its post-mortem, the CIA concluded that the American bombing of Libya was 'indirectly stimulating closer cooperation between Washington and West European countries'. A 'heightened sensitivity to the Libyan terrorist threat among security forces worldwide has prompted increased vigilance and international cooperation in monitoring Libyan operatives, particularly in Western Europe'.[82]

Britain was the last major power to fit into the western counter-assassination community. Until the mid-1980s, other western countries treated the UK as an assassination pariah. It had shared that status, since Franco's death and the democratisation of Spain, with Turkey.[83] Britain and Turkey had terrorist threats that dwarfed those of other European nations. Between the late 1960s and the late 1980s, nearly three thousand people were killed by terrorists in Britain. Over the same period, the Turks lost nearly seven thousand people. The comparative figures for European states were four hundred deaths in Italy, just over a hundred deaths in France and one hundred deaths in West Germany.[84]

Both Britain and Turkey had a specific assassination threat nested within their general terrorism problem. So-called 'active service units' of the PIRA and the INLA posed a direct threat to British officials not only in Britain but also in Europe. Although Turkey's terrorism problems were driven by Kurds, with an admixture of far-left and Islamist groups, its assassination problem derived from an Armenian terrorist group based in Beirut, the Justice Commandos of the Armenian Genocide (JCAG) which specialised in the murder of Turkish diplomats.[85] The general feeling among Western European governments was that Britain and Turkey had brought these disasters upon themselves through repression of ethnic groups.[86] Britain did have some sympathisers within the security forces of European states, but these allies did not always help the cause, often alienating their own political masters.[87]

Of course, Britain was always closer to its western allies than Turkey was to the same countries. The assassination events of late 1984 brought the UK into full alignment with those allies. In October 1984, a very large PIRA bomb exploded near Margaret Thatcher's hotel room in Brighton. A PIRA Active Service Unit had planted the bomb in the hotel in September 1984 and set a timer running to explode when Thatcher would be in residence for the Conservative Party annual conference. The bomb was designed to pancake the floors of the hotel, sending those below to their deaths from falling or from being crushed by rubble. Although her room was wrecked, Margaret Thatcher escaped unhurt: other cabinet ministers, however, were seriously wounded, and hotel guests were killed. The dead included the Conservative MP Sir Anthony Berry. Still dressed in her ballgown, Mrs Thatcher behaved with notable calm. She assembled her cabinet and security officials in a nearby police training college and told them that she would make her scheduled conference speech later in the morning.[88]

However shocking, the Thatcher assassination attempt proved not to be an isolated event. Only nineteen days later, the other female prime minister with a global profile, Indira Gandhi of India, was assassinated by her own Sikh guards. Gandhi was walking through her compound in Delhi to meet the British actor Peter Ustinov. Her senior close-protection officer was talking to Ustinov to prepare the meeting. In his absence, the first Sikh assassin shot her with his revolver. When she fell, the second assassin emptied the magazine of his sub-machine gun into her body. No-one could survive such an onslaught. Other guards arrested the assassins, took them to a guardhouse and shot them, although one survived. There was plainly a conspiracy, but no-one knew how far it reached and if there would be further attacks, particularly on Gandhi's son, Rajiv.[89] The immediate British government reaction was: 'This was a grave event which again demonstrated the onset of a phase of violence in world affairs.'[90] There were operational similarities between Britain and India, not least a protection system run by each capital's police force – the Metropolitan Police's Special Branch and Delhi Police's Special Security District – that was at odds with the national security intelligence service – MI5 and the Intelligence Bureau.[91] One of Margaret Thatcher's first major public engagements after her own brush with death was to attend Gandhi's funeral and to hold talks with Rajiv Gandhi. She took with her the leaders of the opposition parties in parliament as well as her predecessor as prime minister, James Callaghan. During her press conferences, Mrs Thatcher was repeatedly asked about the Brighton bomb and replied by describing the support she had received from Mrs Gandhi.[92] She criticised BBC coverage for giving a platform to Sikh activists denouncing Gandhi as an oppressor.[93] Tellingly, Thatcher also wanted to discuss Ireland with the US Secretary of State, George Shultz, at the Gandhi ceremony.[94] Britain and India co-operated closely on assassination.[95] For other statesmen, too, they came as a pair.[96]

Immediately after the Thatcher attack, Ronald Reagan wrote that, 'in the context of our special relationship, I have directed that my experts be available to work with yours to assist in bringing the perpetrators to justice. If you wish, we can have our experts discuss further cooperative measures when they convene next month in London.'[97] That meeting took place in the wake of the Gandhi assassination. In this case, the president was not engaging in mere political rhetoric. His offer was specifically framed to mean co-operation against the PIRA within the terms of UK–USA intelligence-sharing agreements that bound together GCHQ in Britain and the NSA in America. It was this aspect of intelligence collaboration with regard to Ireland of which the Reagan administration had hitherto been shy, and the British regarded Reagan's offer as a significant breakthrough.[98] Thereafter, British and Americans held 'semi-annual and very frank talks' on counter-terrorism, with the Irish situation included.[99] The Europeans, too, acknowledged that Britain should no longer be regarded as an outlier when it came to assassination.[100]

The broader effects of the mid-1980s counter-assassination effort, as well as some elements of detail, can be pieced together although governments remained notably tight-lipped on the subject.

In Britain, still relatively new in office, Margaret Thatcher had dispensed with the temporary services of the former SAS mercenaries whom her predecessor had employed, and instead deployed military 'guarding teams' to provide security for at-risk British officials overseas. One of the problems with hiring mercenaries for protection was that they could equally well turn their hand to assassination. The French were hardly amused when anti-government forces planning assassinations in Togo threatened to compromise the security of President Mitterrand on a visit to Africa in 1983. Some of those involved were British mercenaries.[101] The responsibility for overseas security thus fell to the British Army and the Ministry of Defence as a permanent commitment of the British state.[102] At the same time, the Home Office expanded Special Branch to provide bodyguard services to a much wider range of British and foreign VIPs in the UK.[103] In 1982, protection became a permanent command within the Met.[104] Other countries adopted parallel measures.[105]

The top level of protection for an overseas dignitary in London was a Special Branch protection team, a Special Branch armoured Jaguar with a specialist driver, a Diplomatic Protection Group fixed post outside the embassy, a DPG motorcycle escort between the embassy and the diplomatic residence, and DPG mobile patrols around all relevant buildings.[106] This level of security was pegged to what the French could offer in Paris.[107]

The system was severely tested by the attack on Shlomo Argov, the Israeli ambassador, inside the Dorchester Hotel in 1982. His Special

Branch team failed to stop the gunman getting through. On the other hand, they hunted down and shot the assassin, and the police rounded up all members of the assassination squad. The government ordered even greater protection in the wake of the Argov attack.[108] The Metropolitan Police raised its highest protection level.[109] The new level of security was pegged to improve on the US offer to foreign diplomats.[110]

At the same time, the US upped its own game on other aspects of security. Notoriously, in March 1981, a gunman had shot and nearly killed President Reagan, showing how ineffective the US Secret Service remained. The reform of US presidential security after the shooting was probably more fundamental even than that occasioned by the murder of President Kennedy in 1963.[111] Where the Americans went, others followed. The use of helicopters for VIP assassination security became standard in the mid-1980s, for instance.[112] It was perhaps naive of President Reagan to be surprised that, at an international meeting in New York, the attendance was ten times the guest list, swelled by armed bodyguards from many nations.[113]

In the early summer of 1984, President Reagan visited Britain. Security culture definitively coalesced. The previous year, Vice President George Bush had made a similar visit. According to the UK's 1968 Firearms Act, it was illegal for foreign bodyguards to carry weapons and ammunition in London. The Americans said no bodyguards, no visits by senior members of the Reagan administration. Bush's Secret Service detail had been let in with some – extra-legal – rules of engagement.[114] During the Reagan visit, it became clear that the US was ignoring both the law and the rules of engagement. Three American agents were stopped and searched at Heathrow: they were found not only to be illegally armed under the terms of the act but also to be casually carrying live ammunition in their hand luggage in contravention of the rules. The incident 'did not inspire confidence in the Americans' adherence to the terms of the concession which they were given'.[115] The French, the West Germans and the Dutch formally complained that the Americans were being granted special privileges. Queen Beatrix of the Netherlands was 'furious' that she was forced to visit London without her armed guards. The French said they would ban Mrs Thatcher's armed Special Branch escort team from Paris. By then, such an overseas team comprised four officers, all armed with pistols and one with a compact sub-machine gun.[116] In September 1984, the Foreign Secretary proposed that the British system should be changed.[117] A new bodyguard system that complied with American practice was agreed before the attempt to assassinate Margaret Thatcher in Brighton in October 1984. The prime minister signed off on the 'immediate implementation' of the new protocol a few days after that assassination attempt. Having had one of his bodyguards arrested for carrying an illegal weapon in June 1984, President Mitterrand and his armed protection detail were among the first to be welcomed to London under the new dispensation.[118]

Those who tried to stay outside the international security sphere became seen as outliers. Lack of competent security among the political elite was 'shocking'.[119] The most famous case was that of Olof Palme, the Prime Minister of Sweden. Decades later, the Swedes worked out that Palme had been murdered on a street in Stockholm in 1986 by a lone middle-ranking business executive using an expensive revolver to work out some unknowable existential grudge.[120] They had also fixed on the lone gunman thesis in the late 1980s but accused the wrong man.[121] At the time of the assassination, however, the investigators seriously canvassed just about every known international assassination threat, Palestinian, Kurdish, even Chilean. In the belief that Olof Palme was a towering international statesman, they thoroughly mobilised the entire western assassination security network.[122] In doing so, they also revealed what a dysfunctional western security system might look like. Its 'ineptitude', the Swedish report on the case concluded, 'is difficult to believe'.[123]

Palme himself had refused close protection because he was jealous of his privacy. There was no covert watch on the prime minister either: he was truly alone. Those Swedish ministers who did have bodyguards summoned and dismissed them at will. When the news of Palme's killing reached members of the Swedish cabinet, they blithely called taxis and rode into central Stockholm without protection. On the security side of the Swedish state, it was plain that few had bothered to point out the risks to their political masters. According to British diplomats, it well suited security officials to take long weekends and relaxed holidays with no-one manning the office.[124] The only person who took his own security seriously, took it too seriously. When the police officer in charge of investigating the Palme murder was removed from his position, he arranged a bizarre televised press conference to which he was accompanied by a twenty-strong bodyguard.[125]

On the other hand, the problem with the now standard western system was that it was good at focusing protection on VIPs but was much less effective as far as 'ordinary' people were concerned.[126] The new system made a clear distinction not only between VIPs and 'ordinary people', but also between VIPs and VVIPs. Its devisers knew that the most obvious response to tight security for VVIPs was for assassins to attack lower down the chain of protection.[127] In Germany, left-wing terrorists assassinated businessmen. In France, the main targets were middle-ranking defence officials.[128] Following the death of Indira Gandhi, Sikh assassins found that they could get nowhere near Rajiv Gandhi: lower-ranking Indian politicians became attractive targets. Their victims included the Congress politicians Lalit Malken and Arjun Dass, and the leader of constitutional Sikhism, Harchand Singh Longowal, as well as the high priest of the Golden Temple, Giani Sahib Singh.[129] The former Maharajah of Patiala, a close confidant of the Gandhi family, resigned from Congress due to 'an understandable concern not to increase the risk of being assassinated'.[130] The British security services arrested members of Sikh terror cells in Britain in preparation for a visit by Rajiv Gandhi.[131] However, militant Sikhs hired a former member of the British army to assassinate the Sikh head of Gandhi's Congress Party in the UK, Tarsem Singh Toor.[132]

In 1985, the British state formally established three tiers of VIP-hood. Being put in the middle category caused predictable irritation and back-biting. The armed forces minister, John Stanley, hissed: 'this is fast becoming a joke. Either there is a real threat, in which case immediate action is necessary, or else we should all forget it.'[133] The lowest tier could just expect security briefings.[134] In 1990, the PIRA assassinated Ian Gow, a Conservative MP and Mrs Thatcher's former parliamentary private secretary, by placing a bomb under his car at his Sussex home. Gow was in the lowest category in the three-tier system, falling 'outside the net where some security measures are provided at Government expense'.[135] Ministers who did have protection were very shaken by the spectre of assassination creeping closer to the barely protected, not least because they had little practical to offer.[136]

Western nations had been visibly distinct in their attitude to assassination at the start of the 1980s. By the end of the decade, they looked much the same. 'Standing next to my French and West German colleagues each surrounded by our respective bodyguards,' a British ambassador wrote, 'I reflected, as they did, on the political and personal havoc another well placed device would create.'[137] VVIPs moved seamlessly within an integrated security sphere, anchored by a series of world cities, most notably New York, London and Paris. It was to these cities that 'the protected' were drawn, for various reasons, including finance and health care. The core signifier of the elite was protection provided by the state: VVIPs were those with protection; anyone without protection was, by definition, not a VVIP. Western leaders had constructed a new social reality for themselves. Assassination may have had only a marginal effect on the foreign policies of the major democratic powers in the 1980s. Assassination had, however, proved very effective in shaping the political culture of the west.

11

VERY VERY IMPORTANT PEOPLE
Security, 1991–2001

It was dangerous for a politician to be excluded from the inner circle of assassination security. The most consequential and revealing assassination conspiracies of the 1990s concerned politicians so excluded: the Indian political dynast Rajiv Gandhi and the South African Black politician Nelson Mandela. The best-attested state protective service in the world in the 1990s was neither British nor American, but Indian. The best-attested state assassination service was South African.

In India, Rajiv Gandhi unwittingly created a flaw in his own security. He had personally designed the Indian prime ministerial security system in the wake of his mother's killing, setting up a Special Protection Group (SPG). However, the SPG was for the prime minister alone. Although no-one one doubted that Gandhi was the Indian politician most at risk of assassination, he lost much of his protection when he left office.[1] Only after Gandhi's assassination was full protection extended to former prime ministers.[2]

There were a lot of people who wanted to kill Rajiv Gandhi.[3] The Sikh extremists, who had killed his mother, remained a threat. There were Kashmiri militants from that disputed Indo-Pakistani borderland. There were Nepalese groups, both monarchist and Maoist, who hated Gandhi-inspired interventions by the Indian intelligence service in Nepal's domestic politics. In Sri Lanka, in whose civil war Gandhi had also tried to intervene, terrorist groups on both sides of the ethnic divide, Sinhalese and Tamil, were talking about assassination.[4] The ultimately successful conspiracy against Gandhi was hatched in Jaffna, Sri Lanka, in October 1990 on the basis that it would only be possible to assassinate him before he returned to power.[5] At the time of his death, Gandhi was on course to win the Indian general election.[6]

The Tamil Tigers were clearly capable of mounting a highly organised assassination plot in mainland India. In June 1990, for instance, they sent a six-member assassination squad to Madras, the capital of the state of Tamil Nadu, to kill K. Padmanabha, the exiled head of a rival Tamil terrorist organisation, the EPRLF. The Tigers had a highly evolved intelligence and surveillance network in Madras. The intelligence network provided the assassination squad with an exact accounting of Padmanabha's movements. The assassins waited for their target to return to his apartment, stormed the apartment building armed with assault rifles, shot Padmanabha, and then killed everyone else in his flat. The squad then made their escape from the city in cars, drove, unmolested, over two hundred miles to the coast, rendezvoused with a Tiger boat and returned safely to Sri Lanka. The firearm that killed Padmanabha was eventually recovered from the dead body of one of Gandhi's assassins.[7]

The assassination of Gandhi took place at a political rally in Tamil Nadu in May 1991. The assassin was a young woman wearing a suicide vest constructed using plastic explosive encased in TNT. She approached Gandhi as if to kiss his feet and detonated a fatal explosion. The Tamil Tigers were not the first group to use suicide bombers, but they were the group to use the method most extensively as means of penetrating tight security. Plainly, this was a technique that was available only to a few organisations. The use of a female was merely a tactical twist appropriate to the quasi-religious circumstances. However, the victim, the technique and the assassin all fixed the eyes of other protective services on Sriperumbudur, where Gandhi had died.

Although painfully obvious in retrospect, the nature of the conspiracy against Gandhi took some time to uncover.[8] The Indian police tracked down the surviving members of the assassination squad to Bangalore in August 1991, but they all committed suicide before they could be captured.[9] With all the assassins dead, the Indians turned to the question of who was to blame. This was an issue that would poison Indian politics for the rest of the decade, not least because Sonia Gandhi, Rajiv's widow, became head of Congress, whereas professional politicians, initially P.V. Narasimha Rao, took over the government. The Congress government-appointed commission of inquiry into the assassination only completed its work in 1997.[10]

The investigation of Gandhi's assassination revealed the Indian state as disorganised and sometimes corrupt. However, Indian fear of the state was as nothing to the South African.[11] It had long been suspected that the South African state made a regular habit of assassinating its opponents. Indeed, David Webster, a British academic and anti-apartheid activist, who had spent the 1980s investigating South African state assassinations, identifying sixty, was himself assassinated in Johannesburg in May 1989.[12]

The accuracy of Webster's suspicions was confirmed, and partially resolved, by a political revolution in the five years between 1989 and 1994 that led to Black majority rule and the election of Nelson Mandela as President of South Africa. As far as assassination was concerned, the first telling revelation was delivered by a former Black policeman in October 1989. Already condemned to death by the criminal courts for a 'normal' murder, he confessed that he had once been a professional assassin for the South African state, working in a police death squad commanded by a white Afrikaner, Dirk Coetzee. Coetzee immediately fled to Mauritius, then London, and started making his own confessions in the press.[13] Before Coetzee began talking, there had been 'disquieting pointers' that South Africa was a major force in world assassination, but proof 'was difficult to obtain'; now there was 'hard evidence'.[14]

Part of the problem in unpacking the South African assassination complex was that it affected each part of the state. The secret service, the armed forces and the police had each created assassination units. They stood up, renamed, reconfigured and stood down these units in a deliberately confusing manner. However, personnel flowed easily: a police unit could suddenly reappear as a military unit or vice versa. The first commission that the South African government set up to investigate assassination concluded that no action need be taken because the

South African Defence Forces (SADF) had disbanded its assassination unit, the Civil Co-operation Bureau (CCB), in July 1990. In fact, the members of the CCB were merely transferred to the SADF's Directorate of Military Intelligence's Directorate of Covert Collection. The commission had no bearing on the South African Police's (SAP) parallel assassination unit, once commanded by Coetzee, known from its base of operations as 'Vlakplaas'.[15] Vlakplaas continued with its 'counter-revolutionary operations'.[16]

In March 1991, Dirk Coetzee asked for political asylum in Britain on the grounds that he was under threat of assassination by the South African state. In April 1992, two South African military intelligence officers, one female, arrived in London to arrange his assassination. Luckily for Coetzee, the British SIS had an informant in the SAP. The assassins were arrested, held for three days, and then sent back to South Africa.[17] However, the Prime Minister, John Major, claimed that Britain did not have enough evidence to charge them, and he preferred to take up the matter informally with the President of South Africa, F.W. de Klerk.[18]

The assassination that really focused international intention was the killing of Chris Hani. Hani was murdered by a Polish member of the fascist AWB in April 1993. The story of a lone right-wing fanatic did not hold up for more than a day. The assassination weapon was a silenced semi-automatic pistol listed as 'stolen' from the SADF air force in 1990.[19] A week after the assassination, the leader of the small South African Conservative Party was arrested as the mastermind behind the conspiracy, but no-one believed that the trail ended there.[20] Faced with international scepticism about their ability to investigate the assassination, the South African police asked the British and German governments for assistance.[21]

At the time of his death, Hani held numerous roles: he was a member of the National Executive Committee of the African National Congress (ANC), the general secretary of the South African Communist Party, and commander of the ANC's paramilitary organisation, MK. More than that, however, he was the most charismatic leader of the ANC after Mandela. Indeed, many younger radicals preferred him over Mandela.[22] Hani's funeral was a moment of some danger for Mandela – political, and also personal. In the wake of the Hani assassination, the South African government finally offered personal protection details to Mandela and other ANC leaders. They accepted.[23]

The threat to well-protected leaders was less acute but still significant. In the spring of 1998, Bill Clinton's press team prepped the president for a US public television show. It was a soft-ball interview, and the press shop knew the questions beforehand. Q: 'Was there one special moment when the enormity of being President hit you?' A: 'The first time you ordered the use of military force – for retaliation against Iraq for the attempted assassination of President Bush.'[24] For the those inside the security system, the assassination plot to kill former president Bush was just as important as the more publicly impactful mass-casualty bombing of the World Trade Center in February 1993.[25] In retrospect, even that attack had been foreshadowed by the assassination of CIA officers in January 1993. The professionals were very aware of those assassinations because they themselves had to spend 'time in a safe house' as a result.[26] 'The possibility of being personally targeted,' the head of the CIA, George Tenet, wrote of the 1990s DCIs, 'was something all of us . . . lived with constantly.'[27]

Iraqi assassination plots were but one facet of the 1990s, but they pressingly reached the president's desk in the spring and early summer of 1993. In the presidential election of November 1992, Clinton had defeated the incumbent, George H.W. Bush. The defeated president, who left office in January 1993, could find some solace in his enduring international fame as a world statesman. In 1990–1, he had crushed Saddam Hussein's attempt to seize and extinguish the small, but massively wealthy, oleaginous kingdom of Kuwait, protected the larger, and even richer, oil monarchy of Saudi Arabia and, through the massive exertion of US armed might, secured America's defining role in the Middle East. Some people were appropriately grateful, hence Bush's post-presidential victory tour of Kuwait in April 1993.

Saddam Hussein was less grateful and ordered the Iraqi intelligence service to assassinate Bush as soon as he put himself within their reach. This was an attempt on a different level from the many Iraqi-sponsored assassinations of the 1980s. Those assassinations had normally been carried out by one of the many terrorist organisations that Iraqi intelligence nurtured in Baghdad, most notably Black June. The Kuwait City plot, however, was not aimed against a dissident in a distant foreign capital but against the former head of state of the main enemy in Iraqi intelligence's near abroad.[28]

Iraqi intelligence certainly had an infrastructure for such attempts. They could smuggle their agents across regional borders with ease. They had a well-organised system for producing assassination weapons: operational sections could choose from a selection of plastic explosives by checking pre-prepared requisition sheets. Luckily for former president Bush, however, the Iraqi assassins were not very effective against hardened targets. Their last major operation had been a complete failure. In 1991, Saddam had ordered the IIS to assassinate the Emir of Kuwait, Jaber al-Saba, then in exile in Saudi following the Iraqi invasion. The job was assigned to an IIS clandestine special operations section known as Unit 999. At least four assassins were sent into Saudi Arabia, three Iraqis and a Palestinian. Their training concentrated on the use of plastic explosives and the construction of car bombs. They were also well used to small arms, one of the assassins being a special forces lieutenant, another a police officer. In a nice touch, the IIS had them sign acknowledgements that their families would be punished if they betrayed the mission.[29]

The problem for the IIS was not that their assassins lacked commitment but that the Saudis and Kuwaitis were only too aware of the threat. There is no record of Unit 999 getting anywhere near royal targets. The same was true for the analogous plot against President Bush in April 1993. The Kuwaiti authorities arrested the assassination squad in possession of its car bomb. Briefed by US intelligence sources, including investigators who had just flown in from Kuwait, the *New York Times* reported in May 1993 that 'none of the 17 suspects in the case, including one who is still at large, ever got near Mr Bush during his three-day visit to Kuwait last month. But Kuwaiti authorities say members of the group, which includes 12 Iraqis, have confessed to having planned to use the car bomb . . . to kill the former President.' The public reporting was an accurate reflection of what the DCI had told Clinton in person.[30]

The Kuwaitis let the Americans do their own forensics and interrogate the assassins. Earlier assassination missions came back to expose the IIS since American investigators could compare their Kuwait City car bomb with those captured during the Gulf War. The bombs were made in the same workshop using the same plastic explosive. In any case, the two senior assassins admitted that the bombs were IIS weapons and that the whole plot had been organised by Iraqi intelligence.

In Congress there was a bipartisan consensus that the evidence against Saddam was as strong, if not stronger, than that presented to justify the attempt to kill Muammar Qaddafi with retaliatory air strikes in 1986.[31] The comparison with Ronald Reagan did not appeal to Clinton, however. He swithered for weeks, finally plumping for a spectacular but limited response in the form of air strikes on IIS headquarters in Baghdad in late June 1993. His spokesmen announced that 'the strike was an exercise in self-defense under Article 51 of the UN Charter. It was designed to damage terrorist infrastructure of the Iraqi regime, reduce its ability to promote terrorism, and deter further acts of aggression against the United States.'[32] According to Clinton, there was little doubt in his mind when he approved the attack that the orders for the assassination of Bush had come directly from Saddam Hussein. However, he had rejected a counter-attack against the presidential palace or any other location where Saddam might be found. He thought, 'under international law and based on the facts of this particular case, that the best possible target was the target of the intelligence headquarters'. 'I think it sent a very important message,' Clinton concluded.[33]

Clinton's response to the Bush assassination plot set a pattern that he followed throughout his presidency, favouring limited air strikes in response to threats, air strikes that would cause visible damage, perhaps kill people, but demonstrably avoid attacking enemy leaders. Indeed, the perils of targeting individuals were demonstrated only a few months after the attack on Baghdad when US special forces attempted to snatch the Somali militia leader Mohammed Farah Aideed. This attempt was a humiliating failure for the US military: their incompetence led to the loss of two helicopters and the filmed slaughter of US troops.[34] In the short term, although the Baghdad attack might have deterred thoughts of another presidential-level assassination – and although it was realised that Bush's visit to Kuwait had been a unique moment of vulnerability, unlikely to be repeated – it certainly did not stop Iraqi assassinations, merely pushing them back into the familiar territory of dissident elimination.[35]

Iraq was not even the main procurer of assassination in the 1990s. America's allies pointed out that the accolade should be shared equally by Sunni militants and the Shia government of Iran. A rash of assassinations of Saudi diplomats, beginning in the late 1980s, had been traced back to Iran by 1990, after a triple assassination in Bangkok. Each Saudi diplomat had been killed separately outside their home as they got in from work. The assassination weapons were very old-school: 6.35mm semi-automatic pistols.[36] Iranian assassins murdered several Kurdish dissidents in Berlin during 1992. The German authorities put out arrest warrants for named Iranian intelligence officers. The Germans claimed that the commissioners of the assassination were the 'special operations committee' of the Iranian government and even convicted the Iranian intelligence minister, Ali Fallahian, of conspiracy to murder, albeit in absentia.[37] A few weeks before the Iraqi plot against Bush became the focus of attention, one of Clinton's briefers told him baldly that 'Iran is the most active state sponsor of terrorism we face today. Iranian agents assassinate Iranian dissidents residing abroad.' Like the Iraqis, the Iranians were very active in London. Their most prominent potential victim was the British novelist Salman Rushdie, who had offended the late Ayatollah Khomeini with a literary sally against Shia Islam and received a religious death sentence in return. Unusually, the British state brought a private individual inside its VVIP protection system as a result. With some regret, the British government was vocal in criticising Iran for its assassination programme: it urged the Americans to be equally outspoken.[38] In his advocacy of the 'dual containment' of both Iraq and Iran, Tony Lake, Clinton's National Security Advisor, labelled them both 'backlash states'. The US attack on Iraq in response to the Iraqis' attempted assassination of President Bush was aimed equally, Lake claimed, towards Iran.[39]

The gravest threat, at presidential level, to one of America's key allies came from neither Iranians nor Iraqis but from Sunni Islamists. The Islamists' potential victim, Hosni Mubarak, the President of Egypt, pointed this out to western governments repeatedly and with vigour: he had been sitting next to his predecessor, Anwar Sadat, when the latter was assassinated by Islamists in 1981. He had no desire to be next.[40] The Egyptians claimed that the Americans were aiding and abetting the Islamists.[41]

The truth of some of Mubarak's charges became painfully apparent as an offshoot of the investigation into the World Trade Center (WTC) bombing in 1993. The godfather of the bombing, Sheikh Omar Abdel Rahman, was a known conspirator in the assassination of Anwar Sadat: a CIA officer, operating under consular cover in Khartoum, had nevertheless issued him with a US visa, a failing that the Americans put down to their own incompetence.[42] The Egyptian General Intelligence Service had succeeded in placing an agent amongst Rahman's followers. They knew that the sheikh's next plot was to assassinate Mubarak at the Waldorf Astoria in New York during the visit he planned to make to the USA in April 1993. Forewarned, the Egyptian head of state cancelled. The details subsequently became public during the trials of the WTC plotters. When the Americans laid their hands on the operational leader of the bombers, they discovered that *his* preferred follow-up to the World Trade Center bombing would have been the assassination of Pope John Paul II when His Holiness visited Manila in 1995.[43]

The temporary closure of their US operation did not mean that the Islamists gave up the plan to assassinate Mubarak. They finally struck in June 1995 when he was in the Ethiopian capital, Addis Ababa, for a meeting of the African Union. Mubarak was travelling through the city centre when assassins opened fire on his limousine with assault rifles. Fortunately for Mubarak, the armour plating of his limousine worked: the bullets bounced off the car although it was hit numerous times. Instead, the assassins killed Ethiopian policemen patrolling the route. The Ethiopians and Mubarak's security detail returned fire, killing two assassins. Mubarak immediately identified the conspirators as operating from Khartoum by friendly arrangement with the government of Omar al-Bashir. The Egyptians took their accusations to the United Nations in a fashion that was convincing enough to the five permanent members to win a Security Council resolution imposing sanctions on Sudan. The case brought a previously obscure name into full international gaze:

Osama bin Laden was identified as the leading Islamist leader operating from Sudan. With the Sudanese now under scrutiny, bin Laden agreed to leave the country for Afghanistan in May 1996.[44]

In August 1998, bin Laden's Al-Qaeda group bombed the US embassies in Nairobi and Dar es Salaam. President Clinton chose to repeat the same tactic that he had used against Saddam Hussein in 1993: missile strikes against the organisation responsible, Al-Qaeda, in Sudan. The president was nevertheless careful to cite bin Laden's record as a procurer of assassination. He was 'no lone terrorist, but the leader of a well-armed organization . . . [that] had already plotted other atrocities around the world, including the assassination of the Pope and the President of Egypt'. 'The time had come to take action,' Clinton concluded. Of course, Clinton had noticeably not taken any action in the face of assassination plots against non-American world leaders, something of which his terrorism specialists in the White House were only too painfully aware.[45]

Those who thought Clinton was reaping the reward for softness on terror urged him to revisit the ban on the US itself carrying out assassinations. If bin Laden was at the root of the problem, there was no point attacking training camps: the US should just kill him. One of the many problems Clinton faced, however, was that he could not assassinate Osama bin Laden, even if he wanted too. The US intelligence community did not have the ability to locate individual targets on a reliable basis. Even when they could, given their experience with Mohammed Farah Aideed, few believed that US special forces could carry out operations in territory much less permissive than Somalia. As the head of the CIA admitted, 'It's not as easy as folks might think to find people.'[46] The President's Intelligence Oversight Board noted that the CIA certainly collaborated with people who 'ordered, planned, or participated in' assassinations, but this was in their old stamping grounds of Central America, rather than anywhere currently useful.[47] As Clinton remarked, 'we should be able to do better'.[48]

At a higher end of the technical spectrum, the USAF and the USN had very sophisticated cruise missiles, but those missiles had been designed to carry nuclear warheads against the Soviet Union in the 1980s: they could hit buildings, as they did in 1993, but not individuals. Tony Lake, Clinton's National Security Advisor, described the uncertainty surrounding Clinton's 1993 attack on the Iraqi intelligence service building: 'when we hit Baghdad,' Lake said, 'we had no way of knowing[,] because it was nighttime, what the effects of the Tomahawk raids would be'. As Lake evoked the scene in the White House, 'everybody is sitting around in the President's little dining room off the Oval Office, waiting for word of some sort'. For want of anything better, they watched TV, where 'all the talking heads are out there pontificating when they had no clue what had happened, even less than we did'.[49]

This did not mean that the United States could not develop technological means to carry out assassinations in the medium term. In 1995, the CIA started deploying an unmanned surveillance aircraft in the Balkans. This 'drone', as it was nicknamed, had the fearsome official designator Predator. The drone was a sophisticated piece of equipment. It was piloted from thousands of miles away by a USAF unit based in Nevada. But the Predator could not actually hurt anyone in 1998. As the Director of Central Intelligence commented, 'we didn't know how important the UAVs [unmanned aerial vehicles] were going to be.'[50] It was not until late 2000, at the back end of the Clinton administration, that Clinton's counter-terrorism adviser in the White House, Richard Clarke, and the head of the CIA's Counterterrorism Center, Cofer Black, persuaded George Tenet to allow them to commission an armed version of the Predator. The purpose of the new weapon was specifically to give the president the ability to assassinate bin Laden and other Al-Qaeda leaders in Afghanistan. The new drone used the same guided missile system as a US army attack helicopter. However, it was only ready for use after George Bush junior had been inaugurated as President in January 2001.[51]

Bill Clinton himself was never in a realistic position to become a procurer of assassination, even if he had wanted to be one. Instead, he put the issue more in moral terms. Clinton declined to rescind the presidential ban against assassination. He reassured Slobodan Milošević of Serbia that 'we won't assassinate him'.[52] However, at the same time, the CIA made explicit an existing caveat in their protocol discouraging CIA officers from consorting with known assassins, allowing a senior officer to OK deals with such individuals whenever he cared to do so.[53] Clinton authorised US intelligence agencies to take covert action to capture bin Laden, with the rider that they could kill him if he resisted. Clinton frequently returned to and tweaked this directive. First, he extended its scope to bring other Al-Qaeda leaders within the rules laid down for bin Laden. Subsequently, he gave permission for US forces to shoot down any aeroplane or helicopter attempting to fly bin Laden out of Afghanistan. According to George Tenet's later testimony, 'almost all of the "authorities" President Clinton provided us with regard to Bin Ladin [sic] were predicated on the planning of capture operations'. The only circumstances in which he might legitimately have been killed was during a capture that went wrong. The point, of course, remained moot since no-one ever had a practical opportunity to decide.[54]

Even leaving aside Saddam Hussein and Osama bin Laden, assassination frequently affected Bill Clinton's presidency.[55] Clinton presided over the commemoration of the twenty-fifth anniversary of the murder of Bobby Kennedy at the same time as he was dealing with the attempted assassination of President Bush. The Kennedy saga truly gripped the Clinton *équipe*. They returned repeatedly to the loss of Bobby Kennedy as a personal touchstone in their lives.[56] The Director of Central Intelligence, Jim Woolsey, thought that sentimentalism over the assassination threat to some personal allies influenced Clinton's decision-making.[57]

A few months after the attack on Iraq, Clinton made a deal with Yitzhak Rabin and Yasser Arafat on Palestine. Two years after that, Clinton attended Rabin's funeral after the Israeli prime minister was assassinated over the deal. After Rabin's loss in November 1995, the Clinton administration's Near East diplomacy slowly fell apart.[58]

Clinton warned the graduating class at West Point that they would be unleashed on a world 'plagued' by 'the random violence of the assassin and the terrorist', a world he compared to that existing in the early years of the twentieth century: confusing and possibly heading for detonation.[59] In this sense, the broader western world just became more American, or America just became like the rest of the world – they all lived in the assassins' 'global village'.[60]

Thus, governments tweaked and further embedded the security systems they had mutually devised in the 1980s. Both the US president and the British prime minister, for example, settled into the back seats of new limousines ordered by their predecessors. Clinton took delivery of three Cadillac Fleetwood 'beasts' from Michigan in 1993. John Major received his new Jaguar-Daimlers starting in 1992.[61] The British cars were armoured by S. MacNeillie & Son of Walsall, who put in 1,200lb of steel armour into each. The attack on Hosni Mubarak in Addis Ababa demonstrated that this international armouring standard – the Egyptians used German Mercedes – worked even against rifle bullets.[62]

Potential assassins tried new methods to work around the kind of security now afforded a head of government. In February 1991, a PIRA active service unit lobbed a mortar bomb into the garden of 10 Downing Street. The mortar, in this case home-made and mounted in a Ford Transit van, was never likely to prove an accurate assassination weapon. It was, however, effective at demonstrating that the PIRA still wished to kill the prime minister, and also in showing that they could get within 200 yards to launch an attack.[63] Robin Butler, who had taken the lead in transforming prime ministerial security as Margaret Thatcher's principal private secretary, was by then in the cabinet room in his own right as cabinet secretary. He recorded his shock. 'We didn't even know it was a mortar,' Butler said; 'the French windows at the end of the room were burst open by the blast. My first impression was that men were going to dash in with masks and sub-machine guns.'[64] Inevitably, the British carried out 'yet another security review' of the prime minister's arrangements, resulting in his surveillance screen being pushed out even further.[65] John Major concluded that there was a wider problem and transferred the responsibility for counter-terrorism in the UK emanating from Ireland from the Metropolitan Police to MI5.[66]

According to the head of the Indian prime ministerial protection service, standard world practice was now to use three security teams. The area security team made sure that there were no physical avenues of attack or any chance of sabotage. The isolation security team ensured that no-one could approach the protectee without being identified, screened and checked. Close security was the personal protection team itself. In the Indian case, the three teams added up to nearly five hundred people.[67]

The Indians noted that there were always challenges in keeping large protection operations at peak performance. There was a risk that personal security officers would be used 'for mere ornamental purposes to feed the ego of the VIP or to impress others'.[68] Even high-status systems could be penetrated. The hitherto highly regarded security division of Shin Bet, the main Israeli security service, mismanaged each layer of protection, thereby leaving Yitzhak Rabin, one of the most threatened political leaders in the world, wide open to his assassin. In addition to incompetence, Israeli VIP protection failures proved that not having enough men on hand could be fatal.[69]

The political dangers of the ever-greater precautions political leaders took against assassination remained the same as those identified in the 1980s.[70] Rajiv Gandhi's international peers had warmed to him as one of their own – he was educated at Cambridge and married to an Italian – but according to their diplomats he was isolated, both physically and morally, 'from ordinary life in India'.[71] As Bill Clinton remarked in November 1993, 'one of the greatest things a president has to guard against all the time is just becoming isolated from the feelings, the concerns, the conditions of daily life that all other Americans have to confront'.[72] He promised not to 'allow the fight against domestic and foreign terrorism to build a wall between me and the American people'.[73]

Nevertheless, at the same moment, the president agreed to the urgings of the Director of Secret Service to close Pennsylvania Avenue, the route that ran from the White House to the Capitol. He framed this as an anti-terrorist measure, 'to preserve our freedom'. However, Clinton had the grace also to admit that it was the inner political elite and their servants who were being protected, not the users of Pennsylvania Avenue, 'which had been routinely open to traffic for the entire history of our Republic'.[74]

Around the turn of the century western politicians were confident that they had already absorbed assassination. If there was a theme, it was the settling of old debts. The last assassination of the twentieth century to garner significant international attention was that of the Spanish judge José Francisco Querol, blown up as he was being driven through Madrid. The bomb that slew Querol also killed his driver and bodyguard while injuring over sixty passers-by. This was not new: the Basque terrorist group ETA had been assassinating the representatives of the Spanish state with large bombs since the murder of Carrero Blanco in 1973.[75]

A few months before Querol's death, the left-wing Greek terrorist group 17N assassinated the British defence attaché in Greece, Brigadier Stephen Saunders, as he drove himself through the Athenian rush hour. 17N had been shooting western intelligence officers, as well as representatives of the Greek state, since the murder of the CIA's Richard Welch in 1975. In both cases, the assassinations proved to be the organisation's last. It is hard to be sure if the mass protests launched after Querol's death, as opposed the very different climate facing terrorists after 9/11, had more influence on ETA's decision to declare a 'permanent ceasefire' in June 2002. It is easier to be precise in the case of 17N. The assassination of Saunders led to significant support to the Greek counter-terrorist branch from the UK.[76] In June 2002, a member of 17N accidentally blew himself up while handling explosives in the port of Piraeus. He was carrying a Smith & Wesson pistol stolen from a policeman murdered by 17N in 1984. The pistol had subsequently been used as the murder weapon in two further assassinations. The capture of the terrorist and his weapon led the police to 17N's operating base, right under their noses in central Athens. The G3 rifle used to assassinate Stephen Saunders was part of their haul. Thereafter, the police rounded up the leaders of 17N in quick succession. Fifteen people were convicted of multiple killings at the end of 2003. 17N assassination ended because the assassins had been defeated; this was nothing to do with a new world order.[77]

Equally, the first assassinations of the new millennium appeared both predictable and familiar. In January 2001, a group of disgruntled army officers assassinated the President of the Congo, Laurent Kabila. As a young man, Kabila had been an ardent supporter of Patrice Lumumba. His own death hardly provoked the accusations of the west that had surrounded his one-time mentor's. Kabila was the victim of an internal Congolese power struggle: his dynasty was secured when his son, Joseph, succeeded him as president.[78]

A case with more obvious international implications was that of Zoran Đinđić. Serbia's first democratically elected prime minister had left the country in the 1990s to avoid assassination by the country's then leader Slobodan Milošević. He returned in October 2000 to help overthrow Milošević. In June 2001, he took the decision to extradite Milošević to The Hague to face trial for war crimes.[79] Milošević's threat did not die with his removal from Serbia, however. In March 2003, a rifle-armed sniper shot the heavily protected Đinđić from the upper storey of a building in Belgrade. Plainly, Đinđić had been wrong to trust all those around him.[80] The assassination was a joint endeavour between former Serbian state security officers, a pro-Milošević militia known as the Red Berets, and a criminal clan. It was possible for an individual to be a member of all three.[81] It emerged during the Đinđić investigation that the same coalition had secretly assassinated the former president of Serbia, Ivan Stambolić, in August 2000. The assassins had concealed the murder by disposing of Stambolić's body in acid once they had shot him. These assassinations had everything to do with internal Serbian feuds from the past.[82]

The most notorious assassin of the later twentieth century also ended up with a bullet in his head for reasons that probably had little to do with the new world order. In August 2002, the Iraqi government announced that Abu Nidal had died by his own hand in Baghdad. According to the Iraqis, Abu Nidal had shot himself when he realised the plot he was brewing against Saddam Hussein had been uncovered. There was inevitably speculation that if Nidal had turned against Hussein, he was unlikely to have held the gun himself. If Nidal's death was an assassination, few lamented his passing. As the widow of the Black June's last victim, a Jordanian diplomat killed in Beirut, commented, 'God finally punished Abu Nidal. He got what he deserved . . . first he was inflicted with cancer and then he was killed in mysterious circumstances.'[83]

12

WHO SHOULD PULL THE TRIGGER?
Assassination in the Twenty-First Century

The great powers reshaped the international system after 2001, not least through inter-state wars. The world of assassination was in turn reshaped by the transformation. Nevertheless, a handful of assassinations came, albeit in retrospect, to be seen as prefiguring the new world.

In December 2000, an Israeli military sniper shot and killed Thabet Ahmed Thabet in the town of Tulkarem in the West Bank. This killing took place three months into the so-called 'second Intifada', a violent Palestinian uprising against Israeli military rule.[1] What made Thabet's death stand out from those of other Palestinians was his dual role as secretary-general of Fatah in Tulkarem and an official of the Palestinian Authority's Ministry of Health. Israel claimed he had a third role: terrorist leader. However, the Israelis did not leave the matter there. Shin Bet, the intelligence agency which had targeted Thabet for elimination, announced that it had neither made a mistake nor done anything wrong. The Israel Defense Forces (IDF), who supplied the sniper, turned the case over to their own lawyers, with instructions to demonstrate that the Israeli state had been quite within its rights to kill Thabet in an ambush.

The IDF house lawyers came back with their arguments within a couple of months. They began with the claim that the international law of armed conflict was no longer fit for purpose: it had evolved to govern declared war between states. No-one declared war on anyone in the twenty-first century. The lawyers then claimed that 'killings were legal' if the target was a terrorist, no arrest was possible and civilian casualties were minimised. The IDF was clearly marking its own homework, but the opinion was granted official status by Israel's Attorney General and subsequently upheld in the Israeli courts.[2]

The new Israeli declaratory policy went even further, however, in establishing that pre-emptive assassination should be regarded as superior to reactive assassination. Israel had been a purveyor of state-sponsored assassination since the 1950s, and an intensive practitioner since the 1970s. Since the 1980s, no-one had seriously pretended otherwise. The Prime Minister, Ehud Barak, had first caught public attention as a successful assassin.[3] The new policy did, nevertheless, constitute an important change: this was no 'quasi-appropriation, quasi-repudiation and subtle evasion' but rather a full-throated endorsement of assassination as state policy.[4] Neither were the Israelis merely playing with words. As they announced their new policy, IDF helicopter gunships hunted down – it took three hours – and killed Massoud Ayad, an officer of Force 17, Yasser Arafat's bodyguard, in Gaza.[5]

In August 2001, the helicopter gunships came back for Abu Ali Mustafa, the head of the PFLP faction of the PLO. Israeli intelligence telephoned Mustafa to make sure he was in his office, the office window was lit up with a laser designator and two helicopters used air-to-ground missiles to kill their victim.[6] Notably, the Israeli line received no support from Israel's western allies, even the US and the UK. The British foreign office minister Ben Bradshaw remarked that 'Britain cannot accept the targeted assassination by Israel of Palestinian militants. . . . These assassinations create an environment in which atrocities are seen as justified and lead to further violence.'[7]

Western states still saw Israel as an outlier: US officials had not developed a different view by the time the Tajik-Afghan mujahideen and warlord Ahmed Shah Massoud was assassinated by Al-Qaeda on 9 September 2001. Massoud was an old Cold War contact of the Americans. In the late 1990s, he and the CIA explored the mutual advantage of getting rid of Osama bin Laden. Massoud was fighting a civil war against the Taliban government of Afghanistan and bin Laden was the main source of the government's effective foreign fighters. In May 1998, the CIA's Counterterrorism Center put up a plan to have their Afghan ally capture bin Laden. Senior officers in the CIA's clandestine service immediately recognised that this would be tantamount to an assassination plot. The DCI briefed President Clinton's National Security Advisor on the existence of the plan, fully acknowledging that, if it proved practicable, a likely result would be bin Laden's death. The Americans decided to go no further.[8] Massoud returned to the charge in December 1999 with proposals for a rocket attack on bin Laden's training camp. Once more, CIA officers characterised the idea as a potential assassination attempt and rejected the Afghan idea. When CIA case officers went to meet Massoud in Afghanistan, they told him that they wanted intelligence rather than direct action.[9] The CIA knew that it was not the main ally of Massoud's Northern Alliance: that was the Iranian intelligence services.[10]

The Americans seemed further along the track towards readopting assassination when it came to new weapons. However, the lack of focus on the drone as a tool of assassination was clear here too.[11] Drone development remained the purview of the United States Air Force, which regarded pilotless aircraft as potentially important for what it called ISR – Intelligence, Surveillance and Reconnaissance – and as anti-tank weapons. For the latter role, drones could be equipped with an anti-tank guided missile known as the Hellfire. There were few serious arguments for stripping control of the weapons system away from America's conventional forces.[12]

Over the summer of 2001, however, the newly elected Bush administration did start pushing drones as a potential assassination weapon. The Deputy National Security Advisor, Steve Hadley, ordered the Department of Defense to ensure that the weapon, when developed, should be accurate enough to hit something smaller than a tank. At the same time, officials and lawyers formally discussed if the US could target and kill named individuals for political purposes without calling those killings assassinations. On one level, there was no problem. A sitting president could simply withdraw the existing Executive Order banning assassination. However, the Bush administration did not wish to incur the potential political costs, domestically or internationally, of publicly endorsing assassination. Thus, to carry out assassinations without calling them assassinations, the American government would need to retain the conspiratorial approach.

Like the Israelis, albeit in secret, American leaders cut the Gordian knot by having their own lawyers declare that targeted killing in self-defence was not assassination.[13] According to John Bellinger, the legal adviser to the State Department, the existing Executive Order was merely intended to 'stop political assassinations'. As Bellinger reported the lawyers' reasoning, 'assassination didn't mean just killing somebody. Assassination was a particular kind of killing, an illegal killing, because it was for a political purpose or something like that. So for a defensive purpose or a military purpose, the assassination ban would not be triggered.' According to the Americans, assassination only referred to a certain kind of political murder. Nevertheless, politicians would continue to make political decisions about their carved-out category of not-assassination.[14]

The Bush government was hardly in a hurry to embrace its newly created world of legal opportunity. Having come into power in January 2001, Bush had his first serious discussion about assassination with his advisers on 4 September 2001: the 'big issue' for the 'principals' was 'who would pull the trigger'.[15] Only the Treasury Secretary, Paul O'Neill, was uncomfortable with the whole idea that the United States should be killing named individuals. The meeting finished with the participants agreeing that when the missile-armed drone was ready, they could more reasonably take some decisions.[16]

Of course, the Bush administration was playing with time that it did not have. The linked Al-Qaeda plots, first to assassinate Massoud and then to fly passenger jet airliners into major American buildings, had been brewing for months. The assassination element of the plot was prepared in the UK, Belgium and France. The Moroccan assassins set out from London, travelling on Belgian passports.[17]

The day before 9/11, the Americans saw Al-Qaeda's decapitation of the Afghan resistance as a setback rather than a severe blow.[18] When President Bush reconvened with his cabinet-level national security principals on 15 September 2001, the world seemed a very different place. Terrorists had piloted two passenger aircraft into the World Trade

Center in Manhattan, causing it to collapse. A third airliner had hit the Pentagon in Washington and a fourth jet had crashed in Pennsylvania during a passenger attack on the terrorists. Everyone on the aeroplanes had died, along with over three thousand people on the ground. Now it was clear why Al-Qaeda had killed Massoud, the only man who had put forward serious proposals to attack Osama bin Laden in Afghanistan. With Massoud gone, George Tenet, the DCI, proposed a plan to start hunting and killing Al-Qaeda members with no geographical limits. According to President Bush, he gave specific permission to 'kill Al-Qaeda operatives', while acknowledging that what he now directed was 'a significant departure from America's policies over the past two decades'.[19] The CIA would 'work from the dark side ... get mean, dirty, and nasty', his Vice President, Dick Cheney, added.[20] However, the first assassination attempt the CIA made with the new drone technology – now accelerated into operational service, in May 2002 – was not aimed at an Al-Qaeda operative but rather the Afghan warlord Gulbuddin Hekmatyar. The attack missed.[21]

Twenty-first-century assassination moved into the first of what became three phases: a short phase in 2001–2, a much longer and more dramatic period between 2002 and 2011, and the current era. In the first phase, new technology made relatively little impact. The world of assassination did not wait for the Americans to sort out their new techniques. Others were pushing ahead with the old. In October 2002, Islamist assassins murdered Laurence Foley, a US diplomat serving in Jordan. The killers ambushed Foley outside his home in Amman with some ease. This was particularly alarming since Amman was regarded as a high-security posting. In this case, the Jordanian security authorities captured the assassins and identified them as part of a group run by an obscure Islamist called Abu Musab al-Zarqawi.[22]

The first successful Islamist assassination of an Afghan leader who had helped overthrow the Taliban government occurred over the summer of 2002. Suborned guards employed by the Ministry of Public Works killed Vice President Haji Abdul Qadir, the only prominent Pathan in the Northern Alliance.[23] The first attempted assassination of the new President of Afghanistan, Mohammed Karzai, followed in

September 2002. In this case, the would-be assassin was an Afghan soldier serving in the guard of the Governor of Kandahar.[24]

A much longer and more clearly defined second phase of 'quasi-appropriation' took shape at the end of 2002 and lasted until 2011. This new phase was based on the Americans' belief that they now had not only the legal right but also the capability to target and kill their enemies. There would be less of a conspiratorial aspect, at least within government: orders to kill individuals would flow down well-established chains of command. However, the American government also chose to keep a policy of 'subtle evasion' in place. According to the Secretary of Defense, Donald Rumsfeld, Bush inaugurated the new phase in October 2002 with an attempt to kill the leader of the Taliban, Mullah Omar. Nevertheless, Rumsfeld still acted as a cut-out for the president, giving orders in person to military subordinates without specifying he had received an explicit 'green light'.[25]

The campaign deliberately stretched beyond conventional war zones. In early November, a drone killed an Al-Qaeda leader called Qaed Salim Sinan al-Harethi in Yemen. The US had secured prior approval from the government of Yemen for the attack. In this case, it was Rumsfeld's deputy, Paul Wolfowitz, who took credit, describing the killing of al-Harethi in a television interview as 'a very successful tactical operation'. However, President Bush regarded Wolfowitz's statement as a step too far. The president's press secretary, Ari Fleischer, commented, 'There are going to be things that are done that the American people may never know about.'[26]

Bush's own public formulation was that although his preferred policy was to have allies arrest enemies of the US – in ways which subsequently became controversial in their own right – 'many others have met a different fate'. 'Let's put it this way,' he commented, 'they are no longer a problem to the United States and our friends and allies.'[27] Bush saw both the US military and the CIA as conduits for action. In December 2002, he signed an executive order giving the CIA prior approval to kill twenty-five named targets whenever they had the opportunity to do so.[28]

President Bush took a direct and personal interest in assassination that went beyond merely accepting the advice of subordinates or the formal exercise of his presidential authority. This became especially apparent when his government moved on from its campaign in Afghanistan to prepare for the invasion of Iraq – on the dual, but false, grounds that Iraq harboured Al-Qaeda and posed an imminent threat of passing nuclear, biological or chemical weapons to terrorists. Both President Bush and Vice President Cheney claimed that Saddam Hussein's sponsorship of assassination was also significant. Saddam had, above all, 'made an assassination attempt on a former president, my father', Bush wrote.[29] Throughout his decision-making on Iraq, Bush frequently consulted with his father, including on the issue of attempts to kill Saddam Hussein.[30] The younger President Bush made his personal grudge against Saddam plain at a Republican fundraising event held at his ranch in Texas in September 2002, claiming that 'there's no doubt his [Saddam's] hatred is mainly directed at us. There's no doubt he can't stand us. After all, this is the guy who tried to kill my Dad at one time.' Earlier in the month, he had brought up the Kuwait City assassination plot during a speech to the UN. It fell to Donald Rumsfeld to run the evasive line, issuing a statement that America's intent was not to kill Saddam Hussein but to remove him from power.[31] Nevertheless, the American attack on Iraq in March 2003 certainly began with an unsuccessful attempt to kill Saddam Hussein.[32]

However, it was by no means clearer in the second phase than it had been in the first that American-style assassination would be more effective than assassination in the hands of weaker rivals. One of the Taliban's responses to their overthrow was to mount a sustained assassination campaign in southern Afghanistan against those who made the appearance of collaborating. Their main targets were Islamic religious figures, policemen and aid workers. The EU estimated that up to thirty people were assassinated per month. The Americans tended to dismiss these deaths as unimportant, but other western observers pointed out that industrial-scale assassination was successfully making a mockery of their claim that Afghanistan was pacified.[33]

When the Americans moved on to Iraq, they faced a similar problem. Just before the American invasion, Islamist assassins, working in this instance in the interest of Saddam Hussein, killed Shakat Haj Mushir, founder of the PUK, the Kurdish armed political party that effectively controlled north-eastern Iraq. The assassins lured Mushir to a meeting with promises of defection. As he leant over to sign a letter, they shot him in the head.[34]

To the south, al-Zarqawi, the organiser of the assassination of Laurence Foley in October 2002, had evolved his tactics. He now attempted to merge assassination with mass-casualty terrorism. In August 2003, his group used a truck bomb to kill the UN envoy to Iraq, Sérgio Vieira de Mello, in the UN building in Baghdad. He used the same tactic to assassinate Ayatollah Muhammed Baqr al-Hakim, the most senior Shia in Iraq, in Najaf.[35] The huge truck bomb attacks did not replace smaller-scale attacks, however. Hakim's son, Moqtada al-Sadr, survived an assassination attempt two days after his father's death: the assassins machine-gunned his car.[36]

The first member of the interim Iraqi governing council to be assassinated, Aquila al-Hashemi, was ambushed as she drove to work in Baghdad.[37] The official in charge of the 'de-Baathification' of Iraq, Muhammed al-Hakim of the Supreme Council of the Islamic Revolution in Iraq (SCIRI), was assassinated outside his home. In December 2003, SCIRI itself, through its armed wing, the Badr Brigades, began a campaign of assassination of former Saddam-era officials: a dozen such men were killed within a few weeks. They were usually shot outside their homes or offices. The assassins used motorbikes in Najaf and cars in Baghdad, observers noted. Intelligence officials were even more worried when they confirmed that the SCIRI assassins had been trained by the Iranians.[38]

As a bad assassination year for the Americans, 2003 was topped off by an attempt on the life of their chief administrator in Iraq, Paul Bremer. His very heavily protected convoy was hit first with a roadside bomb and then gunfire. No Americans were hurt, but the investigation of the attack revealed that the Coalition Provisional Authority was riddled with informers working with the assassins.[39]

At the beginning of 2004, US security officials admitted to themselves that they had not really known what they were doing barrelling into the world of assassination. Compared to their enemies and rivals, they were 'sluggish'. The Departments of Defense and State and the CIA spent more time fighting each other in Washington than properly equipping their assassins/operators in the field. According to the US Secretary of Defense, Robert Gates, 'it was a mess'.[40] At a conference in Tampa, Florida, the American state agencies agreed to try and create a 'killing machine'. The focus of their efforts would be an organisation called Task Force 714, based in Afghanistan but operating over the whole area of the US military command CENTCOM. TF 714 itself brought together detachments of various military units. The intelligence agencies would co-locate with TF 714. A US army officer, Stanley McChrystal, took command.[41]

It was not until April 2004, however, that McChrystal was able to assemble his officers at their Bagram base in Afghanistan, and not until August 2004 that the commander of US Army special forces in Iraq suggested they needed to operate a FIND-FIX-FINISH[i.e. kill]-EXPLOIT-ANALYZE (F3EA) loop. As McChrystal conceded, such mnemonics were hardly earth-shaking innovations in American military art, but it was telling that no-one had thought beforehand that 'hunting individuals required very fast and very precise execution'.[42]

Meanwhile, America's clients continued to die. In June 2004, the international community declared that Iraq was once more a sovereign nation, ruled by a government led by Prime Minister Ayad Allawi. Allawi's first cabinet meeting was devoted to the very pressing question of how its members were going to survive. The cabinet's conclusions bespoke their own profound scepticism about the new Iraqi state: they agreed to each take care of their own security arrangements, based on family or tribal supporters. As the Minister for Human Rights, Bakhtiar Amin, commented, 'the Iraqi security services have been infiltrated by bad elements. I can't [gamble] my life using anyone from an institution that could be compromised. I have only good and loyal people [drawn from his Kurdish Peshmerga fighters] who I trust.'[43]

Those without good and loyal people, and some with, continued to suffer. In December 2004, the deputy communications minister was shot dead: eight of his bodyguards were wounded.[44] A few days later, the same thing happened to the governor of Baghdad, Ali al-Haidari: his motorcade got stuck in Baghdad traffic and assassins using assault rifles killed him and six of his bodyguards.[45] Prime Minister Allawi himself survived an attempt to assassinate him by means of driving a suicide bomb into his motorcade: although he was unhurt many of the policemen protecting him were injured.[46]

However, none of the killings in Afghanistan or Iraq focused world attention to the same level as the murder of the Lebanese politician Rafiq Hariri in February 2005. The assassination of 'Mr Lebanon' attracted the most thorough-going international investigation of a twenty-first-century assassination, with contributions from Germany, France, the Netherlands, Switzerland, the UK and Japan.[47] The UN Tribunal on Lebanon closed its doors in December 2023, having identified the five members of Hezbollah who had arranged the assassination: one of them was already dead; the other four remained at large. It could certainly be argued that the two-decades-long inquiry was an elephant that birthed a gnat. Nevertheless, it demonstrated how a non-superpower would procure an assassination, assemble the assassins, choose the techniques and orchestrate the cover-up in the modern age.[48]

Very few western investigators ever seriously doubted that Bashar al-Assad, the dictator of Syria, procured the assassination of Rafiq Hariri.[49] In January 2005, the Bush administration had sent its Deputy Secretary of State, Richard Armitage, to Damascus explicitly to warn Assad not to assassinate Hariri.[50] The US ambassador to Syria, Ryan Crocker, described the Assad government as a 'totally evil regime'.[51] The plan to assassinate Hariri was hatched in December 2004. He had not 'done' anything to provoke an attack after he resigned as Lebanon's prime minister in October 2004: on the contrary, he had sought reasonable relations with Syria. Hariri was simply so much more charismatic than either Assad or pro-Syrian Lebanese politicians that he inevitably got in the way.[52] According to American informants, Assad was quite satisfied with his handiwork.[53]

The two functionaries charged with arranging the assassination of Syria's opponents in Lebanon were Assad's proconsul in Lebanon, Ghazi Kanaan, and his military aide, General Mohammed Suleiman. Both men were themselves subsequently killed. Kanaan's mysterious death in his Damascus office in October 2005 remains unsolved. General Suleiman was most certainly assassinated: a rifle-armed sniper on a yacht shot him four times in his beach chalet in the Mediterranean resort of Tartus in August 2008.[54]

Assad's men turned to their ally, the Shia armed political party Hezbollah, to carry out the assassination. The actual assassin was a suicide bomber, but the planners of the assassination were a cadre of operatives around Imad Mughniya. Mughniya, although little known to the public, was one of the most notorious terrorists of the late twentieth century, starting his career in the PLO before shifting his allegiance to Hezbollah when it formed in Beirut in the early 1980s. Mughniya was himself assassinated in February 2008 when Mossad planted a bomb inside his Mitsubishi Pajero in a suburb of Damascus.[55]

Hezbollah was assisted by Syria's clients within the Lebanese security state. The Syrian-aligned government of Omar Karami made the assassination easier by withdrawing most of Hariri's protection force.[56] Both the Internal Security Forces and the Lebanese Military Intelligence tracked Hariri's movements and contacts through surveillance and phone-tapping. Indeed, the UN was able to build much of its reconstruction of the assassination conspiracy through telephone records.[57]

Hezbollah was an experienced assassination organisation. The Hariri assassination was but the centrepiece of a planned campaign to kill western-oriented Lebanese leaders. In 2006, the UN identified fourteen such assassinations. Hezbollah was already experimenting with tools and methods before the attack on Hariri.[58] Hariri, however, was a hard target who required special measures. He drove a Mercedes S600 with the highest class of assassination protection. The car was customarily part of a six-vehicle convoy, together with a Toyota Land Cruiser with four rifle-armed policemen (the remnant of the state security force), three further Mercedes each carrying three bodyguards from Hariri's personal protection force (each armed in the same fashion as western close-protection details), and a Chevrolet ambulance with two paramedics.[59] The Mercedes was equipped with jammers designed to interfere with remote-control devices.[60] The technology had just proven its worth by saving President Musharraf of Pakistan's life when Islamist assassins struck.[61]

The Hezbollah planners' solution was to use an extraordinarily large bomb, packed into a Mitsubishi Canter van, placed on the route from Hariri's home to the parliament. Although Hezbollah had access to plenty of plastic explosive, the assassins packed it around with TNT to give the weapon sufficient bulk. There was several thousand pounds of explosive in the van. This was a statement as well as a weapon.[62]

The plan worked as intended. An assassin triggered the bomb as Hariri drew alongside his van. Hariri and all his bodyguards were killed by the blast. Vehicles and debris flew into Beirut harbour, whence they had subsequently to be recovered as evidence by British divers.[63]

A pre-planned cover-up swung into place as soon as Hariri died. The scene was immediately occupied by the Lebanese army and the Operations Division of the internal security forces (ISF). No-one from the investigative police and intelligence service, the Sûreté Générale, attended. The ISF removed the wrecked cars, filled in the crater and reopened the street to traffic within hours, thus preventing forensic investigation. The judge put in charge of the case resigned within weeks after he was presented with case files with no evidence.[64] All this effort concealed the involvement of Hezbollah.[65] It took seven years for the UN to identify the organisation as the assassins.[66]

While attention was focused on Lebanon, the USA was shuffling its killing resources. The CIA shifted into Waziristan, a region on the northwest frontier of Pakistan. TF 714, on the other hand, moved most of its forces out of Afghanistan to Iraq, where it established its new headquarters at Balad.[67] In June 2005, President Bush instructed Stanley McChrystal that his singular and overriding mission was to kill Abu Musab al-Zarqawi.[68] McChrystal admitted that having an effective assassin as a target boosted the standing of America's own assassination force.[69] Zarqawi's was a necessary corpse. It was not enough to kill a man; the killers needed a body as incontrovertible proof that the individual was indeed dead.[70] According to McChrystal, 'Zarkawi was an obsession.' The tempo of special forces operations dropped significantly. The assault troops sat around on quick reaction alert rather than operating on other missions. Nearly all the intelligence staff worked on the Zarqawi hunt. Seventy per cent of surveillance and reconnaissance – aeroplanes, drones, satellites – was devoted to Zarqawi.[71] In June 2006, TF 714 finally found Zarqawi in a village about an hour's drive north of Baghdad. He was killed by the USAF, a manned fighter dropping two 500-pound bombs on his safe house.[72]

Four days before Zarqawi's death, there had been another assassination in Baghdad that had little to do with him. In this case, the victim was a Russian officer, Vitaly Titov, probably a member of the external intelligence service, the SVR, associated with diplomats accredited to Nuri al-Maliki's new Iraqi government. The assassins were Chechens. Just as Zarqawi's killing was a significant waypoint on the American journey to the quasi-appropriation of assassination as state policy, the Titov assassination marked an important shift in the Russian government's similar journey.[73]

In 2003, western observers noticed that Russia, ruled by President Vladimir Putin since 2000, was running a state assassination campaign. In doing so, Putin relied not only on his own intelligence services but also the warlords he had set up as rulers in the Caucasus, most notably in Chechnya. Russian assassination was still cloaked in 2003 but that cloak was wearing thin.[74] In February 2004, the Qataris arrested three operatives of the GRU for assassinating the exiled Chechen leader Zalinkhan Yandarbiev. The GRU's bomb killed Yandarbiev, along with his family, as he left a mosque.[75]

Like the Americans, the Russians did not have it all their own way in terms of assassination. In April 2004, an Islamist assassin detonated his Lada next to the armour-plated Mercedes of Putin's ally, the President of Ingushetia, Murad Zyazikov. The Mercedes saved Zyazikov and his bodyguards: they suffered blast injuries and burns but were not killed.[76] As elsewhere, the assassins' answer was a bigger bomb. Islamists embedded a huge bomb in the concrete of the Dynamo stadium in Grozny. In May 2004, when Putin's Chechen ally Akhmad Kadyrov attended the stadium, for a long-planned celebration of himself, the assassins triggered their explosives with a remote-control device, killing the president and over thirty others in the VIP area.[77]

Also, like Bush, Putin moved from subtle evasion to quasi-appropriation. In March 2006, the Russian duma started to enact legislation to empower him to approve, on his own authority, the extra-judicial killing of anyone overseas whom he defined as an 'extremist'. The parliament put a second, even more far-reaching, law in place after the Titov assassination. Putin publicly ordered Russian 'special services' to 'annihilate' the killers of the diplomat.

Seemingly, the results of Putin's call to arms followed with remarkable rapidity. Within days, the FSB, Russia's security service, claimed that it had assassinated Shamil Basayev, the Chechen leader who had himself organised the assassination of Akhmad Kadyrov in 2004. It is possible that the FSB overstated its role in Basayev's assassination, but it was certainly engaged in an assassination campaign against named Chechen leaders. As for the Americans, it was not enough to kill an individual; the killers needed incontrovertible proof that the individual was dead. When Russian special forces killed the Chechen rebel president, Aslan Maskhadov, in March 2005, they released publicity photographs of his corpse in a pool of his own blood. The FSB killed Maskhadov's successor, Abdul-Khalim Sadulayev, a few days before Basayev's death.[78]

In the wake of these assassinations, Putin welcomed world leaders to the G8 summit in St Petersburg: given the US's killing of Zarqawi and the assassination of Titov in Iraq, there was a general feeling among those present that Putin was making appropriate use of Russian special forces. In 2006, the line that the western powers took was that assassination was not an assassination for a power engaged in counter-insurgency. Neither did such killings have to take place in the country of the insurgency to be part of a military operation. The trouble was that, in the world of 'quasi-appropriation', there was no necessity for anyone to abide by such delimitation.[79]

In October 2006, the Russian journalist Anna Politkovskaya was shot and killed outside her Moscow apartment. The Russian authorities claimed that she had been the victim of criminals; her friends and western investigative journalists immediately riposted that she had been assassinated by the same state agencies who were killing Chechen separatists. The next month, Alexander Litvinenko, a former KGB and FSB agent, who was living as an asylee in London, was assassinated. Litvinenko had been a friend of Politkovskaya. The assassination weapon was particularly noxious: Litvinenko died of radiation poisoning, an isotope of polonium having been administered in his drink. The place and means of the killing brought the assassination well within the arc of the British police and intelligence services. A complex investigation relying on forensic and surveillance evidence established that Litvinenko had been killed by two Russian assassins working for the FSB. The lead assassin was a former KGB officer.[80] The British inquiry eventually concluded 'that the FSB operation to kill Mr Litvinenko was probably approved by Mr Patrushev [the head of the FSB] and also by President Putin'.[81]

London was also the starting point for the most publicised assassination of the following year. In July 2007, the exiled leader of the Pakistan People's Party (PPP), based in London, Benazir Bhutto, decided she would return to Pakistan. This was part of an Anglo-American plan to stabilise Pakistan by creating a 'dream team' of Pervez Musharraf as president and the charismatic, westernised Bhutto as prime minister. The problem with this plan was that it ran the severe risk of getting one or both principals assassinated.[82]

A suicide bomber, whom a Scotland Yard forensic team subsequently identified as 'a teenage male, no more than 16 years old', assassinated Bhutto as she left a rally in Rawalpindi in December 2007.[83] It was clear that there had been multiple assassination teams in play since Bhutto had survived a previous attempt in October 2007: then the assassins had used two external car bombs.[84]

The cover-up for the assassination was immediate and extensive.[85] The Pakistani police and army hosed down the assassination site, preventing any proper crime scene investigation.[86] Pakistani police did not conduct a criminal investigation – they merely adopted the opinions that the intelligence services instructed them to adopt. The UN was in little doubt that these were deliberate and considered acts, endorsed by President Musharraf.[87]

The Pakistani and American governments both named the Waziri warlord and Pakistani Taliban commander Baitullah Mehsud as the procurer of Bhutto's assassination. At the instigation of Bhutto's widower, the new prime minister of Pakistan, the United States in turn made multiple attempts to assassinate Mehsud using drones based in Pakistan.[88] A drone attack in February 2009 missed him but killed more than thirty other people. The Americans finally hit Mehsud in August 2009. Almost as soon as Mehsud was dead, the CIA shut up their, by now highly publicised, drone base at Shamshi in Pakistan and moved it to a new operating station in Afghanistan.[89]

Various parties were unsettled by Bhutto's death. Most pressingly, Mohammed Karzai in Afghanistan inevitably focused on who might be coming for him.[90] Karzai rarely left his heavily fortified palace in

Kabul. Neither Karzai nor some foreign diplomats wished to attend Afghanistan's Independence Day parade in April 2008 on the grounds that an assassination attempt was almost inevitable. The Americans reassured Karzai that, unlike Bhutto, he had an 800-strong Presidential Protective Service that they themselves had trained. And indeed, those trained guards saved Karzai's life when Taliban assassins opened fire on the parade. Nevertheless, Afghan dignitaries, as well as western generals and diplomats, were photographed desperately running away or crawling on their hands and knees, visually demonstrating that 'things in Afghanistan were not as good as they should have been'. The British ambassador, Sherard Cowper-Coles, admitted to having been 'more scared than I ever had been'.[91]

At the same time, new fronts were added to the assassination struggle. In early 2007, Shia assassination squads killed Americans for the first time. They kidnapped four soldiers from a base in Karbala, drove them out of the city and shot them in the head. The Bush administration imposed a no-kill order on Shia – the allies of the Iraqi government – even though TF 714 reported that the Shia assassins were run by the Quds Force of the Iranian Islamic Revolutionary Guards Corps (IRGC).[92]

The Somali Sunni Islamist group Al-Shabaab also launched an assassination campaign. In July 2006, Al-Shabaab assassins shot and killed the Somali cabinet minister Abdallah Isaaq Deerow in the temporary capital of Baidoa.[93] Deerow was a close ally of President Cabdullaahi Yuusuf Axmed. In September 2006, Al-Shaabab made their first suicide bomber assassination attempt against Axmed, also in Baidoa.[94] There was no hold on pursuing Sunni assassins: TF 714 hunted down and killed the founder of Al-Shabaab, Aden Hashi Ayrow, in May 2008. The killing 'represented an important step in TF 714's ability to contribute in even difficult, denied areas'.[95]

The failure of the Bhutto gambit, and the assassination events that followed, set the stage for Barack Obama to inject new thinking on assassination. In August 2008, he attacked the Bush administration for failing to 'take a shot' at Osama bin Laden. Obama made an election commitment to go after bin Laden in Pakistan. Some of his advisers warned that the USA had already destabilised Pakistan. It was Obama himself who insisted, 'I want to say we'd take him out.'[96]

Obama was not just mouthing campaign rhetoric: America was exponentially more capable of 'taking the shot' than it had been in 2005. Obama would have at his disposal both the US military and CIA killing programmes. In mid-2007, the US military had had twenty-four drones devoted to assassination. By the time Obama took office, in 2009, they had about 180 assassination drones.[97] The drones themselves were much more lethal. In 2007, the US military began deploying a new generation of armed drones: the new systems had fifteen times the payload of the older versions.[98] Barack Obama both wanted to kill named individuals and had the ability to do so with this 'incredibly lethal machine'.[99]

Obama's innovation was not just to kill more effectively but to talk about that killing in a new way. This was the step from 'quasi-appropriation' to appropriation. The Bush approach seemed just too messy to Obama: he wanted criteria for killing permanently baked into American statecraft. He told his chief White House assistant for homeland security and counter-terrorism, John Brennan, to supply him with such a system. Brennan's office would process all proposals to kill an individual, at least outside the military areas of operations in Afghanistan and Iraq, and the president would approve the killing in a face-to-face meeting. Obama's goal was to have a system 'that would optimize our ability to take effective lethal action'. He remarked that 'We can't criticize others for conducting such strikes if we don't explain how and when we use them ourselves.' However, it proved very difficult to articulate the rules without sounding both murderous and inane.[100]

As Obama's subordinates struggled to come up with a convincing public explanation as to why assassination was good if carried out by states according to American rules, other states continued to make their own dispositions. In April 2009, Dubai arrested Russian assassins for conspiring to murder Sulim Yamdayev, one of Ramzan Kadyrov's main Chechen rivals. Kadyrov was the son and successor of the assassinated Akhmad Kadyrov. Also in Dubai, a team of eleven Mossad assassins killed Mahmoud al-Mabhouh, the founder of Hamas's military forces. They smothered him in his hotel room. Most of the assassins were filmed extensively by Dubai CCTV. Maintaining a long Mossad tradition, several British passports were linked to the assassination squad.

The British expelled the Mossad head of station in London in frustration.[101] According to Robert Gates, 'the Israelis' assassination of a Hamas leader in Dubai in January 2010, however morally justified, was strategically stupid because the incompetently run operation was quickly discovered and Israel fingered as responsible, thus costing Israel the quiet cooperation of the UAE on security matters.'[102]

The effort to institutionalise killing eventually 'splintered' the Obama team. Stanley McChrystal, supported by Robert Gates, warned Obama that drone killings were only 'effective where they complement, not replace, the capabilities of the state security apparatus . . . they are not scalable in the absence of underlying infrastructure, intelligence, and physical presence.' Gates was 'both astounded and amused . . . as Joe Biden; his National Security Advisor, Tony Blinken . . . and others presumed to understand how to make CT work better than Stan did.' Obama removed McChrystal and Gates.[103]

In the third phase of twenty-first-century assassination, beginning in 2011, governments embraced the public appropriation of the killing of named individuals. The spokesmen of such governments claimed that public appropriation negated any claim that they were involved in assassination. There was no conspiracy, no cover-up, thus no assassination. There could hardly be a more straightforward form of appropriation than to hunt down a target in a foreign country, send troops into that country with no warning to its government, shoot the individual in the head, exfiltrate his corpse for DNA testing, trumpet responsibility, release photographs of the dead man, and then film the body being thrown into the ocean.

One of the criticisms that President Obama had made of President Bush was that during the latter's administration the killing machine had worked its way through victims as it located them, rather than locating the political figureheads of Al-Qaeda, Osama bin Laden and his deputy, Ayman al-Zawahiri, and then killing them. It was two years into the Obama presidency, however, before the Director of the CIA could report that one of either bin Laden or al-Zawahiri might be hiding in the Pakistani city of Abbottabad.[104] Leon Panetta was also forced to admit that the president could not rely on his secret services to kill politically important targets: Obama would have to turn to the killing machine built by Stanley McChrystal. Notably, drones were never seriously considered for America's most important assassination. The two main options Obama's advisers devised were the use of special forces to shoot the target from point-blank range or the obliteration of the target building to ensure that no human could survive. The second option was rejected because killing the man had little practical significance: a killing could only have political significance if proof of death was trumpeted around the world.[105]

Despite the very public killing of Osama bin Laden in early May 2011, the Obama administration did, nevertheless, maintain something of a dance around the regular diet of other killings that continued in its shadow.[106] It was not until April 2012 that President Obama instructed Brennan to make a clear and unambiguous statement of US policy. 'Yes,' Brennan told the Wilson Center, 'in full accordance with the law, and in order to prevent terrorist attacks on the United States and save American lives, the United States Government conducts targeted strikes against specific al-Qaida terrorists.'[107] He went on to say that his statement was 'an admission that up to that time, the American government had refused to make' although it was the 'world's worst kept secret', nothing more than a 'charade'.[108] Obama himself only followed Brennan onto the record once he had successfully secured re-election to the presidency.[109]

In July 2016 the Office of the Director of National Intelligence released official figures for US drone strikes from the point that Obama took office to the end of 2015 (i.e. when he had another year in office to run). The Director of National Intelligence claimed 473 drone strikes had killed about 2,500 enemies.[110] Of course, not all those killed were the primary target of the strikes. However, it can be surmised that there was a target for most strikes, whether slain or not. The press was briefed that the primary purpose of the strikes was action 'against individual terrorist targets'.[111] However, the official figures excluded drone strikes in Afghanistan, Iraq and Syria, and thus did not cover many things that the force built by Stanley McChrystal and his successors had achieved. The US government acknowledged that non-governmental and news organisations had tried to make their own estimates by totting up attacks as they were reported, and those estimates tended to be higher. They conceded that 'figures ... should be considered in the light of inherent limitations on the ability to determine the precise number of combatant and non-combatant deaths given the non-permissive environments in which these strikes occur'.[112] Subsequently, Joe Biden concluded that, to an extent, Obama had been too sanguine about the likely effects of targeted killings. Biden was not concerned about the legality of US killings per se because his team adopted the logic of the Bush, Obama and Trump administrations that targeted killings were not assassinations under US law. The investigators nevertheless found that 'standards and procedures' were not 'rigorous' enough, leading to excessive civilian casualties.[113]

As before, it was not altogether clear if such 'targeted strikes' meant that the US was winning its assassination war even after the end of the 'charade'.[114] James Clapper, the US Director of National Intelligence, 'would observe that the truth regarding the global terrorism threat in 2012 was complicated. Years of drone strikes and commando raids had decimated al-Qaida in Afghanistan, and the bin Laden raid had provided us with valuable intelligence that the CIA and Defense Department had exploited to put the network that remained on the decline. But the ideology that al-Qaida exemplified didn't need bin Laden or even al-Qaida itself to spread.'[115] A few days after Brennan made another speech reinforcing the reality of US practice, Taliban assassins murdered Burhanuddin Rabbani in Kabul. Rabbani was the most significant surviving Islamist mujahideen who had thrown his lot in with Karzai.[116] In February 2012, a Taliban assassin killed two American military officers, Darin Loftis and Robert Marchanti, in their office within the Afghan Interior Ministry building in Kabul. The assassin used the old-fashioned technique of shooting the Americans with a 9mm self-loading pistol. According to the American head of intelligence for the International Security Assistance Force in Afghanistan, it was a 'haunted time'.[117]

The 'haunted time' was not confined to Afghanistan. Libya provided the best-publicised illustration that senior American leaders had underestimated assassination's burden.[118] As in Afghanistan, a combination of external intervention and internal unrest had effectively destroyed the Libyan state. An armed militia murdered one of the architects of modern assassination, Muammar Qaddafi, in October 2011. Of more concern to the western powers was the murder of the US ambassador to Libya, Christopher Stevens, in Benghazi in September 2012. The US government rapidly concluded that Stevens's murder had not been an assassination, but rather the result of a violent mob intent on killing Americans simply because they were Americans.[119] Nevertheless, the killing was spoken of by officials as an assassination, and the subsequent investigation revealed how vulnerable US and other western officials remained.[120]

At the same time as they were investigating the spike in assassinations in Afghanistan and Libya, the CIA reported that 'the use of political assassinations as a form of statecraft by the Russian Federation' was becoming ever more noticeable. Western governments, particularly the British, had been notably ineffective in countering what was by now an indisputable campaign.[121] Reporters estimated that the Russian intelligence services had assassinated approximately eight victims in the UK between 2003 and 2012.[122] The president of Russia between 2008 and 2012, Dmitry Medvedev, subsequently turned the vulnerability of London into a threatening 'joke' against the British press: 'be careful,' he warned. 'After all, a lot of things happen in London.'[123]

The British inquiry into the assassination of Andrei Litvinenko published its report in 2015.[124] In March 2018, the Russians carried out an even more brazen assassination on British soil. Two GRU assassins flew into Heathrow, stayed in east London, attempted to assassinate the defector Sergei Skripal in Salisbury, and then departed the same way they had come. The British authorities finally expelled twenty-three Russian intelligence officers from the UK. The British government also had considerable success in persuading its European allies to do the same, not least because the GRU could be shown to have been running hostile operations in western Europe too.[125] In the wake of a further assassination in Berlin's Little Tiergarten in 2019, the French identified a GRU 'operations hub' in the Alps. In all, European countries expelled about 150 Russian intelligence officers operating under diplomatic cover.[126]

However, even the unmasking of the Russian assassination network in Western Europe could only dominate the headlines for so long. Less than a month after the Prime Minister of Great Britain, Theresa May, officially announced the identity and affiliation of the Russian assassins, Saudi Arabian intelligence officers from two separate agencies lured the émigré Jamal Khashoggi into the Saudi consulate in Istanbul and killed him by dismemberment. The Turks published the identities of the assassination squad and despatched audio recordings of the assassination to the governments of the United States, Britain, France and Germany. The former British Foreign Secretary, Boris Johnson, described the assassination as a 'savage killing by heavies from Crown Prince MbS [Muhammed bin Salman's] own security team'.[127]

At the same moment though, the Israeli assassination campaign had come to be regarded as a proportionate response to threat.[128] In November 2019, an IDF F-15 jet killed the commander of Palestinian Islamic Jihad in Gaza, Baha Abu al-Ata.[129] One of the things that made al-Ata such a desirable target was his closeness to the Iranian IRGC.[130] In January 2020, the successor organisation to TF 714 finally assassinated the head of the Quds Force of the IRGC, Qassem Soleimani, in Baghdad. Soleimani was what was now called a 'personality target'.[131] According to President Trump's son-in-law, Jared Kushner, some diplomats still wanted to avoid 'unwanted attention' for such killings but 'that ship has sailed'.[132]

At the time this book was finished, in late 2024, the best contemporary illustration of Kushner's point was Ukraine. In 2016, Ukrainian assassins killed Arseny Pavlov, the leader of a pro-Russian separatist Donetsk militia. They blew up the lift in Pavlov's apartment block with Pavlov, and his bodyguard, within. This was merely the most publicised assassination of a Ukrainian campaign against separatist leaders working for Russia. Ukraine was a lower-capability power than the US and its close allies. Accordingly, it used more old-fashioned techniques in its assassinations. Nevertheless, Ukraine adhered to the Obama norms: quasi-appropriation to open celebration. Like the US, and Israel, Ukraine adopted the practice of being more open about the assassinations carried out by its military and relatively closed-mouthed about those attempted by its security service, the SBU.[133]

This alignment with US norms was hardly surprising since the CIA, under the direction of John Brennan, forged a close alliance with both the SBU and Ukrainian military intelligence, HUR, in 2016. The CIA's embrace of Ukrainian intelligence was striking because both SBU and HUR were notorious for being riddled with Russian sympathisers.

Nevertheless, with American money and training, both intelligence agencies created special operations units, the Fifth Directorate and Unit 2245, respectively. At the time of their formation, the CIA warned the Ukrainian services that assassination was a 'red line'. The CIA was interested in operations to penetrate the Russian signals network. The Ukrainians ignored the red line. The Fifth Directorate and Unit 2245 were capable of complex assassination plots from the outset. They began carrying out assassinations as soon as they became operational.

During the first Trump presidency, the Ukrainians did not even need to be coy about their intentions. Their relationship with the CIA deepened and broadened and expanded to include Britain's SIS and Dutch intelligence. When the Russians invaded Ukraine in 2022, Kyiv's assassination plans and units were already fully formed. HUR, CIA and SIS collaborated in activating partisan networks in Russian-occupied territory. One of the main roles of the partisans was the assassination of Russian collaborators.[134]

Ukraine also carried out assassinations in Russia itself. In August 2022, the Russian propagandist Darya Dugina died when her Toyota Land Cruiser was destroyed by an in-car bomb. In this case, the Ukrainians denied responsibility and claimed that it was the Russian secret services that had assassinated Dugina for criticising President Putin. In October 2023, however, US intelligence sources briefed the US press that Ukraine had assassinated Darya Dugina. Most observers assumed that the assassins had killed the wrong target, Dugina's father, the much more prominent ultra-nationalist Alexander Dugin, having got into a different car.[135] There was clearly no mistake when the SBU assassinated Lieutenant-General Igor Kirillov in Moscow in December 2024. The Ukrainians briefed the press that Kirillov, the head of Russia's radiation, biological and chemical protection forces, had overseen the use of chemical weapons on their troops. The SBU assassin used an electric scooter rigged with explosive which he parked outside Kirillov's apartment building. He detonated the scooter when the general and his aide emerged to drive to work. The Ukrainians also assassinated Mikhail Shatsky, a civilian cruise missile designer, just outside Moscow. He was shot.[136]

WHO SHOULD PULL THE TRIGGER?

In late 2023, the SBU and HUR assassinated several pro-Russian Ukrainian politicians. An assassin shot Oleg Tsaryov in Yalta in late October 2023, but he survived. The SBU did not announce their responsibility but briefed the press that they had made the attack.[137] In November 2023, HUR assassinated the Russian collaborationist politician Mikhail Filiponenko, using an in-car bomb. HUR made absolutely no bones about their responsibility or the purpose of the assassination. The assassination was a warning that 'traitors to Ukraine and collaborators with terrorist Russia in temporarily occupied territories . . . will receive just retribution!' HUR posted these statements on YouTube and the social media app Telegram to make sure everyone got the message. 'The hunt continues!' HUR added for good measure.[138] The SBU carried out the most high-profile of these collaborationist assassinations a few weeks later, shooting the former Ukrainian MP and 2019 presidential candidate Illya Kyva in the village of Suponevo near Moscow. The SBU briefed the press off the record that they were responsible for the assassination, but it was left to HUR to make a public statement on behalf of their sister service: 'Yes, we can confirm Kyva is no more. This fate will befall other traitors of Ukraine and puppets of Putin's regime.'[139]

The perceived balance between assassination as a threat and assassination as an opportunity for democratic powers plainly shifted in the twenty-first century. However, the burden of assassination has stayed much the same as it has been since the 1980s. The security systems of the 1980s and 1990s merely took on an even more institutionalised form. The main development of the twenty-first century was the marginal spread of such security systems to lower-level political operatives.

When talking about autocratic regimes, western commentators were happy to point to baroque security as an indicator of incipient political failure. In April 2023, for instance, western intelligence unveiled a defector from the Russian Federal Protection Service (FSO). The defector, Captain Gleb Karakulov, confirmed that President Putin had his own parallel railway network allowing him to travel unmolested between his homes near Moscow and the resort of Sochi, some one thousand miles. Karakulov claimed that 'our president has lost touch with the world. . . . He has been living in an information cocoon for the past couple of years, spending most of his time in his residences, which the media very fittingly call bunkers. He is pathologically afraid for his life. He surrounds himself with an impenetrable barrier of quarantines and an information vacuum. He only values his own life and the lives of his family and friends.' The atmosphere around Putin was that of an oriental court, complete with food tasters.[140]

This picture of Putin was clearly a deliberate act of propaganda. However, US policymakers in the twenty-first century made the same connection between extreme security and political failure even when speaking of politicians to whom they were broadly sympathetic. When the Director of the CIA, Leon Panetta, visited President Mubarak of Egypt in 2009, he took it as a worrying sign that Mubarak was protected by legions of security guards: 'the approach to his office was cleared for blocks, emphasizing the distance between Egypt's president and his people'.[141] Panetta's predecessor at CIA, Michael Hayden, and the US ambassador to Iraq, Ryan Crocker, agreed that their newly installed puppet in Iraq, Nuri al-Maliki, was a man warped by his fear of assassination. What al-Maliki had been doing for most of his adult existence, Crocker said, 'was running for his life literally, one step ahead of the assassination squads who caught and killed many of his colleagues . . . and many members of his own family. . . . You trusted no one. You talked to no one.' Maliki was, as a result, suspicious, secretive and uncommunicative.[142]

Such observations by US officials underplayed what fear of assassination had done to their own body politic. When Benazir Bhutto returned to Pakistan in 2007, her partisans in Washington and London estimated that an overall security force of twenty thousand would be necessary to keep the most threatened woman in the world safe from assassination. In January 2009, such were American fears that their first Black president might be assassinated that ninety-nine agencies deployed forty thousand security personnel for Barack Obama's inauguration.[143]

This was not just an impersonal bureaucracy at work: presidents intervened personally and regularly in their own security. Both George Bush and Barack Obama insisted that heads of the Secret Service whom they did not think up to the job should resign.¹⁴⁴ According to George Bush, after US special forces killed Saddam Hussein's adult children in 2003, he subsequently 'received intelligence that Saddam had ordered the killing of Barbara and Jenna [Bush's daughters] in return for the death of his sons'.¹⁴⁵ The US system placed increasingly more stress on the presidential dynasty. In November 2023, the security detail of President Biden's twenty-nine-year-old granddaughter opened fire on a car thief in Georgetown, Washington. The protection of adult grandchildren went far beyond what the American elite had imagined would be necessary even in the 'assassination decade' of the 1960s.¹⁴⁶

Despite these extraordinary precautions, there was still a demand for more. A 2015 Congressional report on the Secret Service concluded that it was 'in crisis', despite increases in both funding and personnel. As a result, the US government expanded the service by 25 per cent between 2015 and 2021.¹⁴⁷ The Secret Service was merely the best-known of a nexus of White House agencies, including the White House Military Office (which has its own security group), the Presidential Airlift Group and the White House Medical Unit. Some lawmakers believed an oriental court atmosphere grew in this nexus.¹⁴⁸

The Americans expanded the practice and principle of protection throughout the federal bureaucracy during the twenty-first century. By 2015, bureaucrats spoke of the 'federal protective force community' made up of over 150 organisations.¹⁴⁹ The old State Department SY, for instance, was transformed into the Diplomatic Security Service, now referred to as DS. It oversaw embassies that looked 'like a modern version of the crusader fortresses which dot the landscape of the Holy Land . . . designed to fill the same function for the American diplomats working inside . . . who are protected against any conceivable terrorist threat'.¹⁵⁰ DS still worked through the Regional Security Officer (RSO) system. In very dangerous countries, such as Iraq, one could expect to find a team of RSOs. Their protectees now fell under many headings: US diplomats, non-government personnel engaged in quasi-diplomatic work, other US federal officials and employees, visiting dignitaries and, indeed, anyone the RSO deemed worthy of protection. The maximum protection for an ambassador was a protective detail provided by DS's own special agents, reinforced by Site Security Teams.¹⁵¹

However, DS could no longer protect its many clients with personnel from within the federal bureaucracy, so the High Threat Protection Division of Overseas Protection Operations started hiring mercenaries. Most close protection was organised by a US mercenary detail leader. Under him were the personal protective details of US mercenaries commanded by a shift leader. Each shift leader commanded a force of three fully armoured SUVs. The detail leader retained a Quick Reaction Force mounted in a modern armoured vehicle capable of carrying ten armed and armoured men with a heavy machine gun or automatic grenade launcher. Under the detail leader too came a support force: mercenary US medics, armourers and dog teams. Base guards could be non-US mercenaries. Locals were only to be employed as interpreters.[152] Other countries matched US precautions, albeit with their own cultural tweaks.[153]

There was some pushback in the US State Department against such extreme levels of security becoming the norm. Obama-era officials in Washington felt that diplomats surrounded by shooters gave the message that Americans were both hated and fearful. A deputy assistant of state said that it was 'embarrassing' that Libya, recently liberated from the Qaddafi dictatorship, required so much security. As a result, the State Department discontinued the ambassador's sixteen-man Site Security Team, lent by the Department of Defense. When Christopher Stevens travelled from Tripoli to Benghazi, he had two DS bodyguards. The Benghazi mission had three DS special agents. The five DS agents were neither alert nor equipped when they were attacked. Less obviously, the CIA had sent in a team of nine heavily armed security officers to their nearby compound after an assassination attempt on the British ambassador. Six of the CIA men, in two armoured vehicles, attempted to save the diplomats, but Ambassador Stevens was dead before the CIA arrived. The inquiry into the death of Stevens became heavily politicised. However, the Obama administration did accept the argument that 'high-risk missions' must always operate on the assumption of imminent attack.[154]

The very real dangers faced by those who were denied security, or refused the offer, undermined any broader critique of too much security. In 2002, the European political class was transfixed by the assassination of the Dutch politician Pim Fortuyn in Hilversum. Fortuyn had made a name for himself as an anti-Islamist, although he was, in fact, shot dead by a militant vegan.[155] The prominent British political commentator Peter Riddell wrote that 'the assassination of politicians . . . and more frequent threats, have created permanent security barriers, increasing the gap between leaders and voters. This has already happened in Britain, the United States and Israel. And now the same looks like happening in The Netherlands, traditionally one of the most open and informal of countries.'[156] In fact, it took the murder of another Dutchman, the filmmaker Theo van Gogh, stabbed to death by a Muslim in Amsterdam in 2004, to cement the change in the Netherlands.[157] The successor to Fortuyn's populist mantle, Geert Wilders, thereafter lived a strange half-life in a government-provided secret home, protected by the Dutch security forces. In 2017, the Dutch government supplemented his security detail from the national police's Safety and Security Service (DBB) with the army's Special Security Missions Brigade (BSB), the military police unit that protected officials and politicians in dangerous environments overseas.[158]

The Dutch and British protective systems were very similar, with a national police protective unit at home and a military police unit overseas. In 2006, the Metropolitan Police created Protection Command, as part of its Specialist Operations Directorate. Like the Dutch DBB, the British now brought together their political, diplomatic and royal protection under one roof. Informally, senior politicians had been equated with royalty since the 1980s. That parity was formalised in the twenty-first century. Thus, various revelations made by the Duke of Sussex, a semi-detached member of the British royal family, in the 2020s also cast light on the political security system. A grant of protection was formalised under a committee, known as RAVEC (Royal and VIP Executive Committee), meeting in the Home Office. Royalty and senior politicians came together as 'role-based' protectees, then there were 'other VIPs', and finally 'occasional' protectees, granted security as the committee decided. A royal who had withdrawn from public duties was thus equated to a disgraced émigré, such as the former Russian oligarch Boris Berezovsky. Both the oligarch and the royal explicitly made the case that private security was far inferior to state security, although the balance between practicality and prestige in their reasoning was hard for outsiders to judge.¹⁵⁹ For those firmly in the state system, comparative security became a matter of comfortable political humour about whose was biggest.¹⁶⁰

For a VVIP, the lone killer, or even an assassin activated by an online conspiracy, was normally not much of a threat. Tony Blair did comment at the end of his prime ministership, however, that 'It's far more likely I'll shake hands with a group of kids today and somebody does something crazy than on a day in Iraq. I don't mean it's more dangerous in Redditch than Baghdad, it means if I am to be assassinated it's more likely to be in circumstances where I am out mixing with people but my people are not anticipating danger.'¹⁶¹

The most notorious example of 'people not anticipating danger' rested with the security detail of President Chen Shui-bian and Vice President Annette Lu of Taiwan. When their principals were shot while campaigning in Tainan in 2004, the security detail failed to notice that they had been hit.¹⁶² Such was the speculation that the Taiwanese government had to import forensics experts from the US to confirm that Chen had been shot in the stomach and Lu in the leg. President Chen dismissed the head of presidential security.¹⁶³

The town of Handlová proved to be the Slovak equivalent of Redditch. In May 2024, a seventy-one-year-old man shot Robert Fico, the Prime Minister of Slovakia, while he was on an official visit to the town. The would-be assassin fired five rounds at point-blank range from a self-loading pistol. Several of the bullets hit Fico: he was seriously wounded. Anyone with access to YouTube could watch the assassination attempt. The first thing that struck such observers was the haplessness of Fico's substantial security detail. Fico's 'people' were plainly not anticipating danger. This was an assassination attempt that should never have taken place.¹⁶⁴

Butler, Pennsylvania, was the US analogue of Redditch and Handlová. In July 2024, a rifle-armed sniper shot former president Donald Trump; a bullet grazed his ear, but he was not seriously wounded. All the major US news organisations were covering Trump's political rally: as a result, the film of the event was of even higher quality than that in the Fico case and was also accompanied by excellent audio. The Secret Service was plainly not sufficiently anticipating danger. The former president took himself into cover before his bodyguards reached him. A counter-sniper team had not spotted the rifleman on the roof of a nearby building, although they shot and killed him after he opened fire. Butler was a clear demonstration of what might happen if a politician's massively resourced security was 'complacent', showed 'repeated evidence of a lack of critical thinking' and 'did not perform at the elite levels needed'.[165] On the other hand, the security perimeter did work. Unlike in Handlová, the would-be lone assassin, a twenty-year-old American male, could not get close to his victim with a handgun. He took long-range shots from outside the speaking venue and missed, albeit barely.[166]

The most notable senior Western European politician to fall victim to a lone killer merely emphasised the danger of rejecting security. In 2003, a man stabbed Anna Lindh, the Swedish foreign minister, to death in a Stockholm department store. On the model of Olaf Palme, she had chosen to have no security while pursuing her private life.[167]

In terms of a world-renowned politician, the most prominent victim was the former Japanese prime minister, Abe Shinzo. In July 2022, a lone killer shot him in the back with a zip gun at a political rally in Nara. Abe was most certainly a VVIP. Japan did have a specialist unit for prime ministerial – including former prime ministerial – protection on the same model as European countries, in its case the Security Police of the Tokyo police force. However, by choice, Abe only had one specialist bodyguard with him at the rally, a handful of local officers from Nara prefecture were providing general security, and crowd control was the job of workers from Abe's Liberal Democratic Party.[168]

Whereas VVIPs had the most to fear from highly organised assassins using innovative methods, such as surface-to-air missiles, mere VIPs, on the edges of the security sphere, had a vested interest in moving within it.[169] For instance, the US Marshals' Service, one of the oldest members of the US 'federal protection community', protected two VVIPs, the Deputy Attorney General and the Secretary of Education. These two individuals had permanent protective details provided by the thirty-six-agent Office of Protective Operations. By contrast, VIPs – numbering 32,000 people, mainly judges – were looked after by the forty-three-strong Office of Protective Security, reinforced on a part-time basis by up to 200 Deputy US Marshals. The marshals reported that they were struggling to protect their VIPs. They calculated that they needed to increase their protective staff by 430 per cent to meet the case load.[170]

The three security spheres – VVIP, VIP and 'ordinary people' – were graphically illustrated by a terrorist attack in London in March 2017. An Islamist terrorist began by attacking unprotected citizens and tourists, using a car to run them down on Westminster Bridge. He then attempted to get into the area within parliament where VIP MPs parked their cars. He murdered the unarmed policeman on the gate with a knife. Protection Command close-protection officers attending their VVIP minister in the parking area then summarily shot the terrorist dead.[171]

The immediate, and relatively easy, response was to further harden the perimeter protection around MPs at work, making civilian access to the legislature even more difficult. The MPs themselves were just as concerned, however, by the risk they faced in their constituencies. There had been a measurable increase in attacks on lower-level politicians in many countries from 2014.[172] For instance, a year before the Westminster attack, the British Labour MP Jo Cox had been murdered near Leeds by a right-wing extremist using a shotgun and a knife. In June 2019, a far-right militant murdered the German CDU politician Walter Lübcke, the president of Kassel council, by shooting him in the head in his front garden. Kassel had been the site of a notorious Organisation Consul assassination attempt against the then council leader in the 1920s, but Lübcke was the first German politician to be assassinated by the Right since the Second World War.[173] In January 2024, the German government published figures showing that attacks on politicians had doubled since 2019.[174] The interior minister observed that because Germany had so many parliaments – seventeen – 'the police cannot be everywhere at once but they can adjust their protection concepts'.[175]

In October 2021, an Islamist stabbed the British Conservative MP David Amess to death in his Essex constituency. In 2024, his daughter filed a legal claim against the Home Office and the police for failing to protect him.[176] The British government finally agreed to fund private bodyguards for MPs in February 2024.[177] Other European countries did much the same.[178] In March 2024, the US Federal Election Commission proposed a change in its own regulations to allow candidates in federal elections to use their political campaign funds to pay for bodyguards and the hardening of their homes. The direction of travel in democracies is clear for the foreseeable future: they will remain under pressure to provide more security for the political elite.[179]

CONCLUSION

The assassination of Archduke Franz Ferdinand, heir to the throne of the Habsburg empire, started the First World War. Franz Ferdinand's death also marked the start of a new era of assassination. His assassins were members of a terrorist organisation backed by a state intelligence agency. The assassination weapon was a self-loading pistol. The assassination at Sarajevo had terrible consequences. It was only with careful thought thereafter that states could dismiss assassinations as the work of unattached groups of fanatics.

From the middle of the twentieth century, the intelligence agencies of the democratic nations themselves flirted with assassination. They developed specialist tools such as silenced weapons. State-sponsored assassination spilled over into the post-war world, as did the belief that the western powers were enthusiastic commissioners of assassination.

As modern terrorism developed in the 1970s, assassination became part of that more general phenomenon. This was, seemingly, the age of non-state assassins. However, those assassins were often financed, trained and employed by states antithetical to the western world. The assassins initially used the methods of their forerunners. The favoured assassination weapon remained the pistol-calibre small arm; but by the 1980s, states began to supply terrorists with plentiful quantities of plastic explosive. Before the 1970s, assassination by explosive device had often been attempted, but usually had failed. Dynamite and TNT killed many bystanders but relatively few actual targets. Plastic explosive changed that equation to some extent. Nevertheless, the pistol remained the weapon that most often hit the target into the twenty-first century.[1]

During the Cold War, the USA devoted billions of dollars to the development of pilotless guided weapons.[2] From 2003, the USA increasingly used such systems to locate and kill selected targets. There was thus a twenty-first-century revolution in assassination weapons. Even when assassination was carried out by more traditional means, it often rested on a huge infrastructure of signals and geospatial intelligence. The United States now regularly kills specific named enemies with guided missiles, usually fired from a pilotless aircraft. Lesser powers have had to make do with twentieth-century methods of killing. However, more and more countries have gained access to precise guided weapons. The full consequences of the twenty-first-century revolution in assassination are yet to be seen; however, assassination will remain the preserve of states.

Beyond the centrality of the state, the detailed study of modern assassination leads to the observation that existing lists of 'significant' assassinations, based on the charismatic power of famous political leaders, are likely to be off beam. The 1960s American trinity of the assassinated – President John F. Kennedy, Dr Martin Luther King and Senator Robert F. Kennedy – have, probably, had the most words written about them. Those words try to capture the imagined lost future of American liberalism. In effect, commentators can write whatever they want about that imagined future because it never came to pass. President Ronald Reagan had it about right when he created Dr Martin Luther King Day in 1983. 'In 1968 Martin Luther King was gunned down by a brutal assassin,' Reagan said, 'his life cut short at the age of 39. But those 39 short years had changed America forever.'[3] What King had done could be described; what he might have done to avoid the souring of American society in the late 1960s was speculation. Much the same could be said about the South Asian trio of Gandhi, Aung San and Liaquat Ali Khan. Who knows if the component parts of the former British Raj could have avoided bloody religious communal conflict, and at times openly declared war, if the charismatic leaders of the independence struggle had survived to guide their nations. The politicians in control of India in

1948 and 1968 confined themselves to sedulously broadcasting the Hindu identity of Gandhi's assassin in the certainty that any word of a Muslim assassin would trigger a 'very severe commotion in the country'.[4]

If one were to pick provably significant assassinations, the list would be somewhat different. It would go something like this. The assassination of Sir Lee Stack in 1924 provoked the British government to divorce the Sudan from Egypt. As a result, when Britain wound up its African empire, Sudan became an independent country. At a 'single stroke', one nation decided the future of two others 'abruptly by an act of force'.[5] At the time, the British Labour Party denounced the British government's handling of Sudan as worse than the Austro-Hungarians' handling of Sarajevo. As their spokesman Charles Trevelyan put it, 'We all remember the Note of Austria to Serbia . . . was generally reprobated in this country as a great deal too violent . . . it was issued nearly a month after the murder of the Archduke and that the serious accusations which were being made against the Serbian government were based upon the findings of a criminal inquiry . . . there had been no criminal inquiry into this case before the Government made their accusation against the Egyptian Government.'[6] Applauding his words, the German press called Austria's July 1914 ultimatum to Serbia 'a model of decent clemency' when compared to Britain's ultimatum to Egypt.[7]

The assassination of Zhang Zuolin in 1928 changed the balance of power in northern China and destabilised both the Chinese and Japanese political systems: they were only stabilised by civil war, world war and millions of deaths.

The assassination of Reinhard Heydrich in 1942 was of little practical significance, although it was a tragedy for those Czechs whom the Germans massacred in the wake of the killing. The death of a man of demonstrably monstrous evil, however, provided a template for 'honourable assassination' carried out by righteous democrats. Thereafter, it was to make an absolute argument against western democracies carrying out assassinations hard to sustain.

The assassination of Indira Gandhi in 1984 sparked communal violence in India. In the longer term, Gandhi's assassination, and the narrowly unsuccessful assassination attempt on Margaret Thatcher a few weeks previously, marked the formalisation of the western security

CONCLUSION

system and the concept of the Very Very Important political leader who must be hived off not only from her own citizenry but also from her lower-level political operatives. At the beginning of the twentieth century, Max Weber had described the political system of the modern state as a balancing act between leader, political operatives (including MPs), the bureaucracy and the citizenry. From 1984 onwards, democratic political leaders knowingly entered a close survival relationship with their security bureaucracies, thus fundamentally altering that balance.

The adaptation to new assumptions about assassination was traumatic. It involved western leaders acknowledging their lack of power to act effectively in the international arena. Their analysis of assassination conspiracies involved the explicit, if reluctant, admission that western countries had become a vulnerable and penetrated group of polities.

Cutting across the grain of many Whiggish assumptions about political development, the later twentieth-century system of independent democratic nation-states proved vulnerable when compared to the previous imperial system. The reach of the imperial powers of the pre-Second World War period had been long. Many assassins were captured. The end of assassination was often bloody retribution: the execution of assassins was standard practice. In the post-Second World war era, on the other hand, it did prove possible for assassins to generate crises through the relentless assassination of middle- or lower-ranking officials. The imperialist democrats valued sangfroid more than their successors.

The nearer one gets to the present, the harder it becomes to identify assassinations of enduring importance. The death of Abu Musab al-Zarqawi in 2006, however, marked the public proof that the US government had constructed its own 'killing machine'. Thereafter, US presidents could, and would, regularly order the killing of adversaries, including US citizens, with a near-certainty that those orders would be carried out. Confident that US domestic law allowed them to avoid the word assassination altogether, American leaders spoke more and more openly about the selective killing of political adversaries.

However, historically, the direct results of assassination have almost always disappointed the assassins. If one looks simply at the well-attested results achieved by the democratic procurers of assassination, the killing has hardly lived up to expectations. The French state's assassination campaign against Algerians did nothing to delay France's defeat in Algeria. At the same time, its blowback saw Frenchmen assassinating Frenchmen. The post-war American assassination campaigns rarely had any positive results. Furthermore, they discredited individuals, organisations and the federal state itself, making it harder for the US to achieve its strategic Cold War goals.

The US government seems content with its twenty-first-century killing machine but has racked up an unenviable record of losing armed conflicts while it has been in operation. The US's close ally Israel was disappointed when its habit of 'mowing the grass' – regularly assassinating militant Palestinian leaders – left it blind to a strategic surprise in October 2023, when it was attacked from the tiny Palestinian enclave of Gaza. The Israelis used assassination after 7 October 2023 on the same model and with the same intensity that the US had pioneered during their defeats in Iraq and Afghanistan.[8] Both US and Israeli leaders faced countervailing threats of assassination, but such threats mainly served to highlight how impotent – at the least in the short term – were those facing a 'killing machine' without one of their own.[9] The asymmetric ability of highly protected political leaders to kill on demand nevertheless risks making them less strategically imaginative.

These observations lead to some potentially counter-intuitive conclusions, at least if one is approaching assassination from the political science tradition of trying to count attacks, the post-Kennedy US tradition of assassination investigation, or even from the tumult of twenty-first-century events. There have been two relatively short moments when assassination has been especially salient for international politics, the first running from 1914 to 1928, the second from 1979 to 1986. In the first period, assassination really did shape the fate of very large portions of the earth's surface, and what might be described as a robust political theory of assassination was articulated by Max Weber. More subtly, in the second period, western governments created a counter-assassination system based on shared assumptions and often co-operation. That counter-assassination system has remained in place, indeed spread and deepened, for decades. It is only when the western counter-assassination system is replaced by something else that the modern age of assassination will come to an end.

NOTES

Introduction

1. American Embassy, Santiago to Secretary of State, Washington, Tel. 7775, 7 November 1986, Department of State Freedom of Information Act Virtual Reading Room [hereafter SDRR].
2. State Department, The Letelier Dispute: Background and Factual Summary, 22 December 1988, SDRR.
3. Robert Pastor [NSC Staff], Memorandum for Zbigniew Brzezinski and David Aaron: Conversation with our Ambassador to Chile, George Landau, 28 June 1978, SDRR.
4. American Embassy, Santiago to Secretary of State, Washington, Tel. 09212, 21 September 1976 & DIA, Washington to RUCRDIB/DIACURINTEL, Chile: Letelier Assassination Aftermath, 28 September 1976, SDRR.
5. CIA, Directorate of Operations, Information Report, 20 August 1974, SDRR.
6. American Embassy, Santiago to Secretary of State, Washington, Tel. 7539, 30 October 1979, SDRR.
7. FBI, Attempted Assassination of Bernardo Leighton, October 6, 1975, Rome, Italy, 9 April 1980, SDRR.
8. American Embassy, Santiago to Secretary of State, Washington, Tel. 06268, 21 August 1987.
9. The Letelier Dispute: Background and Factual Summary, 22 December 1988.
10. American Embassy, Buenos Aires to Secretary of State, Washington (RSO [Regional Security Officer] [George] Beckett to SY), Tel. 0698, 30 January 1975, SDRR.
11. CIA, Former Chilean Ambassador Killed by Bomb in Washington, 21 September 1976, SDRR.
12. The Letelier Dispute: Background and Factual Summary, 22 December 1988.

13. Ibid.
14. Secretary of State, Washington to American Embassy, Caracas, Tel. 024363, 29 January 1979; Secretary of State, Washington to American Embassy, Santiago, Tel. 027763, 29 January 1986, SDRR.
15. Catherine Royle (Santiago) to James Ayres (SAMD, FCO), 18 June 1990, FCO 7/8008, The National Archives, London [hereafter TNA].
16. Terence Todman (ARA) Action Memorandum to the Secretary: The Letelier–Moffitt Assassination Investigation, 8 February 1978, SDRR.
17. The Letelier Dispute: Background and Factual Summary, 22 December 1988.
18. Department of State, Bureau of Intelligence and Research, Report No. 864: South America's Southern Cone – Bloc in Formation? 6 October 1977, SDRR.
19. CIA National Foreign Assessment Center, Latin America Weekly Review, 23 March 1978, SDRR.
20. American Embassy, Santiago to Secretary of State, Washington, Tel. 2314, 30 March 1978, SDRR.
21. Secretary of State, Washington to American Embassy, Caracas, Tel. 103547, 6 May 1977; Acting Chief, Latin American Division, CIA, Memorandum for Director of Central Intelligence: Request for Exception to Agency 'No Comment' Policy Concerning DDO Activities and Relationships, 23 August 1978; Secretary of State, Washington to American Embassy, Stockholm, Tel. 028274, 21 February 1979, SDRR.
22. American Embassy, Santiago to Secretary of State, Washington, Tel. 06363, 24 August 1978, Letelier/Moffitt Assassination Case: Manuel Contreras, *Chile and the United States*, Digital National Security Archive [hereafter DNSA].
23. Secretary of State, Washington to American Embassy, Buenos Aires, Tel. 209192, 23 August 1975, SDRR.
24. American Embassy, Buenos Aires [Legal Attaché] to Director [of the FBI], 28 September 1976, *Argentina, 1975–1980*, DNSA.
25. Secretary of State, Washington to American Embassy, Asunción, Tel. 089326, 24 March 1977, SDRR.
26. US Information Agency, Washington DC to American Embassy, Santiago, 13 July 1978, SDRR.
27. Viron Vaky (ARA), Briefing Memorandum to the Secretary: Letelier/Moffitt Assassination Case: Related Foreign Policy Issue, 18 September 1978, SDRR.
28. Secretary of State, Washington to American Embassy, Santiago, Tel. 201355, 3 August 1979, SDRR.
29. Cyrus Vance, Memorandum for the President: Letelier/Moffitt Case, 19 October 1979; Zbigniew Brzezinski, Memorandum for the Secretary of State: Letelier/Moffitt Case and US Policy to Chile, 27 November 1979; Statement [on the Letelier Case], 30 November 1979, SDRR.
30. [Redacted] to Director [of Central Intelligence], 'Reactions among Military and Carabinero Leaders to the Investigation into Possible Involvement of Chilean Government in Orlando Letelier Assassination', 20 March 1978, SDRR.
31. Letelier/Moffitt Assassination Case: Manuel Contreras.
32. Secretary of State, Washington to American Embassy, Santiago, Tel. 193668, August 1978, SDRR.

33. Robert Pastor, Memorandum for Zbigniew Brzezinski: US Policy to Chile – Reaching the Crunch Point on Letelier, 25 May 1979, SDRR.
34. Alan McPherson, *Ghosts of Sheridan Circle: How a Washington Assassination Brought Pinochet's Terror State to Justice* (University of North Carolina Press, 2019), pp. 281–96.
35. Fiona McCann, 'Pinochet Charged with Killing', *The Times*, 14 June 2004, p. 8.
36. Colin Kidd, 'Assassination Principles in Scottish Political Culture: Buchanan to Hogg', in Caroline Erskine and Roger A. Mason, eds, *George Buchanan: Political Thought in Early Modern Britain and Europe* (Ashgate, 2012), pp. 269–88. Professor Kidd lent me a draft of this essay when I first became interested in assassination: his phrase has stuck with me.
37. Memorandum of Telephone Conversation [Eagleburger and Kissinger], 23 May 1975, *The Kissinger Telephone Conversations: A Verbatim Record of US Diplomacy, 1969–1977*, DNSA.
38. Riyadh to FCO, Tel. 1, 2 January 1990, FCO 8/8179; P. McKearney (British Embassy, Bucharest) to D.A. Jones (Security Coordination Unit, FCO), 27 December 1984, FCO 178/39, TNA.
39. FCO to New Delhi, Tel. 150, 5 February 1985, FCO 178/68, TNA.
40. 'Tony', handwritten note, 14 August 1991 [Weeder's notes inadvertently left in file], DO 35/9415, TNA.
41. Senate Committee on Governmental Affairs, *Investigation of Illegal or Improper Activities in Connection with 1996 Federal Election Campaigns*, Vol. 1, March 1998.
42. President John F. Kennedy Assassination Records Collection, National Archives, Washington. https://www.archives.gov/research/jfk. [hereafter JFK].
43. Murray Havens, Carl Leiden and Karl Schmitt, *The Politics of Assassination* (Prentice-Hall, 1970), p. 4.
44. There is no mention of assassination in the current version of the UK–US extradition treaty, for example, although it was specifically dealt with in its 1931 forebear.
45. David Barron (Acting Assistant Attorney General), Memorandum for the Attorney General: Lethal Operations against Shaykh Anwar Aulaqi, 19 February 2010; US Department of Justice, Office of Legal Counsel, Memorandum for the Attorney General: Applicability of Federal Criminal Laws and the Constitution to Contemplated Legal Operations against Shaykh Anwar al-Aulaqi, 16 July 2010.
46. Michael Hayden, *Playing to the Edge: American Intelligence in the Age of Terror* (Penguin, 2016), p. 124.
47. Patrick Wright (No. 10) to S.J. Barrett (FCO), 27 June 1975, PREM 16/552, TNA; Michael Silvestri, *Policing Bengali Terrorism in India and the World: Imperial Intelligence and Revolutionary Nationalism, 1905–1939* (Springer, 2019), p. 106; Durba Ghosh, *Gentlemanly Terrorists: Political Violence and the Colonial State in India, 1919–1947* (CUP, 2017), pp. 247–52.
48. Ginane Brownell, 'Biljana Srbljanovic on her New Play', *Wall Street Journal*, 22 May 2014.
49. 'The Bhutan Scene: Uneasy End to Isolation', *Financial Times*, 27 May 1969 & T.J. O'Brien (British Embassy, Kathmandu) to I.J.M. [Iain] Sutherland (SAD, FCO), 23 September 1970, FCO 37/531, TNA.
50. Committee of Imperial Defence: Sub-Committee on Arms Traffic, 'Some Considerations on the Traffic in Arms as a Post-war Problem', Memorandum by Lieutenant-Colonel Sir Mark Sykes, Bart, MP, 12 January 1917, CAB 16/44, TNA.

51. *Cmnd.* 3165, *Report by Mr Roderic Bowen, QC, on Procedures for the Arrest, Interrogation and Detention of Suspected Terrorists in Aden*, 14 November 1966.
52. Michael Finch, 'A Total War of the Mind: The French Theory of *la guerre révolutionnaire*, 1954–1958', *War in History*, 25 (2018), pp. 410–34.
53. Nachman Ben-Yahuda, 'Political Assassination Events as a Cross-cultural Form of Alternative Justice', *International Journal of Comparative Sociology*, 38 (1997), pp. 25–47.
54. Department of State, Bureau of Intelligence and Research, Bitburg: A Look Back and Ahead, 7 June 1985, SDRR.

Chapter 1

1. Disraeli was addressing the House of Commons on the assassination of Abraham Lincoln in 1865.
2. The Hon. Auberon Herbert, 'The Ethics of Dynamite', *Contemporary Review*, 65 (1894), pp. 667–87.
3. Sir Eyre Crowe, record of a conversation with Signor Preziosi, 5 November 1923 quoted in note from the Marquess Curzon of Kedleston to Sir R. Graham (Rome), Tel. 297, 7 November 1923, *Documents on British Foreign Policy, 1919–1939*, Ser. 1, Vol. 24 [hereafter *DBFP*].
4. Lisa Traynor, *Archduke Franz Ferdinand and the Era of Assassination* (Royal Armouries, 2018).
5. Danilo Šarenac, 'Why Did Nobody Control Apis? Serbian Military Intelligence and the Sarajevo Assassination', in Mark Cornwall, ed., *Sarajevo 1914: Sparking the First World War* (Bloomsbury, 2015), Chapter 17.
6. Interview with Pavle Bastaitch and Mustafa Golubitch, 1 August 1926, MS 56/2, Durham MSS, Royal Anthropological Institute, London [hereafter Durham MSS].
7. F.R. Bridge, 'The British Elite and the Sarajevo Assassinations', in Mark Cornwall, ed., *Sarajevo 1914: Sparking the First World War* (Bloomsbury, 2015), Chapter 10.
8. 'The Crisis in Hungary', *The Times*, 10 June 1912, p. 8.
9. Barbara Jelavich, 'What the Habsburg Government Knew about the Black Hand', *Austrian Studies Yearbook* (1991), pp. 131–50.
10. Count Berchtold to the Imperial and Royal Ambassadors in London, Paris, Berlin, Rome, Petersburg and Constantinople and to the Imperial and Royal Minister in Bucharest, Addendum I, 23 July 1914, *Austrian Red Book: Official Files Pertaining to Pre-War History, Part I: 28 June to 23 July 1914* (George Allen & Unwin, 1923), Doc. 1 [hereafter *Austrian Red Book*].
11. Samuel Williamson, 'Leopold, Count Berchtold: The Man Who Could Have Prevented the Great War', in Günter Bischof, Fritz Plasser and Peter Berger, eds, *From Empire to Republic: Post World War I Austria* (University of New Orleans Press, 2010), pp. 24–51.
12. John Miller-Melamed, *Misfire: The Sarajevo Assassination and the Winding Road to World War I* (OUP, 2022), pp. 148–85.
13. Jack Levy and William Mulligan, 'Why 1914 but Not Before? A Comparative Study of the July Crisis and its Precursors', *Security Studies*, 30 (2021), pp. 213–44.
14. Miller-Melamed, *Misfire*, pp. 148–85.
15. Williamson, 'Leopold, Count Berchtold'.

16. Count Szapary (St Petersburg) to Count Berchtold, 18 July 1914, *Austrian Red Book*, Doc. 24.
17. Hannes Leidinger, 'The Case of Alfred Redl and the Situation of Austro-Hungarian Military Intelligence on the Eve of World War I', in Günter Bischof, Ferdinand Karlhofer and Samuel Williamson, eds, *1914: Austria-Hungary, the Origins and the First Year of World War I* (University of New Orleans Press, 2014), pp. 35–54.
18. Consul Jones to Sir Edward Grey, 29 June 1914, *British Documents on the Origins of the War, 1898–1914*, ed. G.P. Gooch and Harold Temperley, Volume XI (HMSO, 1926), Doc. 13 [hereafter *BDOW*].
19. Sir M. de Bunsen to Sir Edward Grey, 29 June 1914, *BDOW*, Doc. 21.
20. Tisza's First Memorandum to Franz Josef, 1 July 1914, Ernest Ludwig, 'Martyrdom of Count Stephan Tisza', *Current History*, 21/4 (January 1925), Doc. 1; Relation of the Hungarian Premier Count Tisza, 1 July 1914, *Austrian Red Book*, Doc. 2.
21. Miller-Melamed, *Misfire*, pp. 148–85.
22. Sir M. de Bunsen to Sir Edward Grey, 5 July 1914, *BDOW*, Doc. 37.
23. Autograph Letter from Emperor and King Francis Joseph to Emperor William, 2 July 1914, *Austrian Red Book*, Doc. 1.
24. Levy and Mulligan, 'Why 1914 but Not Before?', p. 241.
25. Sir M. de Bunsen to Sir Edward Grey, 5 July 1914, *BDOW*, Doc. 40.
26. Tisza's Second Memorandum to Franz Josef, 8 July 1914, Ludwig, 'Martyrdom of Count Stephan Tisza', Doc. 2.
27. Max Müller to Sir Edward Grey, 14 July 1914, *BDOW*, Doc. 70.
28. Council of Ministers for Common Concerns: Protocol, 7 July 1914, *Austrian Red Book*, Doc. 8.
29. Councillor von Wiesner (Sarajevo) to Imperial and Royal Department of Foreign Affairs, Telegram, 13 July 1914, *Austrian Red Book*, Doc. 18.
30. Sir Edward Grey to Sir M. de Bunsen, 24 July 1914, *BDOW*, Doc. 61.
31. Sir M. de Bunsen to Sir Edward Grey, 16 July 1914, *BDOW*, Doc. 50.
32. Nathan Orgill, 'Reawakening the Nation: British Journalists and the Interwar Debate on the Origins of the First World War', *Journalism Studies*, 17 (2016), pp. 517–31.
33. Attachments to Sir Maurice de Bunsen to Sir Edward Grey, 15 July 1914, *BDOW*, Doc. 64; Count Berchtold to the Imperial and Royal Ambassadors in London, Paris, Berlin, Rome, Petersburg and Constantinople and to the Imperial and Royal Minister in Bucharest, 23 July 1914, *Austrian Red Book*, Doc. 61.
34. Count Berchtold to Baron von Giesl (Belgrade), 20 July 1914, *Austrian Red Book*, Doc. 27.
35. Count Berchtold to the Imperial and Royal Ambassadors in London, Paris, Berlin, Rome, Petersburg and Constantinople, 20 July 1914, *Austrian Red Book*, Doc. 29.
36. EAC, Minute on Communication by the German Ambassador, 24 July 1914, *BDOW*, Doc. 100.
37. Miller-Melamed, *Misfire*, pp. 148–85.
38. G.P. Gooch to Seton-Watson, 25 October 1914, SEW 17/8/3, Seton-Watson Papers, School of Slavonic and East European Studies, University College London [hereafter SSEES].
39. Paul Miller, '"The First Shots of the First World War": The Sarajevo Assassination in History and Memory', *Central Europe*, 14 (2016), pp. 141–56.

40. Jonathan Steinberg, 'Old Knowledge and New Research: A Summary of the [2011] Conference on the Fischer Controversy 50 Years On', *Journal of Contemporary History*, 48 (2013), pp. 241–50; Christopher Clark, *The Sleepwalkers: How Europe Went to War in 1914* (Penguin, 2013), p. xiii; Annika Mombauer, 'Guilt or Responsibility? The Hundred-Year Debate on the Origins of World War I', *Central European History*, 48 (2015), pp. 541–64.
41. M. Edith Durham, *The Serajevo Crime* (George Allen & Unwin, 1925), p. 23 & p. 64.
42. Edith Durham to Sir Edward Boyle, 10 April 1944, Boyle Papers, MS. 405, Special Collections, Brotherton Library, University of Leeds [hereafter Boyle Papers].
43. Winston Churchill, 'June 28', *The Sunday Dispatch*, 29 June 1941, p. 7.
44. Winston Churchill, *The World Crisis, Volume I, 1911–1914* (Odhams Press, 1938 [1923]), p. 150. Archduke Charles killed by a bomb.
45. T.G. Otte, ' "The Light of History": Scholarship and Officialdom in the Era of the First World War', *Diplomacy & Statecraft*, 30 (2019), pp. 253–87.
46. 'A Day of Fate', Leader, *The Times*, 28 June 1924, p. 13.
47. Report on the Work of the Department of Propaganda in Enemy Countries, November 1918, SEW 4/1/4, SSEES.
48. Minute of a Meeting of the Imperial War Cabinet, 18 December 1918, CAB 23/42/15, TNA.
49. Commission on the Responsibility of the Authors of the War and on Enforcement of Penalties, Report Presented to the Preliminary Peace Conference, 29 March 1919, *American Journal of International Law*, 14 (January–April 1920), pp. 95–154.
50. Executive Committee of Serbian Society to David Lloyd George, 25 June 1917, SEW 5/3/1, SSEES; 'A Nation's Celebration of Supreme Sacrifice' [1917], SEW 5/3/1, SSEES; Hugh and Christopher Seton-Watson, *The Making of a New Europe: R.W. Seton-Watson and the Last Years of Austria-Hungary* (Methuen, 1981), p. 93.
51. Seton-Watson to Arnold Toynbee, 12 February 1929, SEW 17/6/9, SSEES.
52. Wickham Steed, 'Destiny or Devilry', *Observer*, 27 June 1926, p. 7.
53. R.W. Seton-Watson, 'The Murder at Sarajevo', *Foreign Affairs*, 3/1 (1924), pp. 489–509.
54. Even the immensely laudatory *Dictionary of National Biography* entry for Seton-Watson, written by his friend and fellow Serb Society member Henry Wickham Steed, but revised by the Regius Professor of History at Oxford, R.J.W. Evans, in 2004, can be read in this sense.
55. David MacKenzie, 'The "Black Hand" and its Statutes', *East European Quarterly*, 25 (1991), pp. 179–206.
56. Interview with Pavle Bastaitch and Mustafa Golubitch, 1 August 1926.
57. David MacKenzie, *The Black Hand on Trial: Salonika, 1917* (Columbia UP, 1995), p. 72.
58. RWSW (B Section), Intelligence Bureau, Department of Information, Special Memorandum on Pact of Corfu, 14 September 1917, SEW 4/1/3, SSEES.
59. Compton Mackenzie, 'Why Did the Book Society Recommend This?', *Daily Mail*, 12 June 1934, p. 5. Mackenzie, the British secret service head of station in Salonika in 1917, was reviewing Louis Adamic's *The Native Returns*; Edith Durham to Seton-Watson, 8 March 1929, SEW 17/6/9, SSEES.

60. [Pencil notes by SW], 'Col. Cedo Popovic', SEW 9/5/1, SSEES; Dragutin Dimitrijević to the Military Tribunal for Officers, 28 March 1917 in Stoyan Gavrilović, 'New Evidence on the Sarajevo Assassination', *Journal of Modern History*, 27/4 (December 1955), pp. 410–13.
61. Holger Herwig, 'Patriotic Self-Censorship in Germany after the Great War', *International Security*, 12 (Fall 1987), pp. 5–44.
62. Stephan Petzold, 'Fritz Fischer and the Rise of Critical Historiography in West Germany, 1945–1966: A Study in the Social Production of Historical Knowledge', unpublished dissertation, Aberystwyth (2010), pp. 30–31.
63. Wirth to von Preger, 26 November 1921, in Catherine Ann Cline, 'British Historians and the Treaty of Versailles', *Albion*, 20 (1988), pp. 43–8.
64. Harry Elmer Barnes, 'Assessing the Blame for World War: A Revised Judgment Based on All the Available Documents', *Current History*, 20/2 (1924), pp. 171–95; Albert Bushnell Hart [the editor of *Current History*], 'A Dissent from the Conclusions of Professor Barnes', *Current History*, 20/2 (1924), pp. 195–6. Archibald Cary Coolidge [Harvard University, co-editor of *Foreign Affairs*] to Seton-Watson, 22 June 1926, SEW 9/5/4, SSEES; Hamilton Fish Armstrong (Editor, *Foreign Affairs*) to Seton-Watson, 27 December 1926, SEW 17/8/3, SSEES; Hamilton Fish Armstrong to Seton-Watson, 25 July 1927, SEW 17/8/3, SSEES; Bogićević to Edith Durham, 8 June 1927 with M.E. Durham, Note to Bogićević letter, MS 56/1, Durham MSS; Edith Durham to Sir Edward Boyle, 28 October 1938, Boyle Papers, MS. 405.
65. Headlam-Morley, Memorandum, *DBFP, 1919–1939*, Ser. 1A, Vol. 4, Doc. 17.
66. J.W. Headlam-Morley to Seton-Watson, 25 November 1927, SEW 9/3/3, SSEES.
67. Seton-Watson to G.P. Gooch, 27 September 1927, SEW 17/8/3, SSEES; G.P. Gooch to Seton-Watson, 28 September 1927, SEW 17/8/3, SSEES.
68. [James Headlam-Morley], 'Origins of the War', *Times Literary Supplement*, 25 April 1929, p. 325; G.P. Gooch, 'European Diplomacy before the War in the Light of the Archives', 25 October 1938 published in *International Affairs*, 18 (1939), pp. 77–102; John Young, 'Emotions and the British Government's Decision for War in 1914', *Diplomacy & Statecraft*, 29 (2018), pp. 543–64.
69. Statement sent to JMJ for publication, 4 April 1925, SEW 9/2/1, SSEES; J.W. Headlam-Morley (Foreign Office) to Seton-Watson, 25 November 1927, SEW 9/3/3, SSEES; R.W. Seton-Watson, 'Preface to the Czech Edition' [of *Sarajevo*], 28 August 1927, SEW 9/5/4, SSEES; Seton-Watson to Arnold Toynbee, 12 February 1929, SEW 17/6/9, SSEES.
70. Maurice de Bunsen to Seton-Watson, 27 May 1926, SEW 9/5/4, SSEES.
71. Sir Maurice de Bunsen to Edith Durham, 28 June 1928, MS 56/1, Durham MSS.
72. Edith Durham to Sir Edward Boyle, 18 January 1939, Boyle Papers.
73. Edith Durham to Sir Edward Boyle, 15 November 1928, Boyle Papers.
74. Ramsay MacDonald to Edith Durham, 19 February 1925, MS 56/1, Durham MSS.
75. 'Publishing the Archives', Leader, *The Times*, 3 December 1924.
76. G.P. Gooch to Seton-Watson, 25 October 1914, SEW 17/8/3, SSEES; Harold Temperley, 'The Serajevo Murder', Letter to the Editor, *The Times*, 11 January 1926, p. 13; Harold Temperley, 'The Sarajevo Memorial: Some Parallels', Letter to Editor, *Manchester Guardian*, dated 1 February 1930.

77. Seton-Watson to G.P. Gooch, 2 March 1926, SEW 17/8/3, SSEES; R.W. Seton-Watson, *Sarajevo: A Study in the Origins of the Great War* (Hutchinson, 1926).
78. John Paul Newman, 'Post-imperial and Post-war Violence in the South Slav Lands, 1917–1923', *Contemporary European History*, 19 (2010), pp. 249–65; R.W. S.-W., 'Pasic Nicholas (1846–)', SEW 9/5/2, SSEES.
79. Christian Axboe Nielsen, 'Surveillance, Denunciations, and Ideology during King Aleksandar's Dictatorship, 1928–1934', *East European Politics and Societies*, 23 (2009), pp. 34–62.
80. Alex Devine to Edith Durham, 15 July 1928, MS 56/1, Durham MSS.
81. 'A Divided Nation', *Manchester Guardian*, 13 July 1928.
82. R.W. Seton-Watson, 'The Murder at Sarajevo', pp. 489–509; Edith Durham, Notebook 1, MS 52, Durham MSS; Sidney Bradshaw Fay, 'Serbia's Responsibility for the World War', *Current History*, 23/1 (October 1925), pp. 41–8.
83. M.E. Durham, 'Serajevo Murder', *Manchester Guardian*, 20 December 1924, p. 5; M. Edith Durham, 'Fresh Light on the Serajevo Crime', *Contemporary Review*, 137 (1925), pp. 39–49; Seton-Watson to Cecil Melville, 26 March 1925 and 6 April 1925, SEW 9/3/2, SSEES; Ljuba Jovanović, 'The Murder of Sarajevo [translation of 'After Vidov Dan 1914']', *Journal of the British Institute of International Affairs*, 4/2 (March 1925), pp. 57–69.
84. David Kaufman, 'The "One Guilty Nation" Myth: Edith Durham, R.W. Seton-Watson and Footnote in the History of the Outbreak of the First World War', *Journal of Balkan and Near Eastern Studies*, 25 (2023), pp. 297–321.
85. [Pencil notes by SW], SEW 9/5/1, SSEES.
86. Edith Durham, Notebook 1, MS 52, Durham MSS; 'The Murder at Serajevo', *The Times*, 28 April 1926.
87. 'A World Affront', *Daily Mail*, 31 January 1930, p. 1.
88. Miller, '"The First Shots of the First World War"', pp. 141–56.
89. R.W. Seton-Watson, letter to the editor, *The Times*, 31 January [1930] with notes by Edith Durham, MS 56/2, Durham MSS.
90. [H.M. Stannard], 'War Guilt: A Study in Detection', *Times Literary Supplement*, 16 February 1946, p. 1.
91. Winston Churchill, 'How the War Began', *Picture Post*, 5 August 1939, pp. 11–18.
92. Winston Churchill, 'June 28', *Sunday Dispatch*, 29 June 1941, p. 7.

Chapter 2

1. Winston Churchill, 'The Aftermath', *The Times*, 11 February 1929, pp. 13–14. Churchill certainly admired his own phrase and repeated it for years to come.
2. Max Weber, 'The Profession and Vocation of Politics' [October 1919] and 'The President of the Reich', 15 March 1919, in Peter Lassman and Ronald Speirs, eds, *Weber: Political Writings* (CUP, 1994), pp. 309–69, pp. 304–8; Howard Becker, 'Max Weber, Assassination, and German Guilt: An Interview with Marianne Weber' [Becker was an OSS officer: the interview took place on 5 June 1945], *American Journal of Economics and Sociology*, 10 (1951), pp. 401–5.
3. Nicholas Hopkins, 'Charisma and Responsibility: Max Weber, Kurt Eisner, and the Bavarian Revolution of 1918', *Max Weber Studies* (2008), pp. 185–211.
4. Robert Gerwarth, 'The Central European Counter-Revolution: Paramilitary Violence in Germany, Austria and Hungary after the Great War', *Past & Present*, 200 (2008), pp. 175–209.

5. Joachim Schröder, 'Max Weber in Munich (1919/20): Science and Politics in the Last Year of his Life', *Max Weber Studies*, 13 (2013), pp. 15–37.
6. Mark Jones, *Founding Weimar: Violence and the German Revolution of 1918–1919* (CUP, 2016), pp. 233–6.
7. Mark Jones, 'Political Violence in Italy and Germany after the First World War' in Chris Millington and Kevin Passmore, eds, *Political Violence and Democracy in Western Europe, 1918–1940* (Palgrave Macmillan, 2015), pp. 14–30.
8. Jones, *Founding Weimar*, pp. 233–6.
9. Douglas Alder, 'Assassination as Political Efficacy: Two Case Studies from World War I', *East European Quarterly*, 12 (1978), pp. 209–31.
10. John Boyer, 'Silent War and Bitter Peace: The Revolution of 1918 in Austria', *Austrian History Yearbook*, 34 (2003), pp. 1–56.
11. Intelligence Bureau, Department of Information, Weekly Report on Austria-Hungary and Poland, 26 May 1917, SEW 4/1/1, SSEES.
12. Béla Bodó, 'Paramilitary Violence in Hungary after the First World War', *East European Quarterly*, 38 (2004), pp. 129–72; Tamás Révész, 'Soldiers in the Revolution: Violence and Consolidation in 1918 in the Territory of the Disintegrating Kingdom of Hungary', *Hungarian Historical Review*, 10 (2021), pp. 737–67.
13. Elina Ablovatski, *Revolution and Political Violence in Europe: The Deluge of 1919* (CUP, 2021), p. 51 & p. 58.
14. Wolfgang Mommsen, 'Max Weber and the Regeneration of Russia', *Journal of Modern History*, 69 (1997), pp. 1–17; Timofey Dmitriev, 'Max Weber and Peter Struve on the Russian Revolution', *Studies in East European Thought*, 69 (2017), pp. 305–28.
15. Anna Geifman, *Death Orders: The Vanguard of Modern Terrorism in Revolutionary Russia* (Praeger, 2010), p. 32 & p. 36.
16. Anna Geifman, *Thou Shalt Kill: Revolutionary Terrorism in Russia, 1894–1917* (Princeton University Press, 1993), pp. 228–40.
17. Samuel Hoare, 'The Death of Rasputin', 1 January 1917, Templewood Papers, Add. 9863, Box 1, Special Collections, Cambridge University Library.
18. Ibid., 2 January 1917, Templewood Papers.
19. Geifman, *Thou Shalt Kill*, pp. 91–6 & p. 248.
20. Max Weber, 'Socialism' [June 1918], in Lassman and Speirs, *Weber: Political Writings*, pp. 272–303.
21. Alexander Rabinowitch, 'The Schastny File: Trotsky and the Case of the Hero of the Baltic Fleet', *Russian Review*, 58 (1999), pp. 615–34.
22. Lutz Häfner, 'The Assassination of Count Mirbach and the "July Uprising" of the Left Socialist Revolutionaries in Moscow, 1918', *Russian Review*, 50 (1991), pp. 324–44.
23. R.H.B. Lockhart, 'Memorandum on the Internal Situation in Russia', 1 November 1918, sent under cover of Lockhart to Balfour, 7 November 1918, printed for War Cabinet, CAB 24/73, TNA.
24. John Long, 'Plot and Counter-Plot in Revolutionary Russia: Chronicling the Bruce Lockhart Conspiracy, 1918', *Intelligence and National Security*, 10 (1995), pp. 122–43; Vadim Birstein, 'Soviet Military Counterintelligence from 1918 to 1929', *International Journal of Intelligence and Counterintelligence*, 25 (2012), pp. 44–110.
25. Geoffrey Swain, 'An Interesting and Plausible Proposal: Bruce Lockhart, Sidney Reilly and the Latvian Riflemen, Russia 1919', *Intelligence and National Security*, 14 (1999), pp. 81–102.

26. R.H. Bruce Lockhart, *Memoirs of a British Agent* (Pan, 2002 [1932]), pp. 322–3.
27. Oskar Jaszi, Proof of 'Preface to the English Edition' [of *Revolution and Counter-Revolution in Hungary*], September 1923, SEW 95/3, SSEES; Oscar Jaszi, 'The Stream of Political Murder', *American Journal of Economics and Sociology*, 3 (April 1944), pp. 335–55.
28. Jones, 'Political Violence in Italy and Germany after the First World War' and Annette Finley-Croswhite and Gayle Brunelle, 'Lighting the Fuse: Terrorism as Violent Political Discourse in Interwar France', in Millington and Passmore, *Political Violence and Democracy in Western Europe*, pp. 14–30 & 144–58.
29. Béla Bodó, 'Hungarian Aristocracy and the White Terror', *Journal of Contemporary History*, 45 (2010), pp. 703–24.
30. Robert Gerwarth and Ugur Umit Ungor, 'The Collapse of the Ottoman and Habsburg Empires and the Brutalisation of the Successor States', *Journal of Modern European History*, 13 (2015), pp. 226–48
31. House of Commons, *Debates*, 4 March 1920, vol. 126, cc. 616–617; Athelstan-Johnson (Budapest) to Earl Curzon, Desp. 476, 30 June 1920, *DBFP*, Ser. 1, Vol. 12.
32. Ingo Müller, 'Militärgerichtsbarkeit und Strafjustiz: Der Fall Jorns', in Andreas Braun, Michael Dreyer and Sebastian Elsbach, eds, *Vom drohenden Bürgerkrieg zum demokratischen Gewaltmonopol, 1918–1924* (Franz Steiner Verlag, 2021), pp. 83–9.
33. Francis Gribble, 'The German Political Murders', *Fortnightly Review* (October 1923), pp. 563–73.
34. E.J. Gumbel, *Vier Jahre politischer Mord* (Verlag der Neuen Gesellschaft, 1922), pp. 79–81.
35. Jaszi, 'The Stream of Political Murder'; Gumbel, *Vier Jahre Politischer Mord*, p. 147.
36. Gumbel, *Vier Jahre Politischer Mord*, p. 64.
37. T. Hunt Tooley, 'German Political Violence and the Border Plebiscite in Upper Silesia, 1919–1921', *Central European History*, 21 (1988), pp. 56–98; Jochen Böhler, 'Enduring Violence: The Postwar Struggles in East-Central Europe, 1917–1921', *Journal of Contemporary History*, 50 (2015), pp. 58–77.
38. Gerwarth and Ungor, 'The Collapse of the Ottoman and Habsburg Empires', pp. 226–48.
39. Bill Kissane, 'Was There a Civil War in Anatolia between the Ottoman Collapse in World War I and the Establishment of the Republic of Turkey in 1923', *Journal of Modern European History*, 20 (2022), pp. 452–67.
40. 'Assassination of Turkish Ex-Vizier', *Daily Telegraph*, 16 March 1921, p. 11.
41. Sévane Garibian, '"Commanded by my Mother's Corpse": Talaat Pasha, or the Revenge Assassination of a Condemned Man', *Journal of Genocide Research*, 20 (2018), pp. 220–35.
42. 'Assassination of Essad Pasha', *Daily Telegraph*, 14 June 1920; 'M. Veniselos', *Daily Telegraph*, 14 August 1920.
43. 'Ex-Grand Vizier Shot', *Daily Telegraph*, 7 December 1921, p. 12.
44. Martin Sabrow, 'Terroristische Geheimbündelei versus Demokratisches Gewaltmonopol: Die rechtsradikale Anschlagserie gegen die Weimarer Republik 1921/22', in Braun, Dreyer and Elsbach, *Vom drohenden Bürgerkrieg*, pp. 67–82.
45. Lord D'Abernon (Berlin) to the Marquess Curzon of Kedleston, Tel. 437, 28 August 1922, *DBFP*, Ser. 1, Vol. 16.

46. Sabrow, 'Terroristische Geheimbündelei', pp. 67–82.
47. 'Erzberger's Murder', *Daily Telegraph*, 7 June 1922, p. 11.
48. Robert Gerwarth and John Horne, 'Vectors of Violence: Paramilitarism in Europe after the Great War, 1917–1923', *Journal of Modern History*, 83 (2011), pp. 489–512.
49. Gumbel, *Vier Jahre politischer Mord*, p. 71.
50. Carole Fink, 'As Little a Surprise as a Murder Can Be': Ausländische Reaktionen auf den Mord an Walther Rathenau', in Hans Wilderotter, ed., *Walther Rathenau, 1867–1922: Die Extreme berühren sich* (DHM, nd), pp. 237–46.
51. Carole Fink, 'The Murder of Walther Rathenau', *Judaism*, 44 (1995), pp. 259–70.
52. Brian Crim, ' "Our Most Serious Enemy": The Spectre of Judeo-Bolshevism in the German Military Community, 1914–1923', *Central European History*, 44 (2011), pp. 624–41.
53. 'Fears of a "Putsch" ', *Daily Telegraph*, 27 June 1922, p. 12.
54. Martin Sabrow, *Der Rathenaumord und die deutsche Gegenrevolution* (Wallstein Verlag, 2022), p. 140.
55. Lord D'Abernon (Berlin) to the Earl of Balfour, Tel. 511, 2 July 1922, *DBFP*, Ser. 1, Vol. 20.
56. 'Germany's Reactionaries', *Daily Telegraph*, 3 July 1922, p. 12.
57. Dietfrid Krause-Vilmar, 'Albert Grzesinski und die Neuordnung der preußischen Polizei nach 1924', in Braun, Dreyer and Elsbach, *Vom drohenden Bürgerkrieg*, pp. 83–9.
58. 'Severe Blow to German Reaction', *Daily Telegraph*, 2 December 1922, p. 9.
59. Sabrow, *Der Rathenaumord*, pp. 234–54.
60. Mark Jones, *1923: The Forgotten Crisis in the Year of Hitler's Coup* (Basic Books, 2023), p. 122 & p. 129.
61. Sabrow, *Der Rathenaumord*, pp. 255–65.

Chapter 3

1. D.K. Lahiri Choudhury, 'Sinews of Panic and the Nerves of Empire: The Imagined State's Entanglement with Information Panic, India c. 1880–1912', *Modern Asian Studies*, 38 (2004), pp. 965–1002; Harald Fischer-Tiné, 'Mass-Mediated Panic in the British Empire? Shyamji Krishnavarma's "Scientific Terrorism" and the "London Outrage", 1909' and Kama Maclean, 'The Art of Panicking Quietly: British Expatriate Responses to "Terrorist Outrages" in India, 1912–1933', in Harald Fischer-Tiné, ed., *Anxieties, Fear and Panic in Colonial Settings: Empires on the Edge of a Nervous Breakdown* (Macmillan, 2016), pp. 99–134 & 135–68; Michael Silvestri, *Policing Bengali Terrorism in India and the World: Imperial Intelligence and Revolutionary Nationalism, 1905–1939* (Springer, 2019), pp. 7–8.
2. Michael Carrington, 'Officers, Gentlemen, and Murderers: Lord Curzon's Campaign against "Collisions" between Indians and Europeans, 1899–1905', *Modern Asian Studies*, 47 (2013), pp. 780–819; Simon Ball, *The Guardsmen: Harold Macmillan, Three Friends, and the World They Made* (HarperCollins, 2004), pp. 91–6; Phillips Payson O'Brien, 'The Titan Refreshed: Imperial Overstretch and the British Navy before the First World War', *Past & Present*, 172 (2001), pp. 146–69.
3. Max Montesole, 'The British in Egypt', *Fortnightly Review*, 88 (September 1910), pp. 412–24.

4. D. Petrie, Progress Report, 20 March 1913, R.H. Craddock, Note [on Petrie's progress report], 1 June 1913 and H. Wheeler, Minute, 15 September 1914, Government of India, Home Department, Political Branch) [hereafter HP] D, December 1914, No. 1, Abhilekh Patal, National Archives of India [hereafter NAI].
5. 'The Murder of Sir Curzon Wyllie', *The Times*, 3 July 1909, p. 8; Nicholas Owen, 'The Soft Heart of the British Empire: Indian Radicals in Edwardian London', *Past and Present*, 220 (2013), pp. 143–84.
6. 'The Murder of Mr Jackson: Trial of the Accused, Bombay', *The Times*, 8 March 1910, p. 5.
7. J.C. Nixon, 'Notes on Outrages', Vol. I, September 1917, C.A. Tegart, Cambridge South Asian Archive, Centre of South Asian Studies, University of Cambridge [hereafter Tegart Papers, CSAA], Box 3.
8. Kama Maclean, *A Revolutionary History of Interwar India: Violence, Image, Voice and Text* (Hurst, 2015).
9. 'Mr T.C. Kennedy, RFA' and 'Mr Pringle Kennedy', *Dundee Evening Telegraph*, 3 December 1915, p. 4 and *Aberdeen Journal*, 5 March 1925, p. 8.
10. J.R. Dunlop-Smith to [H.A.] Stuart, 12 September 1908, HPB, December 1908, 96–110, NAI.
11. Silvestri, *Policing Bengali Terrorism in India and the World*, p. 88.
12. 'The Murder of Mr Jackson'; 'The Deccan Murder Conspiracy: Arrests and Seizure of Arms', *The Times*, 27 December 1911, p. 3.
13. 'Premier on the Budget, Land Taxes, the Indian Assassinations', *The Scotsman*, 3 July 1909.
14. Draft Conclusions of a Conference of Ministers at 10, Downing Street on Friday, June 23, 1922, at 11 a.m., HO 144/3689, TNA.
15. Silvestri, *Policing Bengali Terrorism in India and the* World, pp. 7–8.
16. D. Petrie, Report on the Delhi Bomb, 8 November 1914, HPD, December 1914, 1, NAI.
17. Sir Walter Lawrence [Curzon's former private secretary and chief of staff to Prince of Wales during his 1905–6 tour of India] to Sir Louis Dane, 15 January 1913, Mss Eur D1103/4/1, India Office Records, British Library (hereafter IOR, BL).
18. W.M. Hailey [Chief Commissioner, Delhi], Note, 24 December 1912, HPD, December 1914, 1, NAI.
19. D. Petrie, Report on the Delhi Bomb, 8 November 1914; J.C. Nixon, 'Notes on Outrages', Vol. IV, September 1917, Tegart Papers, CSAA, Box 3.
20. D. Petrie, Progress Report, 3 June 1913, HPD, December 1914, 1, NAI; D. Petrie to W.M. Hailey, 21 June 1913, HPD, December 1914, 1, NAI.
21. H. Butler, Note, 27 July 1913, HPD, December 1914, 1 NAI.
22. O'M Creagh [Commander-in-Chief], Note, 1 August 1913, HPD, December 1914, 1.
23. R.H. Craddock, Note, 22 August 1913, HPD, December 1914, 1 NAI.
24. D. Petrie, Report on the Delhi Bomb, 8 November 1914.
25. H. Wheeler, Minute, 15 September 1914, HPD, December 1914, 1, NAI.
26. R.H. Craddock, Note, 22 August 1913.
27. D. Petrie, Note on the Delhi-Lahore Case, 18 March 1914, HPD, March 1914, 27, NAI; D. Petrie, Report on the Delhi Bomb, 8 November 1914.
28. Minute by H. Wheeler, 14 February 1914, HPA, November 1914, 39-43, NAI.

29. J.C. Nixon, 'Notes on Outrages', Vol. V, September 1917, Tegart Papers, CSAA, Box 3.
30. R.H. Craddock, Minute [on Secretary of State's telegram, 17 April], 20 April 1914, HPA, November 1914, 39–43, NAI; Viceroy to Secretary of State, 22 April 1914, HPA, November 1914, 39–43, NAI.
31. Secretary of State for India to Viceroy, 30 April 1914, HPA, November 1914, 39–43, NAI; Lord Crewe [Secretary of State for India] to Count Mensdorff, 29 June 1914 in F.R. Bridge, 'The British Elite and the Sarajevo Assassinations', in Mark Cornwall, ed., *Sarajevo 1914: Sparking the First World War* (Bloomsbury, 2015), Appendix I; Durba Ghosh, 'Gandhi and the Terrorists: Revolutionary Challenges from Bengal and Engagements with Non-Violent Political Protest', *South Asia: Journal of South Asian Studies*, 39 (2016), pp. 560–76; Vinayak Chaturvedi, 'Violence as Civility: V.D. Savarkar and the Mahatma's Assassination', *South Asian History and Culture*, 11 (2020), pp. 239–53.
32. D. Petrie, Report on the Delhi Bomb, 8 November 1914.
33. J.C. Nixon, 'Notes on Outrages', Vol. VII, September 1917, Tegart Papers, CSAA, Box 4.
34. J.G. Cumming (Additional Secretary to the Government of Bengal) to The Secretary to the Government of India, Home Department, 14 July 1917, HPA, August 1917, 201–7, NAI.
35. Sir N.G. Chandavarkar and Justice C.P. Beachcroft, Memorandum by the Advisory Committee, Bengal, 1918: The Cases of Detenus under the Defence of India Act and Regulation III of 1818 (Calcutta, Bengal Secretariat Book-Depot, 1918 – not published), Tegart Papers, CSAA, Box 4.
36. Sir J.H. DuBoulay, Memorandum [Summarising conclusions of Conference], 10 December 1917, HPD, January 1918, 28A; *Cd.* 9190, East India (Sedition Committee, 1918), *Report of a Committee Appointed to Investigate Revolutionary Conspiracies in India*.
37. 'The India Budget', *Manchester Guardian*, 23 May 1919, 9.
38. Michael Silvestri, '"A Fanatical Reverence for Gandhi": Nationalism and Police Militancy in Bengal during the Non-cooperation Movement', *Journal of Imperial and Commonwealth History*, 45 (2017), pp. 969–97.
39. H. McPherson, Minute, 25 June 1920 and C. Kaye, Notes in the Central Intelligence Department, 23 July 1920, HPA, August 1922, 368–73, NAI.
40. Sir Milne Cheetham [Acting Consul General] (Ramleh) to Sir Louis Mallet, 9 September 1912, FO 141/746/1, TNA; Political Section, Ministry of the Interior, Report Respecting Secret Societies, 22 June 1911 reproduced in Eliezer Tauber, 'Egyptian Secret Societies, 1911', *Middle Eastern Studies*, 42 (2006), pp. 603–23.
41. Alexandria to Reuters, Tel. 11, 27 July 1914, HIL 465/6, Abbas Hilmi II Papers, Durham University Library.
42. Rudolph Armster [ex-Khedive's secretary], [Note for the ex-Khedive], [30] August 1915, HIL 289, DUL.
43. Ryder (Special Section, Public Security Department) to Tweedy, 28 June 1922, FO 141/494, TNA; A.W. Keown-Boyd to First Secretary, The Residency, 22 June 1926, FO 141/787, TNA.
44. Martin Thomas, *Empires of Intelligence: Security Services and Colonial Disorder after 1914* (University of California Press, 2007), pp. 109–19.
45. Lt Colonel Ryder to High Commissioner: Report by Judge Percival, 26 March 1919, 27 March 1919, FO 141/753, TNA.

46. N.D. Macnaghten, 'Inquiry along the line from Minia to Assiut into the murder of 9 British officers and NCOs at Deirut and Deir-Moeis on the morning of March 18th, 1919', Assiut, 15 April 1919, FO 141/753, TNA.
47. 'Egyptian Premier's Escape', *Manchester Guardian*, 22 December 1919, 8; 'A list about the political crimes which took place between the years 1910 and 1946', Russell 1/10, GB165-0247, Private Papers Collection, Middle East Centre Archive, St Antony's College, Oxford [hereafter MECA].
48. Richard Adamson, 'The Cairo Conspiracy Trial, 1919–1920', Adamson, GB165-0001, MECA; Ryder Diary, 24 January 1922, Ryder, GB165-0249, MECA.
49. High Commissioner for Egypt to FO, Tel. 76, 19 February 1922, FO 141/494, TNA; Ryder for Director General, Department of Public Security, Minister of the Interior to the Chancery, The Residency, 20 February 1922, FO 141/494, TNA.
50. General Manager, ESR to Wassif Simaika Pasha (Minister of Communications), 15 March 1922, FO 141/494, TNA.
51. Memoirs of Aubrey Mellor, Mellor 1/2, GB165-0409, MECA.
52. High Commissioner for Egypt to FO, Tel. 69, 18 February 1922 and Tel. 103, 4 March 1922, FO 141/494, TNA.
53. High Commissioner to FO, Tel. 289, 18 August 1922, FO 141/494, TNA.
54. W.J. Berridge, 'Imperialist and Nationalist Voices in the Struggle for Egyptian Independence, 1919–22', *Journal of Imperial and Commonwealth History*, 42 (2014), pp. 420–39.
55. Commandant, Cairo City Police [T. Russell] to Minister of the Interior, July 1922, Russell 1/4, MECA.
56. High Commissioner to FO, Tel. 289, 18 August 1922, FO 141/494, TNA.
57. Allenby to Colonel C.F. Ryder, 30 December 1922; Allenby to Ryder, 19 July 1923; Extracts from Memoirs of Colonel Charles Ryder, Ryder, MECA.
58. 'The Rule of the Revolver', *Saturday Review*, 1 July 1922, pp. 4–5.
59. 'Sinn Fein and Private Assassination', *Manchester Guardian*, 16 September 1919, p. 7.
60. 'The Dublin Murder', *Manchester Guardian*, 23 January 1920, p. 9.
61. Tom Bowden, 'The Irish Underground and the Irish War of Independence, 1919–1921', *Journal of Contemporary History*, 8 (1973), pp. 3–23; Charles Townshend, 'The Irish Republican Army and the Development of Guerrilla Warfare, 1919–1921', *English Historical Review*, 94 (1979), pp. 318–45.
62. Inspector M. Lowry (Dublin Metropolitan Police), 'Attempt to Assassinate His Excellency', 20 December 1919, HO 45/10974, TNA.
63. Mark Sturgis, *The Last Days of Dublin Castle: The Mark Sturgis Diaries*, ed. Michael Hopkinson (Irish Academic Press, 1999).
64. Eunan O'Halpin, 'Collins and Intelligence, 1919–1923', in Gabriel Doherty and Dermot Keogh, eds, *Michael Collins and the Irish State* (Mercier Press, 1998), pp. 70–82; Andy Bielenberg and Pádraig Óg Ó Ruairc, 'Shallow Graves: Documenting and Assessing IRA Disappearances during the Irish Revolution, 1919–1923', *Small Wars & Insurgencies*, 32 (2021), pp. 619–41.
65. 'Lord French and "Unauthorised Report" of Interview', *Manchester Guardian*, 8 April 1920; John Borgonovo, *Spies, Informers and the 'Anti-Sinn Féin Society': The Intelligence War in Cork City, 1920–1921* (Irish Academic Press, 2007).
66. C.E. Callwell, *Field-Marshal Sir Henry Wilson: His Life and Diaries* (2 vols, London, 1927), ii, 26 November 1920.

67. 'A Record of the Rebellion in Ireland in 1920–21, and the Part Played by the Army in Dealing with It (Intelligence), [1922], in *British Intelligence in Ireland, 1920–21: The Final Reports*, ed. Peter Hart (Cork UP, 2002).
68. Anne Dolan, 'Killing and Bloody Sunday, November 1920', *Historical Journal*, 49 (2006), pp. 789–810.
69. O'Halpin, 'Collins and Intelligence, 1919–1923', pp. 70–82.
70. Note about Sinn Féin Crimes which occurred in Basil Thomson's time, HO 144/3689, TNA.
71. 'Sir H. Wilson Murdered', *The Times*, 23 June 1922, p. 10.
72. Lord Midleton to Lady Bathhurst, 24 June 1922, PRO 30/67, TNA.
73. 'Anxiety in the Commons: Police Protection for Ministers', *The Times*, 24 June 1922; Peter Hart, 'Michael Collins and the Assassination of Sir Henry Wilson', in *The IRA at War, 1916–1923* (OUP, 2003), pp. 194–222.
74. Note by the Commissioner [Brigadier-General Sir W. Horwood], c. 23 June 1922, HO 144/3689, TNA.
75. 'Draft Conclusions', 23 June 1922, HO 144/3689, TNA.
76. Micheál MacDonnchadha (Acting Secretary to the Provisional Government) to Edward Shortt (Home Secretary), 8 August 1922, HO 144/3689, TNA.
77. Chamberlain to Allenby, Tel. 240, 24 November 1924, FO 141/502, TNA.
78. Allenby to Chamberlain, Tel. 360, 19 November 1924, 10 pm, FO 141/502, TNA.
79. Austen Chamberlain to Lord Allenby, Tel. 220, 21 November 1924, FO 141/494, TNA.
80. Sir Eyre Crowe (PUS, FO) to High Commissioner for Egypt, Tel. 279, 5 December 1924, FO 141/494, TNA.
81. Lord Allenby to Foreign Office, Tels 370 & 371, 20 November 1924, FO141/502; 'The Sirdar's Murder', *The Times*, 22 November 1924, p. 12.
82. Gerald Delany, 'Comments – Part II – Allenby', Allenby 1/4, GB165-0005, MECA.
83. J.H. Percival, 'Points establishing Saad Zaghlul's direct responsibility for the murder of Sir Lee Stack', 22 November 1922, FO 141/502, TNA.
84. Allenby to Chamberlain, Tel. 384, 22 November 1924; Chamberlain to Allenby, Tel. 232, 22 November 1924; Allenby to Chamberlain, Tel. 388, 23 November 1924; Chamberlain to Allenby, Tel. 236, 23 November 1924, FO 141/502; Tom Russell to Frank Moore, 27 February 1925, Russell 1/14, MECA.
85. Cecil Howard [CO, 16th Lancers], [Notes on Allenby], Allenby 1/3, MECA.
86. Commandant, Cairo City Police [T. Russell] to High Commissioner [Allenby], 21 February 1925, Russell 1/6, MECA. Report was sent by Allenby, with his endorsement, to Chamberlain on 1 March 1925, Allenby to Chamberlain, Tel. 159, 1 March 1925. Chamberlain, 'read with the greatest interest'; congratulations all round, Allenby to Russell, 24 March 1925, Russell 1/7, MECA.
87. 'The Murder of the Sirdar: Trial Begun in Cairo', *The Times*, 27 May 1925, p. 15.
88. Shafiq Mansur, 'History of the Secret Societies in Egypt', 18 June 1925, FO 141/502, TNA.
89. 'The Cairo Trial', *The Times*, 8 June 1925, p. 15; High Commissioner to Chamberlain, Tel. 244, 2 July 1925, FO 141/502, TNA.
90. Walford Selby to Archie Wavell, 9 December 1936, Allenby 1/3, MECA.
91. Henderson to Chamberlain, Tel. 500, 6 July 1925 and Henderson to Chamberlain, Tel. 294, 14 August 1925, FO 141/503, TNA.

92. European Department, Ministry of the Interior, The Sirdar Murder Trial: Translated extracts from reports of proceedings appearing in *El Mokattam*, etc., Russell 1/8, MECA.
93. Amir Kumar Gupta, 'Defying Death: Nationalist Revolutionism in India, 1897–1938', *Social Scientist*, 25 (1997), pp. 3–27.
94. C.W. Gywnne, Officiating Joint Secretary to the Government of India to Chief Secretary to the Government of Bengal, 8 September 1923, Tegart Papers, Box 2/8, CSAA; Our Special Correspondent, 'Red Conspiracy in Bengal: Revolutionists' Aims; A Grave Peril', *The Times*, 1 October 1924.
95. India Office, *The Bengal Criminal Law Amendment Act*, 20 February 1925; Silvestri, *Policing Bengali Terrorism in India and the World*, pp. 109–10; Sir Alfred Watson, 'Terrorism in Bengal; A Limited Cult; I – Perverted Patriots', *The Times*, 5 September 1933, p. 11.
96. Report on Newspapers and Periodicals in Bengal, 5/1924, 2 February 1924, Tegart Papers, Box 1, CSAA.
97. Foss [Westcott, Bishop of] Calcutta to Arthur [Westcott], Papers of Foss Westcott, Add. 8316/5/1-248, Special Collections, Cambridge University Library [hereafter Westcott Papers, CUL].
98. J.C. Nixon, 'Notes on Outrages', Vol. VII, September 1917, Tegart Papers, Box 4, CSAA.
99. Report on Newspapers and Periodicals in Bengal, 5/1924, 2 February 1924, Tegart Papers, Box 1, CSAA; 'Indian Jury and the Chowringhee Case', *Amrita Bazar Patrika*, 19 February 1924.
100. 'The Chowringhee Murder Case', *Forward*, 16 January 1924.
101. *The Bengal Criminal Law Amendment Act*, 20 February 1925; Gupta, 'Defying Death', pp. 3–27.
102. [Charles Tegart], [Notes], [early 1926], Tegart Papers 2/8, CSAA.
103. A.M. Stow, Chief Commissioner, Delhi to Secretary to the Government of India, Home Department, 'Review of the Police Administration in the Delhi Province for 1926', 28 July 1927, Home Public, 75/17/1927, NAI.
104. *Note by the Secretary of State for India on Terrorism in India*, 30 November 1933 in Joint Committee on Indian Constitutional Reform, 1933–34, *Report*, Volume I (Part 1), 31 October 1934.
105. F.J. Lowman, Deputy Inspector-General of Police (Intelligence Branch, CID), 'A short note on the Youth Association in Bengal', June 1929, HP, 212/30, NAI.
106. P.C. Bamford, DIB [Delhi Intelligence Bureau], Note, 30 July 1929 in Notes on Measures to be Adopted in the Event of Attempts Being Made to Seduce the Troops and Police in the Course of the Non-Cooperation Movement, HP, 228, 1929, NAI.
107. Gupta, 'Defying Death', pp. 3–27; Maclean, *A Revolutionary History of Interwar India*, p. 31.
108. C.C. Garbett, Chief Secretary to the Punjab Government to M.G. Hallett, Secretary to the Government of India, Home Department, 9 November 1932, HP, 1932, 31/76.
109. David Petrie, Minute, 18 February 1929, HP, 1930, F4/7, NAI.
110. Viceroy to Secretary of State for India, 10 January 1929, HP, 1930, F4/7, NAI; H.W. Emerson and J. Crerar [Home Member, Viceroy's Council], Minutes, 6 & 9 September 1929, HP, 212/30, NAI.

111. Colonel G.H.R. Halland [head of Delhi Police], 'Punjab Patrol: Some Memories of an Indian Police Officer', Halland Papers 1, CSAA.
112. Maclean, *A Revolutionary History of Interwar India*, pp. 164–7; Gupta, 'Defying Death', pp. 3–27.
113. Philip E.S. Finney [Superintendent of Police, Barrackpore, Calcutta], 'Just My Luck: Reminiscences', Finney Papers 1, CSAA.
114. *Note by the Secretary of State for India on Terrorism in India*, 30 November 1933.
115. Gupta, 'Defying Death', pp. 3–27.
116. G.H.R. Halland, 'Punjab Patrol'.
117. 'Sir C. Tegart's Story', *The Statesman*, 3 September 1930; Charles Tegart, Commissioner of Police to Chief Secretary to the Government of Bengal, 25 August 1930, Tegart Papers 2/6, CSAA.
118. Philip E.S. Finney, 'Just My Luck.
119. 'Calcutta Outrage', *Amrita Bazar Patrika*, 28 August 1930.
120. Sir Douglas Gordon, 'Memoirs of Life as a Police Officer in India from 1907–1936', Gordon Papers 1, CSAA; Foss [Westcott, Bishop of] Calcutta to Arthur [Westcott], 7 October 1930, Westcott Papers, CUL.
121. 'India and the Conference', *Manchester Guardian,* 9 December 1930, 15.
122. Special Superintendent R.E.A. Ray, Intelligence Branch, CID, Note on the Insufficiency of the Powers Conferred by the Bengal Criminal Law Amendment Act, 1930 to Deal with Terrorism in Bengal, 19 August 1931, HP, 1932, F4/47, NAI.
123. Maclean, *A Revolutionary History of Interwar India*, pp. 187–8.
124. [Alan] Gordon Walker to [Sir Henry] Craik, 26 January 1932, Papers of Baron Gordon-Walker, GNWR 8/1, Churchill Archives Centre, Churchill College, Cambridge [CAC].
125. H. Williamson [Director, DIB], Minute, 21 April 1931, HP, 4/22, NAI.
126. J.C. French (Lately in Charge of the Midnapore District), 'Midnapore – the Murder Spot: How Indian Terrorism Began and its Constitution', *Saturday Review*, 157: 4084 (3 February 1934), pp. 121–2; Report of the Government of Bengal, 24 December 1931 in Reports to Government of India from Local Governments of Congress Activities, Tegart Papers, Box 4, CSAA.
127. Sir Charles Tegart, *Terrorism in India: A Speech Delivered before the Royal Empire Society* (London, 1932).
128. F.W. Kidd, 'Congress cum Terrorist Activities in Midnapur District in 1930–1931', March 1969, Taylor Papers, CSAA.
129. Silvestri, *Policing Bengali Terrorism in India and the* World, p. 233.
130. S.G. Taylor, 'The Terrorist Movement in Bengal, 1930 to 1934', Taylor Papers, CSAA.
131. Foss [Westcott, Bishop of] Calcutta to Arthur [Westcott], 24 December 1931, Westcott Papers, CUL.
132. S.G. Taylor, 'The Terrorist Movement in Bengal, 1930 to 1934'; Philip E.S. Finney, 'Just My Luck.
133. Superintendent G.E.T.H. Evans 'Report on the Murder of Mr. Burge, District Magistrate, Midnapore, on 2 September 1933', 3 September 1933, HP, 1933, F45/9, NAI.
134. Special Tribunal Judgment, 10 February 1934, HP, 1933, F45/9, NAI.
135. Note by R.N. [Robert] Reid [later Acting Governor of Bengal and then Governor of Assam], Mss Eur F207/12, IOR, BL.
136. 'Indian Terrorist Campaign', *Manchester Guardian*, 2 August 1931, p. 9.

137. Special Superintendent R.E.A. Ray, Note on the Insufficiency of the Powers Conferred by the Bengal Criminal Law Amendment Act, 1930 to Deal with Terrorism in Bengal, 19 August 1931.
138. H. Williamson [Director, DIB], Minute, 28 April 1931, HP, F4/22, NAI.
139. H. Williamson [Director, DIB], Note, 4 August 1931, HP, F4/22b, NAI.
140. Chief Secretary to the Government of Bengal to the Government of India, 'Chittagong Enquiry Report', 23 January 1932; Extract from Note attached to Chief Secretary to the Government of Bengal to the Government of India, 'Chittagong Enquiry Report', 23 January 1932.
141. Minute on Judgment of the Special Tribunal, 21 March 1932, IOR L/PJ/7/332, BL.
142. Silvestri, *Policing Bengali Terrorism in India and the* World, pp. 151–2.
143. Office of the Secretary to the Governor of Bengal, 'An analysis of extremist influence among the Hindu population in Bengal', Mss Eur F207/12, IOR, BL.
144. [Sir John Anderson], [Paper, c. 1932], Mss Eur F207/13, IOR, BL.
145. Secretary of State for India to Government of India, Tel. 400, 4 February 1932, HP, 1932, F4/47/Ii, NAI; Secretary of State for India to Government of India, Tel. 494, 13 February 1932, HP, 1932, F4/47/Ii, NAI; Samuel Hoare, notes on J.C. Curry, *The Indian Police*, Templewood Papers, VII/7, CUL.
146. *Cmd. 4014, Measures taken to counteract the Civil Disobedience Movement and to deal with the Terrorist Movement in Bengal*, February 1932; In the Court of the Special Tribunal at Alipore: Emperor vs. Jitendra Nath Gupta and others, 1 May 1935, HP, 1935, F45/7, NAI.
147. S.G. Taylor, 'The Terrorist Movement in Bengal, 1930 to 1934'; Foss [Westcott, Bishop of] Calcutta to Arthur [Westcott], 9 May 1934, Westcott Papers, CUL; *Congress and Terrorism* (1935) marked up by Anderson, MSS Eur F 207/19, IOR, BL.
148. Civil and Military Conference in July 1934: Appreciation of the Present Situation, HP, 1934, F45/44, NAI; R.E.A Ray, Deputy Inspector-General of Police, Intelligence Branch, CID for the Conference that is to be held in July 1934, 28 June 1934, HP, 1934, F45/44, NAI.
149. Appendix to Notes [for Council of State, Simla, August 1934], HP, 1934, F45/17, NAI.
150. *Note by the Secretary of State for India on Terrorism in India*, 30 November 1933.
151. Lizzie Seal and Alexa Neale, 'The Assassination Cases of Madan Lal Dhingra, 1909 and Udham Singh, 1940 as Social Drama', *British Journal of Criminology*, 20 (2023), pp. 1–17.
152. Leader: 'The Trial of Udham Singh', *The Times*, 6 June 1940, p. 7.
153. DVW (IPI), 'Udham Singh's Defence', 18 May 1940; Hugh Grerson, Senior Medical Officer, HMP Brixton, 'Udham Singh', 6 June 1940; IPI to Dibdin, 24 July 1940, IOR, L/P&J/12/500, BL.
154. Secretary of State to Government of India, Home Department, Tel. 1846, 18 April 1940, IOR, L/P&J/12/500, BL.
155. Secretary of State to Home Department, Government of India (IPI to DIB), Tel. 385, 15 July 1940, IOR, L/P&J/12/500, BL.
156. House of Commons, *Debates*, 8 November 1921; Draft Conclusions of a Conference of Ministers at 10, Downing Street on Friday, June 23, 1922, at 11 a.m., HO 144/3689, TNA; Note by the Commissioner [Brigadier-General Sir W. Horwood], c. 23 June 1922. [filed 22 August 1922], HO 144/3689, TNA; 'The Rule of the Revolver', *Saturday Review*, 1 July 1922, pp. 4–5.

157. Superintendent, Special Branch to ACC, 16 December 1932, MEPO 2/5667, TNA; R.M. Howe (Assistant Commissioner) to Secretary of State for Home Affairs, 1 September 1933, MEPO 2/5667, TNA.
158. 'Mr Burge's Assassination', *The Scotsman*, 14 October 1933, p. 13.
159. Mrs Russell to Father, [March 1919], Russell 1/14, MECA.
160. Commandant, Cairo City Police [T. Russell] to Minister of the Interior, July 1922, Russell 1/4, MECA.
161. Memoirs of Aubrey Mellor, Mellor 1/2, GB165-0409, MECA.
162. B. Biggar, Principal Medical Officer, Egyptian Army et al., 'Murder of His Excellency the Sirdar', 22 November 1924, FO 141/502; Sydney Smith, 'The Identification of Firearms and Projectiles as Illustrated by the Case of the Murder of Sir Lee Stack Pasha', *British Medical Journal* (2 January 1926), pp. 8–10.
163. Sir Douglas Gordon, 'Memoirs of Life as a Police Officer in India from 1907–1936'.
164. B.K., Minute, 10 November 1916, HPA, February 1917, 79-81, NAI; India Office copy of Chief Secretary to the Government of Bengal to the Secretary to the Government of India, 15 July 1916, IOR L/PJ/6/1464, BL.
165. C. Kaye, Director, Intelligence Bureau, Memorandum for the guidance of police officers in connection with the tour of His Royal Highness the Prince of Wales, 9 August 1921, HP, 1921, F4/27, NAI.
166. Philip E.S. Finney, 'Just My Luck: Reminiscences'. Finney was the officer in charge of the security team.
167. Colonel G.H.R. Halland, 'Punjab Patrol: Some Memories of an Indian Police Officer', Halland Papers 1, CSAA.
168. 'Sir C. Tegart's Story', *The Statesman*, 3 September 1930.
169. Philip E.S. Finney, 'Just My Luck: Reminiscences'.
170. *Note by the Secretary of State for India on Terrorism in India*, 30 November 1933.
171. Philip E.S. Finney, 'Just My Luck: Reminiscences'.
172. Foss [Westcott, Bishop of] Calcutta to Arthur [Westcott], 11 December 1930, Westcott Papers, CUL.
173. P.E.S. Finney, Superintendent of Police, Rangpur, 'General Police Arrangements in Connection with the Visit of the Governor to Rangpur, 31st October to 2nd November 1936, Finney Papers 1, CSAA.
174. Sir Douglas Gordon, 'Memoirs of Life as a Police Officer in India from 1907–1936'.
175. H. Quinton, 'Terrorism in Bengal: A Memory', Quinton Papers, CSAA; Extract from Note attached to Chief Secretary to the Government of Bengal's to the Government of India, 'Chittagong Enquiry Report', 23 January 1932.
176. *Note by the Secretary of State for India on Terrorism in India*, 30 November 1933.
177. Thomas, *Empires of Intelligence*, pp. 240–41.
178. Charles Tegart, Diary, 22 December 1937, Tegart 4/6, GB165-0281, MECA.
179. Silvestri, *Policing Bengali Terrorism in India and the* World, p. 312.
180. Edward Mackie (*The Statesman*) [Calcutta] to Charles Tegart, 6 January 1939, Tegart 4/2b, MECA.
181. Harold MacMichael (High Commissioner for Palestine) to Malcolm MacDonald (Secretary of State for the Colonies), 20 January 1939, Tegart 4/2b, MECA.
182. Charles Tegart, Diary, 3 January 1938, Tegart 4/6, MECA.
183. Michael Cohen, 'Sir Arthur Wauchope, the Army and the Rebellion in Palestine, 1936', *Middle Eastern Studies*, 9 (1973), pp. 20–34.

184. M.E. Yapp, ed., *Politics and Diplomacy in Egypt: The Diaries of Sir Miles Lampson, 1935–1937* (British Academy, 1997), 12 November 1937; Charles Townshend, 'The Defence of Palestine: Insurrection and Public Security, 1936–1939', *English Historical Review*, 103 (1988), pp. 917–49; Matthew Hughes, *Britain's Pacification of Palestine: The British Army, the Colonial State and the Arab Revolt, 1936–1939* (CUP, 2019), pp. 31–2.
185. Charles Tegart, Diary, 10 January 1938, Tegart 4/6, MECA.
186. Ibid., 23 December 1937, Tegart 4/6, MECA.
187. Eldad Harouvi, *Palestine Investigated: The Criminal Investigation Department of the Palestine Police Force, 1920–1948* (Sussex Academic Press, 2016), pp. 77–8; John Knight, 'Securing Zion? Policing in British Palestine, 1917–1939', *European Review of History*, 18 (2011), pp. 523–43.
188. Asher Maoz, 'Historical Adjudication: Courts of Law, Commissions of Inquiry, and "Historical Truth"', *Law and History Review*, 18 (2000), pp. 559–606.
189. MacKereth's Despatch from Damascus, 14 September 1937 reprinted in Elie Kedourie, 'The Bludan Conference on Palestine, September 1937', *Middle Eastern Studies*, 17 (1981), pp. 107–25.
190. Matthew Hughes, 'A History of Violence: The Shooting in Jerusalem of British Assistant Police Superintendent Alan Sigrist, 12 June 1936', *Journal of Contemporary History*, 45 (2010), pp. 725–43.
191. DSP (CID) [A. T. Barker], Note, 17 December 1937, Tegart 2/3, MECA.
192. Memorandum to DIG (CID): Murder of Mr L.Y. Andrews, OBE, and British Constable P.R. McEwan, 29 September 1937; DSP (CID) to DIG (CID) [Kingsley-Heath], 11 December 1937; DSP (CID) [A. T. Barker], Note, 17 December 1937, Tegart 2/3, MECA.
193. Charles Tegart, Diary, 29 December 1937, Tegart 4/6, MECA.
194. Ibid., 21 December 1937, Tegart 4/6, MECA.
195. Sir Charles Tegart to W.D. Battershill, 31 January 1939, Tegart 2/4, MECA.
196. Hughes, 'A History of Violence', pp. 725–43; idem, 'Demobilised Soldiers and Colonial Control: The British Police in Mandate Palestine and After', *Journal of Modern European History*, 13 (2015), pp. 268–84.
197. Minute by Donald MacGillivray to Sir Harold MacMichael, 14 September 1938, MacGillivray 1/2, GB165-0193, MECA.
198. Matthew Hughes, 'Terror in Galilee: British–Jewish Collaboration and the Special Night Squads in Palestine during the Arab Revolt, 1938–39', *Journal of Imperial and Commonwealth History*, 43 (2015), pp. 590–610.
199. Minute by Donald MacGillivray to Sir Harold MacMichael, 14 September 1938.

Chapter 4

1. Richard Bach Jensen, *The Battle against Anarchist Terrorism: An International History* (CUP, 2014).
2. Director, US Bureau of Investigation (J. Edgar Hoover) to W.H. Moran (Chief, US Secret Service), 16 February 1933, Federal Bureau of Investigation Files, 1933–1944, Serial 1, Box 1, Franklin D. Roosevelt Presidential Library and Museum, Hyde Park, NY [hereafter FDRL].
3. Frank Getty, 'Assassination Seldom Resorted to in America as Political Weapon', *Washington Post*, 7 January 1934, Special Articles, p. 1.

4. 'Third Attack on American Presidents', *New York Times*, 7 September 1901, p. 6.
5. Jensen, *The Battle against Anarchist Terrorism*, p. 455.
6. 'M'Kinley Bodyguard Dead', *New York Times*, 1 July 1908, p. 7.
7. 'Would Give Cabinet Rights in Congress', *New York Times*, 14 October 1915, p. 11.
8. Robert Pinkerton, 'Detective Surveillance of Anarchists', *North American Review*, 173 (November 1901), pp. 609–17.
9. Frederick Kaiser, 'Presidential Assassinations and Assaults: Characteristics and Impact on Protective Procedures', *Presidential Studies Quarterly*, 11 (1981), pp. 545–58.
10. Jay Childers, 'The Democratic Balance: President McKinley's Assassination as Domestic Trauma', *Quarterly Journal of Speech*, 99 (2013), pp. 156–79.
11. Pinkerton, 'Detective Surveillance of Anarchists', pp. 609–17.
12. '5 Pointed Out as Assassins of Archbishop', *Washington Post*, 27 December 1933, p. 14.
13. John Callan O'Laughlin (former Asst. Secretary of State), 'Roosevelt to Have Keen Guards in Cairo', *New York Times*, 23 March 1910, p. 4.
14. 'President Crosses City Under Guard', *New York Times*, 7 September 1903.
15. 'Roosevelt Usually Carried a Revolver', *New York Times*, 15 October 1912, p. 3.
16. Stephen Schwab, 'Sabotage at Black Tom Island: A Wake-up Call for America', *International Journal of Intelligence and Counterintelligence*, 25 (2012), pp. 367–91.
17. 'President Rode in Lane of Steel', *New York Times*, 6 March 1917, p. 1.
18. 'President Travels in Plain Pullman Going to Chicago', *New York Times*, 4 December 1924, p. 1; Harlan Miller, 'Over the Coffee: President's Bodyguard', *Washington Post*, 21 July 1938, p. 13; 'Heavy Guard Kept around Roosevelt', *New York Times*, 22 September 1939, p. 18.
19. Carleton Beals, 'Calles Keeps his Grip in Mexican Confusion', *New York Times*, 2 September 1928, p. 98; Frederic J. Haskin, 'Taft and Diaz', *Washington Post*, 16 October 1909, p. 4.
20. 'Convention Method is Urged on Mexico', *New York Times*, 16 August 1928, p. 24; Sarah Osten, 'Out of the Shadows: Violence and State Consolidation in Postrevolutionary Mexico, 1927–1940', *Latin Americanist*, 64 (2020), pp. 169–99.
21. 'As Mexicans Look At It' [Leader], *New York Times*, 19 July 1928, p. 20.
22. Frederick Palmer, 'Cabrera's Guatemalan Despotism', *New York Times*, 26 February 1909, p. 6.
23. Warren Irvin, 'Despite Shootings, Mexico Wants Peace', *New York Times*, 9 February 1930, p. XX3.
24. 'Castillo Asks for Protection', *New York Times*, 2 February 1914, p. 2; Guatemala in Grip of Reign of Terror', *New York Times*, 5 April 1920, p. 11; T.R. Ybarra, 'Career of Cabrera, Last of the Dictators', *New York Times*, 18 April 1920, p. XX3.
25. 'Not a Revolutionist Nor Ill, Says Castro', *New York Times*, 31 December 1912, p. 1.
26. Secretary of State to Minister in Nicaragua (Hanna), 20 April 1931, *Foreign Relations of the United States* [hereafter *FRUS*], 1931, II.
27. Richard V. Oulahan, 'Hoover Denounces Sandino as Outlaw', *New York Times*, 22 April 1931, p. 1.
28. 'Sandino is Killed by Managua Guard', *New York Times*, 23 February 1934, p. 1; Michel Gobat, *Confronting the American Dream: Nicaragua under US Imperial Rule* (Duke University Press, 2005), pp. 264–5.

29. Minister in Nicaragua (Lane) to Secretary of State, 16 July 1934, *FRUS*, 1935, *The American Republics*, IV.
30. Minister in Costa Rica to Secretary of State, 12 April 1934, *FRUS*, 1934, *The American Republics*, V.
31. Minister in Nicaragua (Lane) to Secretary of State, 26 September 1935, *FRUS*, 1935, *The American Republics*, IV.
32. Christy Thornton, '"Our Balkan Peninsula": The Mexican Question in the League of Nations Debate', *Diplomatic History*, 46 (2022), pp. 237–62.
33. Dimitri Lazo, 'Lansing, Wilson, and the Jenkins Incident', *Diplomatic History*, 22 (1998), pp. 177–98.
34. 'Carranza a Failure like his Predecessors', *New York Times*, 23 May 1920, p. 2.
35. 'Mexico Frees American', *New York Times*, 1 May 1938, p. 37.
36. Michael Smith, 'The Mexican Secret Service in the United States, 1910–1920', *The Americas*, 59 (2002), pp. 65–85.
37. 'Find Bomb at Juarez', *Los Angeles Times*, 23 September 1909, p. 15.
38. 'Taft Escaped Peril', *Washington Post*, 16 October 1909, p. 5.
39. '3,000 Troops for Taft', *New York Times*, 12 October 1909.
40. 'Taft Escaped Peril', *Washington Post*, 16 October 1909, p. 5.
41. Smith, 'The Mexican Secret Service in the United States, 1910–1920', pp. 65–85.
42. William Dirk Raat, 'The Diplomacy of Suppression: *Los Revoltosos*, Mexico, and the United States, 1906–1911', *Hispanic American Historical Review*, 56 (1976), pp. 529–50.
43. Manifesto enclosed in Marion Letcher to [Secretary of State] Philander Knox, 3 April 1912 quoted in Frederick Turner, 'Anti-Americanism in Mexico, 1910–1913', *Hispanic American Historical Review*, 47 (1967), pp. 502–18.
44. 'Huerta Restores Quiet but Foreigners May Send Families Away', *New York Times*, 25 February 1913, p. 1.
45. 'The Mexican Crisis', *New York Times*, [Leader] 24 February 1913, p. 10.
46. 'H.L. Wilson Fears Chaos', *New York Times*, 19 October 1913, p. 9.
47. 'Tells Vivid Story of Madero Murder', *New York Times*, 1 February 1914, p. 2.
48. 'Lind Accuses H. L. Wilson?', *New York Times*, 22 November 1915, p. 8.
49. 'Wilson Demands Light on Killing', *New York Times*, 24 February 1913, p. 1.
50. 'President Firm against Huerta', *New York Times*, 1 August 1913, p. 1.
51. 'Hale Blamed for Mexican Irritation', *New York Times*, 13 August 1913, p. 2.
52. Kenneth Grieb, *The United States and Huerta* (University of Nebraska Press, 1969).
53. Phillips O'Brien, 'The American Press, Public, and the Reaction to the Outbreak of the First World War', *Diplomatic History*, 37 (2013), pp. 446–75.
54. 'President Firm against Huerta'.
55. 'Official Report of the Murder', *New York Times*, 21 July 1923, p. 6; Dirk Raat, 'US Intelligence Operations and Covert Action in Mexico, 1900–1947', *Journal of Contemporary History*, 22 (1987), pp. 615–38.
56. Samuel Brunk, 'Remembering Emiliano Zapata: Three Moments in the Posthumous Career of the Martyr of Chinameca', *Hispanic American Historical Review*, 78 (1998), pp. 457–90.
57. Julia Young, 'The Calles Government and Catholic Dissidents: Mexico's Transnational Projects of Repression, 1916–1929', *The Americas*, 70 (2013), pp. 63–91; Smith, 'The Mexican Secret Service in the United States, 1910–1920', pp. 65–85.

58. 'Carranza a Failure like his Predecessors'.
59. 'Olvera Sees Chance for Peace in Mexico', *New York Times*, 18 July 1920, p. 28.
60. 'Lays Death Plot to Calles, Obregon', *New York Times*, 31 August 1928, p. 9.
61. 'Says Huerta Fled, Fearing Assassins', *New York Times*, 11 April 1926, p. 7.
62. 'Dr. Castillo Blames Obregon's "Violence"', *New York Times*, 18 July 1927, p. 2.
63. James Horn, 'US Diplomacy and the "Specter of Bolshevism" in Mexico, 1924–1927', *The Americas*, 32 (1975), pp. 31–45.
64. Young, 'The Calles Government and Catholic Dissidents', pp. 63–91.
65. Pedro Castro Martínez, 'El asesinato del general Álvaro Obregón: las caras de un imaginario dividido', *Iztapalapa*, 61 (2008), pp. 143–68.
66. 'Obregon Declared Hostile to Calles', *New York Times*, 22 October 1927, p. 3.
67. Osten, 'Out of the Shadows', pp. 169–99.
68. 'Obregon Puts Blame on "Reactionaries"', *New York Times*, 25 November 1927, p. 32.
69. Gema Kloppe-Santamaria, 'Martyrs, Fanatics, and Pious Militants: Religious Violence and the Secular State in 1930s Mexico', *The Americas*, 79 (2022), pp. 197–222.
70. Robert Weis, 'The Revolution on Trial: Assassination, Christianity and the Rule of Law in 1920s Mexico', *Hispanic American Historical Review*, 96 (2016), pp. 320–53.
71. 'Capital Stirred by Assassination', *New York Times*, 18 July 1928, p. 1.
72. Ambassador in Mexico (Morrow) to Secretary of State, 23 July 1928, *FRUS*, 1928, III.
73. Carleton Beals, 'The Diplomat Who Won the Mexicans', *New York Times*, p. SM4.
74. 'Capital Stirred by Assassination'.
75. 'Six Sought Here as Obregon Slayers', *New York Times*, 28 August 1928, p. 1; 'New Clues Aid Hunt for Six Mexicans', *New York Times*, 30 August 1928, p. 8.
76. 'Alleges Plot to Kill Obregonista Leaders', *New York Times*, 12 August 1928, p. 13; Weis, 'The Revolution on Trial', pp. 320–53.
77. Kloppe-Santamaria, 'Martyrs, Fanatics, and Pious Militants', pp. 197–222.
78. '10 Mexicans on Trial for Plot on Obregon', *New York Times*, 10 January 1930, p. 3.
79. Weis, 'The Revolution on Trial', pp. 320–53.
80. Jaymie Heilman, 'The Demon Inside: Madre Conchita, Gender, and the Assassination of Obregón', *Mexican Studies*, 18 (2002), pp. 23–60.
81. 'Coaches are Dynamited', *New York Times*, 11 February 1929, p. 1.
82. Weis, 'The Revolution on Trial', pp. 320–53.
83. 'The Land of Violence' [Leader], *Washington Post*, 7 February 1930, p. 6.
84. 'Assassination of Calles Foiled on Coast', *New York Times*, 2 January 1937, p. 1.
85. 'Armed Peasants Join Guards', *New York Times*, 1 December 1940, p. 40.
86. George Brodnax (Operative in Charge of the Atlanta Office, US Secret Service), Signed Statement, County of Fulton, State of Georgia, 20 February 1933, Federal Bureau of Investigation Files, 1933–1944, Serial 1, Box 1, FDRL.
87. Schuyler Patterson, 'Safeguarding the President: A Rigid Task for Vigilant Men', *New York Times*, 19 February 1933, p. XX1.
88. 'Panama's President Escapes Assassins', *New York Times*, 2 February 1934, p. 11.
89. 'Roosevelt Returns under Heavy Guard', *Washington Post*, 18 February 1933, p. 3.

90. 'Chiefs Want Plans of Roosevelt Cut', *Washington Post*, 17 February 1933, p. 2.
91. C.D. McKean (Special Agent in Charge, FBI) to Director, US Bureau of Investigation (J. Edgar Hoover), 16 February 1933, and V.W. Hughes, Memorandum for the Director, 20 February 1933, Federal Bureau of Investigation Files, 1933–1944, Serial 1, Box 1, FDRL.
92. Gerardo Machado (Presidente de la Republica de Cuba) to Franklin Delano Roosevelt, nd, Franklin D. Roosevelt, Papers as President: The President's Personal File, Part 1, PPF 1, Box 21, File PPF 1 (J), FDRL.
93. Raymond Buell, 'Cuba as a New Test of Platt Amendment', *New York Times*, 12 May 1929, p. XX13.
94. Jules Benjamin, 'The *Machadato* and Cuban Nationalism, 1928–1932', *Hispanic American Historical Review*, 55 (1975), pp. 66–91.
95. 'Two Try to Slay President of Cuba', *New York Times*, 25 February 1931, p. 15.
96. 'Soldier Describes Cuban Bomb Plot', *New York Times*, 1 March 1931, 28.
97. 'Reign of Terror in Cuba Called Halted by Arrests', *Washington Post*, 24 May 1932, p. 3.
98. 'Mined Building Kills Two Cuban Policemen', *New York Times*, 29 January 1932, p. 7.
99. 'Secret Police Head is Slain in Havana', *New York Times*, 10 July 1932, p. 1.
100. 'Strong Arm Chief is Slain in Havana', *New York Times*, 12 March 1933, p. F20.
101. 'Soldiers Guard Havana after 4 Assassinations', *Washington Post*, 28 September 1932, p. 1.
102. 'Soldiers Guard Havana', p. 1.
103. Chargé in Cuba (Edward Reed) to Secretary of State, 29 September 1932, *FRUS, 1932, The American Republics*, V.
104. 'Four Machado Aides Sentenced to Death', *New York Times*, 6 March 1934, p. 8.
105. Chargé in Cuba (Edward Reed) to Secretary of State, 7 October 1932, *FRUS, 1932, The American Republics*, V.
106. Russell B. Porter, 'Amid Cuba's Gayety Stalks the Terror', *New York Times*, 30 April 1933, p. SM5.
107. Ambassador in Cuba (Welles) to Secretary of State, 11 August 1933, *FRUS, 1933, The American Republics*, V.
108. 'Wild Disorder in Havana', *New York Times*, 13 August 1933, p. 1.
109. Ambassador in Cuba (Welles) to Secretary of State, 5 September 1933, *FRUS, 1933, The American Republics*, V.
110. 'Cuba Orders Inquiry in Wave of Killings', *New York Times*, 3 May 1936, p. 38.
111. '"Plot" on Long is Referred to Cummings', *Washington Post*, 18 September 1935, p. 1.
112. 'Observers See '36 Threat if Long Survives', *Washington Post*, 10 September 1935, p. 1.
113. 'Frenzied Puerto Ricans', *Washington Post*, 26 July 1938, p. X5.
114. '2 in Puerto Rico Kill Police Head', *New York Times*, 24 February 1936, p. 1.
115. 'Frenzied Puerto Ricans', p. X5.
116. 'Puerto Ricans Fire Upon Gov. Winship', *New York Times*, 26 July 1938, p. 1; 'Heavy Guard Kept around Roosevelt', *New York Times*, 22 September 1939, p. 18.
117. 'Puerto Rico Frees 5 Seized in Shooting', *New York Times*, 10 June 1937, p. 6.
118. 'Frenzied Puerto Ricans', p. X5.
119. *Report of the Commission of Inquiry on Civil Rights in Puerto Rico*, 22 May 1937.

120. James Kirkham, Sheldon Levy and William Crotty, *Assassination and Political Violence: A Report to the National Commission on the Causes and Prevention of Violence*, Vol. 8 (US GPO, 1969), pp. 58–61.
121. Oral History Interview with Robert G. Nixon, 5 November 1970, Harry S. Truman Library and Museum, Independence, Missouri.
122. Kirkham, Levy and Crotty, *Assassination and Political* Violence, xvii.

Chapter 5

1. David Scott, 'Government by Assassination', *Maclean's Magazine*, 1 June 1936, pp. 15–19.
2. Oleg Benesch, 'The Samurai Next Door: Chinese Examinations of the Japanese Martial Spirit', *Extrême Orient-Extrême Occident*, 38 (2014), pp. 129–68; John Person, 'Between Patriotism and Terrorism: The Policing of Nationalist Movements in 1930s Japan', *Journal of Japanese Studies*, 43 (2017), pp. 289–318.
3. Memorandum by the Chief of the Division of Far Eastern Affairs (Hornbeck), 6 March 1936, *FRUS*, 1936, *The Far East*, IV.
4. Rana Mitter, 'Presentism and China's Changing Wartime Past', *Past & Present*, 234 (2017), pp. 263–74.
5. 'A Damnable Weapon', *North-China Herald*, 28 July 1931, p. 113.
6. 'Young Marshal's Bodyguard', *North-China Herald*, 26 August 1930, p. 301.
7. Paul Dull, 'The Assassination of Chang Tso-Lin', *Far Eastern Quarterly*, 11 (1952), pp. 453–63.
8. Arthur Waldron, 'The Warlord: Twentieth-Century Chinese Understandings of Violence, Militarism and Imperialism', *American Historical Review*, 96 (1991), pp. 1073–1100.
9. Rana Mitter, *China's War with Japan, 1937–1945: The Struggle for Survival* (Penguin, 2014), p. 49.
10. Hugh Byas, 'Says Chang Tso-lin Forced Japan's Hand', *New York Times*, 1 May 1932, p. E8.
11. Danny Orbach, *Curse on This Country: The Rebellious Army of Imperial Japan* (Cornell University Press, 2017), p. 168; 'Attempt on Baron Tanaka', *North-China Herald*, 23 June 1928, p. 508.
12. 'Putnam Weale Has New Theory to Explain Assassination of Late Marshal Chang Tso-lin', *China Press*, 15 August 1928, p. 1. Simpson wrote as 'Putnam Weale'.
13. 'Attempted Assassination of Lenox Simpson', *China Weekly Review*, 4 October 1930, p. 189; 'The Outrage', *North-China Herald*, 7 October 1930, p. 5; Sir Miles Lampson (Peking) to Sir John Simon, Tel. 1158, 24 August 1933, *DBFP*, Ser. 2, Vol. 11.
14. Orbach, *Curse on This Country*, p. 181.
15. Byas, 'Says Chang Tso-lin Forced Japan's Hand', p. E8.
16. Memorandum of a Conversation between the Ambassador in Japan (Grew) and Major General Frank R. McCoy, 12 July 1932, *FRUS*, 1932, *The Far East*, IV.
17. Orbach, *Curse on This Country*, pp. 161–88.
18. John Morris, 'Hundred Wealthy Japanese Marked for Death by Gang of Assassins', *Washington Post*, 15 January 1922, p. 49.
19. Harukata Takenaka, *Failed Democratization in Pre-War Japan* (Stanford University Press, 2017), p. 106.
20. Morris, 'Hundred Wealthy Japanese Marked for Death by Gang of Assassins', p. 49.

21. Orbach, *Curse on This Country*, pp. 194–5.
22. Sir F. Lindley (Tokyo) to Sir John Simon, Tel. 236, 20 May 1932, *DBFP*, Ser. 2, Vol. 10.
23. Ambassador in Japan (Forbes) to Secretary of State, 20 November 1931, *FRUS*, 1931, *The Far East*, III.
24. Orbach, *Curse on This Country*, p. 218.
25. Chargé in Japan (Neville) to Secretary of State, 20 May 1932, *FRUS*, 1932, *The Far East*, IV.
26. Chargé in Japan (Neville) to Secretary of State, 7 April 1932, *FRUS*, 1932, *The Far East*, IV.
27. Sir John Simon (Geneva) to Ramsay MacDonald, 26 April 1932, *DBFP*, Ser. 2, Vol. 10.
28. 'Hugh Byas is Dead', *New York Times*, 7 March 1945 and 'Mr Hugh Byas', *The Times*, 7 March 1945, p. 7.
29. John Morris, 'Japan's "Divine Mission"', *Tribune*, 10 March 1944; Hugh Byas, *Government by Assassination* (Alfred Knopf, 1942), p. vii.
30. 'Political Assassination in Japan', Leader, *Manchester Guardian*, 16 May 1932, p. 8.
31. Stephen Large, 'Nationalist Extremism in Early Shōwa Japan: Inoue Nisshō and the "Blood-Pledge Corps Incident", 1932', *Modern Asian Studies*, 35 (2001), pp. 533–64.
32. Sir F. Lindley (Tokyo) to Sir John Simon, Desp. 139, 11 March 1932, *DBFP*, Ser. 2, Vol. 10.
33. Chargé in Japan (Neville) to Secretary of State, 7 April 1932, *FRUS*, 1932, *The Far East*, IV.
34. Ibid.
35. 'The Assassination Cult in Japan', *China Weekly Review*, 2 April 1932, p. 137.
36. Sir F. Lindley (Tokyo) to Sir John Simon, Desp. 139, 11 March 1932, *DBFP*, Ser. 2, Vol. 10.
37. Large, 'Nationalist Extremism in Early Shōwa Japan', pp. 533–64.
38. Sir F. Lindley (Tokyo) to Sir John Simon, Desp. 271, 19 May 1932, *DBFP*, Ser. 2, Vol. 10.
39. Sir F. Lindley (Tokyo) to Sir John Simon, Desp. 278, 26 May 1932, *DBFP*, Ser. 2, Vol. 10; Ambassador in Japan (Grew) to Secretary of State, 30 June 1932, *FRUS*, 1932, *The Far East*.
40. International Military Tribunal for the Far East, Judgment of 12 November 1948 in John Pritchard and Sonia Zaide, eds, *The Tokyo War Crimes Trial* (Garland, 1981), vol. XXII; Minister in Switzerland (Wilson) to Secretary of State, 9 February 1933, *FRUS*, 1933, *The Far East*, III; Ambassador in Japan (Grew) to Acting Secretary of State, 15 November 1933, *FRUS*, 1933, *The Far East*, III.
41. Takenaka, *Failed Democratization in Pre-War Japan*, p. 1; Ambassador in Japan (Grew) to Secretary of State, 16 August 1940, *FRUS*, 1940, *The Far East*, IV.
42. Hugh Byas, 'Socialism Spurs Japanese Unrest', *New York Times*, 27 August 1933, p. E2; Ambassador in Japan (Grew) to Secretary of State, 17 November 1932, *FRUS*, 1932, *The Far East*, IV; Ambassador in Japan (Grew) to Secretary of State, 3 December 1932, *FRUS*, 1932, *The Far East*, IV.
43. Orbach, *Curse on This Country*, p. 235.
44. Ambassador in Japan to Secretary of State, 5 March 1936, *FRUS*, 1936, *The Far East*, IV.

45. Memorandum by the Second Secretary of Embassy in China [Peiping] (Salisbury), 21 October 1935, *FRUS*, 1935, *The Far East*, III; Person, 'Between Patriotism and Terrorism', pp. 289–318.
46. Judgment of Tokyo War Crimes Trial, 12 November 1948.
47. Orbach, *Curse on This Country*, p. 240.
48. Ibid., p. 251.
49. Ambassador in Japan (Grew) to Secretary of State, 19 March 1936, *FRUS*, 1936, *The Far East*, IV.
50. Memorandum by the Chief of the Division of Far Eastern Affairs (Hornbeck), 6 March 1936, *FRUS*, 1936, *The Far East*, IV.
51. Memorandum by the Adviser on Political Relations (Stanley Hornbeck), 27 August 1941, *FRUS*, 1941, *The Far East*, IV; Memorandum by the Under Secretary of State (Sumner Welles), 13 October 1941, *FRUS*, *Japan 1931–1941*, II; William Langdon, Division of Far Eastern Affairs, Memorandum, 25 October 1941, *FRUS*, 1941, *The Far East*, IV.
52. Editorial note on Sir R. Clive (Tokyo) to Mr Eden, Tel. 57, 26 February 1936, *DBFP*, Ser. 2, Vol. 20.
53. 'Terrorists Hire Murder [Abundance of Luck] Society', *North-China Herald*, 30 September 1936, p. 571; Li Ling, 'Terrorism in Chinese History: Assassinations and Kidnapping', *Contemporary Chinese Thought*, 42 (2010), pp. 35–64; Benesch, 'The Samurai Next Door', pp. 129–68.
54. Gary Bass, *Judgement at Tokyo: World War II on Trial and the Making of Modern Asia* (Picador, 2023), p. 434.
55. CICB, HQ SACSEA, The Japanese Intelligence Service, 15 October 1945, KV 3/296, TNA.
56. Far East Combined Bureau, Singapore, FESS Intelligence: Japanese Intelligence Service, 1st Edition, 1 October 1940, 12 November 1940, KV 3/295, TNA.
57. Wen-hsin Weh, 'Dai Li and the Liu Geqing Affair: Heroism in the Chinese Secret Service during the War of Resistance', *Journal of Asian Studies*, 48 (1989), pp. 545–62; Strategic Services Unit, Japanese Intelligence Organizations in China, 4 June 1946, CIA.
58. CICB, HQ SACSEA, The Japanese Intelligence Service, 15 October 1945.
59. DP (Sir David Petrie, Director-General, Security Service) to Colonel C.E. Dixon (HQ, SACSEA, Singapore): Japanese Intelligence Organisations in the Far East, 21 January 1946, KV 3/296, TNA.
60. Maruyana Shizuo, 'The Nakano School: Memoirs of a Member of the Tokumu Kikan', 30 April 1948, KV 3/297, TNA (translated by the US and sent to MI5).
61. Frederic Wakeman, 'A Revisionist View of the Nanjing Decade: Confucian Fascism', *China Quarterly*, 150 (1997), pp. 395–432.
62. Joseph Yick, 'Juntong and the Ma Hansan Affair: Factionalism in the Nationalist Secret Service, 1946–1949', *Modern China*, 21 (1995), pp. 481–505.
63. Xu Youwei and Philip Billingsley, 'Behind the Scenes of the Xi'an Incident: The Case of the Lixingshe', *China Quarterly*, 154 (1998), pp. 283–307.
64. Weh, 'Dai Li and the Liu Geqing Affair', pp. 545–62.
65. Lloyd Eastman, 'Fascism in Kuomintang China: The Blue Shirts', *China Quarterly*, 49 (1972), pp. 1–31.
66. Frederic Wakeman, 'American Police Advisers and the Nationalist Chinese Secret Service, 1930–1937', *Modern China*, 18 (1992), pp. 107–37.

67. Frederic Wakeman, 'Policing Modern Shanghai', *China Quarterly*, 115 (1988), pp. 409–40.
68. Sir Miles Lampson (Peking) to Sir John Simon, Tel. 1158, 24 August 1933, *DBFP*, Ser. 2, Vol. 11; Keith Schoppa, *Blood Road: The Mystery of Shen Dingyi in Revolutionary China* (University Press of California, 1995), p. 159.
69. Tang Leang-Li, 'Wang Ching-wei – Leader of China Renascent', *China Press*, 21 March 1933, p. 10; 'Wang Ching Wei Scores Political Murders Here', *China Press*, 22 February 1930, p. 1; Edmund Fung, 'Anti-Imperialism and the Left Guomindang', *Modern China*, 11 (1985), pp. 39–76.
70. Strategic Services Unit, 'Japanese Intelligence Organizations in China', 4 June 1946; Mitter, *China's War with Japan, 1937–1945*, p. 291.
71. 'Quadruple Political Murder', *North-China Herald*, 25 February 1925, p. 303.
72. 'Will the War of Words Become a War of Bullets?', *China Weekly Review*, 1 March 1930, p. 8.
73. 'The Pistol as a Political Argument is Unconvincing', *China Press*, 17 March 1931, p. 16.
74. So Wai Chor, 'The Making of Guomindang's Japan Policy, 1932–1937: The Roles of Chiang Kai-shek and Wang Jingwei', *Modern China*, 28 (2002), pp. 213–52.
75. 'Wang Gives 1st Interview Since Attack', *China Press*, 17 November 1935, p. 1.
76. Mitter, *China's War with Japan, 1937–1945*, p. 356.
77. Counselor of Embassy in China [Nanking] (Peck) to Secretary of State, 17 June 1936, *FRUS*, 1936, *The Far East*, IV; Note on Sir A. Cadogan (Shanghai) to Foreign Office, Tel. 70, 1 November 1935, *DBFP*, Ser. 2, Vol. 20.
78. Mitter, *China's War with Japan, 1937–1945*, p. 61.
79. 'Foreign Vice-Minister Assassinated', *North-China Herald*, 1 January 1936, p. 14; Ambassador in China (Johnson) to Secretary of State, 26 December 1935, *FRUS*, 1935, *The Far East*, III; 'Liu Lu-yin Allegedly Implicated in Political Assassinations', *China Weekly Review*, 6 March 1937, p. 12.
80. Yun Xia, *Down with Traitors: Justice and Nationalism in Wartime China* (University of Washington Press, 2017), p. 52.
81. Wai Chor So, 'Race, Culture, and the Anglo-American Powers: The Views of Chinese Collaborators', Modern China, 37 (2011), pp. 69–103, at 87–8.
82. 'Wang Ching-wei Escapes Murder Attempt', *North-China Herald*, 29 March 1939, p. 530.
83. Frederic Wakeman, *Spymaster: Dai Li and the Chinese Secret Service* (University of California Press, 2003), p. 338.
84. Mitter, *China's War with Japan, 1937–1945*, p. 218.
85. Stephen MacKinnon, 'Toward a History of the Chinese Press in the Republican Period', *Modern China*, 23 (1997), pp. 3–32; Sei Jeong Chin, 'The Historical Origins of the Nationalization of the Newspaper Industry in Modern China: A Case Study of the Newspaper Industry, 1937–1953', *China Review*, 13 (2013), pp. 1–34; idem, 'Print Capitalism, War, and the Remaking of the Mass Media in 1930s China', *Modern China*, 40 (2014), pp. 393–425.
86. Michael Miller, *Shanghai on the Métro: Spies, Intrigue, and the French between the Wars* (University of California Press, 1994).
87. Wakeman, 'Policing Modern Shanghai', pp. 409–40.
88. Colonel G.H.R. Halland, 'Punjab Patrol: Some Memories of an Indian Police Officer', Halland Papers 1, CSAA.

89. [British and American defence commanders], Draft aide-mémoire, 14 May 1940, FO 371/24663, TNA.
90. 'S.M.C. Asks Consular Body for Aid', *North-China Herald*, 24 July 1940, p. 124.
91. Wakeman, 'Policing Modern Shanghai', pp. 409–40.
92. Brian Martin, 'The Green Gang and the Guomindang State: Du Yuehsheng and the Politics of Shanghai, 1927–1937', *Journal of Asian Studies*, 54 (1995), pp. 64–92.
93. DP (Sir David Petrie, Director-General, Security Service) to Colonel C.E. Dixon (HQ, SACSEA, Singapore): Japanese Intelligence Organisations in the Far East, 21 January 1946.
94. V [Valentine Vivian, SIS], 'Communist Activities in China, Federated Malay States, etc. (The "Noulens Case")', 7 March 1932, FO 1093/92, TNA; Frederick Litten, 'The Noulens Affair', *China Quarterly*, 138 (1994), pp. 492–512; Heather Streets-Salter, 'The Noulens Affair in East and Southeast Asia: International Communism in the Interwar Period', *Journal of American-East Asian Relations*, 21 (2014), pp. 394–414.
95. 'Reign of Terror Again?', *North-China Herald*, 27 August 1927, p. 362.
96. Xia, *Down with Traitors*, p. 52.
97. Wakeman, 'American Police Advisers', pp. 107–37.
98. 'Fresh Example of Terroristic Methods', *North-China Herald*, 24 September 1927, p. 526.
99. 'Political Murder in Shanghai', *North-China Herald*, 16 November 1929, p. 258.
100. Patricia Stranahan, 'Strange Bedfellows: The Communist Party and Shanghai's Elite in the National Salvation Movement', *China Quarterly*, 129 (1992), pp. 26–51.
101. Lawrence Sullivan, 'Reconstruction and Rectification of the Communist Party in the Shanghai Underground', *China Quarterly*, 101 (1985), pp. 78–97.
102. DS Golder, Shanghai Municipal Police Special Branch, Report on Assassination of Detective Superintendent Wong Ping of the Soong Wu Military HQ, 22 April 1932, Shanghai Municipal Police Files, 1894–1945, Reel 11, *Archives Unbound* [hereafter SMP Files].
103. 'Bureau Secret Service Chief Head Murdered at Local Hotel', *China Weekly Review*, 2 September 1933, p. 29.
104. 'Triple Murder in Hospital', *North-China Herald*, 3 October 1934, p. 12.
105. 'Assassinations since the Revolution', *North-China Herald*, 4 March 1930, p. 372.
106. 'Kwauk Replaces Lo as Director, *China Press*, 2 August 1931, p. 2.
107. 'Station Attack Not First for Soong', *China Press*, 24 July 1931, p. 2.
108. 'Seven Alleged Bomb-Tossers Handed Over', *China Press*, 12 August 1936, p. 9; J.F. Brenan (Shanghai) to Sir John Simon, Desp. 21, 17 February 1932, *DBFP*, Ser. 2, Vol. 9.
109. Xia, *Down with Traitors*, p. 46; Eastman, 'Fascism in Kuomintang China', pp. 1–31.
110. Xia, *Down with Traitors*, p. 58.
111. Strategic Services Unit, 'Japanese Intelligence Organizations in China', 4 June 1946, CIA.
112. Frederic Wakeman, *The Shanghai Badlands: Wartime Terrorism and Urban Crime, 1937–1941* (CUP, 2002), pp. 6–8; Bernard Wasserstein, *Secret War in Shanghai: Treachery, Subversion and Collaboration in the Second World War* (I.B. Tauris, 2017), pp. 52–4.

113. Consul General at Shanghai (Gauss) to Secretary of State, 11 March 1938, *FRUS*, 1938, *The Far East*, III.
114. 'High Police Officer Killed', *North-China Herald*, 24 August 1938, p. 326.
115. 'Another "Ta Tao" Official Slain', *North-China Herald*, 6 July 1938, p. 20.
116. 'Attempted Assassination of Zau Reveals Devilishly Clever Plot', *China Press*, 19 October 1938, p. 1.
117. 'Principal in Murder of Chao Tih-Chao Brought to Shanghai from Hofei', *China Press*, 10 November 1930, p. 1.
118. 'Marquis Li Shot and Killed in Shanghai', *China Weekly Review*, 25 February 1939, p. 399.
119. 'Pro-Japanese Minister Slain in Shanghai', *Washington Post*, 20 February 1939, p. 2; 'Shanghai Faces Reprisals by Japan after 53rd Slaying', *Washington Post*, 22 February 1939, p. 5.
120. Sir Archibald Clark Kerr to Greenway (Chungking), Tel. 146, 22 February 1939, *DBFP*, Ser. 3, Vol. 8.
121. Sir R. Craigie (Tokyo) to Viscount Halifax, Tel. 438, 16 May 1939, *DBFP*, Ser. 3, Vol. 9.
122. Sir Archibald Clark Kerr to Greenway (Chungking), Tel. 146, 22 February 1939.
123. Jamieson (Tientsin) to British Embassy (Shanghai), Tel. 205, 11 April 1939, *DBFP*, Ser. 3, Vol. 9.
124. Jamieson (Tientsin) to Viscount Halifax, Tel. 214, 11 April 1939, *DBFP*, Ser. 3, Vol. 9; Viscount Halifax to Sir Archibald Clark Kerr (Shanghai), Tel. 409, 30 May 1939, *DBFP*, Ser. 3, Vol. 9.
125. Foreign Office Memorandum [for Cabinet], 21 August 1939, *DBFP*, Ser. 3, Vol. 9.
126. 'Shanghai Assassinations Laid to Chungking', *New York Times*, 25 February 1939, p. 7.
127. 'Another Assassination', *China Press*, 13 April 1939, SMP Files; Sir H. Phillips (Consul-General at Shanghai) to British Embassy (Shanghai), Tel. 60, 12 April 1939, *DBFP*, Ser. 3, Vol. 9.
128. 'Attempt on Police Chief', *North-China Herald*, 5 July 1939, p. 19.
129. DI Pan Lien-pih, SMPSB, 'Assassination of Cheng Hai Dao, Acting Chief of the Chinese Staff of the French Police – Arrest of Suspects', 22 October 1939, SMP Files.
130. 'Supt. Tan Shao-Liang Killed', *North-China Herald*, 17 April 1940, p. 92; 'Senior Chinese Detective Shot', *North-China Herald*, 1 May 1940, p. 177; Hayter (Shanghai) to HM Ambassador (Chungking), Tel. 124, 1 May 1940, FO 371/24663, TNA.
131. Lieutenant Commander A.S.D. Ryder, Staff Officer (Intelligence), Shanghai to Director of Naval Intelligence: Japanese Intelligence Services – Changes, 25 February 1938, KV 3/295, TNA.
132. A.H. George (Consul-General) to Ambassador, Shanghai, Desp. 501, 6 August 1940, FO 371/24663, TNA; A.H. George (Consul-General) to Ambassador, Shanghai, Desp. 543, 22 August 1940, FO 371/24663, TNA.
133. 'Council Appeases Both Japanese and Puppet Gangsters', *China Weekly Review*, 16 November 1940, p. 351.
134. 'Terrorist Attacks Laid to One Gang', *North-China Herald*, 6 September 1939, p. 402.
135. DI Crawford, SMP Special Branch Report, 10 January 1940, SMP Files.

136. DI Crawford, SMP Special Branch Report, 5 February 1940, SMP Files.
137. 'Thugs Make Attempt to Kill Phillips', *China Weekly Review*, 13 January 1940, p. 247.
138. K.M. Bourne (Commissioner of Police) to Secretary and Commissioner General (Shanghai Municipal Council), 27 April 1940, FO 371/24663, TNA; W.G. Hayter (British Embassy, Shanghai) to Sir Robert Cragie (Ambassador, Tokyo), Desp. 213, 3 May 1940, FO 371/24663, TNA.
139. A.H. George (Consul-General) to Ambassador, Shanghai, Desp. 614, 23 September 1940, FO 371/24663, TNA.
140. 'Murder Shocks Local Circles', *North-China Herald*, 25 December 1940, p. 498.
141. K.M. Bourne (Commissioner of Police) to Secretary and Commissioner General, 'Activities of 76 Jessfield Road', 23 April 1940, FO 371/24663, TNA.
142. K.M. Bourne (Commissioner of Police) to Secretary and Commissioner General, 27 April 1940, FO 371/24663, TNA.
143. British Consulate-General, Shanghai to Ambassador (British Embassy, Shanghai), Desp. 268, 2 May 1940, FO 371/24663, TNA.
144. A.H. George (Consul-General) to Ambassador, Shanghai, Desp. 318, 20 May 1940, FO 371/24663, TNA; Japanese Embassy to Department of State, 23 August 1940, *FRUS, Japan 1931–1941*, I.
145. A.H. George (Consul-General) to Ambassador, Shanghai, Desp. 543, 22 August 1940, FO 371/24663, TNA; Xia, *Down with Traitors*, p. 72.
146. 'S.M.C. Issues a Survey of 1940', *North-China Herald*, 22 January 1941, p. 128.
147. '"Mayor" Still Visits Home', *China Press*, 2 November 1938, p. 1.
148. 'Attempt Made on Life of Local "Mayor"', *China Press*, 26 November 1938, p. 1.
149. 'Fu's Missing Servant Still Holds Key to Mystery of Mayor's Murder', *China Weekly Review*, 19 October 1940, p. 228.
150. A.H. George (Consul-General) to Ambassador, Shanghai, Desp. 652, 29 October 1940, FO 371/24663, TNA.
151. Douglas Robertson, 'Wang Group Split on Finance Issue', *New York Times*, 18 December 1940, p. 14.
152. Xia, *Down with Traitors*, p. 55.
153. 'Gang of Gunmen Rounded Up', *North-China Herald*, 5 March 1941, p. 371.
154. Xia, *Down with Traitors*, p. 55.
155. Sir Miles Lampson (Peking) to Sir John Simon, Tel. 1158, 24 August 1933.
156. 'Journalists [sic] Escapes Death', *North-China Herald*, 21 August 1940, p. 291.
157. 'The Murder Feud', *North-China Herald*, 26 March 1941, p. 476.
158. Paul Cornish, 'Weapons and Equipment of the Special Operations Executive', in Mark Seaman, ed., *Special Operations Executive: A New Instrument of War* (Routledge, 2006), pp. 22–32.

Chapter 6

1. Frank Getty, 'Assassination Seldom Resorted to in America as Political Weapon', *Washington Post*, 7 January 1934, Special Articles, p. 1; Frederic Ogg, 'Assassination of Rumania's Premier', *Current History*, 39 (1934), pp. 619–26.
2. Ramazan Hakki Oztan, 'Republic of Conspiracies: Cross-Border Plots and the Making of Modern Turkey', *Journal of Contemporary History*, 56 (2021), pp. 55–76.
3. Sir G. Ogilvie-Forbes to Mr Eden, No. 888, 6 October 1937, *DBFP*, Ser. 2, Vol. 19.

4. G. Lowell Field, 'Comparative Aspects of Fascism', *Southwestern Social Science Quarterly*, 20 (January 1939), pp. 349–60.
5. Rubén Gallo, 'Who Killed Trotsky?', *Princeton University Library Chronicle*, 75 (2013), pp. 109–18.
6. Andrew Barros, 'A Window on the "Trust": The Case of Ado Birk', *Intelligence and National Security*, 10 (1995), pp. 273–93.
7. James Harris, *The Great Fear: Stalin's Terror of the 1930s* (OUP, 2016), p. 122.
8. William J. Makin, 'Stalin Dodges Death! How Russia Protects a Dictator', *Chicago Daily Tribune*, 15 October 1939, p. G4.
9. Katherine Foshko, 'The Paul Doumer Assassination and the Russian Diaspora in Interwar France', *French History*, 23 (2009), pp. 383–404; Sophie Cœuré and Frédéric Monier, 'Paul Gorgulov Assassin de Paul Doumer (1932)', *Vingtième Siècle*, 65 (2000), pp. 35–46.
10. Sidney Reilly, *Adventures of a British Master Spy: The Memoirs of Sidney Reilly* ([1932]; Biteback, 2014).
11. Harris, *The Great Fear*, pp. 121–5.
12. Matt Lenoe, 'Did Stalin Kill Kirov and Does it Matter?', *Journal of Modern History*, 74 (2002), pp. 352–80.
13. Matthew E. Lenoe, *The Kirov Murder and Soviet History* (Yale UP, 2010), p. 471 & p. 497.
14. Protocol of interrogation of Leonid Nikolaev, 1 December 1934, Lenoe, *The Kirov Murder and Soviet History*, Document 36.
15. Ibid., Document 36.
16. Protocol of interrogation of Karl Pauzer [b. 1891, Chekist since 1919], member of Kirov's security detail, [5–6 December 1934], Lenoe, *The Kirov Murder and Soviet History*, Document 86.
17. Harris, *The Great Fear*, pp. 121–5.
18. Chargé in the Soviet Union (Henderson) to Secretary of State, 1 September 1936, *FRUS, The Soviet Union, 1933–1939*.
19. Gallo, 'Who Killed Trotsky?', pp. 109–18.
20. Jonathan Haslam, *Near and Distant Neighbours: A New History of Soviet Intelligence* (OUP, 2015).
21. Donald Rayfield, 'The Exquisite Inquisitor: Viascheslav Menzhinky as Poet and Hangman', *New Zealand Slavonic Journal* (2003), pp. 91–109.
22. Excerpt from Genrikh Yagoda's closing statement, Moscow trial, March 1938, Lenoe, *The Kirov Murder and Soviet History*, Document 106.
23. Chief of Sûreté, Lausanne to Commissioner of the Metropolitan Police, 13 September 1937, KV 2/1898, TNA.
24. Sir Percy Sillitoe [written by Morton-Evans] to G.T.D. Patterson [British Embassy, Washington], 17 October 1949, KV 2/1898, TNA.
25. Extract from MI6 letter enclosing note on the death of Walter Krivitsky, 11 April 1941, KV 2/1898, TNA.
26. Extract from SIS Report re RIS activities in Holland, 1930–1949, 5 April 1950, KV 2/805, TNA.
27. Christopher Andrew and Vasili Mitrokhin, *The Mitrokhin Archive: The KGB in Europe and the West* (Penguin, 2000), p. 100.
28. Pavel and Anatoli Sudoplatov, *Special Tasks* (Little, Brown, 1995), p. 67.
29. Gallo, 'Who Killed Trotsky?', pp. 109–18.
30. Lenoe, *The Kirov Murder and Soviet History*, pp. 543–4.

31. Report by 'Glan', 18 November 1940, Vassiliev Yellow Notebook 2, Wilson Center Digital Archive [hereafter WCDA].
32. P.J. Wacks, Memorandum for Edward Tamm, 14 February 1941, Walter G. Krivitsky, File 100-11146, FBI Freedom of Information Act Digital Library [hereafter FBI].
33. Edward Tamm, Memorandum for the Director, 11 February 1941, File 100-11146, FBI.
34. B.E. Sackett, SAC, to Director, 20 February 1941, File 100-11146, FBI.
35. Report to Dep. Chief of the 3rd department, 1st directorate of the NKGB, USSR State Security, Major Cde Prudnikov, Vassiliev Black Notebook, WCDA.
36. 'Who Killed Krivitsky?', *Washington Post*, 13 February 1966, E1.
37. É. Girard, '*Adjonctions Texte anglais*' and John Cullen (Assistant General Editor, Methuen) to Émile Giraud, 14 February 1947, COL187bis/169/2, United Nations Library & Archives, Geneva (hereafter UNL).
38. Matteo Millan, '*Squadrismo*: Disciplining Paramilitary Violence in the Italian Fascist Dictatorship', *Contemporary European History*, 22 (2013), pp. 551–73.
39. Mauro Canali, 'The Matteotti Murder and the Origins of Mussolini's Totalitarian Fascist Regime in Italy', *Journal of Modern Italian Studies*, 14 (2009), pp. 143–67.
40. Millan, '*Squadrismo*', pp. 551–73.
41. Philip Morgan, '"The Trash Who Are Obstacles in our Way": The Italian Fascist Party at the Point of Totalitarian Lift Off, 1920–21', *English Historical Review*, 127 (2012), pp. 303–44.
42. Benedetta Carnaghi, 'Mussolini's Four Would-be Assassins: Emergency Politics and the Consolidation of Fascist Power', *Journal of Modern Italian Studies*, 27 (2022), pp. 1–18.
43. Millan, '*Squadrismo*', pp. 551–73.
44. Japanese Ambassador (Rome) to Foreign Minister (Tokyo), Tel. 77, 27 July 1928 [Decrypt], HW 12/109, TNA.
45. Arnaldo Cortese, 'Anarchist Is Seized in Rome Bomb Plot', *New York Times*, 6 February 1931, p. 10.
46. Millan, '*Squadrismo*', pp. 551–73.
47. [Guy Liddell], 'The Liquidation of Communism, Left Wing Socialism & Pacifism in Germany' (Visit to Berlin 30.3.33–9.4.33), KV 4/111, TNA.
48. Anke Hoffstadt and Richard Kühl, '"Dead Man Walking": Der "Fememörder" Paul Schulz und seine "Erschieß" am 30. Juni 1934', *Historische Sozialforschung*, 34 (2009), pp. 273–85.
49. Sir Eric Phipps (Berlin) to Sir John Simon, Desp. 794, 5 July 1934, *DBFP*, Ser. 2, Vol. 6.
50. Robert Machray, 'International Anarchy: Meaning of the Marseilles Murders', *Saturday Review*, 27 October 1934, p. 300; Ralph Stevenson (Foreign Office) to Major Abraham (League of Nations Secretariat), 31 July 1934, R3734/2C/12738/5425, UNL.
51. Sir John Simon to Mr Hadow (Vienna), Tel. 53, 26 July 1934, *DBFP*, Ser. 2, Vol. 6.
52. Mr Hadow (Vienna) to Sir John Simon, Desp. 145, 26 July 1934, *DBFP*, Ser. 2, Vol. 6.
53. Note by Edith Durham, MS 56/2, Durham MSS.
54. Jean-Pierre Vallé, 'L'assassinat politique du roi Alexandre Ier de Yougoslavie: Un tournant dans la censure des actualités cinématographiques sous la IIIe République', *Hypothèses*, 20 (2017), pp. 221–35.

55. James Sadkovich, *Italian Support for Croatian Separatism, 1927–1937* (Garland, 1987), pp. 120–1.
56. Miller, *Shanghai on the Métro*, pp. 87–8.
57. Vallé, 'L'assassinat politique du roi Alexandre Ier de Yougoslavie', pp. 221–35.
58. Frédéric Monier, 'Défendre des "terroristes" dans la France de 1935: L'avocat des "oustachis croates"', *Le Mouvement social*, 240 (2012/13), pp. 105–20.
59. Stanislao Pugliese, 'Death in Exile: The Assassination of Carlo Rosselli', *Journal of Contemporary History*, 32 (1997), pp. 305–19.
60. Sir Percy Loraine (Angora) to Sir John Simon, Tel. 37, 2 November 1934, *DBFP*, Ser. 2, Vol. 12.
61. Radu Ioanid, 'Nicolae Iorga and Fascism', *Journal of Contemporary History*, 27 (1992), pp. 467–92.
62. Raul Carstocea, 'Breaking the Teeth of Time: Mythical Time and the "Terror of History" in the Rhetoric of the Legionary Movement in Interwar Rumania', *Journal of Modern European History*, 13 (2015), pp. 79–97; Mihai Stelian Rusu, 'Staging Death: Christofascist Necropolitics during the National Legionary State in Romania, 1940–1941', *Nationalities Papers*, 49 (2021), pp. 576–89; Ilarion Tiu, 'Terrorism as Political Tool: The Assassination of Romanian Prime Minister Armand Calinescu by Legionnaires, 21st September 1939', *Cogito*, 5 (2013), pp. 61–9.
63. David Irving, *The Trail of the Fox* (E.P. Dutton, 1977), p. 29.
64. Peter Hoffmann, 'Hitler's Personal Security', *Journal of Contemporary History*, 8 (1973), pp. 25–46.
65. Heinz Pannwitz, 'Attentat auf Heydrich', March 1959, *Vierteljahrshefte für Zeitgeschichte*, 33 (1985), pp. 673–706.
66. Hoffmann, 'Hitler's Personal Security', pp. 25–46.
67. Fred Taylor, ed., *The Goebbels Diaries, 1939–1941* (G.P. Putnam's Sons, 1983), 9 November 1939; Henrik Eberle and Matthias Uhl, eds, *The Hitler Book: The Secret Dossier Prepared for Stalin* (John Murray, 2005).
68. Ron Roizen, 'Herschel Grynszpan: The Fate of a Forgotten Assassin', *Holocaust and Genocide Studies*, 1 (1986), pp. 217–28.
69. Ambassador in Germany (Wilson) to Secretary of State, 10 November 1938, *FRUS*, 1938, *The British Commonwealth, Europe, Near East, and Africa*, I.
70. Lester Diary, 16 November 1938, Diary of Seán Lester, Volume 1, Private Archives, UNL.
71. Geoffrey Household, *Rogue Male* (NYRB, 2007 [1939]); idem, *The Europe that Was* (Orion Books, 2014 [1979]); 'Geoffrey Household: Novelist who Tracked his Prey', *The Times*, Obituary, 6 October 1988, p. 18; Maurice Pearton, 'SOE in Romania', in Mark Seaman, ed., *Special Operations Executive: A New Instrument of War* (Routledge, 2006), pp. 123–36.
72. Ward Thomas, 'Norms and Security: The Case of International Assassination', *International Security*, 25 (Summer 2000), pp. 105–33.
73. Comment to Press, 22 November 1939, FO 1093/200, TNA.
74. Summary of Events [22 November 1939], FO 1093/200, TNA.
75. Ian Fleming, 'Intrepid: Silhouette of a Secret Agent', *Sunday Times*, 21 October 1962, p. 25.
76. WP (40) 271, 19 July 1940, PREM 3/418/1, TNA.
77. Lord Selborne to Prime Minister, 10 April 1942, HS 8/897, TNA; J. Hanbury-Williams and E.W. Playfair, 'Report to the Minister of Economic Warfare on the Organisation of SOE', 18 June 1942, HS 8/1021, TNA.

78. [Valentine Vivian, SIS] to J.B. Curry, MI5, 10 July 1941, KV 2/805, TNA.
79. Christopher Neumaier, 'The Escalation of German Reprisal Policy in Occupied France, 1941–42', *Journal of Contemporary History*, 41 (2006), pp. 113–31.
80. Gaël Eismann, 'Le Militärbefehlshaber in Frankreich et la genèse de la "solution finale" en France (1941–1942)', *Vingtième Siècle*, 132 (2016), pp. 43–59.
81. Gaël Eismann, 'Maintenir l'ordre: Le MBF [Militärbefehlshaber in Frankreich] et la sécurité locale en France occupée', *Vingtième Siècle*, 98 (2008), pp. 125–39.
82. Pannwitz, 'Attentat auf Heydrich', pp. 673–706.
83. *Sonderkommission Attentat H, Schlussbericht: Attentat auf den Stellvertretenden Reichsprotektor und Chef der Sicherheitspolizei und des SD SS-Obergruppenführer Reinhard Heydrich*, 25 September 1942, in Vojtěch Šustek, *Atentát na Reinharda Heydricha: Edice historických dokumentů, sv.* 1 (Scriptorium, 2012), Document I/107; Heinz Pannwitz, 'The Assassination of Reinhard Heydrich' [March 1959], translated from the German and annotated by Stanislav Berton, July 1984, PANN, SSEES; Joint SOE/PWE Survey of Resistance in Occupied Europe, [August 1942], HS8/283, TNA.
84. Edith Durham to Sir Edward Boyle, 28 October 1938, Boyle Papers.
85. Pannwitz, 'Attentat auf Heydrich', pp. 673–706.
86. *Sonderkommission Attentat H, Schlussbericht*.
87. David Stafford, *Churchill and Secret Service* (Abacus, 2001), p. 281.
88. *Sonderkommission Attentat H, Schlussbericht*.
89. Pannwitz, 'The Assassination of Reinhard Heydrich'.
90. F.E. Keary, Major P.W. Auster and Major G.I. Klauber, Czechoslovak Section History, 1940–1945, HS 7/108.
91. Pannwitz, 'Attentat auf Heydrich', pp. 673–706.
92. Pannwitz, 'The Assassination of Reinhard Heydrich'.
93. Stafford, *Churchill and Secret Service*, p. 283.
94. Selborne to Prime Minister, Quarterly Report of SOE Activities, March–June 1942, HS 8/250, TNA.
95. *Sonderkommission Attentat H, Schlussbericht*.
96. [Terence Cuneo, Death of Heydrich], INF 3/24, TNA.
97. 'Suicide Skymen Killed Heydrich', *Daily Mail*, 2 June 1945, p. 1.
98. F.E. Keary, Major P.W. Auster and Major G.I. Klauber, Czechoslovak Section History, 1940–1945.
99. William Mackenzie, *The Secret History of SOE: Special Operations Executive, 1940–1945* ([1948]; St Ermin's Press, 2000), pp. 318–20.
100. History of SOE in the Arab World, September 1945, HS 7/86, TNA.
101. Adam Leong Kok Wey, *Killing the Enemy: Assassination Operations during World War II* (I.B. Tauris, 2015), Chapter 6.
102. AFHQ to USFOR, Tel. 3295, WO 204/4147, TNA.
103. Captain Jacky Porter, 'History of Massingham', 15 September 1945, HS7/169, TNA.
104. SOE Progress Report for Period Ending 4th January 1943, HS 8/223, TNA.
105. History of OSS/SOE Relations, HS 7/283, TNA; T.C. Wales, 'The "Massingham" Mission and the Secret "Special Relationship": Co-operation and Rivalry between the Anglo-American Clandestine Services in French North Africa, November 1942 to May 1943', *Intelligence & National Security*, 20 (2005), pp. 44–71.
106. Note for President and Draft Speech, 24 December 1942, Franklin D. Roosevelt, Master Speech File, Box 70, FDRL.

107. JCS to Algiers, Tel. 489, 26 December 1942, Franklin D. Roosevelt, Papers as President: Map Room Papers, 1941–1945, Box 49, FDRL.
108. Halifax to Eden, Desp. 232, 1 April 1943, HS 8/16, TNA.
109. Minute by Oliver Harvey, 24 April 1945, FO 371/49149, TNA.
110. John Lisle, *The Dirty Tricks Department: The Untold Story of the Real-Life Q Branch, the Masterminds of Second World War Secret Warfare* (History Press, 2023), p. 74.
111. OSS, Special Operations Field Manual – Strategic Services (Provisional), Field Manual No. 4, 23 February 1944, CIA.
112. Walter Brackman to MO Division, OSS: Activities in the ETO, 28 April 1945, CIA.
113. Saul Padover, 'Patterns of Assassination in Occupied Territory', *Public Opinion Quarterly* (Winter 1943), pp. 680–93.
114. WR.E, Counter Intelligence War Room, 'German Terrorist Methods', 2 April 1945, KV 3/414, TNA.
115. HQ Twelfth Army Group to SHAEF Main, 20 and 22 December 1944, WO 219/40A, TNA.
116. Lieutenant E.D. Phillips, 'GC&CS Air and Military History, Vol. XIII, The German Police', HW 11/13, TNA.
117. Klaus Schwabe, *Setting up the Right Kind of Government: American Occupation Experiences in Aachen before Germany's Surrender* (Aachener Geschichtsverein, 2000).
118. Memorandum by AD/A: FOXLEY, 10 October 1944, HS 8/201, TNA. [The minutes for 27 June 1944 remain redacted.]
119. SOE (44) 50, Minutes of Meeting of SOE Council, 30 June 1944, HS 8/201, TNA.
120. SIS, Report from U.35, dated 4.7.44, KV 3/291, TNA.
121. OSS R&A Branch, 'The Attempt of Hitler's Life and its Consequences', 27 July 1944, CIA.
122. SOE Handbook: Missions in Neutral Countries, nd, HS 3/227, TNA.
123. Dr. Geschke to *Adjutantur SS-Obergruppenführer* Heydrich, *Betrifft: Schutzmassnahmen für Jungfern-Breschan*, 14 May 1942, in Šustek, *Atentát na Reinharda Heydricha*, Document I/12.
124. Field Interrogation Report on Horst Kopkow, Neumünster, 7 June 1945, KV 3/109, TNA.
125. SHAEF G-2 Counter Intelligence Sub-Division Evaluation and Dissemination Section, EDS Report No. 33, The Reichssicherheitsdienst and the Schutzdienst, 26 June 1945, KV 3/36, TNA.
126. Hoffmann, 'Hitler's Personal Security', pp. 25–46.
127. Alaric Searle, *Wehrmacht Generals, West German Society, and the Rearmament Debate, 1949–1955* (Praeger, 2003), p. 165.
128. German and Austrian Section, Research Department, Foreign Office, '20th July (1944) Plot Personalities (Traced up to 31st December, 1948)', January 1949, FO 371/76732, TNA.
129. Franklin L. Ford, 'The Twentieth of July in the History of the German Resistance', *American Historical Review*, 51/4 (July 1946), pp. 609–26.
130. Sönke Neitzel, ed., *Tapping Hitler's Generals: Transcripts of Secret Conversations, 1942–45* (Frontline, 2007), Doc. 158.
131. HQ Twelfth Army Group to SHAEF Main, 22 December 1944, WO 219/40A, TNA.

132. Field Interrogation Report on Horst Kopkow, Neumünster, 7 June 1945.
133. Winifried Heinemann, 'Das Ende des Staatsstreichs: Die Niederschlagung des 20. Juli 1944 im Bendlerblock', *Vierteljahrsshefte für Zeitgeschichte*, 68 (2020), pp. 1–23.
134. Neitzel, *Tapping Hitler's Generals*, Doc. 158.
135. Japanese Ambassador, Berlin to Tokyo, 25 July 1944, GC&CS Summary Report 740, 29 July 1944, HW 13/173, TNA; Neitzel, *Tapping Hitler's Generals*, Doc. 151 [August 1944].
136. OSS R&A Branch, 'The Attempt on Hitler's Life and its Consequences', 27 July 1944; Ford, 'The Twentieth of July in the History of the German Resistance', pp. 609–26; Hugh Trevor-Roper, 'Admiral Canaris' [1950, 1968], reprinted in *The Secret World: Behind the Curtain of British Intelligence in World War II and the Cold War*, ed. Edward Harrison (I.B. Tauris, 2014), pp. 48–65.
137. Memorandum by AD/A: FOXLEY, 10 October 1944.
138. AD/X to New York, Tel. 2979, 'Captain E.H. Bennett', 16 March 1945, WCDA.
139. Lt. Col. J.G. Beevor, GSOI (Plans) and A/Comdr SO (M), Personal Attacks, [1945], HS 7/64, TNA.
140. AD/X.1 to AD/E, 'Operation Chalgrove', 8 February 1945, HS 6/674, TNA.
141. Report of Wilhelm Borstelmann, 10 May 1945, HS 6/674, TNA.
142. Briefing Instructions for Operation Chalgrove attached to X/GER. to AD/X.1, 9 February 1945, HS 6/674, TNA.
143. OC Group "C" STS to X/Ger, 'Operational Weapons', 22 February 1945, HS 6/674, TNA.
144. Euphemia Base for Thornley and Ince, 30 May 1945, HS 6/674, TNA.
145. SIS, VCSS's Lectures, 16 May 1946, HS 7/1, TNA.
146. Calder Walton, *Spies: The Epic Intelligence War between East and West* (Abacus, 2023), p. 165.

Chapter 7

1. Nachman Ben-Yehuda, 'Conflict Resolution in an Underground Group: The Shamir-Giladi Clash', *Studies in Conflict and Terrorism*, 12 (1989), pp. 199–212.
2. Measures Undertaken by MI5 in Collaboration with Home Office (Immigration Branch) and Special Branch for Security Control of Jews Travelling to UK ex-Middle East, KV 3/437, TNA.
3. PIC Paper No. 2 (Revised), Jewish Illegal Organisations in Palestine, 8 November 1944, FO 921/154, TNA.
4. Eldad Harouvi, *Palestine Investigated: The Criminal Investigation Department of the Palestine Police Force, 1920–1948* (Sussex Academic Press, 2016), p. 139.
5. Report of a Conference between Representatives of the United Nations Special Commission on Palestine and the Commander and Two Other Representatives of the Irgun Zvai Leumi, 24 June 1947, UNSCOP, GB165-0290, MECA.
6. History of SOE in the Arab World, September 1945, HS 7/86, TNA; Steven Wagner, 'Whispers from Below: Zionist Secret Diplomacy, Terrorism and British Security Inside and Outside of Palestine, 1944–47', *Journal of Imperial and Commonwealth History*, 42 (2014), pp. 440–63.
7. 'Report on the attempt to assassinate the High Commissioner of Palestine', WO 201/189, TNA.
8. Harouvi, *Palestine Investigated*, p. 129 & p. 132.

9. Killearn to FO, Tel. 257, 29 July 1945 & A. J. Kellar (MI5) to C.G. Eastwood (Colonial Office), 24 August 1945, CO 733/456/12. The Stern Gang subsequently murdered the agent.
10. Paper by Brigadier Clayton (for Sir Walter Smart), 14 November 1944, FO 141/1001, TNA; PIC Paper No. 2 (Revised), Jewish Illegal Organisations in Palestine, 8 November 1944.
11. Minute by J.S. Bennett, 31 August 1944, FO 921/147, TNA.
12. Killearn Diary, 18 November 1944, Killearn 5, MECA.
13. Cairo (Minister Resident's Office) to Foreign Office, Tel. 2408, 8 November, CAB 104/254, TNA.
14. Shone (Cairo) to Foreign Office, Tel. 2298, 8 November 1944, CAB 104/254, TNA.
15. Shone (Cairo) to Foreign Office, Tel. 2300, 8 November 1944, PREM 4/51/11, TNA.
16. T.W. Russell, Commandant Cairo City Police, to Mahmoud Ghazali Bey, Director General, Public Security, Ministry of the Interior, 15 November 1944, CAB 104/254, TNA.
17. John Martin to Prime Minister, 20 November 1944, PREM4/51/11, TNA. The drafting of this note was begun on 16 November 1944 and its implications were discussed with the Colonial Secretary.
18. WSC to Foreign Secretary, 3 December 1944, PREM 4/51/11, TNA; Major N.K. Branch, 'Trial of Lord Moyne's Assassins', 12 January 1945, FO 141/1006, TNA.
19. J.S. Bennett to Sir William Croft, 2 December 1944, FO 921/154, TNA; Sir K. Cornwallis (Baghdad) to Foreign Office, Tel. 950, 13 November 1944, CAB 104/254, TNA; Killearn Diary, 18 November 1944, Killearn 5, MECA.
20. Jerusalem to Colonial Office, Tel. 544, 30 November 1944, FO 921/154, TNA.
21. High Commissioner Palestine to Secretary of State, 20 November 1944, FO 921/154, TNA.
22. J.S. Bennett to Sir William Croft, 2 December 1944, FO 921/154, TNA.
23. Palestine: Illegal Jewish Military Organisations, Cunningham 5/4, GB165-0072, MECA; Harouvi, *Palestine Investigated*, p. 157.
24. Armstrong to Greenwood, 10 November 1944, CAB 104/254, TNA.
25. Killearn Diary, 14 November 1944, Killearn 5, MECA.
26. Alan Cunningham (High Commissioner) to Bernard Paget (C-in-C, MEF), 26 November [1946], Cunningham 5/4, MECA.
27. Record of meeting in the Chief Secretary's Office, 26 April 1946, Cunningham 5/4; Minutes of Security Conference, 23 February 1947, Cunningham 4/1, MECA.
28. Defence Security Office, Palestine and Transjordan to SIME (Lt-Col. Maurice Oldfield), 19 November 1946, KV 3/444, TNA.
29. Lt-Col. S.J. Sales, Defence Security Officer Palestine and Transjordan to A.J. [Alex] Kellar (MI5, London), 18 September 1946, KV 3/444, TNA.
30. Motti Golani, ed., *The End of the British Mandate in Palestine, 1948: The Diary of Sir Henry Gurney* (Palgrave Macmillan, 2009), pp. 1–5.
31. David Cesarani, 'The War on Terror that Failed: British Counter-insurgency in Palestine 1945–1947 and the "Farran Affair"', *Small Wars & Insurgencies*, 23 (2012), pp. 648–70.

32. Palestine to Secretary of State for Colonies, Tel. 1137, 13 June 1947, CO 537/230/2, TNA.
33. Bruce Hoffman, *Anonymous Soldiers: The Struggle for Israel, 1917–1947* (Vintage, 2016), pp. 250–51, 322, 336–42, 404–09, 439–40.
34. Cesarani, 'The War on Terror that Failed'.
35. Diary of Guy Liddell, 31 October 1949, KV 4/471, TNA.
36. 'Governor Stabbed on Tour in Sarawak', *The Times*, 5 December 1949, p. 4.
37. 'The Sarawak Crime: Mr Anthony Brooke's Statement', *The Times*, 10 December, p. 3; 'Late Governor of Sarawak', *The Times*, 19 December 1949, p. 3.
38. 'Murder of Governor of Sarawak: Malay Youths on Trial', *The Times*, 6 January 1950, p. 3; 'Sarawak Conspiracy Charges: Reference to Mr Brooke', *The Times*, 10 January 1950, p. 3; 'The Sarawak Murder: Ten Malays Charged with Conspiracy', *The Times*, 7 January 1950, p. 5; 'Sarawak Murder: Nine Death Sentences for Abetting', *The Times*, 17 February 1950, p. 3.
39. John Higham (Colonial Office) to R.H. Scott (FO), 6 February 1950, FO 371/84678, TNA.
40. C.W. Dawson (OAG, Sarawak) to Higham, 13 October 1949, FO 371/84678, TNA.
41. Dawson to Higham, 12 January 1950, FO 371/84678, TNA.
42. Dawson to Sir Thomas Lloyd, 14 December 1949, FO 371/84678, TNA.
43. Higham to Aikman (Sarawak), 22 February 1950, FO 371/84678, TNA.
44. Malcolm MacDonald (Commissioner-General for the UK in South East Asia) to Foreign Secretary, 28 March 1950, FO 371/84678, TNA.
45. 'Investigation into the Murder of HE the Late High Commissioner, Sir Henry Gurney, on 6 October 1951', CO 537/7283, TNA.
46. Simon Smith, 'General Templer and Counter-Insurgency in Malaya: Hearts and Minds, Intelligence, and Propaganda', *Intelligence and National Security*, 16 (2001), pp. 60–78.
47. OAG, Federation of Malaya (M.V. del Tufo) to Secretary of State for the Colonies, No. 83, 30 October 1951, CO 537/7284.
48. MacDonald to Lyttelton, Tel. 736, 31 January 1952, CO 1022/101, TNA.
49. [Sir Hubert Rance], 'The Assassination of Aung San', 19 July 1947, Mss Eur 362/14, BL; [Sir Hubert Rance], 'Memoirs', Part II, Section 1, MSS F169/20.b, BL; Maruyana Shizuo, 'The Nakano School: Memoirs of a Member of the Tokumu Kikan', 30 April 1948, KV 3/297, TNA.
50. [Rance], 'The Assassination of Aung San'; [Rance], 'Memoirs'.
51. Governor of Burma to Secretary of State for Burma, Tel. 283, 19 July 1947, DO 35/2191, TNA.
52. [Rance], 'The Assassination of Aung San'.
53. Richard Aldrich, 'Legacies of Secret Service: Renegade SOE and the Karen Struggle in Burma, 1948–50', *Intelligence and National Security*, 14 (1999), pp. 130–48; IPI/EBP [Paddy Bamford] to R.G. Micklethwait, F.3 (MI5), 15 June 1945, KV 2/3432, TNA.
54. Rance to Listowel, 'Appreciation of the events that led to the assassination of Aung San and 6 members of the Executive Council', 28 July 1947, Mss Eur F 169/13, BL.
55. Thakin Nu's Broadcast, 22 July 1947; Governor of Burma to Secretary of State for Burma, Tel. 309, 25 July 1947; Governor of Burma to Secretary of State for Burma, Tel. 316, 28 July 1947; Governor of Burma to Secretary of State for Burma, Tel. 318, 28 July 1947, IOR, M/4/2679, BL.

56. HQ FARELF to War Office, Isum No. 316, 7 November 1947; Governor of Burma to Secretary of State for Burma, No. 20, 8 November 1947; Governor of Burma to Secretary of State for Burma, Tel. 540, 18 November 1947; Bo Yet La to General Briggs, IOR, M/4/2744, British Library.
57. A.C.B. Symon (High Commissioner, Delhi) to [Philip] Noel-Baker (Secretary of State for Commonwealth Relations), Despatch 25, 'Assassination of Mahatma Gandhi', 11 March 1948, PREM 8/741, TNA.
58. Governor-General's Personal Report, No. 8, 3 February 1948, Mss Eur D714/86, IOR, BL.
59. *Report of Commission of Inquiry into Conspiracy to Murder Mahatma Gandhi*, Part II, Volume 4, in S. Padmavathi & D.G. Hariprasath, eds, *Mahatma Gandhi Assassination: J.L. Kapur Commission Report* (Notion Press, 2017); Durba Ghosh, *Gentlemanly Terrorists: Political Violence and the Colonial State in India, 1919–1947* (CUP, 2017), p. 253.
60. William Gould, 'Hindu Militarism and Partition in 1940s United Provinces: Rethinking the Politics of Violence and Scale', *South Asia: Journal of South Asian Studies*, 42 (2019), pp. 134–51; Governor-General's Personal Report, No. 8, 3 February 1948.
61. *Report of Commission of Inquiry into Conspiracy to Murder Mahatma Gandhi*, Part II, Volume 4.
62. Ibid., Part I, Volume 1 & Part I, Volume 2; Note by Inspector-General T.G. Sanjevi, Investigation into the Assassination of Mahatma Gandhi, Papers of Sardar Patel, NAI.
63. Sardar Vallabhbhai Patel [Home Minister] to Pandit Jawaharlal Nehru, Prime Minister of India, 27 February 1948, Investigation into the Assassination of Mahatma Gandhi, Papers of Sardar Patel, NAI.
64. *Report of Commission of Inquiry into Conspiracy to Murder Mahatma Gandhi*, Part I, Volume 2.
65. Terence Shone to Philip Noel-Baker, SSCR, Despatch 81, 5 May 1948, FO 371/69732, TNA; G.V. Bedekar, Deputy Secretary to the Government of India to Chief Secretaries of all Provincial Governments, 28 July 1948, Ministry of States, Political Branch, File No. 74-P/48, NAI.
66. Sardar Vallabhbhai Patel [Home Minister] to Syama Prasad Mookerji, Minister for Industry & Supply, 6 May 1948, Investigation into the Assassination of Mahatma Gandhi, Papers of Sardar Patel, NAI.
67. V.T. Dehejia (Secretary to the Government of Bombay, Home Department) to the Secretary to the Government of India, Ministry of States, 10 November 1948, 389-P, 1948, NAI.
68. Syama Prasad Mookerji [Minister for Industry & Supply] to Sardar Vallabhbhai Patel [Home Minister], 4 May 1948, Investigation into the Assassination of Mahatma Gandhi, Papers of Sardar Patel, NAI.
69. *Report of Commission of Inquiry into Conspiracy to Murder Mahatma Gandhi*, Part II, Volume 4.
70. 'Text of the U'ren Report on Liaquat Murder', *Dawn*, 26 June 1955, DO 35/5409, TNA.
71. Report of the Commission of Enquiry, *The Assassination of Mr Liaquat Ali Khan* (Karachi: Manager of Publications, Government of Pakistan, 1951), DO 35/3188, TNA.
72. 'Text of the U'ren Report on Liaquat Murder'.
73. Begum Liaquat Ali Khan's Statement on the U'ren Report of 1955, 3 August 1955, DO 35/5409, TNA.

74. Ronen Yitzhak, 'The Assassination of King Abdallah: The First Political Assassination in Jordan. Did it Truly Threaten the Hashemite Kingdom of Jordan?', *Diplomacy & Statecraft*, 21 (2010), pp. 68–86.
75. CIA Office of Current Intelligence, Intelligence Memorandum: The Soviet Attitude toward the Situation in Iran since the Assassination of Razhara, 30 April 1951, *National Security Agency: Organization and Operations, 1945–2009*, DNSA; Joint Intelligence Committee, JIC (51) 88 (Final), 'Review of the Middle East and North Africa', 27 June 1952, CAB 158/13, TNA; Soli Shahvar, 'A Soviet View on the Assassination of the Iranian Prime Minister, Haj 'Ali Razmara, in the Context of the Early Years of the Cold War', *Iranian Studies*, 56 (2023), pp. 309–20.
76. Donald Wilber, Clandestine Service History: Overthrow of Premier Mossadeq of Iran, November 1952–August 1953, March 1954. Published by *The New York Times*, 18 June 2000.
77. CIA, Memorandum for the President of the United States: The Iranian Situation, 1 March 1953, *CIA Covert Operations* IV, DNSA.
78. CIA Information Report: Anti-Mossadeq Activities, 30 April 1953, *CIA Covert Operations* IV, DNSA; CIA Information Report: Miscellaneous Information Concerning Tudeh Party, 10 July 1953, *CIA Covert Operations* IV, DNSA.
79. Wilber, Overthrow of Premier Mossadeq.
80. SSCI, Testimony of Richard Bissell, 11 June 1975, JFK.
81. Mason Cargill, Memorandum to David Belin: Search of Files for Materials Relevant to Assassination Plans, 1 May 1975, *CIA Covert Operations* II, DNSA.
82. Rory Cormac, *Disrupt and Deny: Spies, Special Forces, and the Secret Pursuit of British Foreign Policy* (OUP, 2018), pp. 109–19.
83. David French, *Fighting EOKA: The British Counter-Insurgency Campaign on Cyprus, 1955–1959* (OUP, 2015), p. 90.
84. Jim House and Neil MacMaster, *Paris 1961: Algerians, State Terror, and Memory* (OUP, 2006), p. 48.
85. Martin Thomas and Pierre Asselin, 'French Decolonisation and Civil War: The Dynamics of Violence in the Early Phases of Anti-colonial War in Vietnam and Algeria, 1940–1956', *Journal of Modern European History*, 22 (2022), pp. 513–35.
86. French, *Fighting EOKA*, p. 108; Alban Mahieu, 'Les effectifs de l'armée française en Algérie, 1954–1962', in Jean-Charles Jauffret and Maurice Vaïsse, eds, *Militaires et guérrilla dans la guerre d'Algérie* (Éditions Complexe, 2001), pp. 39–48. Calculations by the author.
87. [SDECE], Operations Conducted since 1 January 1956, WCDA.
88. Damien Van Puyvelde, 'French Paramilitary Actions during the Algerian War of Independence, 1956–1958', *Intelligence and National Security*, 36 (2021), pp. 898–909.
89. [SDECE to Secrétariat général des Affaires africaines et malgaches et de la Communauté], Note Relating to the Designation of an Objective, 1 August 1958, WCDA.
90. Matthew Connelly, *A Diplomatic Revolution: Algeria's Fight for Independence and the Origins of the Post-Cold War Era* (OUP, 2002), p. 202.
91. [SDECE], Operations Conducted since 1 January 1956.
92. David French, 'Toads and Informers: How the British Treated their Collaborators during the Cyprus Emergency, 1955–59', *International History Review*, 39 (2017), pp. 71–88.

93. Governor, Cyprus to Colonial Office, Tel. 436, 26 March 1958, FCO 141/4442, TNA; Governor, Cyprus to Colonial Office, Tel. 1685, 4 October 1958, FCO 141/4493, TNA; Chief Superintendent R.A.P.H. Dutton, Report on Famagusta Allegations: Murder of British Serviceman's Wife, 10 October 1958, FCO 141/4493, TNA; Governor, Cyprus to Colonial Office, Tel. 2138, 1 December 1958, FCO 141/4493, TNA; French, *Fighting EOKA*, p. 262, pp. 267–8.
94. Jacques Valette, 'Le début de la guerre terroriste en Algérie: les attentats de la Toussaint, 1954', *Guerres mondiales et conflits contemporains*, 260 (2015), pp. 79–92; Rabah Aissaoui, 'Fratricidal War: The Conflict between the Mouvement national algérien (MNA) and the Front de libération nationale (FLN) in France during the Algerian War (1954–1962)', *British Journal of Middle Eastern Studies*, 39 (2012), pp. 227–40.
95. Thomas and Asselin, 'French Decolonisation and Civil War', pp. 513–35.
96. Marc André, 'Les groupes de choc du FLN: Particularités de la guerre d'indépendance algérienne en métropole', Revue historique, 669 (2014), pp. 143–78; Aissaoui, 'Fratricidal War', pp. 227–40; Neil MacMaster, 'The "Silent Native": Attentisme, Being Compromised, and Banal Terror during the Algerian War of Independence, 1954–1962', in Martin Thomas, ed., The French Colonial Mind, Volume 2: Violence, Military Encounters, and Colonialism (University of Nebraska Press, 2012), pp. 283–303.
97. André, 'Les groupes de choc du FLN', pp. 143–78.
98. House and MacMaster, *Paris 1961*, p. 194.
99. André, 'Les groupes de choc du FLN', pp. 143–78.
100. Simon Robbins, 'The British Counter-Insurgency in Cyprus', *Small Wars & Insurgencies*, 23 (2012), pp. 720–43; French, *Fighting EOKA*, p. 282.
101. Sir Robert Armitage, 'Mission Impossible in Central Africa, 1956–1961', Papers of Sir Robert Armitage, MSS Afr. s. 2204, 2/4, Special Collections, Bodleian Library, Oxford [hereafter Bodleian].
102. Brian Simpson, 'The Devlin Commission (1959): Colonialism, Emergencies and the Rule of Law', *Oxford Journal of Legal Studies*, 22 (2002), pp. 17–52; John Darwin, 'The Central African Emergency, 1959', *Journal of Imperial and Commonwealth History*, 21 (1993), pp. 217–34; Philip Murphy, 'A Police State? The Nyasaland Emergency and Colonial Intelligence', *Journal of Southern African Studies*, 36 (2010), pp. 765–80.
103. *Cmnd. 814, Report of the Nyasaland Commission of Enquiry*, July 1959 [Devlin Report].
104. *Cmnd. 815, Nyasaland: Despatch by the Governor relating to the Report of the Nyasaland Commission of Enquiry*, 21 July 1959.
105. [Nyasaland] Special Branch, The Emergency Conference of the Nyasaland African Congress held at Blantyre on the 24th/25th January 1959, 13 February 1959, CO 1035/143, TNA; Summary of Reports of Recent Developments in Nyasaland, 2 March 1959, CO 1035/143, TNA; Weekly Review of Current Intelligence, 3 March 1959, CO 1035/143, TNA; [Nyasaland] Special Branch, Note on the Congress Plan of Sabotage, Violence and Murder – Including Evaluation of Sources, 19 March 1959, CO 1035/148, TNA.
106. Memorandum of Conversation [between the Foreign Secretary and the Secretary of State]: Countering UAR Pressure against the British Position in Aden, 27 April 1964, US Declassified Documents Online [hereafter USDDO]; Local

Intelligence Committee, Aden, The National Front for the Liberation of the Occupied South or The National Liberation Front (NLF), 25 January 1965, CAB 191/12, TNA; JIC (65) 5th, 4 February 1965, CAB 159/43; Confidential Annex to JIC (65) 38th, 16 September 1965, CAB 159/44, TNA.
107. Connelly, *A Diplomatic Revolution*, p. 209 & p. 179.
108. James McDougall, 'The Impossible Republic: The Reconquest of Algeria and the Decolonization of France, 1945–1962', *Journal of Modern History*, 89 (2017), pp. 772–811.
109. House and MacMaster, *Paris 1961*, pp. 176–7.
110. Alexander Harrison, *Challenging De Gaulle: The OAS and the Counterrevolution in Algeria, 1954–1962* (Praeger, 1989), p. 79 & pp. 117–18.
111. House and MacMaster, *Paris 1961*, p. 177 & p. 109.
112. Victor Delaporte, 'Aux origines de la Cour de sûreté de l'État', *Vingtième Siècle*, 140 (2018), pp. 137–52.
113. Guy Pervillé, 'Le terrorisme urbain dans la guerre d'Algérie, 1954–1962', in Jauffret and Vaïsse, *Militaires et guérrilla dans la guerre d'Algérie*, pp. 447–67; Raymond Noël, Édouard Chollier, Roger Dejean and Claude Merviel, 'Les brigades de recherche et de contre-sabotage (BRCS) en Algérie, 1956–1962', *Guerres mondiales et conflits contemporains*, 208 (2002), pp. 91–117.
114. Martin Thomas, *Fight or Flight: Britain, France, and their Roads from Empire* (OUP, 2014), p. 334.
115. Delaporte, 'Aux origines de la Cour de sûreté de l'État', pp. 137–52.
116. CIA, Special National Intelligence Estimate 22-3-62: Consequences of the Death or Assassination of De Gaulle, 7 September 1962, USDDO.
117. Todd Shepard, *The Invention of Decolonization: The Algerian War and the Remaking of France* (Cornell University Press, 2006), pp. 134–5.
118. Memorandum for the Record: Minutes of Special Group Meeting, 25 August 1960, *CIA Covert Operations* IV, DNSA; Summary of Facts: Investigation of CIA Involvement in Plans to Assassinate Foreign Leaders [Rockefeller Commission: David Belin Assassination Study, 5 June 1975], *CIA Covert Operations II*, DNSA; William Hyland, Director of Intelligence and Research, Department of State, Memorandum for the Record, 20 October 1975, *CIA Covert Operations II*, DNSA; Stuart Reid, *The Lumumba Plot: The Secret History of the CIA and a Cold War Assassination* (Knopf, 2023), pp. 384–9.
119. Emmanuel Gerard and Bruce Kuklick, *Death in the Congo: Murdering Patrice Lumumba* (Harvard UP, 2015), pp. 194–203.
120. Ibid., pp. 209–10.
121. Susan Williams, *Who Killed Hammarskjöld? The UN, the Cold War and White Supremacy in Africa* (Hurst, 2020), p. 110.
122. Reid, *The Lumumba Plot*, pp. 384–9.
123. J.K.E. Broadley, Minute for Duty Officer, WCAD, 21 December 1962, FO 371/167430, TNA; James Murray to Guy Millard, 25 January 1963, FO 371/167430, TNA; Usumbura to FO, Tel. 13, 15 January 1963, FO 371/167430, TNA.
124. W.B.L. Monson to Forster, 5 May 1967, FCO 31/161, TNA.
125. Thomas Hughes (INR) to Secretary of State, Intelligence Note: Implications of Second Attempt on Nkrumah's Life, 2 January 1964, *CIA Covert Operations III*, DNSA.
126. Tom Keeble (High Commission, Accra) to Victor Martin (CRO), 21 August 1962, DO 195/73, TNA.

127. E.G. Le Tocq (HC, Accra) to Mark Allen (CRO), 2 July 1959, DO 35/9415, TNA; Horace Castell, 'Day Roundup Bomb', Reuters, 2 August 1962, DO 195/73, TNA.
128. McMullen to Martin, 21 August 1962, DO 195/73, TNA.
129. Geoffrey de Freitas (British High Commissioner, Accra) to Duncan Sandys (Secretary of State for Commonwealth Relations), Desp. 24, 27 October 1962, DO 195/73, TNA.
130. Tom Keeble (High Commission, Accra) to Victor Martin (CRO), 21 August 1962.
131. McMullen to Walker (Accra), 23 November 1962, DO 195/73, TNA; Handwritten minute, 31 August 1962, DO 195/73, TNA; R.G. Holden to SLO Central Africa, 20 September 1962, KV 2/4076, TNA; Hastings Banda to Kwame Nkrumah, 14 January 1963 [intercept available to MI5, 24 January 1963], KV 2/4077.
132. Geoffrey de Freitas (British High Commissioner, Accra) to Duncan Sandys (Secretary of State for Commonwealth Relations), Desp. 24, 27 October 1962; Roger Hilsman (Director, INR) to Secretary of State, Intelligence Note: Reports of Opposition Plotting in Ghana, 6 December 1962, USDDO.
133. Thomas Hughes (INR) to Secretary of State, Intelligence Note: Implications of Second Attempt on Nkrumah's Life, 2 January 1964; W. Averell Harriman (Under Secretary of State for Political Affairs), Memorandum for the President: Ghana, 3 April 1964, USDDO.
134. 'Spain Begins an Investigation in Khides [sic] Slaying', *New York Times*, 15 January 1967; Simon Dawbarn (British Interests Section, Algiers) to John Macrae (NEAD, FO), 20 January 1967, FCO 39/14, TNA; A.L. Southern (Rabat) to R.H. Baker (North and East African Department, Foreign Office), 7 March 1967, FCO 39/14, TNA.
135. John Cooley, 'Algerian Coup Attempt Called Off', *Christian Science Monitor*, 20–22 July 1968.
136. Nick Fenn (Algiers) to Terence Wood (North and East African Department, Foreign Office), 2 May 1968, FCO 39/14, TNA.
137. Sevki Kiralp, 'Cyprus between Enosis, Partition and Independence: Domestic Politics, Diplomacy and External Interventions, 1967–1974', *Journal of Balkan and Near Eastern Studies*, 19 (2017), pp. 591–609.
138. Nicosia to FCO, Tel. 796, 19 November 1968, FCO 9/830, TNA.
139. D.S.L. Dodson (British Embassy, Athens) to Robin Edmonds (SED, FCO), 1 November 1968, FCO 9/830, TNA.
140. Olver (Nicosia) to Goodison, 25 March 1974, *Documents on British Policy Overseas (DBPO)*, Ser. 3, Vol. 5.
141. David Beattie (British High Commission, Nicosia) to P.R. [Robin] Fearn (SED, FCO), 25 November & 9 December 1970, FCO 9/1183, TNA.
142. House of Lords, 11 September 1972, *Debates*, vol. 335, cc. 4–9.
143. FCO to Bermuda, Tel. 28, 26 March 1973, FCO 63/1103, TNA.
144. Governor Bermuda to FCO, Tel. 172, 10 September 1972, FCO 63/947, TNA; I.A.C. Kinnear (Acting Governor, Bermuda) to D.A. Scott (FO), 26 September 1972, FCO 63/947, TNA; 'Governor Shot in Bermuda', *Daily Telegraph*, 12 March 1973.
145. Bermuda (Kinnear) to FCO, Unnumbered Tel., 11 March 1973, PREM 15/1313; Caribbean Department, FCO – Bermuda: Visit of Sir Edwin Leather, Governor of Bermuda, November 1973, PREM 15/1313.

146. Bermuda to FCO, Tel. 137, 23 May 1973, FCO 63/1103, TNA; Bermuda to FCO, Tel. 138, 23 May 1973, FCO 63/1103, TNA; Sir Duncan Watson (DUS) to Coles: Bermuda – Murder Investigations, 30 May 1973, FCO 63/1103, TNA
147. [SBO to MoD], CARIBSITREP No. 97: Murder of Sir Richard Sharples and ADC [11 March 1973], FCO 63/1102, TNA; Quito Swan, *Black Power in Bermuda: The Struggle for Decolonization* (Palgrave Macmillan, 2010).
148. Caribbean Department, Brief for Sir Alec Douglas-Home's Talk with Sir Edward Richards (PM of Bermuda), 27 March 1973, FCO 63/1103; TNA; Hamilton to FCO, Tel. 38, 30 November 1977, FCO 44/1463, TNA.
149. W.E. Quantrill (Hong Kong & General Department) to News Department: Capital Punishment: Bermuda, 23 November 1977, FCO 44/1463, TNA; Hamilton to FCO, Tel. 44, 3 December 1977, FCO 44/1464, TNA; Draft Letter from Foreign Secretary to Prime Minister, 3 December 1977, FCO 44/1464, TNA; Antony Duff to Michael Palliser (PUS, FCO): Executions in Bermuda, 20 December 1977, FCO 44/1465, TNA; P.C. Duff (West Indian and Atlantic Department) to Private Secretary/Secretary of State: Notes for Supplementaries, 5 December 1977, FCO 44/1464, TNA.

Chapter 8

1. CIA, Memorandum: Garrison and the Kennedy Assassination, 26 April 1967, USDDO.
2. Howard Osborn (Director of Security, CIA), Memorandum for Executive Secretary, CIA Management Committee: 'Family Jewels', 16 May 1973, CIA.
3. Inspector General, CIA, Memorandum for the Record: Report on Plots to Assassinate Fidel Castro, *CIA Covert Operations* III, [1967], DNSA.
4. SSCI, Testimony of William Harvey, 25 June 1975, JFK.
5. Memorandum for the Record: Minutes of Special Group Meeting, 11 August 1960, 12 August 1960, *CIA Covert Operations* IV, DNSA.
6. Inspector General, CIA, Memorandum for the Record: Report on Plots to Assassinate Fidel Castro; Naval Intelligence Report No. 28, Spring 1971, DEFE 63/45, TNA.
7. US House of Representatives, *Final Report of the Select Committee on Assassinations*, No. 95-1828 (GPO, 1979).
8. John McCone to DCI, 14 April 1967, *Cuban Missile Crisis*, DNSA; Jim Connor, Memorandum for Donald Rumsfeld: The Intelligence Community, 12 September 1975, *CIA Covert Operations* II, DNSA; [White House], Comparison between Rockefeller Commission Report and Other Executive Branch Material, [1975], USDDO; William Hyland, Director of Intelligence and Research, Department of State, Memorandum for the Record, 20 October 1975, *CIA Covert Operations II*, DNSA; Gregory Diamond, ed., *The Unexpurgated Pike Report: Report of the House Select Committee on Intelligence* (McGraw-Hill, 1992).
9. Memorandum of a Conversation: President Gerald R. Ford, Dr Henry Kissinger, Lt General Brent Scowcroft, 4 January 1975, Gerald R. Ford and Foreign Affairs Microfilm Collection, Reel 7, *Archives Unbound*.
10. Piero Gleijeses, 'The Death of Francisco Arana: A Turning Point in the Guatemalan Revolution', *Journal of Latin American Studies*, 22 (1990), pp. 527–52.

11. CIA, 'A Study of Assassination' [from training file for PBSUCCESS], [1952], *Death Squads, Guerrilla War, Covert Ops, and Genocide*, DNSA.
12. [CIA], Memorandum from [Redacted] to Chief, [Redacted]: Guatemalan Communist Personnel to be Disposed during Military Operations of Calligeris [General Carlos Castillo Armas], [September 1952], *Death Squads, Guerrilla War, Covert Ops, and Genocide*, DNSA; CIA Memorandum: Current Planning of Calligeris Organization, Report No. 22, 12 December 1952, *CIA Covert Operations* IV, DNSA.
13. [CIA], Briefing Notes [on Guatemala planning], 3 February 1954, USDDO; [CIA], C/[Redacted] to [Redacted]: All Staff Officers, Memorandum: Selection of Individuals for Disposal by Junta Group, 31 March 1954, *Death Squads, Guerrilla War, Covert Ops, and Genocide*, DNSA.
14. Weekly PBSUCCESS Meeting with [Redacted] [CIA x State], 9 March 1954, *Death Squads, Guerrilla War, Covert Ops, and Genocide*, DNSA.
15. [CIA], C/[Redacted] to Chief/Project, Memorandum: Provocation Plans, 1 June 1954, *Death Squads, Guerrilla War, Covert Ops, and Genocide*, DNSA.
16. Acting Chief, Psychological and Paramilitary Operations Staff, Memorandum for Chiefs, All Area and IO Divisions: The End of the Communist Regime in Guatemala, 9 July 1954, *CIA Covert Operations* IV, DNSA.
17. Luca Trenta, *The President's Kill List: Assassination and US Foreign Policy since 1945* (Edinburgh University Press, 2024), p. 112.
18. James Doolittle, William Franke, Morris Hadley and William Pawley, 'Report on the Covert Activities of the Central Intelligence Agency', 30 September 1954, CIA.
19. J.D. Esterline, Memorandum for Chief, WHD: Material for Possible Use in Discussion with Mr Pawley [Former US ambassador in Peru, Brazil, now petroleum and mining in Dominican Republic, based in Miami], 12 February 1960, *CIA Covert Operations* IV, DNSA.
20. CIA, [Study of Dominican Republic Operations], [1966], *CIA Covert Operations* III, DNSA.
21. Trenta, *The President's Kill* List, p. 120.
22. [Study of Dominican Republic Operations].
23. Director to [Redacted] Operational Immediate, 2 May 1961, *CIA Covert Operations* III, DNSA.
24. [Study of Dominican Republic Operations].
25. Central Intelligence Bulletin Daily Brief, 3 June 1961, CIA.
26. Trenta, *The President's Kill List*, p. 125.
27. [Study of Dominican Republic Operations], [1966], DNSA.
28. McGeorge Bundy [National Security Advisor], Memorandum for the President, 25 February 1961, CIA.
29. SSCI, Testimony of Richard Bissell, 11 June 1975, JFK.
30. Inspector General, CIA, Memorandum for the Record: Report on Plots to Assassinate Fidel Castro.
31. SSCI Transcript: Testimony of DCI William Colby, 21 May 1975, JFK.
32. CIA, *Official History of the Bay of Pigs Operation, III: Evolution of CIA's Anti-Castro Policies, 1959–January 1961* (December 1979), JFK.
33. Memorandum for the Record: Minutes of Special Group Meeting, 11 August 1960.
34. Inspector General, CIA, Memorandum for the Record: Report on Plots to Assassinate Fidel Castro.

35. John Peters, Memorandum for the Record: Preliminary Debriefing Report on AMPANIC-7 Activities in Cuba, 26 November 1960, *CIA Covert Operations* IV, DNSA.
36. *History of the Bay of Pigs Operation*.
37. A. Gromyko [Foreign minister] and M. Za[k]harov [Chief of general staff], Draft Resolution for CC CPSU, 24 June 1961, *Cuban Missile Crisis Revisited*, DNSA.
38. Journal of S.M. Kudryavtsev, 12 July 1961, WCDA.
39. George Lauder (Acting Deputy Chief, Latin America Division, DDO), Memorandum for the Inspector General: Latin America Division Task Force Report of Possible Cuban Complicity in the John F. Kennedy Assassination, 29 June 1977, JFK.
40. US Congress, House Select Committee on Assassinations, Draft Staff Report on the Evolution and Implications of the CIA-sponsored Assassination Conspiracies against Fidel Castro, [12 March 1979], *CIA Covert Operations* III, DNSA.
41. Study of Dominican Republic Operations.
42. [Inspector General, CIA, Memorandum for the Record: Report on Plots to Assassinate Fidel Castro.]
43. George Lauder (Acting Deputy Chief, Latin America Division, DDO), Memorandum for the Inspector General: Latin America Division Task Force Report of Possible Cuban Complicity in the John F. Kennedy Assassination, 29 June 1977.
44. DCI, Special National Intelligence Estimate 85-61, 28 November 1961, *Cuban Missile Crisis*, DNSA.
45. Inspector General, CIA, Memorandum for the Record: Report on Plots to Assassinate Fidel Castro.
46. Inspector General, CIA, Memorandum for the Record: Report on Plots to Assassinate Fidel Castro.
47. William Harvey, Memorandum for Deputy Director (Plans): Operation Mongoose, 14 August 1962, *Cuban Missile Crisis Revisited*, DNSA.
48. George Lauder (Acting Deputy Chief, Latin America Division, DDO), Memorandum for the Inspector General: Latin America Division Task Force Report of Possible Cuban Complicity in the John F. Kennedy Assassination, 29 June 1977.
49. SSCI, Testimony of William Harvey, 25 June 1975.
50. Memorandum for Chief, BGRHYTHM, Washington: BGFIEND Notes for Discussion with Ascham, 27 July 1951 [forwarded to Chief EE], *CIA Covert Operations* IV, DNSA; MGB Action Memorandum, undated (1953), Dmitrii Volkogonov, *Izvestia*, 11 June 1993, WCDA.
51. C [Sir John Sinclair], 'The Khokhlov Case', 7 May 1954, PREM 11/772, TNA.
52. Bonn to FO, Tel. 330, 22 April 1954, PREM 11/772, TNA.
53. Record of a Meeting between the Prime Minister, Mr Anthony Nutting, Sir Ivone Kirkpatrick, Mr Rennie, 1 May 1954, PREM 11/772, TNA; Stanley Grogan (Assistant to the DCI), Memorandum for the Record, 20 November 1956, CIA.
54. [SIS], V.M. Petrov: Intelligence Report Assassination of Trotsky, 2 May 1955, KV 2/505, TNA.
55. Washington to FO, Tel. 774, 21 April 1954, PREM 11/772, TNA.
56. Chief, EE to Chief of Station, Germany, 6 January 1960, CIA.
57. Counterintelligence Information Report: Anatoliy Mikhaylovich GOLITSYN, 24 July 1971, JFK.

58. Chief, Soviet Russia Division, Memorandum for the Director of Central Intelligence: Stefan Bandera's Death and PP Exploitation Thereof, 1 December 1959, CIA.
59. Christopher Andrew and Vasili Mitrokhin, *The Mitrokhin Archive: The KGB in Europe and the West* (Penguin, 2000), p. 471; SR/CI/Research, Memorandum for Warren Commission: Soviet Use of Assassination and Kidnapping, 28 February 1964, JFK.
60. CIA, 'Soviet Executive Action (A Preliminary Survey)', October 1961, JFK.
61. John McCone to McGeorge Bundy, 5 December 1961, *CIA Covert Operations* IV, DNSA.
62. Acting Chief, SR Division [Tennent Bagley], Memorandum for Assistant Deputy Director, Plans: Contact of Lee Oswald with a member of Soviet KGB Assassination Department, 23 November 1963, JFK; Raymond Rocca, Memorandum for the Record: Conversation with David W. Belin, 1 April 1975, JFK.
63. A. Dobrynin (Soviet Ambassador, Washington) to Moscow, 22 November 1963, WCDA.
64. A. Mikoyan (Washington) to CC CPSU, 25 November 1963, WCDA; CIA, President's Daily Brief, 8 June 1968, CIA.
65. A. Dobrynin (Washington) to CC CPSU, 30 November 1963, WCDA.
66. Secretary of State to American Embassy, Seoul, Tel. 110350, 6 February 1968, USDDO; Holub (Czech Ambassador, Pyongyang) to Ministry of Foreign Affairs, Prague, 9 February 1968, WCDA.
67. Chief, WH Division to Chief of Station, Mexico City, 17 December 1963, JFK.
68. John McCone, Memorandum for the Record: Discussion with President Johnson, November 28th, 10:00 a.m., 29 November 1963, Meeting with the President, 23 November–27 December 1963, McCone Memoranda, Box 1, DiscoverLBJ, Lyndon Baines Johnson Presidential Library and Museum.
69. Memorandum for the Record: Minutes of Special Group Meeting, 13 February 1964, 14 February 1964, JFK.
70. SSCI, Transcript: AMLASH Case Officer, 29 July 1975, JFK.
71. George Lauder (Acting Deputy Chief, Latin America Division, DDO), Memorandum for the Inspector General: Latin America Division Task Force Report of Possible Cuban Complicity in the John F. Kennedy Assassination, 29 June 1977.
72. Susan Darlington, Memorandum for Acting Deputy Chief, WHD for Cuba: Attempted Assassination of Castro June 1965, 11 August 1965, JFK.
73. Brent Scowcroft. Memorandum for the President: Church Committee's 'Warren Commission' Report, 24 June 1976, *Cuba and the US, 1959–2016*, DNSA.
74. Office of Current Intelligence, CIA, Current Intelligence Bulletin, 30 October 1956, *CIA Covert Operations IV*, DNSA.
75. [CIA notes], Rolando CUBELA Secades, born 19 January 1933, JFK.
76. Director to Paris, 18 August 1962, JFK.
77. Memorandum for the Record: Tests of Modified Sights for 7.62 Belgium (FAL) Rifle, 10 June 1964, JFK.
78. CIA, Rolando Cubela Secades, 13 April 1966, *CIA Covert Operations* III, DNSA.
79. SSCI, Transcript: AMLASH Case Officer, 29 July 1975.
80. Inspector General, CIA, Memorandum for the Record: Report on Plots to Assassinate Fidel Castro.
81. Trenta, *The President's Kill List*, p. 172.

82. CIA Chilean Task Force Activities, 15 September–3 November 1970 (Projects [Redacted] and [Redacted], 9 March 1974, SDRR; Memorandum for the Record: ARA/CIA Weekly Meeting, 25 July 1979, 29 July 1979, *Chile and the United States Collection*, DNSA.
83. Memorandum of a Conversation: President Gerald R. Ford, Dr. Henry Kissinger, Lt. General Brent Scowcroft, 5 March 1975, Gerald R. Ford and Foreign Affairs Microfilm Collection, Reel 7; Memorandum for the Record: ARA/CIA Weekly Meeting, 25 July 1979, 29 July 1979, CIA.
84. [NSC], Memorandum for the Record: Meeting Saturday Morning – 9:15, 2 November 1963 – Executive Committee, 4 November 1963, *CIA Covert Operations* III, DNSA.
85. Thomas Ahern, *CIA and the House of Ngo: Covert Action in South Vietnam, 1954–63* (CIA Center for the Study of Intelligence, 2000), p. 214.
86. [NSC], Memorandum of Conference with the President, Subject: Vietnam, 9:15, 2 November 1963, *US Policy in the Vietnam War, Part 1, 1954–1968*.
87. Ahern, *CIA and the House of Ngo*, p. 191.
88. [Notes of a meeting between Lt Col. Conein and Gen. Duong Van Minh], 5 October 1963, *US Intelligence Community, 1947–1989*, DNSA.
89. Ahern, CIA and the House of Ngo, p. 191.
90. Saigon [to CIA], 23 October 1963, CIA.
91. US Embassy, Saigon to Secretary of State, Tel. 900, 3 November 1964, USDDO.
92. R.W. Komer, Memorandum for the President: Vietnam Weekly Civil Side Highlights, 20 April 1967, USDDO.
93. Thomas Ahern, *CIA and Rural Pacification in South Vietnam* (CIA Center for the Study of Intelligence, 2001), pp. 300, 287, 250, 360, 362, 373.
94. S[cott] D. Breckinridge, Principal Co-ordinator, HSCA, Memorandum for Hal Clark, DDS&T: Comments on HSCA Report, 22 June 1979, *CIA Covert Operations* III, DNSA.
95. Minutes of National Security Council Meeting, 15 May 1975, USDDO.
96. Radio TV Reports, *Good Morning America*, 21 November 1975: Senate Investigation into the CIA, USDDO.
97. William Hyland, Director of Intelligence and Research, Department of State, Memorandum for the Record, 20 October 1975.
98. Jack Marsh, Memorandum for the President: Assassination Report, 29 October 1975, USDDO.
99. Howard Wachtel, 'Targeting Osama Bin Laden: Examining the Legality of Assassination as a Tool of US Foreign Policy', *Duke Law Journal*, 55 (2005), pp. 677–710.
100. Memorandum of a Conversation, 4 January 1975.
101. Minutes of National Security Council Meeting, 15 May 1975, USDDO.
102. Telecon, Mr. Elfin [Washington Bureau Chief, *Newsweek*]/Secretary Kissinger, 24 November 1975, *Kissinger Telephone Conversations, 1969–1977*, DNSA.

Chapter 9

1. CIA Directorate of Intelligence, Intelligence Memorandum: Implications of Wasfi Tal's Assassination, 28 November 1971, CIA.
2. J.C. Kay (North African Department) to R.M. Evans (Near Eastern Department), 29 December 1971, FCO 17/1704, TNA.

3. Gore-Booth to M.R. Melhuish (Washington), 13 January 1972; Ramsay Melhuish to David Gore-Booth, 10 February 1972; FCO 17/1704, TNA; Gore-Booth to M.R. Melhuish (Washington), 23 February 1972, FCO 17/1705, TNA.
4. Note for the Record [Jerry Wiggin], 13 May 1980, PREM 19/1299, TNA; Lord Sieff to Prime Minister, with annotations by Margaret Thatcher, 25 April 1984, PREM19/1301, TNA; 'Paris Terrorist Linked with Sieff Shooting', *The Times*, 9 July 1975, 3; CIA [Office of Political Research], International and Transnational Terrorism: Diagnosis and Prognosis, April 1976, USDDO.
5. [CIA], Special Report: 'Black September', 8 November 1972, USDDO.
6. D.A. Gore-Booth, Note for the Record, 19 May 1972, FCO 17/1706, TNA.
7. American Embassy, Khartoum to Secretary of State, Tel. 471, Subject: Khartoum Assassinations, 7 March 1973, *Terrorism and US Policy, 1968–2002*, DNSA.
8. Harold Saunders and Richard Kennedy [NSC], Memorandum for Dr Kissinger: Follow-up on Murders in Khartoum, 15 March 1973, *Terrorism and US Policy, 1968–2002*, DNSA.
9. Memorandum of Telephone Conversation [Nixon and Kissinger], 20:30, 2 March 1973, *Kissinger Telephone Conversations, 1969–1977*, DNSA.
10. Telcon, Haig-Kissinger, 8 January 1974, SDRR; Robert Oakley [NSC Staff], Memorandum for Brent Scowcroft: Visit of President Nimeiri of Sudan – Recommended Meeting with President, 6 May 1976, Gerald R. Ford and Foreign Affairs Microfilm Collection, Reel 4.
11. Brian Jenkins, David Ronfeldt and Ralph Stauch, Dealing with Political Kidnapping (U): A Report Prepared for Department of State and Defense Advanced Research Projects Agency, September 1976, USDDO.
12. Bernard Gwertzman, 'Israeli Attache Shot Dead at Home near Washington', *New York Times*, 2 July 1973, p. 57.
13. Lewis Hoffacker, chairman of the Working Group/Cabinet Committee to Combat Terrorism to Working Group, enclosing draft report, 20 January 1975, *Terrorism and US Policy, 1968–2002*, DNSA; Nicholas Horrock, 'New Senate Panel May Study F.B.I. Drive on Arab Terrorism', *New York Times*, 13 February 1975, p. 15.
14. C.P. Scott to Campbell: Passport Application by Mr David Kimche, 21 May 1974, FCO 93/489, TNA; Memorandum of Conversation [President and Cabinet], 18 June 1976, USDDO; Office of the Vice President, 'Arafat's Responsibility for the Murder of Cleo Noel', October 1985, *Terrorism and US Policy, 1968–2002*, DNSA.
15. American Embassy, Beirut to Secretary of State, Washington, Tel. 2958, [19 June 1977], SDRR.
16. The Assassination of American Diplomats in Beirut, Lebanon: Hearing before the Special Subcommittee on Investigations of the Committee on International Relations, House of Representatives, 27 July 1976, SDRR; S.P. Day (Beirut) to C.D. Powell (NENAD), 5 November 1977, FCO 8/3061, TNA; R.M. Morris to K.J. Stowe, Note for Prime Minister on Arab Terrorist Incidents, 4 August 1978, FCO 8/3230, TNA.
17. Memorandum of Conversation [President and Cabinet], 18 June 1976, USDDO.
18. W.R. Tomkys to Sir Antony Duff, 5 January 1978, FCO 93/1559, TNA; DIA, International Terrorism: A Compendium Volume II – Middle East, July 1979, *Terrorism and US Policy, 1968–2002*, DNSA.
19. Gore-Booth to Laver, 6 September 1972, FCO 17/1706, TNA.

20. C.P. Scott to Campbell: Passport Application by Mr David Kimche, 21 May 1974, FCO 93/489, TNA.
21. Beirut to FCO, Tel. 31, 24 January 1979, FCO 93/2056, TNA.
22. FCO to Beirut, Tel. 32, 24 January 1979, FCO 93/2056, TNA.
23. FCO to Tel Aviv, Tel. 48, 16 February 1979, FCO 93/2056, TNA.
24. D.M. Mitchell (Nationality and Treaty Department) to Powell (NENAD), [February 1979], FCO 93/2056, TNA.
25. Tel Aviv (Robinson) to FCO, Tel. 26, 13 January 1981, FCO 93/2804, TNA.
26. Tel Aviv (Mason) to FCO, Tel. 76, 19 February 1979, FCO 93/2056, TNA.
27. Alan Rothnie (British Ambassador, Jedda) to James Callaghan (Foreign Secretary), 29 March 1975, FCO 8/2959, TNA.
28. M.J. Moore to HoC (Head of Chancery, British Embassy, Jedda), 29 March 1975, FCO 8/2959, TNA; Chancery, British Embassy Jeddah to Middle East Department, FCO, 21 June 1975, FCO 8/2600, TNA.
29. Rothnie to Callaghan, 29 March 1975, FCO 8/2959.
30. H.B. Walker to HE [British Ambassador in Jeddah], 21 June 1975, FCO 8/2600, TNA.
31. Moore to HoC, 29 March 1975, FCO 8/2959, TNA.
32. I.T.M. Lucas (MED) to A.R.L. Carr (MD Stephens & Carter Ltd), 17 April 1975, FCO 8/2600, TNA.
33. M.S. Buckmaster [Viscount Buckmaster] (Guidance and Information Policy Department) to H. St J.B. Armitage (Kuwait), FCO, 28 May 1975, FCO 8/2600, TNA; I.T.M. Lucas (MED) to [M.P.] Weir, 'Death of King Faisal', 1 April 1975 with note by Weir, 2 April 1975, FCO 8/2959, TNA.
34. CIA, Directorate of Operations, Information Report, 20 August 1974, SDRR; AS(SPP), Note on Bangladesh forwarded by A.K. Damodaran, Joint Secretary (PP) to Chairman (PPC), 21 August 1975, Ministry of External Affairs, File No. 4/4/PP/JS/7, NAI; P.J.E. Male to Seaward, 'Call by Deputy High Commissioner for Bangladesh', 20 August 1975, FCO 37/1563, TNA.
35. FBI, Foreign Political Matters – Argentina: Argentine Terrorist Activities, 9 October 1974; HQ Air Force Office of Special Operations, Special Report: Terrorism in Argentina, June 1975, 27 May 1977, SDRR.
36. Working Paper, History of the Montoneros in Argentina from March 1970 to Early April 1977, 27 May 1977, SDRR.
37. American Embassy, Buenos Aires to Secretary of State, Washington (RSO [George] Beckett to SY), Tel. 0698, 30 January 1975, SDRR.
38. History of the Montoneros in Argentina.
39. American Embassy, Buenos Aires to Secretary of State, Washington, Tel. 0823, 6 February 1976; American Embassy, Buenos Aires to Secretary of State, Washington, Tel. 4844, 23 July 1976, SDRR.
40. HQ Air Force Office of Special Operations, Special Report: Terrorism in Argentina, June 1975.
41. Department of State, Memorandum of Conversation: Meeting with *Comisario* Margaride, Chief of Argentine Federal Police, 4 March 1975; J.E. Buchanan, Department of State Bureau of Intelligence and Research, Research Study: Argentina: Renewed Terrorist Violence, 16 April 1975, SDRR.
42. History of the Montoneros in Argentina.
43. American Embassy, Buenos Aires to Secretary of State Washington, Tel. 2969, 21 April 1977, SDRR.

44. Secretary of State, Washington to American Embassy, Buenos Aires, Tel. 209192, 23 August 1975, SDRR.
45. [CIA], Terrorist Links in Latin America: Post-Mortem on the JCR, 29 June 1979, SDRR.
46. Des O'Mahony (British Embassy, San Salvador) to Vic Henderson (M and C Department, FCO), 18 May 1977, FCO 99/50, TNA; Secretary of State, Washington to All Diplomatic Posts: Background Study – 'El Salvador: The Search for Peace', Tel. 240302, 9 September 1981, SDRR.
47. American Embassy, Managua to Secretary of State, Washington, Tel. 00219, 18 January 1978, *Nicaragua, 1978–1990*, DNSA.
48. American Embassy, Managua to Secretary of State, Washington, Tel. 00134, 12 January 1978; American Embassy, Managua to Secretary of State, Washington, Tel. 02233, 15 May 1978, *Nicaragua*, DNSA.
49. CIA, [Cable], January 1979, *Death Squads, Guerrilla War, Covert Ops, and Genocide*, DNSA.
50. American Embassy, Guatemala to Secretary of State, Washington, Fuentes Mohr Assassination: Supplementary Background, Tel. 1510, 7 March 1978, *Death Squads, Guerrilla War, Covert Ops, and Genocide*, DNSA.
51. CIA, Guatemala: Assassination, 26 March 1979, *Death Squads, Guerrilla War, Covert Ops, and Genocide*, DNSA.
52. 'Preventive Steps at Samastipur Spelled Out', *Times of India*, 23 July 1976, p. 6.
53. 'Mathew Probe Panel's Scope Wide: Reddy', *Times of India*, 7 February 1975, p. 1.
54. Intelligence Bureau, 'The Threat of Grave Internal Disturbance and the Need for the Proclamation of an Emergency', 11 July 1975, Ministry of External Affairs, File No. 21/23/75-T, NAI.
55. 'Mathew Panel Report Submitted to Government', *Times of India*, 10 May 1977, p. 1.
56. '2 Chapters of Mathew Probe to be Rejected', *Times of India*, 11 November 1977, p. 1.
57. 'Political Leaders Branding Me Guilty: Indira Gandhi', *Times of India*, 13 January 1978, p. 18.
58. P.J.E. Male to Maurice Smith (Ministry of Overseas Development), 22 September 1975, FCO 37/1564, TNA.
59. JS(BD) [Joint Secretary, Bangladesh] to Heads of Mission, Tel. 26434, 21 August 1975, Ministry of External Affairs, File No. 4/4/PP/JS/7, NAI.
60. Gerard Viratelle, 'A Month after the Counter Coup d'Etat the Fight for Power is Continuing in Dacca', *Le Monde*, 10 December 1975; P.J.E. Male to Maurice Smith (Ministry of Overseas Development), 22 September 1975, FCO 37/1564, TNA.
61. Background to FCO to Dacca, Tel. 34, 30 January 1981, FCO 37/2459, TNA.
62. Select Committee on Race Relations and Immigration: Visit to the Sub-Continent, March 1977, FCO 37/1881, TNA.
63. Ambassador at Kabul to Foreign Secretary, 'Afghanistan Annual Review for 1977: The Year Daoud Missed the Bus?', 31 December 1977, FO 37/2075, TNA.
64. Embassy of India, Kabul, 'Monthly Record of Events, January and February, 1979', 12 March 1979, Ministry of External Affairs, R&I Branch, File No. HI/1012/1/79, NAI.
65. American Embassy, Kabul [Chargé] to Secretary of State, Washington, Tel. 01443, Leak of Embassy Confidential Message to *Washington Post*: My Personal Thoughts, 25 February 1979, *Afghanistan, 1973–1990*, DNSA.

66. Michael Palliser to Tatham, 13 July 1978, FCO 8/3251, TNA.
67. J.W.D. Gray (MAED) to Oliver Wright, 25 July 1983, FCO 9/4316, TNA.
68. Joint Intelligence Committee, JIC (81) 17, 8 December 1981, 'The Threat of Sabotage in the United Kingdom', CAB 186/32, TNA; R.H. Smith (EESD) to Goodison, 30 December 1982, FCO 28/4874, TNA.
69. Sofia to FCO, Tel. 180, 10 April 1991, FCO 28/10629, TNA; Sofia to FCO, Tel. 509, 25 November 1991, FCO 28/10629, TNA; DCS Christopher Bird (Anti-Terrorist Branch, SO13, Metropolitan Police) to James Paver (Central European Department, FCO), Memorandum: Markov Investigation, 25 August 1992, FCO 175/148, TNA; Transcript of interview with Oleg Kalugin on OTV1 (Moscow), 27 November 1993, FCO 175/648, TNA; Moscow to FCO, Tel. 2064, 1 December 1993, FCO 175/648, TNA.
70. M.J. Richardson to Sir Michael Palliser and Palliser to Richardson, 28 July 1978, FCO 8/3230, TNA.
71. David Owen to Merlyn Rees, 13 July 1978, FCO 8/3251, TNA.
72. 'Arab Terrorism: Note of a Meeting held on 1st August 1978', FCO 8/3230, TNA.
73. Netanel Avneri, 'The Iraqi Coups of July 1968 and the American Connection', *Middle Eastern Studies*, 51 (2015), pp. 649–63; Kevin Woods and James Lacey, 'Iraqi Perspectives Project. Saddam and Terrorism: Emerging Insights from Captured Iraqi Documents, Volume I (Redacted)', *Paper P-4287* (IDA, 2007); Kevin Woods and Mark Stout, 'New Sources for the Study of Iraqi Intelligence during the Saddam Era', *Intelligence and National Security*, 25 (2010), pp. 547–87; Magdalena Kirchner, '"A Good Investment?" State Sponsorship of Terrorism as an Instrument of Iraqi Foreign Policy, 1979–1991', *Cambridge Review of International Affairs*, 27 (2014), pp. 521–37.
74. Abu Dhabi to FCO, Tel. 4, 8 January 1977, FCO 93/1559, TNA.
75. US Mission to United Nations, New York to Secretary of State, Washington, Tel. 3304, 18 August 1976, SDRR; M.L. Tait (Baghdad) to C[raig] S.M. Shelton, 29 September 1977, FCO 8/3019, TNA; M.L. Tait (Baghdad) to C.S.M. Shelton (MED), 30 October 1977, FCO 8/3019, TNA; Sanaa to FCO (MED), Tel. 248, 30 August 1977, FCO8/3061, TNA; Secretary of State, Washington to American Embassy, Beirut, Tel. 325370, 27 December 1978, SDRR.
76. CIA [Office of Political Research], International and Transnational Terrorism: Diagnosis and Prognosis, April 1976. USDDO; [CIA], Terrorist Links in Latin America: Post-Mortem on the JCR, 29 June 1979.
77. DIA, International Terrorism: A Compendium Volume II – Middle East, July 1979, *Terrorism and US Policy, 1968–2002*, DNSA.
78. 'The Murder of General Abdul Razzak Nayif', Annex to Weir to PS/PUS, 10 July 1978, FCO 8/3251, TNA.
79. Memo by Commander R. Watts of Special Branch, 11 January 1978 attached to Eddie Guy (Home Office) to Ron Beer (PUSD), 13 January 1978, FCO 93/1559, TNA.
80. Note on a Meeting Held on 21 February: Arab Terrorism Incidents in the United Kingdom, FCO 93/1559, TNA.
81. Weir to PS/PUS, 10 July 1978, FCO 8/3251, TNA.
82. Douglas Little, 'To the Shores of Tripoli: America, Qaddafi, and Libyan Revolution, 1969–1989', *International History Review*, 35 (2013), pp. 70–99.

83. Note on a Meeting Held on 21 February: Arab Terrorism Incidents in the United Kingdom.
84. J.C. Kay (North African Department) to R.M. Evans (Near Eastern Department), 29 December 1971, FCO 17/1704, TNA.
85. SNUFFBOX [MI5] to Metropolitan Police Special Branch, 'Assessment of Current Media Reports of Renewed Libyan Support for the Provisional IRA (PIRA)', April 1984, PREM 19/1300, TNA.
86. P.F. Ricketts to A.J. Coles, 14 May 1984, PREM19/1302, TNA.
87. D.J.R. Hill, 'Qadhafi and the IRA', 2 June 1977, CJ 4/3923, TNA.
88. Little, 'To the Shores of Tripoli', pp. 70–99.
89. Nick Spreckley (Paris) reporting the conclusions of French intelligence sources] to J.C. Kay (North African Department, FCO), 19 November 1971, FCO 39/813, TNA.
90. Note for the Record [Jerry Wiggin], 13 May 1980, PREM 19/1299, TNA.
91. David Hill to Mrs E. Alton, 24 November 1977, CJ 4/3923, TNA.
92. Memorandum of Conversation: President Ford, Henry Kissinger, Amb. Herman F. Eilts, American Ambassador to Egypt, Brent Scowcroft, 9 March 1976, Gerald R. Ford and Foreign Affairs Microfilm Collection, Reel 11; Secretary of State, Washington to US Mission to the European Community, Brussels, Tel. 166565, 6 July 1976 [Text of Report on the Situation on the Middle East and the Maghreb by NATO Expert Working Group, 31 May–2 June 1976], SDRR; Brent Scowcroft [to the President], Meeting with Jaafar Nimeiri, President of the Sudan, 8 May 1976, Gerald R. Ford and Foreign Affairs Microfilm Collection, Reel 4.
93. American Consul, Stuttgart to Secretary of State, Washington, Tel. 626, 13 April 1977, SDRR.
94. American Embassy, Bonn to Secretary of State, Washington, Tel. 06576, 15 April 1977, SDRR.
95. JIC (77) (INT 1) 5, Joint Intelligence Committee (Germany) Minutes, 24 May 1977, CAB 190/89, TNA.
96. American Embassy, Bonn to Secretary of State, Washington, Tel. 06576, 15 April 1977.
97. American Embassy, Bonn (Stoessel) to Secretary of State, Washington, Tel. 15801, 23 September 1977, SDRR; Draft Letter from Home Secretary to Leon Brittan MP, December 1977, FCO 8/3061, TNA.
98. Secretary of State, Washington to US Mission to UN, New York, Tel. 156781, 18 June 1979, SDRR.
99. Reginald Hibbert (UK Ambassador in Paris) to Ian Winchester (Security), 23 May 1979, FCO 33/3848.
100. Madrid to FCO, Tel. 542, 22 December 1973, FCO 9/1815, TNA; Kostis Kornetis, 'Rebel Code? The Transnational Imaginary of "Armed Struggle" in the Fall of Southern European Dictatorships', *European Review of History*, 29 (2022), pp. 469–98.
101. C.J.S. Brearley to Patrick Wright, 21 November 1975, PREM 16/398, TNA.
102. C.A. Whitmore to N.E.A. Moore, 'The IRA Doctrine of Counter Intelligence and Intelligence', 3 December 1971, CAB 163/172, TNA.
103. J.B. Bourn to England, 29 July 1975, CJ 4/1156, TNA.
104. Joint Intelligence Committee, Limited Circulation Annex to JIC (76) 23rd, Minute 3, 24 June 1976, CAB 185/19, TNA; Dublin to FCO, Tel. 246, 3 September 1979, FCO 33/3848, TNA; Brigadier J.M. Glover (Defence

Intelligence Service), 'Northern Ireland: Future Terrorist Trends', 2 November 1978 was leaked to a Republican newspaper, Peter Taylor, *Brits: The War against the IRA* (Bloomsbury, 2002), pp. 218–26; *Co-ordination of the Security Effort in Northern Ireland: The Way Forward*. Report by the Security Co-ordinator to the Secretary of State for Northern Ireland, March 1981, PREM 19/817, TNA.

105. House of Commons, *Debates*, 901/1189-95, 28 November 1975.
106. 'MPs on "IRA Death List in Flat"', *Guardian*, 26 January 1977, p. 4.
107. Dublin to FCO, Tel. 282, 22 July 1976, FCO 87/489, TNA.
108. Joint Intelligence Committee, Limited Circulation Annex to JIC (76) 28th, Minute 2, 29 July 1976, CAB 185/19, TNA.
109. J.K. Hickman to Anthony Crosland (Foreign Secretary), 25 July 1976, PREM 16/1341; Julian Bullard (FCO) to Sir Jock Taylor (The Hague), 18 September 1979. Personal and Confidential hand-written note attached to official correspondence, FCO 33/4157, TNA.
110. Hervey (The Hague) to David Owen, 'Murder of Sir Richard Sykes', 27 April 1979, FCO 33/4157, TNA.
111. Duty Clerk to Prime Minister, 22 Mar. 1979, PREM 16/2244; Brussels to FCO, Tel. 44, 27 March 1979, FCO 33/3848; The Hague to FCO, Tel. 94, 27 March 1979, FCO 33/4157; FCO to Berne, Tel. 19, 26 Apr. 1979, FCO 33/3848, TNA; Secretary of State, Washington to American Embassy, Brussels, Tel. 184563, [17] July 1979, SDRR.
112. Secretary of State, Washington to US Mission to UN, New York, Tel. 156781, 18 June 1979, SDRR.
113. Private Secretary to the Secretary of the Cabinet to Prime Minister, Security Service Report, 25 November 1981, PREM 19/1299, TNA.
114. Andrew Lownie, *The Mountbattens: Their Lives and Loves* (Blink, 2019), pp. 337–8.
115. Private Secretary to the Secretary of the Cabinet to Prime Minister, Security Service Report, 25 November 1981, PREM 19/1299, TNA.
116. Paris to FCO, Tel. 316, 16 June 1979, FCO 33/4157, TNA.
117. American Embassy, London to Secretary of State, Washington, Tel. 14336, 23 July 1979, SDRR.
118. S.M. Pope (Division 1 (B)) to Walsh, 20 July 1978, CJ 4/2525, TNA.
119. Helen Jones (Division 1 (B)) to PS/Secretary of State, 11 July 1978, CJ 4/2525, TNA.
120. Ian Paisley to Roy Mason (Secretary of State for Northern Ireland), 7 February 1979, CJ 4/2526, TNA.
121. Lord Chief Justice Lowry, Judgment in Regina v. Bolan [sic = Bohan] and Temperley, [4 July 1979], CJ 4/2526, TNA.
122. Lieutenant Colonel H.M. Rose (MA to GOC), Minutes of a Meeting at Stormont on 5 February 1979 to Discuss Dunloy, 6 February 1979, CJ 4/2525, TNA.
123. John Young, *Twentieth-Century Diplomacy: A Case Study of British Practice, 1963–1976* (Cambridge, 2008), pp. 122–3, 140, 226; 'Death of a Moderate', Leader, *The Times*, 6 January 1978, p. 13.
124. Douglas Dillon, Memorandum for the President, 25 November 1964, USDDO.
125. Report by Interdepartmental Committee on Internal Security on Defense against the Assassination or Kidnapping of Certain Government Officials, 8 March 1972, USDDO.

126. John Dean, Memorandum for Director James Rowley, United States Secret Service, 27 October 1970, USDDO.
127. William Rogers [Secretary of State], Memorandum for the President, 29 March 1973, *Terrorism and US Policy, 1968–2002*, DNSA.
128. Eugene Rossides, Assistant Secretary of the Treasury, to John Lindsay, Mayor of New York, 19 April 1971, USDDO; Lewis Hoffacker, Chairman of the Working Group/Cabinet Committee to Combat Terrorism to Working Group, enclosing draft report, 20 January 1975.
129. Lewis Hoffacker, Chairman of the Working Group/Cabinet Committee to Combat Terrorism, Memorandum to Members and Participants in the WG/CC to Combat Terrorism: 70th Meeting of the WG/CC to Combat Terrorism, November 13, 1974, 14 November 1974, USDDO.
130. G.L. Angel to R.T. Armstrong (answers to PM's questions), 14 January 1972, HO 287/2205, TNA.
131. Assistant Commissioner, Special Branch to F4 Division Home Office, 16 December 1971, HO 287/2205, TNA; Phillips (Amman) to FCO, Tel. 85, 21 February 1972, FCO 17/1705, TNA.
132. Douglas-Home to Amman, Tel. 5, 4 January 1972, FCO 17/1704, TNA.
133. Carter (Amman) to Gore-Booth, 6 May 1972; D. A. Gore-Booth to J. S. (John) Champion (Amman), 16 June 1972, FCO 17/1706, TNA.
134. P.F. Newman (FCO Marine and Transport Department) to J.K.T. Frost (Department of Trade and Industry), June 1972 on JIC (A) (72) (SA) 93, 18 May 1972; Gore-Booth to Laver, 6 September 1972, FCO17/1706, TNA.
135. A.D. Parsons to H.G. Balfour Paul, 18 October 1972, FCO17/1706, TNA.
136. Balfour Paul to FCO, Tel. 539, 13 October 1972, FCO17/1706, TNA.
137. Curle (PCD) note on '"Sheik" Fools Heath's Guards', *The Sun*, 24 January 1974, FCO 57/655, TNA.
138. Richard Hanbury-Tenison (Brussels) to Lees Mayall (PCD), 10 February 1972, FCO 57/393, TNA.
139. Note of a Meeting Held at the Home Office on 25 January 1972, FCO 57/393, TNA.
140. FCO to Madrid, Tel. 385, 20 December 1973, FCO 9/1815, TNA.
141. Note of a Meeting Held at the Home Office on 25 January 1972, FCO 57/393, TNA.
142. G.L. Angel to R.T. Armstrong, 14 January 1972; Lord Bridges to P.H. Grattan (FCO), 25 September 1972; P. Cradock (Assessments Staff) to Lord Bridges, 26 September 1972, HO 287/2205, TNA.
143. Draft letter from Secretary of State for Northern Ireland to Attorney General (15 December 1978); Home Secretary to Attorney General, 28 December 1978, CJ 4/2525, TNA. Civil servants asked ministers to stop putting their thoughts on paper.
144. K.R.C. Pridham (Security Department) to Crawford (Private Secretary), 1 November 1972, FCO 57/428, TNA; 'Personal Security', 19 December 1974, CJ 4/1156, TNA.
145. Sir Denis Greenhill (Permanent Under Secretary, Foreign Office) to Sir Philip Allen (Permanent Under Secretary, Home Office), 23 October 1972, FCO 57/428, TNA.
146. Summary of the Report of the Working Party on Security and Protection of Foreign Missions, and Meeting Held in Room 613, Horseferry House, on 14

February 1974 to discuss the Report of the Working Party on Security and Protection of Diplomatic Missions, FCO 57/655, TNA.
147. Ivor Lucas to [Michael] Weir, 'Assassination of Qadi Abdullah al Hijri', with additional note by Richard Sykes, 13 April 1977, FCO 8/3060, TNA; John Thomas, Memorandum for Robert Lipshutz: US Secret Service Uniformed Division Coverage, 3 February 1978, USDDO.
148. 'MPs on "IRA Death List in Flat"', *Guardian*, 26 January 1977, p. 4.
149. Ken Stowe to Marcia Williams, 5 April 1976, PREM 16/1270, TNA.
150. Chief Inspector D.S. Paton, Metropolitan Police Special Branch, 'Rt Hon. Sir Harold Wilson: Security of Residence', 15 October 1976, PREM 16/1270, TNA.
151. D.A.V. Allen to K.R. Stowe, 1 November 1976, PREM 16/1270, TNA.
152. D.A.V. Allen to Stowe, 'Protection of Sir Harold Wilson', 30 December 1976, PREM 16/1270, TNA.
153. Marcia Falkender to Prime Minister, 29 December 1977, PREM 16/1270, TNA.
154. Jim Callaghan to Marcia Williams, 4 January 1977, PREM 16/1270, TNA.
155. Memorandum of Telephone Conversation [Nixon and Kissinger], 20:30, 2 March 1973, *Kissinger Telephone Conversations, 1969–1977*, DNSA.
156. Harold Saunders and Richard Kennedy [NSC], Memorandum for Dr Kissinger: Follow-up on Murders in Khartoum, 15 March 1973, *Terrorism and US Policy, 1968–2002*, DNSA; Memorandum of a Telephone Conversation [Ehrlichmann and Kissinger], 9:40, 25 April 1970, *Kissinger Telephone Conversations, 1969–1977*, DNSA; Henry Kissinger, Memorandum for the President: Actions to Combat International Terrorism, 27 November 1972, USDDO.
157. Lewis Hoffacker, Chairman of the Working Group/Cabinet Committee to Combat Terrorism, Memorandum to Members and Paricicipants in the WG/CC to Combat Terrorism: 75th Meeting of the WG/CC to Combat Terrorism, January 22, 1974 [sic], 24 January 1975, USDDO.
158. Ralph Erickson, Assistant Attorney General, Office of Legal Counsel, Memorandum for John Dean: Legal Authority to Protect Public Figures, 27 March 1972, USDDO.
159. Memorandum of a Telephone Conversation [Ehrlichmann and Kissinger], 9:40, 25 April 1970.
160. Memorandum of Telephone Conversation [Kissinger and Clarence Kelly], 4 December 1973, *Kissinger Telephone Conversations, 1969–1977*, DNSA.
161. Robert Lipshutz and Robert Gates (for David Aaron), Memorandum for the President: Security Protection for Dr Brzezinski, [August 1979] and Robert Lipshutz, Memorandum for the President: Security Protection for Dr Brzezinski, 2 August 1979, USDDO.
162. HQ Air Force Office of Special Operations, Special Report: Terrorism in Argentina, June 1975 & J.E. Buchanan, Department of State Bureau of Intelligence and Research, Research Study: Argentina: Renewed Terrorist Violence, 16 April 1975, SDRR; Memorandum to Members and Paricicipants in the WG/CC to Combat Terrorism, 24 January 1975.
163. (RSO [George] Beckett to SY) [Security Briefing for Kissinger's visit], Tel. 0698, 30 January 1975; Meeting with *Comisario* Margaride, 4 March 1975.
164. American Embassy, Buenos Aires to Secretary of State, Washington, Tel. 03227, Threat to Assassinate Col. Samuel Stapleton [US Defence Attaché], May 8,

1975, 9 May 1975; American Embassy, Buenos Aires to Secretary of State, Washington, Tel. 3430, 24 May 1976; American Embassy, Buenos Aires (RSO) to American Embassy, Montevideo, Tel. 0754, 25 January 1980, SDRR.
165. I.S. Winchester (Security) to Chief Clerk, 4 May 1979, FCO 33/3848, TNA.
166. Roger Hervey to Ian Winchester, 25 March 1979, FCO 33/4157, TNA.
167. Secretary of State, Washington to American Embassy, Beirut, Tel. 325370, 27 December 1978, SDRR.
168. American Embassy, Beirut to Secretary of State, Tel. 5307, 19 June 1976, SDRR.
169. Secretary of State, Washington to American Embassy, Panama, Tel. 010987, 14 January 1978, SDRR.
170. I.S. Winchester to Chief Clerk, 4 May 1979.

Chapter 10

1. National Foreign Assessment Center, Patterns of International Terrorism 1980: A Research Paper, June 1981, USDDO.
2. Kenneth Baker, *On Assassinations* (Unicorn, 2020), pp. 9–10 & 54–73.
3. Gilbert Guillaume, 'France and the Fight against Terrorism', *Terrorism and Political Violence*, 4 (1992), pp. 131–5.
4. Michel Wievorka, 'France Faced with Terrorism', *Terrorism*, 14 (1991), pp. 157–70.
5. Parsons to Coles, 29 November 1983, PREM 19/1088, TNA.
6. Prime Minister to Emir of Bahrain, 21 March 1983, PREM 19/1283, TNA.
7. S.L. Egerton to [H.D.A.C.] Miers, 20 October 1982, FCO 8/4730, TNA.
8. [W.I.] Rae to Miers, 3 December 1982, FCO 8/4730, TNA.
9. D.B. Goodsir, 'Abu Nidhal', 11 November 1982, FCO 8/4730; NENAD, 'Middle East Terrorism: Who Are the Killers?', 10 December 1982, PREM 19/1087, TNA.
10. Note of a telephone conversation [between the Director of Public Prosecutions and the Foreign Office], 18 January 1983, FCO 8/5265, TNA.
11. Miers to [Oliver] Wright, 25 May 1983, FCO 8/5265, TNA.
12. Amman to FCO, Tel. 72, 23 March 1983, FCO 8/5265, TNA & State Department to London, President's Response to Prime Minister Thatcher's Letter of March 22, 29 March 1983, USDDO.
13. FCO to Baghdad, Tel. 160, 15 March 1983, FCO 8/5265, TNA; USINT [US Interests Section, William Eagleton], Baghdad [to Secretary of State, Washington], Tel. 1204, Subject: Meeting with Barzan Ibrahim Il-Tikriti, May 1983, SDRR.
14. Baghdad to FCO, Tel. 468, 9 August 1983, FCO 8/5265, TNA.
15. NEA Press Guidance, 'Iraq – "Terrorism List"', 5 October 1983, FCO 8/5265, TNA.
16. Baghdad to FCO, Tel. 734, 24 November 1983, FCO 8/5265, TNA.
17. Baghdad to FCO, Tel. 790, 28 December 1983, FCO 8/5265, TNA.
18. Baghdad to FCO, Tel. 736, 28 November 1983, FCO 8/5265, TNA.
19. Antony Duff to Sir Robert Armstrong, 19 December 1983, PREM 19/1088, TNA.
20. C.W. Long (NENAD) to Egerton: Murder of British Council Representative in Athens, 29 March 1984, FCO 9/4668, TNA.
21. CC (84) 13th Conclusions, 29 March 1984, CAB 128/79, TNA; Christopher Hulse (British Embassy, Athens) to Philip Astley (Security Department, FCO), 15 May 1984, FCO 9/4668, TNA; D.B. Goodsir (Security Department) to R.E. Cavaliero (Deputy Director-General, British Council), 30 May 1984, FCO

9/4668, TNA; Bombay to FCO, Tel. 126, 30 November 1984, FCO 178/39, TNA; Bombay to FCO, Tel. 131, 16 December 1984, FCO 178/39, TNA.
22. Christopher Hulse (British Embassy, Athens) to Graham Burton (Head, Security Coordination Unit [SCU]), 4 September 1984, FCO 9/4668, TNA.
23. P.M. Newton (Security Coordination Unit) to Scaddan, 'JIC Paper on Assassination of Deputy High Commissioner in Bombay', 28 November 1984, FCO 178/39, TNA.
24. Paul Feeney (Home Office Immigration Attaché), 'Preliminary Report on the Assassination of Mr Percy Leonard Norris, Deputy High Commissioner, Bombay', 28 November 1984, FCO 178/39, TNA. Passed to SIS.
25. FCO to Abidjan, Tel. 233, 3 December 1984, FCO 178/39, TNA.
26. Cabinet Meeting: 29 November 1984, Assassination of DHC Bombay, FCO 37/3622, TNA.
27. American Embassy, Seoul to Secretary of State, Washington, Tel. 01186, 29 January 1980, SDRR.
28. Secretary of State, Washington to All Diplomatic Posts: Background Study – 'El Salvador: The Search for Peace', Tel. 240302, 9 September 1981; [State Department], 'American Nuns', [1993], SDRR.
29. Little, 'To the Shores of Tripoli', pp. 70–99.
30. Philippa Drew to Douglas Harding, 2 September 1980, FCO 93/2337, TNA.
31. President Carter, 'Evening Reading', 20 December 1979, 5 February 1980 and 4 April 1980 [Selection of evening reading material for President Carter on foreign relations covering period 2/13/78–5/15/80]; National Foreign Assessment Center, Patterns of International Terrorism 1980: A Research Paper, June 1981.
32. Background Note for Secretary of State: Shooting of a Libyan Dissident & FCO to Tripoli, Tel. 112, 14 April 1980, FCO 93/2359, TNA.
33. Lord Carrington to Prime Minister, PM/80/32, n.d., PREM 19/1299, TNA.
34. Note to Prime Minister, 12 May 1980. Underlining by Margaret Thatcher, PREM 19/1299, TNA.
35. Bernard Gwertzman, 'US Expels Libyans and Closes Mission, Charging Terrorism', New York Times, 7 May 1981, A1.
36. FCO to Tripoli, Tel. 228, 13 June 1980, PREM 19/1299, TNA.
37. Secretary of State for Lord Privy Seal and Mr Hurd, Tel. 17, 13 June 1980, PREM19/1299, TNA.
38. William Casey, Director of Central Intelligence, Lessons of Wilson and Terpil, 25 June 1981, USDDO.
39. Philip Taubman, 'Suspect in Libyan's Shooting is Traced to Farm in England', New York Times, 25 October 1981, p. 1; Private Secretary to the Secretary of the Cabinet to Prime Minister, Security Service Report, 'Panorama Programme of 23 November 1981 Dealing with the Activities of Messrs Wilson and Terpil', 25 November 1981, PREM 19/1299, TNA.
40. Richard Allen, Memorandum for Ed Meese, 20 May 1981, CIA Covert Operations: From Carter to Obama, 1977–2010, DNSA.
41. Paul Wolfowitz, Briefing Memorandum for Judge Clark: Broader Political Implications of Libyan SIG, 25 November 1981 & Paul Wolfowitz, Briefing Memorandum for the Secretary: Talking Points for Your February 25 NSC Meeting on Libya, 23 February 1982, USDDO.
42. Raymond Tanter, Memorandum for Richard Allen: Interagency Meetings on Libya and the NSC Staff Paper – 'Libyan Contingencies and US Options', 13

November 1981; [Department of State], Chronology of Consultations and Public Statements Related to Actions Against Libya, [19 November 1981], USDDO.
43. Richard Allen, Memorandum for Ed Meese, 20 May 1981.
44. Elaine Morton, 'A Public Affairs Strategy for Actions against Libya', 17 November 1981, USDDO; UKDEL NATO to FCO, Tel. 478, 'Bilateral Breakfast with Mr Haig: 11 December: Libya', 11 December 1981 and Washington to FCO, Tel. 3946, 'EC Lunch for Haig: Libya', 27 December 1981, PREM 19/1299, TNA.
45. [NSC], Chronology of Libyan Troublemaking 1980–85, 31 December 1985, Terrorist Targets (6), Oliver North Files, Box 48, Digitized Archives, Ronald Reagan Presidential Library & Museum [hereafter RDA]; Tripoli to FCO, Tel. 353, 11 October 1982 and J.E. Holmes to A.J. Coles, 12 October 1983, PREM 19/1299, TNA.
46. Cairo to FCO, Tel. 552, 20 November 1984, FCO 93/3687, TNA.
47. Adrian Hänni, 'Read It in the Papers, Seen It on TV: The 1981 Libyan Hit Squad Scare as a Case of Simulated Terrorism', *Critical Studies on Terrorism*, 9 (2016), pp. 54–75.
48. Donald Fortier, Vincent Cannistraro, Stephen Rosen, Stephen Sestanovich, Memorandum for Robert McFarlane, 10 January 1982, USDDO.
49. UKDEL NATO to FCO, Tel. 478, 'Bilateral Breakfast with Mr Haig: 11 December: Libya', 11 December 1981.
50. National Security Council Meeting, 8 December 1981, *CIA Covert Operations: From Carter to Obama, 1977–2010*, DNSA.
51. Department X, MfS [STASI], 'Information from Security Services of the BPC', 3 June 1983, WCDA.
52. Richard Northern (British Embassy, Rome) to J. McIver (EED), 28 November 1986, FCO 33/8838, TNA.
53. Ronald Reagan to Margaret Thatcher, draft letter, n.d., USDDO.
54. Ephraim Kahana and Sagit Stivi-Kerbis, 'The Assassination of Anwar al-Sadat: An Intelligence Failure', *International Journal of Intelligence and Counterintelligence*, 27 (2014), pp. 178–92.
55. Ambassador at Manila to Secretary of State for Foreign and Commonwealth Affairs, 'The Murder of Former Senator Benigno Aquino and its Aftermath', 24 December 1985, FCO 15/4333, TNA.
56. Southeast Asia Division, Office of East Asian Analysis, CIA Directorate of Intelligence, 'The Philippines: Implications of the Assassination of Benigno Aquino', 26 August 1983, CIA.
57. Secretary of State, Washington to American Embassy, Seoul, Tel. 289025, 9 October 1983, *The US and the Two Koreas, 1969–2000*, DNSA; [Kenneth Dam], Diary entry, 14 October 1983, SDRR; Secretary of State, Washington to American Embassy, Moscow, Tel. 309819, 29 October 1983, *The US and the Two Koreas, 1969–2000*, DNSA.
58. Draft Report on the Bombing Attack by North Korean Terrorists against the Presidential Party of the Republic of Korea at the Martyrs' Mausoleum in Rangoon, Burma on 9 October 1983, FCO 21/2848, TNA; Far Eastern Department, Rangoon Bombing Incident: Joint Statement by EC Foreign Ministers, Points to Make, 21 November 1983, FCO 21/2516, TNA.
59. State Department Bureau of Intelligence and Research, Analysis: Libya: Qadhafi on a Binge, 20 March 1984, USDDO.
60. Libyan Peoples Bureau – Chronology, February–April 1984. Underlining by Prime Minister, PREM 19/1301, TNA.

61. Hugh Taylor (Home Office), 'Threat to Libyan "Dissidents"', 1 March 1984, PREM 19/1299, TNA.
62. Libyan Peoples Bureau – Chronology, February–April 1984.
63. Anglo-Libyan Crisis: Situation Report as at 1900 Hours', 25 April 1984, PREM 19/1301, TNA.
64. Statement by the Home Secretary, the Rt Hon. Leon Brittan, PREM 19/1300; 'Record of a Telephone Conversation between the Prime Minister in Lisbon and the Home Secretary in London at 0710', 19 April 1984, PREM 19/1300, TNA.
65. Anglo-Libyan Crisis: Situation Report as at 1900 Hours', 25 April 1984, PREM19/1301; Washington to FCO, Tel. 1319, 29 April 1984, PREM 19/1301, TNA.
66. P.F. Ricketts to N. Pantling (Home Office), 12 May 1984, PREM 19/1302, TNA.
67. CIA Directorate of Intelligence, 'Libya: Supplying Terrorist Weapons', 3 December 1984 and State Department, 'Libyan Sanctions', 8 January 1986, *Terrorism and US Policy, 1968–2002*, DNSA.
68. Ronald Reagan, Remarks at the Annual Convention of the American Bar Association, 8 July 1985, RDA.
69. Rohrabacher/BE/PJB, Presidential Address: Insert for International Lions Club Convention, Dallas, Texas, Friday, June 21, 1985, 20 June 1985, 6:30 p.m., Terrorist Targets: Libya (3), Oliver North Files, Box 48, RDA.
70. Oliver North, Memorandum for Robert McFarlane: Speech before the National Strategy Information Center, Inc. (NSIC) on 25 March 1985, 22 March 1985, Terrorism Actions: Pending (03/16/1985-03/31/1985), Oliver North Files, Box 49, RDA.
71. CIA, National Foreign Assessment Center, 'Growing Terrorist Danger for Americans', 23 December 1981, *Terrorism and US Policy, 1968–2002*, DNSA; John Poindexter to Charles Powell [Reagan to Thatcher], 9 April 1986, Libya: El Dorado Canyon (1), James Stark Files, Box 91747, Reagan Library [via Thatcher Foundation].
72. National Security Advisor: Talking Points for Congressional Leadership, [14 April 1986], *CIA Covert Operations: From Carter to Obama, 1977–2010*, DNSA & Telegram for Sir Robert Armstrong from John Poindexter: Response to Libyan Terrorism [Reagan to Thatcher], 8 April 1986, Libya: El Dorado Canyon (1), James Stark Files, Box 91747, Reagan Library [via Thatcher Foundation].
73. American Embassy, London to Secretary of State, Tel. 07877: Oakley Meeting at FCO, 14 April 1986, State Department [via Thatcher Foundation].
74. CC (86th) 15th Conclusions, 15 April 1986, CAB 128/83, TNA & Stephen Sherbourne to Prime Minister, 15 April 1986, THCR 1/10/99, CAC [via Thatcher Foundation].
75. American Embassy, Beirut to Secretary of State, Tel. 2051, Subject: Claims of Responsibility for Assassination of British Hostages, April 1986, British Hostages, Oliver North Files, Box 10, RDA.
76. American Consul, Belfast to Secretary of State, Washington, Tel. 328, 14 May 1987, SDRR.
77. Luca Trenta, *The President's Kill List: Assassination and US Foreign Policy since 1945* (Edinburgh University Press, 2024), p. 233.
78. James Stark [Director, Political-Military Affairs, NSC], Memorandum for Donald Fortier [Deputy National Security Advisor]: Libya Follow-on Targets, 28 April 1986, USDDO.
79. Donald Fortier, Memorandum for the President: Acting against Libyan Support for Abu Nidal, [25 April 1986], *CIA Covert Operations: From Carter to Obama, 1977–2010*, DNSA.

80. Memorandum to ISA (State Department): Foreign Reaction to US Airstrike Against Libya [17 April 1986], USDDO.
81. INR, Remarks to a visiting French counter-terrorist delegation regarding patterns of Middle Eastern terrorist operations in Europe, 17 June 1986, USDDO.
82. CIA Directorate of Intelligence, Libya: Qadhafi's Political Position since the Airstrike, 17 July 1986, USDDO.
83. American Embassy, Madrid to State Department, Washington, Tel. 03706, 24 March 1981, SDRR; H.J. Arbuthnott (Paris) to D.C. Wilson, 25 January 1982, FCO 9/3670, TNA.
84. A.J. Jongman, 'Trends in International and Domestic Terrorism in Western Europe, 1968–1988', Terrorism and Political Violence, 4 (1992), pp. 26–76.
85. Secretary of State, Washington to all European diplomatic posts, Tel. 331293, 26 December 1979; American Embassy, London to Secretary of State, Washington, Tel. 19898, 11 September 1982, SDRR; R.P. Flower (PUSD) to Wright, 29 April 1983, FCO9/4315, TNA; Secretary of State, Washington to ALDAC, Tel. 170375, 19 June 1982; American Embassy, Vienna to Secretary of State, Washington, Tel. 15671, 19 November 1984, SDRR.
86. Paris to FCO, Tel. 316, 16 June 1979, FCO 33/4157, TNA; S.L. Rickard (SIL Division, Northern Ireland Office) to Reynolds, 25 July 1989, FCO 87/3048, TNA; James Lee (COI Radio Technical Services), Transcript of Two Doorstep Interviews Given by the Prime Minister, Mrs Thatcher, in Budapest on Wednesday, 19 September 1990, FCO 87/3207, TNA.
87. Jeremy Shapiro & Bénédicte Suzan, 'The French Experience of Counter-Terrorism', *Survival*, 45 (2003), pp. 67–98.
88. Rory Carroll, *Killing Thatcher: The IRA, the Manhunt and the Long War on the Crown* (HarperCollins, 2023), pp. 207–30.
89. The British High Commissioner at New Delhi to the Secretary of State for Foreign and Commonwealth Affairs, 'The Assassination of Indira Gandhi and its Aftermath', 13 December 1984, FCO 160/101, TNA.
90. CC (84) 35th Conclusions, 1 November 1984, CAB 128/79, TNA.
91. *Report of Justice Thakkar Commission of Inquiry on the Assassination of the Late Prime Minister Smt. Indira Gandhi: Interim Report*, 19 November 1985; Christopher Andrew, *The Defence of the Realm: The Authorized History of MI5* (Penguin, 2010), p. 734.
92. Prime Minister's Press Conference: Saturday 3 November and COI to Dhaka, Tel. 5, 3 November 1984, PREM 19/1663, TNA.
93. Margaret Thatcher to Stuart Young [chairman of BBC board of governors], 2 November 1984, PREM 19/1663, TNA.
94. Washington to FCO, Tel. 3247, 1 November 1984, PREM19/1663, TNA.
95. FCO to New Delhi, Tel. 150, 5 February 1985, FCO 178/68, TNA; New Delhi to FCO, Tel. 926, 8 November 1984, PREM 19/1663, TNA; CC (84) 37th Conclusions, 15 November 1984, CAB 128/79, TNA.
96. [Kenneth Dam], Diary entry, 31 October 1984, SDRR; Ronald Reagan, *The Reagan Diaries*, ed. Douglas Brinkley (HarperCollins, 2007), 21 October 1985; Jock Covey, Memorandum for Robert McFarlane: Jha Meeting, McFarlane's Office, 23 May 1985, USDDO.
97. Ronald Reagan to Margaret Thatcher, [13 October 1984], USDDO.
98. Washington to FCO, Tel. 3247, 1 November 1984, PREM 19/1663, TNA.

99. Nicholas Platt, State Department, Memorandum for John Poindexter: US–UK Bilateral Talks on Terrorism, March 5, 1986, 22 March 1986, UK Meeting on Libya, Syria (May 28 1986) (1), James Stark Files, Box 91750, RDA.
100. Prime Minister's Meeting with Signor Craxi, 18 October at 10 Downing Street, PREM 19/1554, TNA; Record of a Meeting between the Prime Minister and Signor Craxi, Prime Minister of Italy, at 10 Downing Street on Friday 19 October at 1000 Hours, PREM19/1554, TNA; Brussels to FCO, Tel. 53, 13 February 1989, FCO 87/3048, TNA; D.F.G. Farr (RID, FCO) to Private Secretary, 'Speaker Thomas Foley and the IRA', 7 August 1990, FCO 87/3207, TNA.
101. Accra to FCO, Tel. 3, 5 January 1983, FCO 65/2970, TNA; Christian Casteran, 'Un commando de tueurs pendant la visite de Mitterrand au Togo', *Le Matin*, 11 January 1983 and 'Togo: l'histoire du complot des mercenaires', *Le Matin*, 12 January 1983.
102. OD (80) 3rd Meeting, 29 January 1980, CAB 148/189, TNA; Antony Acland to [Roger] du Boulay, 1 December 1981, PREM 19/1698, TNA; FCO to New Delhi, Tel. 868, 27 November 1984, FCO 37/3622, TNA.
103. Cmnd. 8254, *Report of the Commissioner of Police of the Metropolis for the Year 1980*, June 1981; American Embassy, London to Secretary of State, Washington, Tel. 19898, 11 September 1982, SDRR; Record of a Conversation between the British Minister of State for Foreign and Commonwealth Affairs and the Turkish Ambassador at 11am on Friday 24 September 1982 at the FCO, 28 September 1982, FCO 9/3723; D.C. Wilson to Mark Russell, 22 September 1983, FCO 9/4360, TNA.
104. Cmnd. 7932, *Report of the Commissioner of Police of the Metropolis* [David McNee] *for the Year 1979*, June 1980.
105. American Embassy, Canberra to State Department, Washington, Tel. 12514, 17 December 1980; American Embassy, Canberra to State Department, Washington, Tel. 3136, 11 May 1981, SDRR.
106. Turkish Ambassador's Call on Lord Belstead, Friday, 24 September 1982: Points to Make, FCO 9/3723, TNA.
107. Record of a Conversation between the British Minister of State for Foreign and Commonwealth Affairs and the Turkish Ambassador at 11am on Friday 24 September 1982 at the FCO, 28 September 1982, FCO 9/3723, TNA.
108. Nick Browne (Maritime, Aviation and Environment) to Chase, 11 March 1983, FCO 8/5265, TNA; D.C. Wilson (SED) to Mark Russell (Ankara), 22 September 1983, FCO 9/4360, TNA.
109. Colonel P.A.W.G. Durrant (PCD) to Gibson, 28 July 1983, FCO 9/4360, TNA.
110. Secretary of State, Washington to American Embassy, Ankara, Tel. 040450, 13 February 1982, SDRR.
111. Donald Regan, Secretary of the Treasury, Memorandum for General Counsel: Investigation of March 30 Attempt on the Life of President Reagan, 28 April 1981, Assassination Report [3], Edwin Meese Files, Box CFOA 28; [Department of Treasury, Review of Assassination Procedures], D. Office of the Secretary, [1981], Assassination Report [3], Edwin Meese Files, Box CFOA 28; [Department of Treasury, Review of Assassination Procedures], C. United States Customs Service, [1981], Assassination Report [3], Edwin Meese Files, Box

CFOA 28, RDA; Ronald Kessler, *Washington Post* to Larry Speakes, Deputy Press Secretary to the President, 3 March 1983, Draft letter to Ronald Kessler, *Washington Post*, [May 1983], White House Staff Memoranda: Military Office, James A. Baker Files, Box 5; Edward Hickey, Memorandum for James Baker: Ronald Kessler Request for Information Regarding DoD Costs in Support of the President, 11 May 1983, White House Staff Memoranda: Military Office, James A. Baker Files, Box 5; Katherine Camalier, Staff Assistant to James Baker, to Dean Nichols, 14 May 1984, Correspondence and Memos 1984, James A. Baker Files, Box 11, RDA.

112. J. Fewtrell (British High Commission, New Delhi) to Mark Dickinson (SAD, FCO), 17 September 1985, FCO 37/4033, TNA.
113. Reagan, *The Reagan Diaries*, 29 September 1981.
114. Sir Robert Armstrong to C.D. Powell, 17 October 1984, PREM 19/1698, TNA.
115. H.H. Taylor to P. Ricketts, 15 June 1984, PREM 19/1698, TNA.
116. FCO to Islamabad, Tel. 704, 18 August 1988, FCO 37/5182, TNA.
117. Leon Brittan to Geoffrey Howe, 7 September 1984, Sir Robert Armstrong to C.D. Powell, 17 October 1984, Sir Robert Armstrong to Charles Powell, 4 April 1986 and Charles Powell to Sir Robert Armstrong, 6 April 1986, PREM 19/1698, TNA.
118. Charles Powell to Sir Robert Armstrong, 19 October 1984, PREM 19/1698, TNA.
119. Snuffbox [MI5] to FCO, OILNAN 7469, 28 September 1989, FCO 9/6454, TNA; Robert Culshaw (British Embassy, Athens) to Philip Parker (SED, FCO), 29 September 1989, FCO 9/6454, TNA.
120. American Embassy, Stockholm to Secretary of State, Washington, Tel. 01527, 3 March 1986, SDRR.
121. American Embassy, Islamabad to Secretary of State, Washington, Tel. 039920, 1 June 1989, SDRR.
122. Stockholm to FCO, Tel. 74, 13 March 1986, FCO 33/8823, TNA; American Embassy, Stockholm to Secretary of State, Washington, Tel. 02687, 9 April 1986; American Embassy, London to Secretary of State, Washington, Tel. 12083, June 1986, SDRR; Steward Tendler, 'Terrorist Suspects Ordered to Leave', *The Times*, 13 October 1986, p. 2.
123. R. Anderson (WED, FCO) to M. Bradfield (British Embassy, Stockholm,), 28 May 1987, FCO 33/9360, TNA.
124. M. Bradfield (British Embassy, Stockholm) to R. Anderson (WED, FCO), 21 May 1987, FCO 33/9360, TNA.
125. M. Bradfield (British Embassy, Stockholm) to Ray Anderson (WED, FCO), 9 March 1987, FCO 33/9360, TNA.
126. Note for Prime Minister, 15 March 1983, FCO 8/5265, TNA; Robin Butler to David Staff, 17 March 1983, FCO 8/5265, TNA.
127. Note by Officials, 'Assassination and Death or Injury in Service' attached to Ian Gow to Prime Minister, 15 November 1985; Nigel Wicks to Prime Minister, with handwritten note by Margaret Thatcher, 19 November 1985, PREM 19/1429, TNA.
128. Jörg Requate and Philipp Zessin, 'Comment sortir du terrorisme? La violence politique et les conditions de sa disparition en France et en République Fédérale d'Allemagne en comparaison, 1970–années 1990', *European Review of History*, 14 (2007), pp. 423–45.
129. *The Jain Commission Report*, Volume III, August 1997 as published by *India Today*, November 1997; T.C. Wood (SAD) to Mooncie (PUSD), 'JIC Paper:

India: The Punjab', 7 August 1985, FCO 37/4033, TNA; Andrew Hall (British High Commission, New Delhi) to Mark Dickinson (SAD, FCO), 3 December 1985, FCO 37/4033, TNA.
130. Sir Robert Wade-Gery [to SAD, FCO], 5 June 1985, FCO 37/4033, TNA.
131. *The Jain Commission Report*, Volume III, August 1997.
132. *The Jain Commission Report*, Volume III, August 1997 as published by *India Today*, November 1997.
133. I.R. Lee (PS/USofS(DP)) to D Mod Sy [A.G. Rucker, Director of Security, MoD], 'Protection of Private Homes at Public Expense', 22 April 1985, DEFE 23/339, TNA.
134. A.G. Rucker (D Mod Sy) to PS/PUS, 'Protection of Private Homes at Public Expense', 18 January 1985, DEFE 23/339, TNA.
135. J.W. Hodge (Security Department) to PS/PUS, 'PIRA Follow-up to Incidents on the British Mainland', 12 July 1990, FCO 87/3207, TNA; Andrew Turnbull (10 Downing Street) to Colin Walters (Home Office), 16 July 1990, FCO 87/3207, TNA; C.T. Wood (SCD, FCO) to Slater, 'Irish Terrorism: Mr Gow', FCO 87/3207, TNA.
136. G.R. Archer (Republic of Ireland Department, FCO) to PS/Mr Waldegrave, 'PIRA Attacks: Post Cabinet Ministerial Discussion' (ID 1961), 27 September 1990, FCO 87/3207, TNA; G.R. Archer (Republic of Ireland Department, FCO) to PS/Mr Waldegrave, 'PIRA Attacks: Post Cabinet Ministerial Discussion' (ID 1966), 27 September 1990, FCO 87/3207, TNA; P.H. Williams (SED, FCO) to Warren-Gash, 'Shooting of Former Governor of Gibraltar', 19 September 1990, FCO 87/3207, TNA.
137. Allan Ramsey (British Ambassador in Lebanon) to Douglas Hurd (Foreign Secretary), 'The Assassination of President Moawad and Election of President Hraoui', 9 December 1989, FCO 93/5647, TNA.

Chapter 11

1. Cabinet Secretary's meeting, 4 December 1989 in *The Jain Commission Report*, Volume IV, August 1997; RAW assessment: Likely threats to the Security of Shri V.P. Singh and Shri Rajiv Gandhi, former Prime Minister, 9 December 1989 reproduced in *The Jain Commission Report*, Volume III, August 1997; Intelligence Bureau: Threat Assessment in respect of Shri Rajiv Gandhi, Ex-Prime Minister and his family members, 6 February 1990 quoted in *The Jain Commission Report*, Volume III, August 1997; Superintendent of Police (Security), Tamil Nadu cited in *The Jain Commission Report*, Volume IV, August 1997.
2. *The Jain Commission Report*, Volume IV, August 1997, November 1997.
3. RAW assessment, 9 December 1989 quoted in *The Jain Commission Report*, Volume III, August 1997.
4. IB assessment, 12 December 1989 quoted in *The Jain Commission Report*, Volume III, August 1997.
5. Anirudhya Mitra, 'Rajiv Assassination: The Inside Story', *India Today*, July 1991, pp. 22–9.
6. Sir David Goodall (High Commissioner, New Delhi) to Sir John Coles (DUS, FCO), 'Rajiv Gandhi: A Farewell Look', 5 August 1991, FCO 37/5875, TNA.
7. *The Jain Commission Report*, Volume VII, August 1997.

NOTES TO PP. 235–238

8. Percy Cradock to [Stephen] Wall [PM's Private Secretary], 22 May 1991, PREM 19/3248, TNA.
9. New Delhi to FCO, Tel. 1035, 30 July 1991, FCO 37/5875, TNA; New Delhi to FCO, Tel. 1138, 22 August 1991, FCO 37/5875, TNA.
10. Sakina Yusuf Khan, 'Ex-officers Denied Access to Records in Rajiv Case', *Times of India*, 4 June 1995, p. 24.
11. Kevin O'Brien, 'The Use of Assassination as a Tool of State Policy: South Africa's Counter-Revolutionary Strategy, 1979–1992', *Terrorism and Political Violence*, 13 (2001), pp. 107–42.
12. Robert Hughes, MP to Lynda Chalker (Minister of State, FCO), 17 November 1989, Files of the Anti-Apartheid Movement, MSS AAM 1989, Special Collections, Bodleian; Peter Godwin, 'Hit-Squad Death Puts Pretoria in a Corner', *Sunday Times*, 7 May 1989.
13. Anti-Apartheid Movement, Press Release: Anti-Apartheid Movement Calls for Full Investigation and Prompt Action Following Revelations of South African Terror Operations in UK, 17 November 1989, Files of the Anti-Apartheid Movement, MSS AAM 1989, Bodleian.
14. Amnesty International, 'South Africa: Political Killings by Security Force "Death Squads"', 19 January 1990, Files of the Anti-Apartheid Movement, MSS AAM 1988, Bodleian.
15. Justice L.T.C. Harms, *Report of Commission of Inquiry into Certain Alleged Murders* (1990), Files of the Anti-Apartheid Movement, MSS AAM 1988, Bodleian.
16. Commission of Inquiry Regarding the Prevention of Public Violence, *Interim Report on Criminal Political Violence by Elements within the South African Police, the KwaZulu Police and the Inkatha Freedom Party*, 18 March 1994.
17. Harvey Morris and Richard Dowden, 'Agents on a Mission to Kill', *Independent*, 15 July 1992.
18. John Major (Prime Minister) to Robert Hughes, MP, 6 August 1992, Files of the Anti-Apartheid Movement, MSS AAM 1989, Bodleian.
19. Cape Town to FCO, Tel. 81, 20 April 1993, FCO 169/1107, TNA.
20. Address by ANC President, Nelson Rolihlahla Mandela, at the Funeral of Martin Chris Hani, FNB Stadium, 19 April 1993, Files of the Anti-Apartheid Movement, MSS AAM 1989, Bodleian.
21. Pretoria to FCO, Tel. 76, 10 May 1993, FCO 169/1218, TNA and Pretoria to FCO, Tel. 77, 10 May 1993, FCO 169/1107, TNA.
22. Cape Town to FCO, Tel. 76, 14 April 1993, FCO 169/1107, TNA.
23. K. Cunningham (African Department (Southern), FCO) to Chris Burford, 21 April 1993; Douglas Hurd (Foreign Secretary) to Archbishop Trevor Huddleston, 27 April 1993; John Major (Prime Minister) to Archbishop Trevor Huddleston, 10 May 1993, Files of the Anti-Apartheid Movement, MSS AAM 1989, Bodleian; D. Wyatt (African Department (Southern)) to Sir T. Daunt, JIC Meeting on Thursday 22 April: JIC (93) (WSI 16 (Draft), 21 April 1993, FCO 169/1107, TNA; Address by ANC President, Nelson Rolihlahla Mandela, at the Funeral of Martin Chris Hani, FNB Stadium, 19 April 1993; Commission of Inquiry Regarding the Prevention of Public Violence, *Report by the Committee Appointed to Hold a Workshop to Consider Events after the Assassination and during the Funeral of Mr Chris Hani*, 29 June 1993.
24. Questions for President Clinton, *The Presidents: In Their Own Words*, PBS, [28 March 1998], *Clinton Digital Library*, Clinton Presidential Library & Museum [hereafter CDL].

25. Annual Report on Intelligence Community [FY 1993], CDL.
26. Transcript of Anthony Lake Oral History, 21 May 2002, William J. Clinton Presidential History Project, Miller Center, University of Virginia [hereafter Miller Center].
27. George Tenet, *At the Center of the Storm: The CIA during America's Time of Crisis* (Harper Perennial, 2008), p. 43.
28. IIS to Saddam Hussein, 18 March 1993, Extract 10 in Kevin M. Woods and James Lacey for Institute for Defense Analyses Iraqi Perspectives Project, *Saddam and Terrorism: Emerging Insights from Captured Iraqi Documents*, Volume 1 (IDA Papers P-4287, November 2007).
29. IIS Documents, January 1991, Extracts 28, 29, 30, 31, 32 in Woods and Lacey, *Saddam and Terrorism*.
30. Counterterrorism Center, CIA Directorate of Intelligence, Intelligence Memorandum: Iraq: Baghdad Attempts to Assassinate Former President Bush, 12 July 1993 [Secret version of Top Secret briefing to the President by DCI], CIA.
31. Douglas Jehl, 'Evidence against Iraq Cited in a Reported Plot on Bush', *New York Times*, 11 May 1993.
32. History of Department of State: III. Security Policies, CDL.
33. The White House, Office of the Press Secretary, Remarks by the President in Photo Opportunity with President Menem of Argentina, 29 June 1993, CDL.
34. The so-called 'Black Hawk Down' incident, 3 October 1993.
35. Points to be Made on Iraq [Presidential Address, 10 October 1994], CDL.
36. Ankara to FCO, Tel. 31, 15 January 1990 & Ankara to FCO, Tel. 66, 31 January 1990; Charles Hollis (British Embassy, Riyadh) to Bill Henderson (MED, FCO); J.R. Young (MED) to Gore-Booth, 2 February 1990; Riyadh to FCO, Tel. 104, 14 February 1990; FCO to Riyadh, Tel. 95, 21 February 1990, FCO 8/8179, TNA.
37. OVP/NSA News Summary, 15 May 1997, CDL.
38. Clifton Wharton, Department of State, Memorandum for the President: Meeting with Prime Minister John Major of Great Britain, 18 February 1993, CDL.
39. 'Enlargement: Purpose and Practice': Speech by National Security Advisor Anthony Lake, Council on Foreign Relations, New York, 14 December 1993, CDL.
40. CIA, Middle East Brief, 23 April 1994, CDL.
41. Chris Hedges, 'US-Egypt Ties Are Strained in Detention of Islamic Cleric', *New York Times*, 7 July 1993, A1.
42. Thomas Lippman, 'State Dept. Says Screening for Visas Is Often Lacking', *Washington Post*, 14 July 1993.
43. Daniel Schorr, 'Afghan Ties Come Back to Haunt Us: Suspect in Trade Center Bombing is a Product of CIA-Backed Training Camp Who Has Come Home to Roost', *USA Today*, 16 February 1995, White House News Reports, CDL.
44. Mohammed Hussain Sharfi, 'Sudan and the Assassination Attempt on President Mubarak in June 1995: A Cornerstone in Ideological Reverse', *Journal of Eastern African Studies*, 12 (2018), pp. 454–72.
45. Steven Simon to Daniel Benjamin and Richard Clarke, E-mail: Great Work by Planning, 21 August 1998, CDL.
46. Transcript of James Woolsey Oral History, 13 January 2010, Miller Center.
47. David Sherman [NSC] to Dale Avery [NSC], E-mail: RE: Guatemala, 26 February 1999, CDL.

48. Samuel Berger (National Security Advisor), Memorandum for the President: Improving Intelligence Collection against Usama bin Ladin, n.d. [2000], DDSO; Transcript of Samuel Berger Oral History, 24 & 25 March 2005, Miller Center.
49. Transcript of Anthony Lake Oral History, 21 May 2002, Miller Center.
50. Transcript of James Woolsey Oral History, 13 January 2010, Miller Center.
51. Brian Williams, 'The CIA's Covert Predator Drone War in Pakistan, 2004–2010: The History of an Assassination Campaign', *Studies in Conflict & Terrorism*, 33 (2010), pp. 871–92.
52. Memorandum of Telephone Conversation: Telcon with British Prime Minister Blair, 29 April 1999, CDL.
53. David Sherman [NSC] to Dale Avery [NSC], E-mail: RE: Guatemala, 26 February 1999.
54. Tenet, *At the Center of the Storm*, p. 109.
55. Neil Kingsley to Carlos Pascual, E-mail: Shades of Oliver Stone, 26 August 1998, CDL.
56. John Podesta, White House Deputy Chief of Staff, Commencement Address, Knox College, 6 June 1998, CDL; Tim Reid, 'Clinton Forced to Apologise for Staying in Race "in Case of Assassination"', *The Times*, 24 May 2008, p. 35.
57. Transcript of James Woolsey Oral History, 13 January 2010, Miller Center.
58. Transcript of Samuel Berger Oral History, 24 & 25 March 2005, Miller Center.
59. The White House, Office of the Press Secretary, Remarks by the President at United States Military Academy Commencement, 29 May 1993, CDL.
60. The White House, Office of the Press Secretary, Remarks by the President in the Nomination of Judge Louis Freeh as Director of the FBI, 20 July 1993, CDL.
61. Stephen Wall to Prime Minister, 17 January 1992, PREM 19/4027, TNA.
62. Robin Catford to Prime Minister, 18 December 1991, PREM 19/4027, TNA.
63. Stewart Tendler and Richard Ford, 'Terrorist Unit Smuggled in for Downing Street Attack', *The Times*, 9 February 1991, p. 22.
64. Andrew, *The Defence of the Realm*, p. 771.
65. 'Colonel Alastair Mathieson' [Mathieson had been the MI5 officer responsible for security at 10 Downing Street], *The Times*, 20 June 2018, p. 52.
66. Andrew, *The Defence of the Realm*, p. 772.
67. *The Jain Commission Report*, Volume IV, August 1997.
68. *Report of Justice Thakkar Commission of Inquiry on the Assassination of the Late Prime Minister Smt. Indira Gandhi: Interim Report*, 19 November 1985.
69. Eetta Prince-Gibson, 'Israel Assassination Report Berates Security Agency, Top Officials', *Washington Post*, 29 March 1996.
70. Sam Afridi (Office of Speechwriting), Secret Service Building Dedication [3]: [Eulogies Secret Service], Box 1, CDL.
71. Sir David Goodall (High Commissioner, New Delhi) to David Gillmore (DUS, FCO), 1 February 1989, FCO 37/5875, TNA.
72. The White House, Office of the Press Secretary, Remarks by President Clinton and President Ramos of the Philippines in Press Availability, 22 November 1993, CDL.
73. White House, Office of the Press Secretary: Radio Address by the President to the Nation, 20 May 1995, CDL.
74. White House, Office of the Press Secretary (East Lansing, Michigan): Remarks by the President at Michigan State University Convocation, 5 May 1995, CDL.

75. 'ETA's Campaign of Terror', *The Times*, 22 June 2002, p. 6.
76. John Carr, 'Policeman Killed by Gunmen as He Kept Watch on Terror Witness', *The Times*, 20 January 2009, p. 4.
77. George Kassimeris, 'Last Act in a Violent Drama? The Trial of Greece's Revolutionary Organization 17 November', *Terrorism and Political Violence*, 18 (2006), pp. 137–57.
78. Michael Dynes and Nick Long, 'Kabila's Allies Promote Son after Shooting', *The Times*, 18 January 2001, p. 19.
79. Janine di Giovanni, 'Man Who Did Dirty Work Has History of Bravery', *The Times*, 30 June 2001, p. 16.
80. Christopher Condon, 'Two Shots and a Prime Minister Lay Dying', *The Times*, 13 March 2003, p. 1.
81. American Embassy, Belgrade to Secretary of State, Tel. 00730, 28 March 2003, SDRR.
82. 'Serbian Assassins Get 40 Years', *The Times*, 24 May 2007, p. 42.
83. Richard Beeston and Rana Sabbagh-Gargour, 'Abu Nidal Killed Himself over Plot', *The Times*, 7 May 2002, p. 6.

Chapter 12

1. Oldrich Bures and Andrew Hawkins, 'Israeli Targeted Killing Operations before and during the Second Intifada: A Contextualized Comparison', *Small Wars & Insurgencies*, 31 (2020), pp. 569–93.
2. Adam Stahl, 'The Evolution of Israeli Targeted Operations: Consequences of the Thabet Thabet Operation', *Studies in Conflict & Terrorism*, 33 (2010), pp. 111–33.
3. Washington to FCO, Tel. 1030, 20 April 1988, FCO 93/5416, TNA.
4. Simon Pratt, 'Anyone Who Hurts Us: How the Logic of Israel's "Assassination Policy" Developed during the Aqsa Intifada', *Terrorism and Political Violence*, 25 (2013), pp. 224–45.
5. Sam Kiley, 'Israelis Stalk and Kill Hezbollah "Training Chief"', *The Times*, 14 February 2001, p. 18.
6. Daniel Byman, *A High Price: The Triumphs and Failures of Israeli Counterterrorism* (OUP, 2011), p. 315.
7. Ross Dunn, 'Eight Palestinians Die in Airstrike', *The Times*, 1 August 2001, p. 13.
8. *The 9/11 Commission Report* [2006], pp. 113–14.
9. Ibid., pp. 187–8.
10. Ryan Crocker (Ambassador to Syria, Pakistan and Iraq), Oral History 9–10 September 2010, Presidential Oral Histories: George W. Bush Presidency, Miller Center.
11. *The 9/11 Commission Report* [2006], p. 211.
12. *The 9/11 Commission Report* [2006], p. 212.
13. Catherine Philp, 'Trump's Assassination of Iran General Qasem Soleimani Was Illegal, Says UN', *The Times*, 7 July 2020.
14. John Bellinger (legal advisor to the State Department), Oral History Part II, 20 April 2013, Miller Center.
15. *The 9/11 Commission Report* [2006], p. 212.
16. *The 9/11 Commission Report* [2006], pp. 213–14.
17. Zahid Hussain, 'Afghan Warlord "Killed" by Bombers', *The Times*, 11 September 2001, p. 16; Daniel McGrory, 'Iranians Extradite al-Qaeda Murder Suspect to Europe', *The Times*, 28 February 2002, p. 18.

18. INR Intelligence Assessment, Afghanistan: Implications of Masood's Death, 10 September 2001, SDRR; *The 9/11 Commission Report* [2006], p. 214.
19. Andris Banka and Adam Quinn, 'Killing Norms Softly: US Targeted Killing, Quasi-Secrecy and the Assassination Ban', *Security Studies*, 27 (2018), pp. 655–703.
20. Philip Webster, Roland Watson and Michael Dynes, '"We Are at War with Terrorism"', *The Times*, 17 September 2001, p. 1.
21. Brian Williams, 'The CIA's Covert Predator Drone War in Pakistan, 2004–2010: The History of an Assassination Campaign', *Studies in Conflict & Terrorism*, 33 (2010), pp. 871–92.
22. American Embassy, Amman to Secretary of State, Tel. 005101, 27 June 2005, SDRR; Richard Beeston, 'How a Junior Partner in Global Jihad Found his Truly Murderous Calling', *The Times*, 9 June 2006, pp. 6–7.
23. Catherine Philp and Shyam Bhatia, 'Afghans Mourn Murdered Leader as Inquiry Begins', *The Times*, 8 July 2002, p. 14.
24. Dumeetha Luthra, Richard Beeston and Roland Watson, 'Afghan Leader Escapes Assassin', *The Times*, 6 September 2002, p. 1.
25. Donald Rumsfeld, *Known and Unknown: A Memoir* (Penguin, 2011), Chapter 28.
26. Banka and Quinn, 'Killing Norms Softly', pp. 655–703; Michael J. Boyle, *The Drone Age: How Drone Technology Will Change War and Peace* (OUP, 2020), pp. 67–8.
27. James Zirin, 'When States Turn Assassin', *The Times*, 11 February 2003, p. 78.
28. Elaine Monaghan, 'CIA Agents Get Licence to Kill', *The Times*, 16 December 2002, p. 10.
29. George Bush, *Decision Points* (Virgin, 2010), p. 228; Dick Cheney, *In My Time: A Personal and Political Memoir* (Threshold Editions, 2011), pp. 366–7.
30. Bush, *Decision Points*, p. 224.
31. Roland Watson, 'Bush Reveals his Personal Grudge against Saddam', *The Times*, 28 September 2002, p. 20.
32. J5 [Directorate for Strategic Plans and Policy], JS [Joint Staff], [Joint Chiefs of Staff], Draft Working Paper: Chronology of Planning and Execution of Operation IRAQI FREEDOM, 9 May 2003, *Targeting Iraq, Part 1: Planning, Invasion, and Occupation, 1997–2004*, DNSA.
33. Anthony Loyd, 'Shadow of Rebel Killers Spreads across the Border from Pakistan', *The Times*, 20 August 2003, p. 13.
34. Dumeetha Luthra, 'General is Lured to His Death', *The Times*, 10 February 2003, p. 11.
35. Richard Beeston, 'How a Junior Partner in Global Jihad Found his Truly Murderous Calling'.
36. Faleh Jabar, 'Assassination Confirms Fears of Baathist Alliance with al-Qaeda', *The Times*, 1 September 2003, p. 12.
37. Richard Lloyd Parry, 'Living with Death in the City of Fear', *The Times*, 27 September 2003, p. 21.
38. Stephen Farrell, 'Death Squads Terrorise Baathists', *The Times*, 19 December 2003, p. 19.
39. Roland Watson, 'American Chief Tells of Escape in Ambush', *The Times*, 20 December 2003, p. 78; Daniel McGrory, 'Assassination Emerges as al-Qaeda's New Tactic', *The Times*, 31 December 2003, p. 15.

40. Robert Gates, *Duty: Memoirs of a Secretary at War* (W.H. Allen, 2014), Chapter 4.
41. Stanley McChrystal, *My Share of the Task: A Memoir* (Penguin, 2014), Chapter 7.
42. McChrystal, *My Share of the Task*, Chapter 10; Robert Gates (Secretary of Defense), Oral History 8 July 2013, Miller Center.
43. Catherine Philp, 'Assassinations Underline Iraq Security Fears', *The Times*, 14 June 2004, p. 8.
44. Stephen Farrell, 'Man Who Made Iraq's Phones Work Is Latest Murder Victim', *The Times*, 17 December 2004, p. 30.
45. James Hider, 'Governor of Baghdad Shot Dead in Ambush', *The Times*, 5 January 2005, p. 32.
46. 'Leader in Car-Bomb Near Miss', *The Times*, 21 April 2005, p. 40.
47. *Third Report of the International Independent Investigation Commission established pursuant to Security Council resolutions 1595 (2005), 1636 (2005) and 1644 (2005)*, UN Security Council S/2006/161, 14 March 2006, p. 9.
48. 'Justice Served: Lebanon's Special Tribunal Closes', *UN News*, 31 December 2023.
49. *Report of the International Independent Investigation Commission established pursuant to Security Council resolution 1595 (2005)*, UN Security Council S/2005/662, 19 October 2005, p. 43; Nicholas Blanford, 'Explosion Kills Mastermind of Hezbollah's Syrian Adventure', *The Times*, 14 May 2016, p. 40; 'Hariri Assassination: UN-Backed Tribunal Finds One Guilty, Three Acquitted', *UN News*, 18 August 2020.
50. Nicholas Blanford, Richard Beeston and James Bone, ' "Something Was Going to Happen – It Was Going to Be Me or Him" ', *The Times*, 18 March 2005, p. 41.
51. Ryan Crocker (Ambassador to Syria, Pakistan and Iraq), Oral History 9–10 September 2010, Miller Center.
52. *Seventh Report of the International Independent Investigation Commission established pursuant to Security Council resolutions 1595 (2005), 1636 (2005), 1644 (2005) and 1686 (2006)*, UN Security Council S/2007/150, 15 March 2007, p. 12.
53. Sid [Sidney Blumenthal], e-mail memorandum for H [Hillary Clinton]: Syria (Source: Sources with access to the highest levels of the Syrian Government, as well as Western Intelligence and security services), 24 February 2012, SDRR; Cheney, *In My Time*, pp. 479–80.
54. Hannah Strange, 'President's Military Aide Assassinated by Sniper', *The Times*, 5 August 2008, p. 33; Nicholas Blanford, 'UN Indicts Hezbollah Henchmen over the Murder of Lebanese Prime Minister', *The Times*, 1 July 2011, p. 31.
55. Nicholas Blanford, 'Terrorist Mastermind with $25m Price on his Head Dies in Car Blast', *The Times*, 14 February 2008, p. 35.
56. *Report of the International Independent Investigation Commission*, 19 October 2005, p. 42; Blanford, Beeston and Bone, ' "Something Was Going to Happen – It Was Going to Be Me or Him" ', p. 41.
57. *Third Report of the International Independent Investigation Commission*, 14 March 2006, p. 9.
58. *Third Report of the International Independent Investigation Commission*, pp. 9, 14; *Sixth Report of the International Independent Investigation Commission established pursuant to Security Council resolutions 1595 (2005), 1636 (2005) and 1644 (2005)*, UN Security Council S/2006/962, 12 December 2006, pp. 15–16; *Seventh Report of the International Independent Investigation Commission*, 15 March 2007, p. 15.
59. Nicholas Blanford, 'Guards and Armour, But It Wasn't Enough to Keep Hariri Alive', *The Times*, 1 September 2006, p. 40.

60. *Sixth Report of the International Independent Investigation Commission*, 12 December 2006, p. 7.
61. Zahid Hussain, 'Would-Be Assassin Served in Pakistan Air Force', *The Times*, 13 January 2005, p. 42.
62. Nicholas Blanford, 'Army Now a Target after General Killed in Bombing', *The Times*, 13 December 2007, p. 45.
63. Blanford, 'Guards and Armour, But It Wasn't Enough to Keep Hariri Alive', p. 40.
64. *Report of the International Independent Investigation Commission*, 19 October 2005, p. 24; Nicholas Blanford, 'Judge Quits over Murder Dossier as Fears Grow of Cover-Up', *The Times*, 24 March 2005, p. 42.
65. *Report of the International Independent Investigation Commission*, 19 October 2005, p. 43.
66. Blanford, 'UN Indicts Hezbollah Henchmen over the Murder of Lebanese Prime Minister', p. 31.
67. Williams, 'The CIA's Covert Predator Drone War in Pakistan, 2004–2010', pp. 871–92.
68. McChrystal, *My Share of the Task*, Chapter 12.
69. McChrystal, *My Share of the Task*, Chapter 9.
70. McChrystal, *My Share of the Task*, Chapter 15 recounts the efforts to recover evidence for the death of the Taliban leader Dadullah the Lame.
71. McChrystal, *My Share of the Task*, Chapter 12.
72. Sean Naylor, *Relentless Strike: The Secret History of Joint Special Operation Command* (St Martin's Griffin, 2015), p. 287.
73. Robert Service, Report for Litvinenko Inquiry, 8 January 2015, LITV 2/DXB/Z1, TNA.
74. Heidi Blake, *From Russia with Blood: Putin's Ruthless Killing Campaign and Secret War on the West* (HarperCollins, 2019), p. 107.
75. HC 695, *The Litvinenko Inquiry: Report into the Death of Alexander Litvinenko*, 21 January 2016.
76. *The Litvinenko Inquiry: Report*.
77. Clem Cecil, 'Putin Vows Revenge for Murder of Chechen President', *The Times*, 10 May 2004, p. 1.
78. Robert Service, Report for Litvinenko Inquiry, 8 January 2015.
79. Jeremy Page, 'Warlord behind Beslan Siege is Killed in Russian Revenge Attack', *The Times*, 11 July, p. 29.
80. Blake, *From Russia with Blood*, p. 180.
81. *The Litvinenko Inquiry*, 21 January 2016.
82. Ryan Crocker (Ambassador to Syria, Pakistan and Iraq), Oral History 9–10 September 2010, Miller Center; *Report of the United Nations Commission of Inquiry into the facts and circumstances of the assassination of former Pakistani Prime Minister Mohtarma Benazir Bhutto*, 10 April 2010 (Reproduced by Sani Hussain Panhwar, PPP); Jeremy Page and Zahid Hussain, 'After Nine Years in a Dangerous Job, Where Can He Hide Now?' *The Times*, 19 August 2008, p. 7.
83. *Report of the United Nations Commission of Inquiry*, 10 April 2010.
84. Bronwen Maddox and Zahid Hussain, 'Bhutto's Return Ends in Bloodbath as Two Suicide Car Bombs Target her Bus', *The Times*, 24 May 2007, p. 44.
85. American Embassy, Islamabad to Secretary of State, Tel. 005393, 30 December 2007, SDRR.

86. Heraldo Muñoz, *Getting Away with Murder: Benazir Bhutto's Assassination and the Politics of Pakistan* (W.W. Norton, 2014), Chapter 8.
87. *Report of the United Nations Commission of Inquiry*, 10 April 2010.
88. Steve Coll, *Directorate S: The CIA and America's Secret Wars in Afghanistan and Pakistan, 2001–2016* (Penguin, 2008), p. 311 & p. 338.
89. Williams, 'The CIA's Covert Predator Drone War in Pakistan, 2004–2010', pp. 871–92.
90. Sherard Cowper-Coles, *Cables from Kabul: The Inside Story of the West's Afghanistan Campaign* (Harper Press, 2011), Chapter 13.
91. Cowper-Coles, *Cables from Kabul*, Chapter 14.
92. McChrystal, *My Share of the Task*, Chapter 15.
93. Rob Crilly, 'Somalia on the Brink of All-Out War as Minister is Shot Dead', *The Times*, 29 July 2006, p. 45.
94. Ellen Chapin, Stephanie Lizzo and Jason Warner, 'Al-Shabaab's Assassinations: Investigating the Uniqueness of Al-Shabaab's Assassination via Suicide Bombings', *Journal of the Middle East and Africa*, 12 (2021), pp. 321–41.
95. McChrystal, *My Share of the Task*, Chapter 15.
96. Ben Rhodes, *The World As It Is: Inside the Obama White House* (Bodley Head, 2018), Chapter 2.
97. Gates, *Duty*, Chapter 4.
98. Williams, 'The CIA's Covert Predator Drone War in Pakistan, 2004–2010', pp. 871–92.
99. McChrystal, *My Share of the Task*, Chapter 15.
100. John Brennan, *Undaunted: My Fight against America's Enemies, at Home and Abroad* (Celadon, 2022), p. 210 & pp. 217–18.
101. 'A Time to Kill', *The Economist*, 13 February 2010, p. 60.
102. Gates, *Duty*, p. 398.
103. Gates, *Duty*, p. 364.
104. Brennan, *Undaunted*, p. 226.
105. Leon Panetta, *Worthy Fights: A Memoir of Leadership in War and Peace* (Penguin, 2014), Chapter 13.
106. Jeremy Page and Catherine Philp, 'Tribal Areas No Longer Safe for Terrorists, Says US after Death of Top al-Qaeda Man', *The Times*, 2 June 2010, p. 25; Brennan, *Undaunted*, p. 222; Panetta, *Worthy Fights*, Chapter 15.
107. Banks and Quinn, 'Killing Norms Softly', pp. 655–703.
108. Brennan, *Undaunted*, p. 219.
109. Presidential Policy Guidance (PPG): Procedures for Approving Direct Action against Terrorist Targets Located outside the United States and Areas of Active Hostilities, 22 May 2013. [Released by US Department of Justice].
110. Office of the Director of National Intelligence, 'Summary of Information Regarding US Counterterrorism Strikes Outside Areas of Active Hostilities', [July 2016].
111. Spencer Ackerman, 'Obama Claims US Drone Strikes Have Killed up to 116 Civilians', *Guardian*, 1 July 2016.
112. 'Summary of Information Regarding US Counterterrorism Strikes outside Areas of Active Hostilities', [July 2016].
113. *Report on the Legal and Policy Frameworks for the United States' Use of Military Force and Related National Security Operations*, [November 2022] [Released by US Department of Justice]; 'U.S. Kills al-Qaeda Leader Ayman al-Zawahiri in

Drone Strike in Kabul', *Washington Post*, 1 August 2022; Eric Schmitt, Charlie Savage and Azmat Khan, 'Pentagon Makes a Major Shift to Reduce Civilian Bloodshed', *New York Times*, 26 August 2022; Charlie Savage, 'Biden Rules Tighten Limits on Drone Strikes', *New York Times*, 1 July 2023.
114. Jenna Jordan, 'Attacking the Leader, Missing the Mark: Why Terrorist Groups Survive Decapitation Strikes', *International Security*, 38 (2014), pp. 7–38.
115. James Clapper, *Facts and Fears: Hard Truths from a Life in Intelligence* (Penguin, 2018), p. 178.
116. 'The Deadly Envoy', *The Economist*, 24 September 2011, p. 73.
117. Coll, *Directorate S*, pp. 603–10.
118. Sid [Sidney Blumenthal], e-mail memorandum for H [Hillary Clinton]: Conversation with Mahmoud Jibril, 12 March 2012, SDRR.
119. Clapper, *Facts and Fears*, p. 169 & p. 180.
120. Huma Abedin, e-mail to H [Hillary Clinton]: Jeff Update (contains report from Jeff Feltman, Assistant Secretary of State for Near Eastern Affairs, currently in Libya], 21 August 2011; H [Hillary Clinton] to Huma Abedin, e-mail: Gunmen try to assassinate head of Libyan army (AP), 10 December 2011; Sid [Sidney Blumenthal], e-mail memorandum for H [Hillary Clinton]: Latest Libyan Leadership Private Discussions and Plans, 25 October 2012; Cheryl Mills (State Department), e-mail to H [Hillary Clinton]: Inquiry into Libya Attack Is Sharply Critical of State Department (NYT), 18 December 2012; Sid [Sidney Blumenthal], e-mail memorandum for H [Hillary Clinton]: Comprehensive Intel Report on Libya, 4 January 2013; Sid [Sidney Blumenthal], e-mail memorandum for H [Hillary Clinton] (forwarded by Clinton to State Department): Libya internal government discussions, 15 January 2013; Sid [Sidney Blumenthal], e-mail memorandum for H [Hillary Clinton] (forwarded by Clinton to Jake Sullivan, State Department): Libya internal security deliberations, 25 January 2013, SDRR; *Report of the US Senate Select Committee on Intelligence Review of the Terrorist Attacks on US Facilities in Benghazi, Libya, September 11–12, 2012*, 15 January 2014.
121. Blake, *From Russia with Blood*, p. 229.
122. 'The 14 Cases Attracting Attention of Investigators', *The Times*, 14 March 2018, pp. 6–7.
123. Steven Swinford, 'Medvedev Threatens *The Times* over Coverage of Russian General's Killing', *The Times*, 18 December 2024.
124. David Gioe, Michael Goodman and David Frey, 'Unforgiven: Russian Intelligence Vengeance as Political Theatre and Strategic Messaging', *Intelligence and National Security*, 34 (2019), pp. 561–75.
125. Francis Elliott, 'May Gives EU Details of Banished Spies', *The Times*, 22 March 2018, p. 7; 'Salisbury Novichok Poisoning: Russian Nationals Named as Suspects', *BBC News*, 5 September 2018; Mark Urban, *The Skripal Files: Putin, Poison and the New Spy War* (Pan, 2019), Chapter 21.
126. 'Russia "Behind Berlin Murder"', *The Times*, 11 September 2019, p. 28; Oliver Moody and Tom Parfitt, 'Germany Expels Two Russian Spies over Berlin Assassination', *The Times*, 5 December 2019, p. 1.
127. Department of State, Jamal Khashoggi – Timeline, 16 November 2018, SDRR.
128. Michael Evans, 'CIA Wins Back Control of Drone Strikes', *The Times*, 15 March 2017, p. 31; Phoebe Greenwood, 'Anger and Mistrust in Gaza as Hamas Hunts

129. for Israel "Collaborators"', *Guardian*, 19 July 2017; Richard Spencer, 'Israel Hits Hamas Banker after Palestinian Strikes', *The Times*, 6 May 2019, p. 30.
129. Glen Segell, 'Israel's Intelligence-Gathering and Analysis for the Target Assassination of Baha Abu al-Ata (2019)', *Defense & Security Analysis*, 38 (2022), pp. 53–73.
130. Sid [Sidney Blumenthal], e-mail memorandum for H [Hillary Clinton]: Saudi Arabia/Iran/Turkey (Source: Sources with access to the highest levels of the Government of Turkey, and Saudi Arabia, as well as regional and Western Intelligence services), 12 October 2011, SDRR; Catherine Philp, 'Iran "Killed Dissidents" on Dutch Soil', *The Times*, 9 January 2019, p. 27.
131. Kenneth McKenzie, 'I Carried out the Strike that Killed Soleimani: America Doesn't Understand the Lesson of his Death', *Atlantic*, 24 May 2024.
132. Jared Kushner, *Breaking History: A White House Memoir* (Broadside, 2022), pp. 297–301.
133. Maxim Tucker, 'Rebel Leader Killed by Bomb in Rubbish Shoot', *The Times*, 18 October 2016, p. 34.
134. Adam Entous and Michael Schwirz, 'CIA's Ukraine Alliance Deepened over a Decade', *New York Times*, 26 February 2024, A1.
135. Julian Barnes, Adam Goldman, Adam Entous and Michael Schwirtz, 'US Believes Ukrainians Were Behind an Assassination in Russia', *New York Times*, 5 October 2022.
136. Maxim Tucker, 'How Ukraine Uses Mossad Tactics to Hunt Down Russian War Criminals', *The Times*, 20 December 2024 and Marc Bennetts, 'Inside Ukraine's Shadowy Hit Squads Targeting its Russian Enemies', *The Times*, 17 December 2024.
137. Marc Santora, 'Kremlin's Pick to Lead Kyiv Is Shot in Crimea', *New York Times*, 29 October 2023, A6.
138. Snejana Farberov, 'Ukraine Admits Blowing up Putin Ally in Car Bomb, Calls It Warning for "Traitors" and "War Criminals"', *New York Post*, 8 November 2023.
139. Jaroslav Lukiv, 'Ukraine Claims Killing of "Traitor" ex-MP Illya Kyva in Russia', *BBC News*, 6 December 2023.
140. Andrew Roth and Pjotr Sauer, 'Russian Defector Sheds Light on Putin Paranoia and his Secret Train Network', *Guardian*, 5 April 2023.
141. Panetta, *Worthy Fights*, Chapter 13.
142. Ryan Crocker, Oral History 9–10 September 2010; Michael Hayden, *Playing to the Edge: American Intelligence in the Age of Terror* (Penguin, 2016), p. 197.
143. Tim Reid and Damian Whitworth, 'A Force of Thousands with One Objective: Protect the President', *The Times*, 20 January 2009, p. 4.
144. Committee on Oversight and Government Reform, House of Representatives, Report 114-385, *United States Secret Service in Crisis*, 18 December 2015.
145. Bush, *Decision Points*, p. 263.
146. Brandon Drenon, 'Secret Service Agent Assigned to Naomi Biden Fires Gun amid Car Break-In', *BBC News*, 13 November 2023.
147. *United States Secret Service in Crisis*, 18 December 2015.
148. 117th Congress, Second Session, House Report 117-663, *Final Report of the Select Committee to Investigate the January 6th Attack on the United States Capitol*, 22 December 2022; Select Committee to Investigate the January 6th Attack on the US Capitol, US House of Representatives, Interview of Anthony Ornato [Deputy Chief of Operations, White House, and USSS], 29 November 2022.

149. *United States Secret Service in Crisis*, 18 December 2015.
150. Richard Beeston, 'Dangerous Diplomacy', *The Times*, 30 October 2002, p. 51.
151. Cheryl Mills, e-mail to H: Inquiry into Libya Attack is Sharply Critical of State Department (NYT), 18 December 2012.
152. Worldwide Personal Protective Services (WPPS II) Contracts, Task Order Request 2006-0007, Adjustment Number 4, 18 April 2007; Worldwide Personal Protective Services (WPPS II) Contracts, Task Order Request 2009-0012, 9 February 2009, SDRR.
153. Cowper-Coles, *Cables from Kabul*, Chapter 23 and Chapter 2.
154. *Report of the US Senate Select Committee on Intelligence Review of the Terrorist Attacks on US Facilities in Benghazi, Libya, September 11–12, 2012*, 15 January 2014; Cheryl Mills, e-mail to H: Inquiry into Libya Attack is Sharply Critical of State Department (NYT), 18 December 2012.
155. Adam Sage, 'Pim Fortuyn's Killer is Jailed for 18 Years', *The Times*, 16 April 2003, p. 18.
156. Peter Riddell, 'Assassinations Leave Legacy of Bodyguards and Barriers', *The Times*, 7 May 2002, p. 6.
157. Anthony Browne, 'Film-maker is Murdered for His Art', *The Times*, 3 November 2004, p. 3.
158. Cynthia Kroet, 'Geert Wilders Protected by Special Military Unit', *Politico.eu*, 1 March 2017.
159. Tristan Kirk, 'Prince Harry to Appeal after Losing High Court Security Case', *Evening Standard*, 28 February 2024; Blake, *From Russia with Blood*, p. 240.
160. Sasha Swire, *Diary of an MP's Wife: Inside and Outside Power* (Little, Brown, 2020), 1 July 2010.
161. Philip Webster, 'I'm More Likely to be Assassinated Here than in Baghdad, Says Blair', *The Times*, 22 June 2007, p. 7.
162. Oliver August, 'Taiwan's Leader Shot by Gunman', *The Times*, 20 March 2004, p. 22.
163. 'Chen Was Shot', *The Times*, 1 April 2004, p. 20.
164. 'Footage Reveals Moments before Slovakian PM is Shot', *Guardian*, 16 May 2024 (Source: YouTube/RTV Prievidza).
165. US Department of Homeland Security, Report of the Independent Review Panel on the July 13, 2024 Assassination Attempt in Butler, Pennsylvania, 15 October 2024.
166. 'Attempted Assassination of Former President Donald Trump', C-SPAN Classroom, https://www.cspan.org/classroom/document/?2287 [accessed 14 July 2024].
167. Edvard Unsgaard and Reid Meloy, 'The Assassination of the Swedish Minister of Foreign Affairs', *Journal of Forensic Sciences*, 56 (2011), pp. 555–9.
168. Yoshifumi Takemoto and Ju-min Park, 'Abe Assassination Raises Questions about Security for VIPs in Japan', *Reuters*, 8 July 2022.
169. Bush, *Decision Points*, p. 266; John Sakellariadis, 'Iran Has a Hit List of Former Trump Aides', *Politico*, 11 October 2024.
170. Office of the Inspector General, Department of Justice, *Audit of the US Marshals Service Judicial Security Activities* (June 2021).
171. Richard Ford, Dominic Kennedy and John Simpson, 'Killer Was Muslim Convert', *The Times*, 24 March 2017, p. 1; Mark Lucraft, Chief Coroner of

England and Wales, *Inquests Arising from the Deaths in the Westminster Terror Attack on 22 March 2017: Regulation 28 Report on Action to Prevent Future Deaths*, 19 December 2018.
172. Adam Taylor, 'Spate of Global Assassination Attempts Hints at a Violent New Era', *Washington Post*, 4 November 2022.
173. Oliver Moody, 'Fear of Far Right Attacks as Man Held for Killing Politician', *The Times*, 19 June 2019, p. 36.
174. Sarah Marsh and Andreas Rinke, 'Germany Denounces Spate of Attacks on Politicians Recalling "Darkest Era" of Its History', *Reuters*, 4 May 2024.
175. 'German Ministers Demand Tough Response to Political Violence', *Deutsche Welle*, 7 May 2024; 'German Court Upholds AfD "Suspected" Extremist Status', *Deutsche Welle*, 13 May 2024.
176. Lewis Adams, 'Sir David Amess Murder', *BBC News*, 17 January 2024.
177. Steven Swinford, 'MPs to Get Bodyguards and "Surge" Police Patrols', *The Times*, 28 February 2024.
178. Hugh O'Connell, 'Politicians Get 25,000 Euros Each to Boost Security', *Sunday Times*, 15 December 2024.
179. Zach Montellaro, 'Threats Against Politicians are Prevalent. The FEC Wants to Let Campaigns Pay for Security', *Politico*, 27 March 2024; Andrew Solender, 'Hakeem Jeffries Demands "Maximum Protection" for Members after Thanksgiving Bomb Threats', *Axios*, 29 November 2024.

Conclusion

1. Arie Perliger, 'The Role of Civil Wars and Elections in Inducing Political Assassinations', *Studies in Conflict and Terrorism*, 40 (2017), pp. 684–700; Margaret Wilson, Angela Scholes and Elizabeth Brocklehurst, 'A Behavioural Analysis of Terrorist Action: The Assassination and Bombing Campaign of ETA between 1980 and 2007', *British Journal of Criminology*, 50 (2010), pp. 690–707; Francesco Marone, 'A Farewell to Firearms? The Logic of Weapon Selection in Terrorism: The Case of Jihadist Attacks in Europe', *Global Change, Peace and Security*, 33 (2021), pp. 221–40.
2. Paul Gillespie, *Weapons of Choice: The Development of Precision Guided Munitions* (University of Alabama Press, 2006).
3. Ronald Reagan, Remarks on Signing the Bill Making the Birthday of Martin Luther King, Jr. a National Holiday, November 2, 1983, RDA.
4. Commission of Inquiry into Mahatma Gandhi Murder Conspiracy [The Kumar Inquiry]. Proceedings of April 27, 1968, Witness No. 79: Miss Mani Ben Patel, MP, Papers Sent for Gandhi Murder Trial Case, Papers of Sardar Patel, NAI.
5. 'France and Egypt: British Action Criticized', *The Times*, 25 November 1924, p. 14.
6. House of Commons, *Debates*, 15 December 1924, 646-756, FO 141/502, TNA.
7. 'Cynical German Comment: Sympathy with Egyptian Revolutionaries', *The Times*, 25 November 1924, p. 14.
8. 'Iran Vows to Avenge Killing of Hamas Political Leader Haniyeh', *BBC News*, 31 July 2024; Kara Fox, 'Israel Has Killed Multiple Hezbollah Leaders', *CNN*, 23 October 2024; Ian Aikman, 'Israel Confirms It Killed Hamas Leader Haniyeh in Tehran', *BBC News*, 23 December 2024.

9. Brad Dress, 'Israeli Police Say They Thwarted Iranian Assassination Attempt', *The Hill*, 19 September 2024; Renee Maltezou, Cassell Bryan-Low, Yannis Souliotis and Phil Stewart, 'Murder for Hire: Inside Iran's Proxy War with Israel in the West', *Reuters*, 5 October 2024; 'US Charges Iranian Man in Plot to kill Donald Trump, DOJ Says', *Reuters*, 9 November 2024.

BIBLIOGRAPHY

Manuscript Sources

The National Archives, London (TNA)

CAB 16	Committee of Imperial Defence, Ad Hoc Sub-Committees: Minutes, Memoranda and Reports
CAB 24	War Cabinet and Cabinet: Memoranda
CAB 104	Cabinet Office and predecessors: Supplementary Registered Files
CAB 128	Cabinet Conclusions
CAB 158	Joint Intelligence Committee: Memoranda
CAB 159	Joint Intelligence Sub-Committee, later Committee: Minutes
CAB 163	Joint Intelligence Sub-Committee, later Committee: Secretariat Files
CAB 185	Joint Intelligence Committee (A): Minutes
CAB 186	Joint Intelligence Committee (A): Memoranda
CAB 190	Joint Intelligence Committee: Working Groups and Working Parties
CAB 191	Overseas Joint Intelligence Groups: Fragmentary Reports
CJ 4	Home Office and Northern Ireland Office: Registered Files
DEFE 4	Ministry of Defence: Chiefs of Staff Committee Minutes
CO 537	Colonial Office: Kenya Original Correspondence
CO 733	Colonial Office: Palestine Original Correspondence and Other Records
CO 1022	Colonial Office: South East Asia Department Original Correspondence
CO 1035	Colonial Office: Intelligence and Security Departments Registered Files
DO 35	Dominions Office and Commonwealth Relations Office: Original Correspondence
DO 195	Commonwealth Relations Office and Commonwealth Office: West and General Africa Department and successors: Registered Files
FCO 7	Foreign and Commonwealth Office: American and Latin American Departments Registered Files

BIBLIOGRAPHY

FCO 8	Foreign Office and Foreign and Commonwealth Office: Middle East Department Registered Files
FCO 9	Foreign Office and Foreign and Commonwealth Office: Southern European Department Registered Files
FCO 15	Foreign Office and Foreign and Commonwealth Office: South East Asian Department Registered Files
FCO 17	Foreign Office: Eastern Department and successors Registered Files
FCO 21	Foreign Office and Foreign and Commonwealth Office: Far Eastern Department Registered Files
FCO 28	Foreign and Commonwealth Office: Northern Department and East European and Soviet Departments and successors Registered Files
FCO 31	Foreign Office and Foreign and Commonwealth Office: East Africa Department Registered Files
FCO 33	Foreign Office and Foreign and Commonwealth Office: Western Department and Western European Department Registered Files
FCO 37	Foreign Office and Foreign and Commonwealth Office: South Asia Department Registered Files
FCO 39	Foreign Office and Foreign and Commonwealth Office: North and East African Department and successors Registered Files
FCO 44	Foreign and Commonwealth Office: West Indian Department Registered Files
FCO 57	Foreign Office and Foreign and Commonwealth Office: Protocol and Conference Department Registered Files
FCO 63	Foreign and Commonwealth Office: North American and Caribbean and Caribbean Department Registered Files
FCO 87	Foreign and Commonwealth Office: Republic of Ireland Department Registered Files
FCO 93	Foreign and Commonwealth Office: Near East and North Africa Department Registered Files
FCO 141	Foreign and Commonwealth Office and predecessors: Records of Former Colonial Administrations Migrated Archives
FCO 160	Foreign and Commonwealth Office: Diplomatic Reports and Diplomatic Documents
FCO 169	Foreign and Commonwealth Office: Central and Southern Africa Department Registered Files
FCO 175	Foreign and Commonwealth Office: Central European Department Registered Files
FCO 178	Foreign and Commonwealth Office: Security Co-ordination Department Registered Files
FO 141	Foreign Office: Embassy and Consulates, Egypt General Correspondence
FO 371	Foreign Office: Political Departments General Correspondence
FO 921	War Cabinet: Office of the Minister of State Resident in the Middle East Registered Files
FO 1093	Foreign Office: Permanent Under-Secretary's Department: Registered and Unregistered Papers
HO 144	Home Office: Registered Papers, Supplementary
HO 287	Home Office: Police Files
HS 3	Special Operations Executive: Africa and Middle East Group Registered Files

BIBLIOGRAPHY

HS 6	Special Operations Executive: Western Europe Registered Files
HS 7	Special Operations Executive: Histories and War Diaries Registered Files
HS 8	Special Operations Executive: Headquarters Records
HW 11	Government Code and Cypher School: WW2 Official Histories
HW 12	Government Code and Cypher School: Diplomatic Section and predecessors Decrypts of Intercepted Diplomatic Communications
HW 13	Government Code and Cypher School: WW2 Intelligence Summaries based on Sigint
INF 3	Ministry of Information: Official Artwork
KV 2	Security Service: Personal Files
KV 3	Security Service: Subject Files
KV 4	Security Service: Policy Files
LITV 2	Records of the Inquiry into the Death of Alexander Litvinenko on 23 November 2006: Evidence, Correspondence and Report
MEPO 2	Metropolitan Police: Office of the Commissioner Correspondence and Papers
PREM 3	Prime Minister's Office: Operational Correspondence and Papers
PREM 4	Prime Minister's Office: Confidential Correspondence and Papers
PREM 8	Prime Minister's Office: Correspondence and Papers, 1945–1951
PREM 11	Prime Minister's Office: Correspondence and Papers, 1951–1964
PREM 15	Prime Minister's Office: Correspondence and Papers, 1970–1974
PREM 16	Prime Minister's Office: Correspondence and Papers, 1974–1979
PREM 19	Prime Minister's Office: Correspondence and Papers, 1979–1997
PRO 30	Original Records acquired as gifts or on deposit
WO 204	War Office: Allied Forces, Mediterranean Theatre Military HQ Papers
WO 219	War Office: Supreme Headquarters Allied Expeditionary Force Military HQ Papers

India Office Records, British Library, London (IOR, BL)

L/P&J	Public and Judicial Department Records
M	Burma Office Records
Mss Eur	Private Papers (European Manuscripts)

Abhilekh Patal, National Archives of India (NAI)

Government of India, Home Department, Political Branch
Government of India, Home Department, Public Branch
Republic of India, Ministry of External Affairs
Republic of India, Ministry of States, Political Branch
Papers of Sardar Patel

US National Archives

President John F. Kennedy Assassination Records Collection (JFK)

Clinton Digital Library, William J. Clinton Presidential Library & Museum (CDL)

DiscoverLBJ, Lyndon Baines Johnson Presidential Library and Museum

BIBLIOGRAPHY

Digitized Archives, Ronald Reagan Presidential Library & Museum (RDA)

Franklin D. Roosevelt Presidential Library and Museum (FDRL), Hyde Park, NY

Federal Bureau of Investigation Files, 1933–1944
Map Room Papers, 1941–1945
Master Speech File
President's Personal File

Online Collections, Harry S. Truman Presidential Library and Museum

CIA Freedom of Information Act Electronic Reading Room (CIA)

FBI Freedom of Information Act Digital Library (FBI)

Department of State Freedom of Information Act Virtual Reading Room (SDRR)

United Nations Library & Archives, Geneva (UNL)

League of Nations: Bulky Enclosures, 1933–1946
League of Nations: Office of the Secretary General, Administrative Commissions and Minorities Section
League of Nations: Private Archives

Cambridge South Asian Archive, Centre of South Asian Studies (CSAA), University of Cambridge

D. Gordon Papers
G.H.R. Halland Papers
P.E.S. Finney Papers
H. Quinton Papers
S.G. Taylor Papers
C.A. Tegart Papers

Cambridge University Library, University of Cambridge (CUL)

Add. 8316   Papers of Foss Westcott
Templewood   Papers of Sir Samuel Hoare

Churchill Archives Centre, Churchill College, Cambridge (CAC)

GNWR Papers of Baron Gordon-Walker
THCR   Papers of Baroness Thatcher (via Margaret Thatcher Foundation Archive)

Durham University Library, Durham (DUL)

HIL   Papers of Abbas Hilmi II

Brotherton Library, University of Leeds

MS. 405 Papers of Sir Edward Boyle

BIBLIOGRAPHY

Middle East Centre Archive, St Antony's College, Oxford (MECA)

GB165-0001	Adamson Papers
GB165-0005	Allenby Papers
GB165-0072	Cunningham Papers
GB165-0176	Killearn Papers
GB165-0193	MacGillivray Papers
GB165-0247	Russell Papers
GB165-0249	Ryder Papers
GB165-0281	Tegart Papers
GB165-0290	UNSCOP Papers
GB165-0409	Mellor Papers

Bodleian Library, Special Collections, Oxford University (Bodleian)

MSS AAM   Files of the Anti-Apartheid Movement
MSS Afr. s. 2204 Papers of Sir Robert Armitage

Royal Anthropological Institute, London

Durham MSS   Papers of Edith Durham

School of Slavonic and East European Studies, University College London (SSEES)

PANN   Papers of Heinz Pannwitz
SEW   Papers of Robert Seton-Watson

Miller Center, University of Virginia

Transcript of John Bellinger Oral History, Part II, 20 April 2013
Transcript of Samuel Berger Oral History, 24 & 25 March 2005
Transcript of Ryan Crocker Oral History, 9 & 10 September 2010
Transcript of Robert Gates Oral History, 8 July 2013
Transcript of Anthony Lake Oral History, 21 May 2002
Transcript of James Woolsey Oral History, 13 January 2010

Archives Unbound

Gerald R. Ford and Foreign Affairs Microfilm Collection
Shanghai Municipal Police Files, 1894–1945 Microfilm Collection

Digital National Security Archive (DNSA)

Afghanistan: The Making of US Policy, 1973–1990
Argentina, 1975–1980: The Making of US Human Rights Policy
Chile and the United States: US Policy toward Democracy
CIA Covert Operations II: The Year of Intelligence, 1975
CIA Covert Operations III: From Kennedy to Nixon, 1961–1974
CIA Covert Operations IV: The Eisenhower Years, 1953–1961
CIA Covert Operations: From Carter to Obama, 1977–2010

BIBLIOGRAPHY

Colombia and the United States: Political Violence, Narcotics, and Human Rights, 1948–2010

Cuba and the US: The Declassified History of Negotiations to Normalize Relations, 1959–2016

The Cuban Missile Crisis, 1962

Cuban Missile Crisis Revisited: An International Collection from Bay of Pigs to Nuclear Brink

Death Squads, Guerrilla War, Covert Ops, and Genocide: Guatemala and the US, 1954–1999

The Kissinger Telephone Conversations: A Verbatim Record of US Diplomacy, 1969–1977

National Security Agency: Organization and Operations, 1945–2009

Nicaragua: The Making of US Policy, 1978–1990

Targeting Iraq, Part 1: Planning, Invasion, and Occupation, 1997–2004

Terrorism and US Policy, 1968–2002

US Intelligence Community: Organization, Operations and Management, 1947–1989

US Policy in the Vietnam War, Part 1, 1954–1968

The US and the Two Koreas, 1969–2000

United States Declassified Documents Online (USDDO)

Wilson Center Digital Archive (WCDA)

Printed Manuscript Sources

Cd. 9190, East India (Sedition Committee, 1918), *Report of a Committee appointed to Investigate Revolutionary Conspiracies in India*.

Cmd. 4014, *Measures taken to counteract the Civil Disobedience Movement and to deal with the Terrorist Movement in Bengal*, February 1932.

Cmnd. 814, *Report of the Nyasaland Commission of Enquiry*, July 1959.

Cmnd. 815, *Nyasaland: Despatch by the Governor relating to the Report of the Nyasaland Commission of Enquiry*, 21 July 1959.

Cmnd. 3165, *Report by Mr Roderic Bowen, QC, on Procedures for the Arrest, Interrogation and Detention of Suspected Terrorists in Aden*, 14 November 1966.

Cmnd. 7932, *Report of the Commissioner of Police of the Metropolis for the Year 1979*, June 1980.

Cmnd. 8254, *Report of the Commissioner of Police of the Metropolis for the Year 1980*, June 1981.

India Office, *The Bengal Criminal Law Amendment Act*, 20 February 1925.

Joint Committee on Indian Constitutional Reform, 1933–34, *Report*, Volume I (Part 1), 31 October 1934.

HC 695, *The Litvinenko Inquiry: Report into the Death of Alexander Litvinenko*, 21 January 2016.

Mark Lucraft, Chief Coroner of England and Wales, *Inquests Arising from the Deaths in the Westminster Terror Attack on 22 March 2017: Regulation 28 Report on Action to Prevent Future Deaths*, 19 December 2018.

Report of the Commission of Inquiry on Civil Rights in Puerto Rico, 22 May 1937.

The 9/11 Commission Report, 2006.

BIBLIOGRAPHY

Wilber, Donald, *Clandestine Service History: Overthrow of Premier Mossadeq of Iran*, November 1952–August 1953, March 1954 (as published by *New York Times*, 18 June 2000).

Presidential Policy Guidance (PPG): Procedures for Approving Direct Action Against Terrorist Targets Located Outside the United States and Areas of Active Hostilities, 22 May 2013.

US Department of Homeland Security, *Report of the Independent Review Panel on the July 13, 2024 Assassination Attempt in Butler, Pennsylvania*, 15 October 2024.

US Department of Justice, David Barron (Acting Assistant Attorney General), Memorandum for the Attorney General: Lethal Operations Against Shaykh Anwar Aulaqi, 19 February 2010.

US Department of Justice, Office of Legal Counsel, Memorandum for the Attorney General: Applicability of Federal Criminal Laws and the Constitution to Contemplated Legal Operations Against Shaykh Anwar al-Aulaqi, 16 July 2010.

US Department of Justice, Office of the Inspector General, *Audit of the US Marshals Service Judicial Security Activities*, June 2021.

US Department of Justice, *Report on the Legal and Policy Frameworks for the United States' Use of Military Force and Related National Security Operations* [November 2022].

US House of Representatives, *Final Report of the Select Committee on Assassinations*, No. 95-1828, 1979.

US House of Representatives, Committee on Oversight and Government Reform, Report 114-385, *United States Secret Service in Crisis*, 18 December 2015.

US House of Representatives, Select Committee to Investigate the January 6th Attack on the US Capitol, Interview of Anthony Ornato, 29 November 2022.

US House of Representatives, *Final Report of the Select Committee to Investigate the January 6th Attack on the United States*, Report 117-663, 22 December 2022.

US Office of the Director of National Intelligence, 'Summary of Information Regarding US Counterterrorism Strikes Outside Areas of Active Hostilities' [July 2016].

US Senate, Committee on Governmental Affairs, *Investigation of Illegal or Improper Activities in Connection with 1996 Federal Election Campaigns*, Vol. 1, March 1998.

US Senate, *Report of the US Senate Select Committee on Intelligence Review of the Terrorist Attacks on US Facilities in Benghazi, Libya, September 11–12, 2012*, 15 January 2014.

Report of Justice Thakkar Commission of Inquiry on the Assassination of the Late Prime Minister Smt. Indira Gandhi: Interim Report, 19 November 1985.

The Jain Commission Report, August 1997 (as published by *India Today*, November 1997).

Commission of Inquiry Regarding the Prevention of Public Violence, *Report by the Committee Appointed to Hold a Workshop to Consider Events after the Assassination and during the Funeral of Mr Chris Hani*, 29 June 1993.

Commission of Inquiry Regarding the Prevention of Public Violence, *Interim Report on Criminal Political Violence by Elements within the South African Police, the KwaZulu Police and the Inkatha Freedom Party*, 18 March 1994.

BIBLIOGRAPHY

Commission on the Responsibility of the Authors of the War and on Enforcement of Penalties, Report Presented to the Preliminary Peace Conference, 29 March 1919, *The American Journal of International Law*, 14 (January–April 1920), pp. 95–154.

International Military Tribunal for the Far East, Judgment of 12 November 1948, in John Pritchard and Sonia Zaide (eds), *The Tokyo War Crimes Trial* (Garland, 1981), vol. XXII.

United Nations, *Report of the International Independent Investigation Commission established pursuant to Security Council resolution 1595 (2005)*, UN Security Council S/2005/662, 19 October 2005.

United Nations, *Third Report of the International Independent Investigation Commission established pursuant to Security Council resolutions 1595 (2005), 1636 (2005) and 1644 (2005)*, UN Security Council S/2006/161, 14 March 2006.

United Nations, *Sixth Report of the International Independent Investigation Commission established pursuant to Security Council resolutions 1595 (2005), 1636 (2005) and 1644 (2005)*, UN Security Council S/2006/962, 12 December 2006.

United Nations, *Seventh Report of the International Independent Investigation Commission established pursuant to Security Council resolutions 1595 (2005), 1636 (2005), 1644 (2005) and 1686 (2006)*, UN Security Council S/2007/150, 15 March 2007.

United Nations, *Report of the United Nations Commission of Inquiry into the facts and circumstances of the assassination of former Pakistani Prime Minister Mohtarma Benazir Bhutto*, 10 April 2010.

British Documents on the Origins of the War, 1898–1914
Vol. XI

Documents on British Foreign Policy, 1919–1939
Ser. 1, Vol. 12
Ser. 1, Vol. 16
Ser. 1, Vol. 20
Ser. 1, Vol. 24
Ser. 1A, Vol. 4
Ser. 2, Vol. 6
Ser. 2, Vol. 9
Ser. 2, Vol. 10
Ser. 2, Vol. 11
Ser. 2, Vol. 12
Ser. 2, Vol. 19
Ser. 2, Vol. 20
Ser. 3, Vol. 8
Ser. 3, Vol. 9

Documents on British Policy Overseas (DBPO)
Ser. 3, Vol. 5

House of Commons, *Debates*
1920, vol. 126
1975, vol. 901

BIBLIOGRAPHY

House of Lords, *Debates*
1972, vol. 335

Foreign Relations of the United States (FRUS)
1928, III
1931, III
1932, IV
1932, V
1933, III
1933, V
1935, III
1936, IV
1938, III
1940, IV
1941, IV
Japan 1931–1941, II
The Soviet Union, 1933–1939

Austrian Red Book: *Official Files Pertaining to Pre-War History, Part I: 28 June to 23 July 1914*

Newspapers, Magazines and Newsletters

Aberdeen Journal
Amrita Bazar Patrika
Atlantic
Axios
BBC News
Christian Science Monitor
Chicago Daily Tribune
China Press
China Weekly Review
Daily Mail
Daily Telegraph
Deutsche Welle
Dundee Evening Telegraph
The Economist
Evening Standard
Fortnightly Review
Forward
Guardian
Independent
India Today
Maclean's Magazine
Manchester Guardian
Le Matin
Le Monde
New York Post
New York Times

BIBLIOGRAPHY

North-China Herald
North American Review
Observer
Picture Post
Politico
Religio
Reuters
Saturday Review
The Scotsman
The Statesman
Sunday Dispatch
Sunday Times
The Times
The Times of India
Times Literary Supplement
Tribune
UN News
Wall Street Journal
Washington Post

Select list of Books and Articles

Ablovatski, Elina, *Revolution and Political Violence in Europe: The Deluge of 1919* (CUP, 2021).

Ahern, Thomas, *CIA and the House of Ngo: Covert Action in South Vietnam, 1954–63* (CIA Center for the Study of Intelligence, 2000).

——, *CIA and Rural Pacification in South Vietnam* (CIA Center for the Study of Intelligence, 2001).

Aissaoui, Rabah, 'Fratricidal War: The Conflict between the Mouvement national algérien (MNA) and the Front de libération nationale (FLN) in France during the Algerian War (1954–1962)', *British Journal of Middle Eastern Studies*, 39 (2012), pp. 227–40.

Alder, Douglas, 'Assassination as Political Efficacy: Two Case Studies from World War I', *East European Quarterly*, 12 (1978), pp. 209–31.

Aldrich, Richard, 'Legacies of Secret Service: Renegade SOE and the Karen Struggle in Burma, 1948–50', *Intelligence and National Security*, 14 (1999), pp. 130–48.

Ambler, Eric, *The Mask of Dimitrios* (Pan, 1999).

André, Marc, 'Les groupes de choc du FLN: Particularités de la guerre d'indépendance algérienne en métropole', *Revue historique*, 669 (2014), pp. 143–78.

Andrew, Christopher, *The Defence of the Realm: The Authorized History of MI5* (Penguin, 2010).

Andrew, Christopher and Vasili Mitrokhin, *The Mitrokhin Archive: The KGB in Europe and the West* (Penguin, 2000).

Baker, Kenneth, *On Assassinations* (Unicorn, 2020).

Ball, Simon, 'Harold Macmillan and the Politics of Defence: The Market for Strategic Ideas in the Sandys Era Revisited', *Twentieth Century British History*, 6 (1995), pp. 78–100.

——, 'Harold Macmillan and Defence Policy', in Richard Aldous and Sabine Lee (eds), *Harold Macmillan and Britain's World Role* (Macmillan, 1996), pp. 67–96.

——, *The Guardsmen: Harold Macmillan, Three Friends, and the World They Made* (HarperCollins, 2004).

BIBLIOGRAPHY

——, 'Banquo's Ghost: Lord Salisbury, Harold Macmillan and the High Politics of Decolonization', *Twentieth Century British History*, 16 (2005), pp. 74–102.

——, 'The Assassination Culture of Imperial Britain, 1909–1979', *Historical Journal*, 56 (2013), pp. 231–56.

——, *Secret History: Writing the Rise of Britain's Intelligence Services* (McGill-Queen's UP, 2020).

——, 'Assassination from MLK to Mrs T: Contrast and Convergence in the United States and Britain', *Diplomacy & Statecraft*, 33 (2022), pp. 64–85.

Banka, Andris and Adam Quinn, 'Killing Norms Softly: US Targeted Killing, Quasi-Secrecy and the Assassination Ban', *Security Studies*, 27 (2018), pp. 655–703.

Barnes, Harry Elmer, 'Assessing the Blame for World War: A Revised Judgment Based on All the Available Documents', *Current History*, 20/2 (1924), pp. 171–95.

Barros, Andrew, 'A Window on the "Trust": The Case of Ado Birk', *Intelligence and National Security*, 10 (1995), pp. 273–93.

Barton, Mary, 'The British Empire and International Terrorism', *Journal of British Studies*, 56 (2017), pp. 351–73.

Bass, Gary, *Judgement at Tokyo: World War II on Trial and the Making of Modern Asia* (Picador, 2023).

Becker, Howard, 'Max Weber, Assassination, and German Guilt: An Interview with Marianne Weber', *American Journal of Economics and Sociology*, 10 (1951), pp. 401–5.

Bell, Laura, 'Terrorist Assassinations and Target Selection', *Studies in Conflict and Terrorism*, 40 (2017), pp. 157–71.

——, 'Terrorist Assassination and Institutional Change in Repressive Regimes', *Terrorism and Political Violence*, 31 (2019), pp. 853–75.

Benesch, Oleg, 'The Samurai Next Door: Chinese Examinations of the Japanese Martial Spirit', *Extrême Orient-Extrême Occident*, 38 (2014), pp. 129–68.

Benjamin, Jules, 'The *Machadato* and Cuban Nationalism, 1928–1932', *Hispanic American Historical Review*, 55 (1975), pp. 66–91.

Ben-Yehuda, Nachman, 'Conflict Resolution in an Underground Group: The Shamir-Giladi Clash', *Studies in Conflict and Terrorism*, 12 (1989), pp. 199–212.

——, 'Gathering Dark Secrets, Hidden and Dirty Information: Some Methodological Notes on Studying Political Assassination', *Qualitative Sociology*, 13 (1990), 345–71.

——, 'Political Assassination Events as a Cross-Cultural Form of Alternative Justice', *International Journal of Comparative Sociology*, 38 (1997), pp. 25–47.

Berridge, W.J., 'Imperialist and Nationalist Voices in the Struggle for Egyptian Independence, 1919–22', *Journal of Imperial and Commonwealth History*, 42 (2014), pp. 420–39.

Bickers, Robert, 'Death of a Young Shanghailander: The Thorburn Case and the Defence of the British Treaty Ports in China in 1931', *Modern Asian Studies*, 30 (1996), pp. 271–300.

——, 'Shanghailanders: The Formation and Identity of the British Settler Community in Shanghai, 1843–1949', *Past & Present*, 159 (1998), pp. 161–211.

Bielenberg, Andy and Pádraig Óg Ó Ruairc, 'Shallow Graves: Documenting and Assessing IRA Disappearances during the Irish Revolution, 1919–1923', *Small Wars & Insurgencies*, 32 (2021), pp. 619–41.

Birstein, Vadim, 'Soviet Military Counterintelligence from 1918 to 1929', *International Journal of Intelligence and Counterintelligence*, 25 (2012), pp. 44–110.

Blake, Heidi, *From Russia with Blood: Putin's Ruthless Killing Campaign and Secret War on the West* (HarperCollins, 2019).

BIBLIOGRAPHY

Bodó, Béla, 'Paramilitary Violence in Hungary after the First World War', *East European Quarterly*, 38 (2004), pp. 129–72.

——, 'Hungarian Aristocracy and the White Terror', *Journal of Contemporary History*, 45 (2010), pp. 703–24.

Böhler, Jochen, 'Enduring Violence: The Postwar Struggles in East-Central Europe, 1917–1921', *Journal of Contemporary History*, 50 (2015), pp. 58–77.

Borgonovo, John, *Spies, Informers and the 'Anti-Sinn Féin Society': The Intelligence War in Cork City, 1920–1921* (Irish Academic Press, 2007).

Bowden, Tom, 'The Irish Underground and the Irish War of Independence, 1919–1921', *Journal of Contemporary History*, 8 (1973), pp. 3–23.

Boyer, John, 'Silent War and Bitter Peace: The Revolution of 1918 in Austria', *Austrian History Yearbook*, 34 (2003), pp. 1–56.

Boyle, Michael J., *The Drone Age: How Drone Technology Will Change War and Peace* (OUP, 2020).

Brennan, John, *Undaunted: My Fight against America's Enemies, At Home and Abroad* (Celadon, 2022).

Bridge, F.R., 'The British Elite and the Sarajevo Assassinations', in Mark Cornwall (ed.), *Sarajevo 1914: Sparking the First World War* (Bloomsbury, 2015), Chapter 10.

Bruce Lockhart, R.H., *Memoirs of a British Agent* (Pan, 2002 [1932]).

Brunk, Samuel, 'Remembering Emiliano Zapata: Three Moments in the Posthumous Career of the Martyr of Chinameca', *Hispanic American Historical Review*, 78 (1998), pp. 457–90.

Bures, Oldrich and Andrew Hawkins, 'Israeli Targeted Killing Operations before and during the Second Intifada: A Contextualized Comparison', *Small Wars & Insurgencies*, 31 (2020), pp. 569–93.

Burleigh, Michael, *Day of the Assassins: A History of Political Murder* (Picador, 2021).

Bush, George, *Decision Points* (Virgin, 2010).

Byas, Hugh, *Government by Assassination* (Alfred Knopf, 1942).

Byman, Daniel, *A High Price: The Triumphs and Failures of Israeli Counterterrorism* (OUP, 2011).

Caden, Christopher and Nir Arielli, 'British Army and Palestine Police Deserters and the Arab-Israeli War of 1948', *War in History*, 28 (2021), pp. 200–22.

Callwell, C.E., *Field-Marshal Sir Henry Wilson: His Life and Diaries* (2 vols, London, 1927).

Canali, Mauro, 'The Matteotti Murder and the Origins of Mussolini's Totalitarian Fascist Regime in Italy', *Journal of Modern Italian Studies*, 14 (2009), pp. 143–67.

Carnaghi, Benedetta, 'Mussolini's Four Would-be Assassins: Emergency Politics and the Consolidation of Fascist Power', *Journal of Modern Italian Studies*, 27 (2022), pp. 1–18.

Carrington, Michael, 'Officers, Gentlemen, and Murderers: Lord Curzon's Campaign against "Collisions" between Indians and Europeans, 1899–1905', *Modern Asian Studies*, 47 (2013), pp. 780–819.

Carroll, Rory, *Killing Thatcher: The IRA, the Manhunt and the Long War on the Crown* (HarperCollins, 2023).

Carstocea, Raul, 'Breaking the Teeth of Time: Mythical Time and the "Terror of History" in the Rhetoric of the Legionary Movement in Interwar Rumania', *Journal of Modern European History*, 13 (2015), pp. 79–97.

Castro Martínez, Pedro, 'El asesinato del general Álvaro Obregón: las caras de un imaginario dividido', *Iztapalapa*, 61 (2008), pp. 143–68.

BIBLIOGRAPHY

Cesarani, David, 'The War on Terror that Failed: British Counter-Insurgency in Palestine 1945–1947 and the "Farran Affair"', *Small Wars & Insurgencies*, 23 (2012), pp. 648–70.

Chapin, Ellen, Stephanie Lizzo and Jason Warner, 'Al-Shabaab's Assassinations: Investigating the Uniqueness of Al-Shabaab's Assassination via Suicide Bombings', *Journal of the Middle East and Africa*, 12 (2021), pp. 321–41.

Chaturvedi, Vinayak, 'Violence as Civility: V.D. Savarkar and the Mahatma's Assassination', *South Asian History and Culture*, 11 (2020), pp. 239–53.

Cheney, Dick, *In My Time: A Personal and Political Memoir* (Threshold Editions, 2011).

Childers, Jay, 'The Democratic Balance: President McKinley's Assassination as Domestic Trauma', *Quarterly Journal of Speech*, 99 (2013), pp. 156–79.

Chin, John, Abel Escribà-Folch, Wonjun Song and Joseph Wright, 'Reshaping the Threat Environment: Personalism, Coups, and Assassination', *Comparative Political Studies*, 55 (2022), pp. 657–87.

Chin, Sei Jeong, 'The Historical Origins of the Nationalization of the Newspaper Industry in Modern China: A Case Study of the Newspaper Industry, 1937–1953', *China Review*, 13 (2013), pp. 1–34.

——, 'Print Capitalism, War, and the Remaking of the Mass Media in 1930s China', *Modern China*, 40 (2014), pp. 393–425.

Choudhury, D.K. Lahiri, 'Sinews of Panic and the Nerves of Empire: The Imagined State's Entanglement with Information Panic, India c. 1880–1912', *Modern Asian Studies*, 38 (2004), pp. 965–1002.

Churchill, Winston, *The World Crisis, Volume I, 1911–1914* (Odhams Press, 1938 [1923]).

Clapper, James, *Facts and Fears: Hard Truths from a Life in Intelligence* (Penguin, 2018).

Clark, Christopher, *The Sleepwalkers: How Europe Went to War in 1914* (Penguin, 2013).

Cline, Catherine Ann, 'British Historians and the Treaty of Versailles', *Albion*, 20 (1988), pp. 43–8.

Cohen, Michael, 'British Strategy and the Palestine Question, 1936–39', *Journal of Contemporary History*, 7 (1972), pp. 157–83.

——, 'Sir Arthur Wauchope, the Army and the Rebellion in Palestine, 1936', *Middle Eastern Studies*, 9 (1973), pp. 20–34.

Coll, Steve, *Directorate S: The CIA and America's Secret Wars in Afghanistan and Pakistan, 2001–2016* (Penguin, 2008),

Condos, Mark, 'The Indian "Alsatia": Sovereignty, Extradition, and the Limits of Franco-British Colonial Policing', *Journal of Imperial and Commonwealth History*, 48 (2020), pp. 101–26.

Connelly, Matthew, *A Diplomatic Revolution: Algeria's Fight for Independence and the Origins of the Post-Cold War Era* (OUP, 2002).

Cormac, Rory, *Disrupt and Deny: Spies, Special Forces, and the Secret Pursuit of British Foreign Policy* (OUP, 2018).

Cornish, Paul, 'Weapons and Equipment of the Special Operations Executive', in Mark Seaman (ed.), *Special Operations Executive: A New Instrument of War* (Routledge, 2006), pp. 22–32.

Cœuré, Sophie and Frédéric Monier, 'Paul Gorgulov Assassin de Paul Doumer (1932)', *Vingtième Siècle*, 65 (2000), pp. 35–46.

BIBLIOGRAPHY

Cowper-Coles, Sherard, *Cables from Kabul: The Inside Story of the West's Afghanistan Campaign* (Harper Press, 2011).

Darwin, John, 'The Central African Emergency, 1959', *Journal of Imperial and Commonwealth History*, 21 (1993), pp. 217–34.

Davenport, Christian and Molly Inman, 'The State of State Repression Research since the 1990s', *Terrorism and Political Violence*, 24 (2012), pp. 619–34.

Delaporte, Victor, 'Aux origines de la Cour de sûreté de l'État', *Vingtième Siècle*, 140 (2018), pp. 137–52.

Diamond, Gregory (ed.), *The Unexpurgated Pike Report: Report of the House Select Committee on Intelligence* (McGraw-Hill, 1992).

Dmitriev, Timofey, 'Max Weber and Peter Struve on the Russian Revolution', *Studies in East European Thought*, 69 (2017), pp. 305–28.

Dolan, Anne, 'Killing and Bloody Sunday, November 1920', *Historical Journal*, 49 (2006), pp. 789–810.

Dubin, M.D., 'Great Britain and the Anti-Terrorist Conventions of 1937', *Terrorism and Political Violence*, 5 (1993), pp. 1–29.

Dull, Paul, 'The Assassination of Chang Tso-Lin', *Far Eastern Quarterly*, 11 (1952), pp. 453–63.

Durham, M. Edith, *The Serajevo Crime* (George Allen & Unwin, 1925).

——, 'Fresh Light on the Serajevo Crime', *Contemporary Review*, CXXXVII (1925), pp. 39–49.

Eastman, Lloyd, 'Fascism in Kuomintang China: The Blue Shirts', *China Quarterly*, 49 (1972), pp. 1–31.

Eberle, Henrik and Matthias Uhl (eds), *The Hitler Book: The Secret Dossier Prepared for Stalin* (John Murray, 2005).

Eich, Stefan and Adam Tooze, 'The Allure of Dark Times: Max Weber, Politics, and the Crisis of Historicism', *History and Theory*, 56 (2017), pp. 197–215.

Eismann, Gaël, 'Maintenir l'ordre: Le MBF et la sécurité locale en France occupée', *Vingtième Siècle*, 98 (2008), pp. 125–39.

——, 'Le Militärbefehlshaber in Frankreich et la genèse de la "solution finale" en France (1941–1942)', *Vingtième Siècle*, 132 (2016), pp. 43–59.

Elpeleg, Zvi, *The Grand Mufti: Haj Amin al-Hussaini, Founder of the Palestinian National Movement* (Frank Cass, 1993).

Eyerman, Ron, *The Cultural Sociology of Political Assassination: From MLK and RFK to Fortuyn and van Gogh* (Palgrave Macmillan, 2011).

Fay, Sidney Bradshaw, 'Serbia's Responsibility for the World War', *Current History*, 23/1 (October 1925), pp. 41–8.

Field, G. Lowell, 'Comparative Aspects of Fascism', *Southwestern Social Science Quarterly*, 20 (January 1939), pp. 349–60.

Finch, Michael, 'A Total War of the Mind: The French Theory of *la guerre révolutionnaire*, 1954–1958', *War in History*, 25 (2018), pp. 410–34.

Fink, Carole, 'The Murder of Walther Rathenau', *Judaism*, 44 (1995), pp. 259–70.

——, 'As Little a Surprise as a Murder Can Be': Ausländische Reaktionen auf den Mord an Walther Rathenau', in Hans Wilderotter (ed.), *Walther Rathenau, 1867–1922: Die Extreme berühren sich* (DHM, n.d.), pp. 237–46.

Finley-Croswhite, Annette and Gayle Brunelle, 'Lighting the Fuse: Terrorism as Violent Political Discourse in Interwar France', in Chris Millington and Kevin Passmore (eds), *Political Violence and Democracy in Western Europe, 1918–1940* (Palgrave Macmillan, 2015), pp. 144–58.

BIBLIOGRAPHY

Fischer-Tiné, Harald, 'Mass-Mediated Panic in the British Empire? Shyamji Krishnavarma's "Scientific Terrorism" and the "London Outrage", 1909', in Harald Fischer-Tiné (ed.), *Anxieties, Fear and Panic in Colonial Settings: Empires on the Edge of a Nervous Breakdown* (Macmillan, 2016), pp. 99–134.

Ford, Franklin L., 'The Twentieth of July in the History of the German Resistance', *American Historical Review*, 51/4 (July 1946), pp. 609–26.

Foshko, Katherine, 'The Paul Doumer Assassination and the Russian Diaspora in Interwar France', *French History*, 23 (2009), pp. 383–404.

French, David, *Fighting EOKA: The British Counter-Insurgency Campaign on Cyprus, 1955–1959* (OUP, 2015),

——, 'Toads and Informers: How the British Treated their Collaborators during the Cyprus Emergency, 1955–59', *International History Review*, 39 (2017), pp. 71–88.

Fung, Edmund, 'Anti-Imperialism and the Left Guomindang', *Modern China*, 11 (1985), pp. 39–76.

Gallo, Ruben, 'Who Killed Trotsky?', *Princeton University Library Chronicle*, 75 (2013), pp. 109–18.

Gao, Wei, Scott Gilbert and Kevin Sylwester, 'The Effect of Assassinations on Political Institutions: Are the Jones-Olkens Findings Robust?', *Applied Economics Letters*, 20 (2013), pp. 673–6.

Garibian, Sevane, '"Commanded by my Mother's Corpse": Talaat Pasha, or the Revenge Assassination of a Condemned Man', *Journal of Genocide Research*, 20 (2018), pp. 220–35.

Gates, Robert, *Duty: Memoirs of a Secretary at War* (W.H. Allen, 2014).

Gavrilović, Stoyan, 'New Evidence on the Sarajevo Assassination', *Journal of Modern History*, 27/4 (1955), pp. 410–13.

Geifman, Anna, *Thou Shalt Kill: Revolutionary Terrorism in Russia, 1894–1917* (Princeton University Press, 1993).

——, *Death Orders: The Vanguard of Modern Terrorism in Revolutionary Russia* (Praeger, 2010).

Gerard, Emmanuel and Bruce Kuklick, *Death in the Congo: Murdering Patrice Lumumba* (Harvard UP, 2015).

Gerwarth, Robert, 'The Central European Counter-Revolution: Paramilitary Violence in Germany, Austria and Hungary after the Great War', *Past & Present*, 200 (2008), pp. 175–209.

Gerwarth, Robert and John Horne, 'Vectors of Violence: Paramilitarism in Europe after the Great War, 1917–1923', *Journal of Modern History*, 83 (2011), pp. 489–512.

Gerwarth, Robert and Ugur Umit Ungor, 'The Collapse of the Ottoman and Habsburg Empires and the Brutalisation of the Successor States', *Journal of Modern European History*, 13 (2015), pp. 226–48.

Ghosh, Durba, 'Gandhi and the Terrorists: Revolutionary Challenges from Bengal and Engagements with Non-Violent Political Protest', *South Asia: Journal of South Asian Studies*, 39 (2016), pp. 560–76.

——, *Gentlemanly Terrorists: Political Violence and the Colonial State in India, 1919–1947* (CUP, 2017).

Gioe, David, Michael Goodman and David Frey, 'Unforgiven: Russian Intelligence Vengeance as Political Theatre and Strategic Messaging', *Intelligence and National Security*, 34 (2019), pp. 561–75.

BIBLIOGRAPHY

Gleijeses, Piero, 'The Death of Francisco Arana: A Turning Point in the Guatemalan Revolution', *Journal of Latin American Studies*, 22 (1990), pp. 527–52.

Gobat, Michel, *Confronting the American Dream: Nicaragua under US Imperial Rule* (Duke University Press, 2005).

Golani, Motti (ed.), *The End of the British Mandate in Palestine, 1948: The Diary of Sir Henry Gurney* (Palgrave Macmillan, 2009).

Gooch, G.P., 'European Diplomacy before the War in the Light of the Archives', *International Affairs*, 18 (1939), pp. 77–102.

Gould, William, 'Hindu Militarism and Partition in 1940s United Provinces: Rethinking the Politics of Violence and Scale', *South Asia: Journal of South Asian Studies*, 42 (2019), pp. 134–51.

Großklaus, Mathias, 'Friction, not Erosion: Assassination Norms at the Fault Line between Sovereignty and Liberal Value', *Contemporary Security Policy*, 38 (2017), pp. 260–80.

Guillaume, Gilbert, 'France and the Fight against Terrorism', *Terrorism and Political Violence*, 4 (1992), pp. 131–5.

Gumbel, E.J., *Vier Jahre politischer Mord* (Verlag der Neuen Gesellschaft, 1922).

Gupta, Amir Kumar, 'Defying Death: Nationalist Revolutionism in India, 1897–1938', *Social Scientist*, 25 (1997), pp. 3–27.

Häfner, Lutz, 'The Assassination of Count Mirbach and the "July Uprising" of the Left Socialist Revolutionaries in Moscow, 1918', *Russian Review*, 50 (1991), pp. 324–44.

Harouvi, Eldad, *Palestine Investigated: The Criminal Investigation Department of the Palestine Police Force, 1920–1948* (Sussex Academic Press, 2016).

Harris, James, *The Great Fear: Stalin's Terror of the 1930s* (OUP, 2016).

Harrison, Alexander, *Challenging De Gaulle: The OAS and the Counterrevolution in Algeria, 1954–1962* (Praeger, 1989).

Hart, Albert Bushnell, 'A Dissent from the Conclusions of Professor Barnes', *Current History*, 20/2 (1924), pp. 195–6.

Hart, Peter (ed.), *British Intelligence in Ireland, 1920–21: The Final Reports* (Cork UP, 2002).

——, *The IRA at War, 1916–1923* (OUP, 2003).

Haslam, Jonathan, *Near and Distant Neighbours: A New History of Soviet Intelligence* (OUP, 2015).

Havens, Murray, Carl Leiden and Karl Schmitt, *The Politics of Assassination* (Prentice-Hall, 1970).

Hayden, Michael, *Playing to the Edge: American Intelligence in the Age of Terror* (Penguin, 2016).

Heilman, Jaymie, 'The Demon Inside: Madre Conchita, Gender, and the Assassination of Obregón', *Mexican Studies*, 18 (2002), pp. 23–60.

Heinemann, Winifried, 'Das Ende des Staatsstreichs: Die Niederschlagung des 20. Juli 1944 im Bendlerblock', *Vierteljahrshefte für Zeitgeschichte*, 68 (2020), pp. 1–23.

Herwig, Holger, 'Patriotic Self-Censorship in Germany after the Great War', *International Security*, 12 (Fall 1987), pp. 5–44.

Hoffman, Rachel, 'The Age of Assassination: Monarchy and Nation in Nineteenth-Century Europe', in Jan Rüger and Nikolaus Wachsmann (eds), *Rewriting German History: New Perspectives on Modern Germany* (London, 2015), pp. 121–41.

Hoffmann, Peter, 'Hitler's Personal Security', *Journal of Contemporary History*, 8 (1973), pp. 25–46.

BIBLIOGRAPHY

Hoffstadt, Anke and Richard Kühl, ' "Dead Man Walking": Der "Fememörder" Paul Schulz und seine "Erschieß" am 30. Juni 1934', *Historische Sozialforschung*, 34 (2009), pp. 273–85.

Holmes, J., 'Political Violence in Argentina and Regime Change, 1965–1976', *Terrorism and Political Violence*, 13 (2001), pp. 134–54.

Hopkins, Nicholas, 'Charisma and Responsibility: Max Weber, Kurt Eisner, and the Bavarian Revolution of 1918', *Max Weber Studies* (2008), pp. 185–211.

Horn, James, 'US Diplomacy and the "Specter of Bolshevism" in Mexico, 1924–1927', *The Americas*, 32 (1975), pp. 31–45.

House, Jim and Neil MacMaster, *Paris 1961: Algerians, State Terror, and Memory* (OUP, 2006).

Household, Geoffrey, *Rogue Male* (NYRB, 2007 [1939]).

——, *The Europe that Was* (Orion Books, 2014 [1979]).

Hughes, Matthew, 'A History of Violence: The Shooting in Jerusalem of British Assistant Police Superintendent Alan Sigrist, 12 June 1936', *Journal of Contemporary History*, 45 (2010), pp. 725–43.

——, 'Demobilised Soldiers and Colonial Control: The British Police in Mandate Palestine and After', *Journal of Modern European History*, 13 (2015), pp. 268–84.

——, 'Terror in Galilee: British-Jewish Collaboration and the Special Night Squads in Palestine during the Arab Revolt, 1938–39', *Journal of Imperial and Commonwealth History*, 43 (2015), pp. 590–610.

——, *Britain's Pacification of Palestine: The British Army, the Colonial State and the Arab Revolt, 1936–1939* (CUP, 2019).

Huskey, James, 'The Cosmopolitan Connection: Americans and Chinese in Shanghai during the Interwar Years', *Diplomatic History*, 11 (1987), pp. 227–42.

Ingiriis, Mohamed Haji, 'Who Assassinated the Somali President in October 1969? The Cold War, the Clan Connection, or the Coup d'État', *African Security*, 10 (2017), pp. 131–54.

Ioanid, Radu, 'Nicolae Iorga and Fascism', *Journal of Contemporary History*, 27 (1992), pp. 467–92.

Iqbal, Zaryab and Christopher Zorn, '*Sic Semper Tyrannis*? Power, Repression and Assassination since the Second World War', *Journal of Politics*, 68 (2006), pp. 489–501.

——, 'The Political Consequences of Assassination', *Journal of Conflict Resolution*, 52 (2008), pp. 385–400.

Irving, David, *The Trail of the Fox* (E.P. Dutton, 1977).

Jaszi, Oscar, 'The Stream of Political Murder', *American Journal of Economics and Sociology*, 3 (April 1944), pp. 335–55.

Jelavich, Barbara, 'What the Habsburg Government Knew about the Black Hand', *Austrian Studies Yearbook* (1991), pp. 131–50.

Jensen, Richard Bach, *The Battle against Anarchist Terrorism: An International History* (CUP, 2014).

Jones, Benjamin and Benjamin Olken, 'Hit or Miss? The Effect of Assassinations on Institutions and War', *American Economic Journal: Macroeconomics*, 1 (2009), pp. 55–87.

Jones, Mark, 'Political Violence in Italy and Germany after the First World War', in Chris Millington and Kevin Passmore (eds), *Political Violence and Democracy in Western Europe, 1918–1940* (Palgrave Macmillan, 2015), pp. 14–30.

BIBLIOGRAPHY

———, *Founding Weimar: Violence and the German Revolution of 1918–1919* (CUP, 2016).

———, *1923: The Forgotten Crisis in the Year of Hitler's Coup* (Basic Books, 2023).

Jongman, A.J., 'Trends in International and Domestic Terrorism in Western Europe, 1968–1988', *Terrorism and Political Violence*, 4 (1992), pp. 26–76.

Jovanović, Ljuba, 'The Murder of Sarajevo', *Journal of the British Institute of International Affairs*, 4/2 (March 1925), pp. 57–69.

Kahana, Ephraim and Sagit Stivi-Kerbis, 'The Assassination of Anwar al-Sadat: An Intelligence Failure', *International Journal of Intelligence and Counterintelligence*, 27 (2014), pp. 178–92.

Kaiser, Frederick, 'Presidential Assassinations and Assaults: Characteristics and Impact on Protective Procedures', *Presidential Studies Quarterly*, 11 (1981), pp. 545–58.

Kassimeris, George, 'Last Act in a Violent Drama? The Trial of Greece's Revolutionary Organization 17 November', *Terrorism and Political Violence*, 18 (2006), pp. 137–57.

Kaufman, David, 'The "One Guilty Nation" Myth: Edith Durham, R.W. Seton-Watson and Footnote in the History of the Outbreak of the First World War', *Journal of Balkan and Near Eastern Studies*, 25 (2023), pp. 297–321.

Kedourie, Elie, 'The Bludan Conference on Palestine, September 1937', *Middle Eastern Studies*, 17 (1981), pp. 107–25.

Kidd, Colin, 'Assassination Principles in Scottish Political Culture: Buchanan to Hogg', in Caroline Erskine and Roger A. Mason (eds), *George Buchanan: Political Thought in Early Modern Britain and Europe* (Ashgate, 2012), pp. 269–88.

Kiralp, Sevki, 'Cyprus between Enosis, Partition and Independence: Domestic Politics, Diplomacy and External Interventions, 1967–1974', *Journal of Balkan and Near Eastern Studies*, 19 (2017), pp. 591–609.

Kirchner, Magdalena, ' "A Good Investment?" State Sponsorship of Terrorism as an Instrument of Iraqi Foreign Policy, 1979–1991', *Cambridge Review of International Affairs*, 27 (2014), pp. 521–37.

Kirkham, James, Sheldon Levy and William Crotty, *Assassination and Political Violence: A Report to the National Commission on the Causes and Prevention of Violence*, Vol. 8 (US GPO, 1969).

Kissane, Bill, 'Was There a Civil War in Anatolia between the Ottoman Collapse in World War I and the Establishment of the Republic of Turkey in 1923', *Journal of Modern European History*, 20 (2022), pp. 452–67.

Kloppe-Santamaria, Gema, 'Martyrs, Fanatics, and Pious Militants: Religious Violence and the Secular State in 1930s Mexico', *The Americas*, 79 (2022), pp. 197–222.

Knight, John, 'Securing Zion? Policing in British Palestine, 1917–1939', *European Review of History*, 18 (2011), pp. 523–43.

Kolinsky, Martin, 'The Collapse and Restoration of Public Security', in Michael Cohen and Martin Kolinsky (eds), *Britain and the Middle East in the 1930s: Security Problems, 1935–39* (Macmillan, 1992), pp. 147–68.

———, *Britain's War in the Middle East: Strategy and Diplomacy, 1936–1942* (Macmillan, 1999).

Kornetis, Kostis, 'Rebel Code? The Transnational Imaginary of "Armed Struggle" in the Fall of Southern European Dictatorships', *European Review of History*, 29 (2022), pp. 469–98.

Krause-Vilmar, Dietfrid, 'Albert Grzesinski und die Neuordnung der preußischen Polizei nach 1924', in Andreas Braun, Michael Dreyer and Sebastian Elsbach (eds),

BIBLIOGRAPHY

Vom drohenden Bürgerkrieg zum demokratischen Gewaltmonopol, 1918–1924 (Franz Steiner Verlag, 2021), pp. 83–9.

Kushner, Jared, *Breaking History: A White House Memoir* (Broadside, 2022).

Large, Stephen, 'Nationalist Extremism in Early Shōwa Japan: Inoue Nisshō and the "Blood-Pledge Corps Incident", 1932', *Modern Asian Studies*, 35 (2001), pp. 533–64.

Lazo, Dimitri, 'Lansing, Wilson, and the Jenkins Incident', *Diplomatic History*, 22 (1998), pp. 177–98.

Leidinger, Hannes, 'The Case of Alfred Redl and the Situation of Austro-Hungarian Military Intelligence on the Eve of World War I', in Günter Bischof, Ferdinand Karlhofer and Samuel Williamson (eds), *1914: Austria-Hungary, the Origins and the First Year of World War I* (University of New Orleans Press, 2014), pp. 35–54.

Lenoe, Matthew, 'Did Stalin Kill Kirov and Does it Matter?', *Journal of Modern History*, 74 (2002), pp. 352–80.

——, *The Kirov Murder and Soviet History* (Yale UP, 2010).

Levy, Jack and William Mulligan, 'Why 1914 but Not Before? A Comparative Study of the July Crisis and its Precursors', *Security Studies*, 30 (2021), pp. 213–44.

Ling, Li, 'Terrorism in Chinese History: Assassinations and Kidnapping', *Contemporary Chinese Thought*, 42 (2010), pp. 35–64.

Lisle, John, *The Dirty Tricks Department: The Untold Story of the Real-Life Q Branch, the Masterminds of Second World War Secret Warfare* (History Press, 2023).

Litten, Frederick, 'The Noulens Affair', *China Quarterly*, 138 (1994), pp. 492–512.

Little, Douglas, 'To the Shores of Tripoli: America, Qaddafi, and Libyan Revolution, 1969–1989', *The International History Review*, 35 (2013), pp. 70–99.

Loffman, Reuben, '"My Training is Deeply Christian and I Am against Violence": Jason Sendwe, the Balubakat, and the Katangese Secession, 1957–1964', *Journal of African History*, 61 (2020), pp. 263–81.

Long, John, 'Plot and Counter-Plot in Revolutionary Russia: Chronicling the Bruce Lockhart Conspiracy, 1918', *Intelligence and National Security*, 10 (1995), pp. 122–43.

Lotysz, Slawomir, 'Tailored to the Times: The Story of Casimir Zeglen's Silk Bullet-Proof Vest', *Arms & Armour*, 11 (2014), pp. 164–86.

Lownie, Andrew, *The Mountbattens: Their Lives and Loves* (Blink, 2019).

Ludwig, Ernest, 'Martyrdom of Count Stephan Tisza', *Current History*, 21/4 (January 1925), pp. 542–9.

MacKenzie, David, 'The "Black Hand" and its Statutes', *East European Quarterly*, 25 (1991), pp. 179–206.

——, *The Black Hand on Trial: Salonika, 1917* (Columbia UP, 1995).

Mackenzie, William, *The Secret History of SOE: Special Operations Executive, 1940–1945* (St Ermin's Press, 2000).

MacKinnon, Stephen, 'Toward a History of the Chinese Press in the Republican Period', *Modern China*, 23 (1997), pp. 3–32.

Maclean, Kama, *A Revolutionary History of Interwar India: Violence, Image, Voice and Text* (Hurst, 2015).

——, 'The Art of Panicking Quietly: British Expatriate Responses to "Terrorist Outrages" in India, 1912–1933', in Harald Fischer-Tiné (ed.), *Anxieties, Fear and Panic in Colonial Settings: Empires on the Edge of a Nervous Breakdown* (Macmillan, 2016), pp. 135–68.

MacLeod, Alan, *International Politics and the Northern Ireland Conflict: The USA, Diplomacy and the Troubles* (I.B. Tauris, 2016).

MacMaster, Neil, 'The "Silent Native": *Attentisme*, Being Compromised, and Banal Terror during the Algerian War of Independence, 1954–1962', in Martin Thomas (ed.), *The French Colonial Mind, Volume 2: Violence, Military Encounters, and Colonialism* (University of Nebraska Press, 2012), pp. 283–303.

Mahieu, Alban, 'Les effectifs de l'armée française en Algérie, 1954–1962', in Jean-Charles Jauffret and Maurice Vaïsse (eds), *Militaires et guérrilla dans la guerre d'Algérie* (Éditions Complexe, 2001).

Maoz, Asher, 'Historical Adjudication: Courts of Law, Commissions of Inquiry, and "Historical Truth", *Law and History Review*, 18 (2000), pp. 559–606.

Marone, Francesco, 'A Farewell to Firearms? The Logic of Weapon Selection in Terrorism: The Case of of Jihadist Attacks in Europe', *Global Change, Peace and Security*, 33 (2021), pp. 221–40.

Martin, Brian, 'The Green Gang and the Guomindang State: Du Yuehsheng and the Politics of Shanghai, 1927–1937', *Journal of Asian Studies*, 54 (1995), pp. 64–92.

Mattar, Philip, *The Mufti of Jerusalem: Al-Hajj Amin al-Husayni and the Palestinian National Movement* (Columbia UP, 1988).

McChrystal, Stanley, *My Share of the Task: A Memoir* (Penguin, 2014).

McDougall, James, 'The Impossible Republic: The Reconquest of Algeria and the Decolonization of France, 1945–1962', *Journal of Modern History*, 89 (2017), pp. 772–811.

McPherson, Alan, 'Letelier Diplomacy: Nonstate Actors and US-Chilean Relations', *Diplomatic History*, 43 (2019), pp. 445–68.

——, *Ghosts of Sheridan Circle: How a Washington Assassination Brought Pinochet's Terror State to Justice* (University of North Carolina Press, 2019).

Michail, Eugene, 'Western Attitudes to War in the Balkans and the Shifting Meanings of Violence, 1912–1991', *Journal of Contemporary History*, 47 (2012), pp. 219–39.

Millan, Matteo, '*Squadrismo*: Disciplining Paramilitary Violence in the Italian Fascist Dictatorship', *Contemporary European History*, 22 (2013), pp. 551–73.

Miller, Michael, *Shanghai on the Métro: Spies, Intrigue, and the French between the Wars* (University of California Press, 1994).

Miller, Martin, *The Foundations of Modern Terrorism: State, Society and the Dynamics of Political Violence* (CUP, 2013).

Miller, Paul, '"The First Shots of the First World War": The Sarajevo Assassination in History and Memory', *Central Europe*, 14 (2016), pp. 141–56.

Miller-Melamed, John, *Misfire: The Sarajevo Assassination and the Winding Road to World War I* (OUP, 2022).

Mitter, Rana, *China's War with Japan, 1937–1945: The Struggle for Survival* (Penguin, 2014).

——, 'Presentism and China's Changing Wartime Past', *Past & Present*, 234 (2017), pp. 263–74.

Mombauer, Annika, 'Guilt or Responsibility? The Hundred-Year Debate on the Origins of World War I', *Central European History*, 48 (2015), pp. 541–64.

Mommsen, Wolfgang, 'Max Weber and the Regeneration of Russia', *Journal of Modern History*, 69 (1997), pp. 1–17.

Monier, Frédéric, 'Défendre des "terroristes" dans la France de 1935: L'avocat des "oustachis croates", *Le Mouvement Social*, 240 (2012/13), pp. 105–20.

BIBLIOGRAPHY

Morgan, Philip, '"The Trash Who Are Obstacles in our Way": The Italian Fascist Party at the Point of Totalitarian Lift Off, 1930–21', *English Historical Review*, 127 (2012), pp. 303–44.

Müller, Ingo, 'Militärgerichtsbarkeit und Strafjustiz: Der Fall Jorns', in Andreas Braun, Michael Dreyer and Sebastian Elsbach (eds), *Vom drohenden Bürgerkrieg zum demokratischen Gewaltmonopol, 1918–1924* (Franz Steiner Verlag, 2021), pp. 83–9.

Muñoz, Heraldo, *Getting Away with Murder: Benazir Bhutto's Assassination and the Politics of Pakistan* (W.W. Norton, 2014).

Murphy, Philip, 'A Police State? The Nyasaland Emergency and Colonial Intelligence', *Journal of Southern African Studies*, 36 (2010), pp. 765–80.

Naylor, Sean, *Relentless Strike: The Secret History of Joint Special Operation Command* (St Martin's Griffin, 2015).

Neitzel, Sönke (ed.), *Tapping Hitler's Generals: Transcripts of Secret Conversations, 1942–45* (Frontline, 2007).

Neumaier, Christopher, 'The Escalation of German Reprisal Policy in Occupied France, 1941–42', *Journal of Contemporary History*, 41 (2006), pp. 113–31.

Nevo, Joseph, 'Palestinian Arab Violent Activity during the 1930s', in Michael Cohen and Martin Kolinsky (eds), *Britain and the Middle East in the 1930s: Security Problems, 1935–39* (Macmillan, 1992), pp. 169–89.

Newman, John Paul, 'Post-Imperial and Post-War Violence in the South Slav Lands, 1917–1923', *Contemporary European History*, 19 (2010), pp. 249–65.

Nielsen, Christian Axboe, 'Surveillance, Denunciations, and Ideology during King Aleksandar's Dictatorship, 1928–1934', *East European Politics and Societies*, 23 (2009), pp. 34–62.

Noël, Raymond, Édouard Chollier, Roger Dejean and Claude Merviel, 'Les brigades de recherche et de contre-sabotage (BRCS) en Algérie, 1956–1962', *Guerres mondiales et conflits contemporains*, 208 (2002), pp. 91–117.

O'Brien, Kevin, 'The Use of Assassination as a Tool of State Policy: South Africa's Counter-Revolutionary Strategy, 1979–1992', *Terrorism and Political Violence*, 13 (2001), pp. 107–42.

O'Brien, Phillips Payson, 'The Titan Refreshed: Imperial Overstretch and the British Navy before the First World War', *Past & Present*, 172 (2001), pp. 146–69.

——, 'The American Press, Public, and the Reaction to the Outbreak of the First World War', *Diplomatic History*, 37 (2013), pp. 446–75.

Ogg, Frederic, 'Assassination of Rumania's Premier', *Current History*, 39 (1934), pp. 619–26.

O'Halpin, Eunan, 'Collins and Intelligence, 1919–1923', in Gabriel Doherty and Dermot Keogh (eds), *Michael Collins and the Irish State* (Mercier Press, 1998), pp. 70–82.

Orbach, Danny, *Curse on This Country: The Rebellious Army of Imperial Japan* (Cornell University Press, 2017).

Orgill, Nathan 'Reawakening the Nation: British Journalists and the Interwar Debate on the Origins of the First World War', *Journalism Studies*, 17 (2016), pp. 517–31.

Osten, Sarah, 'Out of the Shadows: Violence and State Consolidation in Postrevolutionary Mexico, 1927–1940', *Latin Americanist*, 64 (2020), pp. 169–99.

Otte, T.G., '"The Light of History": Scholarship and Officialdom in the Era of the First World War', *Diplomacy & Statecraft*, 30 (2019), pp. 253–87.

BIBLIOGRAPHY

Owen, Nicholas, 'The Soft Heart of the British Empire: Indian Radicals in Edwardian London', *Past and Present*, 220 (2013), pp. 143–84.

Oztan, Ramazan Hakki, 'Republic of Conspiracies: Cross-Border Plots and the Making of Modern Turkey', *Journal of Contemporary History*, 56 (2021), pp. 55–76.

Padmavathi, S. and D.G. Hariprasath (eds), *Report of Commission of Inquiry into Conspiracy to Murder Mahatma Gandhi: J.L. Kapur Commission Report* (Notion Press, 2 vols, 2017).

Padover, Saul, 'Patterns of Assassination in Occupied Territory', *Public Opinion Quarterly* (Winter 1943), pp. 680–93.

Panetta, Leon, *Worthy Fights: A Memoir of Leadership in War and Peace* (Penguin, 2014).

Pannwitz, Heinz, 'Attentat auf Heydrich', March 1959, *Vierteljahrsshefte für Zeitgeschichte*, 33 (1985), pp. 673–706.

Passmore, Kevin, 'Political Violence and Democracy in Western Europe, 1918–1940', in Chris Millington and Kevin Passmore (eds), *Political Violence and Democracy in Western Europe, 1918–1940* (Palgrave Macmillan, 2015), pp. 1–13.

Pearton, Maurice, 'SOE in Romania', in Mark Seaman (ed.), *Special Operations Executive: A New Instrument of War* (Routledge, 2006), pp. 123–36.

Pentland, Gordon, 'The Indignant Nation: Australian Responses to the Attempted Assassination of the Duke of Edinburgh in 1868', *English Historical Review*, CXXX (2015), pp. 57–88.

——, ' "An Offence New in its Kind": Responses to Assassination Attempts on British Royalty, 1800–1900', *Journal of British Studies*, 62 (2023), pp. 418–44.

Perliger, Arie, 'The Role of Civil Wars and Elections in Inducing Political Assassinations', *Studies in Conflict and Terrorism*, 40 (2017), pp. 684–700.

Person, John, 'Between Patriotism and Terrorism: The Policing of Nationalist Movements in 1930s Japan', *Journal of Japanese Studies*, 43 (2017), pp. 289–318.

Pervillé, Guy, 'Le terrorisme urbain dans la guerre d'Algérie, 1954–1962', in Jean-Charles Jauffret and Maurice Vaïsse (eds), *Militaires et guérrilla dans la guerre d'Algérie* (Éditions Complexe, 2001), pp. 447–67.

Petzold, Stephan, 'Fritz Fischer and the Rise of Critical Historiography in West Germany, 1945–1966: A Study in the Social Production of Historical Knowledge', unpublished doctoral dissertation, Aberystwyth (2010).

Pogge von Strandmann, Hartmut, 'The Historical and Historical Significance of the Fischer Controversy', *Journal of Contemporary History*, 48 (2013), pp. 251–70.

Porath, Yehoshua, *The Palestinian Arab National Movement: From Riots to Rebellion* (Frank Cass, 1977).

Pratt, Simon, 'Anyone Who Hurts Us: How the Logic of Israel's "Assassination Policy" Developed during the Aqsa Intifada', *Terrorism and Political Violence*, 25 (2013), pp. 224–45.

Pugliese, Stanislao, 'Death in Exile: The Assassination of Carlo Rosselli', *Journal of Contemporary History*, 32 (1997), pp. 305–19.

Raat, William Dirk, 'The Diplomacy of Suppression: *Los Revoltosos*, Mexico, and the United States, 1906–1911', *Hispanic American Historical Review*, 56 (1976), pp. 529–50.

——, 'US Intelligence Operations and Covert Action in Mexico, 1900–1947', *Journal of Contemporary History*, 22 (1987), pp. 615–38.

Rabinowitch, Alexander, 'The Schastny File: Trotsky and the Case of the Hero of the Baltic Fleet', *Russian Review*, 58 (1999), pp. 615–34.

Rayfield, Donald, 'The Exquisite Inquisitor: Viascheslav Menzhinky as Poet and Hangman', *New Zealand Slavonic Journal* (2003), pp. 91–109.

Reagan, Ronald, *The Reagan Diaries*, ed. Douglas Brinkley (HarperCollins, 2007).

Reid, Stuart, *The Lumumba Plot: The Secret History of the CIA and a Cold War Assassination* (Knopf, 2023).

Reilly, Sidney, *Adventures of a British Master Spy: The Memoirs of Sidney Reilly* (Biteback, 2014).

Requate, Jörg and Philipp Zessin, 'Comment sortir du terrorisme? La violence politique et les conditions de sa disparition en France et en République Fédérale d'Allemagne en comparaison, 1970 to années 1990', *European Review of History*, 14 (2007), pp. 423–45.

Révész, Tamás, 'Soldiers in the Revolution: Violence and Consolidation in 1918 in the Territory of the Disintegrating Kingdom of Hungary', *Hungarian Historical Review*, 10 (2021), pp. 737–67.

Rhodes, Ben, *The World As It Is: Inside the Obama White House* (Bodley Head, 2018).

Roberts, George, 'The Assassination of Eduardo Mondlane: FRELIMO, Tanzania, and the Politics of Exile in Dar es Salaam', *Cold War History*, 17 (2017), pp. 1–19.

Robbins, Simon, 'The British Counter-Insurgency in Cyprus', *Small Wars & Insurgencies*, 23 (2012), pp. 720–43.

Roizen, Ron, 'Herschel Grynszpan: The Fate of a Forgotten Assassin', *Holocaust and Genocide Studies*, 1 (1986), pp. 217–28.

Rosenfeld, Gavriel, 'Monuments and the Politics of Memory: Commemorating Kurt Eisner and the Bavarian Revolutions of 1918–1919 in Postwar Munich', *Central European History*, 30 (1997), pp. 221–52.

Rumsfeld, Donald, *Known and Unknown: A Memoir* (Penguin, 2011).

Rushdie, Salman, *Joseph Anton: A Memoir* (Jonathan Cape, 2012).

Rusu, Mihai Stelian, 'Staging Death: Christofascist Necropolitics during the National Legionary State in Romania, 1940–1941', *Nationalities Papers*, 49 (2021), pp. 576–89.

Sabrow, Martin, 'Terroristische Geheimbündelei versus demokratisches Gewaltmonopol: Die rechtsradikale Anschlagserie gegen die Weimarer Republik 1921/22', in Andreas Braun, Michael Dreyer and Sebastian Elsbach (eds), *Vom drohenden Bürgerkrieg zum demokratischen Gewaltmonopol, 1918–1924* (Franz Steiner Verlag, 2021), pp. 67–82.

——, *Der Rathenaumord und die deutsche Gegenrevolution* (Wallstein Verlag, 2022).

Sadkovich, James, *Italian Support for Croatian Separatism, 1927–1937* (Garland, 1987).

Sánchez-Cuenca, Ignacio, *The Historical Roots of Political Violence: Revolutionary Terrorism in Affluent Countries* (Cambridge UP, 2019).

Šarenac, Danilo, 'Why Did Nobody Control Apis? Serbian Military Intelligence and the Sarajevo Assassination', in Mark Cornwall (ed.), *Sarajevo 1914: Sparking the First World War* (Bloomsbury, 2015).

Schoppa, Keith, *Blood Road: The Mystery of Shen Dingyi in Revolutionary China* (University Press of California, 1995),

Schröder, Joachim, 'Max Weber in Munich (1919/20): Science and Politics in the Last Year of his Life', *Max Weber Studies*, 13 (2013), pp. 15–37.

Schwab, Stephen, 'Sabotage at Black Tom Island: A Wake-Up Call for America', *International Journal of Intelligence and Counterintelligence*, 25 (2012), pp. 367–91.

Schwabe, Klaus, *Setting up the Right Kind of Government: American Occupation Experiences in Aachen before Germany's Surrender* (Aachener Geschichtsverein, 2000).

BIBLIOGRAPHY

Seal, Lizzie and Alexa Neale, 'The Assassination Case of Madan Lal Dhingra, 1909 and Udham Singh, 1940 as Social Drama', *British Journal of Criminology*, 20 (2023), pp. 1–17.

Searle, Alaric, *Wehrmacht Generals, West German Society, and the Rearmament Debate, 1949–1955* (Praeger, 2003).

Segell, Glen, 'Israel's Intelligence-Gathering and Analysis for the Target Assassination of Baha Abu al-Ata (2019)', *Defense & Security Analysis*, 38 (2022), pp. 53–73.

Seton-Watson, Hugh and Christopher Seton-Watson, *The Making of a New Europe: R.W. Seton-Watson and the Last Years of Austria-Hungary* (Methuen, 1981).

Seton-Watson, R.W., 'The Murder at Sarajevo', *Foreign Affairs*, 3/1 (1924), pp. 489–509.

——, *Sarajevo: A Study in the Origins of the Great War* (Hutchinson, 1926).

Shahvar, Soli, 'A Soviet View on the Assassination of the Iranian Prime Minister, Haj 'Ali Razmara, in the Context of the Early Years of the Cold War', *Iranian Studies*, 56 (2023), pp. 309–20.

Shapiro, Jeremy and Bénédicte Suzan, 'The French Experience of Counter-Terrorism', *Survival*, 45 (2003), pp. 67–98.

Sharfi, Mohammed Hussain, 'Sudan and the Assassination Attempt on President Mubarak in June 1995: A Cornerstone in Ideological Reverse', *Journal of Eastern African Studies*, 12 (2018), pp. 454–72.

Shepard, Todd, *The Invention of Decolonization: The Algerian War and the Remaking of France* (Cornell University Press, 2006).

Silvestri, Michael, '"A Fanatical Reverence for Gandhi": Nationalism and Police Militancy in Bengal during the Non-Cooperation Movement', *Journal of Imperial and Commonwealth History*, 45 (2017), pp. 969–97.

——, *Policing Bengali Terrorism in India and the World: Imperial Intelligence and Revolutionary Nationalism, 1905–1939* (Springer, 2019).

Simpson, Brian, 'The Devlin Commission (1959): Colonialism, Emergencies and the Rule of Law', *Oxford Journal of Legal Studies*, 22 (2002), pp. 17–52.

Smith, Michael, 'The Mexican Secret Service in the United States, 1910–1920', *The Americas*, 59 (2002), pp. 65-85.

Smith, Simon, 'General Templer and Counter-Insurgency in Malaya: Hearts and Minds, Intelligence, and Propaganda', *Intelligence and National Security*, 16 (2001), pp. 60–78.

Smith, Sydney, 'The Identification of Firearms and Projectiles as Illustrated by the Case of the Murder of Sir Lee Stack Pasha', *British Medical Journal* (2 January 1926), pp. 8–10.

So, Wai Chor, 'The Making of Guomindang's Japan Policy, 1932–1937: The Roles of Chiang Kai-shek and Wang Jingwei', *Modern China*, 28 (2002), pp. 213–52.

——, 'Race, Culture, and the Anglo-American Powers: The Views of Chinese Collaborators', *Modern China*, 37 (2011), pp. 69–103.

Stafford, David, *Churchill and Secret Service* (Abacus, 2001).

Stahl, Adam, 'The Evolution of Israeli Targeted Operations: Consequences of the Thabet Thabet Operation', *Studies in Conflict & Terrorism*, 33 (2010), pp. 111–33.

Stampnitzky, Liza, *Disciplining Terror: How Experts Invented "Terrorism"* (Cambridge UP, 2013).

Steinberg, Jonathan, 'Old Knowledge and New Research: A Summary of the [2011] Conference on the Fischer Controversy 50 Years On', *Journal of Contemporary History*, 48 (2013), pp. 241–50.

BIBLIOGRAPHY

Stranahan, Patricia, 'Strange Bedfellows: The Communist Party and Shanghai's Elite in the National Salvation Movement', *China Quarterly*, 129 (1992), pp. 26–51.

Streets-Salter, Heather, 'The Noulens Affair in East and Southeast Asia: International Communism in the Interwar Period', *Journal of American-East Asian Relations*, 21 (2014), pp. 394–414.

Stubbs, Richard, *Hearts and Minds in Guerrilla Warfare: The Malayan Emergency* (OUP, 1989).

Sturgis, Mark, *The Last Days of Dublin Castle: The Mark Sturgis Diaries*, ed. Michael Hopkinson (Irish Academic Press, 1999).

Sudoplatov, Pavel and Anatoli Sudoplatov, *Special Tasks* (Little, Brown, 1995).

Sullivan, Lawrence, 'Reconstruction and Rectification of the Communist Party in the Shanghai Underground', *China Quarterly*, 101 (1985), pp. 78–97.

Šustek, Vojtěch, *Atentát na Reinharda Heydricha: Edice historických dokumentů*, vol. 1 (Scriptorium, 2012).

Swain, Geoffrey, 'An Interesting and Plausible Proposal: Bruce Lockhart, Sidney Reilly and the Latvian Riflemen, Russia 1919', *Intelligence and National Security*, 14 (1999), pp. 81–102.

Swan, Quito, *Black Power in Bermuda: The Struggle for Decolonization* (Palgrave Macmillan, 2010).

Swire, Sasha, *Diary of an MP's Wife: Inside and Outside Power* (Little, Brown, 2020).

Taggar, Yehuda, *The Mufti of Jerusalem and Palestine Arab Politics, 1930–1937* (Garland, 1986).

Takenaka, Harukata, *Failed Democratization in Pre-War Japan* (Stanford University Press, 2017).

Tauber, Eliezer, 'Egyptian Secret Societies, 1911', *Middle Eastern Studies*, 42 (2006), pp. 603–23.

Taylor, Fred (ed.), *The Goebbels Diaries, 1939–1941* (G.P. Putnam's Sons, 1983).

Taylor, Peter, *Brits: The War against the IRA* (Bloomsbury, 2002).

Tenet, George, *At the Center of the Storm: The CIA during America's Time of Crisis* (Harper Perennial, 2008).

Thomas, Martin, *Empires of Intelligence: Security Services and Colonial Disorder after 1914* (University of California Press, 2007).

——, *Fight or Flight: Britain, France, and their Roads from Empire* (OUP, 2014).

——, 'The Imperial Culture of French Security Intelligence from World War to Decolonization War', in Simon Ball, Philipp Gassert, Andreas Gestrich and Sönke Neitzel (eds), *Cultures of Intelligence in the Era of the Two World Wars* (OUP, 2020), pp. 337–64.

Thomas, Martin and Pierre Asselin, 'French Decolonisation and Civil War: The Dynamics of Violence in the Early Phases of Anti-Colonial War in Vietnam and Algeria, 1940–1956', *Journal of Modern European History*, 22 (2022), pp. 513–35.

Thomas, Ward, 'Norms and Security: The Case of International Assassination', *International Security*, 25 (Summer 2000), pp. 105–33.

Thornton, Christy, '"Our Balkan Peninsula": The Mexican Question in the League of Nations Debate', *Diplomatic History*, 46 (2022), pp. 237–62.

Tiu, Ilarion, 'Terrorism as Political Tool: The Assassination of Romanian Prime Minister Armand Calinescu by Legionnaires, 21st September 1939', *Cogito*, 5 (2013), pp. 61–9.

Tooley, T. Hunt, 'German Political Violence and the Border Plebiscite in Upper Silesia, 1919–1921', *Central European History*, 21 (1988), pp. 56–98.

BIBLIOGRAPHY

Townshend, Charles, 'The Irish Republican Army and the Development of Guerrilla Warfare, 1919–1921', *English Historical Review*, 94 (1979), pp. 318–45.

——, 'The Defence of Palestine: Insurrection and Public Security, 1936–1939', *English Historical Review*, 103 (1988), pp. 917–49.

Traynor, Lisa, *Archduke Franz Ferdinand and the Era of Assassination* (Royal Armouries, 2018).

Trenta, Luca, *The President's Kill List: Assassination and US Foreign Policy since 1945* (Edinburgh University Press, 2024).

Trevor-Roper, Hugh, *The Secret World: Behind the Curtain of British Intelligence in World War II and the Cold War*, ed. Edward Harrison (I.B. Tauris, 2014).

Turner, Frederick, 'Anti-Americanism in Mexico, 1910–1913', *Hispanic American Historical Review*, 47 (1967), pp. 502–18.

Unsgaard, Edvard and Reid Meloy, 'The Assassination of the Swedish Minister of Foreign Affairs', *Journal of Forensic Sciences*, 56 (2011), pp. 555–9.

Urban, Mark, *The Skripal Files: Putin, Poison and the New Spy War* (Pan, 2019).

Valette, Jacques, 'Le début de la guerre terroriste en Algérie: les attentats de la Toussaint, 1954', *Guerres mondiales et conflits contemporains*, 260 (2015), pp. 79–92.

Vallé, Jean-Pierre, 'L'assassinat politique du roi alexandre Ier de Yougoslavie: un tournant dans la censure des actualités cinématographiques sous la IIIe République', *Hypothèses*, 20 (2017), pp. 221–35.

Van Puyvelde, Damien, 'French Paramilitary Actions during the Algerian War of Independence, 1956–1958', *Intelligence and National Security*, 36 (2021), pp. 898–909.

von Bülow, Mathilde, 'Myth or Reality? The Red Hand and French Covert Action in Federal Germany during the Algerian War, 1956–1961', *Intelligence and National Security*, 22 (2007), pp. 787–820.

Wachtel, Howard, 'Targeting Osama Bin Laden: Examining the Legality of Assassination as a Tool of US Foreign Policy', *Duke Law Journal*, 55 (2005), pp. 677–710.

Wagner, Steven, 'Whispers from Below: Zionist Secret Diplomacy, Terrorism and British Security Inside and Outside of Palestine, 1944–47', *Journal of Imperial and Commonwealth History*, 42 (2014), pp. 440–63.

Wakeman, Frederic, 'Policing Modern Shanghai', *China Quarterly*, 115 (1988), pp. 409–40.

——, 'American Police Advisers and the Nationalist Chinese Secret Service, 1930–1937', *Modern China*, 18 (1992), pp. 107–37.

——, 'A Revisionist View of the Nanjing Decade: Confucian Fascism', *China Quarterly*, 150 (1997), pp. 395–432.

——, *The Shanghai Badlands: Wartime Terrorism and Urban Crime, 1937–1941* (CUP, 2002).

——, *Spymaster: Dai Li and the Chinese Secret Service* (University of California Press, 2003).

Waldron, Arthur, 'The Warlord: Twentieth-Century Chinese Understandings of Violence, Militarism and Imperialism', *American Historical Review*, 96 (1991), pp. 1073–1100.

Wales, T.C., 'The "Massingham" Mission and the Secret "Special Relationship": Cooperation and Rivalry between the Anglo-American Clandestine Services in French North Africa, November 1942 to May 1943', *Intelligence & National Security*, 20 (2005), pp. 44–71.

Walton, Calder, *Spies: The Epic Intelligence War between East and West* (Abacus, 2023).

Wasserstein, Bernard, *Secret War in Shanghai: Treachery, Subversion and Collaboration in the Second World War* (I.B. Tauris, 2017).

Weber, Max, 'Socialism', 'The President of the Reich' & 'The Profession and Vocation of Politics', in Peter Lassman and Ronald Speirs (eds), *Weber: Political Writings* (CUP, 1994), pp. 272–303, 304–8 & 309–69.

Weh, Wen-hsin, 'Dai Li and the Liu Geqing Affair: Heroism in the Chinese Secret Service during the War of Resistance', *Journal of Asian Studies*, 48 (1989), pp. 545–62.

Weis, Robert, 'The Revolution on Trial: Assassination, Christianity and the Rule of Law in 1920s Mexico', *Hispanic American Historical Review*, 96 (2016), pp. 320–53.

Wey, Adam Leong Kok, *Killing the Enemy: Assassination Operations during World War II* (I.B. Tauris, 2015).

Wievorka, Michel, 'France Faced with Terrorism', *Terrorism*, 14 (1991), pp. 157–70.

Williams, Brian, 'The CIA's Covert Predator Drone War in Pakistan, 2004–2010: The History of an Assassination Campaign', *Studies in Conflict & Terrorism*, 33 (2010), pp. 871–92.

Williams, Susan, *Who Killed Hammarskjöld? The UN, the Cold War and White Supremacy in Africa* (Hurst, 2020).

Williamson, Samuel, 'Leopold, Count Berchtold: The Man Who Could Have Prevented the Great War', in Günter Bischof, Fritz Plasser and Peter Berger (eds), *From Empire to Republic: Post World War I Austria* (University of New Orleans Press, 2010).

Wilson, Margaret, Angela Scholes and Elizabeth Brocklehurst, 'A Behavioural Analysis of Terrorist Action: The Assassination and Bombing Campaign of ETA between 1980 and 2007', *British Journal of Criminology*, 50 (2010), pp. 690–707.

Winder, Gordon. 'Imagining World Citizenship in the Networked Newspaper: *La Nación* Reports the Assassination at Sarajevo, 1914', *Historische Sozialforschung*, 35 (2010), pp. 140–66.

Woods, Kevin and James Lacey, 'Iraqi Perspectives Project. Saddam and Terrorism: Emerging Insights from Captured Iraqi Documents, Volume I (Redacted)', *Paper P-4287* (IDA, 2007).

Woods, Kevin and Mark Stout, 'New Sources for the Study of Iraqi Intelligence during the Saddam Era', *Intelligence and National Security*, 25 (2010), pp. 547–87.

Woolbert, Robert Gale, 'Pan Arabism and the Palestine Problem', *Foreign Affairs*, 16 (1937/8), pp. 309–22.

Xia, Yun, *Down with Traitors: Justice and Nationalism in Wartime China* (University of Washington Press, 2017).

Yapp, M.E. (ed.), *Politics and Diplomacy in Egypt: The Diaries of Sir Miles Lampson, 1935–1937* (British Academy, 1997).

Yick, Joseph, 'Juntong and the Ma Hansan Affair: Factionalism in the Nationalist Secret Service, 1946–1949', *Modern China*, 21 (1995), pp. 481–505.

Yitzhak, Ronen, 'The Assassination of King Abdallah: The First Political Assassination in Jordan. Did it Truly Threaten the Hashemite Kingdom of Jordan?', *Diplomacy & Statecraft*, 21 (2010), pp. 68–86.

Young, John, *Twentieth-Century Diplomacy: A Case Study of British Practice, 1963–1976* (CUP, 2008).

BIBLIOGRAPHY

——, 'Emotions and the British Government's Decision for War in 1914', *Diplomacy & Statecraft*, 29 (2018), pp. 543–64.

Young, Julia, 'The Calles Government and Catholic Dissidents: Mexico's Transnational Projects of Repression, 1916–1929', *The Americas*, 70 (2013), pp. 63–91.

Youwei, Xu and Philip Billingsley, 'Behind the Scenes of the Xi'an Incident: The Case of the Lixingshe', *China Quarterly*, 154 (1998), pp. 283–307.

INDEX

Abdullah, King of Jordan, 157, 173
Abe Shinzo, 279
Abu Ali Mustafa, 251
Abu Hassan 195
Abu Nidal
  Black June, 195
  death of, 249
  French amnesty for Black June, 218
  Iraqi support for Black June, 203–4, 219, 220
Acevedo de la Llata, Concepción (Madre Conchita), 85–6
Adler, Fritz, 36–7
Afghanistan
  assassination during the 1970s, 201–2
  assassinations by the Taliban, 269
  Dubs assassination, 201–2
  Islamist-led assassinations, 254–5, 256, 258–9, 264–5
  Massoud assassination, 251–2, 253
Aideed, Mohammed Farah, 240, 243
Albizu Campos, Pedro, 92, 93, 95
Alexander, Crown Prince (later King)
  assassination of, 128–9, 173
  attempted assassinations of, 27–8, 30
  execution of Apis and Malobabić as assassins, 27–8

  and the Sarajevo assassination, 17, 18, 31–2
Algeria
  assassination complex, 158, 160, 163, 164
  assassinations, post-independence, 167
  assassinations in France by Algerian nationalists, 160, 163, 218
  Darlan assassination, 138–9
  French counter-assassination strategies, 159, 163–4
  independence, 162
Allenby, Lord, 55, 60
Allende, Salvador, 189
Al-Qaeda
  al-Harethi assassination, 255
  Massoud assassination, 251–2, 253
  9/11, 253–4
  in Sudan, 243
  US air attack on, 243
  see also bin Laden, Osama
Al-Shabaab, 265
Amess, David, 280–1
Anarchism, 14, 18, 75, 76, 77
Anderson, John, 66, 67–8
Andrews, Lewis, 73
Aquino, Benigno, 223

INDEX

Arafat, Yasser, 205, 211, 245, 251
Araki Sadao, 100, 102–3
Arana, Francisco, 173
Árbenz, Jacobo, 173, 175–6, 189
Argentina
   Monteneros assassinations, 197–8
   Operation Condor, 7
   US counter-assassination security in, 215
Argov, Shlomo, 218–19, 229–30
Armenia, 43, 227
Armitage, Robert, 161–2
Asquith, Herbert, 49–50, 51–2, 59
al-Assad, Bashar, 259–60
assassination
   as a cause of war, 21–2, 25–6, 32–3, 217–18
   CIA training manual, 173–5
   the cover-up, 1, 5–7
   definitions, 11
   four elements of, 1
   geopolitical contexts, 8–9
   in historical records and archives, 10–11
   impact on states' political culture, 9–10
   in the 1960s, 192
   in the 1970s, 192–3
   'patriotic assassination' concept, 118
   as a political instrument, 9, 282, 285–6
   by the political right, 40–1
   pre-emptive assassination, 251
   pre-1914 Sarajevo, 14
   the procurers, 1–2
   scholarship on, 140
   targeted killing in self-defence concept, 250–1, 252–3, 255–6, 267
   by totalitarian states, 119
   against totalitarian states, 120
   victims of, 12–13
assassination conspiracies, definition, 9
assassins
   Anarchist, 14, 18, 75, 76, 77
   cultural figure, 12
   definitions, 9
   the 'honourable assassin' figure, 120, 144, 284
   state commemorations of, 12, 31
   women assassins, 3
   see also tools of the trade
Aung San, 154, 173, 223, 283–4
Austria
   Dollfuss assassination, 127–8
   post-Great War assassinations, 36–7
Ayad, Massoud, 251

Baker, Kenneth, 217
Bandera, Stepan, 182
Bangladesh, 201
Barak, Ehud, 251
Barthou, Louis, 128–9
Bavarian Republic, 34, 35
Begin, Menachem, 195–6
Belgium
   counter-assassination security, 212–13
   IRA assassinations in, 208
   use of political assassination, 164
Bella, Ben, 159
Berchtold, Leopold, 18, 19, 20, 21, 22
Bermuda, 168–9
Bhutto, Benazir, 264–5, 274
Biden, Joe, 267, 269, 274–5
bin Laden, Osama
   Islamist operations in Sudan, 243
   as a US assassination target, 244–5, 251–2, 254, 265–6, 268
   US embassy bombings, 243
   see also 9/11
Bissell, Richard, 158, 178–9, 184
Black Hand, 17, 19, 24, 29, 31, 32, 135
Black September
   Alon assassination in the US, 194–5
   assassination of the US ambassador in Khartoum, 194
   assassinations of Jordanians, 193
   Mossad assassination of members of, 195–6
Blair, Tony, 278
Borgonovo, Mauricio, 199
Boumedienne, Houari, 167
British empire
   Asquith's 'liberal script' response to assassination, 49–50, 51–2, 60, 65, 69, 74
   assassination threats, 146

INDEX

assassinations by the IRA, 56, 57, 58, 59
Calcutta rules, 69–72
colonial-era assassinations in Egypt, 53–5, 60, 69
colonial-era Hindu extremist assassinations, 48–9, 50, 51, 61–2, 63, 64–5, 66, 68–9
Defence of India Act, 52
Macmillan and, 162
O'Dwyer assassination in London, 68
Palestine, 71–2
Rowlatt Act, 53
security establishment responses, 50–3, 55, 56–8, 60, 61–8, 69, 72, 73, 150
tools of the trade, 69–70
violent opposition to, 47–8
Wyllie assassination in London, 48, 49, 68
Buback, Siegfried, 206
Bulgaria, 202, 203
Bunsen, Maurice de, 20–1, 29
Burma
Aung San assassination, 154, 173, 223, 284–5
Chun Doo-hwan attempted assassination, 223
imperial assassinations, 153
nationalist movements, 154
U Saw attempted assassination, 154
Bush, George H.W., 238–40, 241, 256
Bush, George W.
invasion of Iraq, 256
personal security arrangements, 274–5
targeted killing in self-defence concept, 252–3, 255–6, 261
Byas, Hugh, 101

Callaghan, James, 203, 213, 215, 228
Calles, Plutarco, 83, 84, 85–7
Calvo, Miguel, 89
Carranza, Venustiano, 82–3
Carrero Blanco, Luis, 206–7, 212
Casey, Bill, 172
Castro, Fidel
CIA assassination attempts against, 170, 175, 178, 179–81, 184–6

Cuban counter-intelligence strategies, 185, 189–90
Castro, Raúl, 179, 180, 185
Cavendish, Lord Frederick, 56
Central Intelligence Agency (CIA)
Árbenz planned assassination, 175–6, 189
assassination training manual, 173–5
attempted assassination of Castro, 170, 175, 178, 179–81, 183, 184–6, 189–90
awareness of Black September/ Fatah, 193, 195
CIA–SIS operations in Iran, 157
drone technology, 244, 254, 266, 267, 268–9, 283
formalisation of the assassination organisation, 178–9, 258
formation of, 145
hunt for bin Laden, 244–5, 251–2, 254, 265–6, 268
investigation into Orland Letelier's assassination, 7–8
Kennedy assassination accusations against, 170, 171
and the Latin American assassination complex, 172–3
Ngo brothers assassination, 187, 189
Operation Condor, 7
Schneider assassination, 186, 189
targeting of individuals, 243, 267
Trujillo assassination, 176–8, 180, 189
use of political assassination, 157–8, 170–2, 189–91, 257–8
US–GB–Ukraine collaboration, 271–2
Centro Nacional de Informaciones (CNI), 6–7
Chamberlain, Austen, 30
Chamberlain, Neville, 132–3
Chamorro, Pedro Joaquín, 199
Chen Shui-bian, 278
Chiang Ching-kuo, 210–11
Chiang Kai-shek
assassination plot against, 97
Blue Shirt paramilitary organisation, 104–5

INDEX

KMT assassination organisations, 104–6
'Shanghai Massacre,' 108
son of, 211
and the Tang Youren assassination, 107
and the Wang Jingwei attempted assassination, 106–7
Wang Jingwei's counter-assassination strategy against, 107–8
Chile
　Allende assassination, 189
　Centro Nacional de Informaciones (CNI), 6–7
　Directorate of National Intelligence (DINA), 2–4
　Operation Condor, 7, 8
　Pinochet's assassination of Orlando Letelier, 1–3
　Schneider assassination, 186, 189
　see also Letelier, Orlando
China
　Blue Shirt paramilitary organisation, 104–5
　Civil War, 97
　government by assassination, 96–7
　Plum Blossom Society, 104
　Tang Youren assassination, 107
　Treaty Ports, 108, 114
　Wang Jingwei attempted assassination, 106–7
　'whole China' vision, 97
　Zhang Zuolin assassination, 97–9, 100, 284
　see also Kuomintang (KMT, China); Shanghai
Chun Doo-hwan, 223
Churchill, Winston
　creation of Special Operations Executive, 133
　on political assassination, 119
　on political assassination by Zionists, 148–9
　response to IRA assassinations, 58, 59
　on the Sarajevo assassination, 26, 32–3
　state responses to assassination, 60

Ciganović, Miko, 16, 17, 24
Clinton, Bill
　Bobby Kennedy anniversary, 245
　personal security arrangements, 247
　response to the Bush assassination plot, 238, 240–1, 244
　response to the US embassy bombings, 243
　use of political assassination, 244–5
Coetzee, Dirk, 236, 237
Colby, William, 172, 188–9, 190
Collins, Michael, 56, 57–8, 59–60
Congo
　independence, 164–5
　Kabila assassination, 248
　Lumumba assassination, 165–6
Contreras, Manuel, 2–3, 5, 6–7, 8
counter-assassination security
　attacks against politicians, 276–81, 284–5
　Belgium, 212–13
　Britain, 211–13, 215, 226–9, 228–31, 232–3, 246, 277–8
　failings in, 278–9
　fear of assassination, 247
　France, 159, 163–4, 226
　Germany, 212
　India, 246–7
　against the IRA, 208–9, 212
　Netherlands, 277
　politicians' fear of assassination, 274–5, 277, 285
　presidential protection, 75–6, 77–8, 80, 87–8, 274–5, 278–9
　Russia, 273–4
　Sweden, 231–2
　the US, 210–11, 213–16, 226, 230, 245–6
　for VIPs and VVIPs, 232, 233, 285
Cox, Jo, 280
Croatia, 128–9
Cuba
　assassination under President Machado, 88
　assassination/counter-assassination in the 1930s, 80, 89–90
　Bay of Pigs, 180
　la Porra militia, 89–90

INDEX

Machado attempted assassination, 88–9
see also Castro, Fidel
Cuban National Movement (CNM), 2–6, 7, 8
Cubela, Rolando, 175, 185
Curzon Wyllie, William, 48, 49, 68
Cyprus
  assassination complex, 158, 160, 161
  assassinations, post-independence, 167–8
Czechoslovakia
  communist sabotage in, 134–5
  Heydrich assassination, 13, 134–7, 173, 284
  Masaryk assassination, 173

Dai Li, 105
Darlan, François, 138–9
de Gaulle, Charles, 159, 160, 162, 163–4
Dearborn, Henry, 176
Debré, Michel, 163–4
Dhingra, Madao Lao, 48, 52
Díaz, Porfirio, 80
Dies, Martin, 124
Dimitrijević, Dragutin (Apis), 16–17, 27–8, 29
Đinđić, Zoran, 248–9
Directorate of National Intelligence (DINA), 2–6, 7, 8
Disraeli, Benjamin 14
Dollfuss, Engelbert, 127–8
Dominican Republic
  CIA-backed assassins, 175–6
  Trujillo assassination, 176–8, 180, 189
Dubai, 266–7
Dubs, Adolph, 201–2
Dugina, Darya, 272
Dulles, Allen, 172, 180
Durham, Edith, 26, 29, 30, 31, 32, 128, 135

Edwards, Sheffield, 179
Egypt
  British security establishment responses, 55, 58, 60–1
  colonial-era assassinations in, 53–5, 60, 69

Moyne assassination, 148–9
Mubarak attempted assassination, 241–3, 246, 274
Nasser assassination threats, 158, 159
Sadat assassination, 223, 242
Egyptian State Railways (ESR), 54–5
Ehrhardt, Hermann, 42, 44, 45
Eisenhower, Dwight, 176
Eisner, Kurt, 35, 36
El Salvador, 199
Elizabeth II, Queen 158
Elser, George, 132
Erzberger, Matthias, 43–4
Espinoza, Pedro, 2–3, 5
Ethniki Organosis Kyprion Agoniston (EOKA), 158, 160, 161, 167
Ewart-Biggs, Christopher, 207

Farran, Rex, 150
Farran, Roy, 150
Federal Bureau of Investigation (FBI), 124
Ferdinand, Franz, 12, 21, 173, 175, 282; *see also* Sarajevo assassination
Fernández, Armando, 3–4, 5–6
Fico, Robert, 278
Fleming, Ian, 133
Fletcher, Yvonne, 224
Foccart, Jacques, 159, 163
Foley, Laurence, 254, 257
Ford, Gerald, 7, 190–1
Fortuyn, Pim, 277
France
  amnesty for assassins, 218
  assassination deaths, 227
  assassinations in by Algerian nationalists, 160, 163, 218
  Barthou assassination investigation, 128–9
  communist-led assassination of Germans during WWII, 134
  counter-assassination security, 212, 226
  counter-assassination strategies in Algeria, 159, 163–4
  Darlan assassination, 138–9
  SDECE false-flag organisations, 163–4

397

INDEX

SDECE operations in Algeria, 159
  see also Algeria
French, Lord, 56
Fuentes, Alberto, 199

Gandhi, Indira, 200–1, 227–8, 284
Gandhi, Mohandas
  assassination of, 155, 156, 200, 283–4
  British political negotiations with, 62, 63, 64, 65, 67
  condemnation of assassination as a political tactic, 67, 68
  and Madao Lao Dhingra, 52
  personal security arrangements, 69
Gandhi, Rajiv
  assassination, 234–6
  Indira Gandhi's assassination, 228, 232, 234
  personal security arrangements, 234, 247
Georghadjis, Polycarpos, 167–8
Germany
  Armenian assassinations of Ottoman exiles, 43
  assassination deaths, 227
  Bandera assassination in, 182
  Bavarian Republic, 34, 35
  Buback assassination, 206
  constitutional republic, 35–6
  counter-assassination security, 212
  Lübcke killing, 280
  Organisation Consul (OC), 42, 43–6
  the political right's use of assassination, 41, 42
  post-Great War assassinations, 35–6, 37–8, 41–6
  post-Great War propaganda strategies, 27, 28–9, 31
  response to the Sarajevo assassination, 21–2, 24, 26, 27, 28–9
  Schleyer assassination, 206
  state legitimisation of assassination, 35–6
  use of political assassination, 206
  West German Red Army Faction (RAF), 206

see also Hitler, Adolf; Nazi Germany; Sarajevo assassination
Ghana, 166–7
Gibson, Violet, 126
Goldman, Emma, 76
Gow, Ian, 232
Great Britain
  Amess killing, 280–1
  British response to assassinations by Libya, 221, 222, 224
  British secret service in Russia, 38, 39–40
  counter-assassination security, 211–13, 215, 228–31, 232–3, 246, 277–8
  counter-assassinations against the IRA, 208–9, 212
  Cox killing, 280
  government policy on assassination, 217, 218–19
  Gow assassination, 232
  Heydrich assassination, 13, 134–7, 173, 284
  intelligence operations in the Balkans, 20–1
  Markov assassination, 202, 203
  proposals for the assassination of Hitler, 131–2, 133, 141
  reaction to assassinations by Mossad, 195–6
  state response to assassination, 50, 51–2, 60
  UK–USA intelligence-sharing, 228–9
  understanding of assassination during the 1970s, 192–3, 203, 205, 209–10
  use of émigré assassins in the USSR, 120
  US–GB–Ukraine collaboration, 271–2
  VIP and VVIP protection, 277–8, 280, 285
  see also British empire; London; Secret Intelligence Service (SIS); Special Operations Executive (SOE)
Greece
  Saunders assassination, 248

INDEX

Whitty assassination, 220
Guatemala
  Arana assassination, 79, 173
  CIA-backed assassins, 175–6
  Fuentes assassination, 199
Gumbel, Emil Julius, 42
Gurney, Henry, 151, 152–3

Hamaguchi Osachi, 100
Hammarskjöld, Dag, 165–6
Hani, Chris, 237–8
Hara Takashi, 99–100
Harden, Maximilian, 45
Hardinge, Lord, 48, 50, 70
al-Harethi, Qaed Salim Sinan, 222
Hariri, Rafiq, 259–61
Harvey, William, 178–9, 181, 184
Hashimoto Kingoro, 100
Heath, Edward, 205, 211–12, 213
Heinz-Orbis, Franz Josef, 45
Helms, Richard, 170, 172, 173, 176, 184
Heydrich, Reinhard, 13, 130, 134–7, 173, 284
Hezbollah, 259–61
Hirohito, Emperor, 99, 100, 104
Hitler, Adolf
  anti-assassination security, 127, 130, 141
  attempted assassinations of, 132, 141–3, 173
  Kristallnacht, 131
  mass control tactics, 130–1
  use of political assassination, 127
  Venlo-Munich Affair, 132
Hoare, Samuel, 67, 69
Hoover, J. Edgar, 124
Horthy, Nicholas, 41, 128
Household, Geoffrey, 131, 133
Huerta, Victoriano, 81–2
Hungary
  assassination of Count Tisza, 37
  attempted assassination of Count Tisza, 18
  Horthy's use of assassination, 128
  the political right's use of assassination, 41
  the White Terror, 41
  see also Sarajevo assassination

al-Hussein, Hajj Amin, 73
Hussein, Saddam
  and Abu Nidal, 203–4, 219, 220
  attempted assassination of by the US, 256

imperial assassinations
  in Algeria, 158–60, 162–4, 167
  the Asquith 'script', 49–50, 51–2, 60, 65, 69, 74
  in Bermuda, 168–9
  in Burma, 154
  the Calcutta Rules, 69–72
  in Congo, 164–6
  in Cyprus, 158, 160, 161, 167–8
  in Egypt, 53–5, 60–1, 69–70, 148
  in India, 48, 49, 50–3, 61–8, 70–1, 153, 156
  inevitability of, 47–8
  in Ireland, 56–60
  in London, 48–9, 68–9
  in Malaysia, 151–3
  in newly independent countries, 165–7
  in Nyasaland, 161
  in Pakistan, 156
  in Palestine, 71–4, 146–51
  post-war threats, 146
  by Zionists, 137, 147–9
  see also British empire; Egypt; India
India
  assassinations by the Tamil Tigers, 235
  Bengal Act, 62, 63, 66
  British security establishment responses, 50–3, 61–8, 69
  Calcutta rules, 69–72
  colonial-era Hindu extremist assassinations, 48–9, 50, 51, 61–2, 63, 64–5, 66, 68–9, 155–6
  counter-assassination security, 246–7
  Defence of India Act, 52
  democracy–assassination tensions of the 1970s, 200
  Gandhi assassination, 155, 156, 200, 283–4
  Hardinge attempted assassination, 48, 50–1, 70

INDEX

imperial-era assassinations, 48, 49, 50–3, 61–8, 70–1, 153, 156
Indira Gandhi assassination, 227–8, 284
inquiries into assassinations, 10
killings by British troops, 58
Midnapore assassination campaign, 64–5, 69
Mishra assassination, 200–1
Norris assassination, 220
remembrance of assassins, 12
Rowlatt Act, 53
Indonesia, 152
Inukai Tsuyoshi, 102
Iran
  CIA–SIS operations in, 157, 173
  use of political assassination, 241
Iraq
  Bush attempted assassination, 238–40, 241, 256
  first Gulf War, 238
  Islamist-led assassinations, 256–7, 265
  al-Saba attempted assassination, 239
  support for Black June, 203–4, 219, 238–9
  US air strikes, 240–1, 244
  US invasion, 256
  see also Hussein, Saddam
Ireland
  Anglo-Irish truce, 59
  British counter-assassination, 57
  British police and intelligence organisations in, 56–9
  killings by British troops, 58
  remembrance of assassins, 12
Irgun, 137, 147, 149
Irish Republican Army (IRA)
  arms from Libya, 205, 208, 225
  assassinations by, 56, 57, 58, 59, 207–8, 232
  British counter-assassinations against, 208–9, 212
  mortar bombing of 10 Downing St., 246
  Thatcher attempted assassination, 227, 228
Iron Guard, 130
Irwin, Lord, 63, 64, 65, 67, 71

Israel
  Alon's assassination in the US, 194–5
  Argov attempted assassination, 218–19
  belligerent response to assassination, 217–18
  massacre of Israeli athletes at the Munich Olympics, 193
  Rabin assassination, 245, 247
  remembrance of assassins, 12
  targeted killing in self-defence concept, 250–1, 271
  Thabet assassination, 250
  use of political assassination, 251, 286
  see also Mossad
Italy
  assassination deaths, 227
  the Ceka, 125–6
  invasion of Corfu, 125
  John Paul II attempted assassination, 223
  Matteotti assassination, 125–6, 129
  OVRA (secret police), 126–7
  Rosselli assassination, 129, 133
  SOE assassinations in, 143
  see also Mussolini, Benito

Japan
  Abe assassination, 279
  Cherry Blossom Society, 100–1
  government by assassination, 96–7
  Great Japan movement, 99, 100
  institutionalised assassination capabilities, 104
  Inukai assassination, 102
  Mukden Incident, 104
  Nanjing Incident, 98
  post-Great War assassinations, 99–100
  Shanghai Incident, 111
  Tokyo assassination complex, 101–4, 106
  Young Blood Brotherhood, 101–2
  Zhang Zuolin assassination by the army, 98–9, 100, 284
Jerusalem, 157
John Paul II, Pope 223, 242, 243

INDEX

Johnson, Lyndon B., 183–4, 187–8
Jordan
    Foley assassination, 254, 257
    King Abdullah's assassination, 157, 173
    Tal assassination, 193
Jovanović, Ljuba, 31

Kabila, Laurent, 248
Karzai, Mohammed, 254–5, 264–5
Kasa-Vubu, Joseph, 165
Kennedy, John F.
    actions in Latin America and Vietnam, 186–7
    assassination of, 1, 175, 181, 183–4, 283
    CIA suspected involvement in the assassination of, 170, 171
    inquiry into assassination, 10
Kennedy, Robert F., 1, 171, 180, 245, 283
Khan, Liaquat Ali, 156, 283–4
Khashoggi, Jamal, 271
Khider, Mohammed, 167
Khokhlov, Nikolai, 181–2
Kim Il Sung, 223
King, Martin Luther, 1, 10, 171, 175, 283
Kirillov, Igor, 272
Kirov, Sergei, 121–2, 123–4, 173
Kissinger, Henry
    on Black September/Fatah, 194, 195
    counter-assassination security, 214
    on political assassination, 9, 191
    Schneider assassination, 186
Komer, Robert, 188
Komitet gosudarstvennoy bezopasnosti (KGB), 182, 183, 202
Komoto Daisaku, 99, 100, 104
Korea, 96
Krivitsky, Walter, 123–4, 133
Kube, Wilhelm, 141
Kuomintang (KMT)
    assassination campaigns in Shanghai, 105, 111–14, 116–17, 118
    Juntong, 105, 111–14, 116–17
    Nanjing Incident, 98
    security organisations, 105, 109, 110–11

Zhongtong, 105
    see also Chiang Kai-shek; Wang Jingwei
Kusa, Musa, 221
Kuwait, 238–9

Lampson, Miles, 114, 149
Lane Wilson, Henry, 81–2
Latin America
    assassination during the 1970s, 197–200
    the 'Condor' alliance, 7, 198–9
    US implications in assassinations in, 78–80, 172–3, 197, 220
    see also individual countries
Laval, Pierre, 129
League of Nations, 125, 129
Lebanon
    Hariri assassination, 259–61
    Meloy assassination, 215
Lenin, Vladimir, 38, 40
Lennox-Boyd, Alan, 161
Letelier, Orlando
    car bomb, 4–5
    CIA's investigation into the assassination, 7–8
    the cover-up, 5–7
    DINA–CNM assassination of, 1–2
    the procurers, 1–2
Libya
    arms for the IRA, 205, 208, 225
    British response to assassinations by, 221, 222, 224
    Qaddafi assassination, 269–70
    Ramadan assassination, 221
    Stevens assassination, 270, 276
    US air attack on, 225–6, 239
    US response to assassinations by, 222, 225–6, 240
    use of political assassination, 204–5
    see also Qaddafi, Muammar
Liebknecht, Karl, 35–6, 43
Lincoln, Abraham, 75, 80
Lindh, Anna, 279
Litvinenko, Alexander, 263–4, 270–1
Lloyd George, David, 56, 57, 58–60, 66

INDEX

London
  Argov attempted assassination, 218–19, 229–30
  as an assassination hub, 197, 204, 205, 226
  counter-assassination security, 212–13, 229–30
  Fletcher assassination, 224
  imperial assassinations in, 48–9, 68–9
  IRA assassinations in, 59, 207, 208
  IRA mortar bombing of 10 Downing St., 246
  Iranian agents in, 241
  Litvinenko assassination, 263–4, 270–1
  Markov assassination, 202
  Nafa assassination, 221
  O'Dwyer assassination, 68
  Palestinian assassinations in, 194, 204
  Ramadan assassination, 221
  al-Rifai attempted assassination, 193, 205, 211, 212
  Westminster Bridge terror attack, 280
  Wyllie assassination, 48, 49, 68
Long, Huey, 91–2, 173
Lu, Annette, 278
Lübcke, Walter, 280
Lumumba, Patrice, 1, 165, 248
Luxemburg, Rosa, 36, 43
Lyttelton, Oliver, 152, 153

McChrystal, Stanley, 258, 261, 267, 268
MacDonald, Malcolm, 152, 153
MacDonald, Ramsay, 30
Macedonia, 128–9
Machado, Gerardo, 88–9, 90–1
McKinley, William, 75–6
MacMichael, Harold, 147
Macmillan, Harold, 162
McNamara, Robert, 180
McWhirter, Ross, 207, 217
Madero, Francisco, 81–2, 173
Major, John, 237, 246
Makarios III, Archbishop 160, 167–8
Malay National Union, 151–2

Malaysia
  communist sympathisers, 153
  Gurney assassination, 151, 152–3
  Stewart assassination, 151–2
al-Maliki, Nuri, 274
Mandela, Nelson, 234, 236, 237–8
Mansur, Shafiq, 61
Marcos, Ferdinand, 223
Markov, Georgi, 202, 203
Masaryk, Jan, 173
Massoud, Ahmed Shah, 251–2, 253
Matteotti, Giacomo, 125–6, 129
Meloy, Francis, 215
Mexico
  American–Mexican relations, 80–3, 85
  Calles's political career, 83, 84, 85–7
  Carranza assassination, 83
  Catholic revolt, 83–6
  Civil War, 82–3
  Madero assassination, 81–2, 173
  Obregón assassination, 84–6
  Obregón assassination investigation, 85–6
  Obregón attempted assassination, 83–4
  Portes Gil attempted assassination, 86
  Taft–Díaz double assassination threat, 80–1
  Trotsky assassination, 119–20, 123, 173
Mikoyan, Anastas, 183–4
Milošević, Slobodan, 244, 249
Mirbach, Wilhelm von, 39
Mishra, L.N., 200–1
Mitterrand, François, 218, 229
Mobutu, Joseph-Désiré, 165
Moore, George, 194
Morocco, 158
Mossad
  assassinations of Black September members, 195–6
  al-Mabhouh assassination, 266–7
Mossadeq, Mohammed, 157, 158
Mountbatten, Lord, 155, 208
Moyne, Walter, 148–9
Mubarak, Hosni, 241–3, 246, 274
Mughniya, Imad, 260

INDEX

Munich Olympics, 193
Mushir, Shakat Haj, 256–7
Mussolini, Benito
  assassination of King Alexander, 128, 129
  attempted assassinations against, 126–7, 173
  totalitarians, term, 119
  use of political assassination, 125, 126, 129

Nafa, Mahmoud, 221
Nagata Tetsuzan, 103
al-Naif, Razzak, 204
Nasser, Gamal, 158, 159
Nazi Germany
  assassination of Oppenhoff, 140–1
  communist-led assassination campaigns against in France, 134
  investigation into Heydrich's assassination, 135
  plans for assassinations in liberated Europe, 140
  see also Hitler, Adolf
Nehru, Nawaharlal, 67, 68, 155–6
Netherlands
  Fortuyn assassination, 277
  Sykes assassination, 208, 215
Ngo Dinh Diem, 1, 187, 189
Ngo Dinh Nhu, 187, 189
Nicaragua, 79, 199
Nissho Inouye, 101, 102
Nixon, Richard, 194, 210, 213
Nkrumah, Kwame, 166–7
Noel, Cleo, 194, 213
Norris, Percy, 220
North Korea, 223
Northern Ireland, 207
Novo, Guillermo, 4–5
Nyasaland
  assassination panic, 161, 166
  Devlin Commission investigation, 161–2

Obama, Barack
  drone strikes, 268–9
  hunt for bin Laden, 265–6, 268
  institutionalisation of state-sanctioned killing, 266, 267
  personal security arrangements, 274–5
Obregón, Álvaro, 83–6
O'Dwyer, Michael, 68
Office of Strategic Services (OSS)
  assassination as sabotage terminology, 139–40
  Darlan assassination, 138–9
Okada Keisuke, 103
Operation Condor, 7
Oppenhoff, Franz, 140–1
Organisation Consul (OC), 42, 43–6
Oswald, Lee Harvey, 175, 183, 184
Ottoman empire, 41, 43, 53–4, 55

Padover, Saul, 140–1
Pakistan
  Bhutto assassination, 264–5, 274
  imperial assassinations, 153
  Khan assassination, 156
Palestine
  the assassination complex, 72–4, 146–7
  attempted assassination of Hitler, 143
  Black June, 195, 203–4, 218–19, 238–9
  Black September, 193–5
  British security establishment responses, 71–2, 73, 150
  counter-assassination, 74
  Irgun, 137, 147, 149
  Israeli targeted assassinations, 251
  MacMichael attempted assassination, 147–8
  Stern Gang, 147–8
  Stern Gang assassinations, 149–51
  Thabet assassination, 250
  see also Black September
Palestine Liberation Organization (PLO), 193
Palme, Olof, 231–2, 279
Pašić, Nikola, 17, 18, 24, 27, 30, 31, 32
Patel, Vallabhbhai, 155, 156
Pavelić, Ante, 128
Pawley, William, 176
Paz, Virgilio, 3–4
Petrie, David, 50, 51, 52, 70, 72
Philippines, 223

403

INDEX

Pinkerton, Robert, 76
Pinochet, Augusto, 1–2, 5, 6–7, 8
Politkovskaya, Anna, 263
Pope, Alexander, 54
Portes Gil, Emilio, 86
Princip, Gavrilo, 12, 13, 16, 31; *see also* Sarajevo assassination
Puerto Rico
    anti-American militant nationalism, 80, 92–4
    Blair House attack against Truman, 93–5
Putin, Vladimir, 262, 273–4

Qaddafi, Muammar
    attempted assassinations of, 205, 225–6
    murder, 269–70
    use of political assassination, 204–6, 220–1, 224, 225
    see also Libya
Querol, José Francisco, 247–8

Rabin, Yitzhak, 245, 247
Rahman, Sheikh Omar Abdel, 242
Ramadan, Mustafa Mohammed, 221
Rasputin, 38, 67, 173
Rathenau, Walther, 44–5, 46
Razmara, Ali, 157, 173
Reagan, Ronald
    attempted assassination of, 230
    responses to Libyan assassinations, 221, 222, 224, 225
    UK–USA intelligence-sharing, 228–9
    US–Iraqi relations, 219
Reed, Edward, 90
Reiss, Ignace, 122–3, 124
al-Rifai, Zaid, 193, 205, 211, 212
Riggs, Francis, 92–3
Roosevelt, Franklin D.
    American–Mexican relations, 80
    attempted assassination of, 87–8, 173
    Darlan assassination, 139
    and the Long assassination, 91–2, 173
    and Nicaragua, 79
    presidential protection, 77
    and Puerto Rico, 93
Ros, Leopoldo, 89–90
Rosselli, Galeazzo, 129, 133
Rumania, 130, 131
Rumsfeld, Donald, 218–19, 219, 255, 256
Rushdie, Salman, 241
Russell, Tom, 69, 70
Russia
    Bolshevik assassinations, 38–9
    British secret service in, 38, 39–40
    German ambassador's assassination, 39
    Islamist-led assassinations, 262
    knowledge of the Sarajevo assassination, 19, 20
    Litvinenko assassination, 263–4, 270–1
    Politkovskaya killing, 263
    post-Great War assassinations, 38
    pre-Great War assassinations, 38
    Rasputin, 38, 67, 173
    Socialist-Revolutionary Party (SR), 38, 39–40
    Titov assassination, 262
    Ukrainian assassinations in, 272
    use of political assassination, 262–3, 266, 270–1
    see also Soviet Union

al-Saba, Jaber, 239
Sadat, Anwar, 196, 223, 242
Saionji Kinmochi, 100, 103
Salis, John de, 29
Sandino, Augusto, 79
Sarajevo assassination
    the assassins, 14, 15–16, 31
    Austro-Hungarian response to, 18–22, 24, 25–6, 32, 48, 218
    the conspiracy, 15, 18–21, 23–5
    the cover-up, 15, 25–8
    events of, 14, 15–16, 25
    foreign intelligence on, 19, 20–1
    geopolitical impact of, 14–15, 25–6, 32–3, 34, 282
    investigation into, 14, 15, 23–4, 48
    post-Great War investigation, 25–32
    the procurers, 16–17, 20

INDEX

the Serb State thesis, 18, 20–2, 23, 24, 26–7
tools of the trade, 15, 17, 23
Saudi Arabia
  assassination of King Faisal, 196–7
  Iranian assassinations of Saudi diplomats, 241
  Khashoggi assassination, 271
Saunders, Stephen, 248
Savarkar, V.D., 155, 156
Schleyer, Hans Martin, 206
Schneider, René, 186, 189
Secret Intelligence Service (SIS)
  anti-Bolshevik operations, 120–1
  awareness of Black September/Fatah, 193, 195
  CIA–SIS operations in Iran, 157
  Khokhlov defection, 182
  operations in Egypt, 158
  proposals for the assassination of Hitler, 141
  SOE's merger with, 145
  use of political assassination, 157–8
  Venlo-Munich Affair, 132–3
Serbia
  assassination of King Alexander, 128–9
  Austro-Hungarian mobilisation against, 21–2, 24, 32
  Đinđić assassination, 248–9
  the Great Serb dream, 26–7, 30, 31
  the Serb State thesis, 18, 20–2, 23, 24, 26–7
  see also Sarajevo assassination
Service de documentation extérieure et de contre-espionnage (SDECE), 159, 163–4
Seton-Watson, Robert, 27, 28, 29, 31, 32
Shanghai
  assassination complex, 97, 105, 106, 108–9, 110, 111–12, 117–18
  attempts against *Dadao* officials, 112–13, 114, 115, 117
  Communist assassination threat, 109–11, 118
  international diplomatic responses, 113–14

Japanese-backed assassination campaigns, 111–12, 114–16
  Jessfield Road assassination bureau, 115, 116
  KMT assassination campaigns, 105, 111–14, 116–17, 118
  KMT security organisations, 105, 109, 110–11
  'Shanghai Massacre,' 108
  as a Treaty Port, 108, 114
  Wang Leping assassination, 106, 111
Shanghai Incident, 111
Sharples, Richard, 168–9
Shaw, John, 149, 150, 151
Sieff, Teddy, 194
Sigrist, Alan, 73
Simpson, Lenox, 98, 108
Simpson, Norman, 70–1
Singh, Udham, 68
Slovakia, 278
Soleimani, Qassem, 271
Somalia, 240, 265
Somoza, Anastasio, 79, 199
Soong, T.V. 111
Soustelle, Jacques, 160
South Africa
  Hani assassination, 237–8
  use of political assassination, 236–7
Soviet Union
  assassinations of Nazi officers, 141
  Bandera assassination, 182
  émigré assassins, 120–1
  KGB assassins, 182, 183
  Kirov assassination, 121–2, 123–4, 173
  Krivitsky assassination, 123–4, 133
  NKVD investigation into the Kirov assassination, 121–2
  OGPU (secret police), 120, 122
  Reiss assassination, 122–3, 124
  response to the Kennedy assassination, 183–4
  special tasks operations, 122–3, 124, 181–2, 183, 202
  Trotsky assassination, 119–20, 123, 173
  US threat assessment of, 181, 182–3
  Voykov assassination, 121
  see also Russia

INDEX

Spain
  Carrero Blanco assassination, 206–7, 212
  Querol assassination, 247–8
Spartacists, 35–6
Special Operations Executive (SOE)
  attempted assassination of Hitler, 141
  creation of, 133
  Darlan assassination, 138–9
  involvement in Italian assassinations, 143
  joint British-Czech Heydrich assassination, 13, 134–7, 173, 284
  the Rommel raid in Libya, 137–8
  within the SIS, 145
Srbljanović, Biljana, 12
Sri Lanka, 234–6
Stack, Lee, 60, 61, 69–70, 284
Stalin, Joseph, 118, 121–2
Stashinsky, Bogdan, 182
states
  assassination and political culture, 9–10, 284–5
  commemoration of assassins, 12
  definitions of 'assassination', 11
  modern state concept, 34
Stevens, Christopher, 270, 276
Stewart, Duncan, 151–2
Stimson, Henry, 79, 101
Stürgkh, Karl von, 36–7
Suárez, Dionisio, 4–5
Sudan
  Mubarak attempted assassination, 241–3, 246, 274
  Stack assassination, 60, 61, 69–70, 284
Sun Chuanfang, 108
Sweden
  Lindh assassination, 279
  Palme assassination, 231–2
Sykes, Richard, 208, 215
Syria, 259–60

Taft, William, 80–1
Taiwan, 278
Tal, Wasfi, 193
Talaat Pasha, 43

Tanaka Giichi, 98, 99
Tankosić, Vojislav, 16, 17, 24
Tegart, Mike, 62, 63–5, 66, 70, 72
Tenet, George, 238, 244, 245, 254
terrorism
  assassinations overlap with, 193, 282
  global counter-terrorism, 226
  see also Al-Qaeda
Thabet, Thabet Ahmed, 250
Thakin Nu, 154
Thatcher, Margaret
  attempted assassination of, 227, 228, 284–5
  government policy on assassination, 218–19
  response to Libyan terrorism, 221, 224, 225
  UK–USA intelligence-sharing, 228–9
Thomson, Basil, 57
Tisza, István, 21, 22, 37
Titov, Vitaly, 262
tools of the trade
  car bombs, 4–5
  in the CIA assassination training manual, 173–4, 175
  Claymores, 197–8
  drones, 252, 254, 266, 267, 268–9, 283
  explosives, 4–5, 282–3
  long-range rifles, 175
  poison, 182, 183, 202, 203, 263
  Sarajevo assassination, 15
  suicide bombers, 235
totalitarian regimes, 119, 120
Townley, Michael, 3–4, 5–7, 8
Trotsky, Leon, 119–20, 121, 123, 173
Trujillo, Rafael, 1, 176–8, 180, 189
Truman, Harry, 93–5, 173
Trump, Donald, 278–9
Tshombe, Moishe, 165
Turkey
  as an assassination society, 226–7
  John Paul II attempted assassination, 223
  threat from the Armenian JCAG, 227
  use of political assassinations, 43

INDEX

U Saw, 154
Ukraine
  use of political assassination, 271–3
  US–GB–Ukraine collaboration, 271–2
United States of America
  Alon assassination in, 194–5
  American–Mexican relations, 80–3, 85
  Anarchist assassins in, 75, 76, 77
  belligerent response to assassination, 217–18
  Blair House attack against Truman, 93–5, 173
  counter-assassination security, 210–11, 213–16, 226, 230, 245–6
  cruise missiles, 243–4
  definition of 'assassination', 11
  drone technology, 244, 252, 266, 267, 268–9, 283
  government policy on assassination, 224–5
  inquiry into assassinations, 10
  Krivitsky assassination in, 123–4
  and the Latin American assassination complexes, 78–80, 172–3, 197, 220
  Long assassination, 91–2, 173
  9/11, 253–4
  presidential assassinations, 1, 10, 75–6
  presidential protection, 75–6, 77–8, 80, 87–8, 274–5, 278–9
  response to assassinations by Libya, 222, 225–6, 240
  response to the Darlan assassination, 139
  Roosevelt attempted assassination, 87–8
  Soviet assassination threat assessment, 181, 182–3
  stance on Black June, 219
  state response to assassination, 75, 76–7
  Taft–Díaz double assassination threat, 80–1
  targeted killing in self-defence concept, 252–3, 255–6, 268–9
  Task Force 714, 258, 261, 267, 285, 286
  UK–USA intelligence-sharing, 228–9
  UN delegate protection measures, 210–11
  understanding of assassination during the 1970s, 192–3, 209–10
  US–Mexico border protection, 80, 81
  VIP and VVIP protection, 275–6, 279–80, 285
  World Trade Center bombing, 238, 242
  al-Zarqawi assassination, 261, 263, 285
  see also Central Intelligence Agency (CIA); Federal Bureau of Investigation (FBI); Office of Strategic Services (OSS)

Vasconcelos, José, 78, 79
Vázquez Bello, Clemente, 90
victimology, 12–13
Vietnam
  assassination complex, 186, 188
  Ngo brothers assassination, 1, 187, 189
  US assassination operations in, 188–9
Villa, Pancho, 83
Voykov, Pyotr, 121

Walker, Liliana, 3, 6
Wang Jingwei
  assassination attempt against, 106–7
  exile in Japan, 107
  Jessfield Road assassination bureau, 115, 116
  use of political assassination, 105–6, 107–8
Wang Leping, 111
weapons *see* tools of the trade
Weber, Marianne, 35
Weber, Max, 34–5, 39, 40, 285
Webster, David, 236
Welch, Richard, 9

INDEX

Welles, Sumner, 88, 91
Whitty, Kenneth, 220
Wilson, Harold, 213
Wilson, Woodrow, 77–8, 80, 82, 87
Winship, Blanton, 92–3
Wolfowitz, Paul, 222, 255

Yasuda Zanjiro, 100
Yemen, 255
Young, George, 157

Zagallai, Faisal, 222
Zaghlul, Saad, 54, 60–1
Zapata, Emiliano, 83
al-Zarqawi, Abu Musab, 254, 257, 261, 263, 285
Zhang Xueliang (Young Marshal), 97, 105
Zhang Zuolin (Old Marshal), 97–9, 100, 284
Zyazikov, Murad, 262